SAP PRESS e-books

Print or e-book, Kindle or iPad, workplace or airplane: Choose where and how to read your SAP PRESS books! You can now get all our titles as e-books, too:

▸ By download and online access
▸ For all popular devices
▸ And, of course, DRM-free

Convinced? Then go to **www.sap-press.com** and get your e-book today.

SAP® Gateway and OData

 **PRESS**

SAP PRESS is a joint initiative of SAP and Rheinwerk Publishing. The know-how offered by SAP specialists combined with the expertise of Rheinwerk Publishing offers the reader expert books in the field. SAP PRESS features first-hand information and expert advice, and provides useful skills for professional decision-making.

SAP PRESS offers a variety of books on technical and business-related topics for the SAP user. For further information, please visit our website: *www.sap-press.com*.

Anil Bavaraju
SAP Fiori Implementation and Development
2016, 569 pages, hardcover and e-book
www.sap-press.com/3883

Goebels, Nepraunig, Seidel
SAPUI5: The Comprehensive Guide
2016, approx. 725 pp., hardcover and e-book
www.sap-press.com/3980

Paul Hardy
ABAP to the Future
2015, 727 pages, hardcover and e-book
www.sap-press.com/3680

James Wood
Getting Started with SAP HANA Cloud Platform
2015, 519 pages, hardcover and e-book
www.sap-press.com/3638

Carsten Bönnen, Volker Drees, André Fischer, Ludwig Heinz,
Karsten Strothmann

SAP® Gateway and OData

Bonn • Boston

Editor Sarah Frazier
Acquisitions Editor Kelly Grace Weaver
Copyeditor Julie McNamee
Cover Design Graham Geary
Photo Credit Shutterstock.com/267240731/© Noppol Wongvichai
Layout Design Vera Brauner
Production Graham Geary
Typesetting SatzPro, Krefeld (Germany)
Printed and bound in the United States of America, on paper from sustainable sources

ISBN 978-1-4932-1263-7

© 2016 by Rheinwerk Publishing, Inc., Boston (MA)
2nd edition 2016

Library of Congress Cataloging-in-Publication Data
Names: Bönnen, Carsten, author.
Title: SAP Gateway and OData / Carsten Bönnen, Volker Drees, André Fischer, Ludwig Heinz, and Karsten Strothmann.
Other titles: OData and SAP NetWeaver Gateway
Description: Second editon. | Bonn ; Boston : Rheinwerk Publishing, 2016. | Revised edition of: SAP Gateway and OData. | Includes bibliographical references and index.
Identifiers: LCCN 2016001817| ISBN 9781493212637 (print : alk. paper) | ISBN 9781493212644 (ebook) | ISBN 9781493212651 (print and ebook : alk. paper)
Subjects: LCSH: SAP Gateway. | Open Data Protocol.
Classification: LCC QA76.76.S27 B66 2016 | DDC 006.3/3--dc23 LC record available at http://lccn.loc.gov/2016001817

Contents at a Glance

Dear Reader,

Face it: you're madly in love with data. You can't leave home without it, you play with it every day on your computer, and you carry it with you wherever you go. You're smitten. You're whipped. You can't get enough of it. No need to be ashamed. 'Cause, I'll tell you secret: I love data too.

Connecting business data with the modern user, SAP Gateway is SAP's answer to the busy-bodied wireless (or eternally plugged-in) world. And if SAP Gateway is the bridge to data, then OData is the concrete holding it all together, giving developers the power to liberate SAP data and play matchmaker between data and its users. With this book, you'll learn how OData and SAP Gateway can be harnessed to build mobile, social, web, and enterprise applications for popular platforms and devices. So, what do you say? Let's spread the love.

What did you think about the second edition of *SAP Gateway and OData*? Your comments and suggestions are the most useful tools to help us make our books the best they can be. Please feel free to contact me and share any praise or criticism you may have.

Thank you for purchasing a book from SAP PRESS!

Sarah Frazier
Editor, SAP PRESS

Rheinwerk Publishing
Boston, MA

sarahf@rheinwerk-publishing.com
www.sap-press.com

Contents

PART III   Application Development

PART IV Administration

Foreword by Bernd Leukert

Increasing amounts of data have been generated in the past few years and continue to be generated today. Everyone is constantly producing and releasing data, and we are used to having everything available at our fingertips. This is where the digital transformation starts. In fact, about 90% of all global data has been generated in just the past two years, and the worldwide amount of data is to increase tenfold until 2020.

Digitization is rapidly changing how we do business. It changes the way companies create value, interact with their customers and the entire partner ecosystem, and position themselves in established and new markets. This affects the entire value chain of a company down to the suppliers.

To benefit fully from the disruptive power of the digital (r)evolution, the only adequate answer is continuous and profound innovation—whether in a company's organizational structure, processes, or IT systems. To be successful in today's digital economy, companies, no matter the size, have to innovate and rethink their business and business models. They have to drive this change actively by embracing the digital future, and software is and will be the ultimate support for that.

One of the enablers for businesses is SAP Gateway, which is a technology that provides a simple way to connect devices, environments, and platforms to SAP software based on market standards, thus allowing the implementation of new business models. The framework enables the development of innovative solutions with an intuitive user interface, bringing the power of SAP business software to social and collaboration environments, mobile and tablet devices, and rich Internet applications. It offers connectivity to SAP applications using any programming language or model without the need for SAP knowledge by leveraging REST services and OData/ATOM protocols.

When we launched SAP Gateway in 2011, we massively enhanced the extensibility and connectivity of what users could do with our solutions. We enabled them to use the tools of their choice to create, build, and deliver new applications, while at the same time not disrupting existing IT landscapes. Today, the maturity of SAP Gateway is proven: more than 15,000 customers bet on SAP Gateway for bringing unprecedented choice and openness.

Customers aren't the only ones betting on SAP Gateway. Major parts of SAP S/4HANA are based on top of the SAP Gateway framework, providing OData services for SAP S/4HANA's SAPUI5-based services.

This second edition of *SAP Gateway and OData* provides you with a comprehensive guide. I promise you'll be surprised to see what you can do using SAP Gateway without even knowing SAP programming languages.

You'll not only get to know the principles, standards, and technologies, but you'll also learn how SAP Gateway serves as a basis to tackle the challenges of today's digital transformation.

I wish you an inspiring and enjoyable read.

Bernd Leukert
Member of the Executive Board of SAP SE, Products & Innovation

Introduction

Barely 25 years ago, we all started surfing the World Wide Web. Around the same time, we started using mobile phones on a regular basis. At that time, however, not many people thought about bringing those two technologies together. Even fewer people expected the combination to become as popular as it is today.

If you remember that time, you'll know that companies like Google didn't even exist. Amazon wasn't around yet, and everyday devices such as iPods, iPhones, or iPads weren't even invented. Even Nokia—for years to come one of the leading companies for mobile phones—was just getting started, and look how their role has changed. When you remember—and we assume some of you do—the past 25 years, you can easily see how fast things move in the IT area.

Let's fast forward to today. In today's world, not only can you surf the web using your PC, you can also use your smartphone, tablet, phablet, TV, or gaming console—to name only a few. Because of this, we face the challenge of providing business applications that address a virtually end-less number of consumption channels. Furthermore, to remain competitive, we see a necessity to implement social and technological trends alike.

This book is about a product that enables you to implement those trends for SAP Business Suite applications: SAP Gateway. The book takes you on a tour to learn everything you need to know about SAP Gateway. If you are new to SAP Gateway and its concepts, you should take this tour from Chapter 1 to Chapter 16 in one read. If you already understand some of the concepts and technologies involved, we did our best to allow you to take detours, start in the middle of things, and jump around if you like. To make the tour as convenient as possible for you, the book is structured not only in simple chapters but also into several overarching parts.

Part I: Getting Started

The first part of the book consists of four chapters that cover the basics of SAP Gateway. This is the recommended starting point if you want to be informed about SAP Gateway and its related concepts, such as Open Data Protocol (OData).

Introduction to SAP Gateway

Chapter 1 gives you a high-level introduction to SAP Gateway and explains the motivation behind the product. It then provides a basic positioning of the product in the context of other SAP products.

Introduction to OData

OData is the industry standard used by SAP Gateway. We introduce it in detail in **Chapter 2**.

Architecture and integration

Chapter 3 provides you with a solid introduction to the architecture of SAP Gateway, including its backend concepts and integration with other SAP interfaces.

Deployment options, installation, and configuration

Chapter 4 closes the first part of the book by discussing the deployment options of SAP Gateway as found today in real-life system landscapes.

Part II: Service Creation

If you are an experienced traveler and know your way around SAP Gateway and OData, you may have skipped the first part of the book completely. Then again, maybe you worked your way through the first part of the book and just learned about SAP Gateway and OData. No matter which is the case, in this second part, you'll learn everything you need to know about service creation for SAP Gateway.

Introduction to OData service creation

Chapter 5 explains the end-to-end development tools and development cycle for creating SAP Gateway services. It introduces you to both of the main methods of service creation: service development and service generation. Chapter 5 is the basis for the other chapters in the second part of the book.

Service development

Service development is the topic of **Chapter 6**. In this chapter, you'll learn about service development in the backend with ABAP. The chapter takes a hands-on approach to show you how to develop OData services.

Chapter 7 is about the second method of creating services: service generation. It explains the backend-side generation of OData services.

Service generation

Part III: Application Development

As there are two sides to every coin, SAP Gateway has two sides as well: provisioning (backend services and their development) and consumption (usage of backend services in applications). While the second part of our book focused on provisioning, the third part covers consumption. The different chapters take different angles and show the flexibility of SAP Gateway.

Chapter 8 is all about SAPUI5 application development and SAP Fiori. While SAPUI5 is a collection of libraries that developers can use to build applications that run in a browser using HTML5, SAP Fiori is group of business applications levering SAPUI5.

SAPUI5 application development

To build applications, you obviously need a specific development environment. **Chapter 9** is dedicated to the development environment for SAP Fiori—the SAP Web IDE.

SAP Web IDE

Chapter 10 is once again addressing SAP Fiori, but this time the focus is on how to apply extensibility end-to-end. We also cover steps for extending OData services.

Extensibility

One of the most commonly asked questions about application development is how to build mobile applications. **Chapter 11** answers this question and walks you through some examples of mobile application development.

Mobile application development

Chapter 12 is dedicated to social media applications. You'll learn how to develop applications that leverage the power of different social media—from Facebook to Weibo—in combination with OData and SAP Gateway.

Social media application development

In **Chapter 13**, we close Part III of the book with a look at the consumption of OData services from within enterprise applications such as Microsoft Excel and Microsoft SharePoint.

Enterprise application development

Part IV: Administration

Lifecycle management: testing, service deployment, and operations

The fourth part of the book is all about the administration of SAP Gateway. In addition to deploying SAP Gateway, it's important to understand how to roll out software, how to handle errors, and so on, as described in **Chapter 14**.

Security

In theory, the topic of security could have been part of Chapter 14; however, it's so important that it deserves its own chapter. **Chapter 15** is all about the security of SAP Gateway, from authentication to authorization to single sign-on (SSO).

Part V: Roadmap

In the last part of the book, you'll find one chapter: Chapter 16.

Recent and future developments

Chapter 16 provides an outlook on future developments. It takes a deep look into the crystal ball when it comes to topics such as the Internet of Things and gamification.

In addition to all the information contained in this book, we've also provided text versions of the code samples we use. These are available for download on the book's page at *www.sap-press.com/3904*.

Acknowledgments

With this book, you do not hold only the work of five authors in your hands. In addition to countless hours of writing, rewriting, and then rewriting again by the authors, there were many other people involved directly or indirectly. Those people invested hours of their time to read the chapters, comment, criticize, or—in the case of friends and family—endure the authors and their moods and night shifts.

Forewords

First, we would like to extend a very special thanks to Bernd Leukert for his willingness to honor our book with a foreword.

Additional thanks also goes to Martina Bahrke for her support in this effort.

Management

On behalf of Ludwig Heinz, special thanks goes to Norbert Schuster, CFO of Theo Steil GmbH; Daniel Wagner, his former manager at itelligence AG; and to the manager of Customer Solutions & Inventions at itelligence AG, Matthias Kumm.

On behalf of our SAP authors, special thanks goes to Pascal Gibert and Stephan Herbert, who believed in us and the book and supported us in this daring endeavor. Further thanks go to Joav Bally and Thomas Anton. Additional special thanks go to Michael Reh and Vishal Sikka for their support in creating this book.

Colleagues and Special Contributors

Jürgen Kremer, architect for SAP Gateway, is mentioned first for a reason. He has strongly influenced the core part of this book and has significantly improved it with his feedback and ideas. Jürgen, we are very grateful for your excellent contribution.

We would like to thank (in alphabetical order): Martin Bachmann, Wayne Brown, Holger Bruchelt, Suma C V, Fahmi Cheikhrouhou, Suparna Deb, Artur Gajek, Manfred Gaweck, Tobias Griebe, Duong-Han Tran, Judith Hamacher, Ralf Handl, Ran Hassid, Wolfgang Hegmann, Jens Himmelrath, Andreas Hoffner, Christopher Kästner, Felix Köhl, Gerald Krause, Timo Lakner, Oliver Liemert, Hendrik Lock, Thomas Meigen, Tatjana Pfeifer, Daniel Platz, Genady Podgaetsky, Martin Raepple, Elisabeth Riemann, Carlos Roggan, Christoph Scheiber, Claudia Schmidt, Maximilian Schneider, Daniel Schön, Henrike Schuhart, Jin Shin, Jörg Singler, Frank Speidel, Matthias Tebbe, Olaf Tennie, Jirong Wang, Martin Wegmann, Stefan Weitland, Chris Whealy, and Andrew Whitaker.

Special thanks goes to Elisabeth "Lizzie" Riemann for her excellent pictures of some of the authors. Everyone who knows the authors in real life knows what a terrific job she did.

Friends and Family

Very special, warm, and individual thanks are extended from:

▸ Ludwig Heinz to Thomas, Uli, Tobias, Jenny, Alexei, Thorsten, and his whole family who supported and encouraged him all the time.

▸ André Fischer to his wife, Natalie, and his sons, Lars and Timo, for whom he had less time when writing the book—especially during their summer vacation this year—and to his mother, Greta, for her support.

▸ Karsten Strothmann to his partner, Mira, for her encouragement and support during long hours of writing, and to their son, Yann Erik, for his content and happy smile each time his daddy turned his attention to him after hours of having worked on this book.

▸ Volker Drees to his wife, Bettina, and their daughter, Sarah Felicitas, for supporting him in writing this book and accepting the fact that he had to invest many, many hours in it.

▸ Carsten Bönnen to his partner, Susi, who supported him throughout the writing of the book.

In Memoriam

Carsten Bönnen would like to acknowledge the involvement of the two bushi in his life in the creation of this book. Without them, this book would never have happened the way it did. They will never be forgotten.

Final Thanks...

Our final—yet very important—thanks goes to Kelly Grace Weaver and Sarah Frazier, our editors, whose patience, foresight, and ongoing support did a great deal in making this book the best book it could be. Additional thanks go out to all the SAP PRESS people involved in creating this book.

PART I
Getting Started

This chapter introduces SAP Gateway and explains how SAP Gateway addresses the challenges of building business applications based on user interfaces. In addition, the chapter positions SAP Gateway in the context of other SAP products.

1   Introduction to SAP Gateway

In May 2011, SAP launched SAP NetWeaver Gateway (now called SAP Gateway) at SAPPHIRE NOW. Since then, SAP Gateway has become a successful, well-established, and adopted product. It even became part of the standard delivery of SAP NetWeaver (7.40 and higher).

So what is SAP Gateway? The short answer is that SAP Gateway is a technology that improves the reach of SAP business applications. It increases the range of SAP business applications not only in terms of end users but also with regard to the number of developers and addressable environments. With the help of SAP Gateway, SAP business applications, parts of those applications, or simply SAP data can be used by an application developer without prior knowledge of SAP to build—for example—mobile applications.

SAP Gateway or SAP NetWeaver Gateway

As you may have noticed, SAP Gateway is no longer carrying the term "NetWeaver" in its name. This is due to a naming simplification implemented by SAP in 2014. For further details, go to *http://scn.sap.com/community/netweaver/blog/2014/05/30/sap-netweaver-branding-simplification*.

Don't get confused by the fact that you'll still find the old naming in some documents—even the official ones—the naming simplification was implemented only for new releases. So, if you're referring to a specific older release of SAP Gateway, it may still be called SAP NetWeaver Gateway. SAP Gateway and SAP NetWeaver Gateway refer to the same product.

REST and OData   SAP Gateway is able to extend the reach of SAP business applications because it's an open, standards-based framework that can be used by developers to build user-friendly business applications. More technically, SAP Gateway is a RESTful interface based on Atom and OData for the ABAP technology platform, which in turn connects with the SAP Business Suite. SAP Gateway provides a standard-based, centralized interface to the SAP world.

But let's start at the beginning. The motivation for a product such as SAP Gateway is derived from the requirements and challenges that are now placed on modern business applications. In this chapter, we start by looking at these challenges to get a better understanding of what they are. We then consider SAP Gateway as a solution for those challenges. After that, we briefly discuss the installation and deployment options for SAP Gateway. Finally, we take a closer look at how SAP Gateway positions itself in the context of other related SAP products and how it integrates with those products.

> **SAP Gateway and User Interfaces (UIs)**
>
> As you'll see, we'll talk a lot about UIs and applications in this chapter. Although SAP Gateway isn't a UI technology, its capabilities enable developers to have more choices with respect to the UIs they want to use.

1.1   Modern Business Applications

The requirements for business applications have dramatically changed in recent years. In fact, the use of digital media in general is subject to significant changes and, as a result, applications are as well. These changes are observed not only in the private area (the consumer world) but also in the business environment (the enterprise world). End users have become accustomed to a certain way of dealing with digital media and applications, characterized by the constant use of interactive—often intuitive—surfaces for mobile devices, social networks, or almost any application on virtually any device (from mobile phones to televisions to classic PCs).

These experiences in the consumer world lead to expectations in the enterprise world as well. End users have come to expect the same behavior from their business applications as they do from their private applications. And as their use of private applications—especially digital media applications—increases, so will their expectations.

End user expectations

In the wake of this development, IT departments around the world are facing great challenges. These challenges include demands for enhanced end user requirements, which have, as a consequence, led to the necessity of the digital transformations of modern enterprises. In this section, we'll take a look at some of the considerations enterprises must keep in mind for both the UIs and backend infrastructures of their applications.

Digital transformation

1.1.1 User Interfaces

As user expectations change, so must the applications that users work with. Let's consider some of the biggest things to keep in mind when designing the UIs of business applications.

Business application requirements

Intuitiveness

An intuitive UI is essential for applications and digital media in general. In addition to promoting greater acceptance among end users, an intuitive UI increases the effectiveness of these applications. In a time where special knowledge is becoming increasingly important and where experts can be involved in IT processes faster and more easily than ever before, it's important to reduce the training needs for the applications that support the process. Training that is dedicated only to the operation of an application is ineffective and expensive. With an intuitive interface, the need for training can either be avoided in the best case (no training) or at least cut down (shortened training).

Application design

There are other advantages to intuitive UIs as well. Experience shows that intuitive interfaces lead to fewer user errors. Those errors cost money, either as a direct result or through the need for additional process steps to identify and correct these errors. Even ignoring the fact that those errors may endanger enterprises in other ways, it's still mandatory to reduce them to a minimum.

Another point in favor of intuitive UIs is that they increase efficiency and effectiveness in using an application. This is especially true for subject matter experts (SMEs). An intuitive interface can help those experts execute process steps faster and more effectively. For experts, every second saved on a screen is a huge win and, in the long run, saves the company money.

End user acceptance

End user acceptance of an application is also important to consider. The rollout of applications in a company is only the first step—the more important step is the actual use of the application by the end user. If the application isn't understood, it's often not used or not used to the desired extent. Directly or indirectly, this may impact business processes and eventually business success. Improving already rolled-out applications to change that situation will cause additional and unnecessary costs.

Process integration

In this context, it's important to consider that many processes now involve external participants. In the business environment, this may be partners or suppliers on one side or customers on the other. Particularly with a focus on the customer, an intuitive UI is mandatory because acceptance of applications becomes a key differentiator. If a surface isn't intuitive for the end user—in this case, the customer—this may jeopardize the company's success. The best example for this is the current situation in the area of mobile devices, where the importance of intuitive interfaces can't be emphasized too strongly here. In the mobile world, the most successful devices aren't those with the best technology, but those with the most intuitive UI (in combination with a decent technology, of course). The same is true for business-to-consumer (B2C) business applications; an application that isn't immediately understood is rejected by the customer, who will move on to another company providing the same services with a more intuitive UI.

Appeal

Success criteria

An appealing UI is just as important—and not the same as!—an intuitive UI. The surface design of an application relates directly to the end user acceptance and thus the success of the application. It differs from an intuitive interface in that while an intuitive interface may be easy to use, it may still be perceived as ugly by the end user. This may sound irrelevant, but this makes the point even more important because it's often underestimated or completely neglected. An appealing UI dramatically increases acceptance by the end user, especially in combination with an intuitive UI, and this is critical for the success of an application. This applies both to applications used within a company and external-facing applications. While partners still have an intrinsic motivation in the business environment to use applications that are necessary for their business, this is only partly true for customers. In other words, a nonintuitive, nonappealing UI may hinder processes or, in the worst case, prevent sales.

Gamification

The importance of a good UI is emphasized by the recent trend known as *gamification*. For more on this, see Chapter 16.

Business Orientation

Business orientation refers to an application's relevance to the business world, and it's something that often isn't taken into account in the preparation of applications. Instead, technical constraints often determine the UI and functionality of an application. However, these issues aren't relevant for the casual user and the business user. For them, it doesn't matter whether an application is written in Swift, Java, or C#; those users don't care whether the frontend was implemented using HTML5, Flash, or Silverlight. What is important to end users is the use of an error-free, reliable application running on their device and facilitating their activities.

In addition to reliability, design and adaptability of an application are important for business orientation. Business users want to access their data, which means they want to see only the data in applications that are relevant for them. This can be implemented by including end users in the development process via a variety of approaches (e.g., design thinking). Independent from the approach used, it's important to find a common language among the different people involved, for example,

Business user

33

designers, backend and frontend developers, business process experts (BPX), SMEs, and end users.

Innovation

Process adaptation

Innovation is one of the key drivers of business success today. To introduce innovation effectively in a company, it's important that processes adapt rapidly to innovation. For IT departments, it's just as imperative to implement those processes rapidly.

The aspect of innovation is relevant for business orientation as well and thus exists in the same context. Depending on the industry, the business world is changing with dramatic speed. Reflecting these changes in enterprises is only possible when the applications and processes involved can be changed easily, and innovations can be implemented quickly.

Technology lifecycle

Both devices and technologies today come with a much shorter lifecycle than a few years ago, and finding a common denominator between them isn't easy. To illustrate the problem, consider the current bring your own device (BYOD) strategy many companies are following today. As the name suggests, this policy means that employees can bring their own devices, which are usually mobile phones or tablets, to use for work. It's easy to see that this multiplicity of devices is a big problem for IT departments, both when it comes to rolling out applications as well as to the maintenance and management (including security aspects) of the private devices.

> **Digital Transformation**
>
> So, what does the buzzword "digital transformation" actually imply? In short, digital transformation is the process of changing from a traditional—partially digital—entity into an end-to-end digitally integrated entity. These entities can be enterprises but aren't limited from entire industries and even economies. Enterprises that have made this transformation successfully show much faster innovation cycles than those who haven't.
>
> Enterprises in the sports and health sector are good examples. Pick any major brand and you'll soon realize that it has moved from simply selling goods to building communities and digital services around those goods. Instead of just wearing a shirt with that company's logo, you can now use digital services

based on wearables that allow you to improve your health and fitness and at the same time strengthen your bond with that specific company. This is especially true for enterprises that started as digital entities from the get-go. The digital transformation has implications for all of the mentioned challenges in this chapter. For further details please see Chapter 16.

Availability

The reality of today's business world makes it increasingly important to expand the availability of data and applications. In an ideal world, the end user would have access to any data at anytime, anywhere, and from whatever device he chose to use.

The demand for availability is tightly linked to a major trend: the increase in mobilization in the business world. Employees can work from anywhere using different devices—ranging from mobile phones to tablets—and from specialized devices in production to classic PCs. To exacerbate the problem, specific process steps are often required for applications to be made available on different devices. For example, sales representatives will want to use the same applications on both mobile devices and regular PCs.

From a technology perspective, we see a move from technology for experts (e.g., SAP GUI) to more general approaches (e.g., HTML5) and casual user software (e.g., Microsoft Outlook). | SAP GUI to HTML5

In summary, end users prefer to have any data available at any time and at any place. As a result, there are requirements for a broad range of devices and technologies to meet this demand.

Agility

In this context, agility refers to the adaptability of business applications and thus is closely related to innovation. If a process changes within a company, it's important that this new process is quickly available through the respective applications. Agility is important on another level as well—if certain aspects of an application don't work, users expect it to be fixed. For example, if a new application turns out to be too slow or complex for a sales representative in the field, users will expect rapid changes to address the issue.

Flexible processes

Agility and innovation may initially sound very similar, and, in fact, the two have a lot in common. A look at details, however, shows where the two differ. Agility refers to that part of innovation that is about how flexible processes, applications, and technologies can be adapted to business needs. These needs aren't necessarily driven by innovation. They may simply reflect changed market needs—for example, new standards or laws—or changed end user requirements based on the business environment or usability demands.

In addition, flexible processes are only one side of the coin. In an increasingly globalized world, processes often extend to a variety of people, departments, and even countries. The roles and profiles of the people involved have to be taken into account. While an experienced business expert can work with SAP GUI effectively and quickly, it's much harder for a casual user to do so. In addition, processes often require the use of devices that don't even support specific standard software.

Integration

Business processes often span several departments and potentially large numbers of employees. The profiles of the employees involved in a process can be very different though; from the casual user to the expert user, any role can be involved in the same process. Thus, the challenge is to involve all users with respect to their specific skills and available equipment.

To integrate all people who are involved in a process in an optimal way, it's desirable to allow the persons to stay within their familiar environments. For example, while for one user SAP GUI may be optimal, for the next user, it may be Microsoft Excel.

Backend hiding

In terms of backend systems, integration can also mean "hiding" backend systems. In other words, the end user doesn't have to—and most likely doesn't want to—know which backend system he is working on. For the end user, this simplifies the world; for the IT department, this approach allows changes to the infrastructure without having to roll out those changes to the end user. For the end user, the backend systems become a kind of black box. Changes in this black box aren't relevant to him as long as his frontend still runs smoothly.

> **API Management**
>
> With the rise of the digital transformation and economy (sometimes called the API economy) we see a trend in the importance of application programming interfaces (APIs) and API management. With this trend, the need for an enterprise-ready API management tool becomes more and more important. To reflect on this trend and the implications on SAP Gateway, we added a section on SAP API Management at the end of this chapter and discuss in further in Appendix B.

Maintenance

The wealth of new requirements creates brand new challenges for IT departments in the area of maintenance. Various devices and applications must be maintained. At the same time, end users have higher expectations for maintenance and support. The variety of platforms to be supported requires additional maintenance, which costs money. While the already established platforms represent some security here, the introduction of new applications quickly becomes a problem in terms of maintenance. For IT departments, it's essential that these new applications represent as little additional effort in terms of maintenance as possible. So the task is to create new, flexible, and innovative applications that are also easily supported by IT departments.

Maintenance and support

Security

In the field of security, there are problems similar to those that come with maintenance. The variety of applications, devices, and technologies makes securing them increasingly difficult. Despite all of the flexibility and innovation, it's not acceptable for a company to risk the security of its own data or foreign data. Taking into consideration that—to ensure flexibility—data are often held both on-site and in the cloud, as well as in different and sometimes mobile devices, security is becoming more and more important and poses an increasingly complex problem.

Depending on the market environment, security issues can easily lead to issues with a company's reputation and thus have a direct impact on revenue. Even putting reputation aside, security issues such as data leakage can lead to reduced revenue (e.g., if strategic information reaches a competitor).

Reduced Total Cost of Ownership

Budget considerations

Considering that new challenges and demands are always facing IT, you might expect that there is a bigger budget for the projects related to these challenges. However, the business reality is usually different; the budget is often the same or even less than before. In the long run, the introduction of new devices and applications is supposed to reduce the total cost of IT or generate greater business value that makes up for the costs involved. Despite all identified challenges and the introduction of new technologies and processes, it's generally expected that total cost of ownership (TCO) must not rise or must at least be below the expected profit (return on investment, ROI).

Nondisruptiveness

Zero downtime

Nondisruptiveness affects all stakeholders—from decision makers to IT departments to end users. Decision makers expect a high—if not 100%—availability of business systems because failure can mean stopped business and increased costs. The end user expects a similar high availability because, otherwise, he can't do his work. In turn, IT departments are accountable to the decision makers and end users, and they must ensure nondisruptiveness as a consequence. Thus, a requirement of all involved stakeholders—from executive to end user—is the desire for zero downtime. The installation of new solutions, technologies, or applications must not lead to failures in the system or reduce application availability.

The difference between availability (which we've already discussed) and nondisruptiveness may not be obvious; however, nondisruptiveness differs from availability in that it specifically refers to cases in which new applications, technologies, solutions, or processes are implemented. In our usage here, we define *availability* as the technical implementation of improvements in the availability of processes, and so on, while *nondisruptiveness* is concerned with the implementation of new technologies, and so on, without disturbing the ongoing operations.

Keep in mind that we're talking about enterprise software here. For the casual end user, a downtime of a system might be an annoyance but is seldom critical in terms of financial security or success for enterprise software; however, downtime can be critical to the financial success and the survival of a company.

1.1.2   Infrastructures

Today's business applications have more than just UI challenges—they also face infrastructure challenges. Figure 1.1 shows a typical abstracted infrastructure as found in most companies.

Infrastructure;
Point-to-point
solutions

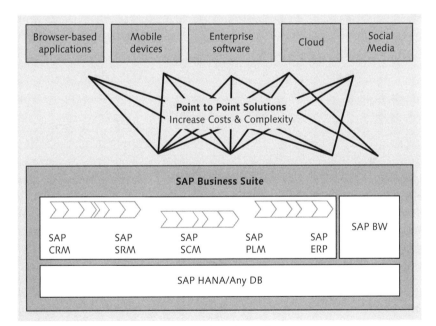

Figure 1.1 Point-to-Point Solutions: Costly and Complex

> **Note**
>
> As an example, Figure 1.1 focuses on SAP backend systems. However, these same types of infrastructure challenges exist even for non-SAP companies.

> In addition, note that these challenges apply to cloud scenarios as well (i.e., if the backend is cloud-based). Hybrid scenarios, for obvious reasons, also apply here (mix of on-premise and on-demand scenarios).

As you can see, business data are stored in one or more—often several—backend systems. The business processes exist in these systems or are mapped there, and access to the backend systems is usually realized using proprietary solutions or access methods (e.g., remote function calls [RFCs] or web services). This infrastructure is complex, to say the least.

In an attempt to simplify this infrastructure, many backend systems now offer a web interface. A web interface already opens the backend systems to a wide range of devices. However, it just takes a look at one of the points mentioned before—integration—to realize that this isn't sufficient. The access methods and interfaces provided by the various backend systems can't be integrated easily because the content of the information provided via HTTP is—in contrast to HTTP as a protocol—not standardized.

Classic infrastructure
A closer look at the infrastructure reveals that in addition to the various backend systems, a variety of devices or channels have to be supported. Despite web enablement of the backend systems, this often leads to a point-to-point scenario in classic infrastructures with classic backend systems. In other words, each backend system must be approached individually. In addition to that, each channel comes with its own requirements; that is, access for each channel can't be realized in the same way. To support a channel, it's necessary to build an individual application for each channel. In a worst-case scenario, this means it's necessary to create an individual application for each channel and each backend system. This approach, though not uncommon, is ineffective, expensive, and potentially insecure.

To support the requirements of today's business applications fully, a solution that unifies access to the backend systems and abstracts the common aspects of the channels is much better. For that kind of solution, it's only necessary to implement channel-specific functionality and rely on common coding for the rest. An additional benefit of this approach is the availability and price of good developers. While backend experts are often scarce and expensive, developers for specific channels and technologies (e.g., Java developers, .NET developers) are more commonly available and less pricey.

One approach to realize this is the use of open standards. Open standards that are implemented in systems or an intermediate layer allow abstraction of the specifics of the backend systems to an extent that the frontend developers only have to worry about the actual application development.

Open standards

A second approach—cloud computing—focuses particularly on the availability and cost. Simplified cloud computing is the outsourcing of data and applications into the network. (We use the term *network* instead of *Internet* because it's possible to implement cloud computing in different network setups, not only the Internet.)

Cloud computing is about using either hardware or software resources provided by or through the network. What makes the approach special is that the resources are provided as services. Accordingly, it's possible to distinguish between the following:

Cloud

▶ **Infrastructure as a Service (IaaS)**
IaaS is the most basic form of cloud computing. In this case, the service provider offers only the infrastructure, without an operating system. Operating systems and software must be installed by the user of the service. A common approach in this area is to create complete system images and upload them to the cloud. The service provider in turn often uses virtual machines to operate the images.

▶ **Platform as a Service (PaaS)**
In this approach, the supplier also provides the operating system and additional software on demand. Thus, the user no longer needs to worry about hardware or software and can concentrate on the actual task in the system.

▶ **Software as a Service (SaaS)**
Finally, this approach goes one step further in that the service provider offers applications directly to the user. All tasks involved when it comes to maintenance of the application are with the service provider.

Public and private cloud

In addition to these three types of cloud computing, there is also a public cloud and a private cloud. While the public cloud is usually an open cloud that is available on a public network—that is, the Internet—a private cloud exists within the confined spaces of a private network, for example, an enterprise. In general, it's also possible to implement a private cloud that can be accessed via the Internet; however, the private cloud is always implemented so that it's only accessible to a specific service user. The private cloud is especially important for implementing the security requirements of many companies.

Hybrid cloud

An interesting combination of a public cloud, private cloud, and on-premise resources are hybrid clouds. Hybrid clouds use a mix of those installations to gain the most flexibility (e.g., moving workloads from a private cloud to a public cloud during peak usages).

Additional Resources

The subject of cloud computing is complex—entire books can and have been written about it. The information presented here is meant only as an introduction. For more in-depth information on cloud computing, we recommend *Operating SAP in the Cloud: Landscapes and Infrastructures* (SAP PRESS, 2016), which can be found at *www.sap-press.com/3841*.

With all of the challenges and different options out there, it's essential to find a solution that works from the perspective of both the UI and the infrastructure.

1.2   SAP Gateway for Modern Business Applications

To briefly summarize the requirements discussed in the previous section, an intuitive and attractive UI for each application type is essential for a successful application. The supporting infrastructure should enable innovation and business orientation, while at the same time allow for high availability and flexibility. In addition, integration, maintainability, and security must be ensured. To top things off, the costs should be kept low, and changes to the infrastructure should happen without disruptions—this includes the rollout of processes and applications.

That description is the exact goal of SAP Gateway. SAP Gateway pro- **REST and OData** vides an open, REST-based interface (Representational State Transfer) that implements simple access to SAP systems via the OData protocol. OData is widely used as an open protocol that was standardized in its most recent version, version 4, and is optimized for UIs and interaction. SAP chose the OData standard for SAP Gateway because it's widely used, well-known, and easy to learn; members of the OASIS OData Technical Committee responsible for development are companies such as IBM, CA, SAP, and Microsoft. (For more on OData, see Chapter 2.)

SAP Gateway provides simple, secure, and controlled access to SAP data via an open standard, abstracting the specifics of the SAP Business Suite systems. Refer back to the point-to-point solutions diagram in Figure 1.1, and now compare that to Figure 1.2, which shows SAP Gateway as a single solution that replaces all other point-to-point solutions.

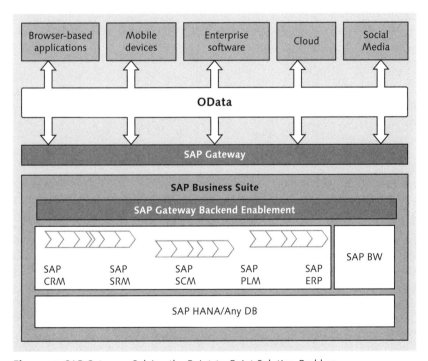

Figure 1.2 SAP Gateway: Solving the Point-to-Point Solution Problem

SAP Gateway layer

As shown in Figure 1.2, SAP Gateway is a layer between the channels (devices, applications, etc.) and the SAP Business Suite systems—more specifically, SAP NetWeaver ABAP-based systems. This layer allows you to mask the sometimes-complex processes and data structures in the SAP Business Suite systems and present them to the outside world in a simplified way. In addition, SAP Gateway unifies access to SAP Business Suite data and processes via the OData protocol and thus opens the SAP world to virtually any developer who understands OData. Knowledge of SAP specifics isn't required.

By addressing non-SAP developers, SAP Gateway makes it possible to keep applications more flexible. For example, if an end user needs an application to access SAP data for Microsoft Office, a Microsoft developer can do the job without detailed knowledge of SAP. The applications can be implemented faster and better because it's now possible for the respective expert to build the application. This is especially important because UI technologies are evolving, so frontend applications change more frequently than backend processes.

> **Note**
>
> Control of the SAP Business Suite data and processes remain with the authorized persons who manage the SAP Business Suite systems. The rights and restrictions of the end user in the SAP Business Suite system are passed to the frontend application. Thus, it's neither intentionally nor accidentally possible for the application developer to gain or provide access to data that doesn't fall within the authorizations of the user.

SAP Gateway workflow

Figure 1.3 shows the workflow for application creation with SAP Gateway. You start by setting up a project for each application, and the project team defines the scenario and the processes to be implemented. Such a project team may consist of a variety of experts, for example, a BPX, a frontend developer, a backend developer, and probably a project manager and designer.

SAP Gateway project interfaces

With SAP Gateway, experts can speak in one language. It's not important to the frontend developer what the backend developer does in detail; in turn, the backend developer doesn't need to know the details of the frontend development. Discussions take place only on the data and processes level. Defined interfaces between the involved stakeholders facilitate discussions between the experts and reduce technology discussions to a minimum. This simplification and facilitation applies to all experts that are involved in a project. As shown in Figure 1.3, experts can then focus on their area of expertise. While the backend developer creates and exposes services to the frontend developer, the frontend developer can focus on the frontend creation. Using OData, the frontend used can be nearly any device and technology.

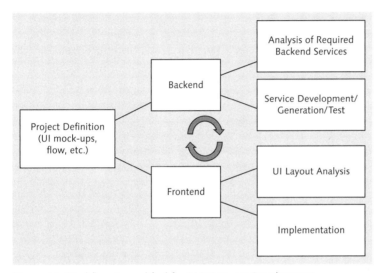

Figure 1.3 Workflow Exemplified for SAP Gateway Development

The approach described here is only one approach. Due to the different configurations of SAP Business Suite systems, it's also possible that a single frontend developer builds applications for the existing data and services, which are already provided in the SAP Business Suite systems. This means development with SAP Gateway scales from individual developers to large project teams.

Project scalability

To summarize briefly, SAP Gateway provides a centralized interface for the SAP world (i.e., for all SAP NetWeaver ABAP-based backend systems) based on open industry standards. By supporting multichannel access instead of focusing only on the mobile channel, the use cases for SAP Gateway applications are vast.

> **Note**
>
> Other SAP technologies support OData as well. Some of them support OData by design, and others use SAP Gateway technology to achieve OData enablement. Overall, it's important to understand that OData is the accepted standard across SAP products.

So does SAP Gateway meet the requirements? Let's have a look at the list:

Multichannel support

- ▶ **Intuitive, appealing UI**
  With SAP Gateway, the frontend developer has the opportunity to completely focus on the application to be developed and to devote maximum attention to the UI. By using specific—partially proprietary—tools for the specific channel, the user paradigm and experience of each channel can be implemented in an optimal way.

- ▶ **Innovation**
  With SAP Gateway application development, the implementation of new processes becomes more flexible. Innovation can be achieved more easily, and SAP Gateway reduces costs for the rollout. Changes need to be made only where change is really taking place. For example, if there is already an application for travel booking on an iPhone, it isn't necessary to touch the backend system to implement the same functionality for Microsoft Kinect. Only the frontend development for the new platform is required, and this frontend development can benefit from the already built applications for other channels.

- ▶ **Business orientation**
  With the flexibility in terms of channel (multichannel support) and developers, it's easy to develop applications that respect the requirements of the business reality the end user is living in. In certain scenarios, it might even be possible for the BPX to build the application.

- ▶ **Availability**
  Multichannel support increases the availability of data and processes. SAP Gateway ensures access to backend data and processes at almost any time.

> **Offline Scenarios**
>
> Offline scenarios pose special situations that have to be considered individually. We'll take a short look at offline scenarios in Appendix A.

▶ **Agility**
Development cycles can be shortened through the use of SAP Gateway. Accordingly, agility increases.

▶ **Integration**
Integration first takes place in the backend, which is now essentially one unit, instead of several. Then it takes place in the frontend, which profits from the use of standards. More specifically, each frontend that supports the standard can directly benefit from it. Frontends that don't understand or support the standard in any way normally can be integrated through individual applications.

▶ **Maintenance and security**
The security of data remains with the administrators of the backend systems, and the same applies to maintenance of the backend systems. Maintenance of the frontend systems is different, though, because it's dependent on the channel used. For specific needs in this area, SAP offers, for example, the SAP Mobile Platform, which allows remote maintenance of mobile applications.

▶ **Costs**
By shortening the development cycle and allowing the experts to focus on their respective areas of expertise, development costs can be reduced. In addition to already mentioned aspects, the main reason for this benefit is a reduction in friction between the different stakeholders. In addition, the implementation of SAP Gateway is relatively cheap and easy; if you're already an SAP customer, you may already have the relevant licenses. As we discuss in more detail in Chapter 4, SAP Gateway comes preinstalled with SAP NetWeaver 7.40 or can be implemented without disruption in an existing landscape.

▶ **Nondisruptiveness**
Finally, as you'll see in the next section, the installation and deployment for SAP Gateway is simple and nondisruptive.

In short, SAP Gateway is SAP's answer to developing business applications that provide the UIs and backend infrastructures required by today's modern users. In addition, SAP Gateway can be an essential part of any infrastructure that enables digital transformation.

1.3   Installation and Deployment

If you want to use SAP Gateway in production and already own the relevant licenses, you can download the SAP Gateway package from the SAP Service Marketplace at *http://support.sap.com/swdc* by choosing INSTALLATIONS AND UPGRADES • BROWSE OUR DOWNLOAD CATALOG • SAP NETWEAVER AND COMPLEMENTARY PRODUCTS • SAP GATEWAY • SAP GATEWAY 2.0. Note that this is only necessary with SAP NetWeaver versions prior to 7.40 SPS 02; starting with this release, SAP Gateway doesn't have to be downloaded but is instead included in the SAP NetWeaver release. However, for some scenarios, the download of additional plug-ins might be necessary. Those plug-ins can be found on the SAP Support Portal (*http://support.sap.com*) as well.

SAP Developer Centers

If you simply want to test SAP Gateway as a developer or in any other function, you can access SAP Gateway easily by visiting the Resources for SAP Developers site at *http://developers.sap.com* and choosing EXPLORE && DISCOVER • TOOLS & SDKS • SAP GATEWAY. Using SAP Developer Centers—the center for SAP Gateway is only one among many—you can easily get access to SAP products for development purposes. In addition, you'll get access to SAP product information and opportunities for free training. The RESOURCES FOR SAP DEVELOPERS site will link you to the different developer center pages and give you access to communities that will support you in your development efforts. In addition, it's a good starting point to understand how different products—including SAP Gateway—fit into the overall picture of SAP's product offering.

After you have SAP Gateway downloaded or have gotten it as part of your SAP NetWeaver installation (> 7.40), you're ready for installation and deployment.

Note

This section provides only a brief overview of the installation and deployment process. For a detailed discussion, see Chapter 4.

1.3.1　Installation

Table 1.1 and Table 1.2 list the requirements that must be met to oper- ate SAP Gateway. The minimum hardware requirements are very easy to meet. This has two advantages: cost-effective systems for companies even after scaling and easy installation (even for non-developers such as business experts).

Installation requirements

Entity	Mimimum Requirement
Processor	Dual Core (two logical CPUs) with 2GHz
Main memory/RAM	8GB or higher
Hard disk capacity	80GB primary, or higher

Table 1.1 Minimum Hardware Requirements for SAP Gateway

Entity	Requirement	
SAP NetWeaver Stack	The latest kernel patch for the corresponding SAP NetWeaver version has to be applied.	
	Core Components (GW_CORE and IW_FND)	▸ SAP NetWeaver 7.0 SPS 25 ▸ SAP NetWeaver 7.01 SPS 10 ▸ SAP NetWeaver 7.02 SPS 07 ▸ SAP NetWeaver 7.03 SPS 01 ▸ SAP NetWeaver 7.31 SPS 01
	Core Component (SAP_GWFND) Comprises functional scope of IW_FND, GW_CORE, IW_BEP, and IW_HDB.	▸ SAP NetWeaver 7.40 SPS 01
	Business Enablement Provisioning Component (IW_BEP)	▸ SAP NetWeaver 7.0 SPS 18 ▸ SAP NetWeaver 7.01 SPS 03 ▸ SAP NetWeaver 7.02 SPS 06 ▸ SAP NetWeaver 7.03 SPS 01 ▸ SAP NetWeaver 7.31 SPS 01

Table 1.2 Minimum Software Requirements

Entity	Requirement	
	Content Adapter Components (IW_PGW) Screen Scraping Component (IW_SCS)	▸ SAP NetWeaver 7.0 SPS 18 ▸ SAP NetWeaver 7.01 SPS 03 ▸ SAP NetWeaver 7.02 SPS 06 ▸ SAP NetWeaver 7.03 SPS 01 ▸ SAP NetWeaver 7.31 SPS 01 ▸ SAP NetWeaver 7.40 SPS 01
	Content Adapter Component (IW_SPI)	▸ SAP NetWeaver 7.02 SPS 06 ▸ SAP NetWeaver 7.03 SPS 01 ▸ SAP NetWeaver 7.31 SPS 01 ▸ SAP NetWeaver 7.40 SPS 01
	Content Adapter Component (IW_HDB)	▸ SAP NetWeaver 7.02 SPS 09 ▸ SAP NetWeaver 7.03 SPS 01 ▸ SAP NetWeaver 7.31 SPS 01 ▸ Minimal requirement of SAP HANA database version: SAP HANA 1.0 SPS 02
	Content Adapter Component (IW_GIL)	▸ SAP NetWeaver 7.01 SPS 03 ▸ SAP NetWeaver 7.02 SPS 06 ▸ SAP NetWeaver 7.03 SPS 01 ▸ SAP NetWeaver 7.31 SPS 01 ▸ SAP NetWeaver 7.40 SPS 01
	Content Components (IW_CNT and IW_CBS)	▸ SAP NetWeaver 7.02 SPS 07 ▸ SAP NetWeaver 7.03 SPS 01 ▸ SAP NetWeaver 7.31 SPS 01 ▸ SAP NetWeaver 7.40 SPS 01
SAP WEB UIF	Core Component Version (IW_FND 250)	▸ SAP WEB UIF 7.01 SP 01 ▸ SAP WEB UIF 7.31 SP 00
	Optional Core Component (IW_FNDGC [for generic channel]*)	▸ SAP WEB UIF 7.46 SP 00 ▸ SAP WEB UIF 7.47 SP 00

Table 1.2 Minimum Software Requirements (Cont.)

Entity	Requirement	
SAP WEB UIF (Cont.)	Content Adapter Component (IW_GIL)	▸ SAP WEB UIF 7.0 SP 03 ▸ SAP WEB UIF 7.01 SP 00 ▸ SAP WEB UIF 7.31 SP 00 ▸ SAP WEB UIF 7.46 SP 00 ▸ SAP WEB UIF 7.47 SP 00
SAP Backend	SAP Business Suite system	
*This component is only necessary if integration scenarios depending on the generic channel will be upgraded. In a fresh installation, it's not necessary.		

Table 1.2 Minimum Software Requirements (Cont.)

1.3.2   Deployment

Two main deployment options are available for SAP Gateway: the hub deployment and the embedded deployment. However, the hub deployment can be subsequently split into two different deployment scenarios: development on the backend system and development on the hub itself. We'll discuss all three options next.

Embedded versus hub deployment

SAP NetWeaver 7.40

The deployment options for SAP Gateway normally include a decision about where to put which component of the product. However, this changes with SAP NetWeaver 7.40. SAP NetWeaver 7.40 includes SAP Gateway and installs SAP_GWFND as part of the standard installation. SAP_GWFND includes the functional scope of IW_BEP, GW_CORE, IW_FND, and IW_HDB. With SAP NetWeaver 7.40, each system can function either as the hub or backend.

Embedded Deployment

Embedded deployment means that the services are registered and published in the SAP Business Suite backend system. In terms of core components, we talk about IW_FND and GW_CORE for older versions and SAP_GWFND for SAP NetWeaver 7.40 or later.

The main benefit of embedded deployment is that the runtime overhead is reduced by one remote call. The main drawback is that if you use several SAP Business Suite systems, you'll have to configure SAP Gateway

Benefits and drawbacks

for every system. In addition, you can't use an embedded system as a hub for other backend systems; that is, routing and composition can't be used.

As a word of caution, we don't recommend using an SAP Business Suite system with an embedded deployment of SAP Gateway as a hub system for an additional backend system. In that specific scenario, the version of the hub system may be lower than the version of the SAP Gateway backend components on the remote backend system. In many companies, there are strict policies about when to update which systems. This can lead to a situation in which the hub system can't be upgraded, while the backend system already is.

To avoid this situation, use either of the following:

▸ Embedded deployment for your SAP Business Suite systems

▸ Dedicated SAP Gateway hub systems with the latest release version of SAP Gateway

> **Note**
>
> For details on dependencies between IW_BEP and IW_FND, check SAP Note 1830198.

Hub Deployment

This deployment scenario uses a dedicated server—the hub system—for the SAP Gateway functionalities.

Development on the Backend System

The first option of hub deployment is used in situations where the services are deployed on the backend systems and only registered on the server. The SAP Gateway server functionalities are only used on the dedicated server (hub). On the backend system, IW_BEP is deployed (or SAP_GWFND for SAP NetWeaver 7.40 or later).

The benefit of this hub deployment is that the system works as a single point of access to the backend systems. On this system, routing and composition of multiple systems is supported. Using this kind of hub system allows the system to be on a newer release, which enables the use of up-to-date functionality, for example, the latest authentication options or SAPUI5. In this scenario, security is improved because there is no direct access to the backend system. At the same time, the deployment allows direct access to local metadata (Data Dictionary, DDIC) and business data, which reduces runtime overhead.

> **Note**
>
> The hub system shouldn't be an SAP Business Suite system; instead, it should be an SAP NetWeaver ABAP Application Server (AS). This is true for both hub deployment options.

Development on the Hub

The second option of hub deployment should be used in situations where either access to the backend system is restricted (i.e., the backend system may not be touched) or development on the backend isn't possible. It should also be used on releases prior to SAP NetWeaver 7.40 when an installation of IW_BEP on the backend isn't allowed. In this form of hub deployment, server functionalities are only used on the SAP Gateway hub system, and—in contrast to the first option—service deployment takes place on the hub.

Hub development

The benefits of this hub deployment are that the backend systems don't have to be touched; that is, there's no need to install or upgrade SAP Gateway add-ons on the backend. In addition, services developed by third-party developers don't need a deployment on the backend system.

Benefits

There are also some other drawbacks:

► An additional server is needed for SAP Gateway.

► Access to the backend is limited to remote-enabled interfaces, for example, RFCs, Business Application Programming Interfaces (BAPIs), SAP Business Warehouse (BW) Easy Queries, and Service Provider Interface objects. These interfaces might not be optimal for usage on the hub.

► Generic Interaction Layer (GenIL) objects can't be accessed remotely, and there is no direct local access to metadata (DDIC) and business data.

Summary

As you can see from this short overview, SAP Gateway deployment is—especially with SAP NetWeaver 7.40 or later—simple and not cost intensive. The different options allow an installation in nearly every setup or infrastructure. However, the choice for a deployment largely depends on the requirements of the infrastructure in which SAP Gateway is installed. (Again, for a detailed discussion of an SAP Gateway deployment, see Chapter 4.)

> **Note**
>
> For further discussion of the pros and cons of embedded versus hub deployment, we recommend the following: *http://help.sap.com/saphelp_nw74/helpdata/de/3E/B1EA508F88BB7EE10000000A445394/content.htm.*

1.4   SAP Gateway and Related Products

When the first edition of this book was written, SAP Gateway was the only product in the market that allowed access to SAP Business Suite using REST and OData. This has changed, as some SAP products have adopted and integrated SAP Gateway technology to gain access to SAP Business Suite using REST and OData. The integration of SAP Gateway technology stresses the importance of SAP Gateway as a product and shows that SAP Gateway has a huge impact on many classic and brand-new scenarios involving SAP business systems.

Let's take a look at some related products and how they compare to SAP Gateway.

> **Note**
>
> The following comparison and positioning of SAP Gateway and other SAP products provides a basic understanding of SAP Gateway in the context of other SAP products. It's not an official SAP position and doesn't claim to be complete.

1.4.1 SAP Gateway for Microsoft

Before SAP Gateway was launched in 2011 at SAPPHIRE NOW, Microsoft—together with SAP—released a product that was already based on a predecessor of SAP Gateway: Duet Enterprise. Duet Enterprise was officially launched on February 1, 2011, and marked a new level of collaboration between Microsoft and SAP. Today the circle closes with the offering of SAP Gateway for Microsoft (GWM).

Product comparison

GWM was built to address SAP and Microsoft interoperability. Because over 90% of SAP customers already use Microsoft products, SAP and Microsoft interoperability is of some importance. GWM provides a flexible framework that allows you to build applications that use SAP content from Microsoft.

Microsoft interoperability

Therefore, if you're familiar and working with Microsoft technology, you can stay with what you know and use GWM to build applications based on SAP content. GWM supports all major Microsoft platforms, such as Office 365, Office 2013, Office 2010, Microsoft Azure, and any C#-based application (with GWM SP 03) (see Figure 1.4).

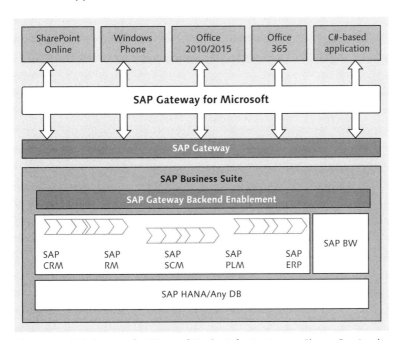

Figure 1.4 SAP Gateway for Microsoft in the Infrastructure as Shown Previously

GWM can be deployed in the cloud—more specifically, the Microsoft Azure cloud. This is true as of GWM SP 03. GWM also supports hybrid scenarios (i.e., a mixture of on-premise and on-demand scenario). This means that you could connect an SAP system to Microsoft using the Microsoft cloud in a secure, scalable, and most importantly nondisruptive way.

As you can see, GWM is partially based on SAP Gateway and can be considered a natural fit to SAP Gateway in SAP Microsoft interoperability scenarios because it takes care of the Microsoft-specific aspects of developing applications for the SAP Business Suite.

GWM benefits It's possible to build applications for Microsoft integration scenarios with SAP Gateway only, but you'll miss out on the advantages that GWM offers, for example, built-in interoperability for the following:

- Single sign-on (SSO)
- Security
- Scalability
- Monitoring
- Templates for different scenarios (e.g., Outlook scenarios)
- Simplified integration into C#-based projects

In summary, GWM eliminates a lot of unnecessary work for the developer with built-in interoperability and thus makes GWM a natural fit for SAP Gateway in SAP Microsoft interoperability scenarios.

1.4.2 SAP Enterprise Portal

SAP Enterprise Portal works as a single point of access to all of your business information—SAP and non-SAP—through a simple web browser. SAP Enterprise Portal is role-based and secure.

SAP NetWeaver Portal? SAP Enterprise Portal?

Due to the same naming simplification that made SAP NetWeaver Gateway become SAP Gateway, the SAP NetWeaver Portal became the SAP Enterprise Portal. As mentioned earlier, you can find additional information here: *http://*

---

scn.sap.com/community/netweaver/blog/2014/05/30/sap-netweaver-brand-ing-simplification.

Note too, that you'll still find the old naming in some documentation, but that doesn't make the documentation obsolete. It just means that the documentation was valid before the naming simplification and most likely still is.

As an integration platform that supports different UI technologies, SAP Enterprise Portal is a natural fit for SAP Gateway. As a complementary product, let's look at the benefits of using SAP Gateway with SAP Enterprise Portal.

Integration platform

First, let's look at some of the requirements customers have today when it comes to SAP Enterprise Portal:

▸ Introduction of new UIs

▸ Mobilization of existing content

▸ Central governance and management of SAP Gateway-based applications

▸ Creation of an external-facing web presence with information from SAP and non-SAP systems while taking advantage of the benefits of SAP Enterprise Portal and SAP Gateway

To fulfill those requirements, the following key capabilities are offered:

SAP Enterprise Portal capabilities

▸ Management of SAP Gateway applications based on existing roles using SAPUI5 iViews (for more on this, see *http://help.sap.com/saphelp_nw74/helpdata/en/fc/5b37515e517262e10000000a44538d/content.htm*)

▸ Usage of SAP Enterprise Portal as a central, scalable, and secure UI integration hub for SAP Gateway applications

▸ Easy deployment of SAP Gateway applications to SAP Enterprise Portal

▸ Development of SAP Enterprise Portal content by developers without traditional SAP skills via the integration of SAP Gateway data sources (see *http://help.sap.com/saphelp_nw74/helpdata/en/07/13829caa59408a82448784dd6428cd/frameset.htm* or *http://help.sap.com/saphelp_nw73/helpdata/en/c5/322d3d85c34704a8121864a31074bb/frameset.htm*)

To sum this up, SAP Gateway allows easy deployment of applications to SAP Enterprise Portal. SAP Enterprise Portal thus provides a role-based, secure, single point of access to these applications, while using existing, scalable infrastructure. Furthermore, SAP Gateway applications can leverage existing portal-based assets (e.g., documents, search, roles).

In short, SAP Gateway and SAP Enterprise Portal in combination are a natural fit, and thus SAP Enterprise Portal officially supports SAP Gateway services consumption since SAP NetWeaver 7.3 SPS 08.

1.4.3 SAP Mobile Platform

Although SAP Mobile Platform also allows access to SAP's business systems through mobile devices, it's different from SAP Gateway in a number of ways. Most notably, SAP Gateway allows multichannel access to the SAP Business Suite, which includes—but isn't limited to—access through mobile devices. In fact, as you can see from Figure 1.5, SAP Mobile Platform actually includes SAP Gateway (Java).

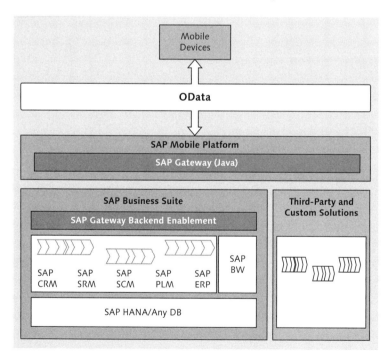

Figure 1.5 SAP Mobile Platform and SAP Gateway

Together, SAP Gateway and SAP Mobile Platform provide complementary functionality based on their core purpose—multichannel and mobile support. The combined usage of SAP Gateway and SAP Mobile Platform leads to the best results—SAP Gateway in enabling OData for your Business Suite and SAP Mobile Platform in mobilizing your applications. However, there are scenarios where SAP Mobile Platform is the main player, and SAP Gateway as such may not even be part of the infrastructure.

SAP Mobile Platform and SAP Gateway

However, SAP Mobile Platform now comes with its own SAP Gateway component, SAP Gateway (Java). This is also sometimes referred to as Integration Gateway. This component facilitates OData provisioning in SAP Mobile Platform 3.0. In some scenarios, this may be beneficial because it can remove the need to install a separate SAP Gateway hub server.

The SAP Gateway component in SAP Mobile Platform 3.0 features the following:

▶ **Design time**

- ▶ Easy OData modeling through an interactive UI
- ▶ OData service implementation: Attribute mapping between source and target (for request and response messages)
- ▶ OData service deployment

▶ **Runtime**

- ▶ Configuration of backend destinations
- ▶ Registration, activation, and deactivation of OData services
- ▶ Destination assignment to provisioned services
- ▶ OData service documents and server log files access

The fact that SAP Mobile Platform 3.0 contains an SAP Gateway component stresses the importance of SAP Gateway and the functionality it provides. With SAP Gateway, SAP Mobile Platform 3.0, and SAP NetWeaver 7.40 (with SAP Gateway included), you have great flexibility in implementing the OData enablement of SAP Business Suite and even in the integration of third-party and custom solutions.

1.4.4 SAP HANA

How does SAP Gateway integrate with SAP HANA? More importantly, why would you want SAP Gateway and SAP HANA to work together?

In-memory

Before we start answering those questions, let's consider what SAP HANA is. SAP HANA converges database and application platform capabilities *in-memory* to transform transactions, analytics, text analysis, and predictive and spatial processing so businesses can operate in real time.

Now let's consider what users expect. SAP HANA's calculation capabilities are one part of the equation; another part of the equation is easy provisioning of SAP Business Suite logic. In general, users expect a way to consume data from SAP HANA as well as data from the SAP Business Suite in a lighter and thus standard way. This is something that the combination of SAP Gateway and SAP HANA can offer. With the combination of those two technologies, it's possible to enrich SAP Gateway object property values with SAP HANA query results. In terms of access, it's possible to explore SAP HANA objects using SAP Gateway, while SAP Gateway allows easy provisioning of data in OData and enables transactional access to the SAP Business Suite.

Total cost of development (TCD)

As a result of these benefits, the combination of SAP Gateway and SAP HANA reduces the total cost of development (TCD) through standard access and provisioning in OData. When it comes to security, the separation of the SAP Business Suite from external consumers allows an enormous improvement and uses a secure infrastructure.

With the latest versions of the SAP Business Suite, *SAP Business Suite on SAP HANA*, and *SAP S/4HANA*, SAP has chosen to leverage the benefits of the SAP Gateway framework running on top of SAP HANA.

1.4.5 SAP Process Integration and SAP Process Orchestration

System-to-system vs. system-to-user

SAP Process Integration (PI) is an enterprise application integration (EAI) platform. Its main purpose is the exchange of information between different systems within a company and especially between a company and third parties (e.g., partners, suppliers).

SAP Process Orchestration (PO) is a combination of SAP PI, SAP Business Process Management (BPM), and SAP Business Rules Management (BRM).

The main difference between SAP Gateway and SAP PI is their respective use cases: while SAP PI is focused on system-to-system communication, SAP Gateway is focused on system-to-user communication.

Today, this assessment is still true, yet we also see some overlap. With SAP PO 7.31 SPS 13 and SAP PO 7.40 SPS 08, SAP Gateway is now part of SAP PO. Similar to SAP Mobile Platform, you can now expose SAP Gateway services from your SAP backend system directly from the SAP PO server. In some scenarios, this may be beneficial because it can remove the need to install a separate SAP Gateway hub server.

SAP Gateway on SAP PO provides the following features:

▶ Single and unified mechanism for exposing services via REST/OData

▶ Single platform for all integration needs

▶ Provisioning of business logic implemented in Java via simple API

SAP Gateway isn't competing with SAP PO and SAP PI—quite the opposite, actually. Both products can benefit from each other. Especially in scenarios where it makes sense to implement SAP PO as the central SAP Gateway hub.

1.4.6 SAP Business Warehouse

SAP BW is one of SAP's business intelligence solutions. It can analyze huge amounts of data and present this data in an intuitive and easily readable way through reports. With the combination of SAP BW and SAP Gateway, it's possible to expose SAP BW data through lightweight consumption using OData and also to create content in this scenario using SAP BW standard tools such as BEx Query Designer or through the multidimensional expressions (MDX) interface. In addition, several benefits can be achieved by combining the two products:

Analyzing data

▶ **Total cost of development (TCD)**
In this scenario, content can be easily created without any coding at all, so it's possible to lower TCD dramatically.

▸ **Multichannel support**
SAP Gateway adds multichannel support, thus exposing existing SAP BW content to virtually any UI channel and broadening the reach of this existing content.

▸ **Consumption tools**
With SAP Gateway consumption tools, it's easily possible to create simple analytical applications on nearly any client.

▸ **Security**
Adding SAP Gateway means adding an additional middle layer and thus protecting the SAP BW system from direct (external) access.

1.4.7 SAP Fiori

SAP Fiori and SAP Gateway

SAP Fiori is the new user experience for SAP products. Its main goal is to apply modern design principles to complex business processes and the involved software products. SAP Fiori focuses on overcoming the challenges mentioned earlier in this chapter and does so based on SAP Gateway.

Because we take a dedicated look at the SAP Fiori in Chapters 8 and 9, we only mention it here briefly to give you a first impression and let you know that it's based on SAP Gateway.

1.4.8 SAP API Management

SAP API Management and SAP Gateway

SAP API Management is a somewhat new addition to SAP's product portfolio. It's sometimes considered a competing product to SAP Gateway, which it isn't. However, it's a very important topic and an interesting addition to any infrastructure in which SAP Gateway is used, so we decided to dedicate a complete appendix to it. We take a detailed look at SAP API Management and SAP Gateway in Appendix B.

1.5 Summary

In this first chapter, we outlined the challenges modern business applications face today. We took a look at the problem that enterprise applications face when it comes to accessing backend systems and introduced the classical point-to-point solution that is often implemented. After identifying the challenges and introducing the point-to-point approach, we showed how SAP Gateway can be a solution to those challenges and simplify the infrastructure for enterprise applications.

A close look at SAP Gateway revealed how it works in general and how it can be installed or used easily by everyone. Finally, we took a look at the positioning in the market and eventually put SAP Gateway in the context of other SAP products.

In the next chapter, we'll move past the basic introductory material and get into some technical details—specifically, we'll introduce you to the OData protocol in the context of SAP Gateway.

In this chapter, you'll learn all about OData—the underlying industry standard that SAP Gateway enables.

2   Introduction to OData

OData is a short and very memorable name for something big: a protocol that is here to open up the data silos of the IT world's big players and that will stay to change IT forever. In this chapter, you'll read about Open Data Protocol (OData) and its foundations (REST). You'll learn about the structure of an OData service and the operations and query options supported by OData. Finally, to show you the importance of this protocol for SAP, we'll provide a short overview of OData in SAP solutions.

In short, this chapter works as an OData jump-start to equip you with the OData background and basics needed for SAP Gateway.

2.1   OData and REST

Because OData is a REST-based protocol, we'll start this chapter with a brief introduction to both.

2.1.1   What Is REST?

A term that you frequently come across when talking about OData is *Representational State Transfer (REST)*. OData requests use the REST model, which was introduced in 2000 by Roy Fielding in his PhD dissertation; Fielding used it to judge the architecture style of software architectures. An architecture is called RESTful if it complies with six architectural constraints:

Six architectural restraints

▶ **Client server architecture**
A uniform interface separates clients from servers, resulting in a separation of concern.

▶ **Statelessness**
No context is stored on the server between requests. Any request from a client contains all required information to service the request.

▶ **Cacheability**
Responses have to define themselves as cacheable or not cacheable to prevent clients from using stale or inappropriate data in response to additional, later requests.

▶ **Layered system**
A client can't tell whether it's connected directly to the end server or to a server along the way.

▶ **Uniform interface**
A uniform interface between clients and servers decouples the architecture.

▶ **Code on demand**
Servers can temporarily extend or customize the functionality of a client by transferring executable code. This constraint is actually optional.

These constraints must be followed for an architecture to be considered RESTful. How you handle the actual implementation is your own choice, as long as you fulfill the mentioned constraints.

REST commands Each REST command is a request of one of the following types, informing the server from the client to perform one of the following operations on the server:

▶ GET
Get a single entry or a collection of entries.

▶ POST
Create a new entry.

▶ PUT
Update an existing entry.

- ▶ DELETE
  Remove an entry.

- ▶ PATCH
  Update single properties of an existing entry.

In a GET request, the response represents the retrieved data as an OData document. In POST and PUT, the client sends its data as an OData document in the request body. With POST, the server returns the created data in the response as an OData document. For DELETE, no document is exchanged.

POST, GET, PUT, and DELETE are supported by Create, Retrieve, Update, Delete (CRUD) interfaces on a server. An OData service might support all four interfaces, but this isn't mandatory. For instance, a service might only support data retrieval through a GET operation.

CRUD support

The most prominent example of a system that fully implements the principles of REST is the World Wide Web. This comes as no surprise because Fielding was a co-writer of the HTTP standard and wrote his dissertation to abstract the design principles from the concrete architecture of HTTP. A RESTful service takes advantage of the way the web works and benefits from its architecture.

> **Note**
>
> A common misconception is to think about REST as some kind of protocol, such as HTTP or Simple Object Access Protocol (SOAP). This is incorrect— REST is a development paradigm, not a protocol.

The key elements of a RESTful architecture are explained next.

Uniform Resource Identifiers

A uniform resource identifier (URI) identifies and locates a resource by the access method used (such as HTTP) and the location inside a network. The basic structure consists of an access method defining a scheme and a scheme-specific-part, which are separated by a colon:

<scheme>:<scheme-specific-part>

Every resource of a service that is important enough for a user to access has to have at least one URI. This URI can be bookmarked so that you can return to it later; you can also paste it in an email or a document. Through the OData protocol, entity sets or single entities are accessible via such URIs. The same is true for results of queries that use the query options of the OData protocol.

Links

HATEOAS   A server exposes a self-describing resource that can be manipulated by a client via a hypermedia link. The formal description of this concept is originally known as *Hypermedia as the Engine of Application State (HATEOAS)*. If we take a closer look at what's behind this intimidating description, we see that it's all about links. Links are well known from HTML, where they allow you to navigate from one web page to another.

As a RESTful protocol, OData offers links that can either read or manipulate the resource itself or navigate to other connected resources. For example, when entering the URI *https://sapes4.sapdevcenter.com/sap/opu/odata/IWBEP/GWSAMPLE_BASIC/SalesOrderSet('0500000000')?sap-ds-debug=true* in your web browser, you'll find the links shown in Figure 2.1 in the payload of the returned XML. To access the URI just mentioned, you have to sign up for the SAP Gateway – Demo Consumption System as described in the SCN document at *http://scn.sap.com/docs/DOC-40986*.

```
<link title="SalesOrder" href="SalesOrderSet('0500000000')" rel="self"/>
<link title="ToBusinessPartner" type="application/atom+xml;type=entry"
href="SalesOrderSet('0500000000')/ToBusinessPartner"
rel="http://schemas.microsoft.com/ado/2007/08/dataservices/related/ToBusinessPartner"/>
<link title="ToLineItems" type="application/atom+xml;type=feed" href="SalesOrderSet
('0500000000')/ToLineItems"
rel="http://schemas.microsoft.com/ado/2007/08/dataservices/related/ToLineItems"/>
```

Figure 2.1 Links of an OData Entity Type

The first link is the self-link that allows the resource (in this case, the sales order) to be manipulated (read, updated, deleted). The two other links offer navigation to related entity sets, namely the business partner to whom this sales order belongs and the sales order line items.

Uniform Interface

One of the main features of RESTful services is that they use existing HTTP verbs against addressable resources identified in the URI. Conceptually, it's a way of performing database-style CRUD operations on resources by using HTTP verbs.

HTTP verbs

Stateless Communication

All RESTful services, including OData, use stateless communication. Stateless communication means that a client has to provide all information in a request so that it can be processed by the server. Session states held by the server don't exist; session information is stored on the client instead.

Multiple Representations of a Resource

Any RESTful server (e.g., SAP Gateway) can deliver different representations of a resource (e.g., XML or JavaScript Object Notation, JSON). The advantage is that, for example, JSON can be more easily consumed by JavaScript clients.

XML or JSON

2.1.2 What Is OData?

OData is a REST-based data access protocol originally released under the Microsoft Open Specification Promise (OSP) for querying and updating data, which has since become an OASIS standard with its latest version. OData builds on broadly known and used industry standards such as Atom Publishing Protocol (AtomPub), XML, and JSON, which makes it easier to understand and use. It's consistent with the way the web works and follows its core principles, allowing for a new level of data integration and interoperability across traditional platform and manufacturer boundaries. It's easy to understand, extensible, and provides consumers with a predictable interface for accessing a variety of data sources. In short, OData can be seen as Online Database Connectivity (ODBC) for the web. It opens up the silos of traditional IT and increases the value of data by allowing for easier and broader data access.

MIX07 conference — OData started back in late April of 2007 at the Microsoft MIX07 conference. An incubation project code-named "Astoria" was started to find a way to transport data across HTTP to architect and develop web-based solutions more efficiently. The project goal was to "enable applications to expose data as a data service that can be consumed by web clients within a corporate network and across the Internet." Even then, most of the core concepts of OData were used: HTTP, URIs to identify the various pieces of information reachable through a service, and the usage of simple formats such as XML or JSON for the representation of data exchanged in interactions.

MIX10 conference — The next big milestone on the Microsoft side was the 2010 MIX Conference, where OData was officially announced by Doug Purdy of Microsoft during the keynote address. The name Open Data Protocol was chosen to indicate that the protocol is supposed to remain as open as possible, following the Open Data Philosophy. This school of thought follows the idea that certain data should be freely available to everyone to use and republish without restrictions from copyrights, patents, or other mechanisms of control. Microsoft first provided an OData software development kit (SDK) for download and announced that it would start to build OData support into a number of products, including SharePoint 2010 and Excel 2010. The OData protocol was consequently released under the OSP, which basically allows free usage of the protocol, inviting everyone to use it as a standard. In other words, OData can be used freely without the need for a license or contract.

SAP Gateway — In parallel, realizing a growing need for easy-to-use, non-ABAP developer access to its systems, SAP started to invest in SAP Gateway in 2009 to enable large communities of developers outside the classic SAP development community.

OASIS Standard — In 2012, Microsoft, Citrix, IBM, Progress Software, SAP, and WSO2 jointly submitted a proposal for the standardization of OData based on the OData 3.0 specification to the Organization for the Advancement of Structured Information Standards (OASIS). *OASIS* is a nonprofit, international consortium that drives the development, convergence, and adoption of open standards for the global information society. The consortium has more than 5,000 participants representing more than 600 organizations and individual members in 100 countries. On March 17, 2014, the OASIS international open standards consortium announced the approval of OData 4.0 and the OData JSON Format 4.0.

OData now officially became for the IT industry what it unofficially already was before—the generally accepted *lingua franca* used by the members of the IT industry for software interoperability across all platforms and borders.

In the years since the announcement of Project Astoria at Mix '07, a rich ecosystem has developed around OData. This ecosystem is a growing community of data producers and consumers using OData to exchange data. *OData consumers* are applications that consume data exposed using the OData protocol and can vary greatly in sophistication, from something as simple as a web browser to custom applications that take advantage of all the features of the OData protocol. The most prominent OData consumer is probably Microsoft Excel.

Consumers and producers

OData producers are services that expose their data using the OData protocol. Applications that expose OData include a number of household names such as Microsoft SharePoint, IBM WebSphere, Microsoft Dynamics, as well as open-source projects such as Drupal or Joomla. On top of that, there is an ever-growing number of live services that serve up information via OData to the public. You can, for example, browse Wikipedia via DBpedia. A detailed list of selected producers can be found on the OData website at *www.odata.org/ecosystem*.

The OData community knows that there is a problem; that is, in this day of big data, an increasing amount of information is coming from an increasing amount of sources that needs to be accessed on an increasing variety of devices (Figure 2.2).

This problem needs a solution. As a web protocol for querying and updating data, as well as applying and building on web technologies such as HTTP, AtomPub, and JSON to provide access to information from a variety of applications, OData is that solution.

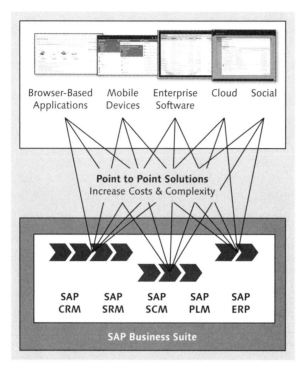

Figure 2.2 The Challenge of Multichannel Access

Abstract model and protocol
OData primarily defines two things: an abstract data model and a protocol that allows any client to access information exposed by any data source. As a result, OData allows mixing and matching providers and consumers following one of the fundamental OData ideas: any client can access any data source. The obvious benefits of this are that it offers a simple and uniform way of sharing data on the protocol level, enables a broad integration across products and platforms, and basically only requires an HTTP stack to integrate with any OData producer.

The OData protocol follows five design principles:

▶ **Data store variety**
Select mechanisms that support diverse data stores. In particular, don't assume a relational data model.

▶ **Backwards compatibility**
Clients and services that speak different versions of the OData protocol should interoperate, supporting everything allowed in lower versions.

▶ **REST principles**
Adhere to these unless there is a good and specific reason not to.

▶ **Graceful degradation**
It should be easy to build a very basic but compliant OData service, with additional work necessary only to support additional capabilities.

▶ **Simplicity**
Address the common cases and provide extensibility where necessary.

Using OData, structured data can be exchanged in both directions between a client and a server. A client uses an HTTP request on a server resource and receives a response. This request is placed by calling a service. A service defines the resources that can be accessed, the relevant HTTP operations, and the format of documents that represent those resources in requests. The representation is in an XML and/or JSON format.

There are four main building blocks of a technical OData implementation:

▶ **OData data model**
The OData data model provides a generic way to organize and describe data.

▶ **OData protocol**
The OData protocol lets a client make requests to and get responses from an OData service. In essence, it's just HTTP-based RESTful CRUD interactions along with an OData-defined query language. Data sent by an OData service can be represented either in the XML-based format or in JSON.

▶ **OData client libraries**
The OData client libraries facilitate the creation of software that accesses data via the OData protocol. Using a specific client library (e.g., from Microsoft) isn't strictly required, but it does make life a lot easier for developers. However, a developer is always free to create an OData client from scratch—it's just code.

▶ **OData services**
Finally, OData services are what implement the OData protocol and expose an endpoint that allows access to data. In effect, OData services use abstractions of the OData data model to translate data between its underlying form into the format sent to the client.

OData also offers a number of very intuitive URI conventions for navigating, filtering, sorting, and paging. This turns OData into a powerful query language—a *SQL light* for the web.

It's important to note that by using these building blocks in an OData implementation, any consumer sees only the data model provided by the OData service. The raw underlying data are wrapped and kept away from the consumer to keep the internal data structure unexposed.

2.2 Structure of an OData Service

Building blocks of an OData service | Now that you have a little background, it's time to get an introduction to the technical details of OData. As you'll recall from the previous section, OData services are what implement the OData protocol and expose an endpoint that allows access to data. The structure of an OData service is comprised of the following building blocks:

▶ **Service document**
A service document represents a service by exposing all resources that can be accessed through the service, their URIs, names, and operations.

▶ **Service metadata document**
The service metadata document exposes all metadata of a service. It exposes the model, types, actions, relations, and detailed semantics information of that part of the model.

Further, these two types of documents are in turn comprised of different elements:

▶ **Entity**
An entity is a potentially empty resource that has either zero content
elements or one content elements. The content element contains one
to many properties. At least one key field is required. Entities can be
addressed individually via key values or as collections via query
options.

▶ **Entity type**
An entity type describes a collection and has a name. In many cases,
the names of the collection and the entity type are equal or related by
some convention. Entity types have a structure defined by their properties and are also associated with a key, which is formed from a subset of the properties of the entity type. The entity key is needed to
define associations between the entity types.

▶ **Entity set**
An entity set represents a potentially empty resource of entries. The
cardinality is 0:many. Several entity sets can be based on the same
entity type. For example, there might be a service that has the entity
sets `EmployeeSet`, `ContactSet`, and `ManagerSet`, which can all be based
on the same entity type called `Person`. If an entity set is addressed by
means of key values, the `GET_ENTITY` method of the entity set has to be
implemented.

▶ **Property**
A property is a typed element that represents a primitive typed data
element, structured data, or a link to another resource. Properties correspond to columns of a table.

▶ **Navigation property**
Entity types may include one or more *navigation properties*. A navigation property is a specific type of property containing a link that presents an association instance. These correspond to links that point to
other tables and table entries, depending on the cardinality of the
underlying association. The navigation property derives its name
from the fact that it allows navigation from one entity (the entity type
that declares the navigation property) to others (anything from 0).

Similar to properties, navigation properties are specified in a separate element called `NavigationProperty`; this defines the navigation property name, the association being used, and the direction.

▶ **Association**

An association defines a relation between entity types. Recursive relations are allowed. Every association includes two association ends, which specify the entity types that are related and the cardinality rules for each end of the association.

Data model

The relationship between all of these elements is encapsulated in the *data model* of the OData service. The OData Model Editor plug-in (discussed in Chapter 9, Section 9.6) in the SAP Web IDE allows developers to create the entity relationship model of an OData service using the code assist and auto complete features. Then the data model can be visualized, as shown in Figure 2.3.

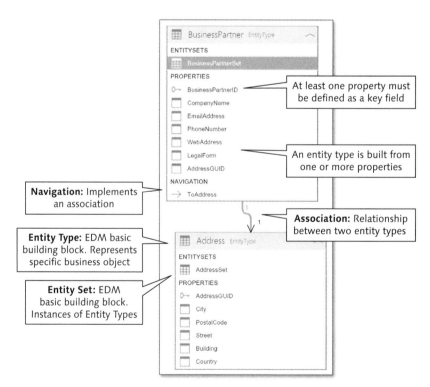

Figure 2.3 Entity Data Model Created with OData Model Editor Plug-In of SAP Web IDE

To explain all of these elements with respect to SAP, we'll use a sample service that has been built using the Service Builder, which is the main tool for service creation in SAP Gateway. (We go into more detail about the Service Builder in Chapter 5.) The service provides access to demo data based on the SAP Enterprise Procurement Model (EPM), which is a frequently used demo scenario.

> **Note**
>
> The GWSAMPLE_BASIC service used in this section is available as part of the SAP Community Network (SCN) trial edition of SAP NetWeaver AS ABAP 7.4 that is available via SCN and via the demo system of the SAP Gateway Developer Center in SCN.

The sample service is based on the data model shown in Figure 2.4. This data model assumes that you want to expose a service to access business partners, sales orders, sales order line items, products, and the contacts of business partners.

Sample data model

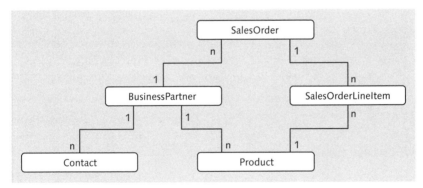

Figure 2.4 Data Model Sample Service GWSAMPLE_BASIC

As we mentioned, two types of documents are associated with each OData service: the *service document* and the *service metadata document*. In this section, we'll take a look at both of these for our sample service, and we'll show you how the pieces and parts described earlier are reflected in this example.

> **Note**
>
> This section is only an overview of OData services. In Chapter 5, Chapter 6, and Chapter 7, we provide detailed explanations of the steps involved in creating services.

2.2.1 Service Document

Let's explore the structure of an OData service by starting with the service document. The OData service document primarily lists all entity sets of an OData service. The service document is available at the service root URI and can be formatted either in Atom or JSON. The base URI of the service document is actually pointing to the service document itself. In our example, we'll call the root URI of the service document using the `sap-ds-debug=true` query parameter.

> **sap-ds-debug=true**
>
> Using the `sap-ds-debug=true` query parameter, the server responses of an SAP Gateway server are rendered as an HTML page with active links. No matter whether you choose XML or JSON as the output format, the server response is rendered in a user-friendly manner that can be displayed in any browser. Another advantage of using this query parameter is that the user is able to follow all links in the server response, allowing for web-like navigation.

After you have access to the demo system provided by the SAP Gateway Developer Center, the service document of the sample service is accessible through the following URI:

https://sapes4.sapdevcenter.com/sap/opu/odata/IWBEP/GWSAMPLE_BASIC/

Entity sets   Looking at the service document (Figure 2.5), you'll see one or more collection tags (`<app:collection>`) that define the relative URL and title of an individual collection or entity set ❶. The service document contains a list of all entity types that can be accessed in this service. For each entity set, a relative link is marked with *href* that points to the respective entity set. The sample service GWSAMPLE_BASIC contains the five collections: `ProductSet`, `BusinessPartnerSet`, `ContactSet`, `SalesOrderSet`, and `SalesOrderLineItemSet`.

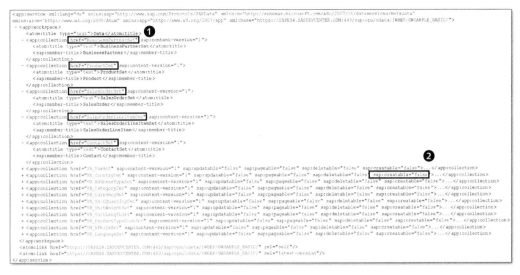

Figure 2.5 Service Document GWSAMPLE_BASIC

You'll also notice that the service document contains some SAP-spe- **SAP annotations**
cific metadata ❷. The annotations `sap:creatable`, `sap:updatable`, and
`sap:deletable` state whether the collection allows adding, changing,
or removing member resources. The annotation `sap:searchable`
denotes whether the content of a collection can be searched using a
Google-like search. Note that the SAP-specific annotations only show
up in the service document and service metadata document if their
value is set to a nondefault value. Default values are, for example, `true`
for `creatable` and `false` for `searchable`. (For more details about this,
we recommend *http://scn.sap.com/docs/DOC-44986*.)

In our sample service, the `VH_CountrySet` and the other collections that
provide value helps are marked as `sap:creatable="false"` (see Listing
2.1).

```
<app:collection href="VH_CountrySet" sap:content-
version="1" sap:updatable="false" sap:pageable="false" sap:dele
table="false" sap:creatable="false"><atom:title type="text">VH_
CountrySet</atom:title>
<sap:member-title>VH_Country</sap:member-title></
app:collection>
```

Listing 2.1 VH_CountrySet Marked as sap:addressable=false

In this example, an exception is raised if a consumer tries to create a new country by sending an HTTP POST request to the VH_CountrySet entity set. (This is implemented via the Search Help Generator, which we discuss in more detail in Chapter 5 and Chapter 7.) This exception tells the consumer that the countries can't be created but only retrieved using a query or read request.

Absolute URI   By combining the base URI of the sample GWSAMPLE_BASIC service— *http://<host>:<port>/sap/opu/odata/IWBEP/GWSAMPLE_BASIC/*—with the relative link *href="BusinessPartnerSet"* that points to the Business-PartnerSet collection, the client is able to construct the absolute URI allowing him to retrieve the entries of the BusinessPartner collection. The following URI points to the business partner entity set of our sample service:

https://sapes4.sapdevcenter.com/sap/opu/odata/IWBEP/GWSAMPLE_BASIC/BusinessPartnerSet?sap-ds-debug=true

Entering this URI in a browser will deliver the XML response shown in Figure 2.6. If you've accessed the service document using the sap-ds-debug=true query parameter, you can browse the content of the service document by clicking the hyperlink (e.g., BusinessPartnerSet).

Here's what you can see in the BusinessPartnerSet entity set:

▸ The <feed> element defines a collection of zero or more <entry> elements. The content thus corresponds to a table.

▸ The <entry> element contains the data for one member of the feed's collection. Its content thus corresponds to a row of a table. Notice that each <entry> element contains one or more <link> elements.

▸ Each <entry> element always contains a self-reference, which is a <link> element marked with either rel="self" or rel="edit". It contains the relative URL for reading the current entry from the collection.

▸ The primary key information of each entry is rendered into the response in brackets right after the name of the entity set. If the primary key consists of only one property, the value is provided right away without the property name (e.g., BusinessPartnerSet('0100000001')).

If the primary key consists of multiple properties, the primary key is provided by a comma-separated list of name/value pairs.

▶ Inside an `<entry>`, you find one or more `<properties>` tags that correspond to single table columns.

▶ The `sap:searchable=true` annotation denotes that the content of a collection can be searched. The `atom:link` with `rel="search"` points to an OpenSearch description document that describes how to do free-text (Google-like) search on the collection via the custom `"search="` query option.

▶ In the response, you find an additional relative link in each entry, for example: *href="BusinessPartnerSet('0100000000')/ToSalesOrders"*. Following this link provides an XML response that lists the sales orders of the selected business partner. Such links are called *navigation properties*.

```
<feed xmlns:m="http://schemas.microsoft.com/ado/2007/08/dataservices/metadata"
xml:base="https://SAPES4.SAPDEVCENTER.COM:443/sap/opu/odata/IWBEP/GWSAMPLE_BASIC/"
xmlns:d="http://schemas.microsoft.com/ado/2007/08/dataservices" xmlns="http://www.w3.org/2005/Atom">
  <id>https://SAPES4.SAPDEVCENTER.COM:443/sap/opu/odata/IWBEP/GWSAMPLE_BASIC/BusinessPartnerSet</id>
  <title type="text">BusinessPartnerSet</title>
  <updated>2015-12-08T20:21:33Z</updated>
- <author>
    <name/>
  </author>
  <link title="BusinessPartnerSet" href="BusinessPartnerSet" rel="self"/>
- <entry m:etag="W/"datetime'2015-10-12T23%3A41%3A54.4490000'"">
    <id>https://SAPES4.SAPDEVCENTER.COM:443/sap/opu/odata/IWBEP/GWSAMPLE_BASIC/BusinessPartnerSet('0100000000')</id>
    <title type="text">BusinessPartnerSet('0100000000')</title>
    <updated>2015-12-08T20:21:33Z</updated>
    <category scheme="http://schemas.microsoft.com/ado/2007/08/dataservices/scheme"
      term="/IWBEP/GWSAMPLE_BASIC.BusinessPartner"/>
    <link title="BusinessPartner" href="BusinessPartnerSet('0100000000')" rel="edit"/>
    <link title="ToSalesOrders" type="application/atom+xml;type=feed" href="BusinessPartnerSet('0100000000')/ToSalesOrders"
      rel="http://schemas.microsoft.com/ado/2007/08/dataservices/related/ToSalesOrders"/>
    <link title="ToContacts" type="application/atom+xml;type=feed" href="BusinessPartnerSet('0100000000')/ToContacts"
      rel="http://schemas.microsoft.com/ado/2007/08/dataservices/related/ToContacts"/>
    <link title="ToProducts" type="application/atom+xml;type=feed" href="BusinessPartnerSet('0100000000')/ToProducts"
      rel="http://schemas.microsoft.com/ado/2007/08/dataservices/related/ToProducts"/>
  - <content type="application/xml">
    - <m:properties xmlns:m="http://schemas.microsoft.com/ado/2007/08/dataservices/metadata"
        xmlns:d="http://schemas.microsoft.com/ado/2007/08/dataservices">
      - <d:Address m:type="/IWBEP/GWSAMPLE_BASIC.CT_Address">
          <d:City>Walldorf</d:City>
          <d:PostalCode>69196</d:PostalCode>
          <d:Street>Dietmar-Hopp-Allee</d:Street>
          <d:Building>16</d:Building>
          <d:Country>DE</d:Country>
          <d:AddressType>02</d:AddressType>
        </d:Address>
        <d:BusinessPartnerID>0100000000</d:BusinessPartnerID>
        <d:CompanyName>SAP</d:CompanyName>
        <d:WebAddress>http://www.sap.com</d:WebAddress>
        <d:EmailAddress>do.not.reply@sap.com</d:EmailAddress>
        <d:PhoneNumber>0622734567</d:PhoneNumber>
        <d:FaxNumber>0622734004</d:FaxNumber>
        <d:LegalForm>AG</d:LegalForm>
        <d:CurrencyCode>EUR</d:CurrencyCode>
        <d:BusinessPartnerRole>01</d:BusinessPartnerRole>
        <d:CreatedAt>2015-02-13T13:48:59.0000000</d:CreatedAt>
        <d:ChangedAt>2015-10-12T23:41:54.4490000</d:ChangedAt>
      </m:properties>
    </content>
  </entry>
+ <entry m:etag="W/"datetime'2015-02-13T13%3A49%3A59.0000000'""> ... </entry>
+ <entry m:etag="W/"datetime'2015-02-13T13%3A48%3A59.0000000'""> ... </entry>
+ <entry m:etag="W/"datetime'2015-02-13T13%3A48%3A59.0000000'""> ... </entry>
+ <entry m:etag="W/"datetime'2015-02-13T13%3A48%3A59.0000000'""> ... </entry>
```

Figure 2.6 Result Query Entity Set BusinessPartnerSet

Now you're able to read, understand, and use an XML document for an entity set as a response from any OData service.

2.2.2 Service Metadata Document

$metadata   As we defined earlier, the service metadata document exposes all metadata of a service, including the model, types, actions, relations, and detailed semantics of the model (see Figure 2.7). The service metadata document URI can be constructed easily by appending the string *$metadata* to the service root URI. The service metadata document of the OData sample service is thus accessible via the following URI:

http://<host>:<port>/sap/opu/odata/IWBEP/GWSAMPLE_BASIC/ $metadata

Figure 2.7 Service Metadata Document GWSAMPLE_BASIC

The purpose of the service metadata document is to enable consumers to discover the shape of an OData service, the structure of its resources, the known links between resources, and the service operations exposed. SDKs use this information to generate proxies that developers then use to access a service in their development environment of choice. This OData service information is encapsulated in the service metadata document via the *entity data model* (*EDM*) for a given service. The EDM describes the organization and relationship of the data resources that are modeled as entity types within a particular business scenario. For this, the service metadata document uses an XML-based language called the *Conceptual Schema Definition Language* (*CSDL*).

Figure 2.8 shows the `BusinessPartner` entity type contained in the service metadata document.

Entity types

```
<EntityType sap:content-version="1" Name="BusinessPartner">
 - <Key>
       <PropertyRef Name="BusinessPartnerID"/>
   </Key>
    <Property Name="Address" Nullable="false" Type="/IWBEP/GWSAMPLE_BASIC.CT_Address"/>
    <Property sap:updatable="false" sap:creatable="false" Name="BusinessPartnerID" Nullable="false" Type="Edm.String" sap:label="Business Partner ID" MaxLength="10"/>
    <Property Name="CompanyName" Nullable="false" Type="Edm.String" sap:label="Company" MaxLength="80"/>
    <Property Name="WebAddress" Type="Edm.String" sap:label="Web Address" sap:semantics="url" sap:filterable="false" sap:sortable="false"/>
    <Property Name="EmailAddress" Nullable="false" Type="Edm.String" sap:label="E-Mail" MaxLength="255" sap:semantics="email"/>
    <Property Name="PhoneNumber" Type="Edm.String" sap:label="Phone No." MaxLength="30" sap:semantics="tel"/>
    <Property Name="FaxNumber" Type="Edm.String" sap:label="Fax Number" MaxLength="30"/>
    <Property Name="LegalForm" Type="Edm.String" sap:label="Legal Form" MaxLength="10"/>
    <Property Name="CurrencyCode" Nullable="false" Type="Edm.String" sap:label="Currency Code" MaxLength="5" sap:semantics="currency-code"/>
    <Property Name="BusinessPartnerRole" Nullable="false" Type="Edm.String" sap:label="Bus. Part. Role" MaxLength="3"/>
    <Property sap:updatable="false" sap:creatable="false" Name="CreatedAt" Type="Edm.DateTime" sap:label="Time Stamp" Precision="7"/>
    <Property sap:updatable="false" sap:creatable="false" Name="ChangedAt" Type="Edm.DateTime" sap:label="Time Stamp" Precision="7" ConcurrencyMode="Fixed"/>
    <NavigationProperty Name="ToSalesOrders" ToRole="ToRole_Assoc_BusinessPartner_SalesOrders" FromRole="FromRole_Assoc_BusinessPartner_SalesOrders"
        Relationship="/IWBEP/GWSAMPLE_BASIC.Assoc_BusinessPartner_SalesOrders"/>
    <NavigationProperty Name="ToContacts" ToRole="ToRole_Assoc_BusinessPartner_Contacts" FromRole="FromRole_Assoc_BusinessPartner_Contacts"
        Relationship="/IWBEP/GWSAMPLE_BASIC.Assoc_BusinessPartner_Contacts"/>
    <NavigationProperty Name="ToProducts" ToRole="ToRole_Assoc_BusinessPartner_Products" FromRole="FromRole_Assoc_BusinessPartner_Products"
        Relationship="/IWBEP/GWSAMPLE_BASIC.Assoc_BusinessPartner_Products"/>
</EntityType>
```

Figure 2.8 Entity Type Definition: BusinessPartner

In our sample service, there are several entity sets, for example, `Sales-OrderLineItemSet`, `BusinessPartnerSet`, and `ContactSet` (Figure 2.9). The `EntityContainer` lists all of the entity sets belonging to one service.

Entity sets

```
<EntityContainer Name="/IWBEP/GWSAMPLE_BASIC_Entities" sap:supported-formats="atom json xlsx" m:IsDefaultEntityContainer="true">
    <EntitySet sap:content-version="1" Name="BusinessPartnerSet" EntityType="/IWBEP/GWSAMPLE_BASIC.BusinessPartner"/>
    <EntitySet sap:content-version="1" Name="ProductSet" EntityType="/IWBEP/GWSAMPLE_BASIC.Product"/>
    <EntitySet sap:content-version="1" sap:updatable="false" Name="SalesOrderSet" EntityType="/IWBEP/GWSAMPLE_BASIC.SalesOrder"/>
    <EntitySet sap:content-version="1" Name="SalesOrderLineItemSet" EntityType="/IWBEP/GWSAMPLE_BASIC.SalesOrderLineItem"/>
    <EntitySet sap:content-version="1" Name="ContactSet" EntityType="/IWBEP/GWSAMPLE_BASIC.Contact"/>
    <EntitySet sap:content-version="1" sap:updatable="false" sap:pageable="false" sap:deletable="false" sap:creatable="false" Name="VH_SexSet
    <EntitySet sap:content-version="1" sap:updatable="false" sap:pageable="false" sap:deletable="false" sap:creatable="false" Name="VH_Countr
    <EntitySet sap:content-version="1" sap:updatable="false" sap:pageable="false" sap:deletable="false" sap:creatable="false" Name="VH_Addres
  + <AssociationSet sap:content-version="1" sap:updatable="false" sap:deletable="false" sap:creatable="false" Name="Assoc_BusinessPartner_Sa
  + <AssociationSet sap:content-version="1" sap:updatable="false" sap:deletable="false" sap:creatable="false" Name="Assoc_VH_Currency_Sales
  + <AssociationSet sap:content-version="1" sap:updatable="false" sap:deletable="false" sap:creatable="false" Name="Assoc_BusinessPartner_Co
  + <AssociationSet sap:content-version="1" sap:updatable="false" sap:deletable="false" sap:creatable="false" Name="Assoc_VH_UnitQuantity_S
  + <FunctionImport Name="RegenerateAllData" m:HttpMethod="POST" ReturnType="/IWBEP/GWSAMPLE_BASIC.CT_String">
  + <FunctionImport Name="SalesOrder_Confirm" EntitySet="SalesOrderSet" m:HttpMethod="POST" ReturnType="/IWBEP/GWSAMPLE_BASIC.
  + <FunctionImport Name="SalesOrder_Cancel" EntitySet="SalesOrderSet" m:HttpMethod="POST" ReturnType="/IWBEP/GWSAMPLE_BASIC.S
</EntityContainer>
```

Figure 2.9 Entity Set Definition: SalesOrderLineItemSet, BusinessPartnerSet, and ContactSet

Associations   Associations between entity types are also part of the schema. They are listed one after the other in the metadata document (e.g., the `Assoc_BusinessPartner_SalesOrders` association between the `BusinessPartnerSet` and `SalesOrderSet` entity types, as shown in Figure 2.10).

```
<Association sap:content-version="1" Name="Assoc_BusinessPartner_SalesOrders">
    <End Type="/IWBEP/GWSAMPLE_BASIC.BusinessPartner" Role="FromRole_Assoc_BusinessPartner_SalesOrders" Multiplicity="1"/>
    <End Type="/IWBEP/GWSAMPLE_BASIC.SalesOrder" Role="ToRole_Assoc_BusinessPartner_SalesOrders" Multiplicity="*"/>
  - <ReferentialConstraint>
    - <Principal Role="FromRole_Assoc_BusinessPartner_SalesOrders">
        <PropertyRef Name="BusinessPartnerID"/>
      </Principal>
    - <Dependent Role="ToRole_Assoc_BusinessPartner_SalesOrders">
        <PropertyRef Name="CustomerID"/>
      </Dependent>
    </ReferentialConstraint>
</Association>
```

Figure 2.10 Association between the BusinessPartner Entity Type and the SalesOrder Entity Type

Navigation properties   Finally, the `BusinessPartner` entity type has three navigation properties named `ToContacts`, `ToProducts`, and `ToSalesOrders` (Figure 2.11). The `ToContacts` navigation property makes it possible to navigate from a `BusinessPartner` instance to all of the contacts that are defined in the backend system for this business partner. The `ToSalesOrders` navigation property, on the other hand, lets you navigate from a `BusinessPartner` instance to all sales orders that belong to this business partner.

```
<NavigationProperty Name="ToSalesOrders" ToRole="ToRole_Assoc_BusinessPartner_SalesOrders"
    FromRole="FromRole_Assoc_BusinessPartner_SalesOrders"
    Relationship="/IWBEP/GWSAMPLE_BASIC.Assoc_BusinessPartner_SalesOrders"/>
<NavigationProperty Name="ToContacts" ToRole="ToRole_Assoc_BusinessPartner_Contacts"
    FromRole="FromRole_Assoc_BusinessPartner_Contacts"
    Relationship="/IWBEP/GWSAMPLE_BASIC.Assoc_BusinessPartner_Contacts"/>
<NavigationProperty Name="ToProducts" ToRole="ToRole_Assoc_BusinessPartner_Products"
    FromRole="FromRole_Assoc_BusinessPartner_Products"
    Relationship="/IWBEP/GWSAMPLE_BASIC.Assoc_BusinessPartner_Products"/>
```

Figure 2.11 Navigation Properties of the BusinessPartner Entity Type

2.3   OData Operations

When discussing data access, people typically talk about CRUD or CRUD-Q ("Q" is for *query*) and indicate the operation to be executed. (`Query` is a kind of `Read` operation and therefore the "Q" isn't always mentioned explicitly.) As already described in Section 2.1.1, OData uses the REST commands POST, GET, PUT, or DELETE, which map to CRUD. The

OData protocol defines conventions for all of these CRUD operations, but it's not mandatory for every OData service to support all four operations. In this section, we'll explain each operation and give some context for their use.

2.3.1 Create

The Create operation is used whenever you want to create data on the backend server. This is data that wasn't present before, for example, a new sales order or a new business partner. The related HTTP method is POST. If the Create operation is successful, you receive the HTTP 201 (created) response code, along with the entity that was created. Via the metadata, you can specify whether an entity set is creatable or not. This information is reflected in the metadata document and allows the consumer to act accordingly (e.g., if the application is of the type Player). But there is no default handling of this annotation by the framework; instead, the service implementation has to handle it according to the metadata definition (see Chapter 5 and Chapter 6 for more details about service implementation).

POST

2.3.2 Read

The Read operation is the most frequently used operation. Typically, applications primarily read data instead of updating data—for example, a lunch menu application that doesn't include any option to provide feedback about the menu provided. This data can be of any kind, such as customizing, master data, transaction data, and so on. The related HTTP method for the Read operation is GET. A successful Read operation has the HTTP 200 (OK) status code.

GET

Read operations can be classified into two different kinds: Query and Single Read.

Query Operation

A Query operation is usually the entry point into an application. The purpose of a query is to read a set of entities. So the result of a query is

Read a set of entities

always an entity set—irrespective of whether the result is empty (no entity), a single entity, or multiple entities. A `Query` operation is usually combined with a filter that reduces the number of results. An example of such a `Query` operation is the retrieval of a list of sales orders, optionally filtered by a certain sales area, a status, and/or a date.

Similar to the `Create` operation, you can control the `Query` operation via the metadata if an entity set can be directly read (`sap:addressable`). If an entity set isn't addressable, it may not be accessed via a `Query` operation. This is used if you only want to allow access via a navigation property. For example, you might not allow a consumer to fetch the list of all sales orders in the system but just allow access to the sales orders of a certain business partner by using the respective navigation property.

In the metadata definition of an entity set, you can also set the REQUIRES FILTER flag to force a consumer to provide a mandatory filter when accessing the entity set; that is, a consumer may not access the collection without a filter. Similar to the other metadata annotations, the SAP Gateway framework doesn't handle this. Instead, the service implementation needs to handle it accordingly (see Chapter 5 and Chapter 6 for more details about service implementation).

Single Read Operation

After you've fetched a set of entities, you can use the provided self-link to navigate to the details of the entities. For that, you can use the `Single Read` operation. The major difference to the `Query` operation is that you specify the primary key of the entity you want to read. So you're accessing an instance with the primary key versus querying for entities that might or might not result in a single unique instance.

The key information has to be passed in brackets right after the name of the collection. If the primary key consists of only a single property, the name of the property doesn't have to be provided. If the primary key consists of multiple properties, the property names have to be provided along with the values. But you don't need to worry about the concatenation of that information because the self-links provided by the SAP Gateway server in the entity set already take care of it.

2.3.3   Update

The Update operation is used whenever you want to change an existing entity. As such, you have to provide the same key information as in the Single Read operation, explained earlier, to uniquely identify the entity you want to update.

Change an existing entity

The HTTP method for the Update operation is PUT. If the Update operation is successful, you receive the HTTP 204 (no content) status. You're intentionally not getting the entity back as part of the HTTP request because the consumer typically knows the current state of the entity, and therefore the SAP Gateway server doesn't need to send it back.

PATCH

Instead of PUT, it's possible to leverage the PATCH operation that allows you to perform a partial update. The PATCH method is supported by the framework and first calls the GETDETAIL method to retrieve all properties that won't be updated, then merges those values with the ones that are sent via the PATCH request, and finally performs an update using the standard update method of an entity set.

Because the consumer knows the key of the entity, it is, of course, possible to perform a Single Read operation after the Update operation to fetch the updated entity. This might be required if the server, for example, does any calculation. It's not a good practice to misuse the Create operation for update requests just to receive the entity back as part of the response.

Similar to the other operations, there is an annotation in the metadata document that shows the ability to update an entity (Updatable).

2.3.4   Delete

Finally, the Delete operation is used whenever you want to delete an entity. Equal to the Update operation, you have to provide the primary key of the entity you want to erase. The related HTTP method is DELETE. A successful Delete operation has the HTTP 204 (no content) status code.

Via the sap:deletable annotation, you can specify whether entities of an entity set can be deleted or not. As before, the service implementation has to make sure that the actual operations are in line with the metadata definition (see Chapter 5 and Chapter 6 for more details about service implementation).

2.4 OData Query Options

OData specifies a simple yet powerful query language that allows a client to request arbitrary filtering, sorting, and paging. Via query string parameters, a client is able to express the amount and order of the data that an OData service returns.

Query options are essential to reducing or influencing the result set provided by the SAP Gateway server. In many cases, you don't want a huge collection to be returned as is (e.g., the list of all products in the backend system) if the result set isn't already filtered based on the user assignment; for example in an SAP Customer Relationship Management (CRM) scenario, the service implementation probably only returns the business partners that are assigned to your user, not all existing business partners in the entire SAP CRM system.

In this short introduction, we're focusing on the most important query options only, as listed in Table 2.1.

Operation	Query Option
Filtering and projecting	`$filter` and `$select`
Sorting	`$orderby`
Client-side paging	`$top`, `$skip` and `$inlinecount`
Counting	`$count`
Inlining	`$expand`
Formatting	`$format`

Table 2.1 Most Important OData Query Options

We'll illustrate the different query options by querying the sample data set that contains a list of business partners (subset taken from the EPM sample content provided with SAP NetWeaver) as shown in Table 2.2.

BusinessPartner ID	CompanyName	LegalForm	City
100000000	SAP	AG	Walldorf, Germany
100000001	Becker Berlin	GmbH	Berlin, Germany
100000002	DelBont Industries	Ltd.	Wilmington, Delaware
100000003	Talpa	GmbH	Hannover, Germany
100000004	Panorama Studios	Inc.	Hollywood, California
100000005	TECUM	AG	Muenster, Germany
100000006	Asia High tech	Inc.	Tokyo, Japan
100000007	Laurent	S.A.	Paris, France
100000008	AVANTEL	S.A.	Mexico City, Mexico
100000009	Telecomunica-ciones Star	S.A.	Buenos Aires, Argentina
100000010	Pear Computing Services	Inc.	Atlanta, Georgia
100000011	Alpine Systems	AG	Salzburg, Austria
100000012	New Line Design	Ltd.	Manchester, England
100000013	HEPA Tec	GmbH	Bremen, Germany
100000014	Anav Ideon	Ltd.	Bismarck, North Dakota
100000015	Robert Brown Entertainment	Ltd.	Quebec, Canada
100000016	Mexican Oil Trading Company	S.A.	Puebla, Mexico
100000017	Meliva	AG	Köln, Germany
100000018	Compostela	S.A.	Mendoza, Argentina
100000019	Pateu	S.A.R.L.	Lyon, France
...	...	...	...
100000044	Sorali	AG	Karlsruhe, Germany

Table 2.2 Subset of Business Partners Contained in the EPM Demo Data Model

Using this dataset, we'll take a detailed look at all of the query options outlined in Table 2.1.

2.4.1 Filtering and Projecting ($filter and $select)

We'll start with the use case of filtering and projecting on a result set. A mobile application provides a list of business partners. Because not all properties of the BusinessPartnerSet entity set can be displayed on the screen, only the BusinessPartnerID and CompanyName properties are shown in the list. In addition, the user can limit the number of business partners by filtering the company names. Figure 2.12 shows a mockup screen of this application limiting the result by the number of rows and columns retrieved.

Figure 2.12 Mobile Application Using Filtering and Projecting

The subset is determined by selecting only the entries that satisfy the filter expression specified by the $filter query option and by limiting the number of properties being retrieved using the $select query option.

$filter The $filter system query option is one of the most important because it allows you to provide sophisticated filtering along with your service call. Similar to the other query options, you have to implement the filtering of your collection in the service implementation yourself; the framework provides no default filtering. Filters are translated by the framework—wherever possible—into corresponding `Select-Options` for easy handling in the ABAP code of the service implementation (see Chapter 5 and Chapter 6 for more details about service implementation).

The following HTTP request delivers the result shown in Table 2.3:

*https://sapes4.sapdevcenter.com/sap/opu/odata/IWBEP/GWSAMPLE_
BASIC/BusinessPartnerSet?$filter=startswith(CompanyName,'S')*

The result is a list of all companies whose company name starts with the letter "S."

BusinessPartner ID	CompanyName	LegalForm	City
0100000000	SAP	AG	Walldorf
0100000041	South American IT Company	S.A.	Cordoba
0100000042	Siwusha	CJV	Shanghai
0100000044	Sorali	AG	Karlsruhe

Table 2.3 List of all Business Partners Whose Company Name Starts with "S"

Another example is to fetch a business partner from the `BusinessPart-ner` collection with the equal (=) operator using the `BusinessPartnerID` property. For example:

*https://sapes4.sapdevcenter.com/sap/opu/odata/IWBEP/GWSAMPLE_
BASIC/BusinessPartnerSet?$filter=BusinessPartnerID eq '0100000000'*

The result is a list with just one entry, namely the business partner "SAP." You can also combine multiple filter statements with the logical operators `AND`, `OR`, and `NOT`. For example:

*https://sapes4.sapdevcenter.com/sap/opu/odata/IWBEP/GWSAMPLE_
BASIC/BusinessPartnerSet?$filter=BusinessPartnerID eq '0100000000' or
BusinessPartnerID eq '0100000044'*

The result of this is all business partners with the `BusinessPartnerID =` `'0100000000'` or `'0100000044'`, which are the business partners "SAP" and "Sorali."

The `$select` query option allows you to specify the properties you want to receive in the response. By default, the response contains all properties

$select

of the EDM. In some situations, mainly for performance reasons, you might not want all fields to be retrieved or calculated on the backend and sent to the consumer via SAP Gateway. In such cases, you can use the $select query option to specify the exact properties you want. For example, the following HTTP request will result in the data shown in Table 2.4:

https://sapes4.sapdevcenter.com/sap/opu/odata/IWBEP/GWSAMPLE_ BASIC/BusinessPartnerSet?$select=BusinessPartnerID,CompanyName

BusinessPartner ID	Company_Name
0100000000	SAP
0100000001	Becker Berlin
0100000002	DelBont Industries
0100000003	Talpa
0100000004	Panorama Studios
0100000005	TECUM
0100000006	Asia High tech
0100000007	Laurent
0100000008	AVANTEL
0100000009	Telecomunicaciones Star

Table 2.4 Result Set When Projecting via $select

In the service implementation, you can identify the properties that have been specified via the $select query option (see Chapter 5 and Chapter 6 for more details about service implementation). This allows the service developer to only fetch/calculate those fields that have actually been requested. If you're fetching your business data from an underlying remote function call (RFC)/Business Application Programming Interface (BAPI) module, there might not be a significant improvement by reducing the number of properties requested because the RFC/BAPI has to be executed anyway. An improvement can be achieved by fetching fewer fields/structures/tables, if the underlying RFC/BAPI supports this (i.e., if the underlying RFC/BAPI makes use of the ABAP feature to identify which interface fields have been requested using the IS SUP-PLIED expression).

Even if you can't simplify the data retrieval in the backend, the SAP Gateway framework only sends back those properties that have been specified by the $select statement. So, in any case, you can at least reduce the amount of data that is transmitted over the wire by using the $select statement.

This query option can be applied to single entities as well as to feeds (collections).

2.4.2 Sorting ($orderby)

As the name implies, $orderby allows you to sort a result set based on properties of your data model. For each property, you can decide if you want the collection to be sorted as ascending (asc suffix) or descending (desc suffix). Ascending is the default sorting, so the asc appendix doesn't need to be provided explicitly along with the URI. Multiple properties have to be separated by commas, for example, if you want to first sort by using the City property and second by the CompanyName property. Note that navigation properties can't be used for sorting.

The framework doesn't perform the sorting itself. Instead, the sorting has to be done by the data provider implementation. As such, whatever sequence is returned by the related data provider method is kept and sent as a response back to the requestor. For example, the following HTTP request results in the entire collection being sorted by LegalForm and CompanyName as shown in Table 2.5:

Sorted by data provider implementation

https://sapes4.sapdevcenter.com/sap/opu/odata/IWBEP/GWSAMPLE_BASIC/BusinessPartnerSet?$select=BusinessPartnerID,CompanyName, LegalForm&$orderby=LegalForm,CompanyName

BusinessPartner ID	Company Name	Legal Form
0100000043	Danish Fish Trading Company	A/S
0100000011	Alpine Systems	AG
0100000038	Bionic Research Lab	AG
0100000017	Meliva	AG
0100000000	SAP	AG

Table 2.5 Business Partners Sorted by LegalForm and CompanyName

2.4.3 Client-Side Paging ($top, $skip, and $inlinecount)

Client-side paging is very often used in mobile applications where space to display results in lists is limited and where scrolling through result sets is cumbersome. In the example shown in Figure 2.13, the resulting list of business partners will be displayed on several pages if the number of retrieved business partners doesn't fit on one page, where only six entries can be displayed.

Flipping through
pages

When flipping through the pages, the user should be informed how many entries have been found in total (see Figure 2.13, ❶). If, as in our example, the number of entries exceeds the number of entries found, the result should be shown on several pages. The user should be informed of which page he is currently on ❷ and through how many entries he has already navigated ❸.

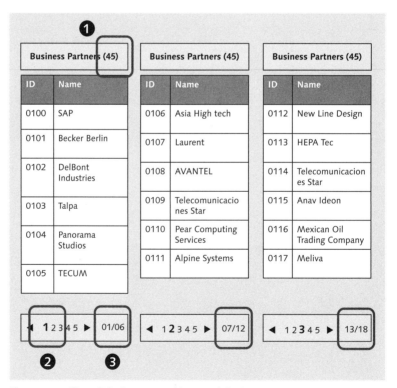

Figure 2.13 Client-Side Paging Used by a Mobile Device

For client-side paging, the client developer can use the following query options:

- `$top`
- `$skip`
- `$inlinecount`

The `$top` query option is typically used along with the `$skip` option, which we'll describe afterwards. Both together are used for client-side paging. `$top` specifies the number of entities you want to receive in your collection. If, for example, `$top=3` is provided, the data provider has to return only the first three entries of the result set. $top

Regarding performance, you should try to feed the `$top` value into, for example, the BAPI or RFC that you use for retrieving the data. Some function modules support the `maxrows` import parameter. Via the `maxrows` parameter, these function modules can reduce the set of data that is fetched from the database. This one is a perfect fit to provide the `$top` value, but don't forget that a `$skip` has been provided as well (in this case, `maxrows` typically is the sum of `$skip` and `$top`). For example, the following HTTP request retrieves the first six business partners of the `BusinessPartnerSet` entity set (see Table 2.6):

https://sapes4.sapdevcenter.com/sap/opu/odata/IWBEP/GWSAMPLE_BASIC/BusinessPartnerSet?$select=BusinessPartnerID,CompanyName, LegalForm&$top=6

BusinessPartner ID	CompanyName	LegalForm
100000000	SAP	AG
100000001	Becker Berlin	GmbH
100000002	DelBont Industries	Ltd.
100000003	Talpa	GmbH
100000004	Panorama Studios	Inc.
100000005	TECUM	AG

Table 2.6 First Six Business Partners Retrieved

$skip   As mentioned before, $skip and $top are usually used together for client-side paging. $skip defines the number of records (not pages) to be skipped at the beginning of the result set. If you provide, for example, $skip=2 as part of the URI, your result set won't contain record 1 and record 2 but will start as of record 3.

$skip and $top are handed over into the service implementation by the framework. The service implementation has to handle the query options. There is no default handling by the framework (see Chapter 5 and Chapter 6 for more details about service implementation).

If the function module used for the data retrieval doesn't contain a maxrows parameter, you should be careful when using $top and $skip. If you can't limit the amount of data that is read from the database tables for each "page" you query from the client, you might perform a lot of unnecessary read statements when paging through the result set. If you've implemented the data retrieval yourself (e.g., accessing your own Z-tables), you're usually more flexible in improving the $select statement (e.g., by using the up to x rows statement when accessing the database).

Other option is to use server-side caching (see Appendix A for more details about the soft state-based query result cache) or to generate OData services based on Core Data Services (CDS) views that support $top and $skip out of the box.

To access the third page of the collection, the following URI has to be issued by the client application as shown in Table 2.7:

*https://sapes4.sapdevcenter.com/sap/opu/odata/IWBEP/GWSAMPLE_*
BASIC/BusinessPartnerSet?$select=BusinessPartnerID,CompanyName,
LegalForm& $skip=12&$top=6

BusinessPartner ID	CompanyName	LegalForm
100000012	New Line Design	Ltd.
100000013	HEPA Tec	GmbH
100000014	Anav Ideon	Ltd.
100000015	Robert Brown Entertainment	Ltd.

Table 2.7 Results for the Third Page Shown by the Mobile Application

BusinessPartner ID	CompanyName	LegalForm
100000016	Mexican Oil Trading Company	S.A.
100000017	Meliva	AG

Table 2.7 Results for the Third Page Shown by the Mobile Application (Cont.)

The `$inlinecount` query option allows you to retrieve a count of the entities that match the filter criteria along with the response data itself. This is in contrast to `/$count`, which only provides the count without the response data and isn't a query option but a resource with its own URI.

The `$inlinecount` option has two values as shown in Table 2.8.

Option	Description
`$inlinecount=allpages`	Provides a count of the number of entities identified by the URI
`$inlinecount=none`	Doesn't contain a count of the number of entities

Table 2.8 $inlinecount Options

A consumer is typically able to count the entities retrieved. Nevertheless, `$inlinecount` has a significant value if it's combined with server- or client-side paging because `$inlinecount` has to reflect the entire collection and not just the result of the current page (this is handled during service implementation). By this, a consumer application can display the total count of entities as well as (optionally) calculate the number of pages related to it (see Chapter 5 and Chapter 6 for more details about service implementation).

Refer to Figure 2.13, where you saw a mockup of an application that displays a list of business partners. It has a count ❶ of business partners (45) along with a page selector that initially shows the result of the first page, together with a total counter. In this example, the URI looks like the following:

*https://sapes4.sapdevcenter.com/sap/opu/odata/IWBEP/GWSAMPLE_*
BASIC/BusinessPartnerSet?$select=BusinessPartnerID,CompanyName&
$inlinecount=allpages&$top=6

The SAP Gateway server "only" provides the first 6 entities as well as the total count of 45. The total number of pages is calculated by the consuming application.

The value for `$inlinecount` is sent by the server in the `<m:count>48</m:count>` count tag, as shown in Figure 2.14.

```
<feed xml:base="https://SAPES4.SAPDEVCENTER.COM:443/sap/opu/odata/IWBEP/GWSAMPLE_BASIC/"
xmlns:d="http://schemas.microsoft.com/ado/2007/08/dataservices" xmlns:m="http://schemas.microsoft.com/ado/2007/08/dataservices/metadata"
xmlns="http://www.w3.org/2005/Atom">
  <id>https://SAPES4.SAPDEVCENTER.COM:443/sap/opu/odata/IWBEP/GWSAMPLE_BASIC/BusinessPartnerSet</id>
  <title type="text">BusinessPartnerSet</title>
  <updated>2015-12-08T21:31:18Z</updated>
- <author>
    <name/>
  </author>
  <link title="BusinessPartnerSet" rel="self" href="BusinessPartnerSet"/>
  <m:count>46</m:count>
- <entry m:etag="W/"datetime'2015-10-12T23%3A41%3A54.4490000'"">
    <id>https://SAPES4.SAPDEVCENTER.COM:443/sap/opu/odata/IWBEP/GWSAMPLE_BASIC/BusinessPartnerSet('0100000000')</id>
    <title type="text">BusinessPartnerSet('0100000000')</title>
    <updated>2015-12-08T21:31:18Z</updated>
    <category scheme="http://schemas.microsoft.com/ado/2007/08/dataservices/scheme" term="/IWBEP/GWSAMPLE_BASIC.BusinessPartner"/>
    <link title="BusinessPartner" rel="edit" href="BusinessPartnerSet('0100000000')"/>
  - <content type="application/xml">
    - <m:properties xmlns:d="http://schemas.microsoft.com/ado/2007/08/dataservices"
        xmlns:m="http://schemas.microsoft.com/ado/2007/08/dataservices/metadata">
        <d:BusinessPartnerID>0100000000</d:BusinessPartnerID>
        <d:CompanyName>SAP</d:CompanyName>
      </m:properties>
    </content>
  </entry>
+ <entry m:etag="W/"datetime'2015-02-13T13%3A48%3A59.0000000'"">...</entry>
+ <entry m:etag="W/"datetime'2015-02-13T13%3A48%3A59.0000000'"">...</entry>
```

Figure 2.14 Location of the Count Value in the HTTP Response to Using the $inlinecount Query Option

2.4.4   Counting ($count)

The `$count` request is used only to retrieve the number of entries in the collection. It doesn't provide anything else—just the number (simple scalar integer value). In this example, the URI looks like the following:

*https://sapes4.sapdevcenter.com/sap/opu/odata/IWBEP/GWSAMPLE_*
BASIC/BusinessPartnerSet/$count

2.4.5   Inlining ($expand)

$expand   The `$expand` query option comes into play whenever you want to read data from multiple entity types using just a single call to the SAP Gateway server, instead of performing multiple calls sequentially or via a batch request. A typical example for this, as shown in Figure 2.15, is the need to read a sales order header entity along with the collection of sales order line items associated to this order header ❶ in just a single call. You might also want to read a business partner alongside all sales order headers that belong to that business partner ❷ or, in an extreme scenario, retrieve all sales order headers together with all sales order line items of a business partner ❸.

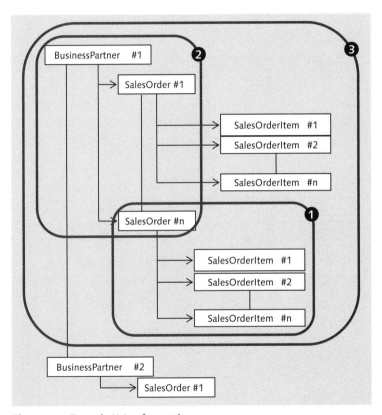

Figure 2.15 Example Using $expand

Because $expand happens along defined navigation routes, you have to define corresponding navigation properties in your model. In this example, we've defined a navigation property ToLineItems to navigate from the SalesOrderSet entity set to the collection of related SalesOrderLineItem entities. The corresponding URI looks like the following:

Define navigation properties

99

*https://sapes4.sapdevcenter.com/sap/opu/odata/IWBEP/GWSAMPLE_*
BASIC/SalesOrderSet('0500000011')?$expand=ToLineItems

The result set returned by the SAP Gateway server looks like that shown in Figure 2.16. The `SalesOrderLineItem` entities can be found in the section marked as `<m:inline>` ... `</m:inline>` ❶. In addition, the data for the sales order header data are retrieved ❷.

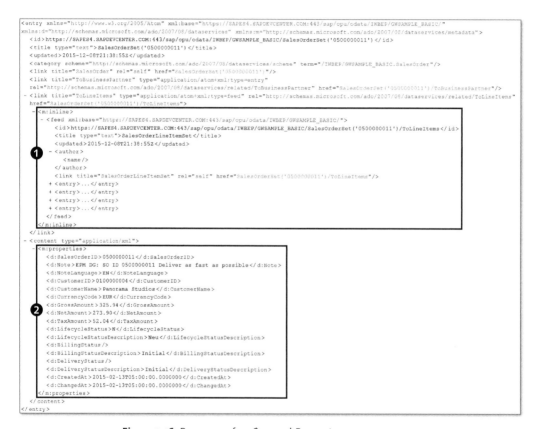

Figure 2.16 Response of an $expand Request

In a simplified way, the result can also be visualized as follows, where the entries that are returned inline are shown as indented list entries:

```
SalesOrder - Entity(SalesOrderID='123')
    SalesOrderLineItem - Entity(SalesOrderID= '123',Item='10')
    SalesOrderLineItem - Entity(SalesOrderID= '123', Item='20')
```

```
SalesOrderLineItem - Entity(SalesOrderID= '123', Item='30')
SalesOrderLineItem - Entity(SalesOrderID= '123', Item='40')
```

Multiple expands are separated by commas. So if you also want to read the business partner information (`ToBusinessPartner` navigation property in a 1:1 relationship to the sales order) alongside the line items, the URI is as follows:

http://<...>/sap/opu/odata/IWBEP/GWSAMPLE_BASIC/SalesOrderSet ('0500000011')?$expand=ToBusinessPartner,ToLineItems

The result can be visualized as follows:

```
SalesOrder - Entity(SalesOrderID='123')
    BusinessPartner - Entity(PartnerID='0815')
    SalesOrderLineItem - Entity(SalesOrderID= '123', Item='10')
    SalesOrderLineItem - Entity(SalesOrderID= '123', Item='20')
    SalesOrderLineItem - Entity(SalesOrderID= '123', Item='30')
    SalesOrderLineItem - Entity(SalesOrderID= '123', Item='40')
    ...
```

The cardinality of the association assigned to the navigation property defines whether the result of the navigation is a feed/collection (in the preceding example, the feed of `SalesOrderLineItem` entities) or a single entry (in the preceding example, the `BusinessPartner` entity).

It's also possible to expand an expanded entity, which means that you can basically navigate along the entire relationship model, following the navigation properties. For example, you can navigate from a `Business-Partner` entity via the `SalesOrderSet` collection to the `SalesOrder-LineItemsSet` collection as depicted earlier in Figure 2.15 ❸. To retrieve all sales orders of one business partner alongside all sales order line items, the consumer has to send the following URL to the server:

Nested expands

http://.../sap/opu/odata/IWBEP/GWSAMPLE_BASIC/BusinessPartnerSet ('0100000000')?$expand=ToSalesOrders,ToSalesOrders/ToLineItems

The result can be visualized as followed:

```
BusinessPartner - Entity(BusinessPartnerID='123')
    SalesOrder  - Entity(SalesOrderID='0815')
        SalesOrderLineItem -
 Entity(SalesOrderID= '0815',Item='10')
        SalesOrderLineItem -
 Entity(SalesOrderID= '0815',Item='20')
        SalesOrderLineItem -
```

```
Entity(SalesOrderID= '0815',Item='30')
   SalesOrder  - Entity(SalesOrderID='0816')
       SalesOrderLineItem -
Entity(SalesOrderID= '0816',Item='10')
       SalesOrderLineItem -
Entity(SalesOrderID= '0816',Item='20')
       SalesOrderLineItem -
Entity(SalesOrderID= '0816',Item='30')
   ...
```

The `$expand` query option allows you to perform nested calls along the navigation properties of the EDM. The SAP Gateway framework automatically executes the corresponding `GET_ENTITYSET`/`GET_ENTITY` method of the related entity type. However, you need to consider the performance and the number of RFCs that have to be performed to retrieve the requested data.

GET_ENTITY_SET
In the first example, we performed an `$expand` of the sales order line items for a single sales order. To retrieve the data of these two entity types (sales order header and sales order line item), the SAP Gateway framework performs the corresponding `GET_ENTITY_SET`/`GET_ENTITY` methods of the underlying service implementation independently of each other. In the given example, this may result in calling the identical RFC module twice because the sales order header and the list of sales order line items are typically retrieved via a `GET_DETAIL` RFC function module (see Chapter 5 and Chapter 6 for more details about service implementation).

GET_EXPANDED_ENTITYSET
To avoid such inefficient calls, it's possible to implement a dedicated method in the service implementation that retrieves the result of an `$expand` statement with a single call (`GET_EXPANDED_ENTITY`/`GET_EXPAND-ED_ENTITYSET`). The implementation of that method is optional, but it should definitely be considered to avoid unnecessary backend calls and to improve performance.

2.4.6 Formatting ($format)

$format
The `$format` query option defines the format of an OData call as well as the expected response. The following two options of the OData 2.0 specification are supported: XML and JSON. The default is XML, so if you

don't add the `$format` query option, the SAP Gateway server automatically assumes `$format=xml`.

Let's look at the following example of a request that selects all business partners whose company name starts with an "S" and that only retrieves the `BusinessPartnerID` and `CompanyName` properties from the `Business-PartnerSet` that we used earlier. Using the `$format=xml` query option creates the result shown in Figure 2.17, whereas the same query result using the `$format=json` query option is depicted in Figure 2.18.

XML

```
<feed xmlns="http://www.w3.org/2005/Atom" xml:base="https://SAPES4.SAPDEVCENTER.COM:443/sap/opu/odata/IWBEP/GWSAMPLE_BASIC/"
xmlns:d="http://schemas.microsoft.com/ado/2007/08/dataservices" xmlns:m="http://schemas.microsoft.com/ado/2007/08/dataservices/metadata">
  <id>https://SAPES4.SAPDEVCENTER.COM:443/sap/opu/odata/IWBEP/GWSAMPLE_BASIC/BusinessPartnerSet</id>
  <title type="text">BusinessPartnerSet</title>
  <updated>2015-12-08T22:23:54Z</updated>
- <author>
    <name/>
  </author>
  <link title="BusinessPartnerSet" rel="self" href="BusinessPartnerSet"/>
- <entry m:etag="W/"datetime'2015-10-12T23%3A41%3A54.4490000'"">
    <id>https://SAPES4.SAPDEVCENTER.COM:443/sap/opu/odata/IWBEP/GWSAMPLE_BASIC/BusinessPartnerSet('0100000000')</id>
    <title type="text">BusinessPartnerSet('0100000000')</title>
    <updated>2015-12-08T22:23:54Z</updated>
    <category scheme="http://schemas.microsoft.com/ado/2007/08/dataservices/scheme" term="/IWBEP/GWSAMPLE_BASIC.BusinessPartner"/>
    <link title="BusinessPartner" rel="edit" href="BusinessPartnerSet('0100000000')"/>
  - <content type="application/xml">
    - <m:properties xmlns:d="http://schemas.microsoft.com/ado/2007/08/dataservices"
      xmlns:m="http://schemas.microsoft.com/ado/2007/08/dataservices/metadata">
        <d:BusinessPartnerID>0100000000</d:BusinessPartnerID>
        <d:CompanyName>SAP</d:CompanyName>
      </m:properties>
    </content>
  </entry>
+ <entry m:etag="W/"datetime'2015-02-13T13%3A48%3A59.0000000'"">...</entry>
+ <entry m:etag="W/"datetime'2015-02-13T13%3A48%3A59.0000000'"">...</entry>
+ <entry m:etag="W/"datetime'2015-02-13T13%3A48%3A59.0000000'"">...</entry>
</feed>
```

Figure 2.17 Response Using the XML Format

```
{
- d: {
  - results: [
    - {
      - __metadata: {
          id: https://SAPES4.SAPDEVCENTER.COM:443/sap/opu/odata/IWBEP/GWSAMPLE_BASIC/BusinessPartnerSet('0100000000'),
          uri: https://SAPES4.SAPDEVCENTER.COM:443/sap/opu/odata/IWBEP/GWSAMPLE_BASIC/BusinessPartnerSet('0100000000'),
          type: "/IWBEP/GWSAMPLE_BASIC.BusinessPartner",
          etag: "W/"datetime'2015-10-12T23%3A41%3A54.4490000'""
        },
        BusinessPartnerID: "0100000000",
        CompanyName: "SAP"
      },
    + {...},
    + {...},
    + {...}
    ]
  }
}
```

Figure 2.18 Response Using the JSON Format

103

As you can see, there is typically less overhead in a JSON-formatted request/response in contrast to an XML-formatted one. Therefore, it makes sense to use the JSON format whenever the consuming side is capable of handling this format.

Browser-Based Access

It's worth noting here how browsers handle the server responses in either XML or JSON. If you want to display the server responses in the JSON format, we recommend using either Firefox or Google Chrome, where you can install appropriate add-ons that perform a rendering in a user-friendly format.

If you're using Firefox, make sure that the JSONView add-on is installed. If it's not installed, choose TOOLS • ADDONS from the menu bar, and enter "JSON-View" as the search string.

If you choose to retrieve the server response in XML format, which is the default format used by SAP Gateway, the SAP Gateway server returns XML with a MIME type of `application/atom+xml`. Most modern browsers interpret this as an Atom feed and format the results in the manner of a news feed. If the results are shown like a feed, details of the server response are suppressed that we want to explore here.

We thus recommend considering the `sap-ds-debug=true` query parameter, which is very helpful when testing your OData service with any browser. Adding this query parameter to the URL instructs the SAP Gateway hub not only to return plain XML or JSON but also to return a dynamically generated HTML page containing the result along with, for example, HTML navigation links.

Excel support SAP Gateway also supports the `$format=xslx` query option. In this case, the response is the binary representation of an Excel file of type `*.xlsx` that can be downloaded by the consumer. The same can be achieved by sending the HTTP header `accept = application/vnd.openxmlformats-officedocument.spreadsheetml.sheet`.

Note that the format XLSX is only supported if the SAP Gateway server is on a SAP NetWeaver 7.40 release and higher and that several restrictions apply (e.g. no support for `$expand`) as outlined in the SAP Gateway foundation (SAP_GWFND) documentation.

2.5   OData in SAP Solutions

Because OData is extensible, you can enrich standard OData requests and responses with extra information. OData for SAP products is an OData extended by SAP to better fit business needs. It contains SAP-specific metadata that helps the developer consume SAP business data, such as descriptions of fields that can be retrieved from the ABAP Data Dictionary (DDIC).

The following are examples of OData for SAP applications:

Examples of OData for SAP

▶ Human-readable, language-dependent labels for all properties (required for building user interfaces [UIs]).

▶ Free-text search, within collections of similar entities, and across collections using OpenSearch.

▶ Semantic annotations, which are required for applications running on mobile devices to provide seamless integration with the contacts, calendar, and telephone functionalities. The client needs to know which OData properties contain a phone number, a part of a name or address, or something related to a calendar event.

Not all entities and entity sets will support the full spectrum of possible interactions defined by the uniform interface, so capability discovery helps clients avoid requests that the server can't fulfill. The metadata document tells whether an entity set is searchable, which properties may be used in filter expressions, and which properties of an entity will always be managed by the server.

As a result, the OData data format enhanced by SAP annotations makes SAP business information both human-readable and self-describing. The barrier for consuming SAP business data and functionality is lowered to where no specialized knowledge of an SAP system is required. Backend data is decoupled from the consumption in the frontend. A new group of developers with little to no SAP background can develop against SAP systems with minimal training. These developers are able to pick the technology of their choice to access SAP data and SAP functionality in a convenient way. In the end, this allows not only for the creation of new applications but also for the enrichment of already-existing applications with SAP data and functionality for a large number of target platforms and technologies (Figure 2.19).

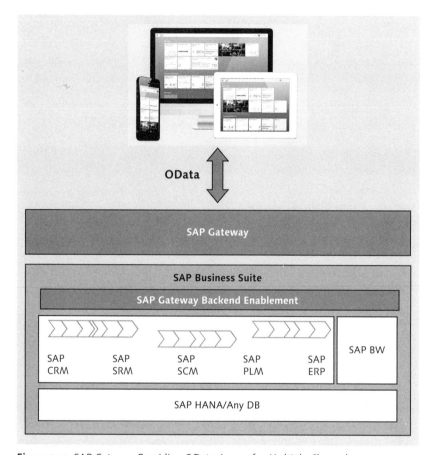

Figure 2.19 SAP Gateway Providing OData Access for Multiple Channels

Both ABAP and non-ABAP solutions

Almost all OData provisioning and consumption at SAP is done using SAP Gateway, and a number of very diverse products and solutions base major or minor parts of their features and functionalities on OData via SAP Gateway. This includes both ABAP-based solutions and non-ABAP solutions.

In this section, we take a look at some of the diverse SAP solutions that benefit from OData.

2.5.1   Mobile Productivity Applications

Mobile has been very important for SAP for a while. SAP mobile applications can be downloaded using typical channels such as Android Market, Blackberry App World, iTunes, or Microsoft Marketplace. Applications target scenarios such as mobile HR support for managers (SAP ERP Human Capital Management [SAP ERP HCM] Manager Insight), support for hospitals (SAP Electronic Medical Record [EMR]), or access to customer financial profiles for sales reps (SAP Customer Financial Fact Sheet).

A significant amount of SAP's mobile applications use OData based on SAP Gateway for communicating with mobile devices, often in close collaboration with SAP Mobile Platform. The latter, for example, provides workflow notifications to mobile consumers, allows for device-specific handling of push notifications, and provides a reverse proxy.

2.5.2   SAP Fiori

SAP Fiori is a collection of applications providing a simple, intuitive user experience across a number of selected SAP business transactions. These transactions have been selected by the frequency of usage and the business value for end users. SAP Fiori has a consistent design across all of the different supported transactions and, even more important, across all of the different interaction channels and platforms SAP Fiori targets—desktop, tablet, and mobile. An SAP Fiori application is used the same way across devices and looks mostly the same but with optimizations depending on the device that's being used to consume it.

SAP Fiori is based on SAP Gateway and OData for its SAP Business Suite connectivity. As a frontend technology, it relies on SAPUI5/HTML5. For more information on SAP Fiori and SAPUI5, see Chapter 8, Chapter 9, and Chapter 10.

SAPUI5/HTML5

2.5.3   SAP Jam

SAP Jam is an enterprise social network that combines the platform of SAP Jam with the features of SAP StreamWork. SAP Jam provides the basis for social learning, onboarding, and other talent processes. It improves these

SAP Success-Factors

processes by allowing employees to more easily find the content and experts to help them with their business needs. Furthermore, employees can discuss and learn from each other in communities. Features such as simple video and screen capture, polling, activity feeds, and public and private groups enable new approaches to doing business. SAP Jam builds on the same profile and organization data available in other SAP SuccessFactors modules.

In a further step to open up to the outside world, SAP Jam allows for OData provisioning and OData consumption:

▸ The OData-SAP Jam API allows for easy OData provisioning. It offers easy creation of social business applications using mashups between SAP Jam and SAP Gateway.

▸ Business events and other business attributes can be consumed via SAP Gateway and are then displayed in the SAP Jam feed.

2.5.4 SAP Enterprise Portal

SAP Enterprise Portal allows for the generation of basic UIs based on OData. This is done using an Eclipse-based assistant that analyzes fields and relations of an OData service and then supports the definition of a basic application. The generated application is based on the *list detail pattern*, which means that you can branch into details by starting from a list of values.

iViews   In addition, it's possible to create iViews that display SAPUI5 applications in SAP Enterprise Portal. These are based on the application integration iView template *com.sap.portal.appintegrator.sap*.

2.5.5 SAP Gateway for Microsoft

Microsoft integration   SAP Gateway for Microsoft (GWM) is a product that makes it even easier to integrate SAP Gateway-based OData services into Microsoft-based products. The relevant data are still stored in the SAP backend; however, various Microsoft products such as Microsoft Excel, Microsoft SharePoint, or Microsoft Azure can be used as the UI. Visual Studio developers can leverage the enterprise-ready functionalities that are generated by the GWM add-in. Without needing specific SAP know-how, the .NET developer can leverage security, single sign-on (SSO) (e.g., X.509, Security Assertion Markup Language [SAML] 2.0, etc.), centralized configuration (e.g., controlled via group policies), and logging (e.g., integration in SAP Solution Manager).

2.5.6 SAP Solution Manager

SAP Solution Manager is one of the crucial components of an SAP environment because it offers support throughout the entire lifecycle of SAP solutions, from the business blueprint to the configuration to production processing. A one-stop shop approach with respect to tools, methods, and preconfigured contents is what makes SAP Solution Manager so unique. One of SAP Solution Manager's main goals is to allow for a timely reaction to problems. To achieve this, monitoring is essential. Using mobile applications either on Android or iOS, IT environments can now be monitored on the go. To allow for this mobile monitoring, SAP Gateway comes preinstalled with newer versions of SAP Solution Manager. The mobile application can either communicate directly using OData or, alternatively, if the SAP Mobile Platform is available, via the SAP Mobile Platform and then using OData to connect to SAP Gateway.

2.5.7 SAP HANA

SAP HANA is SAP's fastest selling product of all time. This in-memory data platform is deployable as an on-premise appliance or in the cloud. It's best suited for performing real-time analytics, as well as developing and deploying real-time applications. At the core of this real-time data platform is the SAP HANA database, which is fundamentally different from any other database engine in the market today.

SAP HANA allows for both real-time analytics and real-time applications. In respect to analytics, it supports operational reporting (real-time insights from transactional systems such as SAP ERP), data warehousing (SAP Business Warehouse [BW] on SAP HANA), and predictive and text analysis on big data. With respect to real-time applications, it's good for, for example, core process accelerators (transactional data are replicated in real time from SAP ERP into SAP HANA for immediate reporting, and then results can even be fed back into SAP ERP), planning and optimization applications (e.g., sales planning, cash forecasting), and sense and response applications that provide real-time insights in big data (e.g., smart meter applications).

OLAP and OLTP   All of this is possible due to SAP HANA's secret sauce: Online Analytical Processing (OLAP) *and* Online Transaction Processing (OLTP). Other database management systems (DBMSs) on the market are typically either good at transactional workloads or analytical workloads—but not both. When transactional DBMS products are used for analytical workloads, they require you to separate your workloads into different databases (OLAP and OLTP). You have to extract data from your transactional system (SAP ERP), transform that data for reporting, and load it into a reporting database (SAP BW). The reporting database still requires significant effort in creating and maintaining tuning structures, such as aggregates and indexes, to provide even moderate performance. Due to its hybrid structure for processing transactional workloads and analytical workloads fully in-memory, SAP HANA combines the best of both worlds.

SAP HANA offers numerous possibilities for improving business processes, and the usage of OData enhances this potential. To allow for the most flexible consumption of information via OData, SAP HANA allows for two different models: the usage of SAP Gateway with the SAP Business Suite running on top of an SAP HANA database (*SAP Business Suite on SAP HANA*) or usage of the native SAP HANA OData support via *SAP HANA Extended Application Services* (*SAP HANA XS*).

SAP Business Suite on SAP HANA

SAP Business Suite on SAP HANA has worked on optimizing the code of the SAP Business Suite to leverage a number of SAP HANA-specific features. Because SAP Business Suite on SAP HANA is still based on the same code line as the classical SAP Business Suite, there wasn't a complete redesign as in SAP S/4HANA.

With SAP Business Suite on SAP HANA, customers are able to benefit from the following optimizations:

▶ **SAP HANA Live**
SAP HANA Live leverages the real-time operational reporting capabilities of SAP HANA directly on the data of your SAP Business Suite on SAP HANA system.

▶ **SAP Fiori Smart Business cockpits**
SAP Fiori Smart Business cockpits allow you to get real-time insights in your business processes using OData services leveraging SAP HANA Live.

▶ **Free-text searches**
It's now possible to perform a Google-like search in SAP ERP by leveraging SAP Gateway-powered OData services. This can help customer service, for example, by reducing the response times to your customers.

SAP HANA Extended Application Services

SAP HANA XS was introduced with SAP HANA SPS 5. The core concept of SAP HANA XS is to deeply embed a full-featured application server, web server, and development environment within the core parts of the SAP HANA database. This allows for outstanding performance and access to SAP HANA core features. With SAP HANA XS, you can now build and deploy your application completely within SAP HANA, providing a lower cost of development and ownership. To facilitate creating applications, SAP HANA Studio comes with all of the necessary tools.

The SAP HANA XS programming model allows you to generate OData services from any existing SAP HANA table or view. The process is simple and straightforward. From within an SAP HANA project, you can create a service definition document (*xsodata*). Within this document, you can specify the name of the source table/view, an entity name, and, optionally, the entity key fields.

SAP HANA XS OData services are great because they provide a large amount of functionality with minimal amounts of development effort.

They currently come with a few limitations, however: only the OData service framework is read. On the other hand, they are quick. Upon activation, there is an executable service that is ready to test. The generated service supports standard OData parameters such as $metadata for introspection, $filter, $orderby, and so on. It also supports Atom/XML and JSON.

2.5.8   SAP S/4HANA

SAP S/4HANA is SAP's new flagship product. This SAP ERP innovation is based on SAP HANA and SAP NetWeaver 7.50 ABAP technology. SAP S/4HANA leverages the SAP Gateway framework that is part of the SAP NetWeaver 7.50 stack and comes in two versions:

▶ **Cloud-based**
The SAP Gateway stack isn't visible to the customer because customers aren't allowed to build their own OData services using Transaction SEGW or perform any other deep-dive custom development.

▶ **On-premise**
Customers have complete freedom to create OData services or any other kind of repository objects. As in SAP Business Suite, it's possible to develop OData services as described in this book.

As a customer or partner, you can leverage the knowledge of OData service development that we provide in this book in SAP Business Suite systems as well as in on-premise SAP S/4HANA systems.

2.5.9   SAP-Certified Partner Solutions

One of the strengths of SAP Gateway is its openness, which is highly beneficial for SAP's large ecosystem. Many SAP partners have already developed SAP Gateway-based solutions or are in the process of doing so. For these solutions, SAP offers a certification. An overview of certified SAP Gateway-based partner solutions can be found on the SAP Partner Finder website (*go.sap.com/partner/find.html*).

2.6   SAP Gateway OData Features

As the core of SAP's OData strategy, SAP Gateway provides OData access for multiple channels and is regularly extended. As of this writing (April 2016), the current version of SAP Gateway (SAP Gateway in SAP Net-Weaver 7.50 SP 1) supports the OData features listed in Table 2.9.

OData Feature	Description
Atom	Atom is an XML-based document format that describes lists of related information known as *feeds*.
JSON	JSON is a lightweight data interchange format based on a subset of the JavaScript programming language standard.
OpenSearch description	The OpenSearch description document format can be used to describe a search engine so that it can be used by search client applications.
HTTP status code	HTTP status codes are defined in exceptional cases via the service implementation.
CRUD	The HTTP POST, GET, UPDATED, and DELETE requests are performed on resources.
Read (media resources)	The binary association of a media link entry is read. The media link entry can either point to an internal binary in a table, for example, or to an external link that must be set in the data provider.
CUD (media resources)	Create, update, and delete media resources are associated with a media link entry.
Batch handling	Batch requests allow the grouping of multiple operations into a single HTTP request payload.
Repeatable requests/ idempotency	Any kind of operation can be repeated by providing a request ID. A repeated request is processed by the idempotency framework (fallback). This can be used to avoid multiple executions of a certain operation.

Table 2.9 Overview of Selected OData Features Supported by SAP Gateway

OData Feature	Description
Deep insert	This operation creates an entity with deep data in an inline format, for example, to create a parent/child relationship simultaneously.
Expand	A URI with an $expand system query option indicates that entries associated with the entry or collection of entries identified by the resource path section of the URI must be represented inline.
Merge/patch	An update request sent via HTTP method MERGE/PATCH indicates that a subset of the entry's properties is sent to the server and should be merged with those fields that aren't present in the request.
Paging	The $top and $skip system query options identify a subset of the entries in the collection of entries.
Filter	The $filter system query option identifies a subset of the entries in the collection of entries.
Order by	The $orderby system query option specifies an expression for determining what values are used to order the collection of entries.
Select (handled by OData client generically)	The $links option specifies that the response to the request contains the links between an entry and an associated entry or a collection of entries.
Skip token (server-driven paging)	The request response contains an `<atom:link rel="next">` element for partial representations of the collection of entries.

Table 2.9 Overview of Selected OData Features Supported by SAP Gateway (Cont.)

OData Feature	Description
Multiorigin/ multidestination	A service may need to connect to multiple backend systems, and the backend calls are done in parallel.
XSRF token-based protection mechanism	The protection against cross-site request forgery (XSRF) attacks is ensured via a token-based exchange mechanism in the HTTP request/response header between the client and the server.

Table 2.9 Overview of Selected OData Features Supported by SAP Gateway (Cont.)

2.7 What's New with OData 4.0?

As previously mentioned in this chapter (see Section 2.1.2), the OData protocol has become an OASIS standard with the release of OData 4.0. At the time of this writing (April 2016), SAP Gateway doesn't currently support OData 4.0. According to the SAP Gateway roadmap, however, SAP plans to support OData 4.0 in the future.

Although most—if not all—that we discuss about OData does also apply to OData 4.0, we want to give an outlook of which new features you can expect with the planned OData 4.0 support in SAP Gateway. In the following subsections, we'll concentrate on those features in OData 4.0 that will be most important for SAP products. A complete list of the changes in OData 4.0 compared to OData 2.0 can be found in the documentation at *www.odata.org/documentation*.

2.7.1 New JavaScript Object Notation Format

JSON is now the recommended and default format used by OData 4.0 services. The new JSON format has been redesigned completely in OData 4.0. The amount of data that is transferred over the wire has been reduced to the bare minimum. All unnecessary metadata has been removed so that the payload more or less only contains name-value pairs. This way, it's possible to achieve a reduction of the payload size up to 60% (see Figure 2.20).

```
d: {
-   __metadata: {
        id: https://ldailgly.wdf.sap.corp:44356/sap/opu/odata/IWBEP/GWSAMPLE_BASIC/ProductSet('HT-1000'),
        uri: https://ldailgly.wdf.sap.corp:44356/sap/opu/odata/IWBEP/GWSAMPLE_BASIC/ProductSet('HT-1000'),
        type: "/IWBEP/GWSAMPLE_BASIC.Product",
        etag: "W/"datetime'2015-10-22T09%3A43%3A25.0000000'""
    },
    ProductID: "HT-1000",                                    V2 Payload Product Details
    TypeCode: "PR",
    Category: "Notebooks",
    Name: "Notebook Basic 15",
    NameLanguage: "EN",
    Description: "Notebook Basic 15 with 2,80 GHz quad core, 15" LCD, 4 GB DDR3 RAM, 500 GB Hard Disc, Windows 8 Pro",
    DescriptionLanguage: "EN",
    SupplierID: "0100000000",
    SupplierName: "SAP",
    TaxTarifCode: 1,
    MeasureUnit: "EA",
    WeightMeasure: "4.200",
    WeightUnit: "KG",
    CurrencyCode: "EUR",
    Price: "956.00",
    Width: "30.000",
    Depth: "18.000",
    Height: "3.000",
    DimUnit: "CM",
    CreatedAt: "/Date(1445507005000)/",
    ChangedAt: "/Date(1445507005000)/",
-   ToSalesOrderLineItems: {
    -   __deferred: {
            uri: https://ldailgly.wdf.sap.corp:44356/sap/opu/odata/IWBEP/GWSAMPLE_BASIC/ProductSet('HT-1000')/ToSalesOrderLineItems
        }
    },
-   ToSupplier: {
    -   __deferred: {
            uri: https://ldailgly.wdf.sap.corp:44356/sap/opu/odata/IWBEP/GWSAMPLE_BASIC/ProductSet('HT-1000')/ToSupplier
        }
    }
}
```

```
{
    @odata.context: "$metadata#ProductList/$entity",
    ProductID: "HT-1000",                                    V4 Payload Product List
    TypeCode: "PR",
    Category: "Notebooks",
    Name: "Notebook Basic 15",
    NameLanguage: "EN",
    Description: "Notebook Basic 15 with 2,80 GHz quad core, 15" LCD, 4 GB DDR3 RAM, 500 GB Hard Disc, Windows 8 Pro",
    DescriptionLanguage: "EN",
    SupplierID: "100000000",
    SupplierName: "SAP",
    TaxTarifCode: 1,
    MeasureUnit: "EA",
    WeightMeasure: 4.2,
    WeightUnit: "KG",
    CurrencyCode: "EUR",
    Price: 956,
    Width: 30,
    Depth: 18,
    Height: 3,
    DimUnit: "CM",
    CreatedAt: "2015-10-22T09:43:25Z",
    ChangedAt: "2015-10-22T09:43:25Z"
}
```

Figure 2.20 OData 2.0 versus OData 4.0 Payload Size: Product Details

2.7.2 Powerful Query Language

Through the enhanced query language capabilities in OData 4.0, it's possible to request exactly the desired subset of data with fewer roundtrips than in OData 2.0. Let's look at two examples of the new query language capabilities.

Analytical query options such as `groupby` also come as part of OData 4.0 (see Figure 2.21). Therefore, the result set can be significantly smaller than the source. An example is shown in the following syntax:

Aggregation

```
GET Sales?$apply=groupby((Product),aggregate(Amount with sum as
Total))
```

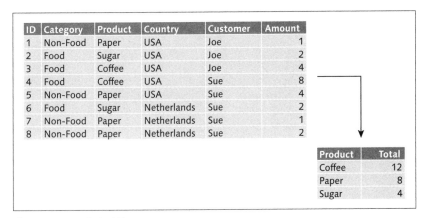

Figure 2.21 Analytical Features

In OData 4.0, it's possible to filter expanded entities on each level. Think about a scenario where you would like to retrieve one or more business partners located in one city (e.g., Walldorf) alongside those sales orders that have a gross amount larger than a certain threshold, with the objective of retrieving only those sales order items that contain the product HT-1041.

$filter and $expand

The corresponding request in OData 4.0 looks as follows:

```
/BusinessPartnerList?$filter=Address/City eq 'Walldorf'&
$expand=BP_2_SO($filter=GrossAmount ge 1100;
$expand=SO_2_SOITEM($filter=Product/ProductID eq 'HT-1041'))
```

The simplified results of the request are shown in Figure 2.22, where we've marked the values that fit the filter conditions.

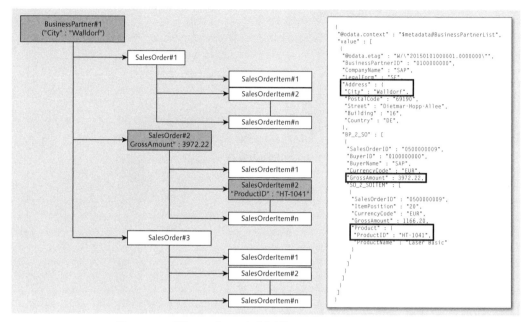

Figure 2.22 Filter on Expanded Entities

2.7.3 Cross-Service Navigation

Whereas in OData 2.0, it was only possible to have navigation properties that point from one entity set to a second entity set in the same OData service, you can now have navigation properties that point to an entity of a referenced service.

Cross-service navigation can, for example, be used for reusing services. Think about an OData service used as a search help that can be leveraged by several other OData services. The portioning of services also helps speed up consumer applications because it allows for a lazy loading of huge service models.

2.7.4 Actions and Functions

There is now a clear separation between nonmodifying and modifying requests that can't be expressed via normal CRUD-Q requests. Whereas the new `edm:Action` element defines the signature of an action describing a modifying request that goes beyond a simple CUD request, the `edm:Function` element defines the signature of a function that can be used to query data in a way that can't simply be expressed with a classic OData query option.

2.7.5 Vocabularies and Annotations

In OData 4.0, vocabularies and annotations will play an important role. SAP Gateway already supports SAP-specific annotations, such as `sap:updatable`, `sap:creatable`, and so on, and will also support OData 4.0 annotations.

2.8 Summary

In this chapter, we've introduced you to OData, which is the underlying protocol that SAP Gateway enables. Although the chapter isn't meant to be a comprehensive discussion of the topic, you should now have a basic understanding of what it is and how it works. To close out our discussion, we'll leave you with some tips and tricks for working with OData.

---

10 OData Dos and Don'ts

- ▶ *Do* think in REST terms.
- ▶ *Do* use the OData system query options `$filter`, `$top`, `$skip`, and `$orderby`.
- ▶ *Do* provide a usable set of filterable properties.
- ▶ *Do* make your properties concrete and readable.
- ▶ *Do* use the right data type for your properties.
- ▶ *Do* use media resources and media link entries instead of binary properties.
- ▶ *Do* follow links provided by the server; *don't* construct links in your client application.
- ▶ *Don't* invent your own custom query options.
- ▶ *Do* strive for high-quality services (e.g., in respect to usability and performance).
- ▶ *Don't* construct URIs in your client application; follow the links provided by the server.

This chapter explains the architectural concepts of SAP Gateway and provides a high-level look at its integration with other SAP interfaces. It lays the foundations for later chapters by introducing a certain part of the theoretical groundwork required for SAP Gateway development.

3   Architecture and Integration

Extended scope

SAP Gateway has a clear goal to open up classic SAP systems to non-ABAP developers. Initially, the scope of SAP Gateway was limited to so-called "lightweight consumption" use cases. To achieve and facilitate these use cases, SAP Gateway provided a platform for provisioning and consumption of services and diverse tools for developing content to be consumed. Now, the definition of gateway principles and their implementation across SAP has broadened the usage of SAP Gateway by allowing for additional usage scenarios, such as analytical consumption.

On the following pages, you'll gain an understanding of the architectural concepts behind gateway principles, an overview of SAP Gateway's architecture, and information about what data sources SAP Gateway can use to integrate with your SAP systems.

3.1   Gateway Principles

Timeless software

At the beginning of enterprise software, systems had been designed as both monolithic and self-contained. With the evolution of enterprise software into a landscape of many systems for various purposes, the challenge of how to connect these systems into end-to-end processes and experiences became obvious. The multisystem landscape is a reality today and, in many cases, even desirable to separate different aspects of running businesses. However, the introduction of middle-tier layers in enterprise landscapes for improved system connection also introduced high cost, complexity, proprietary solutions, and many silo-like approaches for exposing data to the middle tier and connecting systems to each other.

To ease the multisystem landscape complexity, SAP has created a set of *timeless software principles* for how enterprise software systems should be engineered. Timeless software is a systematic and layered approach to how a system of record should be efficiently exposed and how it should interface with the overall system landscape, development tools, runtime engines, and the lifecycle of software.

A differentiation was made between aspects that are local to a system and that adapt the behavior of a given system or platform (platform adaptation) and the needs of a given consumer and the necessary infrastructure to serve a specific consumer (consumer adaptation). This separation makes sense because in an ideal landscape, platform adaptation is coupled to a certain system of record and required once for every system. Consumer adaptation for a specific channel (e.g., mobile, portals, social, UIs, analytics) is required only once per landscape and not for every individual system.

SAP's gateway principles are a set of architectural concepts, methods, design patterns, and standards describing how an enterprise system should make its data and functions available for consumption. They aim to provide access to systems of record by multiple channels and for multiple consumers. Gateway principles are used as guidance for platform adaptation in systems of record and for enabling developers to build timeless applications on top of these platforms. Furthermore, they are applicable for different application domains (e.g., lightweight, analytical, or social consumption).

Elemental gateway principles include the following:

- **Openness**
  Services can be consumed from any device and any platform, and they can create any experience.

- **Timelessness**
  Services work with almost any SAP Business Suite version.

▸ **Ease of consumption**

Application programming interfaces (APIs) are easy to consume, and no internal SAP knowledge is required for the consumption of services.

▸ **User focus**

User interaction scenarios are a main driver for the architecture.

▸ **Division of work**

Non-SAP developers can consume services without any ABAP skills; they can work on the client development almost fully independent of the SAP Gateway service development.

SAP Gateway, in its current form, is based on gateway principles, architectural concepts, design patterns, and standards for diverse application flavors.

3.2   Architecture

From a bird's-eye view, SAP Gateway's architecture consists of three tiers: the SAP Business Suite tier, the SAP Gateway Server tier, and the consumer tier (Figure 3.1).

Three-tier architecture

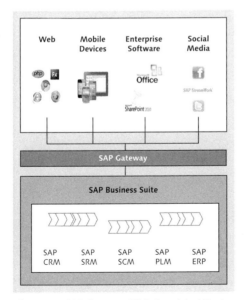

Figure 3.1 SAP Gateway High-Level Architecture

Each tier serves a clearly defined purpose and bundles components needed to fulfill this purpose.

With this approach, lifecycles of the existing SAP Business Suite implementation and the client application environment are decoupled, and concerns are separated. As a result, the dependencies between systems are reduced to a minimum so that upgrades, updates, and deployments have no cross impact. The resulting outcome is a highly flexible landscape architecture that addresses a broad range of possible applications and scenarios.

Consumer tier

The consumer tier is where the actual consumption of SAP Gateway services takes place; with respect to consumption, this serves as the access point. Consumers are any UI-centric clients consuming OData protocol-compliant resources that are exposed by SAP Gateway. This exposure can either happen directly or indirectly, via additional infrastructure components (e.g., via SAP Mobile Platform or SAP API Management). Typical consumers of SAP Gateway services include mobile devices and SAP Fiori.

SAP Gateway tier

Not surprisingly, the SAP Gateway tier holds the major part of SAP Gateway functionalities and components, including the core components. It serves a number of purposes:

▸ Functions as the man in the middle between the backend and the consumer based on runtime components, metadata components, and the OData library.

▸ Provides tools for the development and creation of SAP Gateway services.

▸ Offers everything needed for operating an SAP Gateway landscape, such as logging, tracing, performance analysis tools, and globalization support.

SAP Business
Suite tier

The SAP Business Suite tier is where business application data is located; it remains the system of record with respect to data. In addition, it holds the business logic of the SAP Business Suite, which means that for most applications, it holds by far the biggest part of the business logic. With respect to SAP Gateway-specific components, the SAP Business Suite tier consists of the SAP_GWFND software component, which is included in SAP NetWeaver as of SAP NetWeaver ABAP 7.40 SP 02. In earlier versions, the IW_BEP add-on contained business enablement and event provisioning and had to be deployed separately.

Depending on the landscape setup and the usage scenario, the specific setup of SAP Gateway can differ. As we briefly introduced in Chapter 1, there are basically two main deployment options: on a separate SAP Gateway system (hub deployment) and deployment embedded on the SAP Business Suite system (embedded deployment). In addition, to these main options, a mixed deployment is possible. The specific landscape and usage scenario determines which deployment option to choose. (We'll go into more detail about this in Chapter 4.)

As we said, the major part of SAP Gateway lies in the middle tier, but it's important to know which SAP Gateway components can be found in the other tiers as well. Therefore, let's dig deeper and look more closely at the three tiers and their main components in detail, as shown in Figure 3.2. In Section 3.2.4, we'll also devote some time to explaining the add-on structure of SAP Gateway.

Detailed architecture

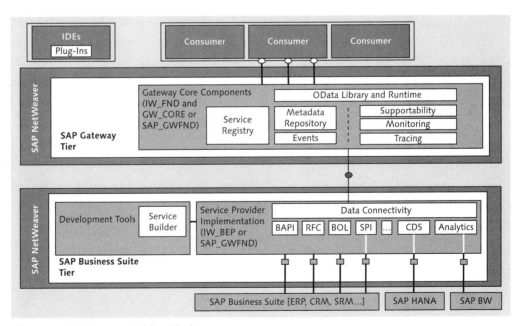

Figure 3.2 SAP Gateway Building Blocks

3.2.1 Consumer Tier

In the consumer tier, two kinds of components can be found: SAP Gateway consumers and integrated development environments (IDEs).

SAP Gateway Consumers

UI-centric clients *SAP Gateway consumers* are components that consume SAP Gateway services. SAP Gateway is primarily designed to provide UI-centric clients (e.g., mobile, native, or web applications, such as SAPUI5/HTML5) access to business data. Clients can access SAP Gateway both directly and indirectly via additional infrastructure components. The SAP Mobile Platform is, for example, one of these additional infrastructure components for mobile scenarios. Duet Enterprise (joint development of SAP and Microsoft) is another one.

SAP Gateway consumers access REST API resources exposed by SAP Gateway via HTTP(S) using the OData protocol. In other words, there's actually not that much to know about SAP Gateway consumers; that, is, as long as a client technology can consume HTTP(S), it can consume SAP Gateway services. Also, if it can construct and parse XML, JSON, or Atom, it can then process the data received. In fact, SAP doesn't make any recommendations or impose any restrictions on which client technology or even development language should be used for the consumption of an SAP Gateway service. Just make sure your client technology of choice has facilities for HTTP(S) communication and can construct and parse an XML or JSON document. Beyond that, SAP Gateway offers full freedom with respect to the client technology. Communication becomes even easier if you use an OData client library that provides a richer developer experience for the client developer. This is because the OData client library performs all the heavy lifting of serialization, deserialization, and validation of the OData payloads.

Integrated Development Environments

IDEs are used to develop SAP Gateway consumers. These development environments are standard and well-known environments such as SAP Web IDE, Eclipse, or Microsoft Visual Studio. Depending on the environment, SAP provides SAP Gateway-specific features and improvements that allow you to easily and quickly create applications that consume SAP Gateway services.

3.2.2 SAP Gateway Tier

The SAP Gateway tier consists of the SAP Gateway core components (refer to Figure 3.2). Once again, the core components stay stable across versions when talking about the specific, individual components. These specific components are packaged in different ways in different versions of SAP Gateway. This means that GW_CORE and IW_FND before SAP NetWeaver 7.40 and SAP_GWFND as of SAP NetWeaver 7.40 contain the same specific core components—just packaged in different ways. In versions newer than SAP NetWeaver 7.40, the core components come via the SAP NetWeaver stack, and no additional software components have to be installed.

Core components

Overall, this tier is the heart of SAP Gateway. At the center of the heart are the *core components* (Figure 3.3). This encompasses several central components:

▶ **Runtime component**
Contains an OData-specific runtime that efficiently processes OData requests and the functionality required to expose OData services.

▶ **OData library**
Contains SAP-specific metadata that helps to consume SAP business data, such as descriptions of fields that can be retrieved from the ABAP Data Dictionary (DDIC).

▶ **Metadata component**
Manages metadata within the SAP Gateway server. The SAP Gateway metadata primarily describes OData models that are exposed as OData service documents and OData service metadata documents. In particular, the metadata component exposes the standardized description of OData services by assembling OData service documents and service metadata documents. The data are then cached in the metadata cache.

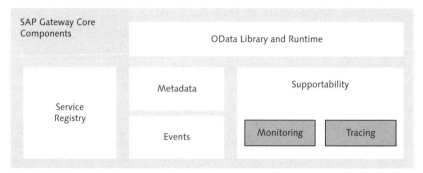

Figure 3.3 SAP Gateway Core Components

In addition to the central core components, a number of other components fall into the category of core components. The *service registry* is the data store that stores the linkage between an OData service and the actual implementation of this service, be it in the SAP Business Suite system or locally in SAP Gateway. Runtime services around *supportability*, *tracing*, and *monitoring* ensure a secure connection between consumers and SAP systems as well as the ability to monitor and trace messages from SAP Gateway components to the SAP Business Suite and back. Finally, *events* are supported to enable push scenarios (e.g., workflow scenarios where a component listens to business events in SAP systems and delivers a set of data descriptions of that event that can then be delivered to the consumer).

> **Generic Channel**
>
> In the initial releases of SAP Gateway, all development was done based on the *generic channel*. This channel was built on top of a generic framework that supported various exposure models. However, the OData channel was introduced with SAP NetWeaver Gateway 2.0 SP 03 and is tailored and optimized to fit the OData protocol specifications. Today, the OData channel is the preferred and strongly recommended option; the generic channel shouldn't be used anymore. Therefore, this book solely focuses on the OData channel where development usually takes place in the SAP Business Suite tier. (We explain the OData channel in much more detail in Chapter 5.)

3.2.3   SAP Business Suite Tier

The SAP Business Suite tier, as you might expect, holds the data and   Business logic
business logic of SAP Business Suite. It consists of development tools
and the service provider implementation. As of SAP NetWeaver ABAP
7.40 SP 02, the development tools and the service provider implementation are based on SAP_GWFND, which comes as standard in systems
based on SAP NetWeaver ABAP 7.40 SP 02 and higher and has replaced
several add-ons that previously needed to be installed in earlier versions.

These add-ons in versions below SAP NetWeaver ABAP 7.40 SP02
included the add-on for SAP Business Suite enablement and event provisioning (IW_BEP), IW_HDB, GW_CORE, and IW_FND.

Development Tools

A set of design-time tools located in the SAP Business Suite tier supports   Service Builder
the development of SAP Gateway services (Figure 3.4).

Figure 3.4 Tools for Service Development

They are very important because without them there would not be a lot
to consume — at least not a lot of things that are suited for specific usage
scenarios. (Most of the time, services are adjusted for a specific usage, if
not generated or developed from scratch to perfectly fit the usage.) The
Service Builder (Transaction SEGW) is the main tool for service creation,
and it provides developers with tools to facilitate this throughout the
entire development lifecycle of a service. The Service Builder provides
an OData-compliant modeling environment for the creation and maintenance of SAP Gateway services. All development artifacts developers
need to create a service are visualized, and wizards enable the creation
of aggregated objects based on remote function calls (RFCs), Business

Object Repository (BOR), and Business Application Programming Interfaces (BAPIs). In addition, it supports the developer when going for a code-based service implementation (For more details about the Service Builder, see Chapter 5.)

Service Provider Implementation

The service provider implementation (Figure 3.5) provides connectivity to SAP Business Suite systems and can connect to a variety of SAP interfaces. This includes BAPIs and RFCs as well as SAP Business Warehouse (BW), Service Provider Interface, or SAP HANA. The service provider implementation is called by the runtime component or metadata component to access services from SAP Business Suite.

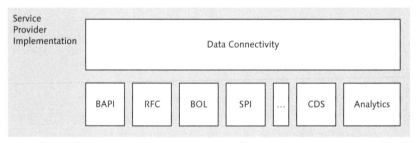

Figure 3.5 Service Provider Implementation

3.2.4 Add-On Structure Evolution

Add-ons   As we explained, SAP Gateway in versions earlier than SAP NetWeaver 7.40 SP 2 essentially consisted of a set of add-ons to the ABAP technology platform. Since then, the deployment of SAP Gateway has been optimized. Add-on structures before and after SAP NetWeaver 7.40 SP 2 differ, with new add-on structures having been simplified and optimized. Most of these former add-ons have become part of the SAP NetWeaver standard. Some additional add-ons for specific use cases remain, however.

Let's start by looking at the evolution of SAP Gateway add-ons/components over time. With SAP Gateway 7.02, there were four add-ons. Starting from SAP NetWeaver 7.40 SP 02, there have been deployment optimizations and targeted changes (Figure 3.6).

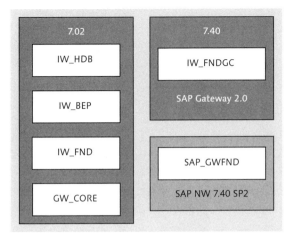

Figure 3.6 New Add-On Structure in SAP NetWeaver 7.40

These deployment optimizations have resulted primarily in two new software components: IW_FNDGC and SAP_GWFND. SAP_GWFND combines the four old add-ons—IW_HDB, IW_BEP, IW_FND, and GW_CORE. IW_FNDGC is only needed to support legacy functionalities for customers that are upgrading from SAP Gateway 2.0 to SAP NetWeaver 7.40 and higher. There are a few older add-ons that aren't recommended anymore (IW_CBS, IW_CNT, and IW_SCS) (Figure 3.7).

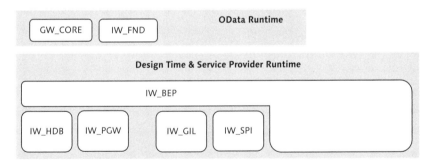

Figure 3.7 Functional View of SAP Gateway Components

As shown in Figure 3.7, for versions older than SAP NetWeaver 7.40 SP 2, there are two SAP Gateway tier framework add-ons (GW_CORE and IW_FND) and four SAP Business Suite tier add-ons (IW_BEP, IW_HDB, IW_GIL, and IW_SPI).

The following looks at the different framework components for the SAP Gateway tier:

- **GW_CORE**
  This contains the functionality required for OData protocols.

- **IW_FND**
  IW_FND, in which FND stands for foundation, holds the framework of the SAP Gateway server. This includes the runtime components, metadata component, and shared services such as monitoring, supportability, and security.

The following describes the SAP Business Suite enablement components:

- **IW_BEP (Business Enablement Provisioning [BEP])**
  This holds the SAP Business Suite enablement and event provisioning.

- **IW_HDB (SAP HANA)**
  This provides a business content adapter for SAP Gateway with SAP HANA that enables OData exposure of SAP HANA views via the ABAP Database Connectivity (ADBC) protocol.

- **IW_GIL (GenIL)**
  This provides a generic OData adapter for content based on the Generic Interaction Layer (GenIL).

- **IW_SPI (Service Provider Infrastructure)**
  This provides a generic OData adapter for content based on the Service Provider Infrastructure.

As of SAP NetWeaver 7.40 SP 2, the SAP_GWFND component combines the four old add-ons (IW_HDB, IW_BEP, IW_FND, and GW_CORE) into one. SAP_GWFND is part of the SAP NetWeaver standard. Consequently, if you have an SAP NetWeaver 7.40 SP 2 (or higher) installation, you can use SAP Gateway without having to install any additional software components.

SAP_GWFND contains the composite functional scope of the combined components. Therefore, it contains the functionality required for the OData protocol and holds the framework of the SAP Gateway server, including the runtime components, metadata component, and shared services such as monitoring, supportability, and security.

As a result, every SAP NetWeaver server that is based on SAP NetWeaver 7.40 SP 2 and higher can take the role of the SAP Gateway hub or the SAP Gateway backend.

There are also optional add-ons that can be installed, that is, the IW_SPI, IW_PGW, and IW_GIL content adapter components. These need only be installed to use specific functionality. Let's take a closer look at these components:

- **IW_PGW (Process Gateway)**
  If you plan on using SAP Fiori approval applications, such as *My Inbox*, and other SAP Fiori approval applications, you'll want to include the IW_PGW (typically referred to as Process Gateway) add-on. This add-on enables exposure for SAP Business Process Management (BPM) and process observer task exposure for SAP BPM and SAP Business Workflow. This add-on has to be installed on the SAP Gateway hub server and requires the IW_BEP add-on to be installed on the SAP Gateway hub as well.

- **IW_GIL (GenIL)**
  This provides a generic OData adapter for content based on the GenIL.

- **IW_SPI (Service Provider Infrastructure)**
  This provides a generic OData adapter for content based on the Service Provider Infrastructure.

3.3   Integration with Other Technologies

As stated in the introduction to this chapter, SAP Gateway has the clear goal to open up classic SAP systems to non-ABAP developers. These classic SAP systems already have a number of ways of exposing data via different channels to the outside world. So the logical way to allow for a broad set of services to be available for easy reuse is to take what is already there as a basis. SAP Gateway therefore provides tools for easy generation of OData services from existing data sources in the SAP Business Suite system by reusing these generic data access options. As a result, developers can use data sources such as RFC/BOR, SAP BW InfoCubes, multidimensional expressions (MDX), SAP BW Easy Query, Core Data Services (CDS), and content built on the GenIL framework and the

Reuse of data sources

Service Provider Infrastructure framework for the creation of SAP Gateway services.

SAP standard concepts versus add-ons Technology-wise, in some cases, standard SAP concepts (e.g., RFCs or BOR, CDS) are used. In other cases, enabling the different generic data access options by SAP Gateway takes place with add-ons (e.g., Service Provider Infrastructure). These add-ons are either local add-ons that are deployed on the respective SAP Business Suite system (e.g., IW_GIL) or remote enabled add-ons (e.g., IW_SPI). Let's take a look at each of these options in a little more detail.

3.3.1 Remote Function Call

An RFC is an SAP standard concept to call a function module running in a system different from the caller's system. The remote function can also be called from within the same system (as a remote call). The ability to call remote functions is provided by the RFC interface system. RFC allows for remote calls between two SAP systems or between an SAP system and a non-SAP system. RFCs consist of two kinds of interfaces, one for calling ABAP programs and one for calling non-ABAP programs. Because SAP Gateway targets opening up an ABAP system, the relevant kind of interfaces for this context are ABAP interfaces.

If an RFC function module is available, an SAP Gateway service can easily be exposed using the SAP Gateway development tools.

3.3.2 Business Object Repository

BAPIs SAP business objects and their BAPIs are managed within the BOR in a structure based on the hierarchy of the SAP Business Suite business application areas. Every single SAP business object type and its methods are identified and described in the BOR. This description includes the SAP business object types, their SAP interface types, and their components, such as methods, attributes, and events. BAPIs are defined as the methods of SAP business object types. To the outside, the SAP business object reveals only its interface.

The BOR contains all SAP business object types, which makes it a perfect basis for generating SAP Gateway services. These services can be easily built using the SAP Gateway development tools.

3.3.3 Service Provider Infrastructure

The Service Provider Infrastructure is an application- and UI-independent layer for business data exposure that is used across the entire SAP Business Suite. Examples include bill of material (BOM) in SAP Product Lifecycle Management (PLM), purchase requisition in Materials Management (MM), and sustainability enhancements for vendors in Financial Accounting (FI).

The Service Provider Infrastructure's main goal is to decouple the UI from the SAP Business Suite completely. It has no dependency on Web Dynpro or any other UI technology. Instead, it works as the backbone for different feeder technologies, such as SAP Interactive Forms by Adobe, and also offers a Floorplan Manager (FPM) integration.

Once again, this broad usage across the SAP Business Suite makes the Service Provider Infrastructure a great source for SAP Gateway OData services. An SAP Gateway OData service can be created easily from a Service Provider Infrastructure object using the Service Builder.

3.3.4 SAP BW InfoCubes

SAP BW, which is used for business intelligence, business planning, analytical services, and data warehousing, is an excellent source of high-quality analytical data.

InfoCubes are the central objects in SAP BW. An InfoCube is a set of relational tables arranged according to the star schema; that is, a large fact table is surrounded by several dimension tables.

Relational tables

3.3.5 Multidimensional Expressions

MDX is a language for querying and manipulating multidimensional data against an Online Analytical Processing (OLAP) database. Microsoft

Query against an OLAP database

135

has moved MDX forward, and it has become an accepted industry standard supported by a number of vendors, including SAP for SAP BW.

SAP Gateway provides an easy way of exposing SAP BW functionalities by using MDX. This exposure is done using the SAP Gateway Analytics Service Generator, which is part of the Service Builder. As the name clearly indicates, this is a generation-based process that doesn't require any coding. MDX is the method of choice for older releases of SAP BW because it has been available since SAP BW 7.0. For newer releases, however, it's recommended to use SAP BW Easy Queries, which are available as of SAP BW 7.30 SP 8 or SAP BW 7.31 SP 5.

3.3.6 SAP BW Easy Query

The recommended approach for exposing data from SAP BW is through SAP BW Easy Query. SAP BW Easy Query is a lot less complex than MDX and has been designed for simplicity and ease of consumption. Actually, all you have to do is set a flag in the BEx Query Designer on the query level. The rest is done by the SAP BW system. Based on queries flagged as SAP BW Easy Query and using SAP Gateway for access, it's possible to expose these as OData services.

3.3.7 Generic Interaction Layer

APIs GenIL is a unifying interface between a client and integrated applications. A client (UI) can use the GenIL to access all APIs of the linked applications without recognizing the API details or the underlying data structures. This means the client doesn't have to be programmed for interaction with each individual application. Instead, it only needs to be programmed for the GenIL application.

As part of the Business Object Layer (BOL), GenIL is frequently used for the SAP Customer Relationship Management (SAP CRM) Web Client UI and also in other SAP Business Suite applications such as SAP ERP Financials and SAP ERP Human Capital Management (SAP ERP HCM).

SAP Gateway allows for the generation of OData services that leverage GenIL. You're therefore able to leverage GenIL objects delivered by SAP and also custom build GenIL objects. The nodes, relations, and queries in the GenIL model are transformed to the corresponding entities in an OData model.

3.3.8   SAP Business Process Management

BPM allows for controlling and automating business processes. It looks at a business from a process perspective rather than an organizational chart perspective and allows for modeling processes end to end. This is extremely beneficial for both analyzing and modeling business processes. BPM supports the entire business process lifecycle—from planning, implementation, and monitoring, right up to optimization.

3.3.9   SAP Business Workflow

To design and execute business processes within SAP application systems, you use SAP Business Workflow. Within SAP Business Workflow, workflow processes are delivered as content in the SAP Business Suite. It's possible to enhance these SAP-provided workflows and create custom versions.

To allow SAP Business Workflow users to handle workflow items on any device or platform, SAP Gateway can expose SAP Business Workflow tasks as OData RESTful services. This allows for a number of new business scenarios, such as workflow inboxes on mobile devices.

3.3.10   Core Data Services

SAP HANA is a platform for real-time analytics and applications. It enables organizations to analyze business operations based on large volumes and a variety of detailed data in real time. In-memory computing, which enables the analysis of very large, nonaggregated data in local memory, is the core technology underlying the SAP HANA platform. The advantages of light-speed data access and analysis can be easily leveraged with SAP Gateway and SAP HANA.

With the availability of the SAP HANA platform, a paradigm shift in the way business applications are developed at SAP has taken place. The database is now where things are supposed to happen to get the best performance.

A *CDS* is an infrastructure used to create the underlying data model that the application services expose to the UI clients. The beauty of CDS is that it simplifies and harmonizes the way data models are defined and consumed—regardless of the consumption technology.

CDS is supported natively on both ABAP and SAP HANA. Technically, CDS is an enhancement of SQL, which provides a Data Definition Language (DDL) for defining semantically rich database tables and views (CDS entities) and user-defined types in the database. The database developer defines the data-persistence and analytic models that are used to expose data in response to client requests via HTTP. The database objects specify what data to make accessible for consumption by applications and how. CDS introduces enhancements over SQL, including annotations to enrich the data models with additional metadata, associations on a conceptual level, replacing joins with simple path expressions in queries, and expressions used for calculations and queries in the data model.

SAP Gateway allows the use of both ABAP and SAP HANA-based CDS views as a basis for creating SAP Gateway services.

3.4   Summary

SAP Gateway's three-tier architecture follows gateway principles and timeless software principles and provides all of the flexibility needed for a wide range of possible use cases—from mobile scenarios to desktop applications to the Internet. At the same time, it offers all of the stability and reliability needed for business-critical use cases. Its main tier is the SAP Gateway tier, where most features and tools can be found. Still, parts of SAP Gateway may reside on the SAP Business Suite tier as well.

SAP Gateway comes with a toolset that allows for the easy creation of SAP Gateway OData services using content and services already available via other SAP technologies. This includes quite a number of SAP standard technologies such as RFC, BOR, Service Provider Infrastructure, CDS, and GenIL.

In the next chapter, we'll round out Part I of the book with a discussion of SAP Gateway deployment, installation, and configuration.

This chapter discusses the methods of deploying SAP Gateway, including how to best install SAP Gateway, the necessary configuration steps for the chosen deployment method, and when to use which method.

4   Deployment Options, Installation, and Configuration

In this chapter, you'll learn the specifics about the different deployment options for SAP Gateway, including the advantages each method provides. We then look at preparations needed for a typical SAP Gateway installation and configuration process, followed by walking through a minimal installation and configuration in what we call a Quick Start Guide. Because this Quick Start Guide just addresses the absolute basics needed to have SAP Gateway up and running, we then present an overview of a standard installation and configuration process and look at selected steps in detail. The chapter closes by discussing the SAP Gateway best practices that are relevant during installation and configuration.

4.1   Introduction to SAP Gateway Deployment

There are basically two ways to look at the SAP Gateway deployment options: from the perspective of SAP Gateway and from an architectural perspective. Both perspectives need to be taken into account to see the full picture. Because the deployment option chosen can have a major impact on performance, we highly recommend selecting your option wisely, based on your system landscape and your intended use case.

Deployment options

In SAP Gateway, there are major differences with respect to deployment, depending on the underlying SAP NetWeaver version. With SAP

NetWeaver 7.40, the add-on structure has been streamlined and further optimized for the OData channel, as compared to prior SAP NetWeaver versions.

Prior to SAP NetWeaver 7.40

Basic SAP Gateway functionalities, if running on releases prior to 7.40, are contained in different add-ons that have to be deployed separately. The SAP Gateway server or hub functionalities require that the GW_CORE and IW_FND add-ons be deployed on the server. IW_BEP has to be deployed on the SAP Business Suite systems for backend enablement (see Table 4.1).

	Core Components	Backend Enablement
Version 7.31 and earlier	GW_CORE IW_FND	IW_BEP
As of version 7.40	SAP_GWFND	SAP_GWFND

Table 4.1 SAP NetWeaver Version and Required SAP Gateway Add-Ons

From SAP NetWeaver 7.40

As of SAP NetWeaver 7.40 and higher, the SAP_GWFND software component is installed as part of the SAP NetWeaver 7.40 standard and includes the functional scope of IW_BEP, GW_CORE, IW_FND, and IW_HDB.

Table 4.2 shows the software components and optional add-ons of SAP Gateway with respect to SAP NetWeaver 7.40.

Name	Type	Version	Notes
SAP_GWFND	ABAP	7.40	Installed as standard in systems based on SAP NetWeaver 7.40 and contains the following: ▶ Runtime components ▶ Metadata component ▶ Shared services, for example, monitoring ▶ OData libraries ▶ Business Enablement Provisioning (BEP) ▶ Business content adapter for SAP Gateway with SAP HANA to enable exposure of SAP HANA views

Table 4.2 Software Components and Optional Add-Ons for SAP Gateway in SAP NetWeaver 7.40

Name	Type	Version	Notes
IW_FNDGC	ABAP	100	Optional. Only to be installed if generic channel services (outdated and not recommended) are still used.

Table 4.2 Software Components and Optional Add-Ons for SAP Gateway in SAP NetWeaver 7.40 (Cont.)

Deployment
The term *deployment*—in this case for versions as of SAP NetWeaver 7.40—describes where SAP Gateway functionality resides because there is no actual deployment needed anymore. Because SAP Gateway components come as part of SAP NetWeaver, it's more of a configuration. We stick to the term deployment here for simplicity reasons and because it has become a set expression.

From an architectural perspective, the big question is whether to go for a hub deployment or for an embedded deployment, as described here:

Hub architecture versus embedded deployment

▸ **Embedded deployment**
In versions before SAP NetWeaver 7.40, SAP Gateway IW_FND and GW_CORE core components were deployed in the SAP Business Suite system. Alternatively, the SAP Business Suite system is based on release 7.40 or higher, where the SAP_GWFND software component is part of the SAP NetWeaver standard and just needs to be configured properly.

▸ **Hub deployment**
In versions before SAP NetWeaver 7.40, SAP Gateway IW_FND and GW_CORE core components are deployed in an SAP Gateway hub system. Alternatively, a 7.40 or higher system is used as the hub system where the SAP_GWFND software component is part of the standard and just needs to be configured properly.

The hub deployment can be further split up into two suboptions, which actually leaves three deployment options. Each of these options has advantages and disadvantages. In this section, we'll discuss all three, compare them, and also discuss the scenario where you might use a mixed deployment that consists of both options.

4.1.1 Hub Deployment with Development in SAP Business Suite

In the case of hub deployment with development in the SAP Business Suite system (Figure 4.1), the SAP Gateway server functionalities are only used on a single dedicated server—the hub system. The SAP Gateway service is thus deployed on the SAP Business Suite systems (where either IW_BEP is deployed for systems prior to SAP NetWeaver 7.40, or the software component SAP_GWFND is configured for SAP NetWeaver 7.40) and is then registered on the SAP Gateway server.

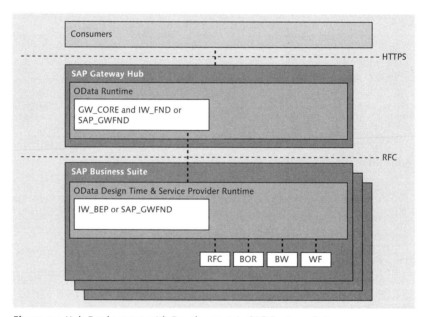

Figure 4.1 Hub Deployment with Development in SAP Business Suite

Deployment use cases

The following are the main use cases for this kind of deployment:

- Production scenarios with a medium-to-high load (e.g., used for the mobile applications delivered by the SAP Business Suite).
- Scenarios where development takes place in the SAP Business Suite system.
- Scenarios where a developer needs to leverage all native interfaces and Data Dictionary (DDIC) structures in the SAP Business Suite systems.

The hub deployment with development in the SAP Business Suite offers the following advantages:

- ▶ Support for routing and composition of multiple systems.
- ▶ Single point of access to multiple SAP Business Suite systems.
- ▶ More flexibility. Hub systems can be based on a newer release (SAP NetWeaver 7.31, SAP NetWeaver 7.40 or SAP NetWeaver 7.50) than any of the connected SAP Business Suite systems that supports additional authentication options (Kerberos, Security Assertion Markup Language [SAML] browser protocol) and can be updated more frequently without too much overhead (service windows, regression tests).

The only disadvantage to this method is that an additional server is needed for SAP Gateway.

There are a few things to consider for the different SAP NetWeaver releases when deciding to go for this SAP Gateway deployment style. For SAP NetWeaver 7.0, 7.01, 7.02, 7.03, and 7.31, you should consider the following:

- ▶ The lifecycle of SAP Gateway content is dictated by the frequency of updates in the SAP Business Suite system.
- ▶ To enable communication between the SAP Gateway system and the SAP Business Suite system, you must install IW_BEP in the backend system.

For SAP NetWeaver 7.40 and 7.50, you should consider the following:

- ▶ The SAP_GWFND component is already installed as part of the standard SAP NetWeaver delivery.
- ▶ The lifecycle of SAP Gateway content is dictated by the frequency of updates in the SAP Business Suite system.

4.1.2   Hub Deployment with Development on the Hub

For hub deployment with development on the hub (Figure 4.2), the SAP Gateway server functionalities are only used on a dedicated server—the hub system. In contrast to the first option (hub deployment with development in the SAP Business Suite systems), this is where service deployment takes place. This option is used if either no development has to be performed on the SAP Business Suite systems, or you can't deploy the IW_BEP add-on in the SAP Business Suite (for releases prior to SAP NetWeaver 7.40). In this specific case, the developer is limited to using the interfaces that are accessible via remote function call (RFC) in the SAP Business Suite systems.

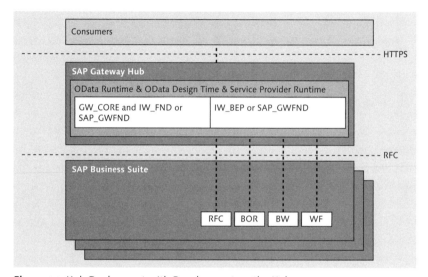

Figure 4.2 Hub Deployment with Development on the Hub

Example

In validated environments (e.g., the pharmaceutical industry), it's a very time-consuming process to change anything in the validated SAP Business Suite systems. Development for these systems is even more restricted. In these scenarios, deployment with development on the hub can be extremely beneficial for using new technologies without disrupting ongoing business-critical processes.

The hub can be located either behind or in front of the firewall. In addition, you can install the optional components for hub deployment in your SAP Gateway system.

The following are the main use cases for a hub deployment with development on the hub:

▶ Scenarios where no deployment of add-ons in the SAP Business Suite system is allowed or wanted.

▶ Scenarios where SAP Gateway add-ons can't be installed in the SAP Business Suite system for security, stability, or incompatibility (due to system release) reasons. In this case, this deployment option is mandatory.

▶ Proof of concept (POC) with SAP Gateway (no changes to existing infrastructure required).

▶ Scenarios where there are multiple SAP Business Suite systems.

▶ Scenarios where the SAP Gateway server is deployed in a demilitarized zone (DMZ).

The following are the advantages of hub deployment with development on the hub:

▶ SAP Gateway capabilities need to be deployed/configured only once within the landscape, which means there is no need to install and/or configure (and upgrade) SAP Gateway add-ons in the SAP Business Suite system.

▶ Content can be deployed without touching the SAP Business Suite system, which means services developed by partners don't need any deployment on the SAP Business Suite systems.

▶ Routing and composition of multiple systems is supported.

▶ The lifecycle of consumer applications is decoupled from the SAP Business Suite system.

▶ Routing and connectivity with SAP Business Suite systems are managed centrally.

▶ Better security is provided because a request is validated at the dedicated box, and consequently potential attacks on the SAP Gateway system won't automatically affect the SAP Business Suite system.

▶ To enable external access and fulfill security requirements, you can locate the SAP Gateway system in a DMZ.

▸ The innovation speed of SAP Gateway and the connected SAP Business Suite systems are independent of each other.

▸ The lifecycle of SAP Gateway content is loosely coupled to the lifecycle of the SAP Business Suite system.

Disadvantages The following are the disadvantages of hub deployment with development on the hub:

▸ An additional server is needed for SAP Gateway.

▸ Access is limited to remote-enabled interfaces (RFC function modules, Business Application Programming Interfaces [BAPIs], SAP BW Easy Queries, Service Provider Interface objects).

▸ Remote-enabled interfaces might not be optimal (e.g., might not offer appropriate filter options).

▸ Generic Interaction Layer (GenIL) objects can't be accessed remotely.

▸ No direct local access to metadata (DDIC) and business data is provided, which means reuse of data is limited to remote access.

▸ OData services delivered by SAP as part of mobile applications or as part of SAP Fiori applications require the deployment of IW_BEP for releases prior to SAP NetWeaver 7.40 on the SAP Business Suite system.

Release considerations There are a few things to consider for the different SAP NetWeaver releases when deciding to go for this SAP Gateway deployment style:

▸ For SAP NetWeaver releases 7.00, 7.01, 7.02, 7.03, and 7.31, you can install the IW_BEP component in each SAP Business Suite system. For SAP NetWeaver release 7.40 and higher, the SAP_GWFND core component is installed as standard and includes the functional scope of IW_BEP.

▸ There will be redundant deployment of metadata or ABAP DDIC structures.

4.1.3 Embedded Deployment

For embedded deployment, the core components for SAP Gateway and any optional components are deployed together in the SAP Business Suite system (see Figure 4.3). For this deployment option, no additional

SAP Gateway server is needed—only an SAP Business Suite system. Development of SAP Gateway services takes place in the SAP Business Suite system.

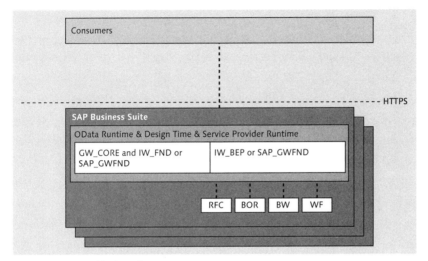

Figure 4.3 Embedded Deployment

The main use cases for an embedded deployment are the following: **Deployment use cases**

▸ For POCs or production environments with a low load.

▸ Scenarios where developers need to leverage all native interfaces of the SAP Business Suite.

The embedded deployment method provides the following advantages: **Advantages**

▸ Less runtime overhead because you save on one remote call.

▸ Direct local access to metadata and business data.

▸ No content merge required for different applications.

▸ No additional, separate SAP Gateway system required, resulting in lower total cost of ownership (TCO) because there is one less system to maintain.

▸ Easy reuse of content in the SAP Business Suite system (e.g., you can reuse structures from the SAP Business Suite system and access local business logic).

The method has the following disadvantages:

- If multiple SAP Business Suite systems are used, SAP Gateway has to be configured on every single system.
- Routing and composition can't be used.
- The upgrade of add-ons in an SAP Business Suite system in larger companies is usually only possible once or twice a year (maintenance windows).
- The innovation speed of SAP Gateway and the SAP Business Suite system need to be synchronized.
- Devices need to be integrated with the SAP Business Suite system on a point-to-point basis.
- The lifecycle of SAP Gateway content is dictated by the frequency of updates in the SAP Business Suite system.
- Cross-system composition isn't advisable.
- A very high number of SAP Gateway service calls can have a performance effect and slow down the SAP Business Suite system. In a production system with a very high number of service calls, this setup isn't advisable.

There is also one release consideration. As of SAP NetWeaver 7.40 and higher, the SAP_GWFND component is already installed as part of the standard SAP NetWeaver delivery, so embedded deployment is possible without any additional effort on every SAP Business Suite system running on top of SAP NetWeaver 7.40 and higher.

4.1.4 Comparison of Deployment Options

As you've seen so far, all three possible deployment options for SAP Gateway have advantages and disadvantages. To help you decide which option to use in your specific scenario, Table 4.3 summarizes and compares the major decision points.

	Embedded Deployment	Hub Deployment: Development on the Hub	Hub Deployment: Development on the SAP Business Suite System
Effort for Installation and Configuration	No additional server is required, and all activities take place in the SAP Business Suite system.	An additional server is required that needs to be ordered and set up. Typically, a trust relationship is set up between the hub and SAP Business Suite.	An additional server is required that needs to be ordered and set up. Typically, a trust relationship is set up between the hub and SAP Business Suite.
Performance	An additional load is placed on the SAP Business Suite system; on the other hand, one remote call is saved.	SAP Gateway server takes the additional load.	SAP Gateway server takes the additional load.
Costs	No additional costs because the existing SAP Business Suite system is used.	Additional SAP Gateway server is needed.	Additional SAP Gateway server is needed.
Maintenance	SAP Gateway depends on the SAP Business Suite system maintenance schedule.	No dependencies between SAP Gateway and SAP Business Suite.	No dependencies between SAP Gateway and SAP Business Suite.
Development Effort/ Limitations	Reuse structures from the SAP Business Suite system, and use access to local business logic.	Access is limited to remote enabled interfaces (RFC function modules, BAPIs, SAP BW Easy Queries, Service Provider Interface objects).	Full access is provided. Reuse structures from the SAP Business Suite system, and access local business logic.
Recommended For	Playground and POCs; production systems only in case of limited to medium load.	POC or production system usage; mandatory when no deployment/ configuration of SAP Gateway in the SAP Business Suite is allowed.	Production system usage; usage in scenarios that use SAP Mobile Platform online applications or SAP Fiori.

Table 4.3 Deployment Comparison

4.1.5 Mixed Deployment Options

Combinations of deployment options

In real-world scenarios, deployment options often build on combinations of the three basic deployment options. Typically, these combinations address shortcomings or special situations in a bigger system landscape environment.

One example is a situation in which an embedded deployment is desired but not initially possible (e.g., because changes in backend systems are only possible during the maintenance windows). Therefore, a first setup includes an SAP Gateway hub deployment with development on the hub that connects to the SAP Business Suite system. This reduces the immediate system impact on the SAP Business Suite system. In a next step, the landscape complexity is then reduced after a piloting phase, meaning the SAP Gateway server is removed from the landscape and replaced by an embedded deployment on the SAP Business Suite system.

Another possible example is a combination of hub deployment and embedded deployment in a single-system landscape across several SAP Business Suite systems, which means that some SAP Business Suite systems use hub deployment, and some use embedded deployment. A system with embedded deployment can therefore also be used as a backend system in a hub deployment.

Combination to be avoided

Avoid using an SAP Business Suite system with embedded deployment as a hub system for additional SAP Business Suite systems (Figure 4.4). This might lead to a situation where the SAP Gateway release of the hub system is lower than the version of the SAP Gateway backend components of the remote SAP Business Suite system. (Such a situation can occur because it might not be possible to upgrade the hub system at the same time as the SAP Business Suite system.) In this case, you won't be able to leverage new features of the higher version.

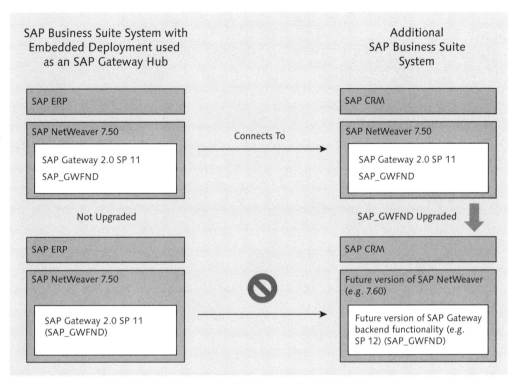

Figure 4.4 Potentially Problematic Upgrade Path Using an Embedded Deployment as Hub for another Backend System

To avoid such a situation, the recommended approach is to use one of the following two options:

Recommended deployment options

▶ Use the embedded deployment option for each of your SAP Business Suite systems.

▶ If you use a hub-based architecture, use a dedicated SAP Gateway hub system that should always run on the latest release of SAP Gateway.

Service Pack Level Equivalence in Mixed Environments
For mixed environments of SAP NetWeaver 7.40 and SAP Gateway 2.0 on top of SAP NetWeaver 7.31 and earlier, you may wonder which service pack level of SAP NetWeaver 7.40 is equivalent to which service pack level of SAP Gateway running on a release prior to SAP NetWeaver 7.40. The answer to this question can be found in SAP Note 1942072: SAP Gateway 2.0 Support Package Stack Definition.

4.2   Preparing for Installation and Configuration

No matter what deployment option has been chosen, before you can start with the actual installation and configuration process, you have to execute several preparation steps. The first step for releases prior to 7.40 is to check whether you fulfill the installation prerequisites. In a next step, you need to get the software. Then it makes sense to note down important information that will be needed during the installation and configuration procedure.

Minimum requirements

To run SAP Gateway, a number of prerequisites need to be fulfilled in terms of both hardware and software. With respect to hardware, the minimum requirements for SAP Gateway are shown in Table 4.4.

Requirement	Specifications
Processor	Dual core or higher, 2GHz or higher
RAM	8GB or higher
Hard disk capacity	80GB primary or higher

Table 4.4 Hardware Requirements

With respect to software, the minimum requirements are a little more complicated; check the newest requirements in the SAP Gateway Installation Guide because these prerequisites are specific for every single add-on. For the main components and SAP Gateway add-ons, the prerequisites (at the time of print) are shown in Table 4.5.

Further Resources
Installation prerequisites for SAP Gateway 2.0 SP 12 can be found at the following:
http://help.sap.com/saphelp_gateway20sp12/helpdata/en/52/ fc994f456a4573957461be15520fe8/content.htm
The SAP Gateway Installation Guide can be found at the following:
http://help.sap.com/saphelp_gateway20sp12/helpdata/en/c3/ 424a2657aa4cf58df949578a56ba80/frameset.htm

Requirements	Specification	
SAP NetWeaver Stack	The latest kernel patch for the corresponding SAP NetWeaver version has to be applied.	
	Core Components GW_CORE and IW_FND	▶ SAP NetWeaver 7.0 SPS 25 ▶ SAP NetWeaver 7.01 SPS 10 ▶ SAP NetWeaver 7.02 SPS 07 ▶ SAP NetWeaver 7.03 SPS 01 ▶ SAP NetWeaver 7.31 SPS 01
	Business Enablement Provisioning (BEP) component (IW_BEP)	▶ SAP NetWeaver 7.0 SPS 18 ▶ SAP NetWeaver 7.01 SPS 03 ▶ SAP NetWeaver 7.02 SPS 06 ▶ SAP NetWeaver 7.03 SPS 01 ▶ SAP NetWeaver 7.31 SPS 01
	Core Component SAP_GWFND (remember, this comprises the functional scope of components IW_FND, GW_CORE, IW_BEP, and IW_HDB)	▶ SAP NetWeaver 7.40 SPS 02
SAP Backend	SAP Business Suite system	

Table 4.5 Software Requirements

For additional information, check on the product availability matrix (PAM) for SAP Gateway at *http://service.sap.com/pam*, and search for SAP Gateway 2.0. Also check SAP Note 1569624 for SAP Gateway.

For releases of SAP NetWeaver 7.40 and higher, you can skip the software download and deployment because SAP Gateway already comes with SAP NetWeaver.

For releases below SAP NetWeaver 7.40, the SAP Gateway download package can be found on the SAP Service Marketplace in the SAP Software Download Center. Go to *http://support.sap.com/swdc,* and navigate to INSTALLATIONS AND UPGRADES • BROWSE OUR DOWNLOAD CATALOG • SAP NETWEAVER AND COMPLEMENTARY PRODUCTS • SAP GATEWAY • SAP NETWEAVER GATEWAY 2.0.

Download package

There you'll find the software under INSTALLATION AND UPGRADE and also the APPLICATION HELP that allows you to download the online documentation in plain HTML format. Alternatively, you can always work with the online documentation at *http://help.sap.com*.

Finally, before starting the actual configuration activities, a number of pieces of information need to be collected about the SAP Gateway host and the overall landscape (see Table 4.6). This will save time later and make things easier.

Required Information	Description
Fully Qualified Domain Name (FQDN)	Name of the SAP NetWeaver Application Server ABAP (AS ABAP) system or the load balancing device (e.g., *server.domain.com*)
Administrator credentials	Login information of the administrator of the SAP NetWeaver AS ABAP to install and maintain the system
HTTP/HTTP(S) ports	HTTP and HTTP(S) port numbers of the central instance of the AS ABAP (e.g., 8000 for HTTP and 8001 for HTTP(S))
SAP system	For each SAP system to which you want to connect the SAP Gateway server, the following information is required: ▶ System ID, system number ▶ Server name ▶ HTTP/HTTP(S) port ▶ Administrator credentials (i.e., user ID and password of an administrative user)

Table 4.6 Information Gathering

4.3   Quick Start Guide

Embedded deployment quick start

The online documentation for SAP Gateway (*http://help.sap.com/nwgateway*) explains all possible configuration options, many of which most people won't even need. Therefore, the idea behind this Quick Start Guide is to get you started quickly with some basic setup. After you have your basic setup running, you can then configure additional features and components as you like. Note that the Quick Start Guide is only valid for the embedded deployment option or for the option of hub deployment with development on the hub, which we've chosen for this guide.

The Quick Start Guide gives you an easy-to-follow overview of the absolutely required steps to set up and configure SAP Gateway. After you've followed the steps, it leaves you with a working SAP Gateway system that you can use as a playground environment or continue to configure to turn the very basic, absolutely minimal configuration into a fully usable production environment.

Important Notes

▶ A sufficiently authorized user is required for this Quick Start Guide to work.

▶ This configuration is extremely basic, and only the absolutely required steps have been performed, so don't use this setup in a production environment without additional configuration (e.g., authorizations, security)! Full details can be found at *http://help.sap.com/saphelp_gateway20sp12/helpdata/en/4c/a670b0e36c4c01ae2b9a042056f9dc/frameset.htm.*

Remember, in the case of embedded deployment and hub deployment with development on the hub, the central components for SAP Gateway and any optional backend components are deployed together in the SAP Business Suite system or the hub system.

Five steps are required to get your initial SAP Gateway setup running— plus an optional step for older SAP Gateway versions:

Setup and configuration steps

1. For versions older than SAP NetWeaver 7.40, deploy SAP Gateway add-ons.

2. Activate SAP Gateway.

3. Create the SAP system alias.

4. Create an SAP Gateway alias.

5. Activate the OPU node.

6. Test your settings.

After you've performed these steps, you should be able to develop a service on the embedded SAP Gateway system and publish it. Let's walk through these steps now.

155

4.3.1 Step 1: Deploy the SAP Gateway Add-Ons for Older SAP NetWeaver Versions

In an SAP NetWeaver 7.40 or 7.50 system, this step can be skipped because the SAP_GWFND software component, which comprises all the functionalities of GW_CORE, IW_FND, and IW_BEP, is already installed as part of the standard.

Transaction SAINT   For a system below SAP NetWeaver 7.40, you first need to deploy the three add-ons—GW_CORE, IW_FND, and IW_BEP—using Transaction SAINT, which is the SAP Add-On Installation Tool.

4.3.2 Step 2: Activate SAP Gateway

Activation in IMG   In the next step, you activate SAP Gateway by starting Transaction SPRO and navigating to the ACTIVATE OR DEACTIVATE SAP GATEWAY node in the implementation guide (IMG) (Figure 4.5).

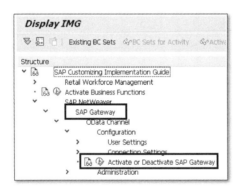

Figure 4.5 Activation of SAP Gateway

4.3.3 Step 3: Create an SAP System Alias

System alias   You now have to create a system alias entry that points from the hub system to the SAP Business Suite system. Because you've chosen an embedded deployment, you'll create a LOCAL system alias entry using the NONE RFC destination. To do so, go to MANAGE SAP SYSTEM ALIASES in the IMG (Figure 4.6) by starting Transaction SPRO and navigating to SAP NETWEAVER • SAP GATEWAY • ODATA CHANNEL • CONFIGURATION • CONNECTION SETTINGS • SAP GATEWAY TO SAP SYSTEM.

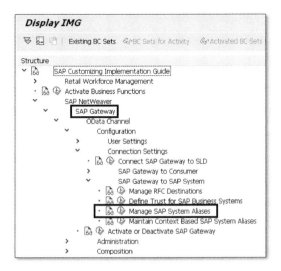

Figure 4.6 Creating the System Alias

This opens the maintenance view, in which you can fill in the values shown in Table 4.7.

Field	Value
SAP SYSTEM ALIAS	LOCAL
DESCRIPTION	LOCAL GATEWAY
LOCAL SAP GW	X
FOR LOCAL APP	(blank)
RFC DESTINATION	NONE
SOFTWARE VERSION	DEFAULT
SYSTEM ID	The SID of your embedded system (i.e., SAP Business Suite)
CLIENT	The client you're working in
WS PROVIDER SYSTEM	(blank)

Table 4.7 Change View Values

After you've entered the values, your screen should look like Figure 4.7.

Figure 4.7 Example System Alias Creation

4.3.4 Step 4: Create an SAP Gateway Alias

SAP Gateway alias   The creation of an SAP Gateway alias is needed to have at least one entry for the SAP Gateway hub in the Service Builder (Transaction SEGW) to allow for registering the services that you're going to develop.

To create an SAP Gateway alias, navigate to a different part in the IMG called SAP GATEWAY SERVICE ENABLEMENT (Figure 4.8). This part contains the SAP Gateway hub-specific customizing settings. Enter the values shown in Table 4.8.

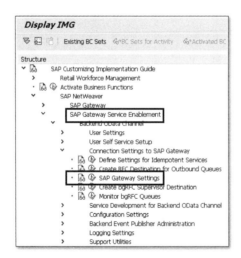

Figure 4.8 SAP Gateway Settings

Field	Value
DESTINATION SYSTEM	GW_HUB
CLIENT	The client you're working in

Table 4.8 Customizing Values

Field	Value
SYSTEM ALIAS	A unique name for the SAP Gateway host, for example, the SID
RFC DESTINATION	NONE

Table 4.8 Customizing Values (Cont.)

Your screen should now look like Figure 4.9.

Change View "SAP Gateway settings": Overview

New Entries

SAP Gateway settings

Destination system	Client	System Alias	RFC Destination
GW_HUB	800		NONE

Figure 4.9 SAP Gateway Settings Overview

4.3.5 Step 5: Activate the OPU Node

In a freshly installed system, you now have to activate the OPU node using Transaction SICF (Figure 4.10).

Transaction SICF

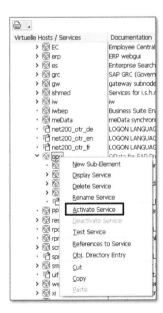

Figure 4.10 Activate Node Using Transaction SICF

Next, a dialog pops up in which you need to confirm that all subnodes will be activated. To do this, click the YES button with the hierarchy symbol (Figure 4.11).

Figure 4.11 Confirmation of Internet Communication Framework Services Creation

Click the REFRESH icon. Now expand the OPU node again (see Figure 4.12), and check whether the changes have been successfully performed.

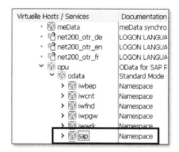

Figure 4.12 Expanding the Node

4.3.6 Step 6: Test Your Settings

Configuration verification

You can now test your settings by developing a simple service using the Service Builder (Transaction SEGW) (see Figure 4.13).

As you can see in Figure 4.13, the name of the destination system of the SAP Gateway alias is shown in the SERVICE MAINTENANCE node in Transaction SEGW.

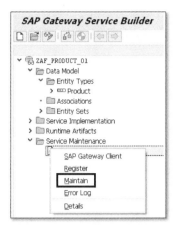

Figure 4.13 Expanding the Node for SAP Gateway Service Builder

When selecting MAINTAIN in the context menu, Transaction /IWFND/ MAINT_SERVICE (Activate and Maintain Service) is started on the hub system (Figure 4.14). Note that the service has been registered for the LOCAL system alias that you've maintained in the process.

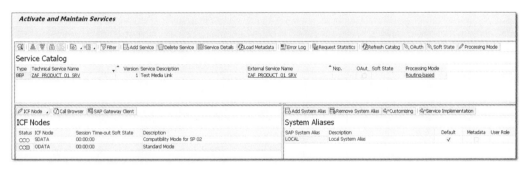

Figure 4.14 Activate and Maintain Services Screen

4.4   Installation and Configuration in Detail

Needless to say, the configuration just discussed in the Quick Start Guide section is extremely basic and should by no means be used in a production environment without additional steps that are absolutely required for usage in a production system. And even for playground or POC systems, additional configurations are recommended and even required in some cases.

Because only the absolutely required configuration steps were executed, and a number of important steps were dropped, the idea of this section is to provide you an overview of what you need to do for a full-blown installation and configuration of SAP Gateway, and to then dig deeper into some of the most important details. Again, a full SAP Gateway configuration guide can be found at *http://help.sap.com/nwgateway*.

Process overview
The installation and configuration process of SAP Gateway consists of five phases (see Figure 4.15):

1. For systems prior to SAP NetWeaver 7.40: the installation and configuration of the SAP Gateway add-ons

2. The basic configuration of SAP Gateway

3. The OData channel configuration

4. The (optional) BEP (IW_BEP) or SAP_GWFND configuration

5. Smoke testing the installation

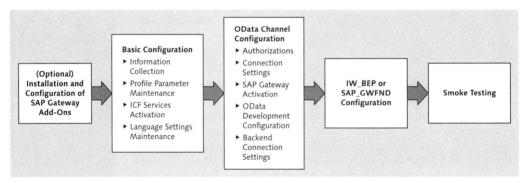

Figure 4.15 Installation and Configuration Process

Each of these phases can be further broken down into several steps. Let's now look into the details of these phases and steps.

4.4.1   Installing the SAP Gateway Add-Ons

As stated earlier, this step is only necessary for systems prior to SAP Net-   Installation
Weaver ABAP 7.40 because the 7.40 release contains the software component SAP_GWFND as part of the standard.

To install the required SAP Gateway add-ons for SAP NetWeaver versions below 7.40 SP 2, you must first download them. Because the
downloaded installation packages have a compressed format, the initial
step of the actual installation process is to unpack them into your local
file system. Next, import the add-ons using the Transaction SAINT
installation tool.

1. Call Transaction SAINT, and choose START.

2. Go to INSTALLATION PACKAGE • LOAD PACKAGES • FROM FRONT END to
   upload the installation files that you've previously downloaded from
   the Service Marketplace.

3. Select the add-on *<add-on> <add-on release>*, and choose CONTINUE. If
   all of the necessary conditions for importing the add-on have been fulfilled, the system displays the relevant queue. The queue consists of
   the add-on package, support packages, and other add-on packages. To
   start the installation process, choose CONTINUE.

4. For more information, call Transaction SAINT, and choose INFO on
   the application toolbar.

5. The system prompts you to enter a password for each add-on component. These passwords can be found in the SAP Gateway Configuration Guide (*http://help.sap.com/nwgateway*).

4.4.2   Basic Configuration Settings

After you've installed the SAP Gateway components, you must config-   Configuration
ure your system. The steps for configuration include executing the basic
customizing for SAP Gateway and describing system configuration activities.

Some tasks are mandatory, and others are optional and depend on specific use cases that you want to enable. With respect to the sequence, the
mandatory basic configuration is the starting point after collecting the

data needed for the configuration process. Then the OData channel configuration takes place.

Preparations   Before starting the actual configuration activities, a number of pieces of information need to be collected about the SAP Gateway host and the overall landscape. (Refer to Section 4.2 for details.)

Now that you've collected the required information, the configuration activities can begin. In a number of areas, settings need to be adjusted to SAP Gateway requirements with respect to values.

First, you need to use Transaction RZ10 to maintain the profile parameters with the values shown in Table 4.9.

Profile Parameter	Value
login/accept_sso2_ticket	1
login/create_sso2_ticket	2

Table 4.9 Profile Parameters

These two profile parameters are only activated after a system restart and are used to enable single sign-on (SSO) from and to the SAP Gateway system.

ICF services activation   In the second step, Internet Communication Framework (ICF) services need to be configured. After the initial installation of an AS ABAP, all ICF services are in an inactive state for security reasons. These services can be directly accessed via HTTP from the Internet. Therefore, unknowingly activated services represent a security risk, which can be mitigated by using suitable methods for restricting access.

Because multiple services can be executed when you call a URL, all relevant service nodes must be activated in a Transaction SICF tree. The URL path gets mapped to ICF subnodes (services) included in the URL. For example, if you want to activate the services for URL */sap/public/icman*, you have to activate the service tree default_host in Transaction SICF. Then, you have to activate services sap, public, and icman separately.

To activate a service, go to Transaction SICF, and select the required ICF service in the tree.

You then use one of the two options to activate the service: either the menu option (SERVICE/HOST • ACTIVATE) or the context menu (choose ACTIVATE SERVICE). You can either activate only a selected service node or the entire subtree (using the tree icon). The SAP Gateway services that need to be activated are shown in Table 4.10.

Service activation options

Service	Comments
/sap/public/opu	This service is needed for loading resources such as images.
/sap/opu/odata with all of its sub-nodes.	OData is the standard mode for all new applications. When creating a service, a new node is created automatically.
/sap/opu/sdata with the following subnodes: ▶ /sap/opu/sdata/iwcnt ▶ /sap/opu/sdata/iwfnd ▶ /sap/opu/sdata/sap	SData is the node used for existing applications. It's called the compatibility mode for SP 02. This is optional unless you're using scenarios based on the outdated generic channel.
If you want to use a web-based scenario, the following nodes on the target system need to be enabled: ▶ /sap/bc/srt/xip/sap ▶ /sap/bc/webdynpro/sap/saml2 ▶ /sap/public/bc ▶ /sap/public/bc/ur ▶ /sap/public/mysssocnt	Web-based scenarios here mean that content is consumed via web services.

Table 4.10 Services to Be Activated

In a third step, the language settings need to be checked and potentially adjusted. As for languages, the SAP Gateway system supports only the intersecting set of the languages of the connected SAP Business Suite backend systems. You can still make sure that your users receive the appropriate language. Follow the specific logon language process for this.

Language settings

> **Logon Language**
>
> For more information about logon languages, we recommend *https://help.sap.com/saphelp_nw74/helpdata/en/48/cae5c9356c3254e10000000a42189b/frameset.htm*.

4.4.3 OData Channel Configuration

OData channel configuration

In the next step, the OData channel configuration has to be maintained. This is a little more challenging due to dependencies on the specific SAP NetWeaver release. For example, the location of the configuration settings for the OData channel and the structure in the IMG can differ depending on the underlying SAP NetWeaver release, as described in the following list:

▸ **SAP NetWeaver releases 7.00 and 7.01**
The OData channel configuration settings are available in the IMG in the system where the IW_FND software component is deployed. In the SAP Reference IMG, navigate to SAP NETWEAVER • GATEWAY.

▸ **SAP NetWeaver releases 7.02 and 7.31**
The OData channel configuration activities are listed in the IMG in the system where the IW_FND software component is deployed. In the SAP Reference IMG, navigate to SAP NETWEAVER • GATEWAY • ODATA CHANNEL.

▸ **SAP NetWeaver release 7.40 and higher**
If you use the SAP_GWFND software component, IMG activities are available under SAP NETWEAVER • SAP GATEWAY and SAP NETWEAVER • SAP GATEWAY SERVICE ENABLEMENT.

In general, a number of steps need to be performed during the OData channel configuration. This includes setting the appropriate authorizations for users, configuring the connection settings for SAP Gateway to the SAP Business Suite systems (including RFCs and system aliases), activating SAP Gateway, setting up the OData channel service development on the SAP Business Suite system (and potentially on the hub system as well), and configuring the connection settings for the SAP Business Suite system to the SAP Gateway server. We walk you through these steps next.

Authorization Configuration

The first task here is to set up an administrator role for SAP Gateway components and assign users to it. After that is done, you can set up one or several user roles and assign users to these as well. To do so, create your own roles or copy existing roles to new custom roles.

To facilitate things, SAP Gateway provides predefined roles as templates for developers, for administrators, and for support use cases. Support templates only have display authorizations and are designed for use by support colleagues.

The three most important kinds of templates are the framework templates (Table 4.11), the OData channel templates (Table 4.12), and the BEP templates (Table 4.13).

Predefined role templates

Template Name	Template for Role
/IWFND/RT_ADMIN	Framework administrator
/IWFND/RT_BOR_DEV	Business Objects Repository (BOR) developer
/IWFND/RT_DEVELOPER	Developer
/IWFND/RT_GW_USER	User
/IWFND/RT_TU_NOTIF	Technical user for notifications

Table 4.11 Framework Templates

Template Name	Template for Role
/IWBEP/RT_MGW_ADM	OData channel administrator
/IWBEP/RT_MGW_DEV	OData channel developer
/IWBEP/RT_MGW_USR	OData channel user
/IWHDB/RT_USER	OData channel SAP HANA integration user
/IWBEP/RT_SUB_USR	On-behalf subscription user

Table 4.12 OData Channel Templates

Template Name	Template for Role
/IWBEP/RT_BEP_ADM	BEP administrator
/IWBEP/RT_BEP_USR	BEP user

Table 4.13 BEP Templates

> **Further Resources**
>
> For more information about templates and creating and assigning roles, we recommend:
>
> *https://help.sap.com/saphelp_gateway20sp12/helpdata/en/c0/af543a0ce04b7 690c196294db1b802/content.htm*

Role creation steps

For creating the three most important roles, namely SAP Gateway developer, SAP Gateway administrator, and SAP Gateway user, only a few steps have to be performed.

For the SAP Gateway developer, create a developer role based on the /IWFND/RT_DEVELOPER and /IWBEP/RT_MGW_DEV templates, which also contain the usual authorizations needed for ABAP development. For the SAP Gateway administrator, create a role for an administrator user with permissions and privileges for several tasks, including the following:

- Creating services
- Analyzing logs and identifying potential issues with the SAP Gateway landscape
- Installing, configuring, and maintaining SAP Gateway components and applications that run on top of SAP Gateway
- Configuring and maintaining users' data, including roles and user mapping

Finally, for SAP Gateway users, you must create roles specific to the user's required tasks. Either you can specify different authorizations for different user roles or have all authorizations bundled in a single user role. For more information, see Chapter 15, Section 15.2.

Connecting SAP Gateway to the SAP Business Suite

Connection settings

In this step, the connection settings have to be maintained. This holds true in both possible directions—SAP Gateway to SAP Business Suite systems and SAP Gateway to consumers.

With respect to the connection settings for the consumers, you have to specify settings when using push flow. (For more details about push flow or notifications, see Appendix A.) After that has been done, you have to configure the SAP Gateway components and define how to interface with the backend system. These activities are again performed in the SAP Reference IMG using Transaction SPRO. Navigate to SAP Net-Weaver • SAP Gateway • OData Channel • Configuration • Connection Settings • SAP Gateway to SAP System.

> **Further Resources**
>
> Detailed information on both how to configure the connection settings for SAP Gateway to consumers and how to configure the settings for SAP Gateway to SAP systems can be found at *https://help.sap.com/saphelp_gateway20sp12/helpdata/en/9d/d9b77a857240d18367b8713a29c1b1/content.htm*.

In the first step, you define the trust relationship between your SAP Business Suite system and the SAP Gateway host by using Transaction SM59 to configure the SAP Business Suite system to be the trusting system and the SAP Gateway host to be the trusted system.

Creating a RFC Destination on the SAP Gateway Host to the SAP System

A type 3 RFC connection from the SAP Gateway host to the SAP Business Suite system is the next thing to set up. To create one, go to Transaction SPRO, and open the SAP Reference IMG. Navigate to SAP NetWeaver • SAP Gateway • OData Channel • Configuration • Connection Settings • SAP Gateway to SAP System • Manage RFC Destinations. There you create the RFC of type 3. It's important to note that you've previously created a trust relationship between the SAP Gateway host and your SAP system.

Creating the SAP System Alias for Applications

In the next step, you need to specify where the SAP system alias should point. Depending on the specific scenario and your system landscape, you accordingly set up the system alias. This system alias is the result of the routing for an inbound request on SAP Gateway and can point to a

System alias creation

remote or a local system. If that system alias is flagged as a local SAP Gateway instance, it means the system that is responsible for processing (managing and storing) the data of an inbound request is the local SAP Gateway instance itself.

To configure the system alias, go to Transaction SPRO, and in the SAP Reference IMG, navigate to SAP NETWEAVER • SAP GATEWAY • ODATA CHANNEL • CONFIGURATION • CONNECTION SETTINGS • SAP GATEWAY TO SAP SYSTEM • MANAGE SAP SYSTEM ALIASES. After selecting CHOOSE NEW ENTRIES, enter the required information for the system alias. This information includes the system alias name, the RFC destination, and the software version, among other things. Check your system alias configuration using CHECK SAP SYSTEM ALIASES to ensure that everything functions properly. Although not mandatory, the system alias should also contain the SAP system ID because it's needed to register an SAP Gateway service from within Transaction SEGW in that backend system.

Activating SAP Gateway

Global activation

Now it's time to activate SAP Gateway in your system. (It's always possible to deactivate it again. In that case, all SAP Gateway services stop running, and an error message is sent to any consumer that calls the services.) To activate SAP Gateway, go to Transaction SPRO, and open the SAP Reference IMG. Navigate to SAP NETWEAVER • SAP GATEWAY • ODATA CHANNEL • CONFIGURATION • ACTIVATE OR DEACTIVATE SAP GATEWAY, and then execute the activation.

Activating Services

Transaction /IWFND/MAINT_SERVICES (Activate and Maintain Services) is used to maintain all registered services on the SAP Gateway server (hub system), to register and activate services, and to delete services. The main screen is divided into an upper and a lower part in which the upper part shows all registered services (SERVICE CATALOG), and the lower part shows the details of the selected service from the service catalog. The details are split into ICF nodes and system aliases.

Settings for OData Channel Service Development on the SAP Business Suite System

OData channel implementations retrieve data from a connected SAP Business Suite system. Both application logic and metadata are hosted there. All SAP Gateway services need to be registered in the backend before being ready for activation on the hub. On the SAP Business Suite system, both models and services need to be maintained (registered). This registration process takes place automatically when generating the runtime artifacts using the Service Builder.

OData channel settings in SAP Business Suite

> **Manual Registration of Services in the Backend**
>
> The registration process can also be started manually, if it hasn't been done during service development, using the Service Builder. If it's necessary to perform the registration process separately, you have to start Transaction SPRO, navigate to SAP NETWEAVER • GATEWAY SERVICE ENABLEMENT • BACKEND ODATA CHANNEL • SERVICE DEVELOPMENT FOR BACKEND ODATA CHANNEL, and then choose either MAINTAIN MODELS or MAINTAIN SERVICES.

After a service has been defined in the SAP Business Suite system, it can be activated on the SAP Gateway system.

Connecting the SAP Business Suite System to the SAP Gateway Server

In this step, the system alias entries in the SAP Business Suite system have to be maintained. The creation of an SAP Gateway alias is needed to have at least one entry for the SAP Gateway hub in the Service Builder (Transaction SEGW) to allow for registering the services that you're going to develop.

Creating a RFC Destination from SAP Business Suite to the SAP Gateway Server

A type 3 RFC connection from the SAP Business Suite system to the SAP Gateway host is the next thing to set up. To create one, go to Transaction SM59. There you create the RFC of type 3. It's important to note that you've previously created a trust relationship between the SAP Business Suite system and your SAP Gateway host.

Maintaining SAP Gateway Settings in the SAP Business Suite System

To configure the settings for the SAP Gateway system in the SAP Business Suite system, go to Transaction SPRO, and, in the IMG, navigate to SAP NETWEAVER • GATEWAY SERVICE ENABLEMENT • BACKEND ODATA CHANNEL • CONNECTION SETTINGS TO SAP NETWEAVER GATEWAY • SAP NETWEAVER GATEWAY SETTINGS. Here you have to enter the values shown in Table 4.14.

Field	Value
DESTINATION SYSTEM	GW_HUB
CLIENT	Client in the SAP Gateway server where SAP Gateway has been activated
SYSTEM ALIAS	A unique name for the SAP Gateway server, for example, the SID
RFC DESTINATION	The name of the RFC destination you've created beforehand

Table 4.14 SAP Gateway Settings: Customizing Values

4.4.4 Business Enablement Provisioning Configuration

Business Enablement Provisioning (BEP) is a component that you enable in your existing SAP Business Suite system to handle the events and actions activated in the SAP system and to publish these events and actions through SAP Gateway. BEP provides functionality to expose data and events as OData-based REST services and is contained, as of SAP NetWeaver 7.40, in the SAP_GWFND component that comes standard with SAP NetWeaver 7.40 and higher. In older releases, BEP is contained in the IW_BEP add-on. You can use BEP to obtain and publish BOR events without writing code, to obtain and send events for SAP Business Workflow, and to send events from your code.

To enable BEP, start by configuring its role templates. Next, you define an event and then the event subscription and notifications. Then specify the connection settings to the SAP Gateway landscape. These settings are available both for BEP and the OData channel.

4.4.5 Smoke Testing

Now that we've finished the installation and configuration, it's important to verify that things work properly. This holds true for all relevant areas—namely, service development, service consumption, and operations. In most cases, there's no need to check on every detail; a smoke test is sufficient for POC and development systems. When a production system is concerned, however, we recommend more detailed tests. Depending on the business case, security topics should be specifically tested. Also, before the go-live, an additional review of the system setup and configuration should be performed.

Installation verification

For smoke testing a POC or development system, we recommend the following steps:

Smoke test procedure

1. Use the SAP Gateway client via Transaction /IWFND/GW_CLIENT to call the CATALOG service that shows the service catalog (*/sap/opu/ odata/IWFND/CATALOGSERVICE/ServiceCollection*).

2. Call one of the registered services, for example, RMT SAMPLE FLIGHT (*/sap/opu/odata/IWFND/RMTSAMPLEFLIGHT/TravelagencyCollection*).

If both of these services return usable data, this confirms that your SAP Gateway installation works on a basic level. (It might be necessary, however, to generate sample flight data by running report SAPBC_DATA_ GENERATOR.)

For smoke testing a production system, the same basic steps just described should be executed to confirm that service calls work and return data. Also, a number of smoke tests should be executed to make sure additional important SAP NetWeaver and SAP Gateway features work. This includes, for example, basic security checks. Which tests

Production systems

make sense depends on your specific setup. Potential tests include the following:

▶ Call SAP Gateway services with different user roles to determine whether the user can see the OData data he is supposed to see.

▶ Call SAP Gateway services with a user who isn't supposed to see data and check the result.

Additional tests recommended As we've already stated, these are only smoke tests. We recommend appropriate tests to ensure your setup works as expected, especially in the performance and security areas.

To run test cases, it's possible to store them for the services you're interested in testing. This can be done using the SAP Gateway client, which offers the feature to store test cases in its test database. The handling of test cases using the SAP Gateway client is described in more detail in Chapter 14.

During quite a number of projects, best practices for SAP Gateway installation and configuration have evolved. In most cases, the official SAP documentation already reflects these lessons learned and points you in the right direction. Let's still have a look at the important best practices and where you can find information to give you additional background.

Deployment bottom line With respect to deployment options, the bottom line is that you should only use an embedded SAP Gateway installation for a production environment in exceptional cases, such as when there is either not a lot of load on the embedded environment, or you're forced to use this setup for other reasons. The strong recommendation is to go for a separate SAP Gateway box to scale better and allow you to always keep the SAP Gateway version up to date.

On the other hand, if you're new to SAP Gateway and want to play around and learn or perform a simple POC, the embedded deployment makes things a lot easier and is the first pick for a straightforward and easy start.

Quick Sizer When you look at sizing your landscape appropriately, SAP helps you with the Quick Sizer tool (*http://service.sap.com/quicksizing*). The Quick

Sizer is a free web-based tool. It's highly recommended that you use this tool early in an SAP Gateway project, not only to make sure you have enough performance to handle all requests but also to do this in an economically smart way. You can find a document that specifically discusses SAP Gateway in the SAP NetWeaver document repository of the Quick Sizer tool.

A number of factors influence system performance, and this isn't limited to the obvious ones such as main memory or the number and kind of CPUs. There are other factors specific to OData and SAP Gateway that you should take into account as well and that can have a major impact. One example is the format of SAP Gateway service calls.

System performance

SAP Gateway 2.0 OData-compliant services implementing the JavaScript Object Notation (JSON) format have a lower overhead than those implementing the AtomPub format, when more than 100 objects are retrieved. So for performance-relevant calls that retrieve more than 100 objects, the recommendation is to use JSON. When fewer than 100 objects are retrieved, the overhead for both AtomPub and JSON is the same.

JSON versus AtomPub

Concerning authorizations, the recommendation is to use SAP's role templates as much as possible to make your life easier.

Role templates

When talking about security, the main recommendation is to not directly expose your SAP Gateway system to the Internet because this opens it up for attacks. Instead use a reverse proxy between the SAP Gateway and the outside world.

Reverse proxy

4.5   Summary

This chapter provided you with background on SAP Gateway's deployment options and an overview of how to perform the setup and configuration. To get you going quickly, a minimal configuration guide was introduced. Additional configuration details and best practices for SAP Gateway system configurations were provided to allow for a well-suited setup in more advanced system environments. With this and SAP's extensive standard documentation, you should be able to start setting up your own SAP Gateway system and tailor it to your specific needs while avoiding potential traps and taking advantage of SAP Gateway's extensive feature set.

With this, we conclude Part I of the book. In this next chapter, we dive into the heart of SAP Gateway: the OData service creation process.

PART II
Service Creation

This chapter explains the end-to-end cycle and the specific tools for creating SAP Gateway services, both for service development and for service generation.

5 Introduction to OData Service Creation

As you'll recall from Chapter 2, OData services are what implement the OData protocol and expose an endpoint that allows access to data. The number of OData services shipped with SAP Gateway is limited and will likely remain rather low because, by nature, OData services are granular and mostly tailored to individual use cases. More commonly, services are shipped as part of products such as SAP Fiori, SAP S/4HANA, or SAP Mobile solutions. A large amount of development time can go into building the right OData service, so understanding this process is essential.

Out-of-the-box OData services

The central interface that is used to define and implement services within SAP Gateway is the Service Builder (Transaction SEGW). After you've created a service in the Service Builder, it can be used directly in any interface. The Service Builder is a one-stop shop with respect to SAP Gateway service development and is supplemented by additional support tools. In certain cases, it even allows you to perform selected steps in third-party tools and then import the results (e.g., usage of an OData modeler for the model definition).

The main objective of this chapter is to give you an overview of the process of service creation, which we then discuss in more detail in Chapter 6 and Chapter 7. To achieve this, in Section 5.1, we give you a brief overview of the two methods used to create OData services in SAP Gateway (service development and service generation) and continue in Section 5.2 to explain the main steps in the process of service creation. In

Section 5.3, we look at the main tool involved in service creation: Service Builder. We then complement this first look at the Service Builder with a quick look at some of SAP Gateway's other tools that support service creation and maintenance. This section will give you an idea of the tools that are available to assist with tasks during the service creation process.

In Section 5.4, we then dig deeper into service creation and look in more detail at the three main steps in service creation: data model definition, service implementation, and service maintenance. Also, we look at additional topics related to service creation such as redefining services and reusing existing SAP Gateway services in extension scenarios to create custom OData services based on OData services that have been delivered by SAP. Finally, we give you an introduction to the development paradigm used for service development: the OData channel (Section 5.5).

5.1 Methods for Creating an OData Service

There are two ways to create OData services with SAP Gateway:

Development versus generation

▸ **Service development**
The classic option is the code-based development of SAP Gateway services. This ABAP-based option is extremely flexible and allows you to develop highly efficient and specialized services, but it also requires some significant technical know-how.

▸ **Service generation**
The second way is the generation of SAP Gateway services. There are four main methods of service generation:

  ▹ *Mapping to a data source*: Allows you to generate a service by mapping the CRUD-Q methods of an entity set to a data source. This is supported for the following data sources

    – Remote function call (RFC)/Business Object Repository (BOR) function modules

    – Search help (only READ and QUERY method)

    – Core Data Services (CDS) views (only READ and QUERY method)

- *Redefinition*: Allows you to define a service based on an existing data source or an existing SAP Gateway service.

- *Referenced data sources*: Allows you to define a service based on a CDS view.

- *Creating CDS views with Eclipse*: Generate an OData service without the Service Builder by creating CDS views using Eclipse and setting the `OData publish:true` option.

Of these two approaches, service generation is the quicker approach and requires a lot less effort. On the other hand, it's more limited, and thus is primarily recommended for developing very straightforward services. Service generation doesn't give you much optimization potential because, without custom coding, you're restricted to what the service generators offer. In most real-world situations, you'll want to opt for service development because the advantages are well worth the effort. Still, if you have search helps, CDS views, Generic Interaction Layer (GenIL) or Service Provider Interface objects, analytical queries such as SAP Business Warehouse (BW) Easy Queries, or a suitable RFC function module or Business Application Programming Interface (BAPI) and are aiming for a quick result, this might be an option for you.

However, with the advent of SAP S/4HANA, OData services based on CDS views can be generated to support the draft infrastructure. As shown in Figure 5.1, option ❶ will become the preferred approach for OData service development. Because this kind of service will also be able to support smart templates for user interface (UI) development, a lot of scenarios in SAP S/4HANA won't require SAPUI5 coding but the development of appropriate CDS views and Business Object Processing Framework (BOPF) objects.

Service creation process

Even when using OData services that are generated from CDS views, the execution of the Service Adaptation Definition Language (SADL) interface can be fine-tuned by implementing its query application programming interface (API) or by adding additional business logic in the data provider extension class. (We'll go into more detail about these specific options in Chapter 7, where we discuss service generation in detail.)

In systems that are based on SAP NetWeaver 7.50, it's still possible to develop OData services using service development and the mapping of data sources (see Figure 5.1, ❷). This way, customers will be able to leverage their existing resources such as ABAP classes and RFC function modules when using SAP Business Suite EHP 8 or higher or when using SAP S/4HANA on-premise.

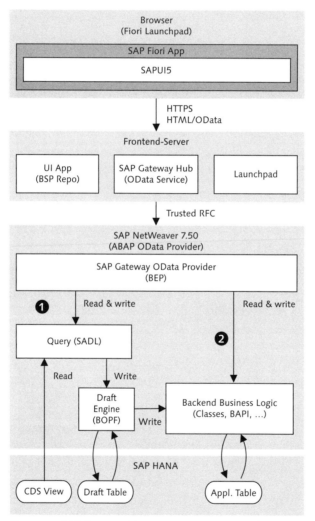

Figure 5.1 SAP Gateway OData Service Provisioning for SAP Fiori: The Transformation to SAP S/4HANA

Whether you're using service development or service generation, you create an OData service by following the SAP Gateway service creation process, as discussed next.

5.2 Service Creation Process Overview

In this section, we'll introduce the general steps in OData service creation and explain how the two methods for creating an OData service (service development and service generation) fit into this process. This explanation of the service creation process is somewhat simplified in an effort to explain it with distinct and sequential steps (a waterfall approach). In reality, some of the steps can also be performed out of order (an incremental approach). We'll go into a bit more detail about this at the end of this section, after presenting the simplified process.

This process consists of three main phases: data model definition, service implementation, and service maintenance. Depending on whether you go for service development or service generation, the individual phases of the service creation process can have different flavors. These flavors result in different paths that can be taken during the actual process.

Before you can start with this process, you have to complete the process of *service definition* as a prerequisite. This is the process of identifying what service to create and specifying its details. Ideally, you've done all of this together with the client developers so that you know exactly what data they require and how this works with the artifacts in the SAP Business Suite that will be the basis for your SAP Gateway service. After you have the service definition, you can start with the three development phases of the service creation process.

In the first phase, *data model definition*, you define the model your service is based on. That is, you define the required artifacts such as entity types, entity sets, associations, and other components that your service will use (refer to Chapter 2 for explanations of these components). After data model definition, you must generate the repository objects and register them in the SAP Business Suite system so that you can proceed with the next main phase, *service implementation*.

Service implementation phase

In the service implementation phase, the operations that are supported by the service are implemented. Here the different tracks for service development and service generation come into play:

▶ For service development, operations that are supported by the service are implemented using ABAP coding.

▶ For service generation, there are four paths depending on the type of generation chosen:

  ▷ If you use data source mapping, service implementation takes place by mapping the OData model to the methods of an RFC function module, search help, or CDS view.

  ▷ If you use redefinition, there is no service implementation step. You only have to perform the model definition step because the implementation of the service is generated based on the customizing that has been performed in the model definition step.

  ▷ If you reference a data source, there is again no service implementation step. Instead, you include one or more existing entity sets and associations of a CDS view into a data model.

  ▷ If you use Eclipse to create a CDS view by setting the `OData.publish:true` option, there is no service implementation step. Based on the CDS view definition, the implementation of the service is generated.

Service maintenance phase

The third phase of the service creation process, *service maintenance*, publishes the service so that it becomes visible in the service catalog of the SAP Gateway system. In effect, this means that the created OData service can then be consumed.

The three phases—data model definition, service implementation, and service maintenance—are depicted in Figure 5.2. Steps that are only performed in service development are marked with one color, and steps that are only executed in service generation are marked with a different color. Steps that have to be performed in both the development and generation of OData services in SAP Gateway are marked with both colors.

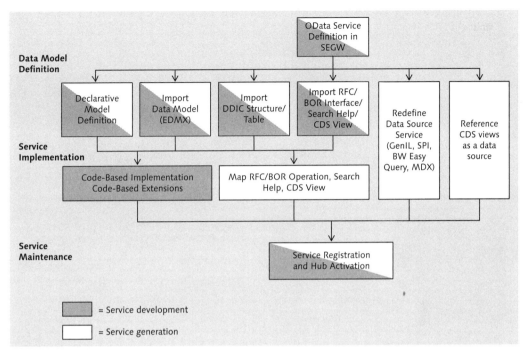

Figure 5.2 Service Creation Process

Although we clearly delineate the two methods of service creation (service generation and service development), it's actually possible to mix these in a way that suits you best. For example, you can create an OData service where one entity set is implemented using the RFC/BOR Generator (service generation), while a second entity set is implemented using code-based implementation (service development). It's also possible to generate a read-only OData service based on an SAP BW query and extend the same via code-based implementation so that it also supports updating business data.

As previously mentioned, we've presented the service creation process in a very structured and clearly sequential way. This waterfall approach allows you to easily understand what the different phases are for. In real-world projects, after you've understood how it works, you can adjust the sequence to what fits you best (within certain boundaries). The one exception to this rule is the service maintenance phase—this is

Incremental service creation process

185

almost always a one-time activity. As soon as a service is registered and activated (published), you don't have to touch these settings anymore, even if the implementation and/or model definition changes.

> **Exception**
>
> The service publication is a one-time activity as long as you don't perform major changes. Registering the service for additional SAP Business Suite systems, for example, is such an activity in which you have to go back to the service maintenance phase. Again, though, changes in the implementation of an already published service or in the data model can be used in the already published service without any further activities.

For all other phases, you'll typically always follow an incremental approach: you build a service—or part of it—execute and test it, and then go back and refine that same service until it fits all of your needs. During the creation of an OData service, you may change the model and/or the service implementation multiple times.

Furthermore, an approach often used in real-world projects is to perform the service implementation and the service maintenance in a different order. Performing the service maintenance with a service implementation stub before the actual service implementation allows you to browse metadata (service document and service metadata document), even if the service itself doesn't yet have any functionality. You've basically started with a service stub and can then fill this stub in an incremental way.

Figure 5.3 depicts the incremental service creation process. It's based on Figure 5.2 and adds incremental steps to the original process. These incremental steps are displayed by the solid line arrows that depict potential transitions among the three phases of data model definition, service implementation, and service maintenance, which are symbolized by the horizontal boxes. The dotted line stands for the one-time activity of service publication as part of the service maintenance phase.

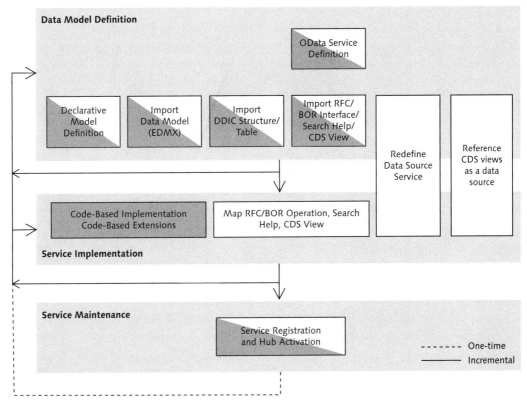

Figure 5.3 Incremental Service Creation

5.3 SAP Gateway Toolset

SAP Gateway provides a set of tools to address all needs from development to testing to operations. For now, we'll skip tools targeted at operating SAP Gateway and focus specifically on tools related to service creation. In this section, we'll take a look at Service Builder—the central, one-stop development tool for SAP Gateway services—and the additional, well-integrated tools that support you during the SAP Gateway service creation process.

5.3.1 Service Builder

Supports development lifecycle of an OData service

The Service Builder contains all relevant functions for modeling and developing OData services in SAP Gateway. This includes both code-based development of services and the generation of OData services. Also, it provides direct access to additional development-related functions such as service registration/activation and service validation. The Service Builder supports the entire development lifecycle of an OData service in SAP Gateway, and you can start it using Transaction SEGW (Figure 5.4).

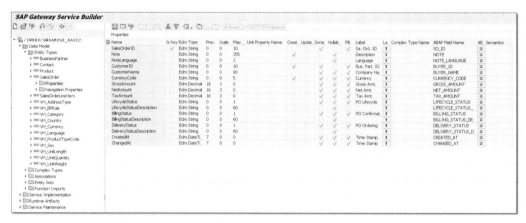

Figure 5.4 Service Builder

Overall, the Service Builder addresses the needs of both experienced and less experienced developers, as well as nondevelopers. Whereas experienced developers can develop their own source code with maximum flexibility in their service implementation, they still can use the built-in OData modeler and other tools to simplify the development process. Less experienced developers will appreciate the ability to use tools that generate OData services without having to write a single line of code.

Service Builder allows for centrally displaying and creating the definition of an OData service. This includes runtime artifacts (model provider class [MPC], data provider class [DPC], model, and service), OData artifacts (entity set, entity type, and properties), as well as data sources and models.

The modeling environment follows a project-based approach, and all relevant data are consolidated in these projects. Development using the Service Builder is therefore organized in projects, and creating a project is the starting point of every service development using the Service Builder. Projects are used to bundle all artifacts that are needed for service development in one central place, thereby providing a means to organize the development process. The Service Builder allows the developer to open several projects at the same time as shown in Figure 5.5 (in this example, ZPRODUCT and ZSALESORDER).

Project-based development

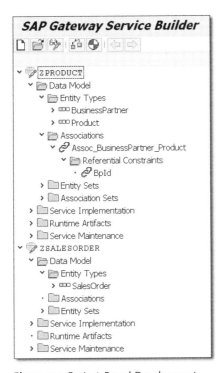

Figure 5.5 Project-Based Development

> **Note**
>
> From a technical system perspective, the Service Builder is used in a system where the Business Enablement Provisioning (BEP) component is installed, which is typically an SAP Business Suite system (refer to Chapter 4 for a discussion of the different deployment options for SAP Gateway). The BEP component is delivered as the IW_BEP add-on until SAP NetWeaver release 7.31.

As of SAP NetWeaver release 7.40 SP 02, the BEP component is included in SAP NetWeaver itself as part of the SAP_GWFND component. As a result, it's possible to perform development of OData services using the Service Builder without additional effort in all systems after they run on top of SAP NetWeaver 7.40 SP 02 or later.

Because the Service Builder is part of the BEP component that is typically (but not necessarily) installed on the SAP Business Suite system, you define the service model (i.e., MPC) as well as the service logic (i.e., DPC) on the same system where the BEP component is deployed. This is important to understand if it comes to referencing other ABAP Repository objects such as Data Dictionary (DDIC) elements (e.g., structures or data elements) that are required when calling, for example, an RFC or BAPI.

Comprehensive support for building OData services

The objective of the Service Builder is to provide comprehensive support for building OData services in a declarative way or by reusing existing business objects in the SAP Business Suite system. However, there are restrictions in what can be declared or generated. Advanced OData features may need to be implemented manually, and certain operations aren't available in a refined business object. The result of what you do in the Service Builder will always be ABAP classes, which are based on the OData channel programming model of SAP Gateway (covered in Section 5.5). You can always drill down to understand what is going on during service execution or tweak the code.

5.3.2 Beyond the Service Builder: Supporting Tools during the Service Creation Process

As stated, the main tool during the service creation process is the Service Builder. At the same time, SAP Gateway provides additional tools that are very useful during the development of SAP Gateway services. These tools allow, for example, for early testing of services or tracing what is happening when calling a service. As such, this section aims to briefly introduce you to some of the functionalities. For a more comprehensive description of the development support and administration toolset of SAP Gateway, see Chapter 14.

SAP Gateway Client

The SAP Gateway client can be used for both testing and troubleshooting and is a Representational State Transfer (REST) client built into SAP Gateway. It can be started from within SAP GUI using Transaction /IWFND/GW_CLIENT. After you've created a service, you can use this tool for a first test, as shown in Figure 5.6.

Testing and troubleshooting

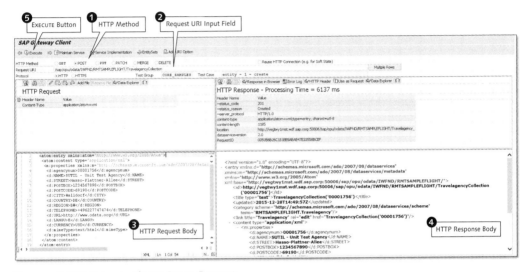

Figure 5.6 SAP Gateway Client: Create Request

First, select an HTTP method such as GET, POST, PUT, PATCH, MERGE, or DELETE ❶. Then enter the URI of your request into the REQUEST URI input field ❷. You can also set a certain HTTP header if needed. The body of an HTTP request can be entered either manually or uploaded from a file ❸. In addition, it's possible to use the REQUEST function to create, for example, an update request based on the response ❹ of a read request that has been issued against the URI before. Finally, perform the HTTP request by choosing EXECUTE ❺.

A very useful feature of the SAP Gateway client is that test cases can be stored in a database. The test case shown in Figure 5.6 is one of more than 70 sample test cases that are delivered in the CORE_SAMPLES test group for the TEA_TEST_APPLICATION and RMTSAMPLEFLIGHT standard test services. Note that the test cases of the CORE_SAMPLES test

Test cases

group have to be manually created from within the SAP Gateway client by selecting ❶ SAP GATEWAY CLIENT and ❷ CREATE CORE SAMPLES from the menu as shown in Figure 5.7.

Figure 5.7 Creating Core Samples from within the SAP Gateway Client

If you've saved a request as a test case, you can add or change the expected HTTP return code. A request can return multiple HTTP return codes that are valid (e.g., 200, 401, 402, and 403). Therefore, multiple statuses, including status ranges separated by a dash, can be entered (e.g., 201 401-403). In addition, it's possible to use payload validation so that the payload of an HTTP response can be compared with the expected result set and not only with the expected HTTP return code.

One or more test cases can then be run using the SAP Gateway client. The results are displayed in a table indicated by a traffic light icon together with the expected and actual HTTP return code.

Error Log

The error log is the second tool the developer will find very useful when it comes to troubleshooting. The error log can be called using Transaction /IWFND/ERROR_LOG in the SAP Gateway server system. There is also an SAP Business Suite system error log with a similar UI available that can be used to analyze errors that occurred in the SAP Business Suite system via Transaction /IWBEP/ERROR_LOG.

The error log is tightly integrated with the SAP Gateway client, so it's possible to rerun a request sent by a consumer that led to errors by selecting REPLAY • SAP GATEWAY CLIENT as shown in Figure 5.8.

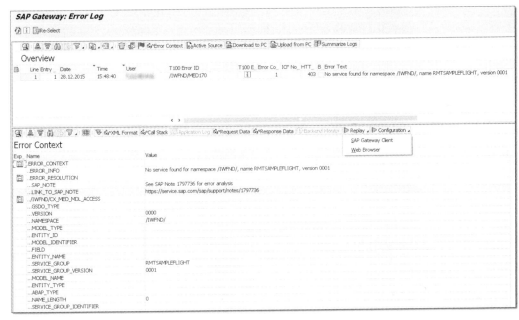

Figure 5.8 Transaction /IWFND/ERROR_LOG

As another way to dig into potential problems, monitoring log entries can be generated for the system log and the application log of SAP Gateway. To access the system log, use Transaction SM21; to access the application log, use Transaction /IWFND/APPS_LOG.

Logging and tracing

SAP Gateway Statistics and Payload Trace

When developing an OData service or a client application, the developer will want to know about the performance of the service. The SAP performance statistics can be obtained by an OData client by adding *?sap-statistics=true* at the end of the request URL or by adding the HTTP request header `sap-statistics=true`. The SAP Gateway framework provides the performance statistic data to the client in the HTTP response header `sap-statistics`. The response time data is also automatically stored by the SAP Gateway framework for every incoming OData request in the SAP Gateway server.

Based on this data, Transaction /IWFND/STATS (SAP Gateway Statistics) provides a detailed statistics view of each service call handled by SAP

Gateway. The data are aggregated on a regular basis so that statistical data for each service can be analyzed easily. In a productive system, the transaction is of great value for the system administrator to check the performance of the OData services (see Figure 5.9).

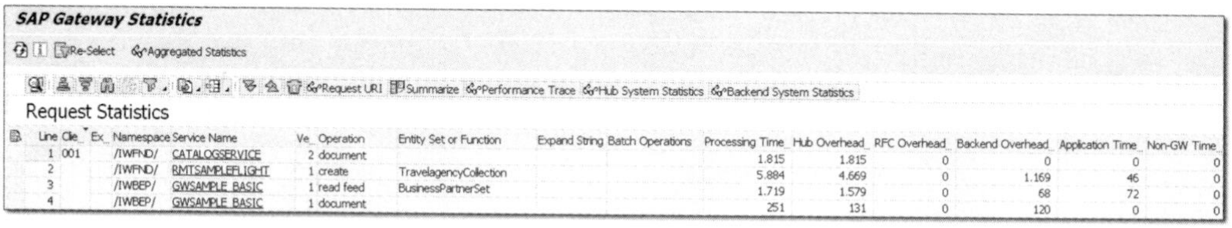

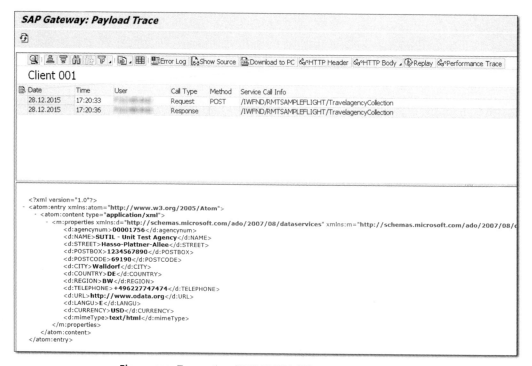

Figure 5.9 Transaction /IWFND/STATS

Via Transaction /IWFND/TRACES, not only you can trace system performance at the service call level for backend and hub systems but also the payload of a request (see Figure 5.10).

Figure 5.10 Transaction /IWFND/TRACES

Using the payload trace, it's even possible to monitor the payload that is sent by the client and the data that the client receives as a response from the server. The traced data can also be used to replay service calls using the SAP Gateway client.

The replay capability can also be used to create test cases in the SAP Gateway client for your service in a convenient way. To use the performance and payload trace, it's necessary to activate those traces.

Payload trace to create test cases

We'll discuss the SAP Gateway statistics transaction and the SAP Gateway performance and payload trace tool in more detail in Appendix A.

Catalog Service

Each SAP Gateway system provides a catalog service that can be used to retrieve a list of all available services on SAP Gateway (Figure 5.11). The catalog service is an OData service, and the list of available services can be accessed via the following URL:

http://<server>:<port>/sap/opu/odata/iwfnd/CATALOGSERVICE/Catalog Collection

```xml
<?xml version="1.0" encoding="UTF-8"?>
<app:service xml:lang="de" xmlns:sap="http://www.sap.com/Protocols/SAPData"
xmlns:m="http://schemas.microsoft.com/ado/2007/08/dataservices/metadata" xmlns:atom="http://www.w3.org/2005/Atom"
xmlns:app="http://www.w3.org/2007/app" xml:base="http://                          /sap/opu/odata/IWFND/CATALOGSERVICE;v=2/">
   - <app:workspace>
         <atom:title type="text">Data</atom:title>
      - <app:collection href="Vocabularies" sap:content-version="2" sap:addressable="false" sap:deletable="false" sap:updatable="false">
            <atom:title type="text">Vocabularies</atom:title>
            <sap:member-title>Vocabulary</sap:member-title>
         </app:collection>
      - <app:collection href="ServiceCollection" sap:content-version="2" sap:deletable="false" sap:updatable="false" sap:searchable="true"
         sap:creatable="false">
            <atom:title type="text">ServiceCollection</atom:title>
            <sap:member-title>Service</sap:member-title>
            <atom:link title="searchServiceCollection" type="application/opensearchdescription+xml"
               href="ServiceCollection/OpenSearchDescription.xml" rel="search"/>
         </app:collection>
      - <app:collection href="TagCollection" sap:content-version="2" sap:updatable="false" sap:creatable="false">
            <atom:title type="text">TagCollection</atom:title>
            <sap:member-title>Tag</sap:member-title>
         </app:collection>
      - <app:collection href="EntitySetCollection" sap:content-version="2" sap:deletable="false" sap:updatable="false" sap:creatable="false">
            <atom:title type="text">EntitySetCollection</atom:title>
            <sap:member-title>EntitySet</sap:member-title>
         </app:collection>
      - <app:collection href="CatalogCollection" sap:content-version="2">
            <atom:title type="text">CatalogCollection</atom:title>
            <sap:member-title>Catalog</sap:member-title>
         </app:collection>
      - <app:collection href="Annotations" sap:content-version="2" sap:deletable="false" sap:updatable="false">
            <atom:title type="text">Annotations</atom:title>
            <sap:member-title>Annotation</sap:member-title>
         </app:collection>
   </app:workspace>
   <atom:link href="http://                          /sap/opu/odata/IWFND/CATALOGSERVICE;v=2/" rel="self"/>
   <atom:link href="http://                          /sap/opu/odata/IWFND/CATALOGSERVICE;v=2/" rel="latest-version"/>
</app:service>
```

Figure 5.11 Service Catalog: Service Document

OpenSearch The catalog service supports OpenSearch. Developers or development tools are thus able to use a free-text search to find services based on the service description that can be retrieved using the following URL: *http://<server>:<port>/sap/opu/odata/iwfnd/CATALOGSERVICE/Service-Collection/OpenSearchDescription.xml*.

5.3.3 ABAP Development Tools for SAP NetWeaver and CDS Views

CDS views – one concept, two flavors A CDS view, as the name indicates, is a view that can be defined to retrieve an application-specific projection on the underlying business data. This is needed because business data are usually distributed across several database tables.

CDS provide a specification for an SQL-based Data Definition Language (DDL). With SAP HANA CDS and ABAP CDS, there are two flavors of this specification available. Whereas SAP HANA CDS views only need to run on top of SAP HANA, ABAP CDS views have to support multiple databases. This is similar to the ABAP Open SQL syntax, which is the last common denominator of the different SQL dialects supported by SAP NetWeaver AS ABAP.

> **Additional Resources**
>
> You'll find a comprehensive and detailed comparison between ABAP CDS views and SAP HANA CDS views at *http://scn.sap.com/community/abap/blog/2015/07/20/cds--one-model-two-flavors*.

Let's look at the example in Listing 5.1 of an ABAP CDS view, which was taken from SAP online documentation at (*http://help.sap.com/saphelp_nw75/helpdata/en/7c/078765ec6d4e6b88b71bdaf8a2bd9f/content.htm*).

```
@AbapCatalog.sqlViewName: 'CUSTOMER_VW'

DEFINE VIEW cust_book_view_entity AS SELECT FROM scustom
    JOIN sbook
    ON scustom.id = sbook.customid
    {
        scustom.id,
        scustom.name,
        sbook.bookid
    }
```

Listing 5.1 Example of an ABAP CDS View

The CDS `cust_book_view_entity` entity creates a join on the two database tables `scustom` and `sbook`, which are part of the SFLIGHT demo data model. As a result, it's possible to access the data via the ABAP Open SQL statement in Listing 5.2.

```
SELECT id name bookid
    FROM cust_book_view_entity
    INTO TABLE @DATA(result_data)
    WHERE ...    .
```

Listing 5.2 Using ABAP CDS Views in ABAP Code

A CDS view can be defined using the Eclipse-based ABAP Development Tools for SAP NetWeaver using the ABAP CDS statement DEFINE VIEW. This will create two objects in the ABAP DDIC, namely an SQL view and the CDS entity, as shown in Figure 5.12.

ABAP Development Tools for SAP NetWeaver

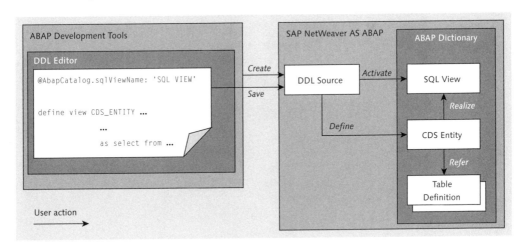

Figure 5.12 ABAP CDS View Building Architecture

> **Note**
>
> The SQL view and the CDS entity are created in the same namespace in the ABAP DDIC. As a result, both names have to be different. In Listing 5.1, the SQL view is therefore denoted as `CUSTOMER_VW`, whereas the CDS entity is denoted as `cust_book_view_entity`.

5.4 Steps in the Service Creation Process

In Section 5.2, we introduced the SAP Gateway service creation process, which consists of three phases: data model definition, service implementation, and service maintenance. You can take different tracks for creating your services depending on whether you go for service development or service generation. Now let's take a closer, more technical look at the different tracks and the individual steps in these tracks. Due to the various options for creating SAP Gateway services, you'll find it useful to refer to Figure 5.2 throughout this section.

5.4.1 Data Model Definition in the Service Builder

The first phase of the service creation process is the data model definition phase. The goal of this phase is to use the Service Builder to create a data model that contains all information about the OData model of a service, such as entity types, complex types, properties, and associations. So, when developing an SAP Gateway service (service development) or when generating an SAP Gateway service by mapping a data source (one specific type of service generation), the first main process step is to create a data model.

> **Note**
>
> When using the second method of service generation, which is to redefine an existing service, the data model isn't defined but rather *redefined* based on the existing business objects. For information about that kind of data model building, see Section 5.4.5.

You can define a data model in several ways with the Service Builder, each of which addresses a specific use case.

The first option is the manual creation of the various components of an OData model, which is called a *declarative model definition*. Entity types, associations, and association sets in this approach are created manually.

Four options for defining an OData model

The second option is the import of data models in the entity data model XML (EDMX) format that have either been defined by the OData Model Editor of the SAP Web IDE or the entity data modeler provided by Microsoft Visual Studio. In addition, it's possible to import the service metadata document of an existing OData service.

The third and fourth options, which are much more convenient for an ABAP developer, are to create entity types by reusing data models that already exist in the SAP Business Suite system. This can be done by the import of DDIC structures/tables or by the generation of new entity types based on an RFC/BOR interface or a search help.

Next, we'll discuss all four options in a bit more detail.

Declarative Data Model

A declarative data model is created manually using the Service Builder. This method is mainly used to create entity types based on manually created properties, which can be based on existing DDIC types. (To model an OData service from scratch in WYSIWYG style, alternative OData modeling tools, such as the SAP Web IDE [see Chapter 9] and Microsoft Visual Studio, are better. However, in these cases, the model has to then be imported into the Service Builder.)

Entity types

Import Data Model via EDMX

Using the import model option, the developer can import a complete OData model stored in an EDMX file, or a metadata document of an existing OData service, into the Service Builder. This includes the definition of entity types, entity sets, associations, and other components. You can import data model files that have been defined by graphical OData modeling tools or service metadata files of an existing OData service. If you perform an import on a service metadata document or an EDMX file for an existing project into the Service Builder, the Service Builder provides the option to reimport the data model files. A dialog will appear that shows which artifacts will be added to and which will be deleted from the data model.

Import Data Model via the Data Dictionary

DDIC type support   To reduce the time required to create entity types and complex types in your data model and to leverage existing data structures in your SAP Business Suite system, you can import the following DDIC types into the Service Builder:

▸ Views

▸ Database tables

▸ Structures

Beautification

When creating an entity type from a DDIC type, the name of the entity type and the names of the properties of the entity type suggested by the Service Builder are derived from the original names of the DDIC type and its fields by removing the underscores and generating a name with camel case notation instead. For example, when using a structure such as BAPI_EPM_PRODUCT_ HEADER, the Service Builder will propose the name BapiEpmProductHeader for the entity type. The same naming convention for proposals is used for the property names of the generated entity type—so that instead of the original field name SUPPLIER_NAME, the field name of the generated entity type becomes SupplierName.

The name of the entity set and its properties should be easy to understand because they are visible to the consumer, and the names of the properties of an entity set are derived from the property names of the underlying entity type.

During the process of importing a DDIC structure or even afterward, the developer can start a process called *beautification*. Through this process, you can reduce the number of properties of an entity type by simply removing single properties from it. In addition, you can maintain the names of the properties of an entity type.

Reducing the number of properties to those that are absolutely necessary and maintaining the names that are visible to the outside world are important for creating services that are easy to consume. Publishing existing DDIC structures as-is to the outside world is usually not very beneficial.

Beautification is discussed in more detail in Chapter 7, Section 7.4.1.

Import Data Model via RFC/BOR

The Service Builder also enables you to create entity types from function module parameters and BAPI parameters. A wizard is provided to guide you through the process. Using the interface of an RFC function module or a BOR interface is beneficial if they are being used to access the data in the SAP Business Suite system. Both code-based implementation and using the RFC/BOR Generator are possible with this approach.

Function module and BAPI parameters

Import Data Model via Search Help

Finally, the Service Builder also allows you to create entity types from Search Helps. Again a wizard is provided to guide you through the process. This wizard even performs the mapping of the READ and QUERY method in the same step so that there's no need for a separate service implementation step.

5.4.2 Service Registration in the SAP Business Suite System

After the data model is defined, it must then be registered. Service registration in the SAP Business Suite manifests the data model definition phase's results. This means that the runtime objects required for an SAP Gateway service are generated using the Service Builder. For the convenience of the developer, the Service Builder also performs the necessary tasks to register the service in the SAP Business Suite.

Service Registration versus Service Maintenance

As you may recall from Section 5.2, the service maintenance phase of service creation involves activating and registering the service on the SAP Gateway server. This isn't to be confused with service registration in the SAP Business Suite system, which is a process that occurs after the data model definition. In this section, we're focusing on service registration in the SAP Business Suite system. In Section 5.4.4, we'll discuss service maintenance.

The difference between service registration and service maintenance is as follows:

▶ Service registration is an activity during service development that results in the creation of artifacts needed for development.

▶ Service maintenance is an activity during the deployment/operation of an SAP Gateway service that activates the service for consumption.

Stub class creation

Based on the data model that has been created, the Service Builder generates a corresponding MPC and DPC, as well as extension classes. The MPC contains the coding that programmatically declares the data model being used by your service. The implementation of the service operations is performed in the DPC. The extension classes that have been generated by the Service Builder can be used to redefine methods of the generated base classes by custom code because the base classes are always regenerated when the model has been changed. (For more information on MPC and DPC, see Section 5.5.)

Service registration

To be used as a service, some configuration steps have to be performed, which are supported by the Service Builder (Figure 5.13).

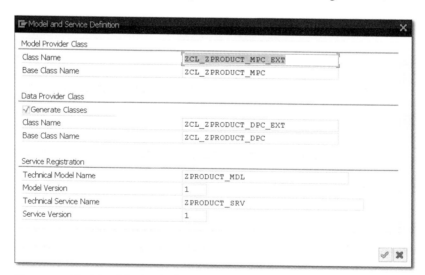

Figure 5.13 Model and Service Definition Using Service Builder

When generating a project for the first time, the developer has to specify the names of the MPC and its extension class and the DPC and its extension class. In addition, the developer has to specify the TECHNICAL MODEL NAME and the TECHNICAL SERVICE NAME. The latter becomes the external service name that is later used for publishing the service on the SAP Gateway.

The MPC and the DPC are thus combined into an SAP Gateway service by means of configuration, not coding. These configuration steps are facilitated for you by the Service Builder when the project is generated for the first time. The model and service definition process is depicted in Figure 5.14. In addition to the MPC (covered in detail in Section 5.5.1) and the DPC (see Section 5.5.2), two additional repository objects for the model and the service are created as part of the registration process of a service in the SAP Business Suite.

MPC and DPC

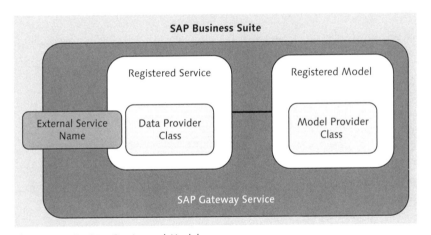

Figure 5.14 Register Service and Model

5.4.3 Service Implementation

During the service implementation phase of the service creation process, operations that are to be supported by the SAP Gateway services are implemented via ABAP code or by mapping the methods of a data source on the properties of an OData model. Operations are executed on the defined data model during runtime and encompass CREATE, READ,

UPDATE, DELETE, and QUERY methods (CRUD-Q methods) when using RFC function modules or BAPIs, or they are limited to READ and QUERY when using Search Help or CDS views.

It's important to note that the service implementation phase applies only to service development and to one of the service generation options: data source mapping. For service generation using redefinition or referencing of a CDS view as a data source, the service implementation step isn't necessary because the implementation of the service will be generated based on the customizing that has been performed in the model definition step.

Next, we'll give you a brief overview of the service implementation phase for both scenarios where the phase is relevant: service development and service generation via data source mapping.

Implementation for Service Development

Remember that during the service registration of the data model definition phase, a data provider extension class was created. Also during the service implementation phase, operations that are to be supported by the SAP Gateway services are being implemented.

To implement the supported SAP Gateway services using ABAP coding, you have to manually redefine the respective methods of the data provider extension class, which should remind you of the CRUD-Q operations:

- `<ENTITY_SET_NAME>_CREATE_ENTITY`
- `<ENTITY_SET_NAME>_GET_ENTITY`
- `<ENTITY_SET_NAME>_UPDATE_ENTITY`

- `<ENTITY_SET_NAME>_DELETE_ENTITY`

- `<ENTITY_SET_NAME>_GET_ENTITYSET`

Access to these methods is offered in a very convenient way by the Service Builder. This takes place by expanding the service implementation node as depicted in Figure 5.15.

Expand CRUD-Q methods

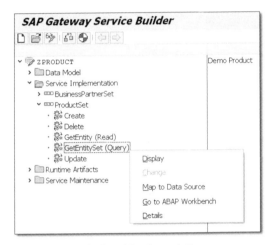

Figure 5.15 Code-Based Implementation

From there, you can navigate to the respective entry of an entity set, expanding all CRUD-Q methods of an entity set. Selecting Go to ABAP Workbench allows the developer to switch seamlessly to the Class Builder (Transaction SE24) to implement an operation.

In addition, it might be necessary to redefine additional methods in the data provider extension class that aren't specific to an entity set such as the CRUD-Q methods mentioned earlier (if, e.g., deep insert should be supported by the OData service).

Implementation for Mapping RFC/BOR Interfaces

The process of implementation for mapping RFC/BOR interfaces is different from that of service development. To start the mapping process, you have to select MAP TO DATA SOURCE in the context menu of a CRUD-Q method of an entity set in the SERVICE IMPLEMENTATION folder (Figure 5.16). The mapping dialog of the Service Builder then allows you to define relations between the interface parameters of a function module or BAPI and the properties of an entity set.

Figure 5.16 Mapping the Methods of an Entity Set to a Data Source

CRUD-Q You can map the CREATE, READ, UPDATE, DELETE, and QUERY (CRUD-Q) methods of each entity set separately. The actual service implementation, that is, the coding in the CRUD-Q methods mentioned earlier, will be generated by the Service Builder based on the mapping you've performed. The Service Builder supports the developer by providing mapping proposals if the entity type has been created by importing a BOR interface or an RFC interface. For example, as shown in Figure 5.17, the Service Builder suggested a mapping between the SoId property in the SalesOrderSet entity set and the SO_ID property of the SOHEADERDATA export parameter of the BAPI_EPM_SO_GET_LIST BAPI. This mapping can automatically be suggested because the entity type on which the SalesOrderSet entity set is based has been created by importing the SOHEADERDATA interface parameter.

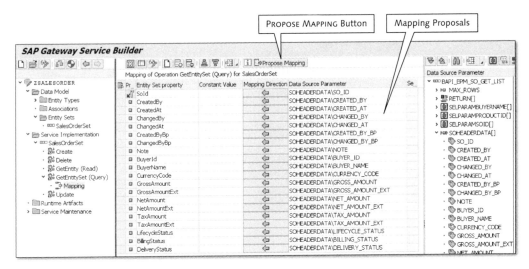

Figure 5.17 Mapping Proposals: RFC Function Module

If additional methods for the entity sets are mapped, the Service Builder checks the already existing mappings and derives proposals for them. If you, for example, started to map the QUERY operation (GET_ENTITYSET) of your entity set and now want to map the READ operation (GET_ENTITY), the Service Builder provides a proposal for those properties that have already been mapped in the GET_ENTITYSET method.

Implementation for Mapping Core Data Services Views

The implementation process for mapping CDS views is different from that of mapping RFC/BOR interfaces. To start the mapping process, you must select MAP TO DATA SOURCE in the context menu of an entity set in the SERVICE IMPLEMENTATION folder, rather than selecting the single CRUD-Q methods.

The mapping dialog in the Service Builder then allows you to define relations between the data source elements of a CDS view and the properties of an entity set (see Figure 5.18), as well as mapping an association of a CDS view to a navigation property of an entity set as shown in Figure 5.19.

Figure 5.18 Mapping a CDS View: Properties

Figure 5.19 Mapping a CDS View: Association to Navigation Property

As a result, the READ and QUERY method of an entity set are mapped. The implementation of CREATE, UPDATE, and DELETE methods (CUD) is still possible via a code-based implementation or via mapping of appropriate RFC function modules to the CUD methods.

Implementation for Mapping Search Help

The implementation for mapping a search help is even easier than mapping RFC/BOR interfaces or CDS views. This is already included in the data model definition step when creating an entity type based on a search help. The wizard that is used to import a search help not only offers to create an entity set but also already performs the mapping of the READ and QUERY method as well (see Figure 5.20).

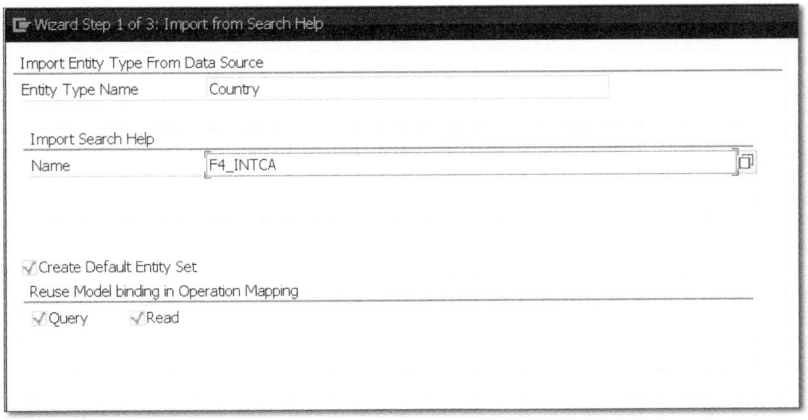

Figure 5.20 Import Search Help Wizard: Automatic Mapping of Query and Read Methods

As with entity sets, where the service implementation is based on CDS views, the implementation of the CUD methods can be performed via a code-based implementation or via mapping of RFC function modules that offer write access.

5.4.4 Service Maintenance

The service maintenance phase primarily consists of the service activation and service registration step in the SAP Gateway system. For SAP Gateway to consume a service using an OData client, this service has to be activated. This activation takes place in the SAP Gateway server and makes the service ready for consumption.

The registration and activation of services in the hub is performed using Transaction /IWFND/MAINT_SERVICE (Activate and Maintain Service).

Activate and maintain service

Transaction /IWFND/MAINT_SERVICE is also used to maintain all activated services on the SAP Gateway server. Services have to be changed if they've been registered in several/additional connected SAP Business Suite systems, or they can simply be deactivated.

Because the Service Builder is the one-stop shop for service development, functionality has been added that allows the developer to directly call the transaction for service maintenance from within the Service Builder. This is even possible for remote systems.

The developer can either select a SAP Gateway system in the SERVICE MAINTENANCE node (Figure 5.21) or can click on the REGISTER button.

Figure 5.21 Registering a Service in the Hub from the SAP Business Suite

---

Service Generation

As outlined earlier in this chapter, when performing service generation via redefinition, referenced data sources, or using Eclipse to create CDS views with the OData.publish:true option, there is no service implementation step. There is only the data modeling phase, and the service can be published afterwards.

5.4.5 Service Generation via Redefinition

As explained in Section 5.2, *redefinition* is the process of generating a service based on an existing data source. This is done using a wizard and combines both the data model definition phase and the service implementation phase into the single phase of redefinition. The resulting generated service has to be registered and activated in the SAP Gateway server system (the service maintenance phase) and can then be consumed. The goal of redefinition is to allow for service creation with less effort.

There are quite a number of existing business objects in an SAP system; SAP Customer Relationship Management (SAP CRM), SAP Product Lifecycle Management (SAP PLM), and SAP Enterprise Asset Management (EAM)—for example—all use a form of business object. Although these business object models have been designed for different use cases, all of them define objects, relations, actions, and queries similar to those that can be found in the OData protocol. It therefore comes as no surprise that a lot of these business objects can be used to generate OData services.

Existing business objects

It's also possible to generate SAP Gateway services from existing SAP Gateway services. This scenario is used if a customer wants to extend an OData service delivered by SAP, for example, the OData service used by a SAP Fiori application. The extensibility of SAP Fiori applications is discussed end to end in Chapter 10.

Extensibility

On top of integrating existing SAP Business Suite business objects, it's also possible to integrate third-party OData services. However, this integration scenario has some technical restrictions.

Third-party OData services

The wizard for generating an OData service using redefinition is almost identical for all integration scenarios. Selecting one of the available options (based on the installed add-on) starts a wizard that guides you through the following three steps:

Redefinition wizard

1. Select the business object.

2. Select artifacts of the data source (data model definition).

3. Generate runtime artifacts and service registration in the backend (service implementation).

In other words, the wizard starts with the data model definition part but automatically performs the steps that belong to the service implementation phase. After the service has been registered and implemented in the SAP Business Suite, it has to be activated in the SAP Gateway server.

The different integration scenarios described in this section are partly based on specific add-ons listed in Table 5.1. If these add-ons have been deployed to the SAP Business Suite system, the related context menu options in the Service Builder are visible as shown in Figure 5.22.

Name of Add-On	Integration Scenario	Remote-Enabled
IW_GIL	Generic Interaction Layer (GenIL)	
IW_SPI	Service Provider Interface	X
SAP_GWFND or IW_BEP	Analytical Queries	X
SAP_GWFND or IW_BEP and IW_FND	OData service (external)	X
SAP_GWFND or IW_BEP	OData service (SAP Gateway)	X

Table 5.1 Add-Ons for Generating a Service Based on an Existing Data Source

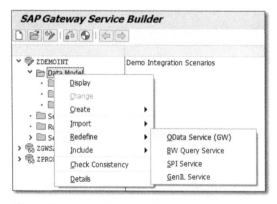

Figure 5.22 Context Menu Options to Create a Data Model Using Redefinition

Most of the scenarios are also remote-enabled, which means that the business object that is to be consumed (e.g., a Service Provider Interface object) doesn't have to exist in the same system in which the BEP component is deployed. As a result, these scenarios can be implemented in the SAP Gateway server (assuming you're using hub deployment with development on the hub).

Next, let's look at the different possible sources for suitable business objects in detail.

Generic Interaction Layer

Integration of GenIL with SAP Gateway offers the possibility of generating OData services based on existing GenIL components. GenIL is meant to be a wrapper around existing business logic. It provides access to all business objects via a unified interface for consuming application logic in the UI layer by using the *Business Object Layer (BOL) API*. The BOL consists of two pieces:

> **GenIL**
> The lower layer is a "dispatcher" that manages GenIL components and their models at runtime and distributes requests from above to the respective components implementing the requested objects.

> **BOL**
> The stateful layer provides optimized performance by avoiding expensive repetitive access to the APIs and thus acts as a buffer for the UI.

While BOL was built for the SAP CRM Web Client, the role of GenIL is different because it can be used for other integration scenarios as well. The consumption of SOAP-based web services using the Web Service tool that directly consumes GenIL is an example of such additional integration.

Similarly, SAP Gateway allows you to generate OData services leveraging GenIL (as shown in Figure 5.23). The nodes, relations, and queries in the GenIL model are transformed to the corresponding entities in an OData model, as shown in Figure 5.24.

Wrapper around existing business logic

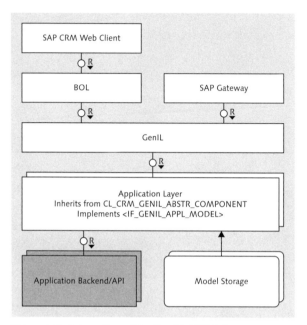

Figure 5.23 Integration of GenIL with SAP Gateway

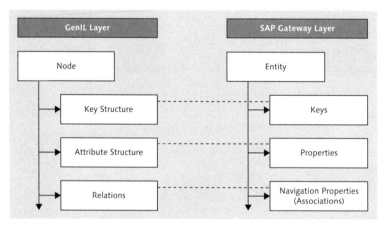

Figure 5.24 Mapping between the GenIL and OData Model

Although BOL (and thus GenIL) are frequently used for SAP CRM Web Client, it has also been used in other SAP Business Suite applications such as SAP ERP Financials and SAP ERP Human Capital Management (SAP ERP HCM). The integration is contained in the IW_GIL add-on.

This must be deployed locally on the SAP Business Suite system (e.g., SAP CRM) on top of the BEP component.

> **Note**
>
> The GenIL integration scenario isn't remote enabled. To use services that are generated based on GenIL objects, the IW_BEP add-on component (SAP_GWFND starting from SAP NetWeaver release 7.40) has to be deployed on the SAP Business Suite system.

Service Provider Interface

The Service Provider Interface was originally developed for SAP Product Lifecycle Management (PLM). Service Provider Interface is a framework generated within the application layer that has different consumers. The framework is currently used not only by the applications for which it was originally developed but also for various other applications within the SAP Business Suite.

Service Provider Interface objects can be called remotely. As a result, it isn't mandatory to deploy the SAP Gateway IW_SPI add-on for Service Provider Interface on the SAP Business Suite system. Because the add-on calls the RFC interface of the Service Provider Interface layer, it can be deployed on the SAP Gateway server system. The IW_GIL add-on instead must be deployed locally on the SAP Business Suite system (e.g., SAP CRM). The integration of Service Provider Interface with SAP Gateway allows Service Provider Interface application building blocks to be provisioned as OData services.

> **Further Resources**
>
> For more information about this topic, we recommend the following:
>
> ▸ SPI wiki on SCN: *https://wiki.scn.sap.com/wiki/display/SPI*
> ▸ SAP Online Help: *http://help.sap.com/saphelp_crm70/helpdata/en/7c/0f77e9f297402aacb48ca7110c7f2a/frameset.htm*

Analytic Queries

Analytic queries are the main tools for consuming analytical data that are embedded in business applications such as the SAP Business Suite and in data warehouses such as SAP BW. While analytic queries in SAP Business Suite provide access to consistent operational data, analytic queries in the SAP BW hub offer access to consistent, highly aggregated data across the enterprise.

SAP Gateway and SAP BW integration allows you to publish SAP BW content as an OData service that has been defined using multidimensional expressions (MDX) or SAP BW Easy Queries. While the MDX approach can also be used for SAP BW systems starting with 7.0, the SAP BW Easy Query approach is only supported for release 7.30 and higher. SAP BW Easy Queries are, however, easier to understand and to handle, so they are recommended.

SAP BW Easy Queries

SAP BW Easy Queries are analytic queries that meet certain criteria. For a given SAP BW Easy Query, an RFC module is created in the system. This is done automatically by the system, based on the available SAP BW query definition. Using this RFC, an SAP BW Easy Query interface can be defined as an OData service.

To release an analytical query as an SAP BW Easy Query, you have to mark the corresponding checkbox in the query properties in the BEx Query Designer (see Figure 5.25).

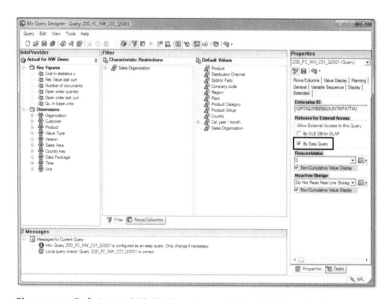

Figure 5.25 Defining an SAP BW Easy Query in the BEx Query Designer

After this has been done, and the query is saved, the generation of the RFC is triggered. General rules that apply for SAP BW Easy Queries are that characteristics are on the rows, key figures are on the columns, and free characteristics aren't mapped to OData.

Dimensions, dimension attributes, and measures are represented as properties of an entity type. The entity type representing the results of an MDX or an SAP BW Easy Query is annotated as `sap:semantics=aggregate`. Table 5.2 shows how SAP BW objects such as dimensions, dimension attributes, and measures are represented in OData. The table shows only the main annotations.

Analytical annotations

SAP BW Objects	OData Representation	SAP Annotation
Cube of type Query	Entity type	`sap:semantics=aggregate`
Dimension	Property	`sap:aggregation-role=dimension`
Dimension attribute	Property	`sap:attribute-for=<dimension name>`
Measure	Property	`sap:aggregation-role=measure`

Table 5.2 Analytical Annotations

External OData Service

OData Services Consumption and Integration (OSCI) is an additional integration scenario that aims at enabling consumption and integration of any OData service. With SP 07 of SAP Gateway 2.0, this functionality is fully integrated with the Service Builder. The integration has to be implemented on the SAP Gateway server system, where the IW_BEP add-on also has to be deployed. This is required because you need the OData library for the consumption of an OData service, and this library only resides on the SAP Gateway server. In addition, you also need IW_BEP for service development on the SAP Gateway server.

OSCI

As of SAP NetWeaver ABAP 7.40 SP 02, this prerequisite will be fulfilled by any SAP NetWeaver ABAP system because the SAP_GWFND software component comprises the required functionality.

OData Service (SAP Gateway)

The Service Builder allows you to generate a service based on an existing OData service in SAP Gateway. This integration scenario can be used to extend an existing service. It creates a new service with the same interface as the original service but with a changed behavior, which is accomplished by redefining methods in the new DPC extension class. The extension of an OData service and an SAPUI5 application delivered by SAP as part of the SAP Fiori reference apps is discussed in detail in Chapter 10.

5.4.6   Service Generation via Referenced Data Sources

With the advent of SAP HANA, there was a paradigm shift in how business applications were developed at SAP. Data provisioning in SAP S/4HANA is based on CDS and OData. This is possible because CDS not only addresses read-only scenarios but also transactional, analytical, and search use cases. Using CDS, it's possible to define semantically reach data models by providing annotations that can be leveraged by Smart Templates. These are smart in a sense that the UI will provide an input field automatically if a property is marked as sap:updatable. CDS views can easily be extended by extending the view. The REFERENCED DATA SOURCE option allows ABAP developers to define dynamic OData services based on CDS view definitions in Transaction SEGW (see Figure 5.26).

Figure 5.26 CDS View as a Referenced Data Source in Transaction SEGW

This means that any change in the underlying CDS view is automatically reflected in the OData service that has been generated using the referenced data source concept. In the Service Builder, you can select a CDS view and select those entities and associations that should be part of the OData Service.

5.4.7 Service Generation via OData.publish:true

Similar to the referenced data sources, `OData.publish:true` allows you to publish CDS views as OData services directly from within the ABAP Development Tools in Eclipse. By setting one simple annotation (`@OData.publish:true`), you can publish a CDS view as an OData service. Technically, a MPC and a DPC are generated, and these classes are registered as an OData service in the SAP Business Suite backend. To publish the registered service, a developer or administrator has to use Transaction /IWFND/MAINT_SERVICE. In contrast to all other options for creating OData services that we've shown thus far, this option doesn't make use of the Service Builder.

It's planned that the `@OData.publish:true` option won't only be suitable for read-only and analytical services but will also be used for transactional services by generating appropriate BOPF objects alongside the OData service. By performing a code-based implementation of those objects, the generated OData service will also support the capability to `create`, `update`, and `delete` business data.

5.5 OData Channel Development Paradigm

Now that we've discussed the basics of the different tracks for the SAP Gateway service creation process, let's look a little closer at the *OData channel development paradigm*, which is a specific approach for service development. This introduction lays the theoretical foundation for Chapter 6, which goes into great detail about service development. The OData channel is part of the SAP Gateway basics if you plan on using service development.

The OData channel for SAP Gateway allows you to develop content by defining object models and registering a corresponding runtime DPC. The advantage of the OData channel paradigm is a certain freedom with respect to development; entire DDIC definitions and local interfaces of the SAP Business Suite can be used to develop SAP Gateway services. In addition, OData query options can be leveraged in the SAP Business Suite systems so that only data that has been requested by the client are selected from the SAP Business Suite system and sent back over the wire. This results in highly optimized services and major performance improvements due to a lower transferred data size.

SAP Gateway services with respect to the OData programming model consist of four components:

Four components of an SAP Gateway service

▶ **MPC**
Implemented to provide the runtime representation of your model definition.

▶ **DPC**
Called at runtime to perform data requests.

▶ **Technical service name**
Used to register the service in the SAP Business Suite system together with the *technical model name*.

▶ **Technical model name**
Used to register the service in the SAP Business Suite system together with the *technical service name*.

The technical service name and technical model name are automatically generated with the MPC and DPC when generating a project using the Service Builder.

5.5.1 Model Provider Class

The MPC is an ABAP class that provides the runtime representation of your model definition; that is, the MPC defines the EDM of a service. As such, all model information that you've defined in your project is generated into the MPC. As a consequence, you have to regenerate the MPC every time you change the model definition in your project. The MPC is important because everything you find in the service metadata document of an OData service published via SAP Gateway has programmatically been defined in the MPC.

Technically, the model definition is actually generated into two classes:

► **Base class**
Technically, the base class is derived from the /IWBEP/CL_MGW_PUSH_ ABS_MODEL superclass and has suffix _MPC.

► **Extension class**
The extension class has the base class as the superclass and has the suffix _MPC_EXT. The extension class will be registered via the technical model name. In the extension class, you can choose which methods to redefine and which methods to inherit from the base class.

In most cases, there's no need for a developer to touch the MPC that has been generated by the Service Builder. The exception to that rule is, for example, if you want to build SAP Gateway services with features that can't (yet) be modeled using SAP Gateway tools. In this case, the developer can redefine methods in the model provider extension class (see Figure 5.27).

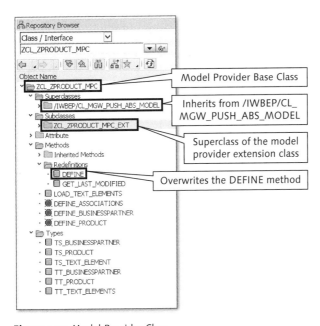

Figure 5.27 Model Provider Class

Model Provider Class Deep Dive

Usually, there's no need for a developer to tap into the coding of the MPC being generated by the Service Builder. Let's still take a closer look at the methods being generated to get a better understanding of the underlying framework.

The `DEFINE` method in the MPC generated by the Service Builder contains calls to the entity type-specific `define_<entity_type>` methods and in addition a call to the `define_Association` method that creates the associations, association sets, referential constraints, and navigation properties.

The `GET_LAST_MODIFIED` method is the basis for a handshake between the SAP Business Suite and SAP Gateway to start a refresh of the cached metadata of the service on the SAP Gateway backend and the SAP Gateway server after the class has been changed. This method shouldn't be changed manually.

In the entity type-specific `DEFINE` methods, the Service Builder generates the coding that creates the parts of the OData model that define the entity types and the entity sets that are based on entity type. The properties are created, and those properties that have been marked as a key field in the Service Builder are set as key fields in the coding:

```
lo_property = lo_entity_type->
create_property( iv_property_name = 'ProductID'
iv_abap_fieldname = 'PRODUCT_ID' ).
lo_property->set_is_key( ).
```

Finally, the entity type is bound to a DDIC structure, and one or more entity sets are created. Note that an entity type that is bound to an existing DDIC structure can leverage conversion exits as well as the labels of the data elements from the DDIC. The medium field label of a data element is used as `sap:label` by default:

```
...
lo_entity_type->
bind_structure( iv_structure_name   =
'BAPI_EPM_PRODUCT_HEADER' iv_bind_conversions = 'X' ).
...
lo_entity_set = lo_entity_type->
create_entity_set( 'Products' )
```

In the `DEFINE_ASSOCIATION` method, you can find the generated code that defines associations, association sets, referential constraints, and navigation properties of an OData model.

5.5.2 Data Provider Class and Data Provider Extension Class

The DPC is an ABAP class that provides all methods required to handle OData requests. It's called at runtime to perform these requests; essentially, we're talking about the runtime representation of your service implementation. For instance, a DPC executes CREATE, READ, UPDATE, DELETE, QUERY, and many more operations.

Again, you can find an extension class (suffix _DPC_EXT) and a base class (suffix _DPC). The data provider extension class inherits from the DPC base class (see Figure 5.28). The DPC extension class is registered via the technical service name. So the extension class is executed in your OData service.

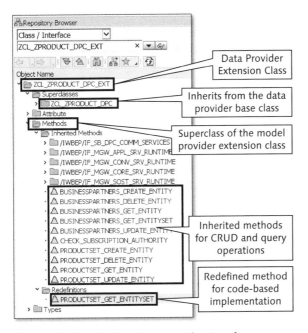

Figure 5.28 Data Provider Extension Class Interface

It's important to note that in the DPC, there are methods that are and are not specific to an entity set.

Entity set-specific methods

Data Provider Class Deep Dive

For each entity set, the Service Builder creates methods that are called by the framework if a CREATE, READ, UPDATE, or DELETE (CRUD) method is sent to this entity set. For an entity set called <ENTITYSET>, the methods created in the base class are shown in Table 5.3.

DPC Method Name	HTTP Verb	Target
<ENTITYSET>_CREATE_ENTITY	POST	Entity set
<ENTITYSET>_DELETE_ENTITY	DELETE	Entity
<ENTITYSET>_GET_ENTITY	GET	Entity
<ENTITYSET>_GET_ENTITYSET	GET	Entity set
<ENTITYSET>_UPDATE_ENTITY	UPDATE or PATCH	Entity

Table 5.3 Entity Set-Specific CRUD Method Implementation in the DPC

There are additional methods available that apply not only for a single entity set but for all of them (nonentity set-specific methods). Examples of these methods are the methods handling $EXPAND statements, deep insert statements, or those that are called when a function import is performed. Let's take a closer look at these examples:

▸ **GET_EXPANDED_ENTITY, GET_EXPANDED_ENTITYSET**
Handling of $expand statements is offered by the SAP Gateway framework out of the box in a generic way after you've modeled the appropriate navigation property and implemented the handling of navigation properties. There might be situations where you instead handle $expand requests by a specific application implementation. Examples are certain BAPIs such as BAPI_EPM_SO_GET_LIST that, along with the header data, also retrieve line items. In this case, when retrieving the sales order header data for a certain sales order, the corresponding sales order items are also read. If the entity set is also called to expand the line items alongside the sales order header, this results in unnecessary database requests.

▸ **CREATE_DEEP_ENTITY**
The counterpart of the $expand statement is the *deep insert* statement, which calls the CREATE_DEEP_ENTITY method. A typical example is the case where a sales order can only be created alongside at least one sales order item. In contrast to the $expand statement, there's no generic handling of a deep insert request. The developer has to implement this method.

▸ **EXECUTE_ACTION**
The EXECUTE_ACTION method is a nonentity set-specific method as well.

It's rather service semantic and is called if a function import into an OData service is called. Function imports allow you to execute functions that can read and/or write data. Function imports are suitable whenever the business scenario requires data to be read or changed that can't be modeled into an entity where you can use the CRUD-Q methods.

5.5.3   Technical Considerations

OData channel development can either take place on the SAP Business Suite system or on the SAP Gateway server, as shown in Figure 5.29. Both options are suited for certain use cases and have their advantages. Wherever you develop, the BEP component has to be installed there, or you have to use a system based on SAP NetWeaver 7.40 or higher.

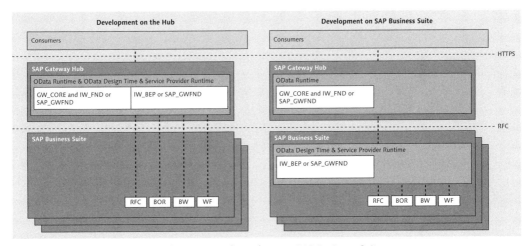

Figure 5.29 OData Channel Development on the Hub or on SAP Business Suite

5.6   Summary

Building OData services with SAP Gateway is done by following the SAP Gateway service creation process. This process is strongly supported and facilitated by the central SAP Gateway service creation tool: the Service Builder. In this chapter, we introduced you to the tool and the process to establish a base of knowledge for the more technical step-by-step instructions in Chapter 6 and Chapter 7, which focus in detail on the processes of service development and service generation. In Chapter 6, you'll also be able to take advantage of the OData channel programming paradigm that you've learned about here.

Service development is one of the two main options for service creation. Although it's more complicated than its counterpart, service generation, it's also more flexible.

6   Service Development

This chapter explains the process of *service development*, which is the backend-side development of OData services using ABAP. After reading this chapter, you'll be able to develop services with the main development tool, the SAP Gateway Service Builder, while making use of the OData channel as the development paradigm.

The steps described in this chapter are in line with the three main steps of service development (data model definition, service implementation, and service maintenance) as explained in Chapter 5. As you'll recall, data model definition, service implementation, and service maintenance don't necessarily have to be performed using a waterfall approach; the data model definition and the service implementation are iterative tasks that will be revisited frequently to let the OData service and its capabilities grow iteration by iteration. This approach is very similar to other programming languages where you start with a first user interface (UI) element and implement its functionality, and then add the next UI element and implement its functionality, and so on.

Data model definition, service implementation, service maintenance

In this chapter, we explain the steps of OData service development as they would occur in a real-world scenario. Figure 6.1 shows the steps of this development process.

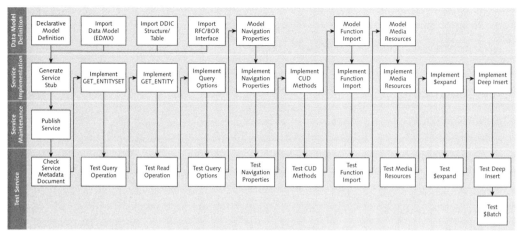

Figure 6.1 Example Development Process

6.1   Data Model Definition

Service Builder   As you've learned from the previous chapters, each OData service consists of a data model definition and a service implementation. At runtime, the model definition results in the service document and the service metadata document, and the service implementation results in the actual functionality of the SAP Gateway service. For an SAP Gateway OData service using the OData channel development paradigm, the model definition is provided via the model provider class (MPC). The service implementation is provided via the data provider class (DPC). The tool that performs both of these tasks is the Service Builder.

> **Manual Service Creation**
>
> You can implement the MPC and DPC manually by using the ABAP Class Builder (Transaction SE24) in ABAP. However, this process can be pretty time consuming and, especially in the case of the MPC, might be a bit error prone. Also on the DPC side, there are some recurring tasks (e.g., mapping a data source and creating CRUD-Q methods for the different entity sets) that are easier with a tool.
>
> From the possible deployment options, you've seen that a remote call into another system out of the SAP_GWFND/IW_BEP component is also possible. In this case, you need to consider that, for example, a certain data element might not be locally available on the SAP_GWFND/IW_BEP system.

There are two main steps in the data model definition: first, create a project, and second, define the actual data model. In this section, we'll walk you through both of these major steps.

6.1.1 Creating a Project

Before you can start with the model definition, you first need to start the Service Builder (Transaction SEGW) and create a new project. A project defines the brackets around all artifacts that are created during your OData service development. The Service Builder allows you to open and work on multiple projects in parallel. Figure 6.2 shows an example of a single Service Builder project.

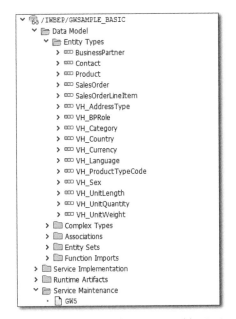

Figure 6.2 Example of a Service Builder Project

The root node is the project itself, which, in this case, is /IWBEP/GWSAMPLE_BASIC (/IWBEP/GWSAMPLE_BASIC is a sample service that is part of the standard shipment as of SAP_GWFND 7.40 SP 08). The first subnode is DATA MODEL. This node takes care of your entire model definition. The SERVICE IMPLEMENTATION subnode actually injects life into your service by mapping data sources (e.g., remote function calls

[RFCs] or Business Application Programming Interfaces [BAPIs]) to your model. It also allows you to manually implement the respective methods using ABAP. RUNTIME ARTIFACTS summarizes all artifacts (or the most important ones) that are generated during your project lifecycle. Finally, SERVICE MAINTENANCE allows you to register and activate your service on the SAP Gateway hub.

When starting the Service Builder the first time, you see an empty window (see Figure 6.3).

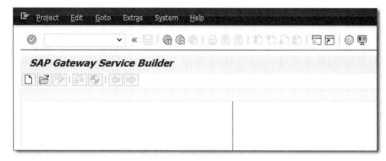

Figure 6.3 Service Builder Start Screen

Create project Choose the CREATE PROJECT button to create a new Service Builder project (see Figure 6.4).

Figure 6.4 Service Builder Create Project Button

Project details This opens the CREATE PROJECT dialog where you need to provide the following (see Figure 6.5):

- ▶ PROJECT
  Special characters and spaces aren't allowed in project names, and they can't start with numbers. Individual words can be separated by

underscores. The maximum length of the project name is 30 characters.

▶ DESCRIPTION
A 60-character, free-text field that describes your project.

▶ PROJECT TYPE
Choose from the following options:

SERVICE WITH SAP ANNOTATIONS: This is the default project type. In this context, *annotations* means standard SAP annotations based on core attributes that can be used to annotate your data model (e.g., `sap:creatable`).

SERVICE WITH VOCABULARY-BASED ANNOTATIONS: This project type allows you to assign one or more vocabularies to your project and, as such, make use of vocabulary-based terms. You can choose from standard vocabularies that are provided out of the box and/or upload your own vocabularies.

ANNOTATION MODEL FOR REFERENCED SERVICE: This project type is used to annotate an existing service. The annotations don't show up with the service metadata itself but can be accessed via `/IWFND/CatalogService;v=2`. These annotations are meant to be read by the consumer (e.g., HTML5 application) to influence the UI behavior.

The default project type is SERVICE WITH SAP ANNOTATIONS, which refers to a project with regular annotations (see Table 6.1).

▶ GENERATION STRATEGY
This option is defaulted to STANDARD. There is currently only one generation strategy that can be chosen here. Depending on the project type, there might be additional generation strategies in the future.

▶ PACKAGE and PERSON RESPONSIBLE
These are the default elements that you already know from other repository objects (e.g., ABAP reports, Data Dictionary [DDIC] tables, etc.). $TMP is used for local developments that you don't want to transport into any target system. If you want to transport the project and its content to any target system, you need to provide a transportable package. Such a package can be created by using the ABAP Development Workbench (Transaction SE80).

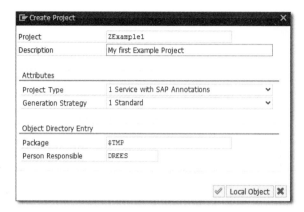

Figure 6.5 Create Project Dialog Screen

ABAP repository entry

The project name becomes an ABAP repository entry, which is why the project name has to fulfill the typical SAP naming conventions (start with a "Z" or a "Y" to separate customer objects from SAP objects). In addition to that, you can also use a registered namespace surrounded by slashes (e.g., /MyNamespace/project) just as you do when, for example, creating your own data element or function module by using the other standard SAP development tools. The object repository entry in this example is R3TR IWPR ZEXAMPLE1. Here, IWPR refers to *Gateway Business Suite Enablement – Service Builder Project* and is, of course, transportable via a regular ABAP Workbench transport request. IWPR only transports the project as such—not the generated artifacts (e.g., MPC or DPC). Those will be separate entries in the transport request with their respective repository object types.

6.1.2 Creating a Data Model

Data model options

As soon as you have a project, you can start building your SAP OData service. The first thing you need to do is create the data model. As introduced in Chapter 5, there are multiple options to build a data model:

▶ Create a declarative data model.

▶ Import a data model via entity data model XML (EDMX).

▶ Import a data model via DDIC.

▶ Import a data model via RFC/Business Object Repository (BOR).

The declarative model definition is typically chosen whenever you start from scratch with your data model definition, which means you have no source from which to derive your data model. Otherwise, you'll use whichever method is appropriate for the data source in question.

Let's discuss each of these options in more detail.

Creating a Declarative Data Model

A declarative data model is created manually. To create your first entity type via this method, right-click on DATA MODEL, and choose CREATE • ENTITY TYPE (see Figure 6.6).

Manual creation

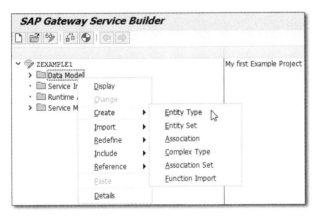

Figure 6.6 Creating a New Entity Type

In the CREATE ENTITY TYPE dialog, you can specify the name of your entity type. The name has to be unique inside your project.

Optionally, you can also mark the CREATE RELATED ENTITY SET checkbox to create a corresponding entity set with an assignment to this entity type in one step. Typically, there is a 1:1 relationship between an entity type and an entity set, but this isn't required; an entity type can be used in many entity sets. For example, a BusinessPartner entity type might be used in entity sets with the name ShipToPartnerSet, SoldToPartnerSet, and so on.

Create a related entity set

In the first example, you'll create a product entity type (see Figure 6.7) with a set of properties. After entering the ENTITY TYPE NAME, select the

CREATE RELATED ENTITY SET checkbox to have the ENTITY SET NAME defaulted and the entity set created with the entity type.

Figure 6.7 Creation of a New Entity Type

After the entity type has been created, the project tree is automatically updated, and the new entity type is highlighted and selected. In the detail section, you see all of the attributes of the entity type (see Figure 6.8).

Figure 6.8 Entity Type Attributes

One of the important attributes is the ABAP STRUCTURE TYPE NAME. Via this optional attribute, you can define a link of your entity type to a DDIC structure or table. This is quite important because it allows you to inherit your property definition (e.g., length and precision) from the underlying DDIC element. In addition, you inherit any labels, including their translations, from the DDIC. This is beneficial if you offer your application in multiple languages and want the application to pick the labels from the exposed metadata (either once during design time or dynamically during runtime via the metadata document) in the respective language. Even if you're running just a single language, this link means that you don't have to maintain your labels in multiple areas. (On the other hand, if the application dynamically fetches its labels from the metadata document, you can't predict how things might look in the final UI. It's entirely up to you which approach you prefer.)

So far, the entity type has no properties. This can be changed by expanding the project tree and double-clicking on PROPERTIES (see Figure 6.9).

Figure 6.9 Properties Node in the Project Tree

On the right-hand side of the project window, the properties grid of the current entity type is shown. Because there is no property so far, the grid is empty after creating a new entity type. By clicking the APPEND ROW or INSERT ROW buttons, you can create a new property for the current entity type.

As mandatory information, you have to provide the NAME and the EDM CORE TYPE of the property (even if you provide a DDIC reference). Each entity type also has to have at least one property marked as the KEY property.

In the current example, you'll create three properties for the product entity type: PRODUCTID, CATEGORY, and NAME. They are all defined as EDM.STRING with individual lengths (see Figure 6.10).

Three properties

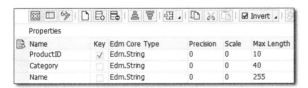

Name	Key	Edm Core Type	Precision	Scale	Max Length
ProductID	✓	Edm.String	0	0	10
Category		Edm.String	0	0	40
Name		Edm.String	0	0	255

Figure 6.10 Entity Type Properties

The property PRODUCTID is marked as a KEY property. So the primary key of the product entity type consists of only one field. The MAX

Key property

LENGTH attribute is defined as 10 for the PRODUCTID, 40 for the CATE-GORY, and 255 for the NAME in this example.

The attribute flags (see Figure 6.11) are described in Table 6.1.

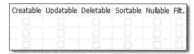

Figure 6.11 Property Attribute Flags

Flag	Annotation	Description/Example
CREATABLE	sap:creatable	This property can be provided by an application when creating an entry resource of this entity type.
		Most of the properties typically have this flag set because they are supposed to be filled when an entry is being created (e.g., `CustomerName`).
		This flag is typically not set in cases where the backend provides the property when an entry is being created (e.g., `SalesOrderNumber` or `BusinessPartnerNumber`).
UPDATABLE	sap:updatable	This property can be provided by an application when updating an entry resource of this entity type.
		The updatable attribute is often in line with the creatable attribute. It's typically set whenever a property of an existing entry can be changed (e.g., `PhoneNumber`).
		It's typically not set whenever a property is calculated by the backend (e.g., `ChangeTimeStamp` or `NetSum`).
DELETABLE	N/A	This attribute has no relevance because individual properties can't be deleted (this has no effect on changing individual properties to their initial state).

Table 6.1 Entity Type Attributes

Flag	Annotation	Description/Example
SORTABLE	`sap:sortable`	The sortable annotation indicates to a consumer if the property can be used in an `$orderby` query option (e.g., `$orderby=CustomerName`).
NULLABLE	`Nullable`	The nullable annotation defines if a property can contain a `Null` value or not. This is very important for `Date` or `Time` fields, for example, if they don't contain a value on the ABAP side; as such, an empty field can't be rendered into an OData response if the nullable annotation isn't set. It's good advice to set the nullable attribute for all nonkey properties to make sure they can carry even empty ABAP values. On the other hand, a consumer considers nullable attributes as being optional, which might not be in line with your business logic. Note that key properties may not contain nullable properties, that is, may not have the value `Null`.
FILTERABLE	`sap:filterable`	The filterable annotation indicates to a consumer if the property can be used in a `$filter` query option (e.g., `$filter=OrderNumber eq '1234'`).

Table 6.1 Entity Type Attributes (Cont.)

The annotations are rendered into the metadata document (see Figure 6.12).

```
- <EntityType Name="Product" sap:content-version="1">
  - <Key>
      <PropertyRef Name="ProductID" />
    </Key>
    <Property Name="ProductID" Type="Edm.String" Nullable="false" MaxLength="10" sap:creatable="false" sap:updatable="false"
      sap:sortable="false" sap:filterable="false" />
  </EntityType>
```

Figure 6.12 Property Metadata with All Flags Set (as an Example)

The creatable, updatable, sortable, and filterable attributes are only used in the metadata document to inform the consumer application about the intended behavior. There is no control via the SAP Gateway framework

Creatable, updatable, sortable, filterable attributes

if a certain property is actually being used the way it's annotated via the metadata. Even if a property isn't marked as updatable, you can still provide the property along with an update request, and the property value will reach the data provider implementation. So it won't be—for example—filtered or handled via an error if you perform an operation that isn't allowed according to the annotations in the metadata document.

As a recommendation, the data provider implementation (DPC) should always behave the same way because the metadata is defining the model. But this isn't a must and unfortunately in many service implementations isn't considered, as most of the services are being developed for individual use cases (e.g., for a dedicated, known consumer application that typically makes them a nonreusable service). Whenever you develop an OData service for reuse, it's strongly recommended to define proper metadata; otherwise, the service consumers have to identify the service capabilities via trial and error, which is obviously not a good practice.

As an example (see Figure 6.13), flag all CREATABLE attributes of the PRODUCTID, CATEGORY, and NAME properties. Later (in the following sections), we'll implement the `Create` operation so that all properties are provided when performing a creation. The UPDATABLE attribute won't be marked for the PRODUCTID because the primary key can't be changed in our example.

SORTABLE isn't marked at all because we won't implement any sorting capabilities. The same holds true for NULLABLE, as none of the properties are optional. FILTERABLE is only set for PRODUCTID and CATEGORY because we'll only provide filter capabilities for these two properties.

Properties												
Name	Key	Edm Core Type	Prec.	Scale	Max Lngth	U	Creatable	Updatable	Sortable	Nullable	Filterable	Label
ProductID	✓	Edm.String	0	0	10		✓	☐	☐	☐	✓	Product Identifier
Category	☐	Edm.String	0	0	40		✓	✓	☐	☐	✓	Product Category
Name	☐	Edm.String	0	0	255		✓	✓	☐	☐	☐	Product Name

Figure 6.13 Maintained Attributes and Labels

The next step is to create an entity set, which is required because the service provisioning as well as the service consumption takes place based on entity sets. An entity set can be created by double-clicking the entity set node in the Project Explorer. This opens the ENTITY SETS section on the right-hand side. You can create new entity sets by using the APPEND ROW or INSERT ROW buttons.

As part of our example, we've created an entity set with the name PRODUCTSET during the creation of the entity type (see Figure 6.14).

Figure 6.14 ProductSet Entity Set (Initial State)

Naming entity sets

There are different approaches for naming an entity set for a given entity type. Some people prefer to add "Collection" to the entity type name (in this example, it would result in `ProductCollection`). Others prefer to use the plural (`Products`). In this example, you'll add "Set" to define the name of the resulting entity set. It's entirely up to you which approach you prefer and how to handle it in your own OData services; just be sure not to mix the approaches within a single OData service.

For each entity set, you also need to specify the underlying entity type name. This is mandatory information. The entity type name can either be typed in manually or chosen from an F4 help dialog. If you've created the entity set during the creation of the entity type, the assignment is already done for you.

Optionally, you can also provide a label. This label is rendered into the metadata document and allows a consumer application to, for example, display a page title.

Entity set attributes

On the entity set level, there are again certain attributes that annotate the capabilities of the related entity set. Similar to the flags on the entity type level, those flags are only part of the meta-information (in this case, in both the metadata as well as the service document). There is no handling or action done via the framework, which means that, for example, if an entity set isn't annotated as creatable, you can still do a POST request and create the related entry resource. Again, make sure that the metadata of the OData service is in line with the actual service provisioning.

Table 6.2 describes the meaning of the entity set attributes.

Flag	Annotation	Description/Example
CREATABLE	sap:creatable	Creation of entries of the related entity type is supported. Creates are handled via HTTP POST requests. For example, you can create a business partner entry.
UPDATABLE	sap:updatable	Updates of entries of the related entity type are supported. Updates are handled via HTTP PUT requests addressing the entry resource you want to update. For example, you can update a product with the product ID "123".
DELETABLE	sap:deletable	Deletions of entries of the related entity type are supported. Deletions are handled via HTTP DELETE requests addressing the entry resource you want to delete. For example, you can delete a sales order line item with the key OrderId='50000',Item='10'.
PAGEABLE	sap:pageable	Client-side paging of this entity set is supported. Client-side paging works via the query parameter. The client can define the page size and the number of entries to be skipped.

Table 6.2 Entity Set Attributes

Flag	Annotation	Description/Example
ADDRESSABLE	`sap:addressable`	This indicates whether the related entity set can be addressed directly via the URI (e.g., `ProductSet`) or whether you have to use a navigation property to address it via a different entry, for example, `SalesOrderSet('1')/Items`. `SalesOrderItemSet` wouldn't be directly addressable because it makes no sense to read all order items across all sales orders without the respective order header.
SEARCHABLE	`sap:searchable`	This indicates whether the service implementation (`QUERY` method) supports a search string. A search string doesn't filter on any properties as such but provides the search string via the URI search parameter, for example, `ProductSet?search='box'`.
SUBSCRIBABLE	`N/A`	This indicates if a consumer can subscribe to changes of the underlying entities. Subscription and notification handling require corresponding system configuration (e.g., bgRFC) as well as user exit implementations or event linkages to send a notification based on a backend event.
REQUIRES FILTER	`sap:requires-filter`	This indicates whether a query requires a filter or not. If a filter is required, you can't execute a query without a filter. For example, `BusinessPartnerSet` fetches all business partners available in the system, which can be quite a lot. Therefore, it makes sense to force a consumer to provide a filter.

Table 6.2 Entity Set Attributes (Cont.)

In our example, we'll set the attributes CREATABLE, UPDATABLE, DELETABLE, PAGEABLE, and ADDRESSABLE (see Figure 6.15).

Figure 6.15 ProductSet Entity Set with Marked Attributes

After the service has been generated and activated (which will be covered in Section 6.2 and Section 6.4), you can see how the attributes are rendered into the metadata document (see Figure 6.16).

```
<?xml version="1.0" encoding="UTF-8"?>
- <edmx:Edmx xmlns:sap="http://www.sap.com/Protocols/SAPData"
    xmlns:m="http://schemas.microsoft.com/ado/2007/08/dataservices/metadata"
    xmlns:edmx="http://schemas.microsoft.com/ado/2007/06/edmx" Version="1.0">
  - <edmx:DataServices m:DataServiceVersion="2.0">
    - <Schema xml:lang="en" xmlns="http://schemas.microsoft.com/ado/2008/09/edm" sap:schema-
        version="1" Namespace="ZEXAMPLE1_SRV">
      - <EntityType sap:content-version="1" Name="Product">
        - <Key>
            <PropertyRef Name="ProductID"/>
          </Key>
          <Property Name="ProductID" sap:sortable="false" sap:updatable="false" sap:label="Product
            Identifier" MaxLength="10" Nullable="false" Type="Edm.String"/>
          <Property Name="Category" sap:sortable="false" sap:label="Product Category" MaxLength="40"
            Nullable="false" Type="Edm.String"/>
          <Property Name="Name" sap:sortable="false" sap:label="Product Name" MaxLength="255"
            Nullable="false" Type="Edm.String" sap:filterable="false"/>
        </EntityType>
      - <EntityContainer Name="ZEXAMPLE1_SRV_Entities" sap:supported-formats="atom json xlsx"
          m:IsDefaultEntityContainer="true">
            <EntitySet sap:content-version="1" Name="ProductSet" EntityType="ZEXAMPLE1_SRV.Product"/>
        </EntityContainer>
        <atom:link xmlns:atom="http://www.w3.org/2005/Atom"
          href="http://SAPGateway:50000/sap/opu/odata/sap/ZEXAMPLE1_SRV/$metadata"
          rel="self"/>
        <atom:link xmlns:atom="http://www.w3.org/2005/Atom"
          href="http://SAPGateway:50000/sap/opu/odata/sap/ZEXAMPLE1_SRV/$metadata"
          rel="latest-version"/>
      </Schema>
    </edmx:DataServices>
  </edmx:Edmx>
```

Figure 6.16 Sample Metadata Document with Entity Set Attributes

This example was relatively easy, as we have just a single entity type assigned to another single entity set. Because you don't have multiple entity types in this example, there's also no need to define any association yet (this will change later).

Read on to see how to import a more sophisticated EDMX file with multiple entity types, entity sets, associations, and related navigation properties.

Importing a Data Model via Entity Data Model XML

It's also possible to import an already existing EDMX file. This can be created via any toolset that is capable of modeling an entity data model (EDM) and exporting it as an EDMX file. One example of such a toolset is the OData Model Editor plug-in in the SAP Web IDE. Another source of EDMX files is any OData service that you have access to, as the metadata document ($metadata) provides a file that can be used as an input. *Entity data model XML*

In this example, you'll use the metadata document of the SAP Gateway sample service /IWBEP/GWSAMPLE_BASIC. To do this, you need to temporarily store the metadata file in your file system. To import a data model from a file, you first create a new project.

Start by creating a new project for importing a data model from a file (see Figure 6.17). *Create new project*

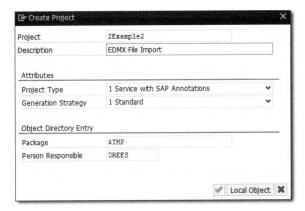

Figure 6.17 Creating a New Project for File Import

After you've created a new project, right-click on DATA MODEL, and choose IMPORT • DATA MODEL FROM FILE (see Figure 6.18).

This opens up step 1 of the FILE IMPORT wizard (see Figure 6.19). In SAP Gateway 2.0 SP 06 and older, the file import was an all-or-nothing functionality. You were only able to replace the entire data model with the imported file. As of SAP Gateway 2.0 SP 07, this functionality has improved, and you're now able to perform a CUSTOM IMPORT that allows you to merge the imported model into your existing model.

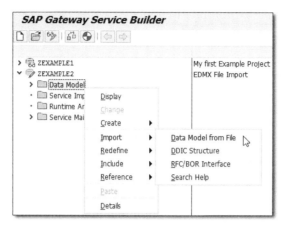

Figure 6.18 Importing a Data Model from File

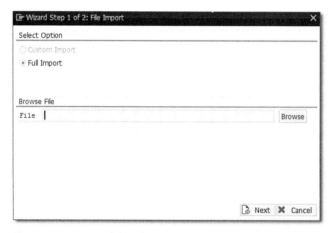

Figure 6.19 Step 1 of the File Import Wizard

Selecting the BROWSE button opens up the SELECT A MODEL FILE FOR IMPORT dialog where you pick the metadata document or EDMX file that you want to import (see Figure 6.20).

After choosing the file, click NEXT in the FILE IMPORT wizard. Depending on your local SAP GUI settings, you might get an SAP GUI security pop-up screen that prompts you to allow access to the specified file. You must allow this; otherwise, the import will be aborted.

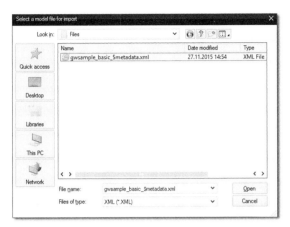

Figure 6.20 Select a Model File for Import Dialog

The file is read and verified to ensure that a valid file was provided. In some cases, the validation might fail if the model file contains, for example, unsupported or unexpected tags or EDM types. In this case, you have to adjust the data model file or choose a different one.

In step 2 of the FILE IMPORT wizard (for a FULL IMPORT), you'll see a preview of what the data model in your project will look like after the wizard is completed (see Figure 6.21). Click FINISH to complete the wizard.

Figure 6.21 Step 2 of the File Import Wizard

File import
successful After the file import has finished, you get a success message: MODEL FILE
IMPORTED SUCCESSFULLY. By default, a model check is triggered that
leads, in the current case (importing the metadata of /IWBEP/GWSAM-
PLE_BASIC), to a number of warnings. This is because the metadata validation of the Service Builder was improved over time to make sure that
whatever you develop during design time properly runs at runtime.
Because the imported EDMX file only contains EDM information but no
DDIC linkage, the derived ABAP data type artifacts might not fit into the
imported model. If warnings or errors occur due to this, you can navigate from the MESSAGES section by double-clicking directly to the erroneous element to correct it.

You can now expand the project tree and explore the imported elements
(see Figure 6.22). For the SAP Gateway sample service, quite a number
of entity types, entity sets, associations, and so on have been imported.

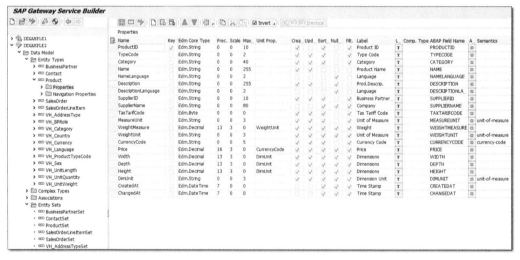

Figure 6.22 Data Model after File Import

> **Note**
>
> The data model from file import only imports the meta-information into your
> service. No service provisioning is imported. This has to be done afterward
> either via the Service Builder or by implementing the related DPC methods in
> ABAP.

After the data model has been imported, you can adjust the model to your needs. You can, for example, delete those elements you don't want to have in your final model. You can also add new elements (e.g., properties) to your model if required. As previously mentioned, you can also reexecute the import of your data model if the source has changed, and you want to apply those changes to your Service Builder project.

Importing a Data Model via the Data Dictionary

The third option to build up an OData model definition is to import a DDIC structure or table. For this, you create a new project (ZEXAMPLE3), right-click on DATA MODEL, and choose IMPORT • DDIC STRUCTURE (see Figure 6.23).

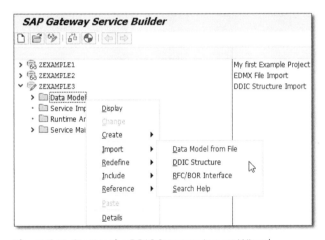

Figure 6.23 Starting the DDIC Structure Import Wizard

This opens step 1 of the IMPORT FROM DDIC STRUCTURE wizard (see Figure 6.24). Although the wizard talks about DDIC structures, it also allows you to import the data definition from the DDIC tables and DDIC views, including CDS views.

By default, your DDIC definition is imported into an entity type. Alternatively, you can select the COMPLEX TYPE radio button to import into a complex type.

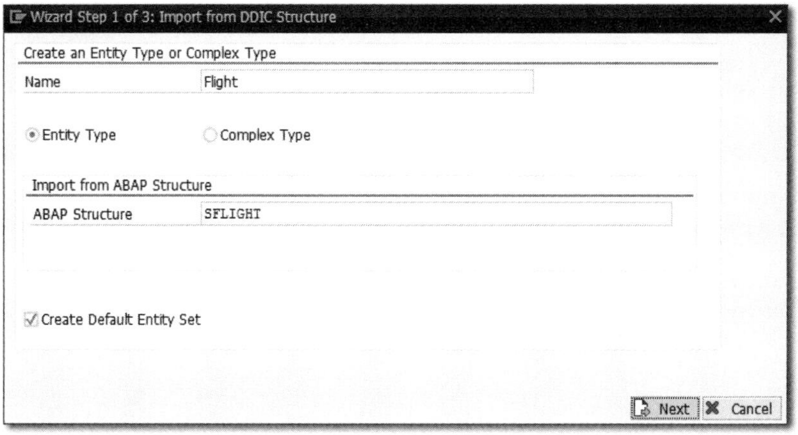

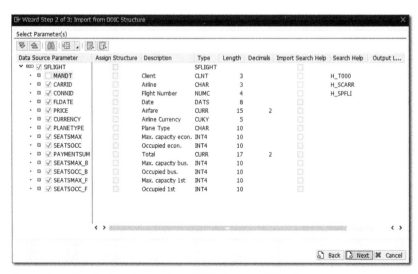

Figure 6.24 Step 1 of the Import from DDIC Structure Wizard

In this example, we enter the entity type name "FLIGHT." The ABAP Structure is still the database table SFLIGHT. By default, the Create Default Entity Set checkbox is marked to create an entity set along with the entity type to link them right away.

After clicking Next, the definition of the provided DDIC object is shown in step 2 of the wizard (see Figure 6.25).

Client field

Figure 6.25 Step 2 of the Import from DDIC Structure Wizard

In this step, you have to select the fields for your DDIC object that you want to import as properties into your data model. Typically, you first mark all fields and then deselect the ones that you don't want imported. For example, the client field (sometimes called MANDT) isn't required in your model because, by default, your login takes place in a specific client, and the ABAP runtime adds the corresponding client information to each database operation.

You also can import related DDIC Search Helps along with the import of the DDIC object itself. They are offered based on the definition in the ABAP DDIC.

After selecting the fields of the DDIC object to be imported, you need to click NEXT. This leads to step 3 of the IMPORT FROM DDIC STRUCTURE wizard (see Figure 6.26), which shows you a summary of the entity type/complex type to be created along with the related properties. First, you want to define the key properties of your entity type (complex types don't have key properties, so all checkboxes are deselected, and the column is grayed out).

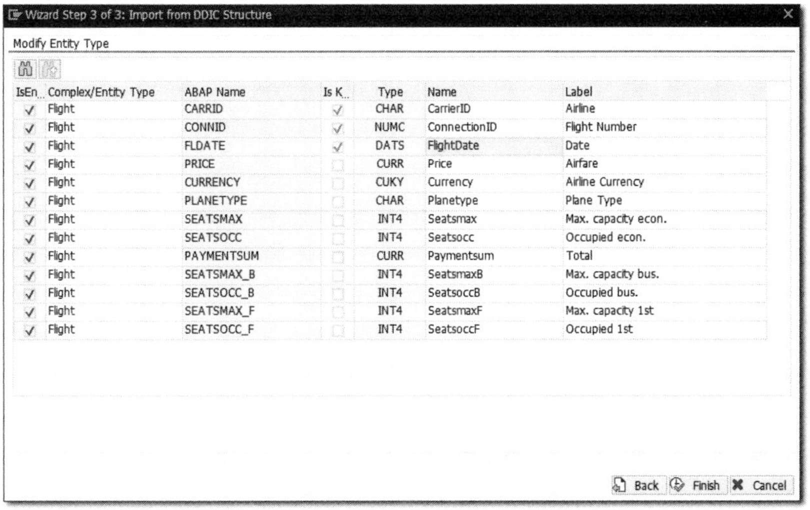

IsEn	Complex/Entity Type	ABAP Name	Is K	Type	Name	Label
✓	Flight	CARRID	✓	CHAR	CarrierID	Airline
✓	Flight	CONNID	✓	NUMC	ConnectionID	Flight Number
✓	Flight	FLDATE	✓	DATS	FlightDate	Date
✓	Flight	PRICE		CURR	Price	Airfare
✓	Flight	CURRENCY		CUKY	Currency	Airline Currency
✓	Flight	PLANETYPE		CHAR	Planetype	Plane Type
✓	Flight	SEATSMAX		INT4	Seatsmax	Max. capacity econ.
✓	Flight	SEATSOCC		INT4	Seatsocc	Occupied econ.
✓	Flight	PAYMENTSUM		CURR	Paymentsum	Total
✓	Flight	SEATSMAX_B		INT4	SeatsmaxB	Max. capacity bus.
✓	Flight	SEATSOCC_B		INT4	SeatsoccB	Occupied bus.
✓	Flight	SEATSMAX_F		INT4	SeatsmaxF	Max. capacity 1st
✓	Flight	SEATSOCC_F		INT4	SeatsoccF	Occupied 1st

Figure 6.26 Step 3 of the Import from DDIC Structure Wizard

In addition, you can adjust the prepopulated property names derived from the individual DDIC field name. This allows you to quickly rename the properties to provide more meaningful names to the developer of a consumer application. For example, field names such as CARRID (or Carrid) are hard to understand by any non-ABAP developer. Instead, you might want to provide CarrierID. In addition, rename Connid to ConnectionID and Fldate to FlightDate.

The last column LABEL allows you to adjust the property labels as well. They are defaulted with the labels derived from the DDIC fields.

Entity type created When you're done, just click FINISH, and the corresponding entity type is created in your project. You can repeat the wizard as many times as you want to add more entity types and entity sets to your project.

The created entity type is automatically associated with the related DDIC structure/table that was used in the wizard (see Figure 6.27).

Figure 6.27 Entity Type with an Associated DDIC Table

As mention earlier, the DDIC structure/table reference allows the framework to pick the property definition from the underlying structure/table field. This includes the data type, length, and precision as well as labels for all installed languages.

After the import has finished, a project check will be executed. When importing the DDIC structure SFLIGHT, you might get some warning messages (see Figure 6.28).

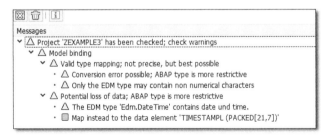

Figure 6.28 Warnings after the DDIC Import

Double-clicking the message navigates you to the related element. For example, the message ONLY THE EDM TYPE MAY CONTAIN NON NUMERICAL CHARACTERS indicates that a data element of type `NUMC` is used during runtime, whereas the EDM data type is a regular string that isn't limited to numbers only. As a consequence, the EDM data type may contain nonnumerical characters that can't be converted into a NUMC field at runtime.

The other warning indicates that an ABAP DATE field, which only stores the date itself but no time information, is mapped to an `Edm.DateTime` property because there is no date-only data type in the OData 2.0 EDM types.

Apparently, there isn't a 100% match between the ABAP data types and the EDM data types. However, the Service Builder tries to map the properties as close as possible when importing from any data source. If the mapping couldn't be executed without the potential loss of data or if there is a chance that problems may occur during runtime, it gives you related warnings or errors.

In our example, it's possible to keep the reported warnings and to generate the runtime artifacts of the OData service (see Section 6.2). The recommended approach is to correct the reported warnings/errors, and ensure the project check reports a green traffic light.

Importing a Data Model via RFC/BOR

The fourth option to import a data model is the RFC/BOR import. BOR allows importing the interface of a BOR method (e.g., `BusinessPartner.CreateFromData`). RFC is a more popular term and allows the import of an RFC interface. BOR methods often point to remote function modules, so BOR and RFC data sources are pretty similar from a Service Builder perspective.

Let's create a new project and perform the import of the remote function module `BAPI_EPM_PRODUCT_GET_LIST`. Start the RFC wizard by right-clicking on DATA MODEL and choosing IMPORT • RFC/BOR INTERFACE (see Figure 6.29).

BAPI_EPM_PRODUCT_GET_LIST

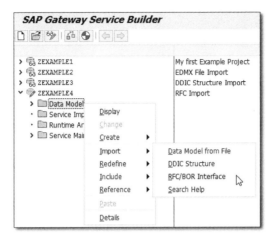

Figure 6.29 Starting the RFC/BOR Import Wizard

On the initial screen, specify the entity type name. In this example, enter "Product." Secondly, you specify whether the BOR/RFC interface you want to import resides in the local system (local from the perspective of the SAP_GWFND/IW_BEP component, which is typically the SAP ERP backend system) or is located in a remote system. In the latter case, you need to also provide the RFC destination to the corresponding system.

BOR or RFC Then, you need to tell the wizard if you want to import the interface of a BOR object or of an RFC module. Finally, you need to provide the name of the object you want to import. Based on the specified type, you get individual F4 help dialogs that allow you search for the object you're looking for. This also works in a remote scenario.

In this example, create the entity type "Product" from the Local system by importing the interface of the RFC with the name "BAPI_EPM_PRO-DUCT_GET_LIST" (see Figure 6.30).

Similar to the other import wizards, a Create Default Entity Set checkbox is available that allows you to create an entity set along with the entity type.

Choose Next when you're done with the first page of the wizard. On the second page (see Figure 6.31), you initially see the collapsed interface of the RFC module or BOR method.

Figure 6.30 Create Entity Type from Data Source Wizard: Step 1

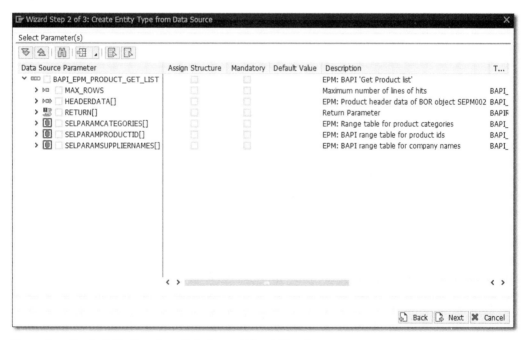

Figure 6.31 Create Entity Type from Data Source Wizard: Step 2

Each interface parameter has an individual icon that describes the type of the following parameters:

- Import parameter
- Export parameter
- Changing parameter
- Tables parameter
- BAPI return parameter
- Select options parameter

The first four parameters (import, export, changing, tables) are the typical parameters that function modules can have. The BAPI return parameter is a special table's parameter based on type BAPIRET2. This parameter has an individual icon because the Service Builder automatically handles the return table if you model the service provisioning with the Service Builder as well (e.g., GetEntitySet (Query) operation). There is no need to define a Return entity type in your data model to expose error information to the consumer; this is automatically done for you by reading the return table and throwing the related exception (e.g., there will be a business error exception thrown in case of an "E" message in the return table). This error results in a corresponding HTTP return code, along with the error long text in the response.

> **Note**
>
> This automatic error handling only takes place if you model the service provisioning via RFC/BOR mapping. If you implement the respective DPC methods yourself in ABAP, you need to verify any return code/return tables yourself and throw the related exception.

Select options or ranges parameters are highlighted with a green icon in square brackets. There is also no need to add ranges tables as entity types into your data model because those should be mapped with corresponding filter parameters in the service implementation and not via individual entity types. Ranges tables are identified based on their DDIC structure with the typical SIGN and OPTION fields as well as a LOW and a HIGH field for the related filter parameter.

The CREATE ENTITY TYPE FROM DATA SOURCE wizard allows you to expand the collapsed interface to browse the underlying parameters, substructures, or nested tables. This example uses a BAPI, which, by definition, can't have a nested interface. Therefore, you only find "normal" fields in the import, export, and table structures. To define an entity type for products, mark the table parameter HEADERDATA[] (see Figure 6.32). After you select the table parameter, the corresponding ASSIGN STRUCTURE checkbox is marked automatically. This checkbox is important because it will associate the underlying DDIC structure with the created entity type. If you deselect the checkbox, no assignment will take place.

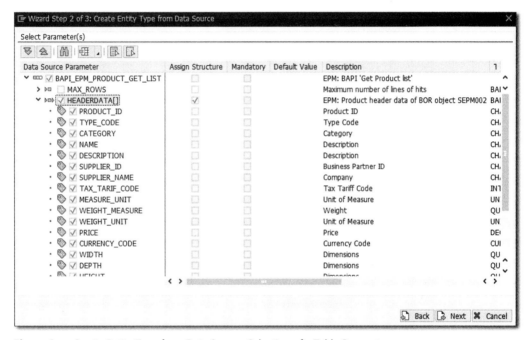

Figure 6.32 Create Entity Type from Data Source: Selection of a Table Parameter

After you're done with the selection of interface parameters, you can choose NEXT. This shows the final screen of the CREATE ENTITY TYPE FROM DATA SOURCE wizard (see Figure 6.33). This is the summary screen where you see which entity sets and/or complex types will be created.

Summary screen

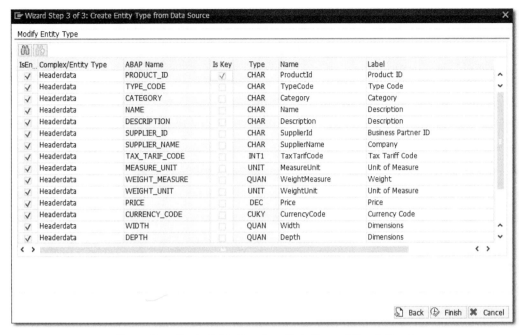

Figure 6.33 Create Entity Type from Data Source Wizard: Step 3

In this example, only the tables parameter HEADERDATA is marked, which automatically selects all fields underneath. Therefore, the wizard only generates a single entity type with the name HEADERDATA and a property for each parameter of the interface table. The entity type name is derived from the node that you've selected.

HEADERDATA The name "Product" that you defined on the first screen of the wizard is ignored in this case because the HEADERDATA node has been selected. If you select all parameters (or a subset) under the node HEADERDATA but not the HEADERDATA node itself, the wizard uses the entity type name defined on the first screen. The reason for this behavior is the capability of the RFC/BOR wizard to create multiple entity types out of multiple interface tables in one step. That's why the name of the interface element is used for the entity type name.

Verify first column Prior to clicking the FINISH button, you should always verify that the very first column (IsENTITY) is marked as expected. In this example, this field is checked for all entries. This is correct and indicates that all properties will end up in an entity type and not a complex type. The name of the resulting entity type is shown in the next (editable) column, COMPLEX/ENTITY TYPE NAME. If you want, you can change the name of the resulting entity type by changing all columns; however, this isn't the recommended approach because it takes time to adjust all properties one by one. It's a lot easier to let the wizard generate the entity type and then just change the name via the project tree.

If the ISENTITY column isn't marked, the properties will end up in a complex type (or in several complex types). This is the case, for example, if you select import or export structures (not tables) of RFC/BOR interfaces.

In addition, you should take a look at the IS KEY column and mark those properties that define the primary key of the resulting entity type (complex types don't have key fields). If you don't mark any property as IS KEY, you'll get a corresponding message because a project check is automatically triggered when you finish the wizard, and an entity type without a primary key is considered an erroneous entity type.

Key column

The next editable column, NAME, defines the name of each generated property in your model. This is what the outside world will see when consuming your OData service. Editing this list allows you to quickly change the name of all properties. Each property also has an ABAP name (see the ABAP NAME column), which isn't editable in this view. The ABAP name is the field name you see on the ABAP side when processing a query or any other operation. This is important to distinguish because the ABAP name—especially when derived from an RFC interface or DDIC structure—sometimes looks a bit cryptic, whereas the property name can be defined in a more consumer-friendly way (e.g., `Sales-OrderID` instead of `VBELN`).

In the last column, LABEL, you can define the label of your property. If an RFC/BOR object uses an underlying DDIC structure, the entity type is bound to the related DDIC element, and thus you don't need to change the label here. If you want to override a label that comes via the DDIC link, you can do this by editing the properties in the properties overview via the project tree (after you've completed the wizard).

Define label

After you click the Finish button, the entity types, entity sets, and/or complex types are created. A project check is executed to check if there are any problems with the current project definition (see Figure 6.34).

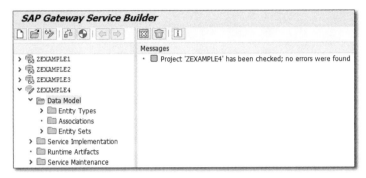

Figure 6.34 Project Check after the RFC/BOR Import

A typical error that is shown after this check is a forgotten primary key definition. If this happens, simply double-click on the error, and you'll be taken to the erroneous element.

In this example, the property type HEADERDATA was created although we've specified "Product" on the first page of the wizard. This is because we've selected the entire HEADERDATA table from the interface and not individual fields. You can easily change the entity type name by double-clicking on it in the project tree and changing it to "Product" in the SAP List Viewer (ALV) grid. Similarly you can navigate to the created entity set and rename it to, for example, "ProductSet."

6.2 Service Registration in the SAP Business Suite System

Four projects If you've followed the examples before, you now have four projects in your Service Builder:

▶ ZExample1
Manually created product entity type.

▶ ZExample2
Imported data model from the /IWBEP/GWSAMPLE_BASIC service.

▸ ZExample3

Imported data model from the SFLIGHT DDIC structure.

▸ ZExample4

Imported data model from the `BAPI_EPM_PRODUCT_GET_LIST` RFC.

You now have to generate the runtime artifacts and register them in the backend system. This is done by generating the project, which is triggered by clicking the GENERATE RUNTIME OBJECTS button (see Figure 6.35).

Figure 6.35 Generate Runtime Objects Button

The first time you click the GENERATE RUNTIME OBJECTS button, you get the model and service definition pop-up screen (see Figure 6.36). Typically, you keep the default values and just click the OK button. But it's important to understand the values that are defaulted as well as the meaning of the respective fields.

Model and Service Definition	
Model Provider Class	
Class Name	ZCL_ZEXAMPLE1_MPC_EXT
Base Class Name	ZCL_ZEXAMPLE1_MPC
Data Provider Class	
✓ Generate Classes	
Class Name	ZCL_ZEXAMPLE1_DPC_EXT
Base Class Name	ZCL_ZEXAMPLE1_DPC
Service Registration	
Technical Model Name	ZEXAMPLE1_MDL
Model Version	1
Technical Service Name	ZEXAMPLE1_SRV
Service Version	1

Figure 6.36 Model and Service Definition Pop-Up Screen

259

All ABAP classes that are generated are named with the pattern `<name-space>CL_<project_name>_<suffix>`. Typically, the namespace is just one of the default namespaces "Z." So in the ZEXAMPLE1 project, the names of the generated classes will start with `ZCL_ZEXAMPLE1`.

MPC

As we explained in Chapter 5, the MPC is an ABAP class that provides the runtime representation of your model definition. As such, all model information that you've defined in your project is generated into the MPC. As a consequence, you have to regenerate the MPC every time you change the model definition in your project.

Extension class and base class

The model definition is generated into two classes: the extension class (with the suffix `_MPC_EXT`) and the base class (with the suffix `_MPC`). Technically, the base class is derived from the `/IWBEP/CL_MGW_PUSH_ABS_MODEL` superclass. The extension class has the base class as its superclass. The extension class is registered via the technical model name, which means that the extension class can define the methods to redefine and the methods to inherit from the base class.

DPC

The same holds true for the DPC. There you also find an extension class (suffix `_DPC_EXT`) and a base class (suffix `_DPC`). The DPCs are responsible for the runtime representation of your service implementation. For instance, the DPCs execute CREATE, READ, UPDATE, DELETE, QUERY, and many more operations.

The DPC base class inherits from the `/IWBEP/CL_MGW_PUSH_ABS_DATA` superclass. The DPC extension class inherits from the DPC base class. The DPC extension class is registered via the technical service name, so the extension class is executed in your OData service.

Extension classes (`MPC_EXT` and `DPC_EXT`) allow you to add your own coding into the model definition as well as the service implementation. This is necessary because certain use cases (e.g., consumption of complex RFC interfaces or handling of deep inserts) can't be entirely defined using the Service Builder.

The extension classes (`MPC_EXT` and `DPC_EXT`) can be changed via the typical development tools (e.g., the ABAP Class Builder), and the Service Builder won't overwrite those extension classes. The regeneration only adds new methods to the classes if necessary (e.g., if you add a new entity set to your project, corresponding CRUD-Q methods are generated into the DPC base class and thus inherited into the DPC extension class). Therefore, you're safe in performing your own development in the extension classes.

Note that the respective CRUD-Q methods, including any manually created redefinitions, are deleted from both the DPC base and the extension class if you remove the related entity set from your project. Therefore, you need to handle deletions of entity sets carefully because they may result in the loss of your redefinitions and thus in the loss of your own ABAP coding.

CRUD-Q

Every OData channel service requires a technical model name and a technical service name on both the backend as well as the SAP Gateway hub server. The backend definitions of the technical model name as well as the technical service name are performed along with the generation of the MPCs and DPCs.

The technical model name basically just points to the MPC extension class. The definition of the technical model name is equal to the backend registration of the model, which can also be performed via the IMG (SAP NetWeaver • SAP Gateway Service Enablement • Backend OData Channel • Service Development for Backend OData Channel • Maintain Models). By default, each model is registered with version 1.

The technical service name points to the DPC extension class and is equal to your external service name (the name under which you'll consume your OData service). Additionally, the technical service name also points to the technical model name because the service implementation needs to have a model definition. The definition of the technical service name is equal to the registration of the service, which can also be performed via the IMG (SAP NetWeaver • SAP Gateway Service Enablement • Backend OData Channel • Service Development for Backend OData Channel • Maintain Services). By default, each service is registered with version 1.

After you click OK in the Model and Service Definition pop-up screen, you're prompted to provide the package name for the generated classes (see Figure 6.37). Typically, you assign your classes to the same package as the project.

Package name

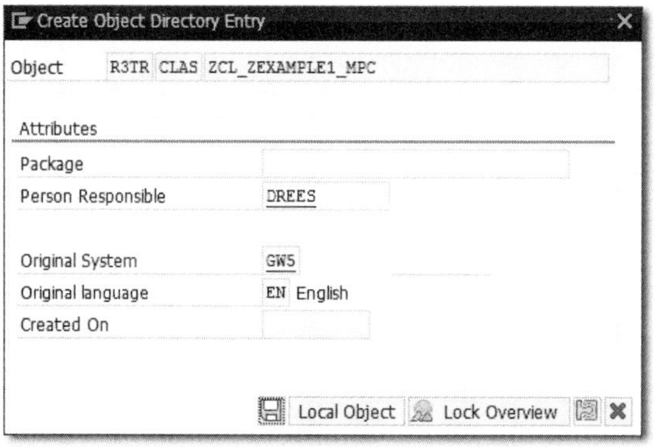

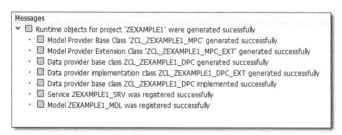

Figure 6.37 Object Directory Entry for the MPC Base Class

After you've provided all information, the generation and backend registration starts. Depending on the number of different RFC interfaces and, more importantly, the size of their interfaces you've defined in your service implementation, the generation might take some time. In the examples here, there is currently no service implementation, so the generation is performed quickly.

Messages window

After the generation has finished, the MESSAGES window appears (Figure 6.38). It should report only green traffic lights, which is your verification that the generation was successful. If the project check or project generation wasn't successful, you'll find corresponding information in the message window.

Messages
> ☐ Runtime objects for project 'ZEXAMPLE1' were generated sucessfully
 · ☐ Model Provider Base Class 'ZCL_ZEXAMPLE1_MPC' generated successfully
 · ☐ Model Provider Extension Class 'ZCL_ZEXAMPLE1_MPC_EXT' generated successfully
 · ☐ Data provider base class ZCL_ZEXAMPLE1_DPC generated successfully
 · ☐ Data provider implementation class ZCL_ZEXAMPLE1_DPC_EXT generated successfully
 · ☐ Data provider base class ZCL_ZEXAMPLE1_DPC implemented successfully
 · ☐ Service ZEXAMPLE1_SRV was registered successfully
 · ☐ Model ZEXAMPLE1_MDL was registered successfully

Figure 6.38 Messages Window after First Project Generation

After the project has been generated, you also see that the RUNTIME ARTIFACTS node in your project is populated. If you expand or double-click the RUNTIME ARTIFACTS node, you see all artifacts that have been generated. In this example, there are the two DPCs, the two MPCs, the model object, and the service object (see Figure 6.39).

Runtime Artifacts				
Name	Generated Artifact Type	Program ID	Object Type	Object Name
ZCL_ZEXAMPLE1_DPC	Data Provider Base Class	R3TR	CLAS	ZCL_ZEXAMPLE1_DPC
ZCL_ZEXAMPLE1_DPC_EXT	Data Provider Extension Class	R3TR	CLAS	ZCL_ZEXAMPLE1_DPC_EXT
ZCL_ZEXAMPLE1_MPC	Model Provider Base Class	R3TR	CLAS	ZCL_ZEXAMPLE1_MPC
ZCL_ZEXAMPLE1_MPC_EXT	Model Provider Extension Class	R3TR	CLAS	ZCL_ZEXAMPLE1_MPC_EXT
ZEXAMPLE1_MDL	Registered Model	R3TR	IWMO	ZEXAMPLE1_MDL
ZEXAMPLE1_SRV	Registered Service	R3TR	IWSV	ZEXAMPLE1_SRV

Figure 6.39 Runtime Artifacts of ZEXAMPLE1

If your project grows, you'll also find new entries in the RUNTIME ARTI-FACTS node. For instance, there will be an ABAP interface for each RFC module/BOR method that you use in the service implementation (e.g., an RFC module that you provide for the query execution). As mentioned before, the resulting model registration is accessible via the IMG (see Figure 6.40).

Runtime artifacts

Display Model

⌂ Model

Model Information	
Technical Model Name	ZEXAMPLE1_MDL
Model Version	1
Model Provider Class	ZCL_ZEXAMPLE1_MPC_EXT
Description	My first Example Project

Figure 6.40 Model Definition of ZEXAMPLE1_MDL

The same holds true for the service registration (see Figure 6.41). The model registration and the service registration together are referred to as the backend registration of an OData channel service.

The generation of the MPCs and DPCs, as well as the backend registration of the model and service concludes the registration of the OData service on the backend.

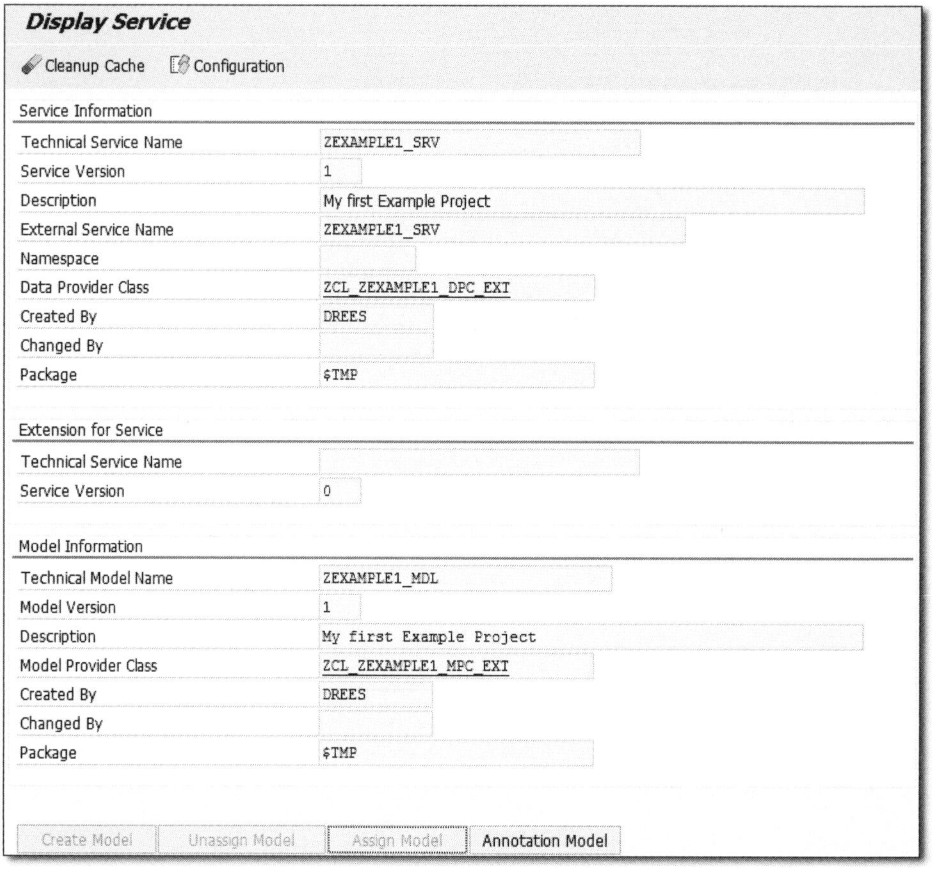

Figure 6.41 Service Definition of ZEXAMPLE1_SRV

6.3   Service Stub Generation

The service implementation actually injects life into the OData service. So far, you've just developed the data model of the OData service. The service implementation connects the data model with the underlying backend business logic (e.g., provided by an RFC function module or any other business logic). This will be explained in detail in Section 6.5.

According to Figure 6.1, shown earlier, at this point, we'll only look at the service implementation stub that was generated by the Service Builder as part of the project generation step in Section 6.2. We're only briefly looking at the service implementation now to consume the OData service in order to see the result of the metadata that was defined in Section 6.1. Every OData Channel service requires an MPC as well as a DPC to function, so we also need to consider the service implementation prior to running the service.

To see the generated DPC, expand the RUNTIME ARTIFACTS node, right-click on ZCL_ZEXAMPLE1_DPC, and select GO TO ABAP WORKBENCH (see Figure 6.42).

DPC

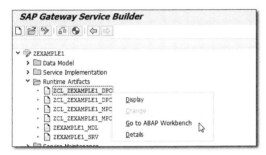

Figure 6.42 Displaying the Generated DPC Base Class Implementation

This opens up the ABAP Class Builder with the DPC base class. The methods shown in black have been redefined; this takes place every time you generate your project (see Figure 6.43).

ABAP Class Builder

Class Interface	ZCL_ZEXAMPLE1_DPC			Implemented / Active			
Properties	Interfaces	Friends	Attributes	Methods	Events	Types	Aliases

□ Parameter 🔍 Exception 📋 📖📑 📇 ... ☐ Filter

Method	Level	Vis...	M...	Description
/IWBEP/IF_MGW_CONV_SRV_RUNTIME~SET_ETAG	Insta...	Pub...		Sets the etag to the HTTP response
/IWBEP/IF_MGW_CONV_SRV_RUNTIME~GET_DP_FACADE	Insta...	Pub...		Gets the Data Provider Facade
/IWBEP/IF_MGW_APPL_SRV_RUNTIME~GET_ENTITY	Insta...	Pub...		Execute a READ request (CReadUD) - ENTRY -
/IWBEP/IF_MGW_APPL_SRV_RUNTIME~GET_STREAM	Insta...	Pub...		Execute a READ request (CReadUD) - ENTRY -
/IWBEP/IF_MGW_APPL_SRV_RUNTIME~EXECUTE_ACTION	Insta...	Pub...		executes a function import
/IWBEP/IF_MGW_APPL_SRV_RUNTIME~UPDATE_ENTITY	Insta...	Pub...		Execute an UPDATE request (CRUpdateD)
/IWBEP/IF_MGW_APPL_SRV_RUNTIME~PATCH_ENTITY	Insta...	Pub...		Execute a PATCH request (CRUpdateD)
/IWBEP/IF_MGW_APPL_SRV_RUNTIME~CREATE_ENTITY	Insta...	Pub...		Execute a CREATE request (CreateRUD)
/IWBEP/IF_MGW_APPL_SRV_RUNTIME~CREATE_DEEP_ENTITY	Insta...	Pub...		Execute a deep insert CREATE request (CreateRUD)
/IWBEP/IF_MGW_APPL_SRV_RUNTIME~DELETE_ENTITY	Insta...	Pub...		Execute a DELETE request (CRUDelete)
/IWBEP/IF_MGW_APPL_SRV_RUNTIME~GET_ENTITYSET	Insta...	Pub...		Execute a READ request (CReadUD) - FEED -
/IWBEP/IF_MGW_APPL_SRV_RUNTIME~GET_EXPANDED_ENTITYSET	Insta...	Pub...		Execute a READ request (CReadUD) - FEED with inlines -

Figure 6.43 DPC Base Class

As an example, double-click the redefined /IWBEP/IF_MGW_APPL_SRV_ RUNTIME~GET_ENTITYSET method name (see Figure 6.44).

```
Method    /IWBEP/IF_MGW_APPL_SRV_RUNTIME~GET_ENTITYSET                    Active
    1   ⊟    method /IWBEP/IF_MGW_APPL_SRV_RUNTIME~GET_ENTITYSET.
    2   ⊟  *&--------------------------------------------------------------------*
    3      *&  Include             /IWBEP/DPC_TMP_ENTITYSET_BASE
    4      *&* This class has been generated on 02.12.2015 16:27:26 in client 001
    5      *&*
    6      *&*       WARNING--> NEVER MODIFY THIS CLASS <--WARNING
    7      *&*   If you want to change the DPC implementation, use the
    8      *&*   generated methods inside the DPC provider subclass - ZCL_ZEXAMPLE1_DPC_EXT
    9   ┕  *&--------------------------------------------------------------------*
   10      DATA productset_get_entityset TYPE zcl_zexample1_mpc=>tt_product.
   11      DATA lv_entityset_name TYPE string.
   12
   13      lv_entityset_name = io_tech_request_context->get_entity_set_name( ).
   14
   15   ⊟ CASE lv_entityset_name.
   16   ⊟  *---------------------------------------------------------------+
   17      *               EntitySet - ProductSet
   18   ┕  *---------------------------------------------------------------+
   19   ◊   WHEN 'ProductSet'.
   20      *    Call the entity set generated method
   21         productset_get_entityset(
   22           EXPORTING
   23             iv_entity_name = iv_entity_name
   24             iv_entity_set_name = iv_entity_set_name
   25             iv_source_name = iv_source_name
   26             it_filter_select_options = it_filter_select_options
   27             it_order = it_order
   28             is_paging = is_paging
   29             it_navigation_path = it_navigation_path
   30             it_key_tab = it_key_tab
   31             iv_filter_string = iv_filter_string
   32             iv_search_string = iv_search_string
   33             io_tech_request_context = io_tech_request_context
   34           IMPORTING
   35             et_entityset = productset_get_entityset
   36             es_response_context = es_response_context
```

Figure 6.44 Generated GET_ENTITYSET Method of the DPC Base Class

Looking at the coding, you can see that there is a big case control structure. For each entity set, a separate submethod is called, which is also created as part of the generation step. This happens for all five CRUD-Q operations for each entity set.

Business exceptions   By default, those methods throw business exceptions (see Figure 6.45). This occurs because the actual service implementation hasn't yet taken place, so an exception is thrown to handle any service call to the respective operation.

Method	PRODUCTSET_GET_ENTITYSET	Active

```
1  ⊟  method PRODUCTSET_GET_ENTITYSET.
2  │    RAISE EXCEPTION TYPE /iwbep/cx_mgw_not_impl_exc
3  │      EXPORTING
4  │        textid = /iwbep/cx_mgw_not_impl_exc=>method_not_implemented
5  │        method = 'PRODUCTSET_GET_ENTITYSET'.
6  └  endmethod.
```

Figure 6.45 Generated PRODUCTSET_GET_ENTITYSET Method of the DPC Base Class

6.4   Service Maintenance

The next step is the registration and activation of the OData service on the SAP Gateway hub, otherwise known as the *service maintenance* phase. This can be done manually by executing Transaction /IWFND/ MAINT_SERVICE and using the ADD SERVICE button on the SAP Gateway hub system; however, it's easier to perform the service registration and activation on the SAP Gateway hub right out of the Service Builder on the backend.

Registration and activation on hub

As a prerequisite, you have to maintain an SAP Gateway hub system in the IMG of the backend system by choosing SAP NETWEAVER • SAP GATEWAY SERVICE ENABLEMENT • BACKEND ODATA CHANNEL • CONNECTION SETTINGS TO SAP GATEWAY • SAP GATEWAY SETTINGS. In this IMG activity, you specify a DESTINATION SYSTEM name, CLIENT, SYSTEM ALIAS, and RFC DESTINATION through which the hub system can be reached. For an embedded deployment (when the backend and SAP Gateway hub are on the same box), you still need to maintain a corresponding entry. In this case, you enter "NONE" as the RFC DESTINATION (see Figure 6.46).

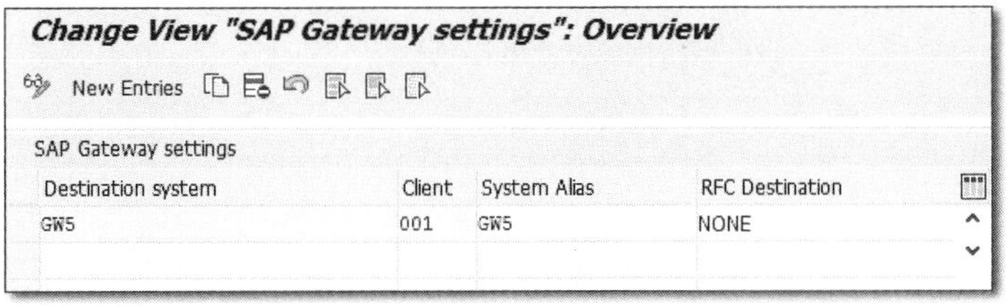

Maintain in IMG

Change View "SAP Gateway settings": Overview

New Entries

SAP Gateway settings

Destination system	Client	System Alias	RFC Destination	
GW5	001	GW5	NONE	

Figure 6.46 Registered SAP Gateway System on the Backend

Make sure to enter an RFC destination for all entries you maintain. Otherwise, the corresponding entry won't show up in the Service Builder UI.

After the SAP Gateway hub system is maintained in the IMG, you find a corresponding entry in each project under the SERVICE MAINTENANCE node. (Make sure to restart the Service Builder transaction each time you change the SAP Gateway settings in the IMG because the Service Builder is caching these values.) The Service Builder shows detailed information on the right-hand side if you double-click the entry (see Figure 6.47).

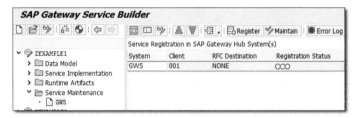

Figure 6.47 Service Registration Status on the SAP Gateway Hub

Now it's time to register and activate the service on the SAP Gateway hub. This is performed by marking the SAP Gateway hub system and clicking the REGISTER button.

The first time you do this, you get a pop-up screen to inform you that the activity will take place on the selected system (see Figure 6.48). In other words, the provided RFC destination will be used to jump into the target SAP Gateway hub system to register and activate your service there, which is why each entry has to have an RFC destination.

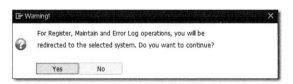

Figure 6.48 Redirect Warning

System alias If you confirm the pop-up screen, the next pop-up screen appears for you to provide the system alias. This system alias is defined on the SAP

Gateway hub system that points to the backend system you're coming from. In an embedded deployment, you typically define an alias in the SAP Gateway IMG that is called LOCAL. This one also uses RFC DESTINA-TION NONE and makes sure that the call stays in the local system. After you've selected the system alias (see Figure 6.49), click the OK button.

Figure 6.49 Alias Definition for the Service Activation

The next pop-up screen again comes from the SAP Gateway hub system and is the same as running Transaction /IWFND/MAINT_SERVICE on the SAP Gateway hub system and clicking the ADD SERVICE button (see Figure 6.50).

Add Service	
Service	
Technical Service Name	ZEXAMPLE1_SRV
Service Version	1
Description	My first Example Project
External Service Name	ZEXAMPLE1_SRV
Namespace	
External Mapping ID	
External Data Source Type	C
Model	
Technical Model Name	ZEXAMPLE1_MDL
Model Version	1
Creation Information	
Package Assignment	$TMP
	Local Object
ICF Node	
⦿ Standard Mode	○ None
☑ Set Current Client as Default Client in ICF Node	
OAuth enablement	
☐ Enable OAuth for Service	

Figure 6.50 Add Service Dialog on the SAP Gateway Hub

Technical service
and model name On this screen, you define a Technical Service Name as well as a Technical Model Name on the SAP Gateway hub side. Those will be
assigned 1:1 to the service name and model name on the backend system defined during the backend registration. The External Service
Name is derived from the technical service name on the backend you've
chosen earlier and can't be changed in this dialog.

You typically leave the default values as they are and only provide a
package name for the repository objects that are created. After you click
the OK button, the service registration and activation on the SAP Gateway hub system takes place, and you're taken back to the Service Builder
on the backend system.

If the service registration and activation were successful, the system
overview screen shown in Figure 6.51 will display a green traffic light.

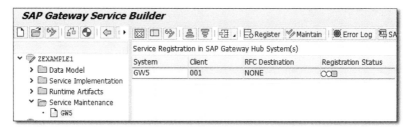

Figure 6.51 Status Change after Successful Service Activation

The OData service is now registered and active on the SAP Gateway hub
system, which means that it can be consumed. The service name in the
URI is the external service name that you've seen in the Add Service
dialog and is derived from the technical service name that you specified
during the first generation of the project in the Service Builder.

Transaction
/IWFND/
GW_CLIENT
You can use the SAP Gateway client (Transaction /IWFND/GW_CLIENT)
on the SAP Gateway hub system to consume the service. The URI is */sap/
opu/odata/sap/ZEXAMPLE1_SRV*. If you execute this URI in the SAP
Gateway client, you get the service document (see Figure 6.52).

If you add /$metadata, you'll get the service metadata document of the
example service (see Figure 6.53).

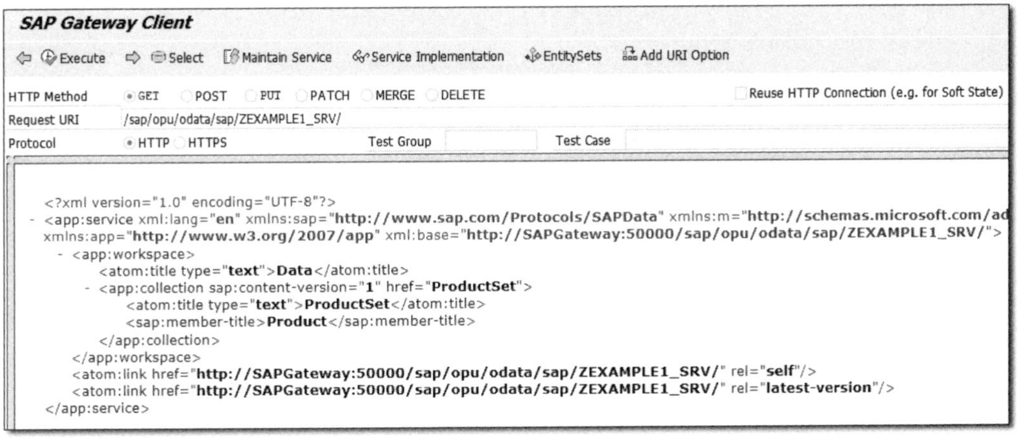

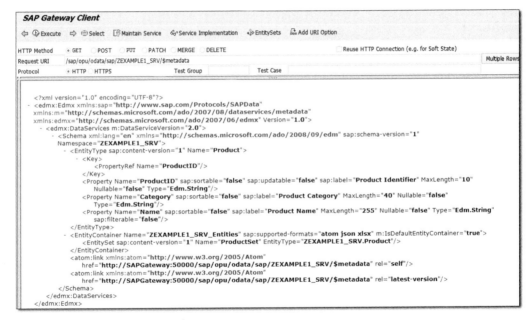

Figure 6.52 Service Document of ZEXAMPLE1_SRV

Figure 6.53 Metadata Document of ZEXAMPLE1_SRV

The service has a single entity set (`ProductSet`), which you can consume as well, but because you haven't done any service implementation so far, it will result in an error message. The service implementation is covered next.

6.5 Incremental Service Implementation and Model Enhancement

Iterative approach

It's now time to implement the service in an iterative approach, as shown earlier in Figure 6.1. Whenever an OData service is consumed, a typical entry point is the execution of a query to fetch the collection/feed of, for example, business partners or products. That's why the `get_entityset` method is typically implemented first in most cases. This allows you to fetch a feed of an entity type and will be explained in detail in Section 6.5.1. From the feed, you receive links to each contained entry resource. That's why the single read (`get_entity`) is typically implemented after the `get_entityset`. Implementing a single read is explained in detail in Section 6.5.2.

Query options

Enriching an OData service with powerful query options can be pretty important because it allows consumers to, for example, only request the required properties (`$select`), filter the result based on different criteria (`$filter`), perform client-side paging (`$top`/`$skip`), calculate the number of entries in a feed along with the feed itself (`$inlinecount`), or sort the feed according to your needs (`$orderby`). All of these query options are explained in detail with code examples in Section 6.5.3.

Navigation properties (also known as navigation links) are important elements of OData services because they define the allowed/foreseen navigations between OData elements. This can, for example, be the navigation from a sales order header (entry) to the corresponding list of sales order line items (feed). The definition and implementation of navigation properties is explained in detail in Section 6.5.4.

If you want to allow write access to your entity set, you also have to implement the `create_entity`, `update_entity`, and the `delete_entity` methods (CUD methods). The detailed implementation of the CUD methods is explained in Section 6.5.5.

In Section 6.5.6, we explain and provide an implementation example for function imports. Function imports are used whenever the known CRUD-Q operations aren't sufficient, and a dedicated function (e.g., confirm order or reject delivery) is required in an OData service.

Media resources can be used to expose binary data such as, for example, graphics to consumers. In Section 6.5.7, we explain how an entity type can be defined as a media link entity type and what you need to consider in this case.

$expand is another powerful feature of OData services that allows you to retrieve multiple entries and/or feeds along the defined navigation properties by using a single service call instead of executing multiple services calls. This typically improves the performance significantly because, for example, less data needs to be determined on the backend. The detailed implementation is explained in Section 6.5.8.

A deep insert is basically the opposite of $expand. Instead of retrieving a nested structure, you can write a nested structure into the SAP Gateway server. This typically substitutes the need to perform several individual create calls. A deep insert can, for example, be used if you want to create a sales order header together with a list (feed) of sales order line items in one single create call. Section 6.5.9 explains in detail how a deep insert can be implemented.

And, finally, Section 6.5.10 provides an introduction into $batch, which is used to bundle multiple independent service calls into one batch call. It can, for example, be used to fetch customizing data that is provided via multiple independent entity sets.

Before you start to implement your own coding, you should regenerate your project to ensure that the MPCs and the DPCs are up to date and match the current state of your project definition. This also ensures that no definition errors are contained in your project (see Figure 6.54).

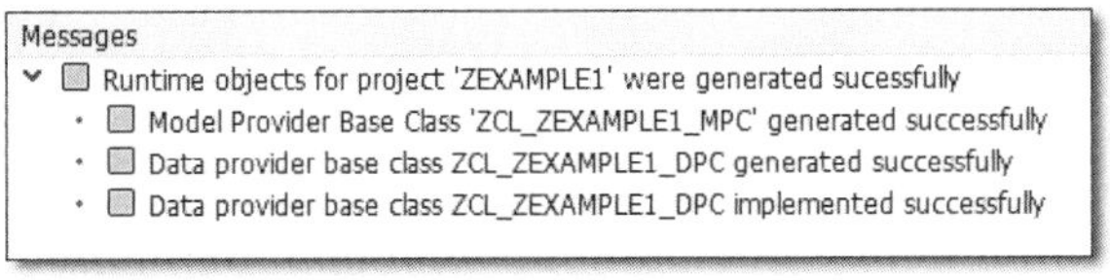

Figure 6.54 Successful Regeneration of the Sample Project

6.5.1 Feed (GET_ENTITYSET)

The get_entityset of the ProductSet entity set is implemented via the Service Builder by expanding the SERVICE IMPLEMENTATION node and the

PRODUCTSET node. Then you right-click on GETENTITYSET (QUERY) and choose GO TO ABAP WORKBENCH (see Figure 6.55).

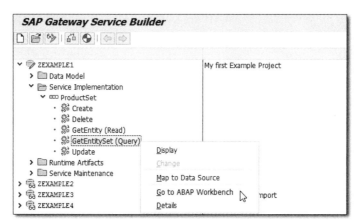

Figure 6.55 Navigating to Query Implementation in the ABAP Workbench

This opens a dialog informing you that the respective method hasn't yet been implemented (see Figure 6.56).

Figure 6.56 Information Screen: Method Not Yet Implemented

Confirming this pop-up screen opens the ZCL_ZEXAMPLE1_DPC_EXT data provider extension class in the ABAP Class Builder (Transaction SE24). Because no method has been redefined yet, all methods are displayed with a blue font. The blue font is an indicator that a method is inherited from the superclass (in this case, the DPC base class) and will be executed there—if not redefined.

Methods derived from interfaces
You'll find quite a number of methods derived from several interfaces in the data provider extension class. The one that we're indirectly looking at first is GET_ENTITYSET of the /IWBEP/IF_MGW_APPL_SRV_RUNTIME interface.

This method is handling all query calls (Get Entityset) of all entity sets of this OData service. That's why this method first needs to distinguish which entity set is being requested. This is where the Service Builder comes into play again; it generates a case structure into each of the five CRUD-Q methods (CREATE_ENTITY, GET_ENTITY, UPDATE_ENTITY, DELETE_ENTITY, GET_ENTITYSET) to handle the individual entity set requested by calling a separate method. In addition to the case structures, the Service Builder generates five separate CRUD-Q methods for each entity set into the DPC base class, which also ends up in the extension class via inheritance.

The separation of the generic five CRUD-Q methods into individual instance methods (protected methods) per entity set provides a clear distinction of the methods required to handle the OData requests. The name is concatenated out of the entity set name as well as the respective CRUD-Q method. If the resulting method name exceeds 30 characters, the name of the entity set will be truncated to guarantee a unique name across the DPC.

The five methods generated in the example project are listed here:

Five methods

- PRODUCTSET_CREATE_ENTITY

- PRODUCTSET_DELETE_ENTITY

- PRODUCTSET_GET_ENTITY

- PRODUCTSET_GET_ENTITYSET

- PRODUCTSET_UPDATE_ENTITY

To implement the Get_Entityset method in the example, you need to redefine the PRODUCTSET_GET_ENTITYSET method.

Set the DPC extension class to edit mode by pressing Ctrl+F1, and scroll down to PRODUCTSET_GET_ENTITYSET (make sure this line is selected). Now click the REDEFINE button. This opens up the ABAP editor and redefines the PRODUCTSET_GET_ENTITYSET method. By default, the ABAP Class Builder generates a code stub that consists of a commented call to the same super method. Replace the existing coding with the lines in Listing 6.1.

```
METHOD productset_get_entityset.

  DATA: ls_headerdata TYPE bapi_epm_product_header,
        lt_headerdata TYPE STANDARD TABLE OF bapi_epm_product_
header,
        ls_product    LIKE LINE OF et_entityset.

  CALL FUNCTION 'BAPI_EPM_PRODUCT_GET_LIST'
*   EXPORTING
*     MAX_ROWS                    =
    TABLES
      headerdata                  = lt_headerdata
*     SELPARAMPRODUCTID           =
*     SELPARAMSUPPLIERNAMES       =
*     SELPARAMCATEGORIES          =
*     RETURN                      =
            .

  LOOP AT lt_headerdata INTO ls_headerdata.
    ls_product-productid = ls_headerdata-product_id.
    ls_product-category  = ls_headerdata-category.
    ls_product-name      = ls_headerdata-name.
    APPEND ls_product TO et_entityset.
  ENDLOOP.

ENDMETHOD.
```

Listing 6.1 Product Set: Get_Entityset Method

Calls function module

As you can see, the sample code performs a call to the underlying business logic (BAPI_EPM_PRODUCT_GET_LIST function module) to retrieve the list of products. This easy example neither supports any filter criteria nor limits the number of items read; you simply fetch all existing Enterprise Procurement Model (EPM) products from the database.

After retrieving the data, you need to map it to the export table. For the Get_EntitySet method, this table is always called ET_ENTITYSET. Looking at the signature, you see that the type of this export table is ZCL_ZEXAMPLE1_MPC=>TT_PRODUCT. This is a generated type in the MPC base class. This is important to know because whenever you add or change any property, you have to make sure to regenerate your project to see this change in the generated MPC.

The mapping of the product list (LT_HEADERDATA) to the export table (ET_ENTITYSET) is pretty straightforward. You could have used the ABAP statement move-corresponding if you had named the productid property with an underscore. Move-corresponding could also have been used if you had implemented the projects that have been generated using a DDIC import or an RFC-interface import because, in those cases, ET_ENTITYSET would have been of the same data type as LT_HEADERDATA. Mapping is also needed if you use the EDMX import option because then the export table would also have been a generated type as in the described case that works with the manually created entity type.

Whenever you encounter any problem in determining the result, you can raise a /IWBEP/CX_MGW_BUSI_EXCEPTION business exception. This terminates the processing and throws the related HTTP error code to the consumer along with the error statements you provide.

Raise business
exception

When you're done with the coding, activate the changes by clicking the ACTIVATION button or by pressing Ctrl+F3 in the ABAP Class Builder. Make sure to activate all changes you've implemented (see Figure 6.57).

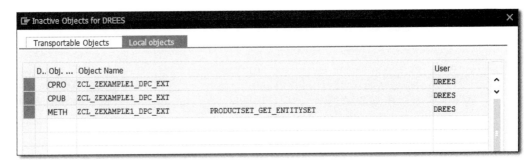

Figure 6.57 Activating All Changes of Your Implementation

The Service Builder project was already generated before, so there's no need to regenerate it.

Via the SAP Gateway client, you can now run the query by executing the */sap/opu/odata/sap/ZEXAMPLE1_SRV/ProductSet* URI. As expected, you get the entity set of product entities (see Figure 6.58).

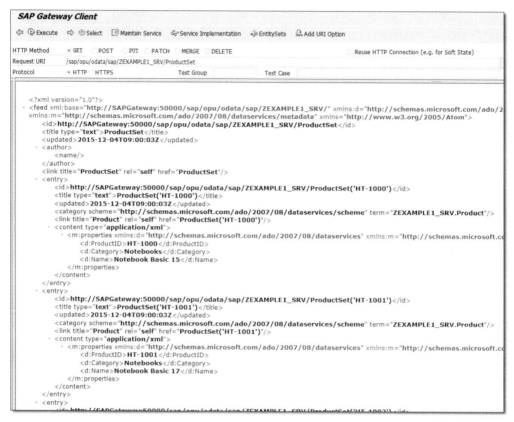

Figure 6.58 ProductSet of ZExample1

As you can see from the result, the OData feed provides a link for each entry that allows you to navigate to the respective entry resource (see the entry-id tag). Because you haven't yet implemented the single read method (get_entity), those links would result in an error if you execute them now.

6.5.2 Single Read (GET_ENTITY)

Similar to the QUERY method, you can easily develop the single read via the ABAP Class Builder. This time, expand the SERVICE IMPLEMENTATION • PRODUCTSET node, right-click on GETENTITY (READ), and choose GO TO ABAP WORKBENCH. An information pop-up screen appears because the method hasn't yet been implemented.

This time, scroll down to the PRODUCTSET_GET_ENTITY method, put the cursor on it, switch to edit mode, and click the REDEFINE button.

Replace the generated code stub with the lines in Listing 6.2.

```
METHOD productset_get_entity.

  DATA: ls_entity     LIKE er_entity,
        ls_product_id TYPE bapi_epm_product_id,
        ls_headerdata TYPE bapi_epm_product_header.

  io_tech_request_context->get_converted_keys(
    IMPORTING
      es_key_values = ls_entity ).

  ls_product_id-product_id = ls_entity-productid.

  CALL FUNCTION 'BAPI_EPM_PRODUCT_GET_DETAIL'
    EXPORTING
      product_id               = ls_product_id
    IMPORTING
      headerdata               = ls_headerdata
*   TABLES
*     CONVERSION_FACTORS       =
*     RETURN                   =
          .

  er_entity-productid = ls_headerdata-product_id.
  er_entity-category  = ls_headerdata-category.
  er_entity-name      = ls_headerdata-name.

ENDMETHOD.
```
Listing 6.2 Product Set: Get_Entity Method

The first thing you need to do in the coding is to determine the values of the key fields to know which entry to provide. The Get_Entity method addresses a single entry resource from the collection. This is done by providing the key properties as part of the URI in parentheses right after the entity set name (e.g., *ProductSet('HT-1000')*).

Determine key fields

The names of the key properties need to be provided as part of the URI if the entity type has more than one key property defined in its metadata. But there's no need to concatenate any URIs manually with property names and key values because the framework takes care of it by generating the respective links automatically.

Access key
properties You access the key properties by looping over the input table IT_KEY_
TAB. However, it isn't recommended to use this table because it provides
the key properties based on the external property name. This is the
name the consumer application sees. The internal (ABAP) name of the
property can be different; this depends on the property definition in
your metadata. In our current example, the external and internal property names are equal, so it doesn't matter. In general, however, it's a
best practice to use only the internal name; for example, a name change
of an external property name also requires changing the related ABAP
code.

> ### Using Internal ABAP Property Names
>
> You should avoid using the external property names and rather make use of
> the internal ABAP property names. This can be achieved by using the io_
> tech_request_context object reference and the provided GET methods
> instead of the simple structure or table import interface parameters (e.g., IT_
> KEY_TAB or IV_SOURCE_NAME). That's why those interface parameters are
> marked as "obsolete" in the parameter description.
>
> This holds true for all methods (e.g., GET_ENTITY, GET_ENTITYSET, CREATE_
> ENTITY, etc.) of the /IWBEP/IF_MGW_APPL_SRV_RUNTIME application inter-
> face.

Conversion exits are also important considerations. By default, conver-
sions are enabled, which means that values are converted to their external representation (e.g., a line-item number "10" without leading zeros
instead of "0000000010") when being exposed. This also takes place for
key fields, which therefore need to be converted back to use them
when, for example, determining a certain entry as in this case.

If you want to retrieve the key values in their external representation,
you can use the get_keys( ) method of the io_tech_request_context
object. You can also use another method called get_converted_keys( ).
As the name indicates, this method provides the converted keys, which
means that the input conversion was executed, and thus we receive the
internal representation (e.g., with leading zeros).

Note that conversion exits are assigned at the property level in the
define method of the MPC. In our current example, we haven't assigned
any conversion exit so far.

The `get_converted_keys( )` method provides you with the key values in the format of your entity type, which is a structure. That's why you define `ls_entity` of type `ZCL_ZEXAMPLE1_MPC=>TS_PRODUCT` or simply like `er_entity`. In contrast, `get_keys( )` provides you the keys in a name/value pair table.

After you've determined the key values needed, you can call the respective function to fetch the data. In this case, use the `BAPI_EPM_PRODUCT_GET_DETAIL` function module to read the product details. The result (`HEADERDATA`) is then mapped into the `ER_ENTITY` return structure field by field because the `productid` internal property name and the field name in the `product_id` BAPI structure are different in our example. If the field names are identical, you can of course use the `move-corresponding` ABAP statement to fill the return structure as described earlier when implementing the `GET_ENTITYSET` method.

The return structure is of type `ZCL_ZEXAMPLE1_MPC=>TS_PRODUCT`, which is generated into the MPC base class.

After activating the changed DPC extension class, you can read the detail of, for example, product HT-1000 by executing the following URI via the SAP Gateway client: */sap/opu/odata/sap/ZEXAMPLE1_SRV/ProductSet('HT-1000')*.

Activate changed DPC class

As expected, you now get a single entry instead of an OData feed (see Figure 6.59).

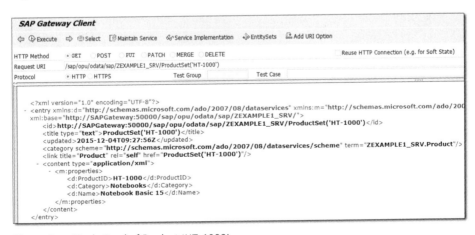

Figure 6.59 Single Read of Product 'HT-1000'

6.5.3 Query Options

Currently, the example service is able to provide an unfiltered list of products (feed/collection) as well as the related entries (get detail, single read). In this section, we'll take a close look at the different query options such as `$select`, `$filter`, `$top`, `$skip`, `$inlinecount`, and `$orderby`. They allow you to select only the properties you want (`$select`), filter the result (`$filter`), perform a client-side paging (`$top` and `$skip`), count the number of records (`$inlinecount`), and/or sort them (`$orderby`).

$select

Handled automatically

The `$select` query option allows you to select the properties you want to receive in your OData feed as well as in your single read. The framework handles `$select` automatically by reducing the list of properties provided to the OData consumer—irrespective of what data the data provider has determined.

If you want to react on a `$select` query option in the way that you, for example, only read and determine the properties that have been requested, you have to do this in the DPC extension class (`Get_Entity/Get_EntitySet` methods). You can access the `$select` properties by using the `io_tech_request_context->get_select( )` method and, in newer versions, the `get_select_with_mandtry_fields( )` method. Both methods provide you with a table for all selected properties. The latter one makes sure that all key properties are also included—even if they haven't been selected in the URI.

Performance improvement

Reacting on a `$select` query option can have a significant performance improvement if you can, for example, avoid the calculation or determination of certain expensive properties (i.e., properties whose calculated values require significant effort, such as with price calculations, availabilities, etc.).

This example won't benefit from considering the `$select` statement anyway because all properties are determined by the underlying function module.

$filter

The $filter query option is the most frequently used query option. It allows you to filter the result set of your Get_EntitySet implementation. By that, you can avoid providing an unfiltered list of all business partners or sales orders to the consumer (which can be quite a huge collection with many entries).

Most frequently used

An entity set can also be annotated as requiring a filter. In this case, you have to provide a $filter query option in the URI. As mentioned earlier, this is just an annotation, and no framework feature checks this.

The example service isn't yet able to handle any filter criteria because you haven't done anything in that regard so far. Looking at the interface of the BAPI_EPM_PRODUCT_GET_LIST function module, you see that it has range filter parameters for categories, product IDs, and supplier names (see Figure 6.60).

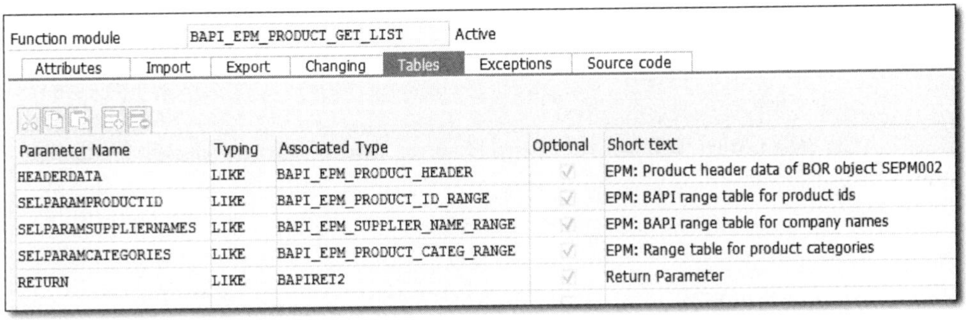

Function module	BAPI_EPM_PRODUCT_GET_LIST		Active	

Attributes	Import	Export	Changing	Tables	Exceptions	Source code

Parameter Name	Typing	Associated Type	Optional	Short text
HEADERDATA	LIKE	BAPI_EPM_PRODUCT_HEADER	✓	EPM: Product header data of BOR object SEPM002
SELPARAMPRODUCTID	LIKE	BAPI_EPM_PRODUCT_ID_RANGE	✓	EPM: BAPI range table for product ids
SELPARAMSUPPLIERNAMES	LIKE	BAPI_EPM_SUPPLIER_NAME_RANGE	✓	EPM: BAPI range table for company names
SELPARAMCATEGORIES	LIKE	BAPI_EPM_PRODUCT_CATEG_RANGE	✓	EPM: Range table for product categories
RETURN	LIKE	BAPIRET2	✓	Return Parameter

Figure 6.60 Interface of BAPI_EPM_PRODUCT_GET_LIST

To make use of a filter parameter, you have to enhance the coding in the Get_EntitySet DPC extension class. Replace the PRODUCTSET_GET_ENTITYSET method with the lines in Listing 6.3.

Enhance coding

```
METHOD productset_get_entityset.

  DATA: lr_filter                TYPE REF TO /iwbep/if_mgw_req_
filter,
        lt_filter_select_options TYPE /iwbep/t_mgw_select_
option,
        ls_filter_select_options TYPE /iwbep/s_mgw_select_
option,
        ls_select_option         TYPE /iwbep/s_cod_select_
```

```
option,
        lt_selparamproductid        TYPE STANDARD TABLE OF bapi_
epm_product_id_range,
        ls_selparamproductid        TYPE bapi_epm_product_id_
range.

  DATA: lt_headerdata              TYPE STANDARD TABLE OF bapi_
epm_product_header,
        ls_headerdata              TYPE bapi_epm_product_header,
        ls_product                 LIKE LINE OF et_entityset.

  lr_filter = io_tech_request_context->get_filter( ).
  lt_filter_select_options = lr_filter->get_filter_select_
options( ).

  LOOP AT lt_filter_select_options INTO ls_filter_select_
options.
    IF ls_filter_select_options-property EQ 'PRODUCTID'.
      LOOP AT ls_filter_select_options-select_options INTO ls_
select_option.
        ls_selparamproductid-sign   = ls_select_option-sign.
        ls_selparamproductid-option = ls_select_option-option.
        ls_selparamproductid-low    = ls_select_option-low.
        ls_selparamproductid-high   = ls_select_option-high.
        APPEND ls_selparamproductid TO lt_selparamproductid.
      ENDLOOP.
    ENDIF.
  ENDLOOP.

  CALL FUNCTION 'BAPI_EPM_PRODUCT_GET_LIST'
*    EXPORTING
*      MAX_ROWS                    =
    TABLES
      headerdata                  = lt_headerdata
      selparamproductid           = lt_selparamproductid
*      SELPARAMSUPPLIERNAMES       =
*      SELPARAMCATEGORIES          =
*      RETURN                      =
              .

  LOOP AT lt_headerdata INTO ls_headerdata.
    ls_product-productid = ls_headerdata-product_id.
    ls_product-category  = ls_headerdata-category.
    ls_product-name      = ls_headerdata-name.
    APPEND ls_product TO et_entityset.
  ENDLOOP.

ENDMETHOD.
```

Listing 6.3 Product Set: Get_Entityset Method with ProductID Filter

The changes introduced in this example take place at the beginning of the coding. Via `io_tech_request_context->get_filter( )`, you first retrieve a reference to the central filter object, which provides a table in a ranges-table-friendly way via `get_filter_select_options( )`, so you can easily map it into a corresponding ranges table. This only works if the `$filter` parameter of the requested URI can be mapped into it. To do this, loop over the select-options table, check for the internal property name, and copy the entries over into a local ranges table that is defined based on the function module interface. Then you also need to uncomment the `selparamproductid` parameter and hand over the local ranges table when calling the BAPI.

Now you need to activate the DPC extension class to actually use the new filter criteria. As an example, you can execute the following URI to filter on products with the `product-id >= 'HT-1000'` and `product-id <= 'HT-1020'`:

/sap/opu/odata/sap/ZEXAMPLE1_SRV/ProductSet?$filter=ProductID ge 'HT-1000' and ProductID le 'HT-1020'

In addition to this, you can enrich the coding to also consider a filter on categories. Besides the data declaration and the mapping for the function module, add the code shown in Listing 6.4 into the loop.

Filter on categories

```
    ELSEIF ls_filter_select_options-property EQ 'CATEGORY'.
      LOOP AT ls_filter_select_options-select_options INTO ls_
select_option.
        ls_selparamcategories-sign   = ls_select_option-sign.
        ls_selparamcategories-option = ls_select_option-option.
        ls_selparamcategories-low    = ls_select_option-low.
        ls_selparamcategories-high   = ls_select_option-high.
      APPEND ls_selparamcategories TO lt_selparamcategories.
    ENDLOOP.
```

Listing 6.4 Product Set: Get_Entityset Method Additional Filter on CATEGORY

In addition to the previous filter, the URI for filtering on `Category = 'Notebooks'` looks like the following:

/sap/opu/odata/sap/ZEXAMPLE1_SRV/ProductSet?$filter=ProductID ge 'HT-1000' and ProductID le 'HT-1020' and Category eq 'Notebooks'

As you can see, filter criteria can become quite complex.

Ranges tables   The filter criteria are mapped into ranges tables by the framework. This allows you to easily process them and assign them to the corresponding ranges-input table of your function module in your `Get_EntitySet` method. The OData framework provides them in a generic table in which each entry represents a property that is used in the filter query option.

Note that the preparation of the ranges tables has certain limitations. Similar to defining an ABAP report with `select-options` fields, you can't cover all use cases. For example, a filter such as `FieldA eq 'A' or FieldB eq 'B'` can't be put into ranges tables because of the `or` operator. It would work if you use `and` instead of `or`, but that is, of course, a different statement with a different result.

For these cases, the filter object provides the `get_filter_string( )` method that returns the actual filter string provided via the `$filter` query option (but not in a ranges-tables style).

Another option is to use the `get_osql_where_clause` method or `get_osql_where_clause_convert` method of the `io_tech_request_context` import parameter, which provides you a string that can be used in a dynamic Open SQL `SELECT` statement.

$top, $skip, and $inlinecount

Client-side paging   The `$top` and `$skip` query options are called client-side paging in that the client (consumer) defines how many entries to receive (`$top`) and how many entries to skip (`$skip`) by the SAP Gateway server. This enables the consumer to implement a paging functionality.

Let's assume the consumer is able to display three products per page. The following URI fetches the first page (products 1–3):

/sap/opu/odata/sap/ZEXAMPLE1_SRV/ProductSet?$top=3&$skip=0

The following URI fetches the second page (products 4–6):

/sap/opu/odata/sap/ZEXAMPLE1_SRV/ProductSet?$top=3&$skip=3

As you can see, the $top value (page size) remains stable if the page size doesn't change, whereas the $skip value provides the number of *entries* to be skipped—not the number of pages.

This allows you to implement quite efficient data accesses to the underlying database because you only need to read the records that are relevant for the requested page. When you're fetching your data via any standard function module (as in this example), you can't really benefit from it because most of the function modules don't support input parameters for top and skip. What you typically find is a MAX_ROWS input parameter that at least limits the number of records returned. But you can only make use of this if no sorting has to be applied on the returned list.

Consider an example with default sorting by the function module and three products per page. To read the product entries for page 5, for example, you can calculate the MAX_ROWS parameter via the following formula:

MAX_ROWS = <page_size> × <page> = 3 × 5 = 15

So you need to read the first 15 records from the database to provide the entries for page 5 (products 13 – 15). The entries for all other pages (products 1 – 12) are read by the RFC module but need to be ignored in the Get_EntitySet processing. This gets worse if the client keeps calling the SAP Gateway server for page 6, page 7, page 8, and so on, because more and more entries need to be fetched that are finally thrown away.

As you can see, client-side paging can cause a significant load on the server. Ultimately, though, it all depends on how access to the underlying database tables has been implemented. If you're accessing your own Z-tables, you can significantly improve your SELECT statements to reduce the server load.

Server load

The values for $top and $skip can be retrieved via the get_top( ) and get_skip( ) methods of io_tech_request_context. The calculation and filtering of the result table has to be done via your own coding. Prior to calling the BAPI_EPM_PRODUCT_GET_LIST function module, you can calculate the max-rows parameter as shown in Listing 6.5.

```
lv_maxrows-bapimaxrow = 0.
lv_top   = io_tech_request_context->get_top( ).
lv_skip = io_tech_request_context->get_skip( ).
IF ( lv_top IS NOT INITIAL ).
  lv_maxrows-bapimaxrow = lv_top + lv_skip.
ENDIF.
```

Listing 6.5 Calculate Max Row Parameters

Lv_maxrows is declared as type bapi_epm_max_rows. Right after the function module, you can apply the $top and $skip options. For that, you need to calculate the start and the end of the table entries you want to copy over into the get_entityset export table, as shown in Listing 6.6.

```
lv_start = 1.
IF lv_skip IS NOT INITIAL.
  lv_start = lv_skip + 1.
ENDIF.

IF lv_top IS NOT INITIAL.
  lv_end = lv_top + lv_start - 1.
ELSE.
  lv_end = lines( lt_headerdata ).
ENDIF.

LOOP AT lt_headerdata INTO ls_headerdata
  FROM lv_start TO lv_end.
  ls_product-productid = ls_headerdata-product_id.
  ls_product-category  = ls_headerdata-category.
  ls_product-name      = ls_headerdata-name.
  APPEND ls_product TO et_entityset.
ENDLOOP.
```

Listing 6.6 Product Set: Get_Entityset Method with External Paging

Max-rows parameter
As mentioned earlier, and as you can see from the coding, the only benefit comes by providing the max-rows parameter, which might reduce the number of records fetched from the database (we don't know that unless we investigate how the function module determines its data). Other than that, $top and $skip just ensure that a subset of the determined data is returned to the consumer.

The $inlinecount query option typically comes into play in combination with $top and $skip. Similar to $count, it's supposed to count the number of entries. The difference is that the value of the inline count is provided along with the OData feed, which is why it's called "inline." The $inlinecount query option has to be provided with the value all-pages to work. If you provide $inlinecount=none, it's handled as if no inline count was provided.

Inline count always counts the entire number of entries—even if the resulting collection contains less because of $top and/or $skip. So, in this case, it destroys the option to use the max-rows input parameter of the function module because you need to receive all entries to be able to count them. You can use the has_inlinecount( ) method of the io_tech_request_context input object to find out if the $inlinecount query option was provided. The adjusted coding right before the function module call looks like the following:

Entire number of entries

```
lv_maxrows-bapimaxrow = 0.
lv_top  = io_tech_request_context->get_top( ).
lv_skip = io_tech_request_context->get_skip( ).
lv_has_inlinecount = io_tech_request_context->has_
inlinecount( ).
IF ( lv_top IS NOT INITIAL ) AND
   ( lv_has_inlinecount EQ abap_false ).
  lv_maxrows-bapimaxrow = lv_top + lv_skip.
ENDIF.
```

And right after the function module call, you can provide the inline count by setting the inlinecount value of the ES_RESPONSE_CONTEXT export structure:

```
IF lv_has_inlinecount EQ abap_true.
  es_response_context-inlinecount = lines( lt_headerdata ).
ENDIF.
```

As an example, the following URI only provides the first 3 entries (first page) but counts the entire collection (in this case, 115 entities):

Provides three entries, counts entire collection

/sap/opu/odata/sap/ZEXAMPLE1_SRV/ProductSet?$top=3&$skip=0&$inlinecount=allpages

The inline count is contained in the OData response via the m:count tag (see Figure 6.61).

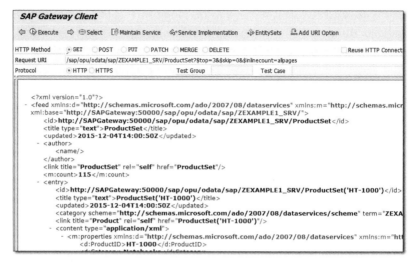

Figure 6.61 Query Result with $inlinecount

$orderby

The $orderby query option allows you to define the sorting of your result set. Order-by parameters are provided by the framework in your Get_EntitySet method via the get_orderby( ) method of io_tech_request_context. It provides a table that contains an entry for each property provided in the $orderby clause with the internal property name.

If you want the collection to be sorted by category (first) and name (second), the URI would look like the following:

/sap/opu/odata/sap/ZEXAMPLE1_SRV/ProductSet?$orderby=Category, Name

In this case, the table received by get_orderby( ) contains the two entries shown in Table 6.3. The Property_Path column comes into play if you, for example, want to sort by a property of a complex type.

Property	Property_Path	Order
CATEGORY	CATEGORY	asc
NAME	NAME	asc

Table 6.3 Content of the Orderby Table

Correspondingly, you get `order = desc` if you provide the related `$orderby` query property with the descending option `desc`. Ascending `asc` doesn't need to be provided in the URI because it's the default sort order.

In combination with `$top` and `$skip`, you should always perform the sorting first and the paging second. Otherwise, the result might be incorrect.

If you combine those query options and also don't execute your own `SELECT` statement, it's even harder to perform an efficient database access because RFC modules usually don't offer any sorting capabilities. In other words, for each page, you always have to read all records, sort them, and then pick the requested page from the result. Such requests have to be handled carefully because they can significantly impact the performance of the server if there are many concurrent calls. In this case, it's more efficient to go for server-side paging, which typically requires the client to cache the entries that were already read.

Server-side paging

6.5.4 Navigation Properties

Navigation properties allow you to navigate from one entry or collection to another entry or collection. A typical example is the navigation from a sales order header (entry) to the list of sales order line items (collection). Navigation properties are always based on associations (relationships) that also define the cardinality. In addition, you can optionally define a referential constraint to specify the foreign key relationship (if possible).

You can see a number of navigation property examples with associations and referential constraints in the ZEXAMPLE2 project into which the metadata of the /IWBEP/GWSAMPLE_BASIC sample service has been imported. To add a navigation property to the ZEXAMPLE1 project, you first need to enter the property NAME "SupplierID" of EDM CORE TYPE "Edm.String" with the MAX LENGTH "10" to the product entity type (see Figure 6.62). Mark the CREATABLE and UPDATABLE attributes.

Navigation property examples

Then you have to regenerate the project and add a mapping line into the `Get_EntitySet` and `Get_Entity` methods.

Properties											
Name	Key	Edm Core Type	Prec.	Scale	Max	U	Crea	Upd	Sort	Null	Filt.	Label
ProductID	✓	Edm.String	0	0	10		✓				✓	Product Identifier
Category		Edm.String	0	0	40		✓	✓			✓	Product Category
Name		Edm.String	0	0	255		✓	✓				Product Name
SupplierID		Edm.String	0	0	10		✓	✓				Supplier ID

Figure 6.62 Product Entity Type with New Property SupplierID

The `SupplierID` is provided via the output table/structure `HEADERDATA`. For the `Get_EntitySet` method (`PRODUCTSET_GET_ENTITYSET`), the required line needs to be added into the loop:

```
ls_product-supplierid = ls_headerdata-supplier_id.
```

For the `Get_Entity` method (`PRODUCTSET_GET_ENTITY`), the required line looks like the following:

```
er_entity-supplierid = ls_headerdata-supplier_id.
```

After activation of the DPC extension class, you can verify whether the `SupplierID` is properly exposed in the OData service (see Figure 6.63).

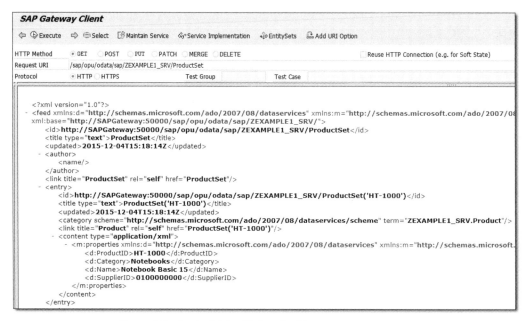

Figure 6.63 Product Set with SupplierID

To navigate from one entity to another, you need a new entity type in the model. For this, you create a new entity type called "Supplier" in the project ZEXAMPLE1 (see Figure 6.64).

Supplier entity type

Properties

Name	Key	Edm Core Type	Prec.	Scale	Max Lngth	U	Crea...	Upd...	Sort...	Null...	Filt.	Label
SupplierID	✓	Edm.String	0	0	10							Supplier ID
SupplierName		Edm.String	0	0	80							Supplier Name

Figure 6.64 New Entity Type: Supplier

For the sake of simplicity, just define two properties `SupplierID` (`Edm.String, Max length=10`) and `SupplierName` (`Edm.String, Max length=80`) for the supplier entity type. The attributes can be left unmarked as we'll only support read access without filtering and sorting.

Also, create a new entity set called SUPPLIERSET (see Figure 6.65), where only the ADDRESSABLE attribute will be marked, as we won't implement any other capability.

Entity Sets

Name	Entity Type Name	L...	L...	S...	Crea...	Upd...	Dele...	Pag...	Add...	Sear...	Sub...	Req...
ProductSet	Product		T		✓	✓	✓	✓	✓			
SupplierSet	Supplier		T						✓			

Figure 6.65 New Entity Set: SupplierSet

Generate and redefine

The next step is to regenerate the project and redefine the new `SUPPLIERSET_GET_ENTITYSET` method of the DPC extension class with the coding in Listing 6.7.

```
METHOD supplierset_get_entityset.

  DATA: ls_bpheaderdata TYPE bapi_epm_bp_header,
        lt_bpheaderdata TYPE STANDARD TABLE OF bapi_epm_bp_
header,
        ls_supplier     LIKE LINE OF et_entityset.

  CALL FUNCTION 'BAPI_EPM_BP_GET_LIST'
    TABLES
      bpheaderdata = lt_bpheaderdata.
```

```
LOOP AT lt_bpheaderdata INTO ls_bpheaderdata.
  ls_supplier-supplierid   = ls_bpheaderdata-bp_id.
  ls_supplier-suppliername = ls_bpheaderdata-company_name.
  APPEND ls_supplier TO et_entityset.
ENDLOOP.

ENDMETHOD.
```
Listing 6.7 Supplier Set: Get_Entityset Method

The SUPPLIERSET_GET_ENTITY needs to be implemented with the coding in Listing 6.8 to fetch an entry based on the provided primary key.

```
METHOD supplierset_get_entity.

  DATA: ls_entity     LIKE er_entity,
        ls_bp_id      TYPE bapi_epm_bp_id,
        ls_headerdata TYPE bapi_epm_bp_header.

  io_tech_request_context->get_converted_keys(
    IMPORTING
      es_key_values = ls_entity ).

  ls_bp_id-bp_id = ls_entity-supplierid.

  CALL FUNCTION 'BAPI_EPM_BP_GET_DETAIL'
    EXPORTING
      bp_id      = ls_bp_id
    IMPORTING
      headerdata = ls_headerdata.

  er_entity-supplierid   = ls_headerdata-bp_id.
  er_entity-suppliername = ls_headerdata-company_name.

ENDMETHOD.
```
Listing 6.8 Supplier Set: Get_Entity Method

Now you need to activate the changes in the DPC extension class. Via the SAP Gateway client, you can execute the following URI to fetch the list of suppliers (see Figure 6.66):

/sap/opu/odata/sap/ZEXAMPLE1_SRV/SupplierSet

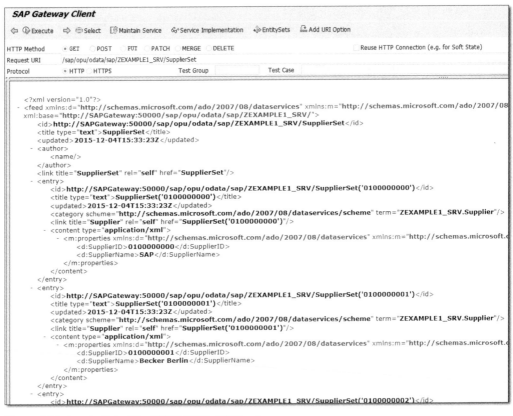

Figure 6.66 SupplierSet of the ZEXAMPLE1_SRV Service

Also verify that the `Get_Entity` implementation is working by executing any of the provided URIs in the collection.

So far, you've added a new entity type and a new entity set with an implementation for the `Get_Entity` and `Get_EntitySet` methods. Now let's define the navigation property. For this, you first need to create an association by double-clicking on DATA MODEL • ASSOCIATIONS in the project tree and clicking the CREATE button in the grid. Each association has to have a NAME, PRINCIPAL ENTITY type, PRINCIPAL ENTITY CARDINALITY, DEPENDENT ENTITY type, and DEPENDENT ENTITY CARDINALITY (see Figure 6.67).

Define navigation property

Figure 6.67 Definition of Assoc_Product_Supplier Association

Because each supplier can deliver 0...n products, set the DEPENDENT ENTITY CARDINALITY (SUPPLIER) to 1 and the PRINCIPAL ENTITY CARDINALITY (PRODUCT) to M. Make sure to use the [F4] value help to see the possible cardinality values.

Now you can define the navigation property by navigating to DATA MODEL • ENTITY TYPES • PRODUCT • NAVIGATION PROPERTIES and clicking the CREATE button to define a navigation property for the product entity type. The navigation property requires a NAME and a RELATIONSHIP NAME (see Figure 6.68). The RELATIONSHIP NAME is the association you've defined before.

Figure 6.68 Navigation Property Definition

For the navigation property NAME, specify "ToSupplier" to use this navigation property to navigate from the product to the related supplier.

Check and regenerate

Now you can check and regenerate the project. After the regeneration, you'll see that the metadata has grown. This isn't only because of the newly added supplier entity type but also because of the association and the navigation property that you've defined.

The navigation property is also visible in the product set (see Figure 6.69) as well as in each product entry. Each entry resource now contains a new link that ends with */ToSupplier*, which allows you to navigate to the related supplier entry.

```
<entry>
    <id>http://SAPGateway:50000/sap/opu/odata/sap/ZEXAMPLE1_SRV/ProductSet('HT-1000')</id>
    <title type="text">ProductSet('HT-1000')</title>
    <updated>2015-12-04T15:39:12Z</updated>
    <category scheme="http://schemas.microsoft.com/ado/2007/08/dataservices/scheme" term="ZEXAMPLE1_SRV.Product"/>
    <link title="Product" rel="edit" href="ProductSet('HT-1000')"/>
    <link title="ToSupplier" type="application/atom+xml;type=entry"
        rel="http://schemas.microsoft.com/ado/2007/08/dataservices/related/ToSupplier" href="ProductSet('HT-1000')/ToSupplier"/>
    <content type="application/xml">
        <m:properties xmlns:d="http://schemas.microsoft.com/ado/2007/08/dataservices"
            xmlns:m="http://schemas.microsoft.com/ado/2007/08/dataservices/metadata">
            <d:ProductID>HT-1000</d:ProductID>
            <d:Category>Notebooks</d:Category>
            <d:Name>Notebook Basic 15</d:Name>
            <d:SupplierID>0100000000</d:SupplierID>
        </m:properties>
    </content>
</entry>
```

Figure 6.69 Navigation Property in the Product Set

This particular navigation property navigates to a supplier entry—not to the collection—because of the definition of the cardinality. In the EPM example, a product always has a unique supplier, whereas a supplier can deliver many products.

If you execute this navigation link for any product, you'll run into an error. This is because the URI with the navigation link only contains the primary key of the product, but the Get_Entity method of the supplier (which is invoked when executing the navigation link) requires the primary key of the supplier. You need to enhance the previous coding a little bit to deal with this issue.

Error at execution

The change that you need to implement now is to derive the SupplierID from the ProductID in the supplier Get_Entity method SUPPLIERSET_GET_ENTITY, as shown in Listing 6.9.

```
METHOD supplierset_get_entity.

  DATA: ls_entity         LIKE er_entity,
        ls_bp_id          TYPE bapi_epm_bp_id,
        ls_headerdata     TYPE bapi_epm_bp_header.

  DATA: lv_source_entity_set_name TYPE /iwbep/mgw_tech_name,
        ls_product                TYPE zcl_zexample1_mpc=>ts_
product,
        ls_product_id             TYPE bapi_epm_product_id,
        ls_prd_headerdata         TYPE bapi_epm_product_header.

  lv_source_entity_set_name = io_tech_request_context->get_
source_entity_set_name( ).
```

```
IF lv_source_entity_set_name EQ 'ProductSet'.
  io_tech_request_context->get_converted_source_keys(
    IMPORTING
      es_key_values = ls_product ).

  ls_product_id-product_id = ls_product-productid.

  CALL FUNCTION 'BAPI_EPM_PRODUCT_GET_DETAIL'
    EXPORTING
      product_id              = ls_product_id
    IMPORTING
      headerdata              = ls_prd_headerdata.

  ls_bp_id-bp_id = ls_prd_headerdata-supplier_id.
ELSE.
  io_tech_request_context->get_converted_keys(
    IMPORTING
      es_key_values = ls_entity ).

  ls_bp_id-bp_id = ls_entity-supplierid.
ENDIF.

CALL FUNCTION 'BAPI_EPM_BP_GET_DETAIL'
  EXPORTING
    bp_id      = ls_bp_id
  IMPORTING
    headerdata = ls_headerdata.

er_entity-supplierid   = ls_headerdata-bp_id.
er_entity-suppliername = ls_headerdata-company_name.

ENDMETHOD.
```

Listing 6.9 Supplier Set: Get_Entity Method with Supplier Determination via the Product BAPI

As you can see, the product detail is read by calling the same BAPI (BAPI_EPM_PRODUCT_GET_DETAIL) as in the PRODUCTSET_GET_ENTITY method. This provides the product details which correspond to the product key that is handed over via the navigation link. The product key is determined by using the get_converted_source_keys method of io_tech_request_context in contrast to using get_converted_keys when accessing the supplier details directly without a navigation step.

The IF statement makes sure that this code snippet is only executed in the navigation property case. In the regular supplier Get_Entity case, this coding doesn't need to be executed.

Activate the changes in the DPC extension class, and execute the follow- **Activate changes**
ing sample URI via the SAP Gateway client:

/sap/opu/odata/sap/ZEXAMPLE1_SRV/ProductSet('HT-1000')/ToSupplier

As a result, you see the supplier entry (with its key and name) that
belongs to the 'HT-1000' product (see Figure 6.70).

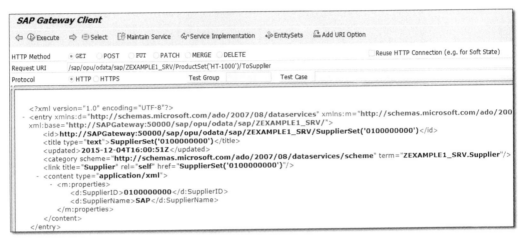

Figure 6.70 ToSupplier Navigation Result of Product HT-1000

According to the OData standard, you find a self-link to the retrieved
supplier entry (.../SupplierSet('0100000000')) in the navigation result.

6.5.5 Create, Update, and Delete Methods

So far we've only read data from the underlying data source by executing the respective GET_LIST and GET_DETAIL function modules via the
Get_EntitySet and Get_Entity methods. In contrast to read access, CRE-
ATE, UPDATE, and DELETE (CUD) methods are *write access* operations
because they typically change the underlying data.

Create

CREATE is used whenever you want to create a new entry into the respective collection. The CREATE operation for the product entity type is handled by the PRODUCTSET_CREATE_ENTITY method in the DPC.

Redefine in the
DPC extension
class Similar to the read methods, you need to redefine this method in the data provider extension class. As an example, use the coding in Listing 6.10.

```abap
METHOD productset_create_entity.

  DATA: ls_headerdata TYPE bapi_epm_product_header,
        ls_product    LIKE er_entity,
        lt_return     TYPE STANDARD TABLE OF bapiret2.

  io_data_provider->read_entry_data( IMPORTING es_data = ls_
product ).

  ls_headerdata-product_id    = ls_product-productid.
  ls_headerdata-category      = ls_product-category.
  ls_headerdata-name          = ls_product-name.
  ls_headerdata-supplier_id   = ls_product-supplierid.
  ls_headerdata-measure_unit  = 'EA'.
  ls_headerdata-currency_code = 'EUR'.
  ls_headerdata-tax_tarif_code = '1'.
  ls_headerdata-type_code     = 'PR'.

  CALL FUNCTION 'BAPI_EPM_PRODUCT_CREATE'
    EXPORTING
      headerdata          = ls_headerdata
*     PERSIST_TO_DB       = ABAP_TRUE
    TABLES
*     CONVERSION_FACTORS =
      return              = lt_return.

  IF lt_return IS NOT INITIAL.
    mo_context->get_message_container( )->add_messages_from_
bapi(
      it_bapi_messages        = lt_return
      iv_determine_leading_msg = /iwbep/if_message_
container=>gcs_leading_msg_search_option-first ).

    RAISE EXCEPTION TYPE /iwbep/cx_mgw_busi_exception
      EXPORTING
        textid          = /iwbep/cx_mgw_busi_
exception=>business_error
        message_container = mo_context->get_message_
container( ).
  ENDIF.

  er_entity = ls_product.

ENDMETHOD.
```

Listing 6.10 Product Set: Create Entity Method

Using the `read_entry_data` method of the `io_data_provider` import object reference, you can retrieve the data that was passed along the `POST` request in the HTTP body. The entry is retrieved in the format of the entity type definition. That's why the `ls_product` structure is of type `ER_ENTITY`.

To successfully call the `BAPI_EPM_PRODUCT_CREATE` function module, some values that aren't part of the data model need to be defaulted (e.g., `measure_unit`). This is the specific logic of the underlying business function.

In this example, we've also introduced some error handling. For the sake of simplicity, we haven't done this in the `Get_EntitySet` and `Get_Entity` cases, although it definitely makes sense there as well. The error handling consists of retrieving the return table from the function module call.

Error handling

Assuming that only errors will be part of table `return`, if the table isn't empty, you first use the `mo_context` member object reference to determine the message container (via `get_message_container( )`) and use the `add_messages_from_bapi` method to log the BAPI messages. Secondly, you raise a `/iwbep/cx_mgw_busi_exception` business exception that will abort the processing, send an HTTP 400 return code to the consumer, and provide the messages as part of the response body.

At the end of the method, you provide the newly created entry back to the framework (`ER_ENTITY`). Typically, you have to call the corresponding `Get-Detail` BAPI to fetch the detail of the newly created entry because some properties might have been changed or calculated. This isn't the case for this example, so you can pass the retrieved entry right back to the framework.

After you've performed the implementation of the `CREATE` method, again activate the DPC extension class. After that, use the SAP Gateway client to verify if the `CREATE` operation works as expected. The `CREATE` operation requires a proper HTTP body with the entry to be created. Instead of putting such an HTTP body together manually, you can click the USE AS REQUEST button in the SAP Gateway client. For this, you first need to execute a `GET` operation to receive a suitable source entry. Then click the USE AS REQUEST button to copy it over to the left-hand side of

Activate the DPC extension class

the SAP Gateway client (see Figure 6.71). The left-hand side is the HTTP REQUEST side, and the right-hand side is the HTTP RESPONSE side.

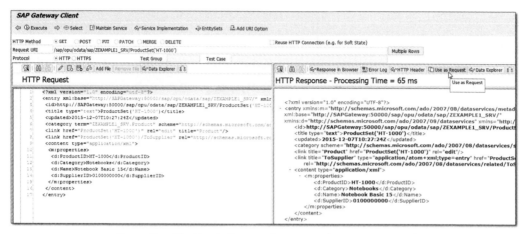

Figure 6.71 The Use As Request Function in the SAP Gateway Client

Before you can execute the CREATE operation, you also need to change the HTTP method from GET to POST. In addition, you need to adjust the URI because the CREATE operation has to be executed on a collection and not on a single entry (make sure to remove the brackets with the primary key). Finally, you may want to adjust the HTTP body, which contains the data of the entry to be created (e.g., make sure to change the product ID and the product name).

Depending on the underlying business logic, the primary key may not need to be provided in the HTTP request body if it's calculated by the function module that was mapped in the CREATE operation. In this example, you have to provide a unique/new product ID because there is no number range that calculates a new ID for you.

HTTP 201   If the CREATE operation was successful (see Figure 6.72), you get an HTTP 201 response. Furthermore, you get the newly created record because the backend server might have determined the primary key of the new entry (not in this example case, however). Therefore, the server has to provide the record, or the client won't be able to access it without the key.

In addition, the client benefits from this if the server determines/calculates properties other than just the primary key because those values are sent along with the response, and the client doesn't need to execute another GET request. This pattern is different in the update case, as you'll see next.

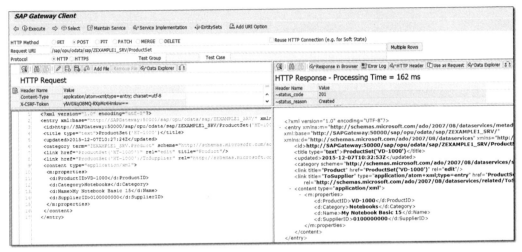

Figure 6.72 Successful CREATE Operation

Update

The UPDATE operation comes into play whenever an existing entry resource needs to be changed. So the URI needs to address the entry as in a Get-Detail case. The UPDATE operation for the product entity type is handled by the PRODUCTSET_UPDATE_ENTITY method in the DPC. Similar to the other methods that you've implemented, you redefine this method in the DPC extension class and apply the coding in Listing 6.11.

```
METHOD productset_update_entity.

  DATA: ls_product     LIKE er_entity,
        ls_entity      LIKE er_entity,
        ls_product_id  TYPE bapi_epm_product_id,
        ls_headerdata  TYPE bapi_epm_product_header,
        ls_headerdatax TYPE bapi_epm_product_headerx,
        lt_return      TYPE STANDARD TABLE OF bapiret2.
```

```
      io_data_provider->read_entry_data( IMPORTING es_data = ls_
product ).

      io_tech_request_context->get_converted_keys(
        IMPORTING
          es_key_values = ls_entity ).

      ls_product_id-product_id = ls_entity-productid.

      CALL FUNCTION 'BAPI_EPM_PRODUCT_GET_DETAIL'
        EXPORTING
          product_id              = ls_product_id
        IMPORTING
          headerdata              = ls_headerdata
        TABLES
*         CONVERSION_FACTORS      =
          return                  = lt_return.

      IF lt_return IS NOT INITIAL.
        mo_context->get_message_container( )->add_messages_from_
bapi(
          it_bapi_messages        = lt_return
          iv_determine_leading_msg = /iwbep/if_message_
container=>gcs_leading_msg_search_option-first ).

        RAISE EXCEPTION TYPE /iwbep/cx_mgw_busi_exception
          EXPORTING
            textid              = /iwbep/cx_mgw_busi_
exception=>business_error
            message_container = mo_context->get_message_
container( ).
      ENDIF.

      ls_headerdata-category    = ls_product-category.
      ls_headerdata-name        = ls_product-name.
      ls_headerdata-supplier_id = ls_product-supplierid.

      ls_headerdatax-product_id  = ls_headerdata-product_id.
      ls_headerdatax-category    = 'X'.
      ls_headerdatax-name        = 'X'.
      ls_headerdatax-supplier_id = 'X'.

      CALL FUNCTION 'BAPI_EPM_PRODUCT_CHANGE'
        EXPORTING
          product_id            = ls_product_id
          headerdata            = ls_headerdata
          headerdatax           = ls_headerdatax
*         PERSIST_TO_DB         = ABAP_TRUE
        TABLES
```

```
*      CONVERSION_FACTORS  =
*      CONVERSION_FACTORSX =
       return             = lt_return.

   IF lt_return IS NOT INITIAL.
     mo_context->get_message_container( )->add_messages_from_
bapi(
       it_bapi_messages        = lt_return
       iv_determine_leading_msg = /iwbep/if_message_
container=>gcs_leading_msg_search_option-first ).

     RAISE EXCEPTION TYPE /iwbep/cx_mgw_busi_exception
       EXPORTING
         textid              = /iwbep/cx_mgw_busi_
exception=>business_error
         message_container = mo_context->get_message_
container( ).
   ENDIF.

   er_entity = ls_product.

ENDMETHOD.
```

Listing 6.11 Product Set: Update Entity Method

This implementation reuses certain elements from the other methods. First, use the `io_data_provider` input object reference to fetch the incoming data from the HTTP body. Then, pick the converted primary key from the `get_converted_keys` method of `io_tech_request_con-text`. With the primary key, read the product instance with the `BAPI_EPM_PRODUCT_GET_DETAIL` function to fill the `ls_headerdata` structure. This time, you check table `return` for any entries (assuming that only errors will be reported in that table, and no success message will be provided) to avoid that an invalid primary key was used in the URI.

After the product instance is read, you apply the incoming properties. You also need to set the X flags in the corresponding X-structure to inform the BAPI of which attributes to update. Next, call `BAPI_EPM_PRO-DUCT_CHANGE` to actually perform the update. Similar to the `CREATE` method, you check table `return` for existing messages and throw an exception in that case. Finally, there is also an `ER_ENTITY` export parameter that should be filled.

Incoming properties

305

After you're done with the implementation of the UPDATE method, you need to activate the DPC extension class. Now you must use the SAP Gateway client to verify whether the UPDATE operation works as expected. To do this, first perform a single read to get a proper HTTP response body that you can copy over to the request side by clicking the USE AS REQUEST button. The URI remains unchanged because the UPDATE operation is always performed on a single entry resource. You only need to switch the HTTP method from GET to PUT. If the update was successful (see Figure 6.73), you only get an HTTP 204 (no content) response.

Figure 6.73 Successful Update Operation

The HTTP code indicates that the response body is empty. This happens on purpose because the assumption is that the client has all information, and thus sending the entry along with the response causes unnecessary overhead. The client can always perform a single read to fetch the entity again if the backend server has calculated any values that the client doesn't have.

Delete

The DELETE operation is typically very simple to implement. It requires redefining the PRODUCTSET_DELETE_ENTITY method of the DPC extension class. You can use the coding in Listing 6.12 as an example.

```
METHOD productset_delete_entity.

  DATA: ls_entity     TYPE zcl_zexample1_mpc=>ts_product,
        ls_product_id TYPE bapi_epm_product_id,
        lt_return     TYPE STANDARD TABLE OF bapiret2.

  io_tech_request_context->get_converted_keys(
    IMPORTING
      es_key_values = ls_entity ).

  ls_product_id-product_id = ls_entity-productid.

  CALL FUNCTION 'BAPI_EPM_PRODUCT_DELETE'
    EXPORTING
      product_id    = ls_product_id
*     PERSIST_TO_DB = ABAP_TRUE
    TABLES
      return        = lt_return.

  IF lt_return IS NOT INITIAL.
    mo_context->get_message_container( )->add_messages_from_
bapi(
      it_bapi_messages            = lt_return
      iv_determine_leading_msg = /iwbep/if_message_
container=>gcs_leading_msg_search_option-first ).

    RAISE EXCEPTION TYPE /iwbep/cx_mgw_busi_exception
      EXPORTING
        textid             = /iwbep/cx_mgw_busi_
exception=>business_error
        message_container = mo_context->get_message_
container( ).
  ENDIF.

ENDMETHOD.
```

Listing 6.12 Product Set: Delete Entity Method

First, again handle the primary key of the entry to be deleted. With this information, call the DELETE function BAPI_EPM_PRODUCT_DELETE right away. Table return is checked again for entries, and an exception is thrown if any entry exists—assuming that you don't receive any success or warning messages in table return.

Primary key

After the activation of the DPC extension class, you can verify whether the implemented DELETE operation works properly. DELETE operations are always executed on a single entry. Therefore, you have to provide a

URI that addresses a single-entry resource. The HTTP method has to be DELETE.

If the DELETE was successful, you get an HTTP 204 (no content) response (see Figure 6.74).

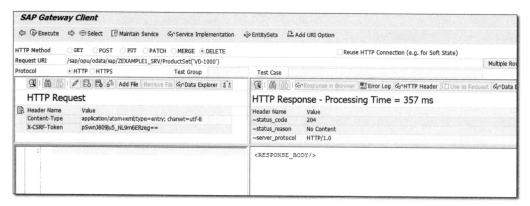

Figure 6.74 Successful DELETE Operation

6.5.6 Function Imports

Function imports or actions are used whenever a function needs to be executed on a business object that doesn't fit into the default CRUD-Q operations. One example is the release of a sales order that might influence a number of properties and in addition also trigger some backend functionality (e.g., start a workflow). Function imports are defined on the service level, so a function isn't executed on a dedicated collection or entry.

Define function import
A function import can be defined by right-clicking on DATA MODEL and selecting CREATE • FUNCTION IMPORT in the Service Builder. This opens up the CREATE FUNCTION IMPORT window, where you first need to provide a name of the function import (see Figure 6.75).

Figure 6.75 Create Function Import Dialog

For each function import, you can define a return kind of the function import. The values listed in Table 6.4 are supported.

Return Kind	Description
Complex type	Data returned as complex type
Entity type	Data returned as entity type
No return	No data returned

Table 6.4 Function Import Return Types

In this example, you want to implement a function import that determines the heaviest products. For that, you first need to enter the WEIGHTMEASURE property and select EDM.DECIMAL, PRECISION 13, and SCALE 3 for the product entity type. Furthermore, add the property WEIGHTUNIT, and select EDM.STRING and MAXLENGTH 3 (see Figure 6.76). You need this to see the weight as well as the weight-unit of each product. The function import itself doesn't need these two additional properties.

Name	Key	Edm Core Type	Prec.	Scale	Max	Unit Property Name	Crea	Upd	Sort	Null	Filt.	Label
ProductID	✓	Edm.String	0	0	10		✓	☐	☐	☐	✓	Product Identifier
Category	☐	Edm.String	0	0	40		✓	✓	☐	☐	✓	Product Category
Name	☐	Edm.String	0	0	255		✓	✓	☐	☐	☐	Product Name
SupplierID	☐	Edm.String	0	0	10		✓	✓	☐	☐	☐	Supplier ID
WeightMeasure	☐	Edm.Decimal	13	3	0	WeightUnit	✓	✓	☐	✓	☐	Weight Measure
WeightUnit	☐	Edm.String	0	0	3		✓	✓	☐	✓	☐	Weight Unit

Figure 6.76 WeightMeasure and WeightUnit of the Product Entity Type

Make sure to adjust the `PRODUCTSET_GET_ENTITYSET`, `PRODUCTSET_GET_ENTITY`, `PRODUCTSET_CREATE_ENTITY` and `PRODUCTSET_UPDATE_ENTITY` methods to also consider both new properties (add related mappings).

The return type of the function import is an entity set because you want to receive the list of heaviest products. A list is used because there could be no product according to the parameter or there could be a set of products that are all heaviest.

If you set the return kind (RET. KIND field) to ENTITY TYPE, you can also specify the return type. In this case, this is the PRODUCT entity type. The

RETURN CARDINALITY specifies how many of the defined return type can occur. The values in Table 6.5 are supported.

Cardinality	Description
0..1	No more than one instance occurs. Zero instances are also permitted. Please note that this return cardinality isn't recommended to be used (see SAP Note 2009874 for details).
1	Occurrence of exactly one instance.
0..n	Occurrence of zero or more instances.
1..n	Occurrence of one or more instances.

Table 6.5 Return Cardinalities

In this example, we choose 0..n for the RETURN CARDINALITY field as there can be a list (including a list with only one entry) or no entries in the result set.

After choosing a cardinality where many (n) entries can be returned (collection), you also need to define the return entity set. In this example, we enter "ProductSet" for RETURN ENTITY SET.

The HTTP method basically defines whether the function import is just reading any data (HTTP GET) or is also manipulating any data (HTTP POST). This is important because a GET may not change any data in the system. A POST method is always protected via a cross-site request forgery (XSRF) token, which isn't the case for GET accesses.

Finally, set the ACTION FOR ENTITY TYPE to PRODUCT to indicate that this function import is related to the product entity type.

After all attributes are specified, you have the function import definition as shown in Figure 6.77.

Function Imports						
Name	Return Type Kind	Return Type	Return Cardinality	Return Entity Set	HTTP	Action for Entity Type
DetermineHeaviestProduct	Entity Type	Product	0..n	ProductSet	GET	Product

Figure 6.77 Definition of a Sample Function Import

In our example, you also need to provide an import parameter for the example function import. This parameter defines the product category of which you want to determine the heaviest product.

Provide import parameter

To define import parameters for function imports, you need to expand the new node FUNCTION IMPORTS • DETERMINEHEAVIESTPRODUCT in the project tree and then double-click on FUNCTION IMPORT PARAMETERS. You can add entries into the grid by using the ADD/CREATE buttons.

In this example, enter a function import parameter called Category. It has the same attributes as the Category property in the product entity type (see Figure 6.78).

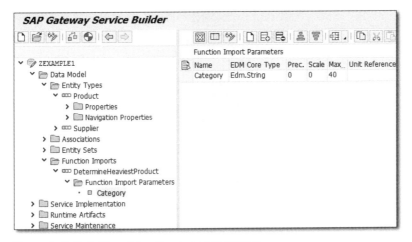

Figure 6.78 Definition of Function Import Parameter

That is all you need to do on the metadata side. You can now check and regenerate the project. The service provisioning (data provider) has to be done manually by redefining the respective method in the DPC extension class. For this, open ZCL_ZEXAMPLE1_DPC_EXT in the ABAP Class Builder, and put it to edit mode. The method you need to redefine is EXECUTE_ACTION (/IWBEP/IF_MGW_APPL_SRV_RUNTIME interface).

Listing 6.13 shows the coding we're using.

```
METHOD /iwbep/if_mgw_appl_srv_runtime~execute_action.

  DATA: lv_action_name   TYPE /iwbep/mgw_tech_name,
        lt_product       TYPE zcl_zexample1_mpc=>tt_product,
```

```
        ls_product            TYPE zcl_zexample1_mpc=>ts_product,
        lt_headerdata         TYPE TABLE OF bapi_epm_product_
header,
        lt_headerdata_orig TYPE TABLE OF bapi_epm_product_
header,
        ls_headerdata         TYPE bapi_epm_product_header,
        lt_categories         TYPE TABLE OF bapi_epm_product_
categ_range,
        ls_categories         TYPE bapi_epm_product_categ_range,
        lv_max_weight         TYPE snwd_weight_measure,
        lv_output             TYPE snwd_weight_measure.

  CONSTANTS: cv_weight_unit_kg TYPE snwd_weight_
unit VALUE 'KG'.

  lv_action_name = io_tech_request_context->get_function_
import_name( ).

  CASE lv_action_name.
    WHEN 'DetermineHeaviestProduct'.
*     Put Category filter together
      io_tech_request_context->get_converted_parameters(
        IMPORTING
          es_parameter_values = ls_product ).

      IF NOT ls_product-category IS INITIAL.
        ls_categories-low    = ls_product-category.
        ls_categories-option = 'EQ'.    "Equal
        ls_categories-sign   = 'I'.    "Including
        APPEND ls_categories TO lt_categories.
      ENDIF.

*     Fetch filtered Products
      CALL FUNCTION 'BAPI_EPM_PRODUCT_GET_LIST'
        TABLES
          headerdata        = lt_headerdata_orig
          selparamcategories = lt_categories.

*     Convert all Weights to KG and determine the highest weigh
t value
      CLEAR lv_max_weight.
      LOOP AT lt_headerdata_orig INTO ls_headerdata.
        CALL FUNCTION 'UNIT_CONVERSION_SIMPLE'
          EXPORTING
            input                    = ls_headerdata-weight_
measure
            unit_in                  = ls_headerdata-weight_
unit
            unit_out                 = cv_weight_unit_kg
```

```
      IMPORTING
        output                  = lv_output
      EXCEPTIONS
        conversion_not_found    = 1
        division_by_zero        = 2
        input_invalid           = 3
        output_invalid          = 4
        overflow                = 5
        type_invalid            = 6
        units_missing           = 7
        unit_in_not_found       = 8
        unit_out_not_found      = 9
        OTHERS                  = 10.

    IF sy-subrc NE 0.  CONTINUE.  ENDIF.
    ls_headerdata-weight_measure = lv_output.
    ls_headerdata-weight_unit    = cv_weight_unit_kg.
    APPEND ls_headerdata TO lt_headerdata.
    IF lv_output > lv_max_weight.  lv_max_weight = lv_
output.  ENDIF.
  ENDLOOP.

*   Put the product(s) with the highest weight into the resul
t table
  SORT lt_headerdata_orig BY product_id.
  LOOP AT lt_headerdata INTO ls_headerdata WHERE weight_
measure = lv_max_weight.
    READ TABLE lt_headerdata_orig INTO ls_
headerdata WITH KEY product_id = ls_headerdata-product_
id BINARY SEARCH.

    CLEAR ls_product.
    ls_product-productid     = ls_headerdata-product_id.
    ls_product-name          = ls_headerdata-name.
    ls_product-category      = ls_headerdata-category.
    ls_product-supplierid    = ls_headerdata-supplier_id.
    ls_product-weightmeasure = ls_headerdata-weight_
measure.
    ls_product-weightunit    = ls_headerdata-weight_unit.
    APPEND ls_product TO lt_product.
  ENDLOOP.

  copy_data_to_ref(
    EXPORTING
      is_data = lt_product
    CHANGING
      cr_data = er_data ).

WHEN OTHERS.
```

```
        CALL METHOD super->/iwbep/if_mgw_appl_srv_
runtime~execute_action
            EXPORTING
                iv_action_name          = iv_action_name
                it_parameter             = it_parameter
                io_tech_request_context  = io_tech_request_context
            IMPORTING
                er_data                  = er_data.

    ENDCASE.

ENDMETHOD.
```

Listing 6.13 Function Import for DetermineHeaviestProduct

In this method, first use a case control structure because every function import of the OData service is handled via this single ABAP method (there is no submethod generated), and you need to distinguish which function import is supposed to be handled. For this, use the `get_function_import_name( )` method of `io_tech_request_context`.

The next step is to determine the import parameter (category) by using the `get_converted_parameters` method of `io_tech_request_context`. This filter parameter is being added to the category ranges table of the function module that you use.

Call function module

Then call the `BAPI_EPM_PRODUCT_GET_LIST` function module to provide the filtered list of products. Because a result may contain products that use different weight units (e.g., g and kg), you first need to convert all weight measures to the same unit. For the sake of simplicity, we'll skip those products where the unit conversion wasn't successful. While looping over the result table, you also identify the highest weight value (`lv_max_weight`).

As soon as you've determined the highest weight, pick those products (as there can be multiple) with their original (unconverted) weight. Then put them into result table `lt_product`. Finally, this table is copied into the `er_data` data reference by the very helpful `copy_data_to_ref` method from the framework.

After you've activated the DPC extension class, you can execute the function import. The URI in the SAP Gateway client could be the following:

/sap/opu/odata/sap/ZEXAMPLE1_SRV/DetermineHeaviestProduct?Category='Keyboards'

From the URI structure, you can see that every function import is executed based on the service itself and not based on a collection or single entry. Parameters are handed over in the regular way of using URL parameters. Multiple parameters are separated by &. Table parameters can't be used (though this functionality is planned for future versions).

From the result of the function import (see Figure 6.79), you can see that a single product was found. The category filter was also used properly.

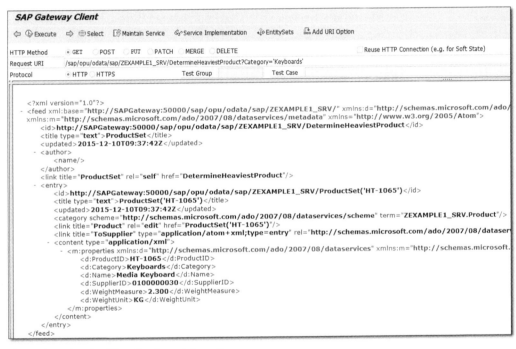

Figure 6.79 Result of Function Import Execution

6.5.7 Media Resources

Media resources are used to expose different binary data, such as graphics and videos, to consumers. A media resource is accessed via a media link entry.

Flag as media To let a regular entity type become a media link entity type, you have to flag it as media via the Service Builder using the M checkbox on the entity type level. The same attribute can also be set manually via coding in the MPC extension class by using the `set_is_media( )` method on the entity type level. As a result, the `HasStream` attribute in the metadata document of the entity type is set to `true`.

As soon as you define an entity type as a media type, you also have to consider two properties:

- **Source URI**
  The source URI property can be used by the consuming application to retrieve the associated media resource itself from the respective location.

  It's recommended to annotate the property that contains the source URI during runtime using the `set_as_content_source( )` method, but this is optional. The framework uses this information during runtime to provide a content tag that consists of the MIME-type (see next point) as well as the URI.

  If no property is defined as the content source, or if the property value is empty at runtime, the framework automatically generates a source tag that uses the `$value` option. This allows the consumer to access the raw value of the entry.

- **MIME type**
  The MIME type describes the type of the media resource (e.g., *image/jpeg*). The property containing the MIME type has to be annotated by using the `set_as_content_type( )` method. It's mandatory to define this. If you don't, you'll get a runtime error when accessing any data.

If the source URI contains an absolute path to the media resource, the consumer can access the resource directly from its location (e.g., *<content-server>:<port>/path/subpath/.../picture.jpg*). But this requires that the consuming application has direct access to that media location, which might not be given by default due to, for example, required authentication or access via firewall.

$value Instead of accessing the resource via an absolute URI, you can also access it via the SAP Gateway server by using the `$value` option to get the raw value of the corresponding entry. This requires implementing the `Get_Stream` method in the DPC extension class, which has to return the corresponding stream. This is very beneficial because a consumer application continues to communicate with the same server (SAP Gateway) instead of connecting/authenticating with multiple destinations or endpoints.

To enhance the ZExample1_SRV service, you first need to add two new properties: one for the source URI and one for the MIME type. As mentioned before, the source URI property is optional.

For our example, enter the property names "PictureURI" (EDM.STRING, MAX LENGTH 255) and "PictureMIMEType" (EDM.STRING, MAX LENGTH 128) to the product entity type (see Figure 6.80).

Properties												
Name	Key	Edm Core Type	Prec.	Scale	Max	Unit Property Name	Crea	Upd	Sort	Null	Filt.	Label
ProductID	✓	Edm.String	0	0	10		✓	☐	☐	☐	✓	Product Identifier
Category	☐	Edm.String	0	0	40		✓	✓	☐	☐	✓	Product Category
Name	☐	Edm.String	0	0	255		✓	✓	☐	☐	☐	Product Name
SupplierID	☐	Edm.String	0	0	10		✓	✓	☐	☐	☐	Supplier ID
WeightMeasure	☐	Edm.Decimal	13	3	0	WeightUnit	✓	✓	☐	✓	☐	Weight Measure
WeightUnit	☐	Edm.String	0	0	3		✓	✓	☐	✓	☐	Weight Unit
PictureURI	☐	Edm.String	0	0	255		✓	✓	☐	☐	☐	Picture URI
PictureMIMEType	☐	Edm.String	0	0	128		✓	✓	☐	☐	☐	Picture MIME Type

Figure 6.80 Properties for Media Resources

In the MPC extension class, you need to redefine the `define( )` method with the code shown in Listing 6.14.

```
METHOD define.

  DATA: lo_entity_type TYPE REF TO /iwbep/if_mgw_odata_entity_
typ,
        lo_property    TYPE REF TO /iwbep/if_mgw_odata_
property.

  super->define( ).

  lo_entity_type = model->get_entity_type( 'Product' ).
  lo_entity_type->set_is_media( ).
  lo_property = lo_entity_type->get_property( 'PictureURI' ).
  lo_property->set_as_content_source( ).
  lo_property = lo_entity_type->get_
property( 'PictureMIMEType' ).
```

```
lo_property->set_as_content_type( ).

ENDMETHOD.
```
Listing 6.14 Redefinition of the Define Method

MPC base class   This code first calls the define method of the superclass (MPC base class) where all definitions defined via the Service Builder take place. Then you make the entity type a media type by calling the `set_is_media( )` method. The `PictureURI` property is set to provide the `content-source`, and the `PictureMIMEType` property is set to provide the `content-type`.

After you've regenerated the project and activated the MPC extension class, you'll find a new tag in the metadata document of your service: `m:HasStream` (see Figure 6.81).

```xml
<?xml version="1.0" encoding="UTF-8"?>
<edmx:Edmx xmlns:sap="http://www.sap.com/Protocols/SAPData"
xmlns:m="http://schemas.microsoft.com/ado/2007/08/dataservices/metadata"
xmlns:edmx="http://schemas.microsoft.com/ado/2007/06/edmx" Version="1.0">
- <edmx:DataServices m:DataServiceVersion="2.0">
  - <Schema xml:lang="en" xmlns="http://schemas.microsoft.com/ado/2008/09/edm" sap:schema-version="1"
      Namespace="ZEXAMPLE1_SRV">
    - <EntityType sap:content-version="1" m:HasStream="true" Name="Product">
      - <Key>
          <PropertyRef Name="ProductID"/>
        </Key>
        <Property Name="ProductID" sap:label="Product Identifier" MaxLength="10" Nullable="false" Type="Edm.String"/>
        <Property Name="Category" sap:label="Product Category" MaxLength="40" Type="Edm.String"/>
        <Property Name="Name" sap:label="Product Name" MaxLength="255" Type="Edm.String"/>
        <Property Name="SupplierID" sap:label="Supplier ID" MaxLength="10" Type="Edm.String"/>
        <Property Name="WeightMeasure" sap:label="Weight Measure" Type="Edm.Decimal" sap:unit="WeightUnit" Scale="3"
          Precision="13"/>
        <Property Name="WeightUnit" sap:label="Weight Unit" MaxLength="3" Type="Edm.String"/>
        <Property Name="PictureURI" sap:label="Picture URI" MaxLength="255" Type="Edm.String"/>
        <Property Name="PictureMIMEType" sap:label="Picture MIME Type" MaxLength="128" Type="Edm.String"/>
        <NavigationProperty Name="ToSupplier" ToRole="ToRole_Assoc_Product_Supplier" FromRole="FromRole_Assoc_Prod
          Relationship="ZEXAMPLE1_SRV.Assoc_Product_Supplier"/>
      </EntityType>
```

Figure 6.81 Media Entity Type

Next, you need to take care of the data provisioning. For this, again adjust the `PRODUCTSET_GET_ENTITYSET`, `PRODUCTSET_GET_ENTITY`, `PRODUCTSET_CREATE_ENTITY`, `PRODUCTSET_UPDATE_ENTITY`, and `EXECUTE_ACTION` methods to also map the new properties.

MIME type   The MIME type is unfortunately not part of the `HEADERDATA` structure and thus needs to be calculated manually. This is often necessary because there isn't always a suitable source field that can be taken from the return structure/table of a certain function. In this example, you'll add this determination to the product `Get_EntitySet` method of the DPC extension class.

Together with the previous examples, the `PRODUCTSET_GET_ENTITYSET` method has grown to what is shown in Listing 6.15.

```abap
METHOD productset_get_entityset.

  DATA: lr_filter                 TYPE REF TO /iwbep/if_mgw_req_
filter,
        lt_filter_select_options  TYPE /iwbep/t_mgw_select_
option,
        ls_filter_select_options  TYPE /iwbep/s_mgw_select_
option,
        ls_select_option          TYPE /iwbep/s_cod_select_
option,
        lt_selparamproductid      TYPE STANDARD TABLE OF bapi_
epm_product_id_range,
        ls_selparamproductid      TYPE bapi_epm_product_id_
range,
        lt_selparamcategories     TYPE STANDARD TABLE OF bapi_
epm_product_categ_range,
        ls_selparamcategories     TYPE bapi_epm_product_categ_
range.

  DATA: lt_headerdata             TYPE STANDARD TABLE OF bapi_
epm_product_header,
        ls_headerdata             TYPE bapi_epm_product_header,
        ls_product                LIKE LINE OF et_entityset.

  DATA: lv_maxrows        TYPE bapi_epm_max_rows,
        lv_top            TYPE int4,
        lv_skip           TYPE int4,
        lv_start          TYPE int4,
        lv_end            TYPE int4,
        lv_has_inlinecount TYPE abap_bool.

  DATA: lr_mr_api TYPE REF TO if_mr_api.

  lr_mr_api = cl_mime_repository_api=>if_mr_api~get_api( ).

  lr_filter = io_tech_request_context->get_filter( ).
  lt_filter_select_options = lr_filter->get_filter_select_
options( ).

  LOOP AT lt_filter_select_options INTO ls_filter_select_
options.
    IF ls_filter_select_options-property EQ 'PRODUCTID'.
```

```
      LOOP AT ls_filter_select_options-select_options INTO ls_
select_option.
        ls_selparamproductid-sign   = ls_select_option-sign.
        ls_selparamproductid-option = ls_select_option-option.
        ls_selparamproductid-low    = ls_select_option-low.
        ls_selparamproductid-high   = ls_select_option-high.
        APPEND ls_selparamproductid TO lt_selparamproductid.
      ENDLOOP.
    ELSEIF ls_filter_select_options-property EQ 'CATEGORY'.
      LOOP AT ls_filter_select_options-select_options INTO ls_
select_option.
        ls_selparamcategories-sign   = ls_select_option-sign.
        ls_selparamcategories-option = ls_select_option-option.
        ls_selparamcategories-low    = ls_select_option-low.
        ls_selparamcategories-high   = ls_select_option-high.
        APPEND ls_selparamcategories TO lt_selparamcategories.
      ENDLOOP.
    ENDIF.
  ENDLOOP.

  lv_maxrows-bapimaxrow = 0.
  lv_top  = io_tech_request_context->get_top( ).
  lv_skip = io_tech_request_context->get_skip( ).
  lv_has_inlinecount = io_tech_request_context->has_
inlinecount( ).
  IF ( lv_top IS NOT INITIAL ) AND
     ( lv_has_inlinecount EQ abap_false ).
    lv_maxrows-bapimaxrow = lv_top + lv_skip.
  ENDIF.

  CALL FUNCTION 'BAPI_EPM_PRODUCT_GET_LIST'
    EXPORTING
      max_rows                  = lv_maxrows
    TABLES
      headerdata                = lt_headerdata
      selparamproductid         = lt_selparamproductid
*     SELPARAMSUPPLIERNAMES     =
      selparamcategories        = lt_selparamcategories
*     RETURN                    =
      .

  IF lv_has_inlinecount EQ abap_true.
    es_response_context-inlinecount = lines( lt_headerdata ).
  ENDIF.

  lv_start = 1.
  IF lv_skip IS NOT INITIAL.
    lv_start = lv_skip + 1.
  ENDIF.
```

```
IF lv_top IS NOT INITIAL.
  lv_end = lv_top + lv_start - 1.
ELSE.
  lv_end = lines( lt_headerdata ).
ENDIF.

LOOP AT lt_headerdata INTO ls_headerdata
  FROM lv_start TO lv_end.
  ls_product-productid     = ls_headerdata-product_id.
  ls_product-category      = ls_headerdata-category.
  ls_product-name          = ls_headerdata-name.
  ls_product-supplierid    = ls_headerdata-supplier_id.
  ls_product-weightmeasure = ls_headerdata-weight_measure.
  ls_product-weightunit    = ls_headerdata-weight_unit.
  ls_product-pictureuri    = ls_headerdata-product_pic_url.

  IF ls_product-pictureuri IS NOT INITIAL.
    CALL METHOD lr_mr_api->get
      EXPORTING
        i_url              = ls_product-pictureuri
      IMPORTING
        e_mime_type        = ls_product-picturemimetype
      EXCEPTIONS
        parameter_missing  = 1
        error_occured      = 2
        not_found          = 3
        permission_failure = 4
        OTHERS             = 5.
  ENDIF.

  APPEND ls_product TO et_entityset.
ENDLOOP.

ENDMETHOD.
```

Listing 6.15 Product Set: Get_Entityset Method with Filters, Client-Side Paging, Inline Count, and MIME Type Determination

In this specific example, the `PictureURI` contains an absolute path to the MIME repository. This is a special feature of the EPM product RFC modules. Therefore, you can use the MIME repository API to determine the MIME type of the picture via the `GET` method.

As a result, you see the `PictureMIMEType` property filled for those entities in the collection that have a valid `PictureURI` (see Figure 6.82). In addition, you see that a `content` tag with the values `type` and `src` is rendered into the result. There is also a new link that points to the entity's raw data (/$value).

```
<entry>
    <id>http://SAPGateway:50000/sap/opu/odata/sap/ZEXAMPLE1_SRV/ProductSet('HT-1000')</id>
    <title type="text">ProductSet('HT-1000')</title>
    <updated>2015-12-10T14:22:00Z</updated>
    <category scheme="http://schemas.microsoft.com/ado/2007/08/dataservices/scheme" term="ZEXAMPLE1_SRV.Product"/>
    <link title="Product" href="ProductSet('HT-1000')" rel="edit"/>
    <link href="ProductSet('HT-1000')/$value" rel="edit-media" type="image/jpeg"/>
    <link title="ToSupplier" href="ProductSet('HT-1000')/ToSupplier" rel="http://schemas.microsoft.com/ado/2007/08/dataservices/
    <content type="image/jpeg" src="/sap/public/bc/NWDEMO_MODEL/IMAGES/HT-1000.jpg"/>
    <m:properties xmlns:m="http://schemas.microsoft.com/ado/2007/08/dataservices/metadata" xmlns:d="http://schemas.microsof
        <d:ProductID>HT-1000</d:ProductID>
        <d:Category>Notebooks</d:Category>
        <d:Name>Notebook Basic 15</d:Name>
        <d:SupplierID>0100000000</d:SupplierID>
        <d:WeightMeasure>4.200</d:WeightMeasure>
        <d:WeightUnit>KG</d:WeightUnit>
        <d:PictureURI>/sap/public/bc/NWDEMO_MODEL/IMAGES/HT-1000.jpg</d:PictureURI>
        <d:PictureMIMEType>image/jpeg</d:PictureMIMEType>
    </m:properties>
</entry>
```

Figure 6.82 Entity with Media Resource Information

Be sure to also adjust the product Get_Entity method (PRODUCTSET_GET_ENTITY) of the DPC extension class with the same logic to also determine the PictureMIMEType property. This ensures that Get_Entity and Get_EntitySet provide the same properties. The final coding is shown in Listing 6.16.

```
METHOD productset_get_entity.

    DATA: ls_entity      LIKE er_entity,
          ls_product_id  TYPE bapi_epm_product_id,
          ls_headerdata  TYPE bapi_epm_product_header.

    DATA: lr_mr_api TYPE REF TO if_mr_api.

    lr_mr_api = cl_mime_repository_api=>if_mr_api~get_api( ).

    io_tech_request_context->get_converted_keys(
      IMPORTING
        es_key_values = ls_entity ).

    ls_product_id-product_id = ls_entity-productid.

    CALL FUNCTION 'BAPI_EPM_PRODUCT_GET_DETAIL'
      EXPORTING
        product_id                = ls_product_id
      IMPORTING
        headerdata                = ls_headerdata
*     TABLES
*       CONVERSION_FACTORS        =
```

```
*      RETURN                  =
              .
   er_entity-productid      = ls_headerdata-product_id.
   er_entity-category       = ls_headerdata-category.
   er_entity-name           = ls_headerdata-name.
   er_entity-supplierid     = ls_headerdata-supplier_id.
   er_entity-weightmeasure  = ls_headerdata-weight_measure.
   er_entity-weightunit     = ls_headerdata-weight_unit.
   er_entity-pictureuri     = ls_headerdata-product_pic_url.

   IF er_entity-pictureuri IS NOT INITIAL.
     CALL METHOD lr_mr_api->get
       EXPORTING
         i_url                = er_entity-pictureuri
       IMPORTING
         e_mime_type          = er_entity-picturemimetype
       EXCEPTIONS
         parameter_missing  = 1
         error_occured      = 2
         not_found          = 3
         permission_failure = 4
         OTHERS             = 5.
   ENDIF.

ENDMETHOD.
```

Listing 6.16 Product Set: Get_Entity Method with MIME Type Determination

The `content-src` tag already provides an absolute path to the picture **Absolute path** itself. A consumer can call this one to retrieve the media resource. But in this example, you want to provide the raw data of the entity that is retrieved when the `/$value` option is used.

For this, you have to implement (redefine) the `/IWBEP/IF_MGW_APPL_SRV_RUNTIME~GET_STREAM` method in the DPC extension class. Provide the coding shown in Listing 6.17.

```
METHOD /iwbep/if_mgw_appl_srv_runtime~get_stream.

   DATA: lv_entityset_name TYPE /iwbep/mgw_tech_name,
         ls_product        TYPE zcl_zexample1_mpc=>ts_product,
         lr_mr_api         TYPE REF TO if_mr_api,
         ls_stream         TYPE ty_s_media_resource.

   lv_entityset_name = io_tech_request_context->get_entity_set_
name( ).
```

```
CASE lv_entityset_name.
  WHEN 'ProductSet'.
    CALL METHOD productset_get_entity
      EXPORTING
        iv_entity_name          = iv_entity_name
        iv_entity_set_name      = iv_entity_set_name
        iv_source_name          = iv_source_name
        it_key_tab              = it_key_tab
        io_tech_request_context = io_tech_request_context
        it_navigation_path      = it_navigation_path
      IMPORTING
        er_entity               = ls_product.

    IF NOT ls_product-pictureuri IS INITIAL.
      lr_mr_api = cl_mime_repository_api=>if_mr_api~get_
api( ).
      CALL METHOD lr_mr_api->get
        EXPORTING
          i_url                 = ls_product-pictureuri
        IMPORTING
          e_content             = ls_stream-value
          e_mime_type           = ls_stream-mime_type
        EXCEPTIONS
          parameter_missing     = 1
          error_occured         = 2
          not_found             = 3
          permission_failure    = 4
          OTHERS                = 5.

      copy_data_to_ref(
        EXPORTING
          is_data = ls_stream
        CHANGING
          cr_data = er_stream ).
    ENDIF.

  WHEN OTHERS.
    CALL METHOD super->/iwbep/if_mgw_appl_srv_runtime~get_
stream
      EXPORTING
        iv_entity_name          = iv_entity_name
        iv_entity_set_name      = iv_entity_set_name
        iv_source_name          = iv_source_name
        it_key_tab              = it_key_tab
        it_navigation_path      = it_navigation_path
        io_tech_request_context = io_tech_request_context
      IMPORTING
        er_stream               = er_stream
        es_response_context     = es_response_context.
```

```
ENDCASE.

ENDMETHOD.
```
Listing 6.17 Service Get-Stream Method

The coding first checks if the current entity set to be processed is a product (similar to the function import, there is no individual method generated, which is why these methods typically start with a case structure).

Next you execute the product `Get_Entity` method to fetch the product details. Because you've implemented the handling for the `PictureURI` property before, the `ls_product-pictureuri` field now contains the value that you need to determine the stream—at least for those products that have a URI. For this, you again use the MIME repository API `GET` method. It provides the actual content and the MIME type. Both need to be put into a specific structure of type `ty_s_media_resource`. At the end, you use the already known `copy_data_to_ref` method to copy the structure into a generic data container.

Execute method

After activating the DPC extension class, you can run the following URI in the SAP Gateway client:

/sap/opu/odata/sap/ZEXAMPLE1_SRV/ProductSet('HT-1000')/$value

As a result, you get the picture of the HT-1000 product (see Figure 6.83).

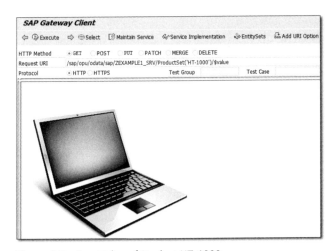

Figure 6.83 Raw Value of Product HT-1000

6.5.8 Expand/Self-Expand

The $expand query option is very powerful and allows you to provide multiple entities and/or entity sets in one single service call, instead of performing several calls subsequently.

Handled by
SAP Gateway
framework
The $expand takes place along the defined navigation properties. The SAP Gateway framework handles this by calling the respective Get_ Entity and/or Get_EntitySet methods of the related DPC and putting the result together into a nested table or structure. The SAP Gateway framework knows the dependencies (associations) between each entity type as defined in the metadata and thus knows which methods to call and how to put the result together.

The only disadvantage you have when letting the SAP Gateway framework do the job is that certain RFCs might be unnecessarily called multiple times. This is because the framework knows the technical dependencies but not the business context of the data handled and thus can't know that a specific RFC might be able to provide the data of the entire tree in one call. To avoid this, you can redefine the DPC framework GET_EXPANDED_ENTITY method (/IWBEP/IF_MGW_APPL_SRV_ RUNTIME interface) or the GET_EXPANDED_ENTITYSET method.

In this example, a navigation property has been defined between the product and the supplier. Instead of performing multiple service calls to first fetch the product and then fetch the supplier, you can use the $expand query option to provide both with a single service call. For this, you can, for instance, use the following URI in the SAP Gateway client to retrieve the details of the HT-1000 product along with the supplier information:

/sap/opu/odata/sap/ZEXAMPLE1_SRV/ProductSet('HT-1000')?
$expand=ToSupplier

In the response, you see that the supplier is provided with an m:inline tag (see Figure 6.84).

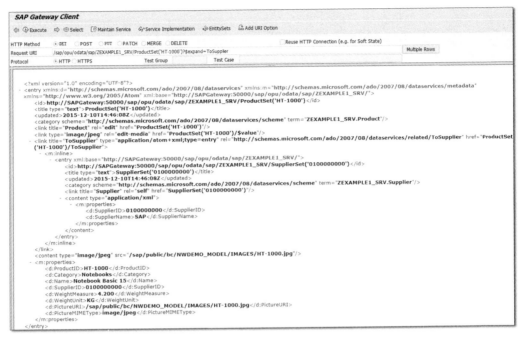

Figure 6.84 Product Details with $expand to Supplier

To demonstrate the redefinition of the GetExpandedEntity method, you first need to enhance the data model. Add another entity type with the name ProductConvFactor to the model. Its properties are shown in Figure 6.85.

Enhance data model

Properties											
Name	Key	Edm Core Type	Prec.	Scale	Max	Unit Property Name	Crea	Upd	Sort	Null	Filt.	Label
ProductID	✓	Edm.String	0	0	10		✓	☐	☐	☐	✓	Product Identifier
SourceUnit	✓	Edm.String	0	0	3		✓	☐	☐	☐		Source Unit
TargetUnit	✓	Edm.String	0	0	3		✓	☐	☐	☐		Target Unit
Numerator	☐	Edm.Int32	0	0	0		✓	☐	☐	☐		Numerator
Denominator	☐	Edm.Int32	0	0	0		✓	☐	☐	☐		Denominator

Figure 6.85 Properties of the ProductConvFactor Entity Type

Create an entity set with the name ProductConvFactorSet that uses the new entity type. Create an association with the NAME ASSOC_PRODUCT_PRODCONVFACTOR that defines a 1:M relationship between the PRODUCT and the PRODUCTCONVFACTOR entity types (see Figure 6.86).

Associations					
Name	E..	Principal Entity	Principal Entity Cardinality	Dependent Entity	Dependent Entity Cardinality
Assoc_Product_Supplier		Product	M	Supplier	1
Assoc_Product_ProdConvFactor		Product	1	ProductConvFactor	M

Figure 6.86 New Association Assoc_Product_ProductConvFactor

Double-click on REFERENTIAL CONSTRAINTS , and add a new entry for the PRODUCTID (see Figure 6.87). Note that the read-only fields are filled as soon as you enter data into the other fields and press ⌑Enter⌑.

Referential Constraints			
Principal Entity	Principal Key	Dependent Entity	Dependent Property
Product	ProductID	ProductConvFactor	ProductID

Figure 6.87 Referential Constraint for ProductID

Create navigation property Create a navigation property for the product entity type with the name TOCONVFACTORS that uses the newly created association (see Figure 6.88).

Navigation Properties		
Name	Relationship Name	ABAP Field Name
ToSupplier	Assoc_Product_Supplier	TOSUPPLIER
ToConvFactors	Assoc_Product_ProdConvFactor	TOCONVFACTORS

Figure 6.88 ToConvFactors Navigation Property

Generate the project to update the MPCs and the DPCs. Because you've added a new entity set to the model, there are five new methods (CRUD-Q) generated into the DPC base class, which are inherited to the extension class.

Redefine the conversion factor `Get_EntitySet` method `PRODUCTCONVFAC-TO_GET_ENTITYSET` in the DPC extension class, and provide the coding shown in Listing 6.18.

```
METHOD productconvfacto_get_entityset.

   DATA: lv_source_entity_set_name TYPE /iwbep/mgw_tech_name,
         ls_product                TYPE zcl_zexample1_mpc=>ts_
product,
         ls_product_id             TYPE bapi_epm_product_id,
         ls_conversion_factors     TYPE bapi_epm_product_conv_
factors,
```

```
        lt_conversion_factors        TYPE STANDARD TABLE OF bapi_
epm_product_conv_factors,
        ls_conv_factor               LIKE LINE OF et_entityset,
        lt_
return                   TYPE STANDARD TABLE OF bapiret2.

  lv_source_entity_set_name = io_tech_request_context->get_
source_entity_set_name( ).

* Is this a navigation from the ProductSet?
  IF lv_source_entity_set_name EQ 'ProductSet'.
    io_tech_request_context->get_converted_source_keys(
      IMPORTING
        es_key_values = ls_product ).

    ls_product_id-product_id = ls_product-productid.

    CALL FUNCTION 'BAPI_EPM_PRODUCT_GET_DETAIL'
      EXPORTING
        product_id               = ls_product_id
*       IMPORTING
*         HEADERDATA             =
      TABLES
        conversion_factors       = lt_conversion_factors
        return                   = lt_return.

    IF lt_return IS NOT INITIAL.
      mo_context->get_message_container( )->add_messages_from_
bapi(
        it_bapi_messages         = lt_return
        iv_determine_leading_msg = /iwbep/if_message_
container=>gcs_leading_msg_search_option-first ).

      RAISE EXCEPTION TYPE /iwbep/cx_mgw_busi_exception
        EXPORTING
          textid                = /iwbep/cx_mgw_busi_
exception=>business_error
          message_container = mo_context->get_message_
container( ).
    ENDIF.

    LOOP AT lt_conversion_factors INTO ls_conversion_factors.
      ls_conv_factor-productid   = ls_conversion_factors-
product_id.
      ls_conv_factor-sourceunit  = ls_conversion_factors-
source_unit.
      ls_conv_factor-targetunit  = ls_conversion_factors-
target_unit.
      ls_conv_factor-numerator   = ls_conversion_factors-
```

```
numerator.
      ls_conv_factor-denominator = ls_conversion_factors-
denominator.
      APPEND ls_conv_factor TO et_entityset.
    ENDLOOP.

  ELSE.
    CALL METHOD super->productconvfacto_get_entityset
      EXPORTING
        iv_entity_name          = iv_entity_name
        iv_entity_set_name      = iv_entity_set_name
        iv_source_name          = iv_source_name
        it_filter_select_options = it_filter_select_options
        is_paging               = is_paging
        it_key_tab              = it_key_tab
        it_navigation_path      = it_navigation_path
        it_order                = it_order
        iv_filter_string        = iv_filter_string
        iv_search_string        = iv_search_string
        io_tech_request_context = io_tech_request_context
      IMPORTING
        et_entityset            = et_entityset
        es_response_context     = es_response_context.
  ENDIF.

ENDMETHOD.
```

Listing 6.18 Product Conversion Factors Set: Get_Entityset Method

Activate DPC
extension class

Activate the DPC extension class. Now you can execute the following URI to list all conversion factors of the HT-1000 product:

*/sap/opu/odata/sap/ZEXAMPLE1_SRV/ProductSet('HT-1010')/
ToConvFactors*

The corresponding expand statement to fetch the product together with the conversion factors is the following:

*/sap/opu/odata/sap/ZEXAMPLE1_SRV/ProductSet('HT-1010')?$expand=
ToConvFactors*

As you can see, this is pretty straightforward and works fine. The only problem is that the preceding $expand statement executes the BAPI_EPM_ PRODUCT_GET_DETAIL function module two times: first to fetch the product detail and second to fetch the list of conversion factors. In this little example, this might not be a problem, but in a real scenario accessing, for example, SAP CRM sales data over multiple entity types, that can have a significant performance impact.

Therefore, it's possible to redefine the GET_EXPANDED_ENTITY and/or GET_EXPANDED_ENTITYSET framework methods as already mentioned earlier. In these methods, you can expand the data yourself and return the result in a nested table or structure. This gives you full flexibility on which expands you want to handle yourself and which you want the framework to handle. You can also handle the $expand partially if you want.

Redefine framework methods

In the following example, you'll handle the $expand of the conversion factors, so navigate into the DPC extension class, and redefine the GET_ EXPANDED_ENTITY method of the /IWBEP/IF_MGW_APPL_SRV_RUNTIME interface. Provide the coding shown in Listing 6.19.

```
METHOD /iwbep/if_mgw_appl_srv_runtime~get_expanded_entity.

* Nested result type
  DATA: BEGIN OF ls_prod_convfactors.
          INCLUDE TYPE zcl_zexample1_mpc=>ts_product.
  DATA: toconvfactors TYPE STANDARD TABLE OF zcl_zexample1_
mpc=>ts_productconvfactor WITH DEFAULT KEY,
        END OF ls_prod_convfactors.

  DATA: ls_product      TYPE zcl_zexample1_mpc=>ts_product,
        ls_product_id   TYPE bapi_epm_product_id,
        ls_headerdata   TYPE bapi_epm_product_header,
        ls_conv_factors TYPE bapi_epm_product_conv_factors,
        lt_conv_factors TYPE TABLE OF bapi_epm_product_conv_
factors,
        ls_conv_factor  TYPE zcl_zexample1_mpc=>ts_
productconvfactor,
        lt_return       TYPE STANDARD TABLE OF bapiret2.

  DATA: lv_entityset_name           TYPE /iwbep/mgw_tech_
name,
        lv_compare_result_prod_convfac TYPE io_expand->ty_e_
compare_result,
        ls_expanded_clause          LIKE LINE OF et_
expanded_tech_clauses.

  DATA: lr_mr_api TYPE REF TO if_mr_api.
```

```abap
lr_mr_api = cl_mime_repository_api=>if_mr_api~get_api( ).

lv_entityset_name              = io_tech_request_context-
>get_entity_set_name( ).
lv_compare_result_prod_convfac = io_expand->compare_to_tech_
names( 'TOCONVFACTORS' ).

* Expand on Product / Conversion Factors?
  IF lv_entityset_name EQ 'ProductSet' AND
    ( lv_compare_result_prod_convfac EQ io_expand->gcs_compare_
result-match_subset OR
      lv_compare_result_prod_convfac EQ io_expand->gcs_compare_
result-match_equals ).

    io_tech_request_context->get_converted_keys(
      IMPORTING
        es_key_values = ls_product ).

    ls_product_id-product_id = ls_product-productid.

    CALL FUNCTION 'BAPI_EPM_PRODUCT_GET_DETAIL'
      EXPORTING
        product_id        = ls_product_id
      IMPORTING
        headerdata        = ls_headerdata
      TABLES
        conversion_factors = lt_conv_factors
        return            = lt_return.

    IF lt_return IS NOT INITIAL.
      mo_context->get_message_container( )->add_messages_from_
bapi(
        it_bapi_messages       = lt_return
        iv_determine_leading_msg = /iwbep/if_message_
container=>gcs_leading_msg_search_option-first ).

      RAISE EXCEPTION TYPE /iwbep/cx_mgw_busi_exception
        EXPORTING
          textid            = /iwbep/cx_mgw_busi_
exception=>business_error
          message_container = mo_context->get_message_
container( ).
    ENDIF.

    ls_prod_convfactors-productid     = ls_headerdata-product_
id.
    ls_prod_convfactors-category      = ls_headerdata-category.
    ls_prod_convfactors-name          = ls_headerdata-name.
    ls_prod_convfactors-supplierid    = ls_headerdata-supplier_
```

```
id.
    ls_prod_convfactors-weightmeasure = ls_headerdata-weight_
measure.
    ls_prod_convfactors-weightunit    = ls_headerdata-weight_
unit.
    ls_prod_convfactors-pictureuri    = ls_headerdata-product_
pic_url.

    IF ls_prod_convfactors-pictureuri IS NOT INITIAL.
      CALL METHOD lr_mr_api->get
        EXPORTING
          i_url              = ls_prod_convfactors-pictureuri
        IMPORTING
          e_mime_type        = ls_prod_convfactors-
picturemimetype
        EXCEPTIONS
          parameter_missing  = 1
          error_occured      = 2
          not_found          = 3
          permission_failure = 4
          OTHERS             = 5.
    ENDIF.

    LOOP AT lt_conv_factors INTO ls_conv_factors.
      ls_conv_factor-productid   = ls_conv_factors-product_id.
      ls_conv_factor-sourceunit  = ls_conv_factors-source_unit.
      ls_conv_factor-targetunit  = ls_conv_factors-target_unit.
      ls_conv_factor-numerator   = ls_conv_factors-numerator.
      ls_conv_factor-denominator = ls_conv_factors-denominator.
      APPEND ls_conv_factor TO ls_prod_convfactors-
toconvfactors.
    ENDLOOP.

    copy_data_to_ref(
      EXPORTING
        is_data = ls_prod_convfactors
      CHANGING
        cr_data = er_entity ).

    ls_expanded_clause = 'TOCONVFACTORS'.
    APPEND ls_expanded_clause TO et_expanded_tech_clauses.

  ELSE.
    super->/iwbep/if_mgw_appl_srv_runtime~get_expanded_entity(
      EXPORTING
        iv_entity_name          = iv_entity_name
        iv_entity_set_name      = iv_entity_set_name
        iv_source_name          = iv_source_name
        io_expand               = io_expand
```

```
        it_key_tab                 = it_key_tab
        it_navigation_path         = it_navigation_path
        io_tech_request_context    = io_tech_request_context
    IMPORTING
        er_entity                  = er_entity
        et_expanded_clauses        = et_expanded_clauses
        et_expanded_tech_clauses   = et_expanded_tech_clauses ).
  ENDIF.

ENDMETHOD.
```

Listing 6.19 Service Get-Expanded-Entity Method for Conversion Factors Expansion

This coding appears a little lengthy but is actually not too complex. The data declaration part defines a nested structure that can hold the product as well as the list of conversion factors. The conversion factors go into a table field with the name `ToConvFactors`, which always has to be equal to the name of the defined navigation property. Then you need some tables/structures to call the RFC module as well as some fields for some framework data.

The `lv_compare_result_prod_convfac` field based on `io_expand->ty_e_compare_result` is very important because it will be used in the `io_expand->compare_to_tech_names` call to determine where you are in the expand tree. As this is a fairly small tree, the comparison will result in match-equals. Inside the `IF` statement, you determine the primary key of the product and call the `BAPI_EPM_PRODUCT_GET_DETAIL` function module only once—retrieving the product `HEADERDATA` along with the table of conversion factors in one shot.

Fill nested structure

Next you need to fill the nested structure that was defined at the beginning with the results of the function module call. The nested structure is copied to the data reference that you return. Lastly, you need to tell the framework that you've actually taken care of the `$expand` by adding a line to `et_expanded_tech_clauses` specifying the navigation property (`ToConvFactors`) that you've handled.

The `else` branch is for all other expands that you want the SAP Gateway framework to handle generically.

6.5.9   Deep Insert

A deep insert is the inversion of $expand. Instead of receiving a nested structure of entries and/or collections, a consumer is able to POST a nested structure to the SAP Gateway server. By doing this, you can, for example, create a sales order header together with the collection of line items with a single service call.

Inversion of $expand

In this example, you'll create a product together with the list of conversion factors by using a deep insert. A product is a single entry, whereas the list of conversion factors is a collection.

Similar to $expand, you need to implement the handling yourself in the DPC extension class. The deep insert is handled by the CREATE_DEEP_ENTITY method of the /IWBEP/IF_MGW_APPL_SRV_RUNTIME framework interface.

If you've followed the media resource implementation steps before, switch the entity type back from a media entity type to a regular entity type. Otherwise, the CREATE_STREAM method needs to handle the deep insert (which of course also works, but isn't the point of this discussion). The easiest way to switch the entity type back to a regular one is to comment the line lo_entity_type->set_is_media( ) in the MPC extension class. After you've changed the MPC extension class, be sure to activate it.

In the DPC extension class, redefine the CREATE_DEEP_ENTITY method of the /IWBEP/IF_MGW_APPL_SRV_RUNTIME interface, and provide the coding shown in Listing 6.20.

```
METHOD /iwbep/if_mgw_appl_srv_runtime~create_deep_entity.

* Nested input/result type
  DATA: BEGIN OF ls_prod_convfactors.
          INCLUDE TYPE zcl_zexample1_mpc=>ts_product.
  DATA: toconvfactors TYPE STANDARD TABLE OF zcl_zexample1_
mpc=>ts_productconvfactor WITH DEFAULT KEY,
        END OF ls_prod_convfactors.

  DATA: lv_entityset_name TYPE /iwbep/mgw_tech_name,
        ls_headerdata     TYPE bapi_epm_product_header,
        ls_conv_factors   TYPE bapi_epm_product_conv_factors,
```

```
        lt_conv_factors    TYPE TABLE OF bapi_epm_product_conv_
factors,
        ls_conv_factor     TYPE zcl_zexample1_mpc=>ts_
productconvfactor,
        lt_return          TYPE TABLE OF bapiret2.

  lv_entityset_name = io_tech_request_context->get_entity_set_
name( ).

  CASE lv_entityset_name.
    WHEN 'ProductSet'.
      io_data_provider->read_entry_data( IMPORTING es_
data = ls_prod_convfactors ).

      ls_headerdata-product_id     = ls_prod_convfactors-
productid.
      ls_headerdata-category       = ls_prod_convfactors-
category.
      ls_headerdata-name           = ls_prod_convfactors-name.
      ls_headerdata-supplier_id    = ls_prod_convfactors-
supplierid.
      ls_headerdata-measure_unit   = 'EA'.
      ls_headerdata-currency_code  = 'EUR'.
      ls_headerdata-tax_tarif_code = '1'.
      ls_headerdata-type_code      = 'PR'.
      ls_headerdata-weight_measure = ls_prod_convfactors-
weightmeasure.
      ls_headerdata-weight_unit    = ls_prod_convfactors-
weightunit.
      ls_headerdata-product_pic_url = ls_prod_convfactors-
pictureuri.

      LOOP AT ls_prod_convfactors-toconvfactors INTO ls_conv_
factor.
        ls_conv_factors-product_id  = ls_conv_factor-productid.
        ls_conv_factors-source_unit = ls_conv_factor-
sourceunit.
        ls_conv_factors-target_unit = ls_conv_factor-
targetunit.
        ls_conv_factors-numerator   = ls_conv_factor-numerator.
        ls_conv_factors-denominator = ls_conv_factor-
denominator.
      APPEND ls_conv_factors TO lt_conv_factors.
      ENDLOOP.

      CALL FUNCTION 'BAPI_EPM_PRODUCT_CREATE'
        EXPORTING
          headerdata          = ls_headerdata
        TABLES
```

```
                conversion_factors = lt_conv_factors
                return             = lt_return.

        IF lt_return IS NOT INITIAL.
            mo_context->get_message_container( )->add_messages_
from_bapi(
                it_bapi_messages           = lt_return
                iv_determine_leading_msg = /iwbep/if_message_
container=>gcs_leading_msg_search_option-first ).

            RAISE EXCEPTION TYPE /iwbep/cx_mgw_busi_exception
                EXPORTING
                    textid             = /iwbep/cx_mgw_busi_
exception=>business_error
                    message_container = mo_context->get_message_
container( ).
        ENDIF.

        copy_data_to_ref(
            EXPORTING
                is_data = ls_prod_convfactors
            CHANGING
                cr_data = er_deep_entity ).

    WHEN OTHERS.
        CALL METHOD super->/iwbep/if_mgw_appl_srv_runtime~create_
deep_entity
            EXPORTING
                iv_entity_name             = iv_entity_name
                iv_entity_set_name         = iv_entity_set_name
                iv_source_name             = iv_source_name
                io_data_provider           = io_data_provider
                it_key_tab                 = it_key_tab
                it_navigation_path         = it_navigation_path
                io_expand                  = io_expand
                io_tech_request_context   = io_tech_request_context
            IMPORTING
                er_deep_entity             = er_deep_entity.
    ENDCASE.

ENDMETHOD.
```

Listing 6.20 Service Create-Deep-Entity Method for Product and Conversion Factors Creation with Error Handling

First, you again define a complex data type `ls_prod_convfactors` that can carry the nested data retrieved with the POST call. In the case structure, make sure that this is a POST on the ProductSet and not on any

Define complex data type

337

other collection. The `others` branch will actually end up in a technical exception because a deep insert isn't generically handled by the framework and thus has to be handled via the redefined `CREATE_DEEP_ENTITY` method.

Besides the product properties, the `ls_prod_convfactors` nested structure has a table field (`toconvfactors`) that contains the table of conversion factors. All of these properties are processed and put into the respective structure/table data fields to be able to call the `BAPI_EPM_PRO-DUCT_CREATE` function module. The error handling is done by checking whether the return table is empty. If the return table has entries, the log is saved, and a business exception is thrown.

Finally, the nested structure is copied to a data reference that hands it back to the framework via the `er_deep_entity` parameter. This is necessary because a `POST` requires the return of the entity created to at least inform the consumer about the primary key of the created entity (and maybe some calculated fields). In this example, there is neither an internal number range that defines the next primary key nor an entity property that is defaulted. Therefore, you can return the same nested structure that you've received (if the `CREATE` BAPI was processed successfully).

Via the SAP Gateway client, you can easily test the deep insert of your service. It's recommended to first perform an `$expand` on any source entity that you want to use as a pattern and to click the USE AS REQUEST button to copy the response body over to the request body.

Adjust product ID   Next, adjust the data because the product ID has to be unique. Also adjust the product ID for the conversion factors. Then you need to change the HTTP method to `POST` and change the URI to `ProductSet`. Finally, you can execute the call; if everything is successful, you get a nested structure of the created data back (see Figure 6.89). As verification, you can perform a `GET` on the newly created product with its conversion factors to see if the nested data was persisted successfully.

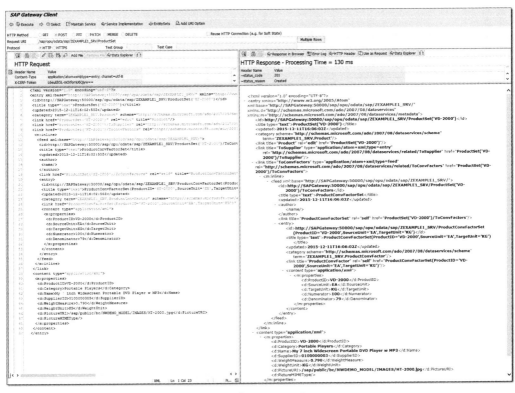

Figure 6.89 Successful Deep Insert of Product and Conversion Factors

6.5.10 Batch

An OData batch request is typically used whenever a consumer wants to perform multiple independent HTTP calls and wants to avoid multiple server roundtrips. A common example is the fetching of customizing data at application start, where you typically request the data of several independent entity sets.

Batch processing just batches up several independent OData service calls into a single (big) call. Those calls can combine read and write accesses. For write access, you need to define related `change-sets` in the request body to define logical units of work (LUWs) for everything that has to be executed either entirely or rolled back in case of any problem.

Combine read and write access

> **Note**
>
> Batch processing can't be used if the individual calls are dependent on each other (e.g., one call requires the results of a preceding call).
>
> As of SAP_GWFND 7.40 SP 13 and SAP Gateway 2.0 SP 12, a new feature called Content ID Referencing was introduced that allows you to perform calls that depend on each other.

A batch call is always performed via the HTTP POST method. The URI for all $batch requests of an OData service is always the same; for example, the URI for this example in the SAP Gateway client looks like */sap/opu/odata/sap/ZEXAMPLE1_SRV/$batch*.

The individual steps to be executed need to be put into the request body. That has the positive side effect that the URIs are also secured if you use the HTTPS protocol.

The OData batch request is a multipart MIME v1.0 message in which each part may have a different content type. The easiest meaningful batch is probably the execution of two get_entity calls. Such a request body looks like the code shown in Listing 6.21.

```
--batch_zmybatch
Content-Type: application/http
Content-Transfer-Encoding: binary

GET ProductSet('HT-1000') HTTP/1.1


--batch_zmybatch
Content-Type: application/http
Content-Transfer-Encoding: binary

GET ProductSet('HT-1001') HTTP/1.1


--batch_zmybatch--
```
Listing 6.21 Sample $batch Request Body

An OData batch request also requires setting the Content-Type request header according to the boundary defined. In the preceding case, the Content-Type needs to be multipart/mixed;boundary=batch_zmybatch.

If you execute this batch request via the SAP Gateway client, you get the details of the HT-1000 and HT-1001 products (see Figure 6.90).

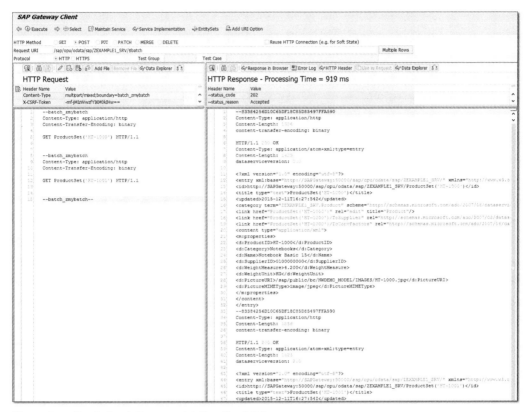

Figure 6.90 Simple Batch Request with Two Read Calls

Note that the `batch_zmybatch` boundary marker is set in the request header, as well as in front of each retrieve operation preceding with `--` in the request body. The `Content-Type` on the header level is set to `multipart/mixed`. Each operation needs to define its `Content-Type`, which in this example is `application/http`.

Boundary marker

Be sure to provide at least two blank lines between each batch operation. Otherwise, you get a malformed service request error. Don't forget to conclude the HTTP request body with the closing boundary marker with preceding double hyphens (`--`) as well as subsequent double hyphens (`--`). The batch operation itself (`GET ProductSet('HT-1000')`

341

HTTP/1.1) needs to define the HTTP operation (in this case, GET) as well as the resource and additional parameter, as in the URI.

Because this simple batch example only consists of retrieve operations, a change-set isn't necessary. Whenever a batch request contains any write operations, you have to provide a change-set.

You can use this, for example, in a regular UPDATE operation that—according to the OData standard—doesn't return the entry resource updated. But you can combine an UPDATE operation together with a GET operation to fetch the details. A corresponding $batch request can look like the code in Listing 6.22.

```
--batch_zmybatch
Content-Type: multipart/mixed; boundary=changeset_zmychangeset

--changeset_zmychangeset
Content-Type: application/http
Content-Transfer-Encoding: binary

PUT ProductSet('HT-1001') HTTP/1.1
Content-Type: application/atom+xml

<atom:entry xmlns:atom="http://www.w3.org/2005/Atom">
<atom:content type="application/xml">
<m:properties xmlns:m="http://schemas.microsoft.com/ado/2007/
08/dataservices/metadata" xmlns:d="http://
schemas.microsoft.com/ado/2007/08/dataservices">
  <d:ProductID>HT-1001</d:ProductID>
  <d:Category>Notebooks</d:Category>
  <d:Name>Notebook Basic 42</d:Name>
  <d:SupplierID>0100000001</d:SupplierID>
  <d:WeightMeasure>4.500</d:WeightMeasure>
  <d:WeightUnit>KG</d:WeightUnit>
  <d:PictureURI>/sap/public/bc/NWDEMO_MODEL/IMAGES/HT-
1001.jpg</d:PictureURI>
  <d:PictureMIMEType>image/jpeg</d:PictureMIMEType>
</m:properties>
</atom:content>
</atom:entry>

--changeset_zmychangeset--


--batch_zmybatch
Content-Type: application/http
```

```
Content-Transfer-Encoding: binary

GET ProductSet('HT-1001') HTTP/1.1


--batch_zmybatch--
```
Listing 6.22 Example Batch Call with Write Operation

This OData batch request first updates the HT-1001 product and then performs a GET request to read the updated entry resource. If there are multiple write operations (CREATE, UPDATE, DELETE) contained in a single change-set, no operation may perform a commit-work because otherwise the all-or-nothing paradigm can't be met. The framework checks this and triggers a short dump if this rule is violated. This check is deactivated if the change-set only consists of a single write operation.

The SAP Gateway framework executes a commit-work at the end of each change-set. At the beginning of each change-set, the SAP Gateway framework executes the CHANGESET_BEGIN method (/IWBEP/IF_MGW_APPL_SRV_RUNTIME interface). This method can be redefined if you want to implement your own handling. It has to be redefined if the change-set contains changes to more than one entity type.

Commit-work

In the change-set-begin method, you can, for example, set a member variable to indicate that a change-set processing is taking place. This information can be used inside an UPDATE method to only store changes in memory or to avoid a commit-work.

The change-set-begin method can also be used to verify if the change-set contains unsupported combinations of entity types. The method has input table it_operation_info, which lists all entity types contained in the current change-set. This allows you to react on combinations you don't want to support by throwing the corresponding exception.

At the end of each change-set, the CHANGESET_END method (same interface) is called. You can redefine it to perform your own change-set end handling where you reset the member variable and perform your database UPDATE and/or commit-work.

6.6   Summary

This chapter provided an introduction to the OData service development using the Service Builder toolset. Following a step-by-step approach, we've modeled, implemented, and executed the OData service.

The model definition was done in a declarative way by creating entity types, entity sets, properties, associations, referential constraints, navigation properties, and function imports. We also looked at the options to import a model definition from an EDMX file, from a DDIC structure/table, and from a BOR/RFC interface.

The service implementation part was entirely done by redefining/overwriting the related methods in the DPC extension class using ABAP. This method works pretty well, although it might sometimes appear to be a bit lengthy. That's why the Service Builder has the capability to generate the service implementation of the CRUD-Q methods by mapping the respective method to a corresponding data source (e.g., RFC module). This will be explained further in the next chapter.

Service generation is another way to create OData services using SAP Gateway. This chapter explains the end-to-end development tools and development cycle for this process.

7   Service Generation

In the previous chapter, we taught you how to develop service implementation logic with custom ABAP code. However, it's also possible to leverage existing interfaces and business objects in the SAP Business Suite to generate OData services without the need to write a single line of code. This process is called *service generation*.

This chapter explains the generation of OData services using the SAP Gateway Service Builder. The generation of OData services from existing interfaces and business objects—such as remote function calls (RFCs), Business Application Programming Interfaces (BAPIs) defined as methods of SAP business object types in the Business Object Repository (BOR), ABAP Core Data Services (CDS) views, Generic Interaction Layer (GenIL) objects, Service Provider Interface building blocks, SAP Business Warehouse (BW) Easy Queries, and so on—takes place by translating existing, predefined interfaces and SAP business objects into more compact and consumable new OData services.

We discuss four use cases in this chapter:

▶ **Generation via RFC/BOR Generator**
The first and most widely used use case is the RFC/BOR Generator. Service generation using the RFC/BOR Generator doesn't require writing code—at least for the basic features. Like service development, service generation using the RFC/BOR Generator takes place in the three main phases—data model definition phase, service implementation phase, and service maintenance phase—as depicted again in Figure 7.1). However, in contrast to service development, where

Service generation
use cases

service implementation is performed via a code-based implementation, the developer has to map the interface of the RFC/BOR interface to the OData service. Although this process step requires detailed knowledge of the underlying RFC function modules, ABAP knowledge is only necessary to the extent required to understand the corresponding data types. (The exception to this rule is when there is no appropriate function module available, and thus it needs to be created, which is also explained and demonstrated in this chapter.)

▶ **Generation via Search Help**

The second use case uses search helps defined in the ABAP Data Dictionary (DDIC). Search helps are used frequently in any SAP Business Suite system in classic Web Dynpro screens that allow the user to select data in a user-friendly way. Because search helps are very helpful in SAPUI5-based applications as well, SAP provided a way to leverage these valuable assets as OData services without the need to write a single line of code.

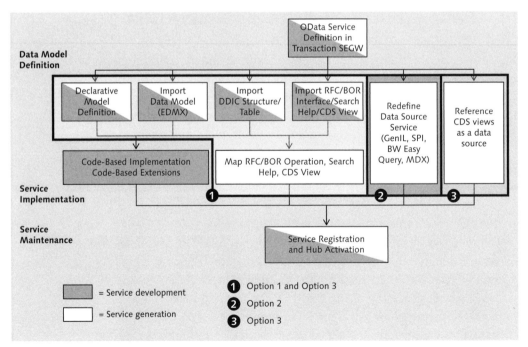

Figure 7.1 Service Generation in SAP Gateway Using the Service Builder (Transaction SEGW)

▸ **Generation via CDS views**
The third use case is to generate an OData service from ABAP CDS views that are delivered, for example, by SAP with SAP S/4HANA or can be built as of SAP NetWeaver 7.40 SP 5. This use case has two options for generating OData services:

  ▹ *Modeled data sources (MDS):* This option came with SAP NetWeaver 7.40 and works similarly to the RFC/BOR Generator or the Search Help generator mentioned previously. As a developer, you must map a business object (an ABAP CDS view) to an entity set that has been created by a DDIC import.

  ▹ *Referenced data sources (RDS):* The second option is called RDS. From the developer's point of view, this is similar to the redefinition process mentioned in the next list item. You only have to select the business object entities and associations. Here, the service implementation is handled via the framework in a generic way.

In the end, both approaches perform an implementation of the query and read method of an OData service. If a CUD method is implemented, this must be done by using either code-based implementation or the implementation of an appropriate Business Object Processing Framework (BOPF) object.

▸ **Generation via redefinition**
The fourth use case is to generate a service based on another SAP business object using redefinition. Compared to using the RFC/BOR Generator, this option is a much easier approach. This involves redefining an existing business object based on GenIL objects, Service Provider Interface objects, and SAP BW Easy Queries or multidimensional expressions (MDX) queries. In contrast to the RFC/BOR Generator, the mapping process in these integration scenarios is more straightforward because the business objects in question are already similar to OData services. When using redefinition, the data model definitions of existing business object entities and methods are mapped to the entity types and sets of an OData service while the implementation is generated on the basis of mapped OData artifacts chosen by the developer.

This chapter includes detailed coverage of the technical basics of selected integration scenarios as well as best practices for efficient OData service generation. The goal is to enable you to generate services with the main development tool, the Service Builder. For this, we've provided examples that make use of the following:

1. RFC/BOR interface

2. Search Help

3. Mapping of CDS views and the RDS approach

4. Redefinition (of an SAP BW Easy Query and a Service Provider Interface building block)

7.1 Generation via RFC/BOR Interface

In Chapter 6, we introduced the process of data model definition by importing the OData model from an RFC/BOR interface. This approach is commonly used because most custom-built SAP Gateway OData services are based on remote function modules. In this section, we'll show you how to implement the service by simply mapping the interfaces of the RFC function modules to the operations of the OData service (as opposed to the code-based approach taken in Chapter 6).

RFC/BOR interface You'll start the service generation process by creating a new project, ZRFC1, in the Service Builder and defining a data model (Section 7.1.1). The model will consist of two entity types: `SalesOrderHeader` and `SalesOrderLineItem`. Both entity type definitions will be imported from the corresponding sample function modules that are part of the *SAP Enterprise Procurement Model (EPM)*. EPM is a test application that serves as a proxy for SAP's real-world SAP Business Suite applications.

Next, you'll define a navigation property between the order header and the line items to navigate from a header entry to its collection of line items. This also allows you to perform an `$expand` call to retrieve the header information along with the corresponding line items in one single service call. The model is depicted in Figure 7.2.

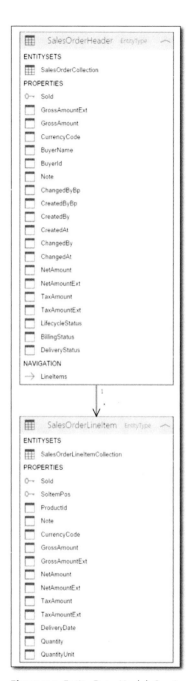

Figure 7.2 Entity Data Model: Service ZRFC1

> **Note**
>
> As we mentioned in Chapter 5, in real-world development scenarios, the sequence in which data model definition, service implementation, and service maintenance are performed will vary and not always follow the waterfall model shown earlier in Figure 7.1.

After the data model is defined, repository objects are generated, and the Service Builder registers the service in the backend (Section 7.1.2). In this step, the model provider class (MPC) is generated. A stub for the data provider class (DPC) is also generated with (empty) methods that have to be implemented by either code-based implementation (as described in Chapter 6) or by mapping (as described in this section). Because the basic service implementation (stub creation) has already been performed, you'll first continue with activating the service to test the service metadata document and the implementation of the different CREATE, READ, UPDATE, DELETE, and QUERY (CRUD-Q) methods (Section 7.1.4). This real-world service creation flow is depicted in Figure 7.3.

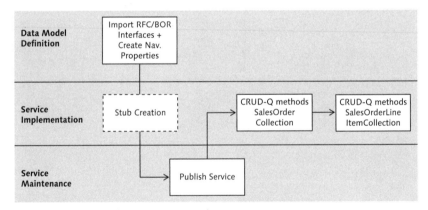

Figure 7.3 Real-World Service Creation Flow: RFC/BOR Generator

CRUD-Q operations
The final service implementation is described in Section 7.1.4 and Section 7.1.5. It's performed via the Service Builder by assigning the corresponding RFC function modules to the respective operation and by mapping the function module fields to the related entity set properties. This allows you to implement full CRUD-Q operations (CREATE, READ, UPDATE, DELETE, and QUERY) as well as navigation property support with-

out writing a single line of ABAP code—at least for the basic operations and as long as a corresponding RFC function module is available. In this example, you'll use a set of five EPM sales order function modules. You'll see that the CRUD-Q operations on the header level can be easily generated, whereas the operations on the item level need certain adjustments.

7.1.1   Data Model Definition

After creating the mentioned project, you first import the data model from the BAPI_EPM_SO_GET_LIST RFC module. This function module is used to retrieve the list of sales order headers. The interface also has an output table for the line items.

When defining a data model based on a function module, the interesting part of the function module is the interface; as such, you use the interface definition to derive the model definition for your entity types. The actual data provided by the function module comes into play when you do the service implementation.

Define a data model

In this new project, right-click on DATA MODEL and choose IMPORT • RFC/BOR INTERFACE. This opens the CREATE ENTITY TYPE FROM DATA SOURCE screen (see Figure 7.4).

Entity type: step 1

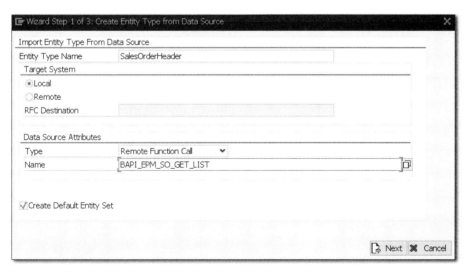

Figure 7.4 Step 1 of the Create Entity Type from Data Source Wizard

For ENTITY TYPE NAME, enter "SalesOrderHeader." Note that this name will only be considered if you select individual fields from the interface in the subsequent step.

For TARGET SYSTEM, use LOCAL to fetch the interface from the local system. It's also possible to provide an RFC DESTINATION to fetch the function module interface from a remote system.

DATA SOURCE ATTRIBUTES specify what data source you're looking for. TYPE can be BOR OBJECT or REMOTE FUNCTION CALL. Note that regular function modules (nonremote) aren't supported. Finally, you have to name the RFC function module from which to fetch the interface. In this case, enter "BAPI_EPM_SO_GET_LIST."

Leave the CREATE DEFAULT ENTITY SET checkbox checked, and choose NEXT.

Entity type: step 2   The wizard now reads the interface definition of the provided data source and shows the result on the second screen of the wizard (see Figure 7.5). On this screen, you select the attributes you want to create as properties in your entity type.

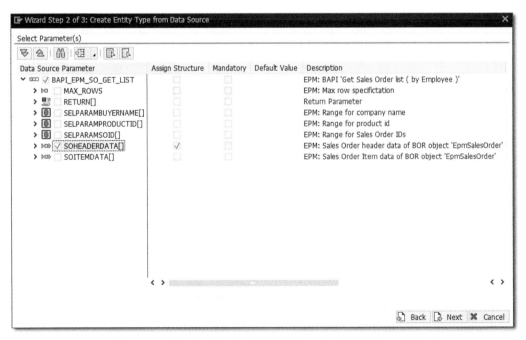

Figure 7.5 Step 2 of the Create Entity Type from Data Source Wizard

Start by selecting the properties for the sales order header entity type. Note that the RFC/BOR import wizard can be used to create multiple entity types and/or complex types in one go. But for the sake of simplicity, we'll call the wizard one by one for each entity type we want to create.

To create the entity type for the sales order header, the corresponding interface table is SOHEADERDATA. You can select the entire table by marking the checkbox next to SOHEADERDATA[] (see Figure 7.5). Although this is the easiest way, it has the minor disadvantage that the entity type name provided on the first page is ignored, and instead the entity type receives the name of the interface table (this is because you can select multiple tables to create multiple entity types in one go). Instead of selecting the entire SOHEADERDATA table, you can also select individual fields by expanding the tree.

When selecting the entire table, the corresponding Assign Structure checkbox is also selected. This is important because it will assign the underlying DDIC structure to the entity type that is being created.

Select the entire table, and choose Next. On the subsequent screen, mark the primary key fields of the entity type you want to create. (If you don't, you'll get an error after completing the wizard; a project check is automatically triggered right after the wizard execution, and an entity type without a primary key is considered an erroneous entity type.)

Entity type: step 3

In this example, mark SO_ID (sales order ID) as the primary key of the sales order header entity type (see Figure 7.6), and choose Finish.

If you've marked the entire table, you need to change the entity type name from Soheaderdata to SalesOrderHeader and the entity set name from SoheaderdataSet to SalesOrderHeaderSet. Also make sure that the entity type has the right ABAP structure assigned to it, that is, BAPI_EPM_SO_HEADER (see Figure 7.7). This is important because it ensures that the related entity properties and MPC type declarations are based on the correct DDIC object.

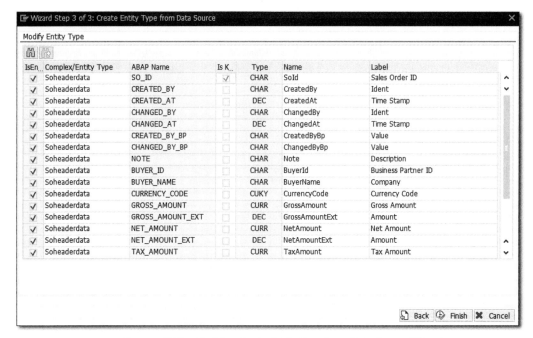

Figure 7.6 Step 3 of the Create Entity Type from Data Source Wizard

Figure 7.7 ABAP Structure Assignment to Entity Type

Now perform the same steps to create an entity type for the sales order line items. The name of the entity type is `SalesOrderLineItem`. It can be imported by using the same `BAPI_EPM_SO_GET_LIST` function module. The interface table is `SOITEMDATA`. The primary key consists of two fields: `SO_ID` and `SO_ITEM_POS`.

Setting SAP Annotations

Make sure to set the respective SAP annotations (creatable, updatable, etc.) for each property imported. It's strongly recommended to set at least the nullable annotation for each nonkey property that isn't mandatory; otherwise, this might lead to problems when executing the service, especially with date/time fields.

For both entity types, corresponding entity sets are generated. Both entity sets have to be renamed to get more meaningful names than the ones that have been derived from the name of the underlying DDIC structure (see Figure 7.8).

Entity sets

Figure 7.8 Entity Sets for Sales Order Header and Line Item Entity Types

The next step is to define an association with a referential constraint. This allows you to create a navigation property that can be used to fetch the line items related to a certain sales order header. The association can be created by navigating to the ASSOCIATION node under DATA MODEL in the project tree. It can also be created by right-clicking on DATA MODEL and selecting CREATE • ASSOCIATION. This opens the CREATE ASSOCIATION wizard that allows you to create an association together with the referential constraint as well as the navigation property.

Association and referential constraint

On the first screen of the CREATE ASSOCIATION wizard, you specify the name of the association and the entity types contained with their respective cardinality (see Figure 7.9). You can also select the CREATE RELATED NAVIGATION PROPERTY checkbox to create a corresponding navigation property. In this example, you're creating the navigation property TOLINEITEMS.

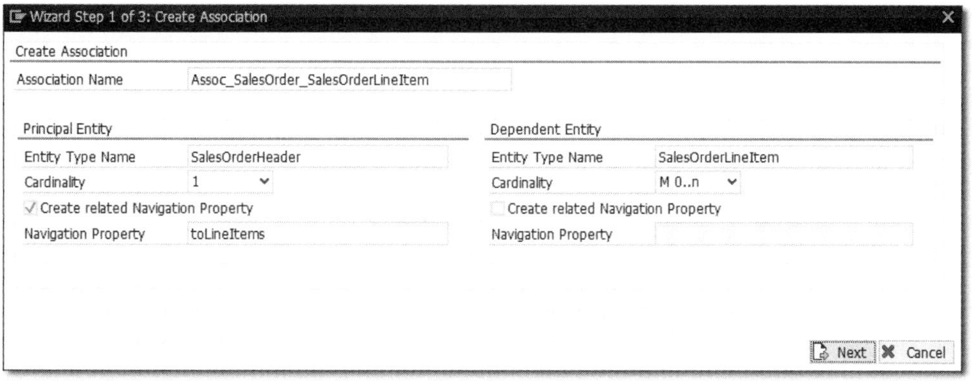

Figure 7.9 Step 1 of the Create Association Wizard

355

On the second screen, you specify the referential constraint by mapping the key fields of the principal entity type to the properties of the dependent entity. In this example, the Principal Entity type is the SalesOrderHeader, and the Principal Key only consists of a single field, SoID. This property is mapped to SoID of the dependent entity type SalesOrderLineItem (see Figure 7.10).

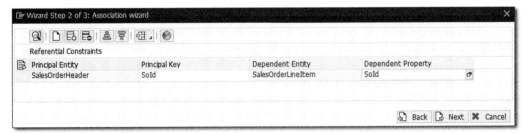

Figure 7.10 Step 2 of the Create Association Wizard

On the third screen, you provide the name of the association set to be created. The name is defaulted based on the name provided for the association. The corresponding entity sets are derived from the related entity types (see Figure 7.11).

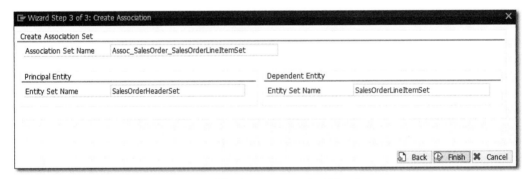

Figure 7.11 Step 3 of the Create Association Wizard

This concludes the model definition of the RFC example. The data model now consists of two entity types, two entity sets, an association with referential constraint, and a navigation property.

7.1.2   Service Registration: Stub Creation

You can now generate the runtime artifacts by clicking the GENERATE button. In the MODEL AND SERVICE DEFINITION pop-up, leave the default values as provided by the Service Builder. This step creates both MPCs and both DPCs, as you've learned from previous chapters. Note that while the MPC contains the model information, the DPC is created as an empty stub. The Service Builder also registers the service on the backend by creating a technical model and a technical service (see Figure 7.12).

Model and service generation

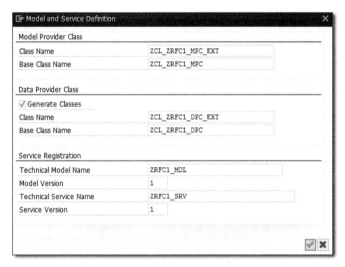

Figure 7.12 Model and Service Generation

7.1.3   Service Maintenance

After the project has been successfully generated and registered on the backend, you can register and activate the OData service on the SAP Gateway hub so that it gets published. For this, you expand the SERVICE MAINTENANCE node in the example project, right-click on the hub entry you want the service to register and activate on, and select REGISTER from the context menu.

Service activation on the hub

After confirming the pop-up stating that this step will be carried out on the SAP Gateway hub system, you provide the system alias that was created before on the hub system (here we choose LOCAL because we're using an embedded deployment).

This opens up the ADD SERVICE pop-up screen where you see the corresponding elements (service name, model name, etc.) that will be created on the SAP Gateway hub system (see Figure 7.13).

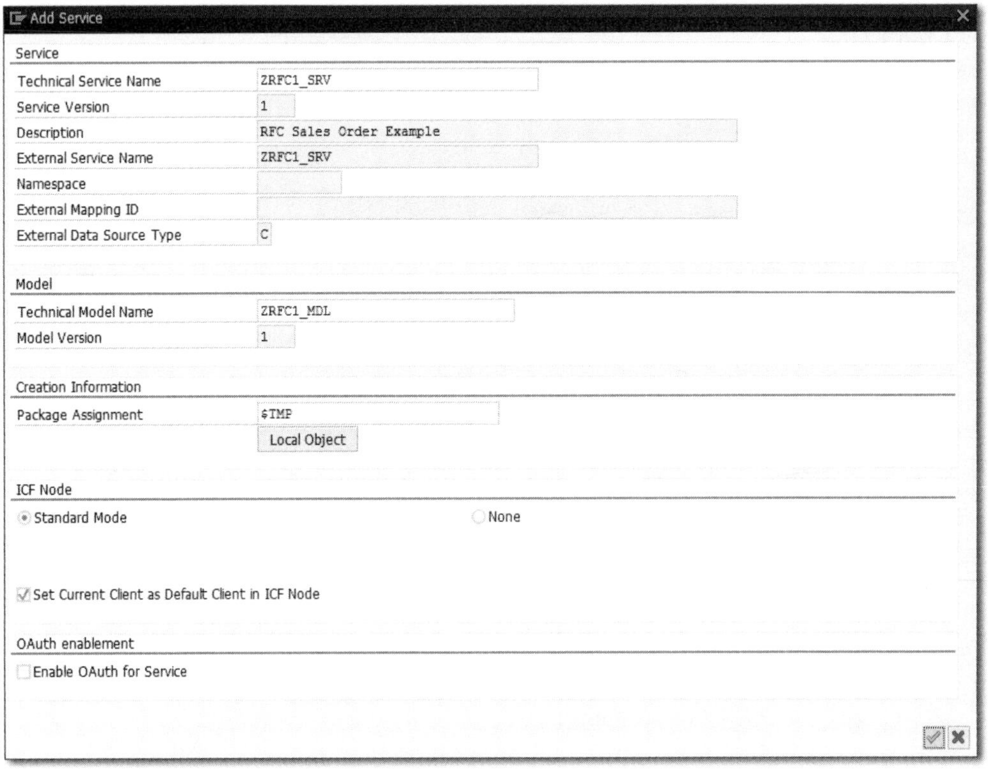

Figure 7.13 Add Service Dialog on the SAP Gateway Hub

Again, leave the default values as they are, and click the LOCAL OBJECT button, which sets the package to $TMP. If you want to transport the repository elements, you need to provide a transportable package.

Note the EXTERNAL SERVICE NAME field under which the service will be activated as an Internet Communication Framework (ICF) service. This name is derived from the technical service name provided during the first generation of the project where the registration of the OData service on the backend took place. It's not possible to change the external service name while registering and activating the service on the SAP Gateway hub.

After confirming the ADD SERVICE dialog, the OData service is activated on the SAP Gateway hub system. You can now use the SAP Gateway client to test the service—at least the metadata, as only an empty stub has been generated for the DPC. The assignment of RFC methods hasn't yet been done.

Test metadata

The URI of the service is */sap/opu/odata/sap/ZRFC1_SRV* and provides the service document. Adding */$metadata* provides the metadata of the OData service. This allows you to verify whether all properties have been derived properly from the provided RFC function module. You also see the key fields, the association, the referential constraint, and the navigation property you've defined in the project (see Figure 7.14).

Figure 7.14 Metadata of the ZRFC1_SRV Service

7.1.4   Service Implementation: SalesOrderHeaderSet

After the runtime artifacts are generated, you can start with the service implementation. The Service Builder has generated empty methods for each CRUD-Q method of an entity set in the DPC as a stub. To start the mapping process, you have to select MAP TO DATASOURCE in the context menu of a CRUD-Q method of an entity set in the SERVICE IMPLEMENTATION folder (Figure 7.15). The built-in mapping tool of the Service Builder then allows you to define mappings between the interface parameters of a function module or BAPI and the properties of an entity set.

Next we'll walk through the mapping process for all CRUD-Q methods of the SalesOrderHeaderSet entity set.

Query

Let's start with the SalesOrderHeaderSet entity set. For this, you expand the SERVICE IMPLEMENTATION • SALESORDERHEADERSET node in the project, right-click on GETENTITYSET (QUERY), and choose MAP TO DATA SOURCE (see Figure 7.15).

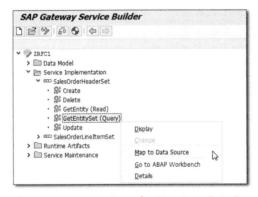

Figure 7.15 Context Menu for Mapping a Data Source

Local or remote system

This opens a dialog where you first need to specify if the data source resides in the local system where IW_BEP or SAP_GWFND are installed, or if the data source is available in a remote system (see Figure 7.16). In the latter case, you need to provide the RFC DESTINATION to the remote system, which is the same as you provided when defining the data model out of an RFC interface.

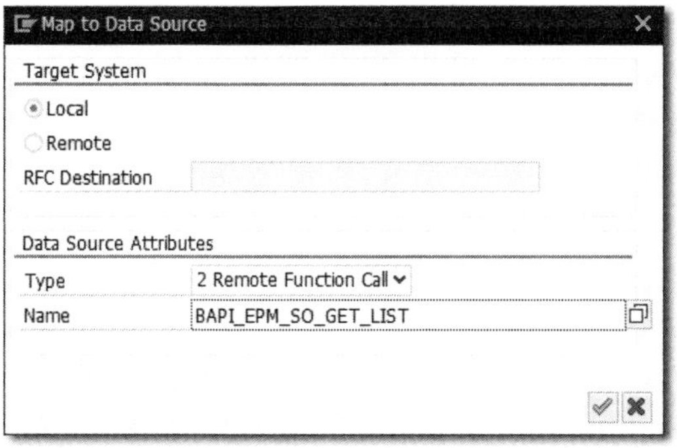

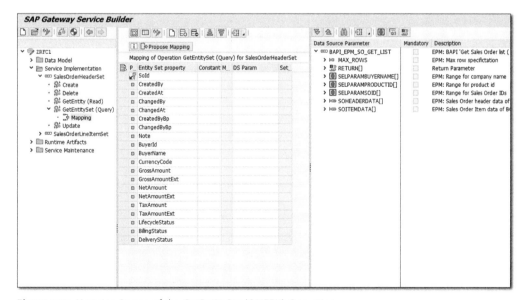

Figure 7.16 Map to Data Source Pop-Up Dialog

In the example, you call the EPM function module from the local system. In the DATA SOURCE ATTRIBUTES section, you first define the type of data source that you want to map to your OData service. The type can either be a BOR object/method or an RFC function module. Regular function modules (non-RFC) aren't supported.

Mapping screen

In this example, you choose REMOTE FUNCTION CALL and BAPI_EPM_SO_GET_LIST for the module that you want to map. After clicking OK, you'll see the prepopulated mapping screen (see Figure 7.17).

Figure 7.17 Mapping Screen of the GetEntitySet (QUERY) Operation

The grid in the middle shows the current mapping of the operation. On the right-hand side, you see the RFC function module that you've provided as well as its interface.

By default, nothing is mapped. Because the model is imported from an RFC interface, it's possible to use the PROPOSE MAPPING button to propose a mapping based on the origin of each property.

The proposal remains empty for those cases where the Service Builder isn't able to propose a mapping based on the property origin (e.g., in a case where you've manually added a property to the corresponding entity type not using the import from RFC). In such cases, you need to perform the mapping manually by dragging the wanted function module parameter from the right-hand side (data source) and dropping it to the entity set property line you want to map the parameter to.

Mapping direction

As soon as you map a parameter, the mapping direction is set. The mapping direction is visualized by an arrow pointing to the left (output) or pointing to the right (input) in the MAPPING DIRECTION column. If the mapping direction can't be defaulted, there will be a question mark icon. The mapping direction icon is a button that you can click to change the mapping direction, providing that the mapped RFC function module parameter supports this (e.g., a function module output parameter can't be mapped with an input direction).

Output mapping direction means that the function module parameter is provided to the consumer (e.g., property value in an entry of a collection). Input mapping means that the property value is handed over to the function module call as an input parameter (e.g., a filter).

Data source parameter

It's mandatory to map all primary key entity set properties with a data source parameter. Otherwise, the project check will display an error. Nonprimary key properties can remain unmapped. This has the same effect as if you deleted the line from the mapping grid, which, of course, doesn't delete the property itself.

> **Note**
>
> The CONSTANT VALUE column isn't relevant for output values. It's relevant only for input values (e.g., an X flag that a certain RFC might require to provide the necessary data).

In this example, the mapping proposal can map all parameters to the corresponding entity set properties of the GetEntitySet (QUERY) operation (see Figure 7.18).

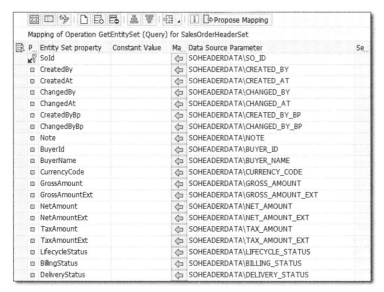

Figure 7.18 Complete Mapping of GetEntitySet (QUERY) Operation

After you're done with the mapping, you should verify that the project and mappings are technically correct and thus avoid runtime errors. The Service Builder checks whether, for example, the data types of the mapped function module fields are compatible.

That's all you need to do to implement the QUERY method in this example. The only thing left is to generate the project. After you've done this successfully, you can run the service by executing the following URI in the SAP Gateway client:

Generate project

/sap/opu/odata/sap/ZRFC1_SRV/SalesOrderHeaderSet

Executing this URI provides an unfiltered list of sales order headers provided by the BAPI_EPM_SO_GET_LIST function module.

So far, you haven't performed any input mapping. Therefore, the QUERY operation doesn't support any filtering capabilities. This can be changed by adding new lines to the mapping of the GetEntitySet (QUERY) operation of the sales order header collection. This, of course, requires suitable input parameters of the RFC function module that is used.

The `BAPI_EPM_SO_GET_LIST` function module has three `SELECT-OPTION` input tables: `SELPARAMSOID`, `SELPARAMBUYERNAME`, and `SELPARAMPRODUC-TID`. The first two (sales order ID and buyer name) are based on the header level; the third one (product ID) is based on the line item level. To use the two `SELECT-OPTION` tables on the header level, you first have to add two new mapping lines to the mapping grid by clicking the APPEND ROW or INSERT ROW buttons.

The entity set property names can either be typed in manually or picked from the F4 value help. In this example, enter "SoId" and "Buyer-Name." Then you can drag and drop the wanted ranges tables from the function module interface to the data source parameter fields of the newly added lines (make sure to drag and drop the entire ranges table and not individual fields). Because you're not mapping regular input fields but `SELECT-OPTION` tables, you get a MAP RANGE pop-up for each `SELECT-OPTION` table you map (see Figure 7.19).

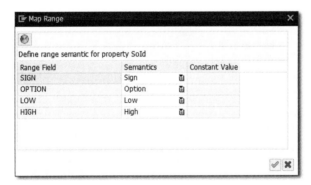

Figure 7.19 Map Range Pop-Up for Mapping SELECT-OPTION Filters

The Service Builder needs to know in which field of the ranges table the SIGN, OPTION, LOW, and HIGH values are located, which is why the pop-up is automatically shown each time you map a ranges table. Typically, the values in this pop-up are properly defaulted and just need to be confirmed.

After you've completed the mapping of the sales order ID and the buyer name SELECT-OPTION tables, the GetEntitySet mapping screen has two new input mappings (see Figure 7.20).

New input mapping

Figure 7.20 Input Mapping of SELECT-OPTION Filters

The green icon with the square brackets indicates that the mapping is based on a ranges table. By clicking on the respective icon, you can open the corresponding map range pop-up to verify the mapping and change it.

Now you need to regenerate the project to actually use the newly mapped filters. As an example, you can execute the following URI to filter on sales orders with the id >= '500000010' and id <= '500000020':

/sap/opu/odata/sap/ZRFC1_SRV/SalesOrderHeaderSet?$filter=SoId ge '500000010' and SoId le '500000020'

Note that we're using the external representation of the sales order ID, which has no leading zeros ('*500000010*') instead of the internal one ('*0500000010*'). This is because the conversion exits are enabled by default, and thus input values (like the filter values) are converted from the external to the internal format.

In addition, you can filter on the buyer name. It's possible to add this to the already existing filter. The URI for filtering on buyer name = "Panorama Studios" in addition to the previous filter looks like the following:

/sap/opu/odata/sap/ZRFC1_SRV/SalesOrderHeaderSet?$filter=SoId ge '500000010' and SoId le '500000020' and BuyerName eq 'Panorama Studios'

As you can see, the filter criteria can become quite lengthy.

The filter criteria are mapped into ranges tables by the framework. This allows you to easily process them and to assign them to the corresponding table RANGES-INPUT of your RFC module in the GetEntitySet method. The OData framework provides them in a generic table in

Filter criteria

which each entry represents an entity set property that is used in the $filter query option.

Note that the preparation of the ranges tables has certain limitations. Similar to defining an ABAP report with SELECT-OPTIONS fields, you can't cover all use cases. For example, a filter such as FieldA eq 'A' or FieldB eq 'B' can't be put into ranges tables because of the or operand. It would work if you use and instead of or, but this of course has a different result.

Single Read

Similar to the QUERY operation, you can easily model the single read via the Service Builder. This time, you expand the SERVICE IMPLEMENTATION • SALESORDERHEADERSET node, right-click on GETENTITY (READ), and choose MAP TO DATA SOURCE.

The target system remains the same (LOCAL) but can of course be different if needed (although it's unlikely that the query and the single read results are coming from different systems). This time, provide "BAPI_EPM_SO_GET_DETAIL" as the RFC function module from which you want to get your data. You again use the PROPOSE MAPPING button to perform the mapping of the function module parameters to the corresponding entity set properties.

Besides the output parameter, you also have to create an input mapping for all key fields (in this example, it's only one key field). This is something the check function of the Service Builder will report as an error if missing (see Figure 7.21).

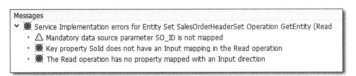

Figure 7.21 Missing Input Mapping Reported in the Message Window

Missing input mapping The missing input mapping can easily be rectified by adding a new line to the mapping screen and selecting SoId as the entity set property via the value help. Now you need to drag and drop the RFC input parameter SO_ID-SO_ID to the data source parameter column. Because this is an import parameter of the RFC module, the mapping direction is automatically set to input. There is no MAP RANGE pop-up and no green brackets shown as in the QUERY operation because you're not mapping a SELECT-OPTIONS table.

The project check now shows a green traffic light to signify that the reported problem was corrected. After generating the project, you can read a single entry of the sales order header collection by executing, for example, the following URI via the SAP Gateway client:

/sap/opu/odata/sap/ZRFC1_SRV/SalesOrderHeaderSet('500000011')

As expected, you now get a single entry instead of an OData feed.

Disable Conversion Exits

If you don't want to use conversion exits, you can disable them using the define method of the MPC. The corresponding coding of the MPC extension class for redefining the define method is the following:

```
METHOD define.
  model->set_no_conversion( abap_true ).
  super->define( ).
ENDMETHOD.
```

After activating this coding, the conversion exit will no longer be called.

Note that this disables the conversion exits for the whole data model. In our current example, this would also disable the conversion exit for the currency fields, which are quite important.

If you want to disable the conversion exit for only a particular property, you can do this via the code shown in Listing 7.1.

```
METHOD define.
  DATA: lo_entity_type TYPE REF TO /iwbep/if_mgw_odata_entity_
typ,
        lo_property    TYPE REF TO /iwbep/if_mgw_odata_
property.

  super->define( ).

  lo_entity_type = model->get_entity_
type( 'SalesOrderHeader' ).
```

```
lo_property = lo_entity_type->get_property( 'SoId' ).
lo_property->disable_conversion( ).
ENDMETHOD.
```
Listing 7.1 Disabling Conversion Exits

So far, the service is capable of fetching filtered and unfiltered collections of sales order headers as well as single sales order header entries. The next step is to implement create, update, and delete capabilities.

Create

The CREATE operation is used whenever you want to create a new entry into the respective collection. In the Service Builder, you can perform the service implementation for the SalesOrderHeaderSet CREATE operation by expanding the SERVICE IMPLEMENTATION • SALESORDERHEADER-SET node, right-clicking on CREATE, and selecting MAP TO DATA SOURCE.

Map to data source This opens up the MAP TO DATA SOURCE dialog where you specify the target system, the data source type, and the name of the data source. In this example, you again choose RFC as the data source, and enter the RFC function module "BAPI_EPM_SO_CREATE".

Again, you use the PROPOSE MAPPING button to perform the mapping of the function module parameters to the respective entity set properties. This time, the default direction is input because all properties have to be moved from the request body to the corresponding input structure of the RFC function module.

The handling of the RFC return table is automatically done by the generated coding. In the case of an error, a corresponding business exception is thrown, and the error text is provided along with the corresponding HTTP code. This also takes place for the other operations but typically comes into focus when writing data into the system.

Mapping proposal If the mapping proposal is correct, you just need to add a new mapping line manually for the order ID that is returned by the Create RFC function module, map it via drag and drop to the SALESORDERID\SO_ID field, and check the mapping. If the mapping isn't correct, the check function of the Service Builder reports an error, such as the missing input mapping you saw in Figure 7.21.

In this example, this information is returned by the field SO_ID of the export structure SALESORDERID. It needs to be mapped to the primary key of the entity type. The mapping direction is automatically set to output. The complete mapping is shown in Figure 7.22.

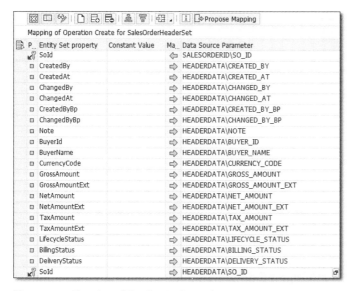

Figure 7.22 Mapping of the Create Operation

After you're done with the mapping of the CREATE operation, check and regenerate the project again. After that, you use the SAP Gateway client to verify whether the CREATE operation works as expected (you can use any other REST client to test the service as well).

The CREATE operation requires the creation of a proper HTTP body with the sales order entry. Instead of putting such an HTTP body together manually, you can select the USE AS REQUEST button in the SAP Gateway client. For this, you first need to execute a GET operation to receive a suitable source entry. Then, you click the USE AS REQUEST button to copy it over to the left-hand side of the SAP Gateway client (the left-hand side is the HTTP REQUEST side, and the right-hand side the HTTP RESPONSE side).

HTTP body

Before you can execute the CREATE operation, you first need to change the HTTP method from GET to POST. In addition, you need to adjust the URI because the CREATE operation has to be executed on a collection and not on a single record (make sure to remove the brackets with the primary key).

Finally, you need to adjust the HTTP body and the property values. In this example, you need to remove all properties apart from Currency-Code, BuyerName, BuyerId, and Note because the underlying RFC function module doesn't allow the other fields to be provided in the CREATE operation. You can also delete the mapping of these properties to make sure the fields aren't provided to the function module call, but then the consumer won't know that the properties are ignored. If you keep the mapping, corresponding error messages are provided to the consumer if those unallowed properties are still provided.

If the CREATE operation is successful (see Figure 7.23), you get an HTTP 201 response.

Figure 7.23 Successful CREATE Operation

Furthermore, you get the newly created record along with the calculated order number derived from the related number range. In addition, there are some other fields that have been calculated/determined by the back-end server (e.g., CreatedAt, CreatedBy, etc.).

You may wonder why the complete entry is returned after the creation, despite the fact that only the sales order ID was mapped as the output property before. This occurs because the RFC/BOR Generator automatically generates a get_entity call at the end of the Create method to retrieve the created entry.

Update

The UPDATE operation comes into play whenever an existing entry needs to be changed. In the Service Builder, you can perform the service implementation for the SalesOrderHeaderSet UPDATE operation by expanding the node SERVICE IMPLEMENTATION • SALESORDERHEADERSET, right-clicking on UPDATE, and selecting MAP TO DATA SOURCE.

This time, you enter "BAPI_EPM_SO_CHANGE" in the MAP TO DATA SOURCE dialog. Similar to the CREATE operation, you perform the mapping by using the PROPOSE MAPPING button.

Map to data source

You also have to inform the RFC function module about the fields you're going to change. This is based on the standard SAP BAPI behavior in which each import structure field has to have a corresponding X structure. This X structure has a flag for each field of the original structure indicating whether the field is to be considered.

In this example, this is the SOHEADERDATAX structure (note the X at the end). The fields of this structure have the same names as the original import structure; the difference is that only the primary key fields (in this example, just SO_ID) are based on the same data element. All other fields point to a default data element BAPIUPDATE, which is a character 1 field.

SOHEADERDATAX

Each property in the OData service that you want to be able to change via the UPDATE operation has to contain an X in the field of the SOHEADERDATAX structure. If there is no X, the field must be blank. For this, you can make use of the constant values on the mapping screen. To achieve this, you need to add one line for each constant you want to provide (see Figure 7.24). Constant values don't have an entity set property because they are a constant for the function module call (input mapping). It's not possible to provide a constant value for an output mapping (which wouldn't make much sense).

Finally, you also need to map the SoId entity set property to the SO_ID\ SO_ID input structure of the RFC function module. When it's all said and done, you're mapping the sales order primary key property three times to be able to call this RFC function module.

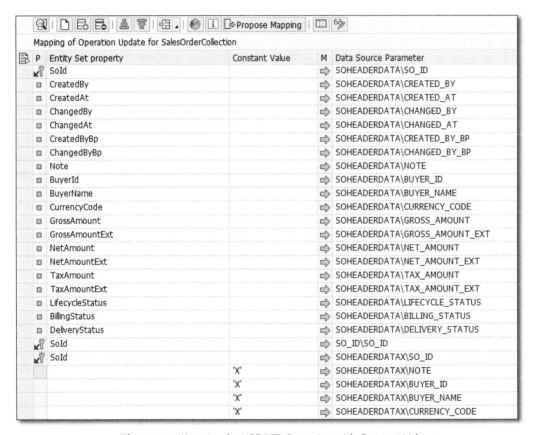

P	Entity Set property	Constant Value	M	Data Source Parameter
	SoId		⇨	SOHEADERDATA\SO_ID
▫	CreatedBy		⇨	SOHEADERDATA\CREATED_BY
▫	CreatedAt		⇨	SOHEADERDATA\CREATED_AT
▫	ChangedBy		⇨	SOHEADERDATA\CHANGED_BY
▫	ChangedAt		⇨	SOHEADERDATA\CHANGED_AT
▫	CreatedByBp		⇨	SOHEADERDATA\CREATED_BY_BP
▫	ChangedByBp		⇨	SOHEADERDATA\CHANGED_BY_BP
▫	Note		⇨	SOHEADERDATA\NOTE
▫	BuyerId		⇨	SOHEADERDATA\BUYER_ID
▫	BuyerName		⇨	SOHEADERDATA\BUYER_NAME
▫	CurrencyCode		⇨	SOHEADERDATA\CURRENCY_CODE
▫	GrossAmount		⇨	SOHEADERDATA\GROSS_AMOUNT
▫	GrossAmountExt		⇨	SOHEADERDATA\GROSS_AMOUNT_EXT
▫	NetAmount		⇨	SOHEADERDATA\NET_AMOUNT
▫	NetAmountExt		⇨	SOHEADERDATA\NET_AMOUNT_EXT
▫	TaxAmount		⇨	SOHEADERDATA\TAX_AMOUNT
▫	TaxAmountExt		⇨	SOHEADERDATA\TAX_AMOUNT_EXT
▫	LifecycleStatus		⇨	SOHEADERDATA\LIFECYCLE_STATUS
▫	BillingStatus		⇨	SOHEADERDATA\BILLING_STATUS
▫	DeliveryStatus		⇨	SOHEADERDATA\DELIVERY_STATUS
	SoId		⇨	SO_ID\SO_ID
	SoId		⇨	SOHEADERDATAX\SO_ID
		'X'	⇨	SOHEADERDATAX\NOTE
		'X'	⇨	SOHEADERDATAX\BUYER_ID
		'X'	⇨	SOHEADERDATAX\BUYER_NAME
		'X'	⇨	SOHEADERDATAX\CURRENCY_CODE

Figure 7.24 Mapping the UPDATE Operation with Constant Values

Check and regen-
erate project
After you're done with the mapping of the UPDATE operation, you can check and regenerate the project again. After that, you use the SAP Gate-

way client to verify whether the UPDATE operation works as expected. Similar to the CREATE operation, you first perform a single read to get a proper HTTP response body that you can copy over to the request side by using the USE AS REQUEST button. The URI remains unchanged, as the UPDATE operation is always performed on a single entry. You only need to change the HTTP method from GET to PUT. If the update was successful, you get an HTTP 204 (no content) response.

The HTTP return code indicates that the response body is empty. This is intentional because the assumption is that the client has all information, and thus sending the entry along with the response causes unnecessary overhead. The client can always perform a single read to fetch the entry again in case the backend server has calculated any values that the client doesn't have.

Delete

In contrast to the UPDATE operation, the DELETE operation is rather simple to implement. In the Service Builder, you can perform the service implementation for the SalesOrderHeaderSet DELETE operation by expanding the SERVICE IMPLEMENTATION • SALESORDERHEADERSET node, right-clicking on DELETE, and selecting MAP TO DATA SOURCE.

The corresponding function module is BAPI_EPM_SO_DELETE. It only requires the primary key to be mapped (see Figure 7.25) as no request body and no X fields are required for this operation. **Primary key**

Figure 7.25 Mapping the DELETE Operation

After the regeneration of the project, you can verify if the implemented DELETE operation works properly. DELETE operations are always executed on a single entry; therefore, you have to provide a URI that addresses a single sales order. The HTTP method has to be DELETE. If the DELETE operation is successful, you get an HTTP 204 (no content) response.

7.1.5   Service Implementation: SalesOrderLineItemSet

After you've performed the mapping for the `SalesOrderHeaderSet` entity set, you'll do the same for the second `SalesOrderLineItemSet` entity set. In this case, we'll show an example where no suitable EPM RFC function module is provided for each method, and explain how to circumvent this issue by developing your own wrapper RFC function model.

Query

For the sales order header, you were able to map all five CRUD-Q operations to the corresponding EPM RFC function modules. This was pretty straightforward because related function modules are available for each operation.

No dedicated RFC function modules

Next, you need to take care of the sales order line items (`SalesOrder-LineItemSet` entity set). For line items, there are no dedicated RFC function modules available in the EPM demo model. Instead, the line items information is provided as part of the corresponding sales order header function modules. That's the reason why the mapping can't entirely be done via the Service Builder. Instead, some of the operations have to be redefined with your own coding.

In the metadata, we've defined a navigation property `toLineItems` that allows you to navigate from a sales order entry to its list of line items. Such a navigation property is also required when using the `$expand` system query option or the deep insert capability described in Chapter 6, Section 6.5.9.

The metadata of the `SalesOrderLineItemSet` entity set has been annotated as not addressable. That means you don't allow any consumer to access the collection directly by, for example, executing the following URI:

/sap/opu/odata/sap/ZRFC1_SRV/SalesOrderLineItemSet

Because you can't prevent the consumer from executing such a URI, you need to make sure that the service implementation is responding to this request appropriately.

The first operation you're going to map to the related data source pro-   Map operation
vider is the `GetEntitySet` (`QUERY`) operation. Because there is no dedicated RFC function module for fetching the list of line items (`QUERY`), you
need to use the sales order header detail `BAPI_EPM_SO_GET_DETAIL` function module, which also provides the list of line items via its table
parameters.

In the project tree, expand the SERVICE IMPLEMENTATION • SALESORDER-
LINEITEMSET node, right-click on GETENTITYSET (QUERY), and select MAP
TO DATA SOURCE. In the dialog pop-up, enter the function module
"BAPI_EPM_SO_GET_DETAIL." Again, make use of the mapping pro-
posal.

Because the sales order header detail function module requires a sales   New mapping line
order ID as an input parameter, you get a corresponding warning mes-
sage after the mapping was executed (which triggers a project check by
default). Therefore, you add a new mapping line where you map the
entity set property `SoId` to the `SO_ID\SO_ID` function module import
parameter (see Figure 7.26). Via the referential constraint that was
defined in the metadata, the framework is able to provide the primary
key from the principal entity type (`SalesOrderHeader SoId`) as filter criteria to the dependent entity type property (`SalesOrderLineItem SoId`).

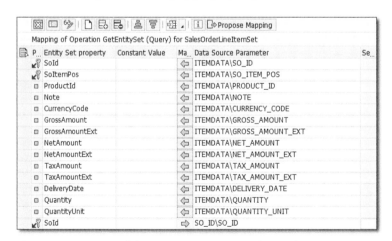

Figure 7.26 Mapping of the Line Item GetEntitySet (QUERY) Operation

375

After generating the project, you're able to use the navigation property to navigate from the sales order header to the list of line items. The list of line items is determined via the filter on the sales order ID. The following is a sample URI: */sap/opu/odata/sap/ZRFC1_SRV/ SalesOrderHeaderSet('500000000')/toLineItems*.

Accessing the list of line items without any filter will result in an error because the RFC function module requires the sales order ID to be provided.

Single Read

Three options

Mapping the single read (GetEntity) operation is a little trickier now because there is no suitable EPM RFC function module that provides a single sales order line item. In such a case, you basically have three options. The first is to create your own (Z-)RFC function module that wraps a suitable standard RFC function module along with the missing ABAP logic that you need, and then map it using the Service Builder, as you've seen before. The second is to use the standard RFC function module and map the fields as close as possible, generate the coding, copy the entire method over to the DPC extension class, and adjust it. The third option is to implement the operation entirely from scratch, as we described in the previous chapter.

The second and the third options are somewhat similar because both implement the operation via the respective method (e.g., Get_Entity) in the extension class. However, the second option has the disadvantage that it suggests a present mapping done via the Service Builder, despite the fact that the generated method isn't actually used anymore (because it was copied over to the extension class method and thus is disconnected from further changes and regenerations). Another disadvantage of the second approach is the following: Suppose you have a BAPI that performs a read request on a sales order. This will have the sales order ID as an input field but won't necessarily have an output field that contains the sales order ID. In this case, it's impossible to perform the mandatory mapping of the sales order ID as an output field.

We'll focus on the first option, which is to develop a wrapper RFC function module, Z_BAPI_EPM_SO_ITEM_GET_DETAIL. For this example, we've created a function group via Transaction SE80 (e.g., ZRFC1).

Wrapper RFC function module

The interface of the wrapper function module consists of two import parameters, one for the sales order ID (SO_ID) and one for the sales order line item position (SO_ITEM_POS). It has one export structure, itemdata, that can hold a single line item. The RETURN table parameter is for the BAPI return table. The coding is shown in Listing 7.2.

```
FUNCTION z_bapi_epm_so_item_get_detail.
*"----------------------------------------------------------------
*"*"Local Interface:
*"  IMPORTING
*"     VALUE(SO_ID) TYPE  SNWD_SO_ID
*"     VALUE(SO_ITEM_POS) TYPE  SNWD_SO_ITEM_POS
*"  EXPORTING
*"     VALUE(ITEMDATA) TYPE  BAPI_EPM_SO_ITEM
*"  TABLES
*"      RETURN STRUCTURE  BAPIRET2 OPTIONAL
*"----------------------------------------------------------------

  DATA: ls_so_id    TYPE bapi_epm_so_id,
        lt_itemdata TYPE STANDARD TABLE OF bapi_epm_so_item,
        ls_return   TYPE bapiret2.

  ls_so_id-so_id = so_id.
  CALL FUNCTION 'BAPI_EPM_SO_GET_DETAIL'
    EXPORTING
      so_id           = ls_so_id
*   IMPORTING
*     HEADERDATA      =
    TABLES
      itemdata        = lt_itemdata
      return          = return.

  CHECK return[] IS INITIAL.
  READ TABLE lt_itemdata INTO itemdata WITH KEY so_item_
pos = so_item_pos.
  IF sy-subrc NE 0.
    CALL FUNCTION 'BALW_BAPIRETURN_GET2'
      EXPORTING
        type   = 'E'
        cl     = 'SEPM_BOR_MESSAGES'
        number = '003'
        par1   = 'Item does not exist'
      IMPORTING
        return = ls_return.
```

377

```
        APPEND ls_return TO return.
    ENDIF.

ENDFUNCTION.
```

Listing 7.2 Coding of the Wrapper RFC to Retrieve Sales Order Item Details

As you can see, the standard EPM `BAPI_EPM_SO_GET_DETAIL` function module is used to retrieve the requested information. This function module returns the entire list of all line items for a given sales order. As a second step, you use the `SO_ITEM_POS` import parameter to pick the requested line item out of the determined `lt_itemdata` line item list. A corresponding message is added to the return table if a nonexistent item position was provided via `SO_ITEM_POS`.

After you've activated the Z-RFC function module, you can map it to the `GetEntity` (`READ`) operation for the `SalesOrderLineItemSet` entity set (see Figure 7.27).

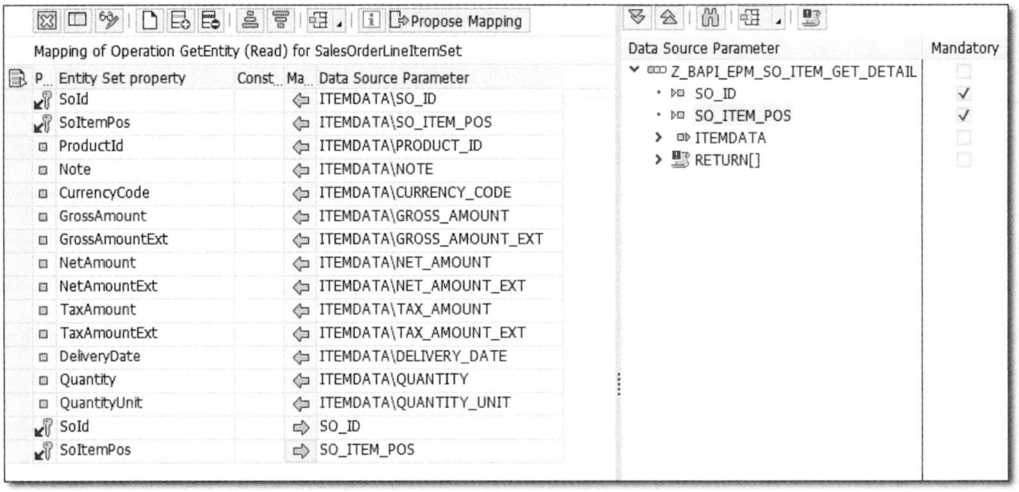

Figure 7.27 Mapping the Line Item GetEntity (READ) Operation

Propose mapping

Note that the PROPOSE MAPPING button can still be used, even though the data model was derived from a different RFC function module. This is because the PROPOSE MAPPING functionality not only checks the function module name but also considers the declaration of the respective fields. In other words, it's always worth trying the PROPOSE MAPPING button.

Don't forget to add two new mapping lines to map (input mapping), as well as the sales order ID and the line item number.

Also note that the RFC function module definitions are cached. So if you keep adjusting your function module interface, you may need to restart the Service Builder transaction to see your interface changes. After generating the project, you can test the single read for the sales order line item with, for example, the following URI:

Cached RFC function module definitions

/sap/opu/odata/sap/ZRFC1_SRV/SalesOrderLineItemSet(SoId= '500000002',SoItemPos='40')

Create

The CREATE operation for the SalesOrderLineItemSet entity set can also be mapped using a wrapper function module. Similar to the single READ operation, you create a new Z-RFC function module called Z_BAPI_EPM_SO_ITEM_CREATE. The interface consists of an import parameter for the sales order ID (SO_ID) and import structures for the line item data (SOITEMDATA) as well as the known X-structure (SOITEMDATAX) with the flags indicating what to do. The PERSIST_TO_DB import parameter defines whether the data should be persisted to the database or just kept in memory. The parameter also defines whether a COMMIT WORK is executed. By default, this parameter is set.

Wrapper function module

Via the SO_ITEM_POS export parameter, you return the created line item position back to the caller. The coding is shown in Listing 7.3.

```
FUNCTION z_bapi_epm_so_item_create.
*"----------------------------------------------------------------
- - - - - - - - -
*"*"Local Interface:
*"  IMPORTING
*"     VALUE(SO_ID) TYPE  SNWD_SO_ID
*"     VALUE(SOITEMDATA) TYPE  BAPI_EPM_SO_ITEM
*"     VALUE(SOITEMDATAX) TYPE  BAPI_EPM_SO_ITEMX
*"     VALUE(PERSIST_TO_DB) TYPE  BAPI_EPM_
BOOLEAN DEFAULT ABAP_TRUE
*"  EXPORTING
*"     VALUE(SO_ITEM_POS) TYPE  SNWD_SO_ITEM_POS
```

```
*"  TABLES
*"      RETURN STRUCTURE  BAPIRET2 OPTIONAL
*"-----------------------------------------------------------
---------

  DATA: ls_so_id         TYPE bapi_epm_so_id,
        lt_soitemdata    TYPE STANDARD TABLE OF bapi_epm_so_
item,
        lt_soitemdatax   TYPE STANDARD TABLE OF bapi_epm_so_
itemx,
        ls_itemdata_new TYPE  bapi_epm_so_item,
        lt_itemdata_new TYPE STANDARD TABLE OF bapi_epm_so_
item.

  ls_so_id-so_id = so_id.
  APPEND soitemdata  TO lt_soitemdata.
  APPEND soitemdatax TO lt_soitemdatax.
  CALL FUNCTION 'BAPI_EPM_SO_CHANGE'
    EXPORTING
      so_id        = ls_so_id
      persist_to_db = persist_to_db
    TABLES
      soitemdata   = lt_soitemdata
      soitemdatax  = lt_soitemdatax
      return       = return.

  CHECK return[] IS INITIAL.
  CALL FUNCTION 'BAPI_EPM_SO_GET_DETAIL'
    EXPORTING
      so_id   = ls_so_id
    TABLES
      itemdata = lt_itemdata_new.

  SORT lt_itemdata_new BY so_item_pos DESCENDING.
  READ TABLE lt_itemdata_new INTO ls_itemdata_new INDEX 1.
  so_item_pos = ls_itemdata_new-so_item_pos.

ENDFUNCTION.
```

Listing 7.3 Coding of the Wrapper RFC to Create Sales Order Item Details

EPM function module

This time, the EPM BAPI_EPM_SO_CHANGE function module is used because the creation of a line item is a change to the related sales order instance. Table SOITEMDATAX has an ACTIONCODE field used to indicate that this is an insert operation. The actual value I is set as a constant value via the mapping of the CREATE operation in the Service Builder (see Figure 7.28).

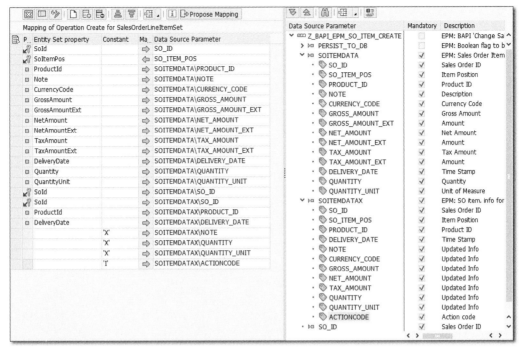

Figure 7.28 Mapping of Line Item CREATE Operation

After the successful creation of the line item (verified by checking if the return table is empty), read the entire list of line items by using BAPI_ EPM_SO_GET_DETAIL; this is the only way to identify the newly created line item position.

Finally, after generating the project, you can test the sales order line item CREATE operation via the SAP Gateway client by performing a POST on the following URI:

/sap/opu/odata/sap/ZRFC1_SRV/SalesOrderLineItemSet

Similar to the other POST requests that you executed before (using the SAP Gateway client), it's recommended to first perform a GET on a line item detail and to click the USE AS REQUEST button as a starting point for the HTTP request body. Adjusting such a defaulted HTTP request is a lot easier than manually creating the request from scratch.

Update

Standard RFC
function module The UPDATE operation can even be mapped using the standard BAPI_EPM_ SO_CHANGE RFC function module. There's no need to implement a wrapper function module in this specific case due to the interface and the ability of the RFC/BOR Generator to handle even table parameters.

The ACTIONCODE in this case is U because you want to update the record (see Figure 7.29).

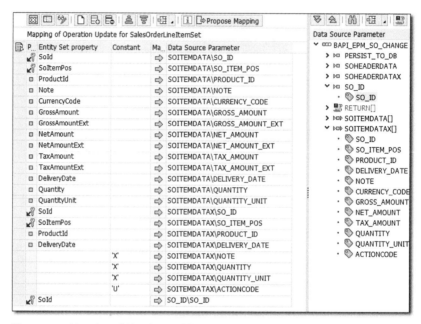

Figure 7.29 Mapping of Line Item UPDATE Operation

After generating the project, you can test the sales order line item UPDATE operation via the SAP Gateway client by performing a PUT request on, for example, the following URI:

/sap/opu/odata/sap/ZRFC1_SRV/SalesOrderLineItemSet(SoId= '500000002',SoItemPos='10')

If everything goes smoothly, the HTTP response is empty, and the HTTP return code is 204 (no content).

Delete

Finally, the line item DELETE operation again requires a wrapper RFC function module because a line item isn't just uniquely identified by its item position but also requires the product ID as well as the delivery date, which is an EPM-specific logic. Accordingly, you must again develop a wrapper Z-RFC Z_BAPI_EPM_SO_ITEM_DELETE function module that first reads the line item detail and then prepares the call to the BAPI_EPM_SO_CHANGE standard function to delete the line item entry.

Wrapper RFC function module

The coding looks like Listing 7.4.

```
FUNCTION z_bapi_epm_so_item_delete.
*"----------------------------------------------------------
---------
*"*"Local Interface:
*"  IMPORTING
*"     VALUE(SO_ID) TYPE  SNWD_SO_ID
*"     VALUE(SO_ITEM_POS) TYPE  SNWD_SO_ITEM_POS
*"     VALUE(PERSIST_TO_DB) TYPE  BAPI_EPM_
BOOLEAN DEFAULT ABAP_TRUE
*"  TABLES
*"      RETURN STRUCTURE  BAPIRET2 OPTIONAL
*"----------------------------------------------------------
---------

  DATA: ls_so_id     TYPE bapi_epm_so_id,
        ls_itemdata  TYPE bapi_epm_so_item,
        lt_itemdata  TYPE STANDARD TABLE OF bapi_epm_so_item,
        ls_itemdatax TYPE bapi_epm_so_itemx,
        lt_itemdatax TYPE STANDARD TABLE OF bapi_epm_so_itemx.

  CALL FUNCTION 'Z_BAPI_EPM_SO_ITEM_GET_DETAIL'
    EXPORTING
      so_id      = so_id
      so_item_pos = so_item_pos
    IMPORTING
      itemdata   = ls_itemdata
    TABLES
      return     = return.

  CHECK return[] IS INITIAL.
  APPEND ls_itemdata TO lt_itemdata.

  ls_itemdatax-so_id       = so_id.
  ls_itemdatax-so_item_pos  = so_item_pos.
  ls_itemdatax-product_id   = ls_itemdata-product_id.
  ls_itemdatax-delivery_date = ls_itemdata-delivery_date.
```

```
   ls_itemdatax-actioncode    = 'D'.
   APPEND ls_itemdatax TO lt_itemdatax.

   ls_so_id-so_id = so_id.
   CALL FUNCTION 'BAPI_EPM_SO_CHANGE'
     EXPORTING
       so_id           = ls_so_id
*      SOHEADERDATA    =
*      SOHEADERDATAX   =
       persist_to_db = persist_to_db
     TABLES
       soitemdata     = lt_itemdata
       soitemdatax    = lt_itemdatax
       return         = return.

ENDFUNCTION.
```
Listing 7.4 Function Module to Delete a Sales Order Line Item

After performing the mapping and generating the project, you can test the sales order line item DELETE operation via the SAP Gateway client by performing a DELETE request on, for example, the following URI:

/sap/opu/odata/sap/ZRFC1_SRV/SalesOrderLineItem-Set(SoId='500000011',SoItemPos='20')

Upon success, this also leads to an HTTP 204 (no content) return code.

7.1.6 Conclusion

As you've seen from the provided example, the Service Builder helps you significantly in modeling your metadata as well as defining your service provisioning. However, there are also situations where you either need to adjust the generated coding or implement some wrapper functions because the RFC/BOR Generator isn't able to cover all possible use cases.

7.2 Generation via Search Help

Similar to RFC function modules that can be mapped to an OData service as a data source, it's possible to leverage Search Helps that are defined in the ABAP DDIC. It's very convenient to generate OData services because a large number of Search Helps are available in the SAP backend systems that can be leveraged in OData service development.

The wizard for creating an entity type based on a Search Help performs both steps: data model definition and service implementation. Therefore, the process of service generation using a Search Help is much simpler than using an RFC function module.

In the first screen of the IMPORT FROM SEARCH HELP wizard, you simply select the appropriate search help (here: F4_INTCA) via [F4] for the NAME field and enter a name for the entity type (here: "Country"). Leave the CREATE DEFAULT ENTITY SET, QUERY, and READ checkboxes marked (see Figure 7.30).

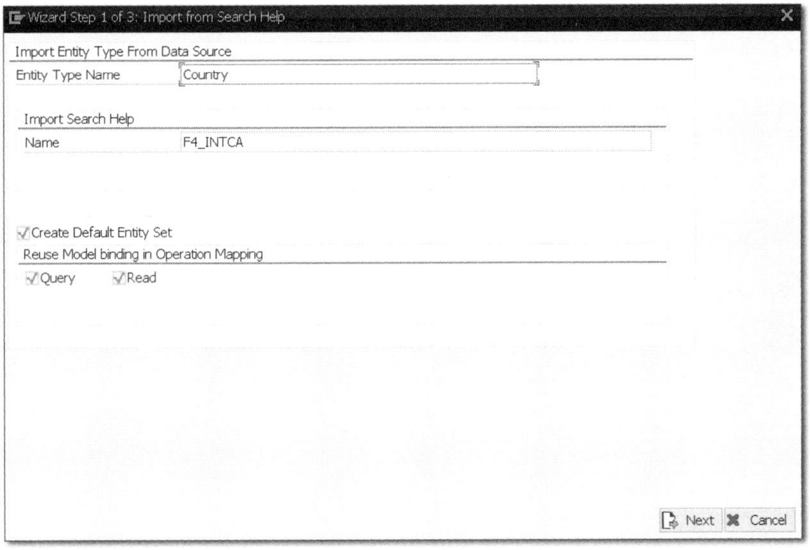

Figure 7.30 Step 1 of the Import from Search Help Wizard

As a result, the Service Builder creates a `CountrySet` entity set, and the service implementation of the `READ` and `QUERY` method is performed automatically via the mapping of the Search Help being used.

In the second screen of the wizard, you can select the fields that should be part of the entity type (see Figure 7.31).

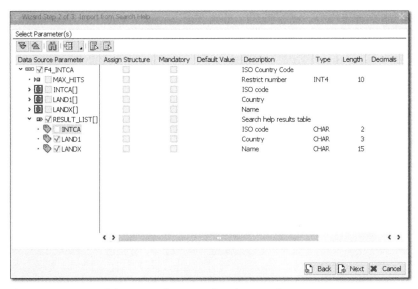

Figure 7.31 Step 2 of the Import from Search Help Wizard

In the third step, you only have to specify the key fields of the entity type and click FINISH (see Figure 7.32).

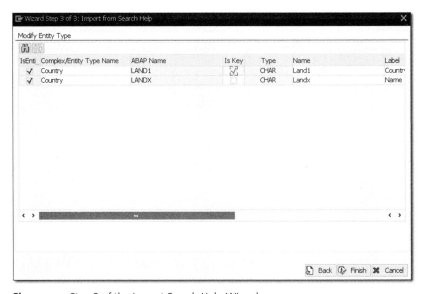

Figure 7.32 Step 3 of the Import Search Help Wizard

After generating the runtime artifacts, the service is now registered in the backend, and you can check the service implementation. As you can see, the wizard has performed the mapping for the READ and QUERY method (see Figure 7.33).

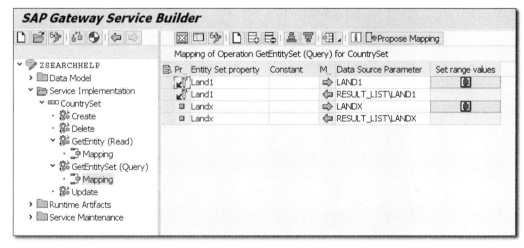

Figure 7.33 Service Implementation via Mapping a Search Help

Because mapping the QUERY method also encompasses mapping the range tables, the $filter is supported out of the box. As a verification, you can use the following URI via the SAP Gateway client to perform a query using a filter:

/sap/opu/odata/SAP/ZSEARCHHELP_SRV/CountrySet?$filter=Land1 eq 'US'

7.3 Generation via CDS Views

Building OData services based on ABAP CDS views is another flexible approach to developing OData services using the Service Builder.

In this section, we'll provide a high-level introduction to ABAP CDS views and use an example to illustrate how to create ABAP CDS views and consume them in an OData service. As the term *view* indicates, the purpose of a CDS view is to access data that might be distributed across several database tables and/or other views, which is also called *projection*.

CDS

As described in Chapter 5, ABAP CDS views are one of the two available flavors of CDS views that are created in the ABAP DDIC. While the other flavor, the SAP HANA CDS views only have to support SAP HANA, ABAP CDS views are more open like Open SQL that supports several databases.

To begin generation via ABAP CDS views, the first thing you need to do is set up the ABAP Development Tools for SAP NetWeaver environment, which is based on Eclipse. This is necessary because ABAP CDS views can't be edited using the traditional ABAP tools (such as Transaction SE80). The necessary information about setting up the ABAP Development Tools can be found on the SAP Development Tools for Eclipse website (*https://tools.hana.ondemand.com/*). On the ABAP tab, you'll find the necessary information about which Eclipse release, Java Runtime Environment (JRE) version, and so on to use. Make sure to choose the right OS/runtime version (32-bit or 64-bit) when downloading the components.

The ABAP Development Tool is installed using the INSTALL NEW SOFTWARE feature inside Eclipse. After you've performed this, you can open the ABAP perspective, as shown in Figure 7.34.

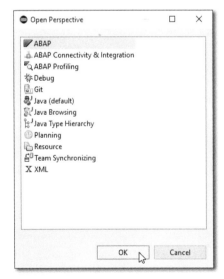

Figure 7.34 Opening the ABAP Perspective in Eclipse

In the ABAP perspective, you first need to create an ABAP project. This involves connecting to an existing SAP NetWeaver ABAP system and gives you access to the contained development objects. The easiest way to create an ABAP project is to click on the little drop-down arrow next to the New icon and choose ABAP Project (see Figure 7.35).

ABAP project

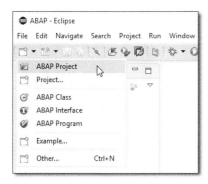

Figure 7.35 Creating a New ABAP Project

In the subsequent dialog box, you can browse your existing SAP GUI connections and choose the one pointing to your SAP Gateway backend system. It's also possible to define a manual connection by providing the system ID, application server, and instance number.

On the next screen, you need to provide the logon information to the ABAP system (client, user, password, and language) and click Finish.

By default, the $TMP package is added to your Favorite Packages. That is sufficient for our example. By right-clicking on Favorite Packages and choosing Add a Package, you can add additional packages. That is required, for example, if you want to transport your development into connected systems.

To create ABAP CDS views, you need to create a Data Definition Language (DDL) source. A DDL source is the underlying ABAP development object for all CDS entities.

DDL Source

To create a DDL source, right-click on $TMP in the navigation tree and select New • Other ABAP Repository Object. In the New ABAP Repository Object wizard, scroll down to Core Data Services, expand the node, and select DDL Source (see Figure 7.36).

Figure 7.36 New ABAP Repository Object Entry

Select NEXT to open the NEW DDL SOURCE wizard where you need to provide a NAME as well as a DESCRIPTION for the DDL source you want to create. The PACKAGE and PROJECT are provided by default based on your current selection (see Figure 7.37).

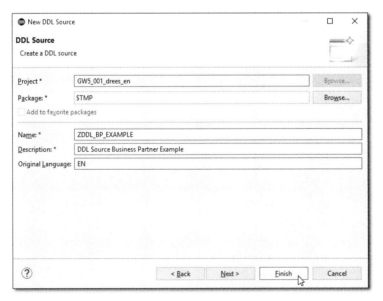

Figure 7.37 New DDL Source Wizard

That is sufficient for the time being. You can choose NEXT to assign a transport request or select a different template than the default one. There are templates for joins (DEFINE VIEW WITH JOIN) and for associations (DEFINE VIEW WITH ASSOCIATION) that can help you develop more complex DDL sources.

After selecting FINISH, the DDL source is created, and the related text editor opens. By default, the name of the ABAP CDS view is set to the name of the DDL source (see Figure 7.38).

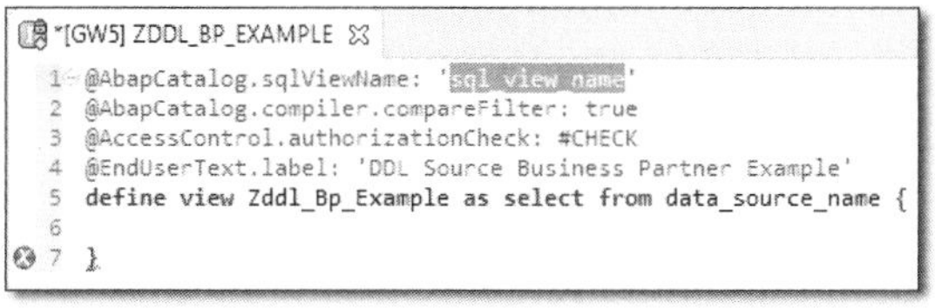

```
*[GW5] ZDDL_BP_EXAMPLE ☒
1  @AbapCatalog.sqlViewName: 'sql view name'
2  @AbapCatalog.compiler.compareFilter: true
3  @AccessControl.authorizationCheck: #CHECK
4  @EndUserText.label: 'DDL Source Business Partner Example'
5  define view Zddl_Bp_Example as select from data_source_name {
6
7  }
```

Figure 7.38 Text Editor after DDL Source Creation

Another element that comes into play when defining a CDS view in the DDL source is the SQL view. For each CDS view, a corresponding SQL view is generated in the ABAP DDIC. The structure of the view is defined by the CDS view. The SQL view allows you to access the data via the KNOWN tools (e.g., Transaction SE11 and Transaction SE16) and Open SQL statements, although it's not recommended to use the generated SQL view in ABAP programs. Instead, you should use the CDS view to make full use of the new CDS features.

SQL view

Note that the name of the SQL view and the name of the CDS view have to be different.

Naming

> **Naming**
>
> When creating ABAP CDS views, you have to distinguish three names:
>
> ▸ **Name of the DDL source**
>   The DDL source contains the ABAP development object. This name appears in the navigation tree under DATA DEFINITIONS.
>
> ▸ **Name of the SQL view**
>   This is the name of the ABAP DDIC SQL view, defined by the @AbapCatalog.sqlViewName annotation at the beginning of the DDL source.

> ► **Name of the ABAP CDS view**
> This is the name defined by the text right after `define view`. You can access this name under your ABAP CDS view (e.g., via the Service Builder).

Let's start our example by changing the highlighted SQL view name (see Figure 7.38). By default, the SQL view name is always called `sql_view_name`, which you can change into `zview_bp_example`. Then, change the actual ABAP CDS view name from `Zddl_Bp_Example` to `ZCDS_BP_Example`.

Begin by accessing a single EPM table and picking a few fields from it. For this, change `data_source_name` to `snwd_bpa`, which is the root table of the EPM business partner. To reduce the typing effort, define an alias by adding `as bp`.

Finally, define a set of three fields: `bp.node_key`, `bp.bp_id`, and `bp.company_name`. The `node_key` is a GUID that is defined as the primary key of the table. Add it to the ABAP CDS view definition; otherwise, all view fields would be considered key fields. The `bp.node_key` receives the prefix `key` to indicate that this field is the primary key of the ABAP CDS view. The resulting CDS view should look like Figure 7.39.

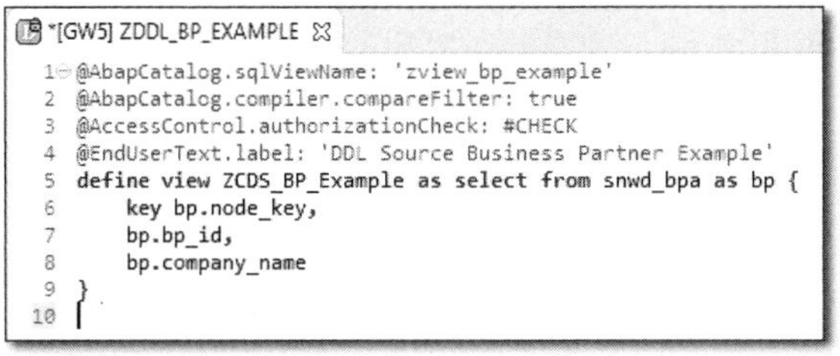

```
[GW5] ZDDL_BP_EXAMPLE ⊠
 1  @AbapCatalog.sqlViewName: 'zview_bp_example'
 2  @AbapCatalog.compiler.compareFilter: true
 3  @AccessControl.authorizationCheck: #CHECK
 4  @EndUserText.label: 'DDL Source Business Partner Example'
 5  define view ZCDS_BP_Example as select from snwd_bpa as bp {
 6      key bp.node_key,
 7      bp.bp_id,
 8      bp.company_name
 9  }
10
```

Figure 7.39 First ABAP CDS View

Note that the client handling (e.g., `MANDT` field) is done implicitly. It's not necessary to add the client field to the definition of the ABAP CDS view. The generated SQL view automatically contains the client field in case the underlying data source (in this case, table `snwd_bpa`) contains one as well.

To active the object, either click the related menu button or press [Ctrl]+[F3], as in the ABAP Development Workbench. Once activated, you can run a data preview by right-clicking on the DDL source name and selecting OPEN DATA PREVIEW (see Figure 7.40).

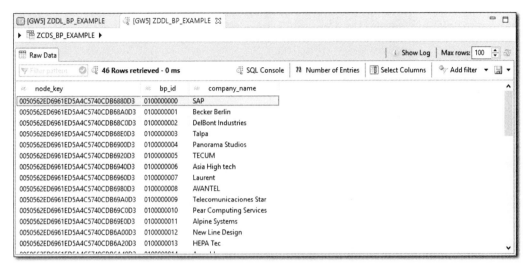

Figure 7.40 Preview of the ABAP CDS View

You can beautify the field names a bit by providing more understandable field names as shown in Listing 7.5.

```
@AbapCatalog.sqlViewName: 'zview_bp_example'
@AbapCatalog.compiler.compareFilter: true
@AccessControl.authorizationCheck: #CHECK
@EndUserText.label: 'DDL Source Business Partner Example'
define view ZCDS_BP_Example as select from snwd_bpa as bp {
    key bp.node_key as BusinessPartnerUUID,
    bp.bp_id       as BusinessPartnerID,
    bp.company_name as CompanyName
}
```

Listing 7.5 Field Names

This simple ABAP CDS view is already sufficient for use as a source for a Service Builder project.

7.3.1 Modeled Data Sources

So far, all the data sources that we've used in the Service Builder projects are *modeled data sources (MDS)*. This is because the entire model down to each property is modeled during design time and generated into the related MPC classes.

MDS for CDS view   The same approach can be followed when adding ABAP CDS views to your data model. For this, create a new project (e.g., ZCDS_MDS), right-click on DATA MODEL, and choose IMPORT • DDIC STRUCTURE. The name of the ABAP STRUCTURE is the name of the generated ZVIEW_BP_EXAMPLE SQL view (see Figure 7.41).

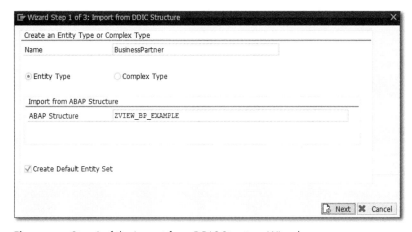

Figure 7.41 Step 1 of the Import from DDIC Structure Wizard

On the second screen of the wizard, select all fields apart from the client field (MANDT). On the third screen, mark the BUSINESSPARTNERUUID as the primary key, and select FINISH. This results in an entity type with three properties, as shown in Figure 7.42.

Name	Key	Edm Type	Prec.	Scale	Max	U	Crea	Upd	Sort	Null	Filt.	Label	L	C	ABAP Field Name
Businesspartneruuid	✓	Edm.Guid	0	0	0							Node Key	T		BUSINESSPARTNERUUID
Businesspartnerid		Edm.String	0	0	10							Business Partner ID	T		BUSINESSPARTNERID
Companyname		Edm.String	0	0	80							Company	T		COMPANYNAME

Figure 7.42 Imported ABAP CDS View Properties

Thus far, we've created an entity type (including an entity set) based on a DDIC source. The actual ABAP CDS view relation comes into play

during service implementation. For this, expand the SERVICE IMPLEMEN-
TATION node in the navigation tree, right-click on BUSINESSPARTNERSET,
and choose MAP TO DATA SOURCE. Note that this time you right-click on
the entity set itself and not on a single operation (see Figure 7.43).

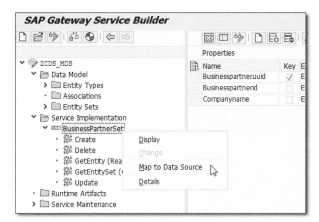

Figure 7.43 Performing Service Implementation

In the MAP TO DATA SOURCE pop-up, you'll find the new entry BUSINESS
ENTITY in the TYPE dropdown. The name of our data source is CDS~ZCDS_
BP_EXAMPLE. The name can be selected by using the F4 value help (see
Figure 7.44).

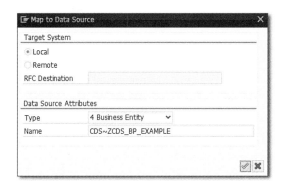

Figure 7.44 Defining the ABAP CDS View as a Data Source

Confirming the popup opens up the MODELED DATA SOURCE mapping screen. Similar to the RFC mapping, you can generate the mapping by clicking the GENERATE MAPPING button (see Figure 7.45).

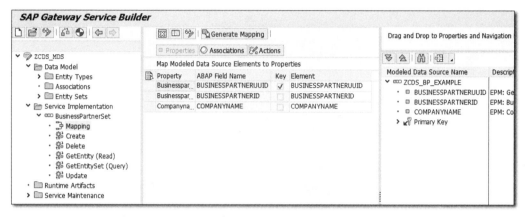

Figure 7.45 Mapping the ABAP CDS View Properties

This concludes the mapping. You can generate and register the OData service and run it using the SAP Gateway client. Executing the URI */sap/ opu/odata/SAP/ZCDS_MDS_SRV/BusinessPartnerSet* in the SAP Gateway client provides you an unfiltered list of business partners.

SADL   The data access at runtime is handled via the *Service Adaptation Definition Language (SADL)* framework, which translates, for example, filter statements into `where` clauses for direct database access. This significantly improves the performance and avoids the need to write ABAP coding to cover all query options. Even filters that couldn't be handled via select options can be executed, such as the following example that uses a `$filter` statement with the `substringof` query option:

/sap/opu/odata/SAP/ZCDS_MDS_SRV/BusinessPartnerSet?$filter=substringof('ech',Companyname) or Businesspartnerid lt '100000001'

If you execute this URI in the SAP Gateway client, you'll obtain the result shown in Figure 7.46.

Figure 7.46 Running OData Service Based on an ABAP CDS View

You can now extend the ABAP CDS view by adding a join to provide the address information. The adjusted DDL source is shown in Listing 7.6.

```
@AbapCatalog.sqlViewName: 'zview_bp_example'
@AbapCatalog.compiler.compareFilter: true
@AccessControl.authorizationCheck: #CHECK
@EndUserText.label: 'DDL Source Business Partner Example'
define view ZCDS_BP_Example
    as select from snwd_bpa as bp
    inner join snwd_ad as adr
    on bp.address_guid = adr.node_key
{
    key bp.node_key as BusinessPartnerUUID,
    bp.bp_id        as BusinessPartnerID,
    bp.company_name as CompanyName,
    adr.city        as City,
    adr.country     as CountryID
}
```

Listing 7.6 Extended CDS View That Returns Business Partners and the Country and City They Are Located In

This adds the `City` and `CountryID` fields to the ABAP CDS view. After you've activated the DDL source, restart the Service Builder, put your project into edit mode, and expand the navigation tree. Right-click on the BUSINESSPARTNER entity type, and choose IMPORT • PROPERTIES (see Figure 7.47). It's necessary to restart the Service Builder because it caches the dictionary objects that have been read, and therefore you wouldn't see your changes without a restart.

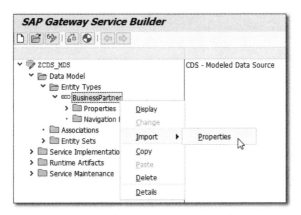

Figure 7.47 Starting the Import Properties Dialog

This opens up the wizard that you've used during the initial definition of the entity type. It allows you to select additional fields from the underlying data source (`ZVIEW_BP_EXAMPLE` SQL view) that haven't been imported so far. Mark the two new fields CITY and COUNTRYID, and complete the wizard (see Figure 7.48).

You also need to revisit the mapping screen under SERVICE IMPLEMENTATION. The GENERATE MAPPING button should add the new mappings. Regenerate your project, and run the OData service in the SAP Gateway client.

As you can see, you have to edit the data model definition and adapt the mapping in the service implementation part in your Service Builder project whenever you want to add new properties, for example.

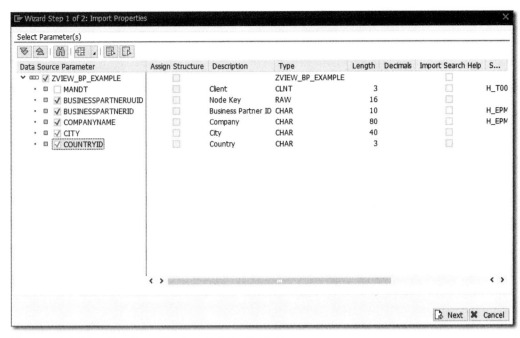

Figure 7.48 Adding New Properties to an Existing Entity Type

7.3.2 Reference Data Sources

Reference data sources (RDS) allow you a more generic approach of exposing ABAP CDS views via OData services.

First, create a new Service Builder project (e.g., ZCDS_RDS). Instead of importing the DDIC structure, right-click on DATA MODEL, and choose REFERENCE • MODELED DATA SOURCE REFERENCE (see Figure 7.49).

RDS

In step 1 of the REFERENCE DATA SOURCE WIZARD screen, choose CDS CORE DATA SERVICES as the MODELED DATA SOURCE TYPE and ZCDS_BP_EXAMPLE as the MODELED DATA SOURCE NAME (see Figure 7.50). The data source name also offers a value help that can be used to find the ABAP CDS view.

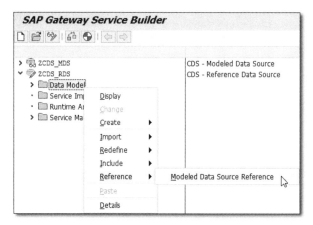

Figure 7.49 Starting the Reference Data Source Dialog

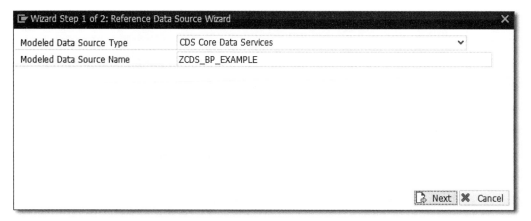

Figure 7.50 Step 1 of the Reference Data Source Wizard

Choosing NEXT analyzes the definition of the provided ABAP CDS view and displays the result on the subsequent screen (see Figure 7.51). Our ABAP CDS view is pretty simple and doesn't contain any association, so no additional elements are shown in the wizard. Click FINISH to add the reference of the ABAP CDS view to our project. You might have noticed that there was no need to select individual properties or to define a key property. This is all derived from the reference to the ABAP CDS view.

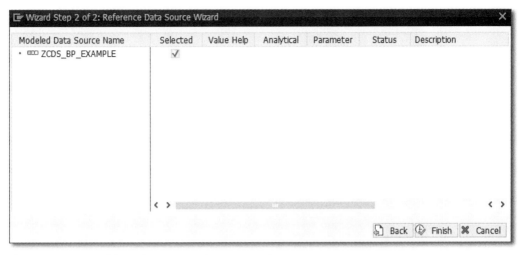

Figure 7.51 Step 2 of the Reference Data Source Wizard

Generate the Service Builder project, and register the OData service on the SAP Gateway hub. You can consume the business partner entity set via */sap/opu/odata/SAP/ZCDS_RDS_SRV/ZCDS_BP_Example*. As you can see, the name of the entity set is automatically set to the name of the ABAP CDS view.

Now add the `Street` and `Building` fields to the ABAP CDS view, and activate it via the ABAP Development Tools in Listing 7.7.

```
@AbapCatalog.sqlViewName: 'zview_bp_example'
@AbapCatalog.compiler.compareFilter: true
@AccessControl.authorizationCheck: #CHECK
@EndUserText.label: 'DDL Source Business Partner Example'
define view ZCDS_BP_Example
    as select from snwd_bpa as bp
    inner join snwd_ad as adr
    on bp.address_guid = adr.node_key
{
    key bp.node_key as BusinessPartnerUUID,
    bp.bp_id         as BusinessPartnerID,
    bp.company_name as CompanyName,
    adr.city         as City,
    adr.country      as CountryID,
    adr.street       as Street,
    adr.building     as Building
}
```

Listing 7.7 CDS View Definition with the New Street and Building Fields

This time, there's no need to restart or regenerate the Service Builder project. Depending on your cache configuration on the SAP Gateway hub, you might need to clear the cache. After that, the new `Street` and `Building` properties automatically appear in the data model and are also filled with the corresponding values (see Figure 7.52).

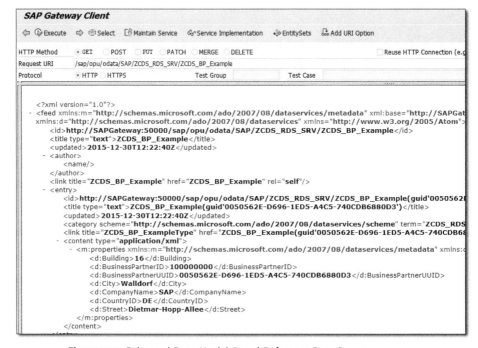

Figure 7.52 Enhanced Data Model-Based Reference Data Source

The next step is to enhance the ABAP CDS view by adding an association. For this, we create a new DDL source, ZDDL_CONT_EXAMPLE, that defines an ABAP CDS view for the EPM contact person (Listing 7.8).

EPM contact person

```
@AbapCatalog.sqlViewName: 'zview_ct_example'
@AbapCatalog.compiler.compareFilter: true
@AccessControl.authorizationCheck: #CHECK
@EndUserText.label: 'DDL Source Contact Example'
define view ZCDS_Cont_Example
    as select from snwd_bpa_contact as cont
    {
        key cont.node_key as ContactUUID,
        cont.first_name as FirstName,
        cont.last_name  as LastName,
```

```
        cont.parent_key as BusinessPartnerUUID
}
```

Listing 7.8 Additional CDS View to Show Navigation

Don't forget to activate the new DDL source in the ABAP Development Tools.

Add a zero to the association ([0..*]) of the business partner ZCDS_BP_ Example ABAP CDS view (Listing 7.9). The association points to the new ZCDS_Cont_Example ABAP CDS view that you've created before. Don't forget to also add contacts to the field list to make the association "visible" to consumers such as the Service Builder.

```
@AbapCatalog.sqlViewName: 'zview_bp_example'
@AbapCatalog.compiler.compareFilter: true
@AccessControl.authorizationCheck: #CHECK
@EndUserText.label: 'DDL Source Business Partner Example'
define view ZCDS_BP_Example
    as select from snwd_bpa as bp
    inner join snwd_ad as adr
    on bp.address_guid = adr.node_key

    association [0..*] to ZCDS_Cont_Example as contacts
    on $projection.BusinessPartnerUUID = contacts.BusinessPartn
erUUID
{
    key bp.node_key    as BusinessPartnerUUID,
    bp.bp_id           as BusinessPartnerID,
    bp.company_name    as CompanyName,
    adr.city           as City,
    adr.country        as CountryID,
    adr.street         as Street,
    adr.building       as Building,

    contacts
}
```

Listing 7.9 CDS View Extended with Association

Now you need to restart the Service Builder to access the new developments. Put the project into edit mode, expand the DATA MODEL • DATA SOURCE REFERENCES • EXPOSURE VIA SADL node, and double-click on EXPOSURE FOR CDS. This opens up the main screen for adding/removing associations and ABAP CDS views. You'll see that the contacts association as well as the new ZCDS_Cont_Example view appears now under the existing ZCDS_BP_Example view (see Figure 7.53).

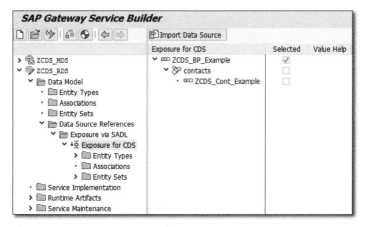

Figure 7.53 New Association and ABAP CDS View

By default, the new association and view aren't selected. This needs to be done manually and is the only change you need to make when using RDSs. After you've selected both new elements, you need to regenerate your project. This adds the new elements to your OData service. In addition, you'll find a `tocontacts` navigation property when consuming the service. It allows you to navigate to the list of contacts associated to a certain business partner.

7.4   Generation via Redefinition

As you saw in Section 7.1, creating an OData service using the RFC/BOR Generator has much in common with the manual development process described in Chapter 6. In both cases, it's necessary to use an entity data model as a basis for the service implementation. Although the RFC/BOR Generator doesn't require the developer to write his own code, the mapping process can become tedious if there's no suitable RFC function module available. On the other hand, the generated services provide a lot of out-of-the-box functionality such as the support of filtering and client-side paging that otherwise has to be implemented manually.

Obviously, it would be nice to be able to generate OData services with a minimized need for manual action, and this is where the integration scenarios supported by the Service Builder come into play. SAP has invested greatly in sophisticated frameworks that allow the modeling of business objects for various use cases. In addition, customers themselves have implemented their business scenarios based on these frameworks or have adapted existing objects delivered by SAP. Fortunately, these business objects can be used to generate OData services, which is a process known as *redefinition*.

The term redefinition stems from the inheritance concept that is available in ABAP objects. ABAP objects allow the method of a superclass to be redefined in a subclass to implement extended functionality while still being able to leverage the functionalities of the base class. An OData service that has been created through the Service Builder using redefinition inherits the functionality of the business object that has been used as a data source.

Redefining a service from an existing business object is available for the following frameworks:

Redefinition

Redefinition frameworks

- ▶ SAP BW
- ▶ Service Provider Interface
- ▶ GenIL
- ▶ Operational Data Provisioning (ODP)

These business objects already have much in common with OData services. Because they support similar concepts, such as entity sets and query methods, it's possible to map these concepts to the entity sets and CRUD-Q methods of an OData service.

In addition, it's possible to create a service via redefinition with the following options:

- ▶ ODATA SERVICE (GW): Built with SAP Gateway.
- ▶ ODATA SERVICE: Built with third-party tools.

The support of these integration scenarios has been implemented within different software components that have been built on top of SAP_GWFND/IW_BEP and are shipped in separate add-ons. While the integration scenario for Service Provider Interface requires the deployment of the IW_SPI add-on, the integration with GenIL requires the IW_GIL add-on. The integration with SAP BW objects and OData services is already included in IW_BEP and SAP_GWFND. Depending on the add-ons that are installed in your system, the redefinition option in the Service Builder will offer different submenu options under REDEFINE. You'll find the SPI SERVICE, GENIL SERVICE, and BW QUERY SERVICE options, as shown in Figure 7.54, depending on the installed add-ons just mentioned.

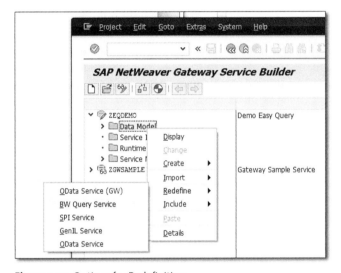

Figure 7.54 Options for Redefinition

Wizard Selecting one of these options starts a wizard that will guide you through the following three steps:

1. Select the business object.

2. Perform service registration in the backend, and deal with transport-related issues.

3. Select artifacts of the data source.

A hands-on description of the generation of an OData service is almost identical for all integration scenarios mentioned earlier. The steps that have to be performed to generate an OData service based on existing services from external frameworks and from existing OData services from SAP Gateway mainly differ in the third dialog, which shows the artifacts of the data source that can be selected.

We've already shown in Section 7.1 how a service can be generated based on the RFC/BOR Generator, so we'll now provide step-by-step instructions on how OData services can be generated based on two business objects:

Redefinition examples

▸ SAP BW Easy Query (Section 7.4.1)

▸ Service Provider Interface (Section 7.4.2)

SAP BW Easy Query and the Service Provider Interface

7.4.1 SAP BW Easy Query

SAP BW Easy Queries provide an external interface for accessing analytic queries in SAP BW. Unlike other external query interfaces in SAP BW, SAP BW Easy Queries intentionally limit the flexibility of data processing to provide an easy way to consume queries. SAP BW Easy Queries thus reduce complexity in certain areas.

Let's look at a use case for the generation of a service based on an SAP BW Easy Query. Suppose that a company wants to offer an application that can be used to provide data about the sales numbers of its products in various countries. The reporting data will be filled dynamically with the query data from the company's SAP BW system.

Business case

In this example, we'll use the SAP demo content for features. Each sample scenario of the SAP demo content contains predefined objects, such as InfoProviders, queries, and workbooks, with prepopulated data. Part of the SAP demo content is a sample scenario based on the SAP NetWeaver Demo Model, which contains several queries—we'll use the one called `0D_FC_NW_C01_Q0001`. (For more details about the SAP demo content, see *http://help.sap.com/saphelp_nw74/helpdata/en/47/addc08e04b1599e10000000a42189c/frameset.htm*.)

> **Note**
>
> In older releases, SAP demo content didn't contain queries marked as SAP BW Easy Queries. Therefore, the existing query just mentioned needs to be copied, marked as an SAP BW Easy Query, and saved with the new technical name `ZOD_FC_NW_C01_Q0001`. This has changed with SP 06 of SAP Gateway

7.40, where several queries of the demo content have been marked as SAP BW Easy Queries.

Follow these steps in SAP BW:

1. Before you start to use SAP BW Easy Query, there are certain system settings that have to be performed in your SAP BW system. These settings are described in SAP Note 1944258.

2. Use the BEx Query Designer (which allows you to look up an existing query model or create a new one) to create or locate the analytic query to be used.

3. Release the analytic query for external access as an SAP BW Easy Query. Here you have to comply with rules for SAP BW Easy Query design. A tabular layout has to be selected. You also have to keep in mind that only single-valued and interval variables are supported, no conditions or exceptions can be used, and there is no support for input-enabled queries used in planning contexts.

The generation of a corresponding OData service for an existing SAP BW Easy Query has to be performed in a system where the IW_BEP add-on has been deployed or in a system that runs on top of at least SAP NetWeaver 7.40 SP 02. This can either be in the SAP BW system or in the SAP Gateway hub system.

As a prerequisite, the SAP_BW component must be based on SAP_BW 7.30 SP 08 and above or SAP_BW 7.31 SP 05 and above.

For this chapter, we're using client 001 of an SAP NetWeaver 7.40 ABAP trial system (*www.sap.com/abaptrial*) where SAP BW sample content has been activated.

Process steps

In the remainder of this section, you'll perform the steps described in the following:

1. Generate an OData service based on the SAP BW Easy Query using redefinition (encompasses the data model definition and service implementation phases).

2. Publish the service on the SAP Gateway system (service maintenance phase).

3. Use the BEAUTIFICATION option to rename the properties of the generated entity set (part of the data model definition phase).

4. Regenerate the service (from the service implementation phase).

The steps and their assignment to the three phases of service creation are shown in Figure 7.55.

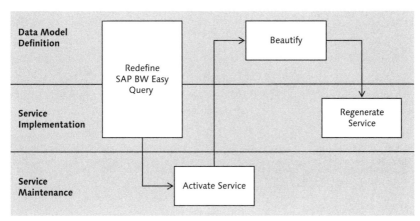

Figure 7.55 Redefining an SAP BW Query Service

Redefine SAP BW Easy Query

After the SAP BW Easy Query is created, you can start to generate an OData service by creating a project in the Service Builder that is called ZEQDEMO.

Create a project

Right-click on the DATA MODEL node, select REDEFINE, and then choose BW QUERY SERVICE as shown in Figure 7.56.

Redefine

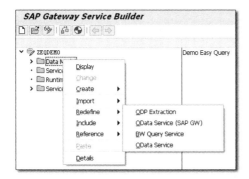

Figure 7.56 Redefining SAP BW Query Service

This starts the wizard for the redefinition of an SAP BW query service, as shown in Figure 7.57. In the first of three screens of the wizard, you

Wizard: Step 1

have to enter several input parameters. In the ACCESS TYPE field, specify which kind of SAP BW query to use. You can choose from CONTROLLER FOR MDX (SAP BW) or CONTROLLER FOR EASY QUERIES (SAP BW). For this scenario, choose the latter because it's the recommended one. In the RFC DESTINATION field, specify the name of the RFC destination pointing to the SAP BW system. For our example, choose NONE because the SAP BW Easy Query is accessed in the same system and client. Leave the CATALOG NAME field blank. For the QUERY NAME field, enter the name of the SAP BW Easy Query, "Z0D_FC_NW_C01_Q0001," which was created beforehand.

Figure 7.57 Redefine Service Wizard: Step 1 of 3

Wizard: Step 2   On the second screen of the wizard, shown in Figure 7.58, you provide a description for the technical model and the technical service that is being created.

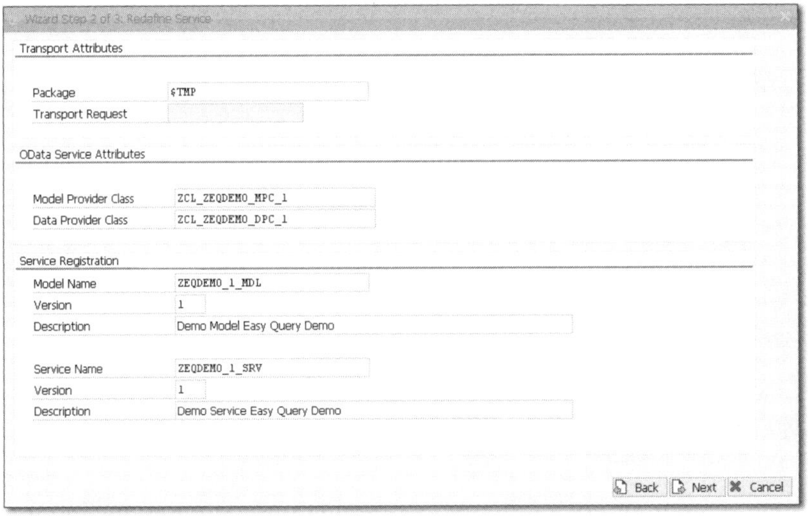

Figure 7.58 Redefine Service Wizard: Step 2 of 3

On the final screen of the wizard, be sure to select all options, as shown in Figure 7.59, and click FINISH.

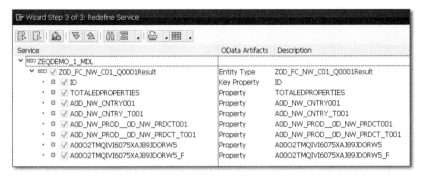

Wizard: Step 3

Figure 7.59 Redefine Service Wizard: Step 3 of 3

Finally, click the GENERATE button to generate an OData service based on an SAP BW Easy Query through redefinition, as shown in Figure 7.60.

Generate and register service

Figure 7.60 Generation of the Redefined Service

In the MODEL AND SERVICE DEFINITION dialog box shown in Figure 7.61, leave the default values, and then click CONTINUE. This step creates both MPC classes and DPC classes, as you've learned from the previous examples. It also registers the service on the backend side by creating a technical model and a technical service.

In the CREATE OBJECT DIRECTORY ENTRY window, click the LOCAL OBJECT button, which sets the package to $TMP. If you want to transport the repository elements, you need to provide a transportable package.

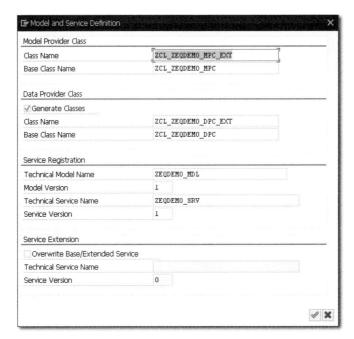

Figure 7.61 Model and Service Generation: SAP BW Easy Query

Activate Service

Service activation

After the project has been successfully generated and registered on the backend, the service must be registered and activated on the SAP Gateway hub system. For this, you expand the SERVICE MAINTENANCE node in the project, right-click on the hub entry you want the service to register and activate on, and select REGISTER from the context menu.

After confirming the warning pop-up, which informs you that this step will be carried out on the SAP Gateway hub system, you provide the system alias that was created before on the hub system that points to the SAP BW system (this pop-up only appears if several system alias entries have been created).

In the ADD SERVICE dialog on the hub, click LOCAL OBJECT to select $TMP as the package for the repository objects of the service that you're now

going to generate, and click OK. If you want to create repository objects
that can be transported, you have to choose an appropriate package.

Afterward, it's possible to test the access to the newly created service. **Test the service**
Expand the SERVICE MAINTENANCE node in the project, right-click on the
hub entry used to publish the service, and select SAP GATEWAY CLIENT
from the context menu. Here you can start the SAP Gateway client as
shown in Figure 7.62.

Figure 7.62 Testing the Activated Service with the SAP Gateway Client

If the service is working properly, the SAP Gateway client displays the
service document as shown in Figure 7.63.

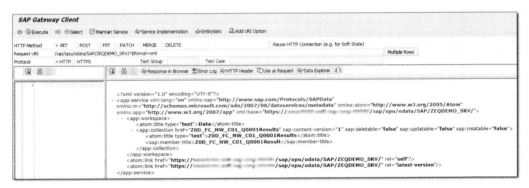

Figure 7.63 Test Service Document

You can retrieve the result of the query by entering the following URI in
the SAP Gateway client:

/sap/opu/odata/sap/ZEQDEMO_SRV/ZOD_FC_NW_C01_Q0001Results

The service responds with a set of entries as shown in Figure 7.64.

```
<entry>
  <id>https://                    /sap/opu/odata/SAP/ZEQDEMO_SRV/Z0D_FC_NW_C01_Q0001Results
  ('2.3_DEMOB')</id>
  <title type="text">Z0D_FC_NW_C01_Q0001Results('2.3_DEMOB')</title>
  <updated>2016-01-07T13:28:14Z</updated>
  <category scheme="http://schemas.microsoft.com/ado/2007/08/dataservices/scheme"
    term="ZEQDEMO_SRV.Z0D_FC_NW_C01_Q0001Result"/>
  <link title="Z0D_FC_NW_C01_Q0001Result" href="Z0D_FC_NW_C01_Q0001Results('2.3_DEMOB')" rel="self"/>
- <content type="application/xml">
  -  <m:properties xmlns:m="http://schemas.microsoft.com/ado/2007/08/dataservices/metadata"
     xmlns:d="http://schemas.microsoft.com/ado/2007/08/dataservices">
        <d:ID>2.3_DEMOB</d:ID>
        <d:TotaledProperties/>
        <d:A0D_NW_CNTRY>DE</d:A0D_NW_CNTRY>
        <d:A0D_NW_CNTRY_T>DE</d:A0D_NW_CNTRY_T>
        <d:A0D_NW_PROD__0D_NW_PRDCT>MOB</d:A0D_NW_PROD__0D_NW_PRDCT>
        <d:A0D_NW_PROD__0D_NW_PRDCT_T>MOB</d:A0D_NW_PROD__0D_NW_PRDCT_T>
        <d:A00O2TMQIVI6075XAJ89JDORW5>16808664.0000000000000</d:A00O2TMQIVI6075XAJ89JDORW5>
        <d:A00O2TMQIVI6075XAJ89JDORW5_F>16.808.664,00 EUR</d:A00O2TMQIVI6075XAJ89JDORW5_F>
     </m:properties>
  </content>
</entry>
```

Figure 7.64 Single Entry: Query Result

SAP BW query results

Log on to the SAP BW client of the ABAP trial system to have a look at the query results that can be retrieved using Transaction RSRT. Enter the name of the query, and choose the query display option HTML. The result is shown in Figure 7.65 for the COUNTRY and PRODUCT CATEGORY drilldowns.

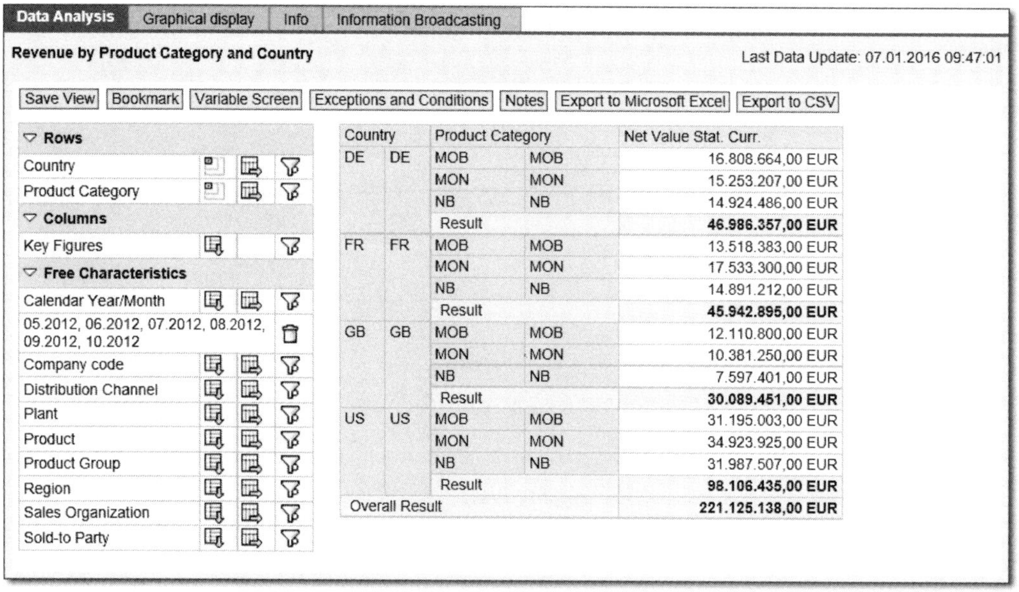

| Data Analysis | Graphical display | Info | Information Broadcasting |

Revenue by Product Category and Country   Last Data Update: 07.01.2016 09:47:01

| Save View | Bookmark | Variable Screen | Exceptions and Conditions | Notes | Export to Microsoft Excel | Export to CSV |

▽ Rows				Country	Product Category		Net Value Stat. Curr.
Country				DE	DE	MOB	MOB	16.808.664,00 EUR
Product Category						MON	MON	15.253.207,00 EUR
▽ Columns						NB	NB	14.924.486,00 EUR
Key Figures						Result		46.986.357,00 EUR
▽ Free Characteristics				FR	FR	MOB	MOB	13.518.383,00 EUR
Calendar Year/Month						MON	MON	17.533.300,00 EUR
05.2012, 06.2012, 07.2012, 08.2012, 09.2012, 10.2012						NB	NB	14.891.212,00 EUR
Company code						Result		45.942.895,00 EUR
Distribution Channel				GB	GB	MOB	MOB	12.110.800,00 EUR
Plant						MON	MON	10.381.250,00 EUR
Product						NB	NB	7.597.401,00 EUR
Product Group						Result		30.089.451,00 EUR
Region				US	US	MOB	MOB	31.195.003,00 EUR
Sales Organization						MON	MON	34.923.925,00 EUR
Sold-to Party						NB	NB	31.987.507,00 EUR
						Result		98.106.435,00 EUR
				Overall Result				221.125.138,00 EUR

Figure 7.65 Transaction RSRT: Query Monitor

Beautify

As you may have noticed (refer to Figure 7.64), the properties of the `Z0D_FC_NW_C01_Q0001Results` entity set that return the query result aren't very easy to grasp. They are defined by the technical names found in the original SAP BW query. However, the properties of the entity set can be renamed and beautified so that they are easier to understand for the non-SAP developer. To do so, start the Service Builder, and open the ZEQDEMO project. Navigate to the entity type Z0D_FC_NW_C01_ Q0001RESULT, and choose REDEFINE ATTRIBUTES. Replace the value in the NAME column with values that are derived from those you find in the LABEL column (Figure 7.66). These are the same names that can be found in the `sap:label` annotations in the service metadata document.

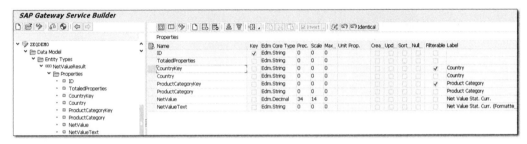

Figure 7.66 Redefining Attributes

Note that properties must not contain special characters such as white spaces. You thus create property names following a camel case notation by removing any special characters such as white spaces or points. Perform the following changes in the NAME column:

No special characters

- Change A0D_NW_CNTRY_T to COUNTRY.
- Change A0D_NW_CNTRY to COUNTRYKEY.
- Change A0D_NW_PROD__0D_NW_PRDCT_T to PRODUCTCATEGORY.
- Change A0D_NW_PROD__0D_NW_PRDCT to PRODUCTCATEGORYKEY.
- Change A00O2TMQIVI6075XAJ89JDORW5 to NETVALUE.
- Change A00O2TMQIVI6075XAJ89JDORW5_F to NETVALUETEXT.

In addition to the property names in the generated entity type, you can redefine the name of the Z0D_FC_NW_C01_Q0001RESULT entity type and the Z0D_FC_NW_C01_Q0001RESULTS entity set to NETVALUERESULT and NETVALUERESULTS, respectively, and then click SAVE.

Regenerate Service

After performing all changes, you can now regenerate the OData service by clicking the GENERATE button. Then you can retrieve the beautified query result in the browser or the SAP Gateway client.

The generated service supports filtering out of the box because the properties used in the row have been marked in the underlying SAP BW Easy Query such that they are provided as TEXT AND KEY. This is why you're able to filter on the NetValueResults entity set using the $filter=CountryKey eq 'US' filter string to limit the result set using the following URI in the SAP Gateway client or in a browser:

/sap/opu/odata/sap/ZEQDEMO_SRV/NetValueResults?$filter=CountryKey eq 'US'&$select=ProductCategory,NetValueText&$format=json

Compare the result shown earlier in Figure 7.65 with the result retrieved with Transaction RSRT shown in Figure 7.67.

```
{
 - d: {
   - results: [
     - {
         + __metadata: {...},
           ProductCategory: "MOB",
           NetValueText: "31.195.003,00 EUR"
       },
     - {
         + __metadata: {...},
           ProductCategory: "MON",
           NetValueText: "34.923.925,00 EUR"
       },
     - {
         + __metadata: {...},
           ProductCategory: "NB",
           NetValueText: "31.987.507,00 EUR"
       },
     - {
         + __metadata: {...},
           ProductCategory: "Overall Result",
           NetValueText: "98.106.435,00 EUR"
       }
     ]
   }
}
```

Figure 7.67 Filtered and Beautified Result

7.4.2 Service Provider Interface

A second example of an integration scenario is the Service Provider Interface. In contrast to SAP BW, query services based on Service Provider Interface also allow you to create, update, and change data in the backend system. Because the Service Provider Interface is remote-enabled, the IW_SPI add-on can also be deployed on the SAP Gateway hub system. As a result of the redefinition process, the nodes, data structure, and ID structure in the Service Provider Interface model are mapped to the corresponding entity types in an OData model.

In this section, we'll use a sample Service Provider Interface object based on the enterprise procurement model that is shipped as part of the SAP Business Suite foundation software component (SAP_BS_FND). The business case is that you want to build an OData service for an application that allows a user to list the business partners of the fictional company ITelo. The application will allow the user not only to list business partners but also to create new business partners, update existing ones, and retrieve the contacts of a business partner. To take advantage of the work already invested in building this business partner service using the Service Provider Interface framework, you can reuse this service to generate an easy-to-consume OData service.

Service Provider Interface

To run this example, you need an SAP Gateway hub system or SAP backend system where the add-ons of Table 7.1 have been deployed.

Software Component	Description
SAP_GWFND/IW_BEP	Backend Event Provider
IW_SPI	Service Provider Infrastructure
SAP_BS_FND	SAP Business Suite Foundation

Table 7.1 Add-Ons Needed to Generate OData Services Based on Service Provider Interface

The system in this example is using an embedded deployment. In the remainder of this section, you'll perform the steps required to generate an OData service based on a Service Provider Interface service:

1. Generate an OData service based on a Service Provider Interface service using redefinition (encompasses the data model definition and service implementation phases).

2. Publish the service on the SAP Gateway system (service maintenance phase).

In contrast to the redefinition of an SAP BW Easy Query, it's not necessary to jump back to the data model definition phase because the names of the entity types, entity sets, and their properties are already readable.

The steps and their assignment to the three phases of service creation are depicted in Figure 7.68.

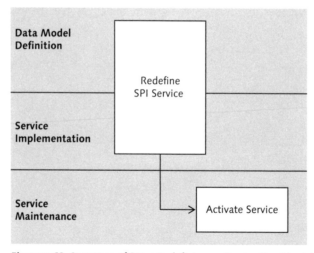

Figure 7.68 Sequence of Steps Redefining an Service Provider Interface Service

Redefine Service Provider Interface Service

Create project   Start by creating a new project in the Service Builder (Transaction SEGW) that is called ZSPIDEMO. In the project tree, right-click on the DATA MODEL node, select REDEFINE, and then choose SPI SERVICE as shown in Figure 7.69.

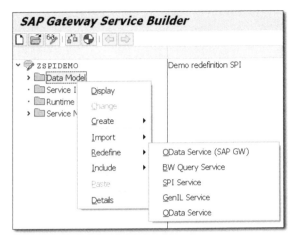

Figure 7.69 Starting Service Generation Based on Service Provider Interface Objects

On the first screen of the wizard (see Figure 7.70), you have to specify the Service Provider Interface object that should serve as a data source, as described in Table 7.2.

Redefine a Service Provider Interface service; Wizard: Step 1 of 3

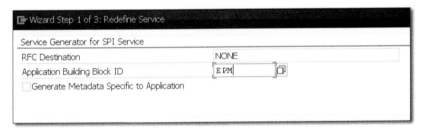

Figure 7.70 Selecting the Application Building Block ID

Field Name	Value
RFC DESTINATION	Specify the name of the RFC destination pointing to the backend system where the Service Provider Interface object resides. In this example, we select NONE.
APPLICATION BUILDING BLOCK ID	Enter "EPM" as the name of the Service Provider Interface object, which is called the *Application Building Block ID*.

Table 7.2 Input Fields (Screen 1 of 3) Redefine Service Wizard for Service Provider Interface Objects

Wizard: Step 2 of 3   On the second screen of the wizard, enter meaningful descriptions in the DESCRIPTION fields of the technical model and the technical service that will be generated by the Service Builder. All other values that are suggested by the Service Builder can be left unchanged, as shown in Figure 7.71.

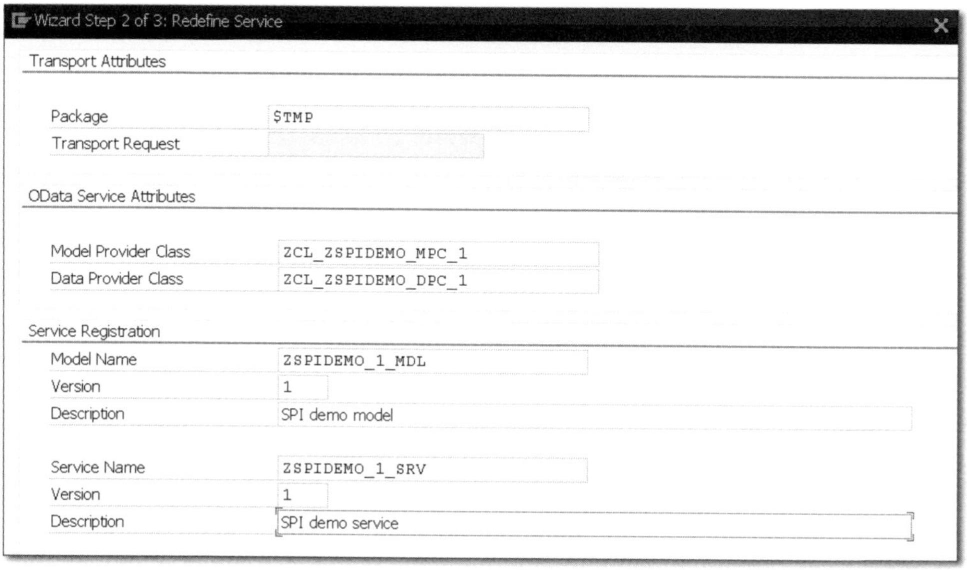

Figure 7.71 Service Registration in the Backend

Wizard: Step 3 of 3   On the third screen of the wizard, you finally have to choose the Service Provider Interface service artifacts, which will be mapped and become part of the OData service.

In this example, select the BUSINESS_PARTNER and CONTACT entity types and the CONTACTOFBUSINESS_PARTNER association as shown in Figure 7.72. Click FINISH.

Generate   In the Service Builder, you now have to choose PROJECT • GENERATE or click the GENERATE button. In the following MODEL AND SERVICE DEFINITION dialog box, leave the default values unchanged, and click CONTINUE as shown in Figure 7.73. In the CREATE OBJECT DIRECTORY ENTRY dialog box, enter "$TMP" as the package name, and click SAVE, or click the LOCAL OBJECT button.

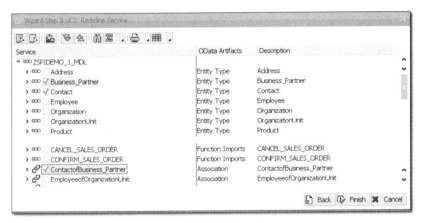

Figure 7.72 Selecting OData Artifacts: Step 3 of 3

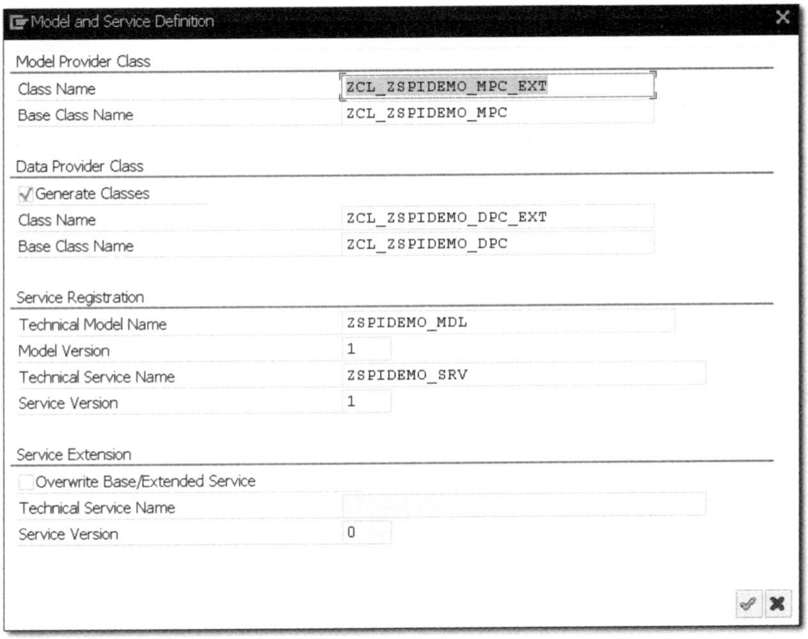

Figure 7.73 Model and Service Definition

Activate Service

After the service has been generated, you need to register and activate the service in the SAP Gateway hub. To do so, expand the SERVICE

Maintenance node in the project, right-click on the hub entry you want the service to activate on, and select Register from the context menu.

In the Select System Alias (Hub to Backend) dialog, select the system alias LOCAL_SPI that has been configured for this Service Provider Interface service redefinition scenario. Because we're using a system that contains the software component SAP_BS_FND, the Software Version of the system alias entry has been set to /IWSPI/BSFND_731 as shown in Figure 7.74

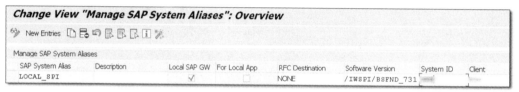

Figure 7.74 System Alias Configuration

In the Add Service dialog, you have to specify the package being used.

SAP System Alias Definition for the Service Provider Interface Integration Scenario

The implementation of the integration scenario for the Service Provider Interface was changed in the past. As a result, it's necessary to specify a software version for the SAP system alias that points to the backend system where the Service Provider Interface service resides. That's why you have to make sure that you've created an appropriate SAP system alias before activating the service.

While creating an SAP system alias, the software version must be selected depending on the version of the software component SAP_BS_FND that is used in the backend system:

▶ If the Service Provider Interface is used in an SAP_BS_FND 702 SP 09 system, choose Default as the Software Version.

▶ If the Service Provider Interface is used in an SAP_BS_FND 731 SP 03 system, choose /IWSPI/BSFND_731 as the Software Version.

Test service

Now you're ready to test the service. Expand the Service Maintenance node in the project, right-click on the hub entry on which you've registered and activated the service, and select SAP GATEWAY CLIENT from the context menu.

Using the SAP Gateway client, you can show that the generated service allows for retrieving a list of business partners, the details of one business partner, and a list of contacts via a navigation property (Figure 7.75). The service even supports the use of filtering options. Therefore, you can perform the following requests using the SAP Gateway client:

▶ Show a list of business partners by entering the following relative URL in the SAP Gateway client:
/sap/opu/odata/sap/ZSPIDEMO_SRV/Business_PartnerCollection

▶ Show the details of one business partner:
/sap/opu/odata/sap/ZSPIDEMO_SRV/Business_PartnerCollection (binary'0050561C01C71ED284BB80D90161152B')/

▶ Show the contacts of the selected business partner using the `Contact-Collection` navigation property:
/sap/opu/odata/sap/ZSPIDEMO_SRV/Business_PartnerCollection (binary'0050561C01C71ED284BB80D90161152B')/ContactCollection?$select=FIRST_NAME,LAST_NAME,EMAIL_ADDRESS&$filter= FIRST_NAME eq 'Karl'&$format=json&sap-ds-debug=true

```
{
 - d: {
   - results: [
     - {
       + __metadata: {...},
         FIRST_NAME: "Karl",
         LAST_NAME: "Muller",
         EMAIL_ADDRESS: "do.not.reply@sap.com"
       }
     ]
   }
 }
```

Figure 7.75 Query Result of Generated Service, Based on Service Provider Interface Integration

7.5   Summary

In this chapter we've shown the four different ways to generate OData services in SAP Gateway:

- RFC/BOR interface
- Search Help
- Using ABAP CDS views via data source mapping and as referenced data sources
- Redefinition

You've learned that by using the RFC/BOR Generator, it's possible to create an OData service in SAP Gateway based on existing RFC function modules without writing a single line of code. But we also showed what needs to be done if no suitable RFC function module is available for each method of your OData service, and how to circumvent this issue by developing your own wrapper RFC function model.

As the second scenario, we showed you how to leverage F4 Search Helps. This is very convenient because it allows you to populate search helps for your SAP Fiori UIs without writing a single line of code.

In addition, you learned about the third approach to generate an OData service based on ABAP CDS views and how to create ABAP CDS views yourself. Here we showed both methods for creating OData services with the help of ABAP CDS views. While the approach using data source mapping is already available with SAP NetWeaver 7.40 the referenced data source option requires the use of SAP NetWeaver 7.50. The use of ABAP CDS views as a referenced data source will become more important in the future because SAP S/4HANA is using ABAP CDS views as the preferred way to model business objects.

Finally, generating OData services using redefinition was shown for the following integration scenarios:

- SAP BW Easy Query
- Service Provider Interface

PART III
Application Development

The dream of developing once and using on different platforms can come true with HTML5 applications. In this chapter, we show you how to easily develop HTML5 applications with SAPUI5 and provide a short introduction to SAP Fiori.

8 SAPUI5 Application Development

Application development has become an increasingly important topic in recent years in both the consumer and business sectors. SAP's user interface (UI) development toolkit for HTML5 and SAPUI5, supports application developers in creating easy-to-use UI applications based on HTML5 and JavaScript. SAPUI5 provides a consistent cross-platform user experience, adapting to the capabilities of whatever device it's run on. SAPUI5 is currently used in the building of SAP Fiori business applications.

In this chapter, we discuss application development using SAPUI5. We begin by introducing the primary building blocks of web development in Section 8.1. From there, we provide an overview of SAP Fiori and SAPUI5 in Section 8.2. *SAP Fiori* is a group of HTML5 business applications provided by SAP that are created using SAPUI5.

SAP Fiori/SAPUI5

The SAPUI5 JavaScript library is growing rapidly. Because all SAP Fiori applications and all instructions in this chapter are based on SAPUI5, remember to use these tutorials as a first step into the SAPUI5 world. If you're going to plan a production application, look at the official SAP web pages (or references in this chapter) to see whether there is a newer version or a newer how-to guide available.

After introducing you to how the building blocks of web development fit together and the basics of SAP Fiori and SAPUI5, we'll walk through how to install SAPUI5 in Section 8.3. Finally, in Section 8.4, we'll show you how to create an SAPUI5 application, both manually and using the Eclipse-integrated deployment option.

> **OpenUI5**
>
> SAPUI5 is now nearly open source and often referred to as *OpenUI5* (although we'll continue to use the term SAPUI5 in this chapter). OpenUI5 is the free version of SAPUI5, which is available under the Apache 2.0 Open Source license. One important reason to open the main functions of SAPUI5 was the growing HTML5 developer community and the corresponding development process of SAPUI5 itself. While the UI development process is totally decoupled from the backend system, it was an important step to open the UI side to the community. However, not everything is opened. There are still some control libraries that are only available in the SAPUI5 version.
>
> For more information, we recommend the following sources:
>
> ▸ *http://openui5.org*
>
> ▸ *https://openui5.hana.ondemand.com*

8.1   Building Blocks of Web Application Development

The three important building blocks for web application development are HTML, Cascading Style Sheets (CSS), and JavaScript. HTML defines the structure and layout of a web document and is the main language of nearly all web content. The visual formatting of that content is normally done with the CSS declarative language for style sheets. Finally, JavaScript is a scripting language for validating user input or communication with web servers; it expands the capabilities of HTML and CSS.

Browser The latest release of HTML, HTML5, has new features such as the ability to play video or audio within web pages, and, in combination with CSS or JavaScript, animation and interactivity. HTML5 isn't only for mobile applications—it can also be used as a normal website for desktop computers or laptops. Although HTML5 is platform-independent, it's not browser independent—meaning it isn't yet an official standard, and no browsers have full HTML5 support today. However, all major browsers, including Edge, Internet Explorer, Firefox, Chrome, Safari, and Opera, continue to add new HTML5 features to their latest releases. Before you start with the development of your new HTML5 application, you have to think about who will benefit from it and which browsers are available for the specific use cases. You can use the *http://html5test.com* website to test your browser to see which HTML5-specifications are supported.

HTML5 Browser Recommendation

We currently recommend the Google Chrome browser for HTML5 development because, as of today, it supports more HTML5 features than Internet Explorer or Firefox. On October 28, 2014, the World Wide Web Consortium (W3C) declared HTML5, finally, as a formal standard.

Features in HTML5 also include mobile device support. Due to its advanced features in this respect, the phrase "HTML5 applications" has become a synonym for *web applications*. In this chapter, we're talking about the creation of web applications using SAPUI5. Usually, these are always-online applications that have direct access to your server, where the data are stored.

Web applications

Now that you have a better understanding of web development and how it's applied to SAPUI5, let's begin looking at one of SAPUI5's most prominent use cases: creating SAP Fiori applications.

8.2 Introduction to SAP Fiori and SAPUI5

The best example of SAPUI5 currently in use is a series of business applications known as SAP Fiori. In this section, we'll start by briefly introducing you to these applications and their SAPUI5 architecture. Then we'll move on to a more general discussion of SAPUI5, including an explanation of how to install the SAPUI5 development toolkit.

8.2.1 SAP Fiori

SAP Fiori was developed in close cooperation with more than 250 customers. Along with them, the most-used software functions in everyday business challenges were identified. SAP Fiori is intended to improve employee productivity, reduce work completion time, and increase the adoption of business processes. Applications from SAP Fiori can be used with any browser that supports HTML5 on desktop and mobile devices.

SAP Fiori applications provide a simple UI and intuitive user experience. The consistent and responsive design automatically adapts to the UI of the calling device and adjusts the layout to fit the screen size.

Keeping simple things simple
The slogan "keeping simple things simple" rings true with SAP Fiori. SAP Fiori can be implemented either as a collection of applications on a single platform or as multiple web applications. You're able to start all existing applications via the SAP Fiori Launchpad that is optimized for the device in use (Figure 8.1).

Figure 8.1 SAP Fiori Launchpad

First release
The first release of SAP applications for SAP Fiori came in 2013, and included 25 applications for common functions such as workflow approvals, information lookups, and self-service tasks. Today, SAP has published more than 750 SAP Fiori apps.

> **Note**
>
> You can find the complete catalog of SAP Fiori apps at *https://fioriappslibrary.hana.ondemand.com/sap/fix/externalViewer/#/home.*

Look and feel
As previously mentioned, the look and feel of SAP Fiori applications are optimized and changed dynamically for the different screen sizes of each

device. While the desktop and tablet views offer all information in one screen, the smartphone view is optimized for smaller screens, and has a totally different, but intuitive, way of navigation that is likely reminiscent of your own native smartphone apps.

There are three types of SAP Fiori applications (Table 8.1).

Application types

Application Type	Description
Transactional	▶ Provides task-based access (e.g., create or change) ▶ Runs on any database and SAP HANA
Analytical	▶ Provides a visual overview for monitoring or tracking purposes ▶ Runs on an SAP HANA database
Fact sheet	▶ Provides an object view or contextual navigation between related objects ▶ Runs on an SAP HANA database

Table 8.1 Application Types

In Figure 8.2, we lay out a high-level overview of SAP Fiori's architecture.

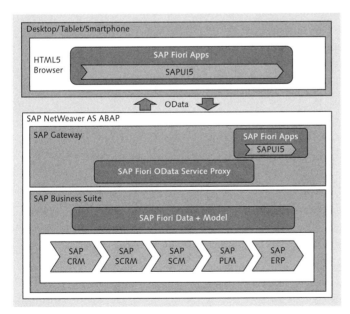

Figure 8.2 SAP Fiori Architecture

Prerequisites

You can find a detailed prerequisites checklist of all required features on the SAP Help site at *http://help.sap.com/fiori*.

From a technical point of view, each SAP Fiori application consists of a data-providing component and a UI component. The SAP Fiori UI component is a normal SAPUI5 application built by SAP, and the data-providing component contains the business logic and SAP Gateway OData service. The SAP Fiori UI component is typically installed on the same system as the SAP Gateway components to avoid the same origin policy issues. This policy limits access to scripts contained in one origin to access data in a second origin. Using a shared reverse proxy, you can also install the SAP Fiori UI component on any other SAP NetWeaver Application Server (AS) ABAP with an installed SAPUI5 for SAP NetWeaver add-on.

Further Resources

For more details about SAP Fiori deployments, we recommend the following:

http://help.sap.com/fiori_bs2013/helpdata/en/40/1b675374bc6655e10000000a 423f68/frameset.htm

Enhancing SAP Fiori applications

Enhancing the functionality of any SAP Fiori application can be done by changing the SAP Business Suite, SAP Gateway OData service, and/or SAPUI5 layers. You don't have to enhance all of the layers each time, so we want to give you a short overview of the criteria for determining which layer has to be enhanced (see Table 8.2). To get a detailed look at the enhancement options, read Chapter 10.

Application Layer	Enhancement
SAP Business Suite	▸ Requires content.
	▸ Business logic doesn't exist on the backend side.
SAP Gateway	▸ Requires content.
	▸ Business logic exists on the backend side but isn't exposed as an OData service by SAP Gateway.

Table 8.2 Application Layers for SAP Fiori

Application Layer	Enhancement
SAPUI5	▸ Requires content. ▸ Business logic exists on the backend side and is exposed as an OData service by SAP Gateway but isn't consumed by the frontend SAPUI5 application.

Table 8.2 Application Layers for SAP Fiori (Cont.)

The easiest option to enhance the SAPUI5 layer is the SAP Web IDE, which is available in a free of charge version on the SAP HANA Cloud Platform (HCP). You can find more details about SAP Web IDE in Chapter 9.

SAP Web IDE

Further Resources

For more information on enhancing the different layers of SAP Fiori applications, the different SAP Fiori application types, and general SAP Fiori application development details, check out *SAP Fiori Implementation and Development* by Anil Bavaraju (SAP PRESS, 2016) at *www.sap-press.com/3883*.

Despite the SAP Web IDE being the easier option, we'll also show you other alternatives to SAPUI5 development and focus on the enhancement of the UI layer of an existing SAP Fiori application in Section 8.4.2 with Eclipse support. If also you want to enhance your OData service from SAP Gateway (second layer), refer to our discussion of service development in Chapter 7.

8.2.2 SAPUI5

The SAP UI development toolkit for HTML5 (SAPUI5) is a collection of libraries that can be easily used by web developers to create desktop and mobile web applications. In fact, SAPUI5 is based on open standards and can use OData to communicate with your SAP Gateway system.

The SAPUI5 runtime is a client-side HTML5 rendering library with a set of UI controls for building both desktop and mobile applications. SAPUI5 provides a lightweight programming model, is based on Java-Script, and can be used together with any other JavaScript library. The

UI design is managed with *Cascading Style Sheets Level 3* (CSS3), which allows you to adopt themes to your own branding in a very effective way. SAP uses the *jQuery* library as a foundation and to add all additionally needed elements to the already proven open-source library.

Model-View-
Controller

SAPUI5 development is based on the *Model-View-Controller* (*MVC*) concept (Figure 8.3). MVC is a pattern for structuring software development in the three independent units:

▸ **Model**
Application data, business rules, functions, logic.

▸ **View**
Rendering, UI, layout.

▸ **Controller**
Application behavior, user actions/input, converting.

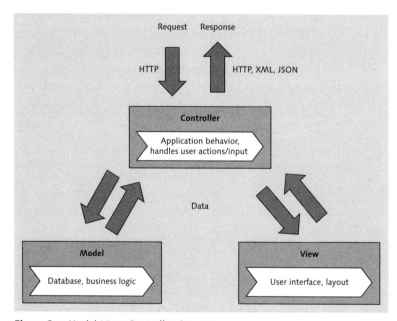

Figure 8.3 Model-View-Controller Concept

According to the MVC paradigm, the coding relevant for the view (UI) is distinguished from the coding for the controller. This makes it easier to connect to non-SAP backends.

You can get a detailed overview of the various SAP development tools packages for Eclipse at *https://tools.hana.ondemand.com/*.

Requirements

SAPUI5 Eclipse Plug-In: Minimum Requirements

▶ Eclipse Kepler (version 4.3) or Luna (version 4.4)

▶ Windows OS (7) 32- or 64-bit, Linux, or Apple Mac OS X 10.6

▶ Java Runtime Environment (JRE) version 1.6 or higher, 32-bit or 64-bit

The SAPUI5 development toolkit is a set of Eclipse-based tools, editors, and wizards that helps you create new projects and supports the development process with code snippets and code completion. A good point to start is on the Demo Kit web page (see Figure 8.4) at:

Deployment

https://sapui5.netweaver.ondemand.com/sdk/#docs/guide/95d113be50a e40d5b0b562b84d715227.html

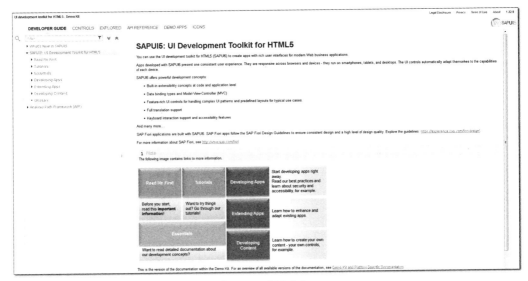

Figure 8.4 SAPUI5 UI Development Toolkit for HTML5 Website

8.3   Installing SAPUI5

Before we get any further, it's time to download and install the development toolkit for SAPUI5. Follow these steps:

Eclipse
1. Download and install Java SE7.

2. Download and start Eclipse (Kepler or Luna).

3. From the Eclipse main menu, choose HELP • INSTALL NEW SOFTWARE.

4. In the WORK WITH field, enter the update site URL where the features are available for installation: "*https://tools.hana.ondemand.com/kepler*" (replace Kepler with Luna if you're using Eclipse Luna), and press Enter .

> **SAP GWPA**
>
> If you want to use the outdated Gateway Productivity Accelerator (GWPA) tool , you have to use Eclipse Juno. Any other version isn't supported, as the tool is deprecated.

The update site lists the features available for SAPUI5 together with their name and version (see Figure 8.5).

5. Select the UI DEVELOPMENT TOOLKIT FOR HTML5 checkbox, and all child elements are selected automatically. The SAPUI5 ABAP REPOSITORY TEAM PROVIDER (DEVELOPER EDITION) checkbox is important for the integrated deployment process to the ABAP repository.

6. Click NEXT. Eclipse downloads the needed plug-ins, and you'll see an overview of the selected items to be installed.

7. Click NEXT again, and read and accept the terms of the license agreement by choosing the radio button and clicking on FINISH.

8. The installation process starts. On completion, Eclipse prompts you to restart. Restart Eclipse.

Now you're able to use the plug-in to create or enhance your SAPUI5 applications. In the next section, we'll create an SAPUI5 application.

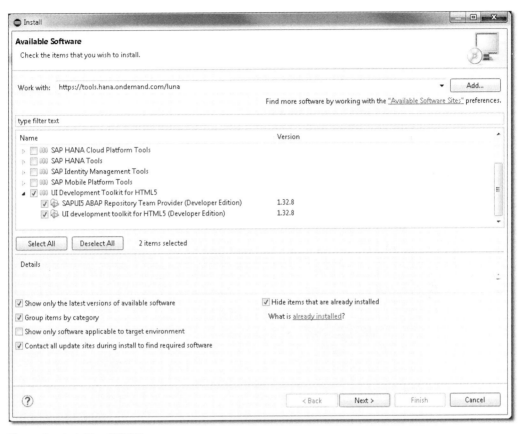

Figure 8.5 Installing SAPUI5

8.4 Creating an SAPUI5 Application

Now that you have a general idea of how SAPUI5 application development works, let's dive into the technical details a bit more. The first step in the SAPUI5 application development process is, of course, to create an application. We discuss the following two options for doing so in this section:

▸ Without the help of any software development kit (SDK), that is, manual creation (Section 8.4.1)

▸ Using the Eclipse development environment (Section 8.4.2)

The quicker way, that is, with the SAP Web IDE, is described in Chapter 9.

Any web application that has been developed by using the SAPUI5 framework can run on the following platforms:

▶ SAP NetWeaver ABAP Server

▶ SAP NetWeaver Java Server

▶ SAP HCP

▶ Open Source Java Application Server

▶ Static Open Source Web Server

When choosing one of the SAP platforms, there are two options for the deployment process, depending on the release version of SAP Net-Weaver:

▶ **SAP NetWeaver 7.00, 7.01, 7.02, and 7.03/7.31 < SPS 04**
Manual deployment process with report /UI5/UI5_REPOSITORY_LOAD.

▶ **SAP NetWeaver 7.03/7.31/and higher**
Eclipse-integrated deployment process with the ABAP Repository Team Provider plug-in.

8.4.1 Manual Creation

Hello World example

In this section, we'll start with our first option: manual creation without an SDK. We'll use a *Hello World* example provided by SAP, which takes only a few minutes to develop. You can use any computer to create this sample application and use nearly every browser to test the created application. The important thing is to know where you can refer to the SAPUI5 JavaScript library on a public server.

> **SAPUI5 JavaScript File**
>
> The SAPUI5 JavaScript file in the script tag *https://sapui5.netweaver. ondemand.com/resources/sap-ui-core.js* is prefilled at the time of writing (April 2016). Try to call this URL in your browser first. If it doesn't work, you need to find another SAPUI5 installation, or you can deploy SAPUI5 directly on one of your own servers.

To create your first SAPUI5 application on your Windows computer, follow these steps:

1. Create a new text document (i.e., right-click on your desktop, and select NEW • TEXT DOCUMENT) and name the file, for example, "HelloWorld.html". The important part is that the file extension is *html*, which you have to use. Therefore, accept the change warning of the change from *.txt* to *.html*, and open the newly created file with the Windows Notepad editor (don't use Microsoft Word).

2. Type the HTML code shown in Listing 8.1 into your editor, and save the file when you're finished.

```
<html>
<head>
    <meta http-equiv="X-UA-Compatible" content="IE=edge" />
    <meta http-equiv="Content-Type" content="text/html;char-
set=UTF-8"/>
    <title>SAPUI5</title>
    <script id="sap-ui-bootstrap"
        src=" https://sapui5.netweaver.ondemand.com/
resources/sap-ui-core.js"
        data-sap-ui-theme="sap_goldreflection"
        data-sap-ui-libs="sap.ui.commons">
    </script>
    <script>
        $(function(){
            $("#uiArea").sapui("Button", "btn", {
                text:"Hello World!",
                press:function(){$("#btn").fadeOut();}
            });
        });
    </script>
</head>
<body class="sapUiBody">
    <div id="uiArea"></div>
</body>
</html>
```

Listing 8.1 SAP Hello World Sample Application

3. That's it! To test your first SAPUI5 application, open the completed HTML file in your preferred browser. You'll see the implemented button with the given label inside your created SAPUI5 application (Figure 8.6).

Figure 8.6 SAPUI5: Hello World Application Button

Hello World   4. Now you can click HELLO WORLD!, and it will fade out (Figure 8.7).

Figure 8.7 SAPUI5: Hello World Application after Clicking the Button

This manual procedure is optimized by SAPUI5 for Eclipse, which is the option we discuss next.

8.4.2   Using the Eclipse Development Environment

Let's now look at the Eclipse development environment option. To create a new SAPUI5 project, follow these steps:

1. Start by opening the FILE • NEW • PROJECT wizard and selecting APPLICATION PROJECT under the SAPUI5 APPLICATION DEVELOPMENT node.

2. Click NEXT, and enter your PROJECT NAME (Figure 8.8).

3. Keep the CREATE AN INITIAL VIEW checkbox selected to create a new view (you're also able to create additional views later on). In addition, you can choose your target library: SAP.UI.COMMONS or SAP.M (browser support for mobile operating systems). In this scenario, select SAP.UI.COMMONS. Click NEXT again.

Create new view   To create a new view (Figure 8.9), you have to specify the view-related data, such as the FOLDER (keep the default), the view NAME of your choice, and the DEVELOPMENT PARADIGM (keep JAVASCRIPT selected).

Figure 8.8 Creating an Application Project for SAPUI5

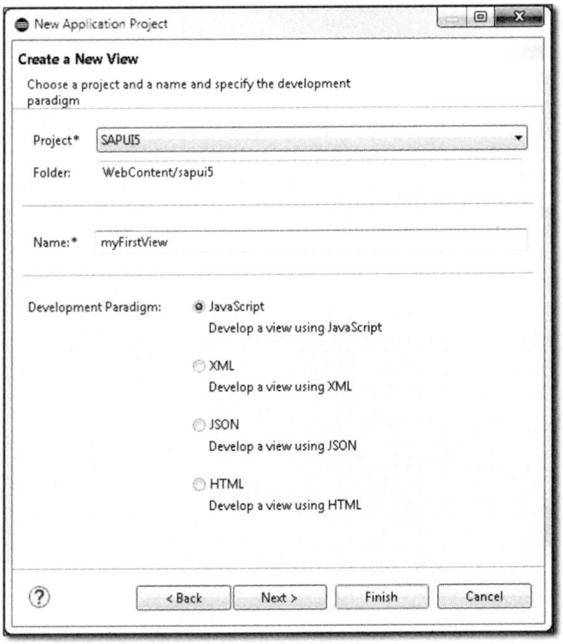

Figure 8.9 Creating a New View

Click NEXT to see the confirmation page with a summary of the selected data on the previous pages. Check the information, and click FINISH if everything is correct. The wizard creates a new SAPUI5 project and opens the *index.html* file, the controller (*myFirstView.controller.js*), and the view (*myFirstView.view.js*) JavaScript files in the preview view (Figure 8.10).

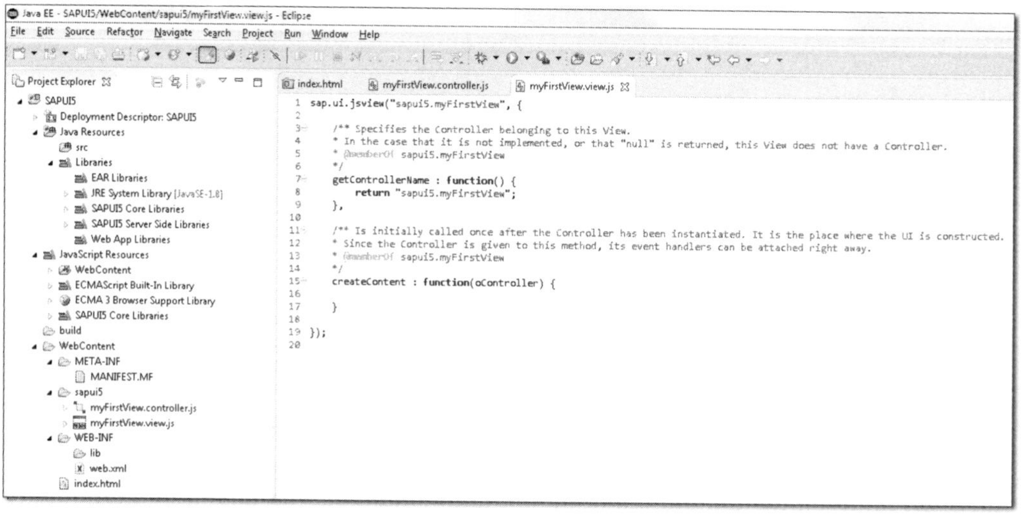

Figure 8.10 New SAPUI5 Project

Add buttons We've already shown how to create a new SAPUI5 application with one button implemented. To add a similar function inside the created Eclipse project, follow these steps:

1. To add a new button to your SAPUI5 application, open the JavaScript view file (*myFirstView.view.js*), insert the code in Listing 8.2, and replace the existing `createContent` function.

```
createContent : function(oController) {
    var aControls = [];
    var oButton   = new sap.ui.commons.Button({
    id    : this.createId("MyFirstButton"),
    text  : "HelloSAPUI5"
    });
    aControls.push(oButton.attachPress(oController.display-
Text));
```

```
    return aControls;
}
```

Listing 8.2 View Function

2. Handle the event `displayText`.

3. Open your JavaScript controller file (*myFirstView.controller.js*), and add the following code:

```
displayText : function(oEvent) {
    alert(oEvent.getSource().getId() + "works!");
}
```

> **Note**
>
> The shown coding works for JavaScript only. If you've selected a different development paradigm, visit the SAP help site to get the right source code:
>
> *http://help.sap.com/saphelp_nw74/helpdata/de/07/d2bdc3ad0e4c62b14123 e6f80dca56/content.htm?frameset=/de/fc/f5e9b5068f4e008779e520e54660 4b/frameset.htm&current_toc=/de/5c/be4e5b4a19479a92b1d32ff23b7b63/ plain.htm&node_id=38*

You can test your new SAPUI5 application in an embedded Jetty server by right-clicking on the project node and choosing RUN AS • WEB APP PREVIEW (Figure 8.11).

Web app preview feature

Figure 8.11 Test SAPUI5 Application in Web App Preview

Everything is configured automatically, and a new tab opens next to the existing ones inside Eclipse. You can also open the URL inside a browser of your choice (Figure 8.12).

To check that the method is working, click the created HELLOSAPUI5 button. An alert pop-up appears with the internal button ID and the defined text message (Figure 8.13).

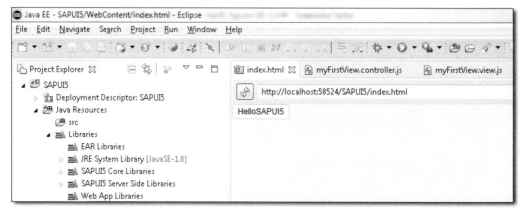

Figure 8.12 Web App Preview with the SAPUI5 Button

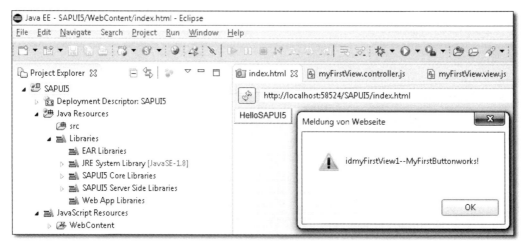

Figure 8.13 Alert Message Inside SAPUI5

If you change anything inside your SAPUI5 project, you have to refresh the application preview with the REFRESH button (the icon with two arrows on the left-hand side of the location bar). You can also test the application in your external default browser by selecting the OPEN IN EXTERNAL BROWSER button (the globe icon on the right-hand side of the location bar).

Further Resources

For more information about how to develop your first application using SAPUI5, we recommend the following:

https://sapui5.hana.ondemand.com/sdk/index.html#docs/guide/23cfd955f581 42389fa7c9097e11559c.html

8.5   Summary

After reading this chapter, you should understand the benefits of HTML5, how to create a new SAPUI5 application inside a text editor, and how to create your first application with SAPUI5 support. You can use the SAPUI5 code snippets to speed up your development process.

HTML5 is the final standard, but the use of the correct browser has a big influence on the look and feel of your application. Take a look at the supported browsers by SAPUI5 on the following web page to make sure you use the right one to test and develop your SAPUI5 application: *https://sapui5.netweaver.ondemand.com/sdk/#docs/guide/BrowserSupport.html*.

If you need further information, you can find more detailed information on the SAP Community Network (SCN). The central place to start with your SAPUI5 development career is the demo kit on the SAP HANA Cloud Platform at *https://sapui5.hana.ondemand.com*.

In the next chapter, we'll look at the SAP Web IDE.

Application development can be optimized by different SAP tools. This chapter walks through the registration and use of SAP's browser-based development tool for SAPUI5: the SAP Web IDE.

9   SAP Web IDE

In addition to the target platform and corresponding development language (SAPUI5; see Chapter 8), supported development tools also play a crucial role in application development. To make the entry into the world of application development as easy as possible, SAP provides some useful standalone plug-ins and a new browser-based development tool for SAPUI5 called the *SAP Web IDE*. The SAP Web IDE is a development environment with a set of embedded tools covering the entire end-to-end development process.

Beginning in 2013, SAP offered a graphical WYSIWYG web editor called the *SAP AppBuilder*. The SAP AppBuilder was a development environment for prototypes only. In 2014, the tool was enhanced and renamed *SAP River RDE* (rapid development environment). The tool was eventually renamed and revamped into the SAP Web IDE.

The SAP Web IDE covers the full spectrum of designing and developing SAPUI5 applications or enhancing existing SAP Fiori apps. It improves the process through helpful templates, wizards, and code or model editors for browser and mobile devices.

The SAP Web IDE is optimized for the needs of any application developer and UI developer and offers an easy and fast consumption of any available OData service. This generates a complete small sample application, including a UI and the coding for the consumption of the given OData service.

In this chapter, we'll provide an overview of the SAP Web IDE and how to access the free trial version on SAP HANA Cloud Platform (HCP) and install the SAP Web IDE locally (Section 9.1), including the needed configuration (Section 9.2). Then we show you how to connect the SAP Web IDE to SAP Gateway (Section 9.2.2). Part of this chapter is also a short introduction to the available OData sample services from *www.odata.org*, the available sample SAP Gateway services provided by SAP, and how to get free access to those (Section 9.3). We show you how to develop a SAPUI5 application (Section 9.4) and which SAP Fiori reference apps are available (Section 9.5). Finally, we'll use the OData Model Editor for creating and changing OData models (Section 9.6).

9.1   Installation and Access

There are two ways to access and install the SAP Web IDE:

On-premise and
on-demand

- ▸ Installing a local version on your desktop (on-premise)
- ▸ Via SAP HCP (on-demand)

In this section, we'll walk through the steps for both options.

9.1.1   Installing On-Premise via the Local Version

You can install a local version of the SAP Web IDE on your desktop PC. This local version is for test and evaluation purposes, and is not updated with the latest features like the SAP HCP version is.

To install the local version of the SAP Web IDE, follow these steps:

1. Go to *https://store.sap.com,* and search for "SAP Web IDE."

2. On the results page, click on the Trial Version button (Figure 9.1).

3. In the dialog box that appears, enter your contact information, accept the terms and conditions, and click Submit to download the local installer.

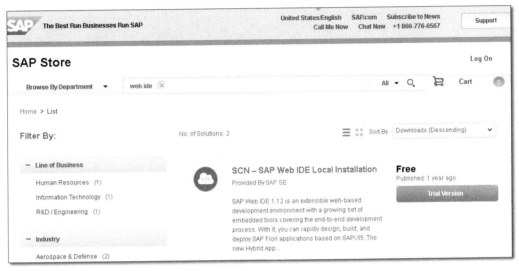

Figure 9.1 SAP Store—SAP Web IDE

4. You'll receive an email with a download link for a 94MB zip file called *SAP_Web_IDE_Local_Inst.zip*. After you've downloaded the setup file, launch it, and follow the instructions.

5. Create a local folder named *SAPWebIDE* on your *C* drive.

6. Download the *Eclipse Orion Application Server* from *http://download. eclipse.org/orion/* in the current stable version, and extract it to the previously created *C:/SAPWebIDE* folder. Eclipse Orion Application server

7. Download the standalone *p2 director* from *www.eclipse.org/downloads/ download.php?file=/tools/buckminster/products/director_latest.zip,* and unzip it to your *D* drive (or any other folder).

Provisioning Platform (p2)

p2 is a technology for provisioning and managing Eclipse- and Equinox-based applications.

8. Before you continue, check your Java version from the command line with `java -version` (Figure 9.2).

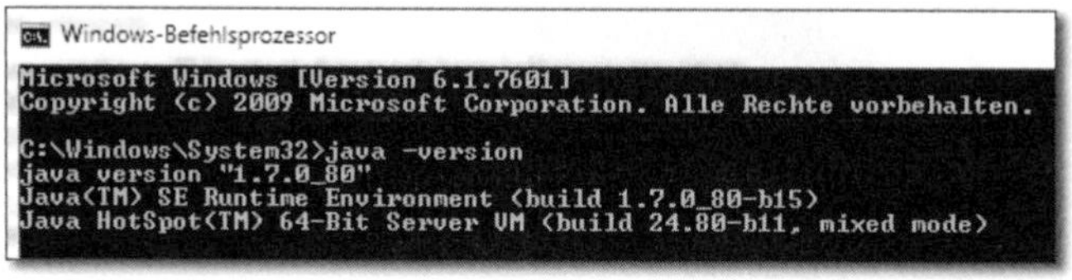

Figure 9.2 Check the Java Version

Java SE 7

Use Java SE 7 (build 1.7.x) instead of version 8 (build 1.8.x) because there are some know problems with version 8. If you already have version 8 installed, please uninstall it, and download the latest Java SE 7 Runtime Environment from *www.oracle.com/technetwork/java/javase/downloads/jre7-downloads-1880261.html*.

JAVA SE   After you've downloaded and unzipped all necessary files to your local storage, you can continue with the installation process by following these steps:

1. Open your command line again, and install the SAP Web IDE package into Eclipse Orion with the help of the p2 director tool. Enter the following command: (Adjust the path to your *updatesite.zip* and/or your Eclipse Orion folder if you've used another path then described. If the path of the zip file or the Eclipse folder contains spaces, surround the path with quotation marks.)

   ```
   director -repository jar:file:D:\updatesite.zip!/
     -installIU com.sap.webide.orionplugin.feature.feature.
     group -destination c:\SAPWebIDE\eclipse
   ```

   Press [Enter] (see Figure 9.3).

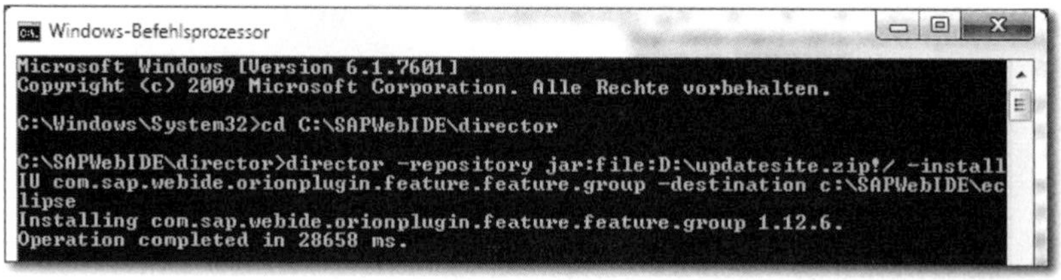

Figure 9.3 Installing the SAP Web IDE Package to Eclipse Orion

2. Before starting Eclipse Orion, navigate to the Eclipse Orion folder at **Orion Port**
   C:\SAPWebIDE\eclipse, and open the *orion.ini* file with a text editor.

3. Search the command line for `-Dorg.eclipse.equinox.http.jetty.`
   `http.port=8080`, and replace the 8080 with, for example, 8090 (Figure
   9.4).

```
orion.ini - Editor
Datei  Bearbeiten  Format  Ansicht  ?
-startup
plugins/org.eclipse.equinox.launcher_1.3.0.v20140415-2008.jar
--launcher.library
plugins/org.eclipse.equinox.launcher.win32.win32.x86_64_1.1.200.v20140603-1326
-consoleLog
-console
-data
serverworkspace
-nosplash
-vmargs
-Dorg.eclipse.equinox.http.jetty.http.port=8090
-Dorg.eclipse.equinox.http.jetty.autostart=false
-Dhelp.lucene.tokenizer=standard
-Xms40m
-Xmx384m
```

Figure 9.4 Changing the Orion Web Port

4. Save the file. Execute the *orion.exe* file to start the Eclipse Orion
   server, and a command shell opens.

5. Open a web browser of your choice, and open the server web page at
   http://localhost:8090/webide/index.html. The Eclipse Orion home page
   is displayed, where you have to sign in with your Orion, GitHub, or
   Google account (Figure 9.5).

Figure 9.5 Orion Web Server Login

451

Orion account 6. If you don't have such an account, we recommend setting up an Orion account at *https://orionhub.org/mixloginstatic/register.html*. You'll receive an email to confirm.

7. Log in with your credentials on the local installation. The SAP Web IDE welcome page will appear after a short loading time (Figure 9.6).

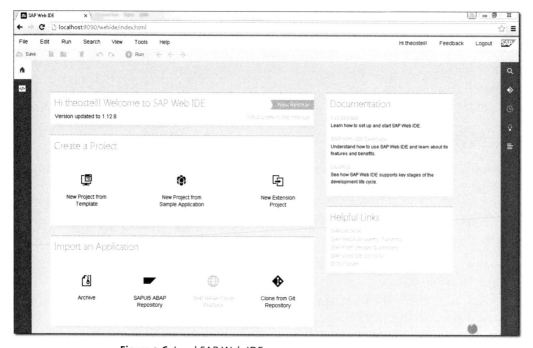

Figure 9.6 Local SAP Web IDE

You're now ready to develop on your local SAP Web IDE installation.

To stop your local SAP Web IDE, first close the web page in your browser, and then open the Eclipse Orion console, enter the `close` command, and press ⌈Enter⌉. Confirm to close the server by pressing ⌈Y⌉. The command line is automatically closed.

Further Resources

For more information on the SAP Web IDE local installation, go to *https://scn.sap.com/docs/DOC-58848*.

9.1.2   Accessing On-Demand via SAP HANA Cloud Platform

The SAP Web IDE is available on SAP HCP without the need for a local installation.   **Free trial account**

As previously discussed in the introduction to this chapter, the SAP Web IDE is a toolset made up of former SAP tools such as SAP AppBuilder, AppDesigner, the Gateway Productivity Accelerator (GWPA), the SAP Fiori Toolkit, and so on. These tools and plug-ins could only be used in the specific environment in question (e.g., iOS or Android) or, like GWPA, as an Eclipse-based developer tool. SAP partly transfers the tools in the SAP Web IDE on SAP HCP to speed up the development process without the need of installation.

> **Further Resources**
>
> You can find all basic information in the SAP HCP documentation at *https://help.hana.ondemand.com/webide/frameset.htm* (Figure 9.7).

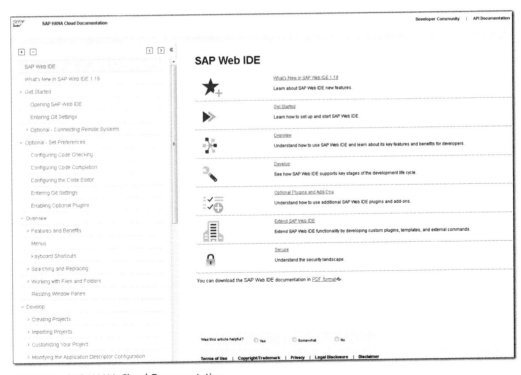

Figure 9.7 SAP HANA Cloud Documentation

SAP HCP is SAP's fundamental technology for any modern applications based on SAP HANA in the cloud. Figure 9.8 provides an architectural layout of the SAP Web IDE environment via SAP HCP. The following important elements are found in this environment:

SAP HCP environment

▶ **SAP HANA Cloud Platform cockpit**
The associated SAP HCP cockpit is the central point for managing all features and applications inside the SAP HCP, like accessing the SAP Web IDE or configuring a remote destination.

▶ **Orion server**
The Orion server provides a number of backend services that the SAP Web IDE relies on.

▶ **Git repository**
The Git repository can be used to control the source code.

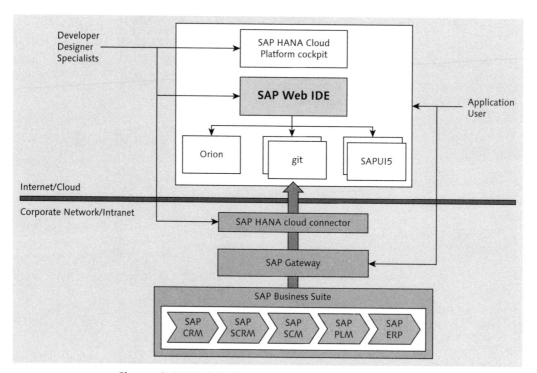

Figure 9.8 SAP Web IDE Environment

- **SAPUI5**

  SAPUI5 is a well-known UI repository and also the base language used for building SAP Fiori applications.

- **SAP HANA cloud connector**

  The SAP HANA cloud connector allows all on-demand functions inside the SAP HCP to be securely connected to your on-premise SAP system.

You can register a free public trial account on SAP HCP by following these steps:

1. Visit *https://account.hanatrial.ondemand.com*, and click on REGISTER (Figure 9.9).

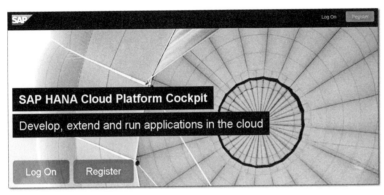

Figure 9.9 SAP HANA Cloud Platform Logon

2. When the REGISTRATION dialog box appears, enter your first and last name, enter your email address, set a password, and choose your contact preferences. Finally, accept the terms and conditions, and click REGISTER.

3. You'll receive an email with a link to activate your account. Click the link within this email to complete your registration process. Your account is automatically created, and a popup appears for you to click CONTINUE to visit the SAP HCP Cockpit (Figure 9.10).

4. Click on SUBSCRIPTIONS in the left menu to access the SAP Web IDE. Click on WEBIDE in the table on the following screen to open the SAP Web IDE (e.g., *https://webide-yourusername.dispatcher.hanatrial.ondemand.com*).

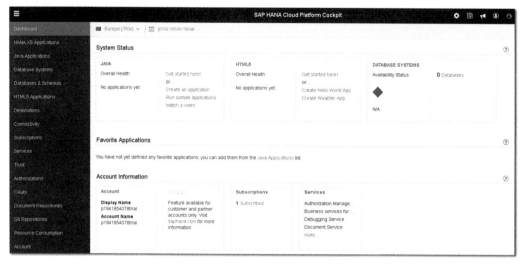

Figure 9.10 SAP HANA Cloud Platform Cockpit

You're now able to use the SAP Web IDE inside the SAP HCP.

In the next section, we'll run through the steps for configuring the connection of both the local installation and SAP HCP so you can connect to SAP Gateway.

9.2 Connecting to SAP Gateway

In the previous section, we looked at how to install a local version of the SAP Web IDE to your desktop as well as how to access and register the SAP Web IDE on SAP HCP. In this section, we'll look at how to configure the local installation and SAP HCP to connect the SAP Web IDE with SAP Gateway.

9.2.1 Connecting the Local Installation to SAP Gateway

Remote systems   This section guides you through how to configure your local SAP Web IDE to connect to a remote system. Later, in Section 9.2.2, we'll show you how to connect the SAP Web IDE on SAP HCP with SAP Gateway to consume OData services.

> **Connecting Remote Systems**
>
> You can define different service destinations to access remote systems. For further information, we recommend the following how-to guide:
>
> www.sdn.sap.com/irj/scn/go/portal/prtroot/docs/library/uuid/d010835c-b539-3210-6eb6-906c58d3c573?QuickLink=index&overridelayout=true&60408715 027671.
>
> In addition, as a prerequisite for connecting to your own ABAP system, you must have at least SAP Basis 7.31 SP 14 or 7.40 SP 8.

Follow these steps to configure the connection:

1. Open a command prompt, and navigate to the DESTINATIONS folder of your Eclipse Orion subfolder in the SAP WEB IDE folder. As described in Section 9.1, the path is *C:\SAPWebIDE\eclipse\config_master\service.destinations\destinations*; therefore, enter the following: "cd C:\SAPWebIDE\eclipse\config_master\service.destinations\destinations" (Figure 9.11).

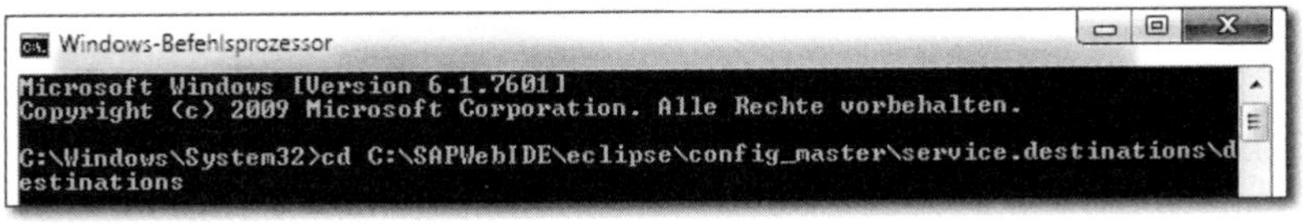

Figure 9.11 Destinations Folder

2. Next, you need to connect to the ES4 demo system. Enter the command line "echo #ServiceDestination > ES4" to create the destination file. Type "notepad es4" to open the created file with the Notepad++ editor. Replace #ServiceDestination with the lines in Listing 9.1, and save the file.

```
Description=ES4                                                Service destination
Type=HTTP
TrustAll=true
Authentication=NoAuthentication
Name=ES4
ProxyType=Internet
URL=https\://sapes4.sapdevcenter.com
WebIDEUsage=odata_abap,ui5_execute_abap,dev_abap
WebIDESystem=ES4
WebIDEEnabled=true
```

Listing 9.1 Destiantion Configuration for the SAP ES4 Demo System

457

3. Close SAP Web IDE, if it was already open, and restart it. You'll probably need to sign in again in your Eclipse Orion server.

Now you can connect your local version of SAP Web IDE to any SAP Gateway system.

9.2.2 Connecting SAP Web IDE on SAP HANA Cloud Platform to SAP Gateway

This section shows you how to connect your SAP Web IDE environment on SAP HCP with any SAP Gateway system to consume OData services. Section 9.4 will show you how to develop an SAPUI5 application with the SAP Web IDE consuming an OData service.

Follow these steps to configure the connection:

1. Open the URL to your on-demand SAP Web IDE in SAP HCP, and log in with your credentials. Click on DESTINATIONS in the left menu, and create a NEW DESTINATION.

2. On the next screen, enter the NAME of your destination and the TYPE ("HTTP"). The destination URL should only be the system domain (*https://sapes4.sapdevcenter.com/*) with a "/" at the end. The SAP Web IDE will automatically concatenate the resource path to the system URL. Enter the PROXY TYPE ("Internet"), AUTHENTICATION method ("BasicAuthentication"), and your NAME and PASSWORD (Figure 9.12).

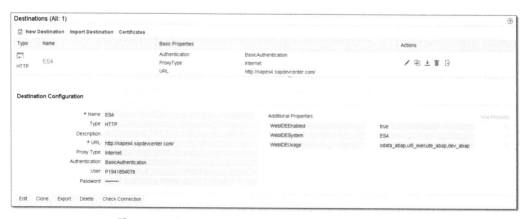

Figure 9.12 Creating a New SAP Gateway Destination

3. Add the following additional properties shown in Table 9.1 by clicking the NEW PROPERTY button.

Parameter	Value
WEBIDEENABLED	TRUE
WEBIDESYSTEM	ES4
WEBIDEUSAGE	ODATA_ABAP,UI5_EXECUTE_ABAP,DEV_ABAP

Table 9.1 Additional Destination Properties

4. Click SAVE to finish your destination configuration. Click on CHECK
CONNECTION to validate your data.

You're now able to connect any service application on SAP HCP to your
configured SAP Gateway system destination.

9.3   OData Sample Services

If you don't have an SAP Gateway system available but want to start
with your first development directly and consume an OData service
or just simply get a preview, you can register for the free SAP Gateway sample service test drive. You can get access to the SAP test drive
for SAP Gateway services on the SCN page at *http://scn.sap.com/docs/
DOC-40986*.

First, you have to sign up for an account to the SAP Gateway – Demo
Consumption Service with your SCN user data (*https://accounts.sap.com/
saml2/idp/sso/accounts.sap.com*). After you're registered for the system,
you should receive an email with your user name and password. From
now on, you can connect to the system via the SAP Gateway Web GUI
from *https://sapes4.sapdevcenter.com* (Figure 9.13).

This is the only way to connect because SAP has disabled connections
from the Windows or Java GUI client due to security reasons. You'll
have read and write authorizations and access to the development tools,
but you're not allowed to develop or change anything yourself.

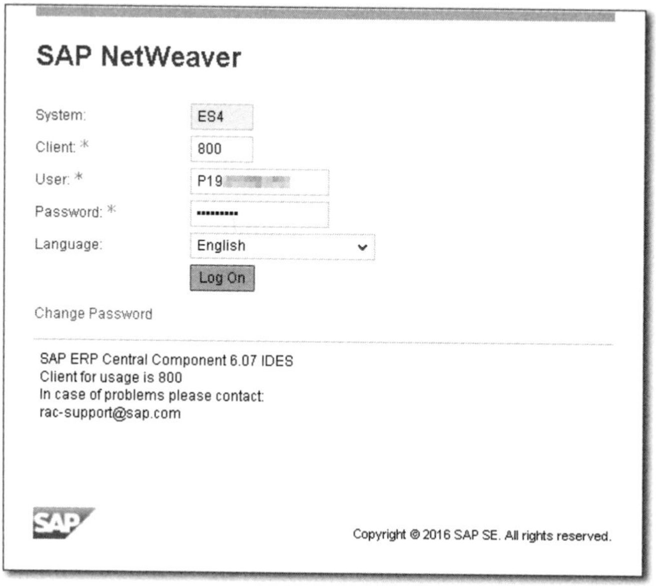

Figure 9.13 SAP ES4 Web GUI

SAP provides a number of typical scenarios to help you become familiar with SAP Gateway. Each available OData service provides the following functionalities at a minimum:

- Metadata document
- Consumption model
- Sample query operation
- Sample read operation

SAP sample services

You're free to use your preferred development environment or web browser to connect to the demo services via the following list of URIs:

- **Enterprise Procurement Model (CRUD-Q)**
  CRUD-Q operations for the entity types BusinessPartner, Contact, Product, SalesOrder, and SalesOrderLineItem:
  https://sapes4.sapdevcenter.com/sap/opu/odata/IWBEP/GWSAMPLE_ BASIC/?sap-ds-debug=true

▸ **Flight example (read-only)**
Access information about the famous SAP flight data:
https://sapes4.sapdevcenter.com/sap/opu/odata/IWFND/RMTSAMPLE-FLIGHT/?sap-ds-debug=true

▸ **Enterprise Procurement Model (read-only)**
Access information about business partner, address data, and more:
https://sapes4.sapdevcenter.com/sap/opu/odata/IWBEP/GWDEMO/?sap-ds-debug=true

SAP will continuously offer additional services covering more and more use cases. A complete list of all available SAP Gateway sample OData services is available on SCN at *http://scn.sap.com/docs/DOC-31221*.

OData.org also provides three useful example OData services:

OData.org sample services

▸ **Northwind service (read-only)**
Access the famous Northwind database:
http://services.odata.org/Northwind/Northwind.svc/

▸ **OData sample service (read-only)**
Access categories, products, and suppliers data:
http://services.odata.org/OData/OData.svc/

▸ **OData sample service (read/write)**
Access categories, products, and supplier data with write functionalities (during a session identified by the URL):
http://services.odata.org/v3/odata/odata.svc

The complete list of OData sample services is available at *www.odata.org/ecosystem/*. Let's now take a look at how to develop a SAPUI5 app with the SAP Web IDE.

9.4 Developing SAPUI5 Applications

The SAP Web IDE accelerates the application building process for desktop and mobile devices in a simplified way. As described in Section 9.2 (on-premise) and Section 9.2.2 (on-demand), you have to connect your SAP Web IDE to an SAP Gateway system to consume any OData service.

In this section, we'll guide you through the development of an SAPUI5 app with the SAP Web IDE inside SAP HCP as this is similar to the local installation but is always updated with the latest features.

Follow these steps:

1. Log on to your SAP HCP Cockpit to access the SAP Web IDE. Click SUBSCRIPTION (Figure 9.14).

Figure 9.14 Subscription SAP Web IDE

Subscription
2. Choose the subscription WEBIDE. The subscription will be loaded and displayed in an overview. You can see the ACTIVE APPLICATION VERSION of the SAP Web IDE, including the direct APPLICATION URL.

3. Click on the URL to open SAP Web IDE. Log on with your credentials to start the developing process. Bookmark the URL for easy access in the future.

4. On the welcome screen, choose NEW PROJECT FROM TEMPLATE (Figure 9.15).

5. Select the default template, SAP FIORI MASTER DETAIL APPLICATION, and click NEXT. Enter a PROJECT NAME (without spaces) and click NEXT again.

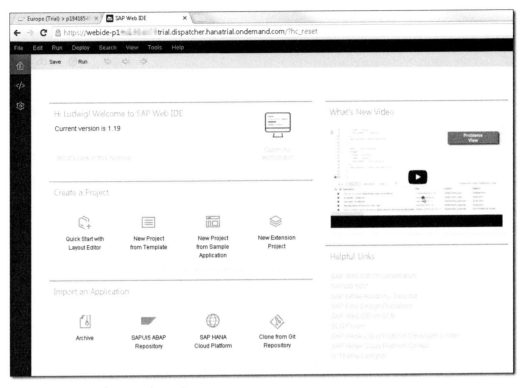

Figure 9.15 SAP Web IDE Welcome Screen

6. Under SOURCE, choose a data connection from a SERVICE CATALOG, WORKSPACE, FILE SYSTEM, or SERVICE URL:

Data connection

 ▶ SERVICE CATALOG: Choose your preferred SAP Gateway system, and select the OData service of your choice (Figure 9.16). If you choose this option, you'll proceed by clicking NEXT.

 ▶ WORKSPACE: Choose a local service from your SAP Web IDE workspace (see Section 9.6).

 ▶ FILE SYSTEM: Upload the service information from a local file to your SAP Web IDE.

 ▶ SERVICE URL: Copy your created SAP Gateway service URL without the host information (*sap/opu/odata/IWFND/RMTSAMPLEFLIGHT/*), enter your credentials if prompted, and wait until you're able to browse through all existing entities on the selected OData service (Figure 9.17). Choose the FLIGHTCOLLECTION entity from the right-hand side DETAILS list, and click NEXT.

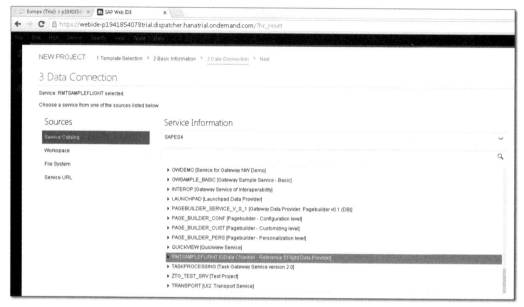

Figure 9.16 Choose OData Service from the Service Catalog

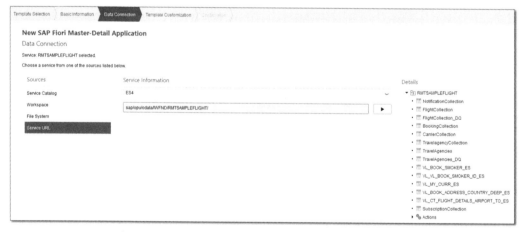

Figure 9.17 SAP Web IDE: Service URL

7. The next step is to customize the chosen template. On this screen, you'll enter the APPLICATION SETTINGS and DATA BINDINGS (Figure 9.18). You can open Figure 9.18 with the named fields and their corresponding position on the SAPUI5 screen. Click NEXT when you're done.

Template customizing

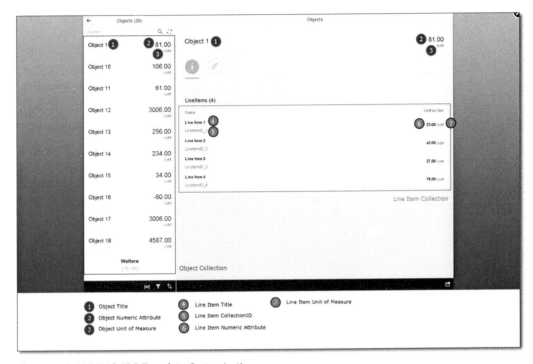

Figure 9.18 SAP Web IDE Template Customization

8. Click FINISH on the confirmation page. Your SAPUI5 application project is generated.

Further Resources

For more information on SAP Web IDE development, go to *https://help. hana.ondemand.com/webide/frameset.htm?6284a94889db4f3cad001ba6742 82f20.html*.

9. Right-click your automatically created project file, and choose RUN • RUN WITH SERVER (Figure 9.19).

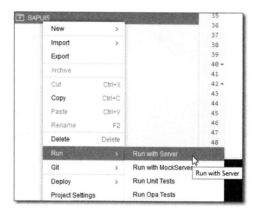

Figure 9.19 SAPUI5 Project with OData Server

A new window opens, where you'll be authenticated, and the SAPUI5 app and the data from the OData service are displayed (Figure 9.20).

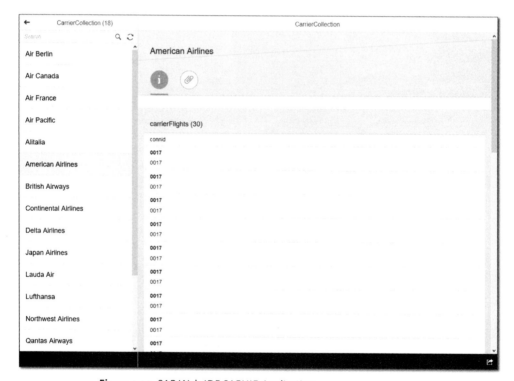

Figure 9.20 SAP Web IDE SAPUI5 Application

In this section, we demonstrated how you can create an SAPUI5 web application in the SAP Web IDE and run it without writing one line of code. For our example, we created a simple master detail SAPUI5 app that consumed an OData service from your SAP Gateway destination.

Extending Applications

It's also possible to extend applications for additional functionality. In Chapter 10, we'll guide you through the extension of an SAP Fiori application.

9.5 SAP Fiori Reference Apps

SAP Fiori reference apps are sample applications that developers and designers can work with to introduce them to developing SAP Fiori applications. The following looks at the benefits each group can take from the reference apps:

- **Developer**
  The sample apps are also for both new and experienced developers. You'll get sample code and examples, which cover all available layers.

- **Designer**
  UI designers will also find examples of the patterns and controls for SAP Fiori. They can also discover the interaction flow of the SAP Fiori business applications.

SAP Fiori reference apps are directly available as integrated samples within the SAP Web IDE and are based on the standard SAP Enterprise Procurement Model (EPM). In this section, we'll walk through the steps to create an SAP Fiori reference app.

Follow these steps:

1. In the SAP Web IDE menu, select FILE • NEW • PROJECT FROM SAMPLE APPLICATION (Figure 9.21).

SAP Fiori reference apps

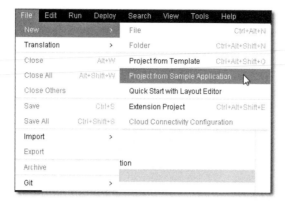

Figure 9.21 Choosing Project from Sample Application

Sample apps

2. You can choose one of the following sample apps:

- ▸ SHOP (full screen app)
- ▸ MANAGE PRODUCTS (master detail app)
- ▸ APPROVE PURCHASE ORDERS (master detail app)

These apps demonstrate the coding development and the user experience design guidelines.

SAP Fiori Apps Reference Library

The SAP Fiori apps reference library provides information about available SAP Fiori apps available, which helps you explore and implement SAP Fiori in your projects: *https://fioriappslibrary.hana.ondemand.com/sap/fix/externalViewer/*.

3. For our example, choose MANAGE PRODUCTS, and click NEXT.

4. Agree to the SAP license agreement, and click FINISH to generate the project. A new project with the default name NW.EPM.REFAAPS.EXT. PROD.MANAGE is created. Click RUN to launch the app.

5. A new popup window opens, where you can choose a file to run (Figure 9.22). Choose either SERVICE or MOCKDATA for the run type:

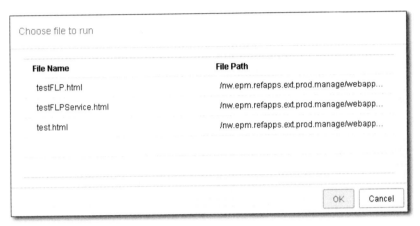

Figure 9.22 SAP Fiori: Choosing the Run Type

6. There are three different start modes available:

- TESTFLPSERVICE.HTML: This starts the same with an OData service connection and therefore data included.

- TESTFLP.HTML: This starts an empty app without any OData service connection, but mockdata included.

- TEST.HTML: This launches an overview test page with two direct links to the other available app pages.

7. Choose TESTFLPSERVICE.HTML, and click OK. The SAP Fiori app is loaded (Figure 9.23).

testFLPService.html

You're now able to create a sample application from the available SAP Fiori apps and browse through the coding. With these sample apps, you can learn how to develop impressive designs and write well-formed coding.

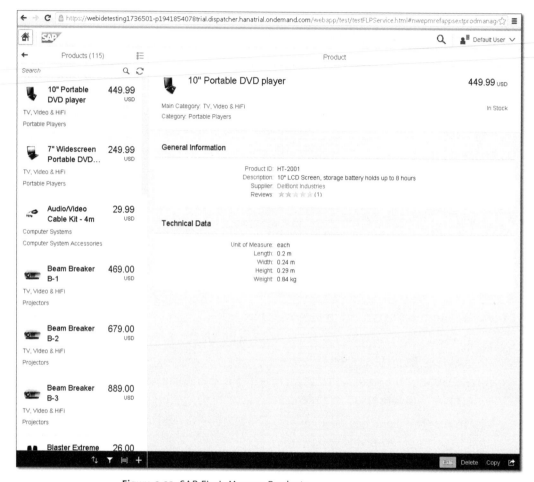

Figure 9.23 SAP Fiori: Manage Products

9.6 OData Model Editor

SAP Web IDE isn't just a helpful tool for application development; it also enables you to create new OData models within a web-based OData Model Editor. You can also change existing OData models and view a relationship model in an easy-to-use graphical modeler.

No ABAP development skills required

This easy-to-use tool allows people with no ABAP development skills to create or change an OData model. The OData Model Editor enables you to speed up the development process, addressing non-SAP developers who want the freedom to concentrate on the data they require in a given business context. After you finish the model creation, you can export the model, so the ABAP developer can use the exported file to generate the service with the SAP Gateway Service Builder.

In this section, we'll walk through how to activate the OData Model Editor in the SAP Web IDE. We'll then discuss how to import files via the OData Model Editor.

9.6.1   Activating the OData Model Editor

To activate the OData Model Editor, follow these steps:

1. Open SAP Web IDE, choose TOOLS • PREFERENCES, and then select OPTIONAL PLUGINS in the left side PREFERENCES pane. Select ODATA MODEL EDITOR, and click SAVE. Refresh your browser to reload the SAP Web IDE application.

   OData model

2. Create a new folder by right-clicking the LOCAL folder in the tree list and selecting NEW • FOLDER. Enter a name for the new folder, and click OK. Right-click the newly created folder, choose NEW • ODATA MODEL FILE, and enter a MODEL NAME (Figure 9.24).

Figure 9.24 OData Model File

3. Click OK. A valid OData *.edmx* file is created.

4. You can access different options to edit the model by right-clicking to place your cursor on the position of the source code you want to edit. Press [Ctrl]+[Spacebar] to access the list of elements that can be used at the cursor position (Figure 9.25).

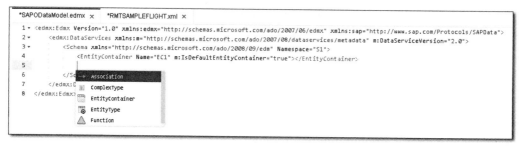

Figure 9.25 Schema-Based Code Assist

Model-Based code assist

5. The model-based code assist provides code suggestions based on your model. Place your cursor between the quotes of the name attribute for a given PROPERTYREF element, and press [Ctrl]+[Spacebar] to see the available name suggestions (Figure 9.26).

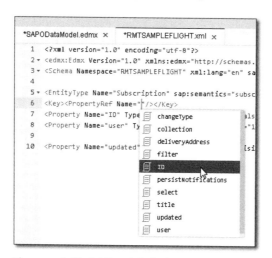

Figure 9.26 Model-Based Code Assist

You're now able to use the SAP Web IDE OData Model Editor!

Next, we'll look at how to use the editor to import files.

9.6.2 Importing Files via the OData Model Editor

The SAP Web IDE OData Model Editor also supports importing files. Following these steps to import a file:

1. You can download an existing metadata XML file from any OData service. Open *https://sapes4.sapdevcenter.com/sap/opu/odata/IWFND/RMTSAMPLEFLIGHT/$metadata* in your browser, and save the file to your local workstation.

2. Right-click the folder where you want to import the file, and choose IMPORT • ODATA MODEL. Click BROWSE, and select a valid XML (or EDMX) file on the IMPORT pop-up screen.

3. Click IMPORT to start the upload process. The file is validated, and any errors are displayed.

4. Switch to the DESIGN tab to open the graphical viewer of the included entities (Figure 9.27).

Opening the graphical viewer

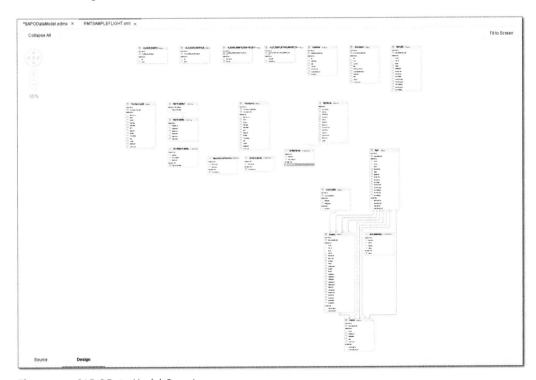

Figure 9.27 SAP OData Model Overview

Now that you've imported a service metadata file into the OData Model Editor and visualized the entities, next you'll create a new SAPUI5 without a connection to a remote system using the earlier imported EDMX file.

To create a new app, go back to Section 9.4 where you chose your data connection, and select WORKSPACE as a service source. Open the folder in your workspace where you've imported the EDMX file, and continue with the wizard as described.

Further Resources

For more information on OData Model Editor development, go to:

https://help.hana.ondemand.com/webide_odatamodeler/frameset.htm?e5c928 9506a7493189948b55c69097db.html

9.7 Summary

The SAP Web IDE is a browser-based tool that provides a lot of functionality, such as OData service consumption and application generation. We also discussed how you can use the OData Model Editor to optimize the entire development process. The SAP Web IDE is very easy to use and will have a huge impact on the development time of your applications and improve the quality of your future application development projects.

Next, in Chapter 10, we'll introduce you to the process of extending existing OData services and applications.

In this chapter, we'll explain the extensibility process end-to-end and demonstrate how OData development comes into play.

10 Extensibility

With SAP Fiori, SAP delivers a large number of applications that use OData services based on SAP Gateway. Beyond the standard business applications, SAP enables you to customize applications to suit individual customer needs. Because simply changing the UI isn't always sufficient in certain scenarios, SAP allows customers to extend the functionality of their applications and the underlying OData service.

SAP Fiori applications use an extensibility concept that provides various options for customers and partners to extend the services and applications delivered by SAP to meet their needs. In this chapter, we'll explain how to extend the underlying OData service of an SAP Fiori application using the SAP Gateway Service Builder, and then we'll describe the extensibility options in SAPUI5 applications using SAP Web IDE.

10.1 Redefining and Extending OData Services

The extensibility of OData services delivered by SAP or a partner in SAP Gateway is based on a process called *redefinition*. By redefining an existing SAP Gateway OData service, you create a new service that inherits all the functionality from the base service. This can be done without writing a single line of code. The data model of the newly created OData service can then be extended.

Redefinition

Examples of such extensions are adding fields ❶ to an entity type (field extensibility) or even adding new entity types and entity sets, associations, and navigation attributes ❷ (node extensibility), as shown in Figure 10.1.

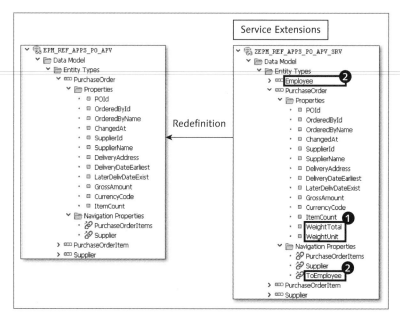

Figure 10.1 Data Model Structure of the Original, Redefined, and Extended Service

In this section, we'll begin by discussing the redefinition process for OData services. We'll then look at two examples of extending services with custom fields and custom entity sets.

10.1.1 Redefinition

SAP-enabled extension options

The development flow when redefining an OData service using Transaction SEGW is depicted in Figure 10.2. Let's walk through the process:

1. The development starts with the creation of a new project, which is the service definition step.

2. The data model definition and service implementation are performed in just one step by selecting REDEFINE • GATEWAY SERVICE from the context menu of the data model folder.

3. After the service has been registered in the backend and published on the SAP Gateway hub, it can be extended.

4. You can now extend the data model by adding fields or entity types to the redefined service. Some extensions may require a code-based implementation (adding additional entity sets), and others may not (adding properties to an existing entity type).

5. After you've extended the service, you have to test the service implementation.

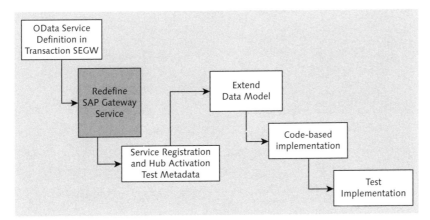

Figure 10.2 SAP Gateway OData Service Extensibility: Development Flow

The process depicted Figure 10.2 is described, step-by-step, in Section 10.3.1. Before digging into the step-by-step instructions, it's important to decide how the generated OData service behaves:

▶ The first option is that the new service that will be created is accessible via its own newly created URL.

▶ The second option is that no new URL is created, so the new service will be accessible via the URL of the base service.

To allow you to make an informed decision regarding these options, we'll explain the two different behaviors of redefined services in more detail.

The first option when using redefinition is that a second service with its own service URL is created. After redefinition of the service, you'll have two service URLs:

477

Service URLs
- ▸ .../ZEXTENDED_SRV
- ▸ .../ZBASE_SRV

If an OData client calls the .../ZEXTENDED_SRV URL, this means that the ZEXTENDED_SRV service implementation of the extended service is used (see Figure 10.3). If an OData client calls the .../ZBASE_SRV URL instead, the service implementation of the ZBASE_SRV base service is used. This behavior is depicted in Figure 10.3.

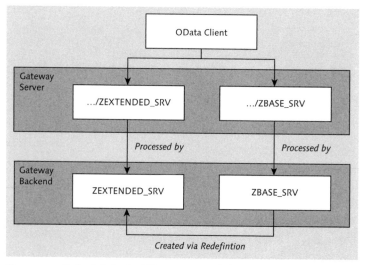

Figure 10.3 Default Behavior When Using Redefinition

The second option when using redefinition is that the base service implementation will be inaccessible afterwards. After the redefinition of the service, you'll only have one service URL—.../ZBASE_SRV.

If an OData client now calls the .../ZBASE_SRV URL, this time the service implementation of the extended service is used. The service implementation of the base service isn't accessible anymore, as depicted in Figure 10.4. The use case for choosing the second option is an SAP Fiori application that must be extended in such a way that the service URL isn't change.

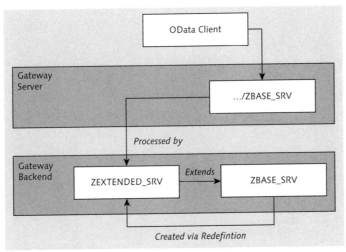

Figure 10.4 Redefinition Behavior When Using the Service Extension Option

So, how does a developer decide whether to use a new URL for the extended service or whether to stick to the existing URL of the base service? The behavior—whether you have two service URLs or just one—is defined in the service registration step (see Figure 10.2). In this step, you generate the runtime objects in the backend and perform the service registration.

In this step, you have two options. If you select the OVERWRITE BASE/EXTENDED SERVICE checkbox, as shown in Figure 10.5, the extended service will be registered using the TECHNICAL SERVICE NAME ZBASE_SRV of the base service. The SAP Gateway Service Builder will warn you that the base service won't be accessible anymore. This is because the technical service name of a service, which is used to create the service URL, can't be changed afterwards. The extended service will thus now use the service URL that has been created for the base service: */sap/opu/odata/sap/ZBASE_SRV*.

If you don't select the OVERWRITE BASE/EXTENDED SERVICE checkbox (the default setting offered by Transaction SEGW), the extended service will be registered using the TECHNICAL SERVICE NAME ZEXTENDED_SRV, as shown in Figure 10.6. The service, if published, will be accessible via a new URI: */sap/opu/odata/sap/ZEXTENDED_SRV*.

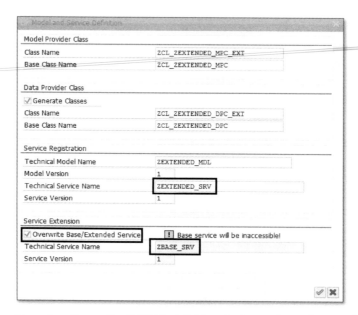

Figure 10.5 Transaction SEGW Redefinition: Settings to Reuse the URL of the Base Service

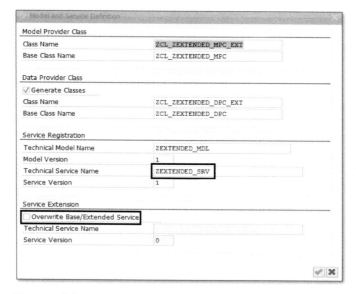

Figure 10.6 Transaction SEGW Redefinition: Settings to Publish an Extended Service via a New URL

> **Note**
>
> You should only use the OVERWRITE BASE/EXTENDED SERVICE option if your system is at least based on SAP Gateway 2.0 SP 9 or SAP NetWeaver 7.40 SP 8.
>
> Because the service URL used by SAP Fiori apps can easily be changed by creating an extension project as described in Section 10.3.2, there's usually no need to this option.

10.1.2 Field Extensibility

Entity types are typically based on a data dictionary DDIC structure that can be extended by adding an append structure to it. Even if such a DDIC structure is extended, the entity type won't be extended automatically. The developer still has to extend the entity type of the service that has been created via redefinition.

But how do newly created properties get populated with data? Additional properties usually must be implemented via a code-based implementation. To do this, you have to redefine the appropriate methods in the DPC_EXT class. However, for SAP Fiori applications, where extensibility is foreseen, a mechanism based on *extension includes* is used, which doesn't require any coding.

Field extensions

Extension includes are empty DDIC structures. SAP Fiori applications use entity types that are based on DDIC structures with extension includes. Extension includes are shipped by SAP as an anchor point for extensions. Customers can create append structures. Application extension fields can be treated generically. Using programming techniques such as MOVE-CORRESPONDING, the code is able to treat additional fields added by customers in their append structures appropriately.

Extension includes

As a result, the extension of a real SAP Fiori application can be relatively simple if, for the extension of an entity type, customers can leverage append structures that they've used to extend SAP database tables.

10.1.3   Node Extensibility

The extension of an OData service isn't limited to adding properties to an existing entity type. New entity types, entity sets, and even navigation properties can be added to the data model as well. However, because no CRUD-Q methods are generated by Transaction SEGW for newly added entity sets, the developer has to redefine generic dispatcher methods such as /iwbep/if_mgw_appl_srv_runtime~get_entity that handle GET_ENTITY calls in the data provider extension class.

Node extensions   Via a select case statement that checks for the name of the entity set being called, the developer can provide custom code or can call the code of the base class for all entity sets that were already part of the base service, as shown in Listing 10.1.

```
method /iwbep/if_mgw_appl_srv_runtime~get_entityset.
  ...
  case lv_entityset_name.
    when '<new entity set>'.
*       do something to get the data
    when others.
        super->/iwbep/if_mgw_appl_srv_runtime~get_
entityset( ... ).
  endcase.
endmethod.
```

Listing 10.1 Sample Code for a Redefined Dispatcher Method

10.2   Extending SAPUI5 Applications

SAPUI5 extensibility   You can extend SAPUI5 applications directly online in the SAP Web IDE (Chapter 9). To do so, you have to create an *extension project*, which alters the functionality or appearance of the original application, while the changes are made only to an extension project. The customized app is the start-up project and launches the SAPUI5 application with the extended objects. This allows the original application to remain unchanged so that there's no need for a modification. The concept of using extension projects is depicted in Figure 10.7.

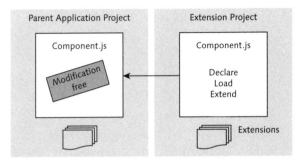

Figure 10.7 SAP Fiori: UI Extensibility Concept

You have different options to extend your SAPUI5 application, depending on which object you want to change.

In general, SAPUI5 supports the following operations:

SAPUI5 operations

- Adding new views
- Adding new navigation paths
- Customizing navigation routes
- Extending views
- Replacing views
- Modifying views
- Extending controllers
- Replacing controllers
- Customizing I18n resource text

The most common scenarios for these operations are the following:

- Adding new fields
- Hiding fields
- Adding new buttons
- Adding custom lists
- Adding custom tabs
- Replacing OData services
- Replacing complete views
- Replacing complete controllers

Figure 10.8 shows the Model-View-Controller (MVC) concept that is used by SAPUI5 applications. The previously mentioned options to extend an SAPUI5 application are changing the data model, the view, or the controller layer of an SAPUI5 application.

The data model of an SAPUI5 application is changed by extending the OData service in SAP Gateway. To extend views, SAP delivers *extension points*, which work as anchor points where you can insert your own coding (i.e., the enhancement points in ABAP). An extension point refers to the SAPUI5 control `<core:ExtensionPoint/>` XML view element.

Views can also be modified by hiding single UI controls whose visibility can be set. On the controller side is the UI controller hook, which is a certain type of extension point of controllers. You can replace a controller, which we'll also show in this chapter.

MVC concept

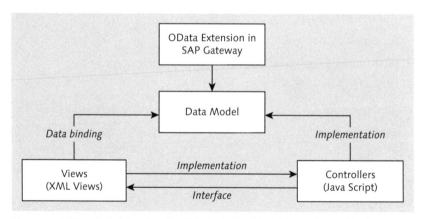

Figure 10.8 SAP Fiori: Extension Possibilities in the Model-View-Controller Concept

> **Warning**
>
> There are limitations when extending SAPUI5 applications. Although SAP ships a new version of an application without overwriting customer-specific extension code, these modifications aren't guaranteed to still work after any app upgrade. We recommend reading "Caveats Regarding Stability Across Application Upgrades" at *https://sapui5.hana.ondemand.com/sdk/#docs/guide/aef3384510724522a07df94ec90d1351.html* for more information.

10.3 Extending SAP Fiori Applications

In this section, we'll extend the SAP Fiori reference app *Approve Purchase Orders*. The Approve Purchase Orders app is a typical approval app that provides you with a list of purchase orders that have been assigned to you and allows you to approve or reject them.

To showcase the concept of extensibility, we'll enhance the Purchase Order Approval app so that the approver sees the total weight ❶ of an order as additional information in the Purchase Order details screen (see Figure 10.9). Furthermore, the approver is shown in the contact details ❷ of the employee who placed the order so that he can contact the person if necessary before approving or rejecting a purchase order.

Extending
SAP Fiori apps

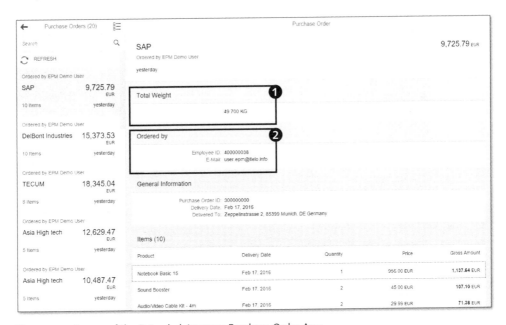

Figure 10.9 Screen of the Extended Approve Purchase Order App

> **Additional Information**
>
> You can find more information about SAP Fiori reference apps in the follow-ing SCN document: *http://scn.sap.com/docs/DOC-59963*.

The example we've chosen (Approve Purchase Orders app) to extend requires the extension of an OData service as well as an SAPUI5 applica-tion of our SAP Fiori reference app. This section is thus divided into two subsections:

- In Section 10.3.1, we'll describe the steps to extend the OData service using the Service Builder.

- In Section 10.3.2, we'll show how to use the SAP Web IDE to extend the SAPUI5 application of the Approve Purchase Orders app.

Let's start by describing what the OData service developer needs to do.

10.3.1 Extending the OData Service

In our example, we want to show data that isn't offered by the OData service of the original SAP Fiori reference app. To retrieve the additional data from the SAP backend system, you have to extend the underlying OData service. While the total weight of a purchase order can be stored in an additional custom field of the `PurchaseOrders` entity set, the con-tact details have to be retrieved from a new `EmployeeSet` entity set. This is because one employee can have placed several purchase orders, so there is a 1:n relationship between these two entities. The total weight of the purchase order will be calculated in the SAP backend by reading the weight of each product for every purchase order line item. Because this is an example of an entity type that doesn't offer extension includes, it shows how to handle field extensibility for any entity set of an SAP Fiori application.

OData service extension For our SAP Fiori app, the OData service will be extended in several ways. You'll start by extending the `Purchase Order` entity type. This entity type will get two additional properties to store the total weight of an order (`WeightTotal`) and the unit of the total weight (`WeightUnit`). In addition, you'll add the `EmployeeSet` entity set with an option to navi-gate from a purchase order entity set to the employee entity set.

Using the `ToEmployee` navigation property, you can retrieve the contact details of an employee that has created a purchase order. The data model structure of the original service and the redefined service is shown in Figure 10.1.

Follow these steps to extend the OData service of the Purchase Order Approval app:

1. Create a new project, ZEPM_REF_APPS_PO_APV, via the Service Builder, and create a new service by redefining the EPM_REF_APPS_ PO_APV _SRV service.

2. Extend the data model by adding the new properties `WeightTotal` and `WeightUnit` to the `PurchaseOrder` entity type.

3. Redefine the `purchaseorders_get_entityset` and `purchaseorders_ get_entity methods` in the data provider extension class, and add code to calculate the total weight for all the selected purchase orders.

4. Extend the data model by adding the `Employee` entity type and the `EmployeeSet` entity set, and add the `ToEmployee` navigation property to the `PurchaseOrders` entity set.

5. Because the Service Builder doesn't automatically create the methods for read (`GET_ENTITY`) and query (`GET_ENTITYSET`) in this case, manually create these methods in the data provider extension class.

6. In the data provider extension class, redefine the `/iwbep/if_mgw_appl_ srv_runtime~get_entity` and `/iwbep/if_mgw_appl_srv_runtime~get_ entityset` methods because the dispatcher methods won't call the manually created methods out of the box.

Creating an Append Structure

The `PurchaseOrders` entity set is based on the `SEPM_REF_APPS_PO_APV_PO` DDIC structure. To add additional fields to the `PurchaseOrders` entity set, you first have to extend the DDIC structure by following these steps:

1. Start Transaction SE11. In the DATA TYPE field, enter the name of the dictionary structure "SEPM_REF_APPS_PO_APV_PO."

2. Click APPEND STRUCTURE, and enter "ZZPO_EXT" in the CREATE APPEND STRUCTURE FOR... pop-up for the APPEND NAME (see Figure 10.10).

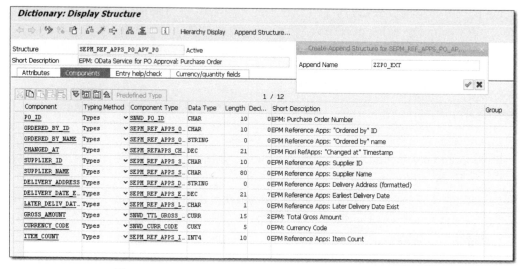

Figure 10.10 Creating the ZZPO_EXT Append Structure

3. Add two fields for the total weight and the unit in which the weight is measured. Enter "Total weight of items in purchase order" as a DESCRIPTION and the values shown in Table 10.1 for the new fields.

Component	Typing Method	Component Type
ZZ_WEIGHT_TOTAL	TYPES	SNWD_WEIGHT_MEASURE
ZZ_WEIGHT_UNIT	TYPES	SNWD_WEIGHT_UNIT

Table 10.1 Fields of the ZZPO_EXT Append Structure

4. Switch to the CURRENCY/QUANTITY FIELDS tab (Figure 10.11). In the line for the ZZ_WEIGHT_TOTAL component, enter "ZZPO_EXT" in the REFERENCE TABLE column and enter "ZZ_WEIGHT_UNIT" in the REF. FIELD column.

5. To activate your changes, choose STRUCTURE • ACTIVATE from the menu. In the CREATE OBJECT DIRECTORY ENTRY popup, enter $TMP for the package, and click SAVE. The extended structure is shown in Figure 10.12.

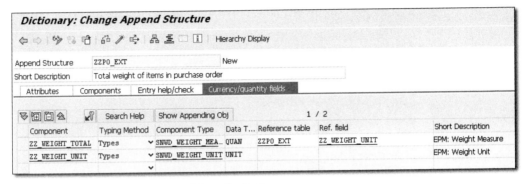

Figure 10.11 Maintaining Currency and Quantity Fields

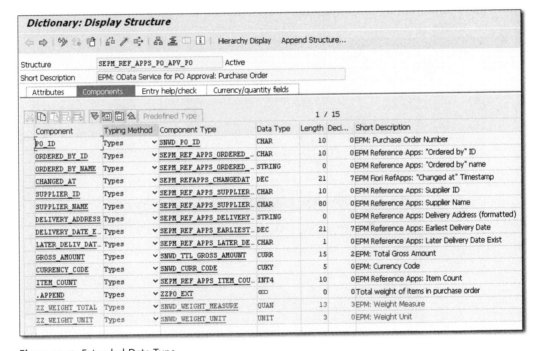

Figure 10.12 Extended Data Type

Redefining the EPM_REF_APPS_PO_APV_SRV OData Service

Next, you'll redefine the OData service by following these steps:

1. Start the Service Builder, and create a new project called ZEPM_REF_ APPS_PO_APV_SRV. Enter the DESCRIPTION "Extension of SAP Fiori   Redefinition

489

Ref App "Approve Purchase Orders"." Right-click on the DATA MODEL node, select REDEFINE, and then choose ODATA SERVICE (SAP GW). This starts the wizard for the redefinition of an SAP Gateway OData service (see Figure 10.13).

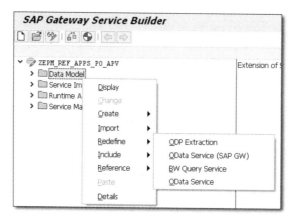

Figure 10.13 Starting the Redefinition of the OData Service

2. Enter "EPM_REF_APPS_PO_APV_SRV" in the TECHNICAL SERVICE NAME field, enter "0001" in the VERSION field, and click NEXT (see Figure 10.14).

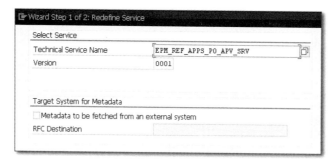

Figure 10.14 Wizard Step 1 of 2: Redefine Service

3. On the second screen of the wizard (see Figure 10.15), select all of the components of the OData model EPM_REF_APPS_PO_APV_MDL for the service EPM_REF_APPS_PO_APV_SRV. After you've select the services, click FINISH.

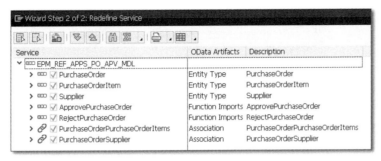

Figure 10.15 Wizard Step 2 of 2: Redefine Service

Registering and Publishing the OData Redefined Service

Next, you need to register the redefined OData service in the backend and publish it on the hub so that it can be extended and tested. Follow these steps:

1. Click the GENERATE button to generate the runtime artifacts and to register the OData service in the backend.

Registering

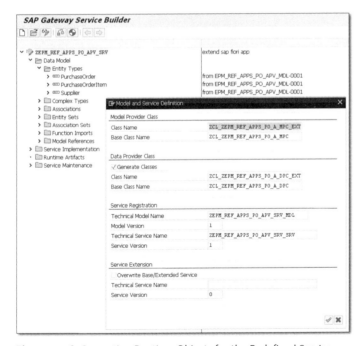

Figure 10.16 Generating Runtime Objects for the Redefined Service

On the MODEL AND SERVICE DEFINITION screen, leave the default values unchanged. Only check the OVERWRITE BASE/EXTENDED SERVICE checkbox if you want to use the existing URL of the base service for the extended service as well and if you don't need to access the original service anymore (see Section 10.1.1 for more details). Click CONTINUE (see Figure 10.16).

2. In the CREATE OBJECT DIRECTORY ENTRY screen, in the PACKAGE field, enter "$TMP," and click CONTINUE, as shown in Figure 10.17.

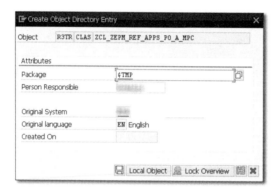

Figure 10.17 Create Object Directory Entry Screen

3. Expand the SERVICE MAINTENANCE folder, and select the entry for the SAP Gateway hub system (here, LOCAL) where the service will be published. Once done, select REGISTER from the context menu, as shown in Figure 10.18.

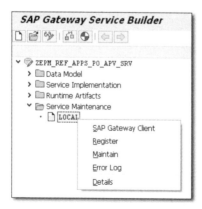

Figure 10.18 Publishing the Redefined Service on the Hub

4. In the SELECT SYSTEM ALIAS (HUB TO BACKEND) dialog, enter "LOCAL"
   in the SYSTEM ALIAS field, as shown in Figure 10.19.

Figure 10.19 Selecting the System Alias That Points from the Hub to the Backend

5. On the ADD SERVICE screen, in the PACKAGE ASSIGNMENT field, enter
   "$TMP," and then click CONTINUE (see Figure 10.20).

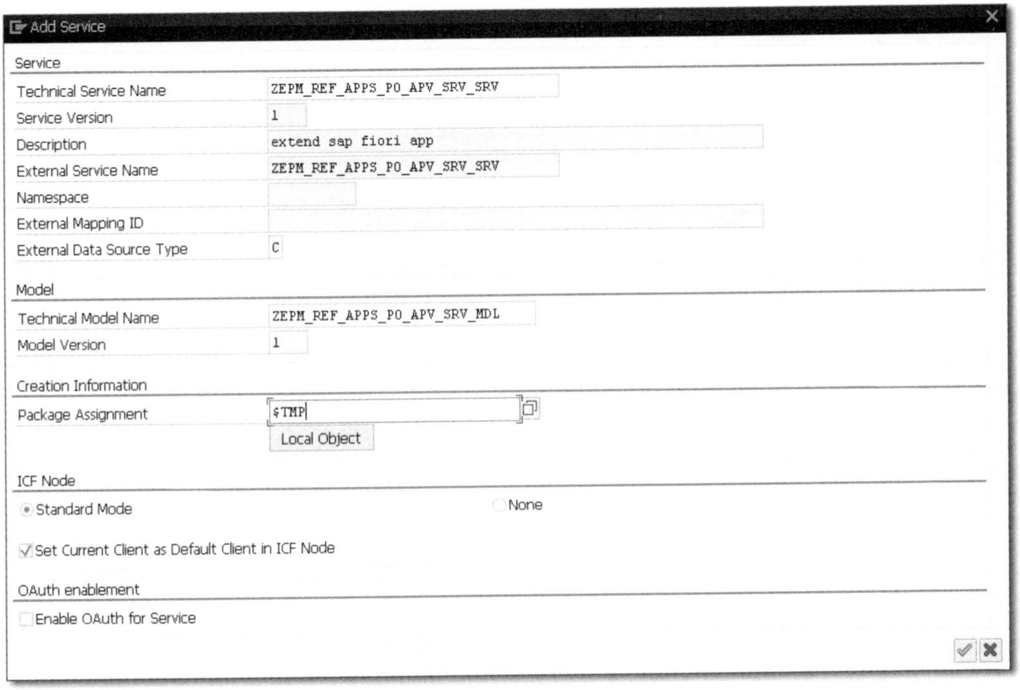

Figure 10.20 Add Service Dialog to Publish the Service on the Hub

You should now test to check whether the redefined service provides
the same data as the service that is used by the SAP Fiori reference application.

Following these steps:

1. From the context menu shown earlier in Figure 10.18, select SAP GATEWAY CLIENT. Confirm the warning that you'll now be redirected to the selected system

2. If you enter the URI "/sap/opu/odata/SAP/ZEPM_REF_APPS_PO_APV_SRV_SRV/PurchaseOrders?$format=json" into the REQUEST URI field, you should get the result shown in Figure 10.21.

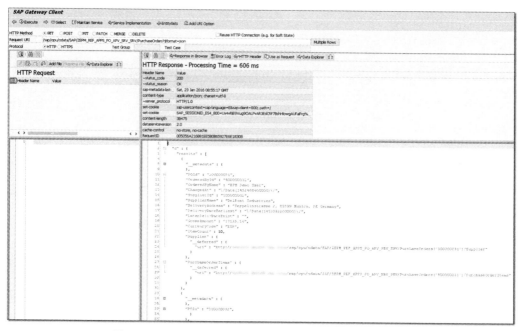

Figure 10.21 Testing the Redefined Service in the SAP Gateway Client

Adding Custom Fields

In this section, you'll extend an entity type with custom fields. Follow these steps:

1. Start the extension of the data model by adding two fields to the Pur-chaseOrder entity type. In your Service Builder project, drill down to the PROPERTIES folder of the PURCHASEORDER entity type, and double-click it.

2. In the right pane, choose the DISPLAY <-> CHANGE mode button, and then click the APPEND ROW button twice to add the WEIGHTTOTAL and WEIGHTUNIT properties, as shown in Figure 10.22.

Figure 10.22 Adding New Properties to the PurchaseOrder Entity Type

3. Enter the values shown in Table 10.2 for the respective columns. Note that for the EDM CORE TYPE and ABAP FIELD NAME fields, you can use F4 to avoid typos. The F4 Help for the ABAP FIELD NAME field will show the ZZ_WEIGHT_TOTAL and ZZ_WEIGHT_UNIT fields that you've added to the SEPM_REF_APPS_PO_APV_PO structure using the ZZPO_EXT append structure.

Name	Edm Core Type	Precision	Scale	Max Lngth	Label	ABAP Field Name
WEIGHT-TOTAL	EDM.DECIMAL	13	3		TOTAL WEIGHT	ZZ_WEIGHT_TOTAL
WEIGHT-UNIT	EDM.STRING			3	UNIT OF MEASURE	ZZ_WEIGHT_UNIT

Table 10.2 New Properties of the PurchaseOrder Entity Type

Don't forget to save and regenerate your Service Builder project.

Service Implementation for the Custom Fields

You now have to redefine the PURCHASEORDERS_GET_ENTITYSET method in the ZCL_ZEPM_REF_APPS_PO_A_DPC_EXT data provider extension class of your redefined service so that the WeightTotal and WeightUnit properties get populated if a GET request is sent to the PurchaseOrderSet entity set.

Redefine the GET_ ENTITYSET method

Custom field The code in Listing 10.2 first calls the `purchaseorders_get_entityset` method of the superclass to get the list of purchase orders via internal table `et_entityset`. It then loops across the internal table and calculates the total weight of the items within the purchase order using the `z_get_total_po_weight` method.

```
method purchaseorders_get_entityset.
data : ls_entityset like line of et_entityset.

    try.
        call method super->purchaseorders_get_entityset
          exporting
            iv_entity_name          = iv_entity_name
            iv_entity_set_name      = iv_entity_set_name
            iv_source_name          = iv_source_name
            it_filter_select_options = it_filter_select_options
            is_paging               = is_paging
            it_key_tab              = it_key_tab
            it_navigation_path      = it_navigation_path
            it_order                = it_order
            iv_filter_string        = iv_filter_string
            iv_search_string        = iv_search_string
            io_tech_request_context = io_tech_request_context
          importing
            et_entityset            = et_entityset
            es_response_context     = es_response_context.
      catch /iwbep/cx_mgw_busi_exception .
      catch /iwbep/cx_mgw_tech_exception .
    endtry.

* filling the fields for total weight and weight unit in the ex
tended entity set

    loop at et_entityset into ls_entityset.
      call method z_get_total_po_weight
        exporting
          po_id        = ls_entityset-po_id
        importing
          weight_total = ls_entityset-zz_weight_total
          weight_unit  = ls_entityset-zz_weight_unit.
      modify et_entityset from ls_entityset.
    endloop.
endmethod.
```

Listing 10.2 purchaseorders_get_entityset

The same `z_get_total_po_weight` method can be used to calculate the new property values when the `GET_ENTITY` method is called (see Listing 10.3).

```
method purchaseorders_get_entity.
try.
        call method super->purchaseorders_get_entity
          exporting
            iv_entity_name         = iv_entity_name
            iv_entity_set_name     = iv_entity_set_name
            iv_source_name         = iv_source_name
            it_key_tab             = it_key_tab
            it_navigation_path     = it_navigation_path
            io_tech_request_context = io_tech_request_context
          importing
            er_entity              = er_entity
            es_response_context    = es_response_context.
      catch /iwbep/cx_mgw_busi_exception .
      catch /iwbep/cx_mgw_tech_exception .
    endtry.

* filling the fields for total weight and weight unit in the ex
tended entity

    call method z_get_total_po_weight
      exporting
        po_id       = er_entity-po_id
      importing
        weight_total = er_entity-zz_weight_total
        weight_unit  = er_entity-zz_weight_unit.
endmethod.
```
Listing 10.3 purchaseorders_get_entity

The `z_get_total_po_weight` method calculates the total weight of the purchase order items using an inner join of the `sepm_ipoie` Core Data Services (CDS) view that contains the purchase order items and `sepm_iproducte`, which contains product information, such as weight. Because the weights of the single items are given in grams and kilograms, the code uses the `UNIT_CONVERSION_SIMPLE` function module to convert all weights to kilogram (see Listing 10.4).

```
method z_get_total_po_weight.

    data: begin of wa,
          purchaseorder     type sepm_ipoie-purchaseorder,
          purchaseorderitem type sepm_ipoie-
```

```
purchaseorderitem,
          product           type sepm_ipoie-product,
          quantity          type sepm_ipoie-quantity,
          weight            type sepm_iproducte-weight,
          weightunit        type sepm_iproducte-weightunit,
        end of wa,
        itab      like sorted table of wa
          with unique key purchaseorder purchaseorderitem ,
        totalweight type sepm_iproducte-weight,
        weight      type sepm_iproducte-weight.

  constants: cv_weight_unit_kg type snwd_weight_
unit value 'KG'.

  select  poi~purchaseorder poi~purchaseorderitem poi~product
 poi~quantity pd~weight pd~weightunit
     into  corresponding fields of table itab
     from  ( sepm_ipoie as poi
              inner join sepm_
iproducte as pd on poi~product = pd~product  )
     where poi~purchaseorder = po_id .

  clear totalweight.

  loop at itab into wa.

*     Convert all Weights to KG
      clear weight.

      call function 'UNIT_CONVERSION_SIMPLE'
        exporting
          input              = wa-weight
          unit_in            = wa-weightunit
          unit_out           = cv_weight_unit_kg
        importing
          output             = weight
        exceptions
          conversion_not_found = 1
          division_by_zero   = 2
          input_invalid      = 3
          output_invalid     = 4
          overflow           = 5
          type_invalid       = 6
          units_missing      = 7
          unit_in_not_found  = 8
          unit_out_not_found = 9
          others             = 10.

      if sy-subrc ne 0.  continue.  endif.
      totalweight = totalweight + wa-quantity * weight.
```

```
    endloop.

    weight_total = totalweight.
    weight_unit = cv_weight_unit_kg.

endmethod.
```
Listing 10.4 Method z_get_total_po_weight

If you now perform a GET request using the following URI with the SAP Gateway client */sap/opu/odata/SAP/ZEPM_REF_APPS_PO_APV_SRV_SRV/ PurchaseOrders?$format=json,* the HTTP response will contain a list of the purchase orders where the newly added properties will be populated with values such as "WeightTotal" : "18.360" and "WeightUnit" : "KG." The result is also shown in Figure 10.23.

```
{
  "__metadata" : {
  },
  "POId" : "300000031",
  "OrderedById" : "400000032",
  "OrderedByName" : "EPM Demo User",
  "ChangedAt" : "\/Date(1452488400000)\/",
  "SupplierId" : "100000002",
  "SupplierName" : "DelBont Industries",
  "DeliveryAddress" : "Zeppelinstrasse 2, 85399 Munich, DE Germany",
  "DeliveryDateEarliest" : "\/Date(1453093200000)\/",
  "LaterDelivDateExist" : "",
  "GrossAmount" : "17135.16",
  "CurrencyCode" : "EUR",
  "ItemCount" : 10,
  "WeightTotal" : "18.360",
  "WeightUnit" : "KG",
  "Supplier" : {
    "__deferred" : {
      "uri" : "http://            /sap/opu/odata/SAP/ZEPM_REF_APPS_PO_APV_SRV_SRV/PurchaseOrders('300000031')/Supplier"
    }
  },
```

Figure 10.23 Result of the Extended PurchaseOrder List

Adding a Custom Entity Set

Next, you'll extend the data model for our app by adding the Employee entity type and the EmployeeSet entity set.

Custom entity set

The EmployeeSet entity set provides a list of employee contact data. The idea is to enhance the SAP Fiori sample application so that the contact details of the orderer alongside with the purchase order details are shown. This way the approver of the purchase order will have the opportunity to easily get in touch with the orderer to discuss any open topics.

499

To add the entity set, follow these steps:

1. From the tree structure of your Service Builder project ZEPM_REF_APPS_PO_APV, right-click on the DATA MODEL folder, and select IMPORT • DDIC STRUCTURE from the context menu, as shown in Figure 10.24.

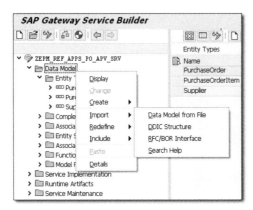

Figure 10.24 Import DDIC Structure SNWD_EMPLOYEES

2. In the first screen of the IMPORT FROM DDIC STRUCTURE, wizard, enter "Employee" in the NAME field, and select SNWD_EMPLOYEES in the ABAP STRUCTURE field. Leave the CREATE DEFAULT ENTITY SET checkbox activated, and click NEXT to continue. As a result, the wizard will create the EmployeeSet entity set and the Employee entity type (see Figure 10.25).

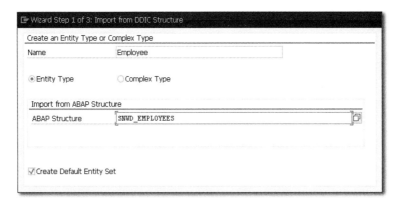

Figure 10.25 Wizard Step 1 of 3: Import from DDIC structure

3. In the second screen of the IMPORT FROM DDIC STRUCTURE wizard, select only the following fields of the data source: SNWD_EMPLOYEE: EMPLOYEE_ID, FIRST_NAME, MIDDLE_NAME, LAST_NAME, PHONE_NUMBER, EMAIL_ADDRESS, and EMPLOYEE_PIC_URL (see Figure 10.26).

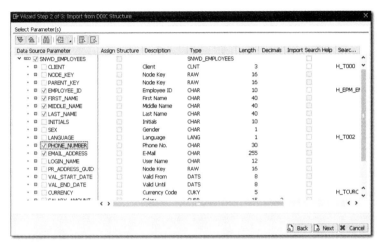

Figure 10.26 Wizard Step 2 of 3: Import from DDIC Structure

4. In the third screen of the IMPORT FROM DDIC STRUCTURE wizard, choose EMPLOYEEID as the key field of the entity type (Figure 10.27).

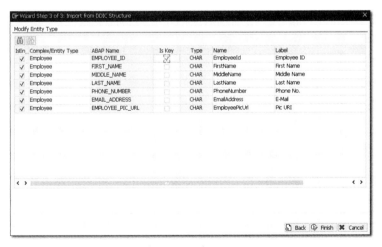

Figure 10.27 Wizard Step 3 of 3: Import from DDIC Structure

Create navigation property You can now create an association between the newly created `Employee` entity type and the `PurchaseOrder` entity type that is part of the redefined data model of our Approve Purchase Orders app. The wizard will guide you through the steps necessary to create an appropriate `ToPurchaseOrders` navigation property in the `EmployeeSet` entity set.

Follow these steps:

1. From the tree structure of your Service Builder ZEPM_REF_APPS_PO_ APV_SRV project, right-click on the DATA MODEL folder, and select CREATE • ASSOCIATION from the context menu (see Figure 10.28).

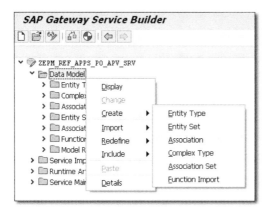

Figure 10.28 Creating an Association Using the Service Builder

2. In the first screen of the wizard (Figure 10.29), specify the name of the association and the entity types with their respective cardinalities. You can also select the CREATE RELATED NAVIGATION PROPERTY checkbox to create corresponding navigation properties.

3. In this case, you'll create the `Assoc_Employee_PurchaseOrder` association. For the PRINCIPAL ENTITY, enter "Employee" in the ENTITY TYPE NAME field, "1" in the CARDINALITY field, and "ToPurchaseOrders" in the NAVIGATION PROPERTY field. For the DEPENDENT ENTITY, enter "PurchaseOrder" in the ENTITY TYPE NAME field, "0..n" in the CARDINALITY field (because one employee can create none or several purchase orders), and "ToEmployee" in the NAVIGATION PROPERTY field.

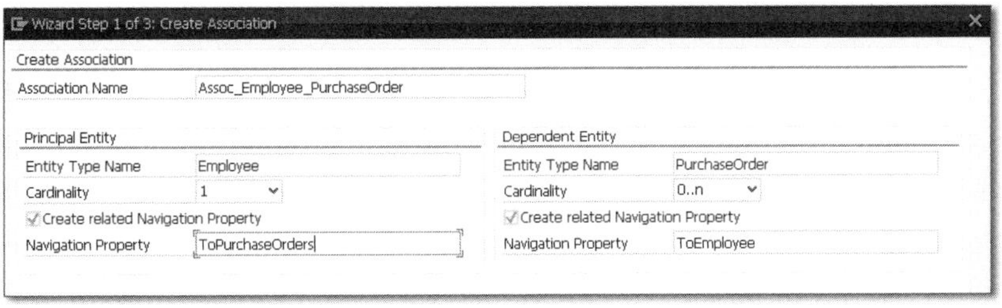

Figure 10.29 Wizard Step 1 of 3: Create Association

4. On the second screen, specify the referential constraint by mapping the key fields of the principal entity type to the properties of the dependent entity. In this example, the PRINCIPAL ENTITY type is EMPLOYEE, and the PRINCIPAL KEY only consists of a single field, EMPLOYEEID. This property is mapped to DEPENDENT PROPERTY ORDEREDBYID of the DEPENDENT ENTITY PURCHASEORDER (see Figure 10.30). Click NEXT to continue.

Figure 10.30 Wizard Step 2 of 3: Create Association

5. On the third screen, provide the name of the association set to be created (Figure 10.31). The name is defaulted based on the name provided for the association. The corresponding entity sets are derived from the related entity types. Leave the default values, and click FINISH.

Figure 10.31 Wizard Step 3 of 3: Create Association

Service Implementation for a Custom Entity Set

After the model of the redefined service has been extended by adding a new entity set, you can now start the service implementation.

Because the Service Builder doesn't create default CRUD-Q methods if an entity set is added to a data model of a service that has been generated via redefinition, you have to manually create two methods: Z_EMPLOYEESET_GET_ENTITY and Z_EMPLOYEESET_GET_ENTITYSET. Those two methods aren't called automatically though.

Custom entity set

Therefore, in addition, you have to redefine the generic /iwbep/if_mgw_appl_srv_runtime~get_entity and /iwbep/if_mgw_appl_srv_runtime~get_entityset dispatcher methods. Via a CASE statement, the system checks whether the new implementations in Z_EMPLOYEESET_GET_ENTITY and Z_EMPLOYEESET_GET_ENTITYSET for the READ and QUERY method of the EmployeeSet entity set should be called. Otherwise, the dispatcher methods in the data provider extension class call the respective methods in the superclass.

You first have to create two methods—Z_EMPLOYEESET_GET_ENTITY and Z_EMPLOYEESET_GET_ENTITYSET—by copying the /IWBEP/IF_MGW_APPL_SRV_RUNTIME~GET_ENTITY and /IWBEP/IF_MGW_APPL_SRV_RUNTIME~GET_ENTITYSET methods.

In the Z_EMPLOYEESET_GET_ENTITYSET method, you first have to rename the ER_ENTITYSET return parameter to ET_ENTITYSET. In addition, you have to change the parameter typing from TYPE REF TO to TYPE (Figure 10.32), and you have to change the type to ZCL_ZEPM_REF_APPS_PO_A_MPC=>TT_EMPLOYEE.

In the Z_EMPLOYEESET_GET_ENTITY method, you only have to change the parameter typing of the ER_ENTITY parameter from TYPE REF TO to TYPE (Figure 10.33). The type has to be changed as well to ZCL_ZEPM_REF_APPS_PO_A_MPC=>TS_EMPLOYEE.

Ty.	Parameter	Type spec.
▶❑	IV_ENTITY_NAME	TYPE STRING OPTIONAL
▶❑	IV_ENTITY_SET_NAME	TYPE STRING OPTIONAL
▶❑	IV_SOURCE_NAME	TYPE STRING OPTIONAL
▶❑	IT_FILTER_SELECT_OPTIONS	TYPE /IWBEP/T_MGW_SELECT_OPTION OPTIONAL
▶❑	IT_ORDER	TYPE /IWBEP/T_MGW_SORTING_ORDER OPTIONAL
▶❑	IS_PAGING	TYPE /IWBEP/S_MGW_PAGING OPTIONAL
▶❑	IT_NAVIGATION_PATH	TYPE /IWBEP/T_MGW_NAVIGATION_PATH OPTIONAL
▶❑	IT_KEY_TAB	TYPE /IWBEP/T_MGW_NAME_VALUE_PAIR OPTIONAL
▶❑	IV_FILTER_STRING	TYPE STRING OPTIONAL
▶❑	IV_SEARCH_STRING	TYPE STRING OPTIONAL
▶❑	IO_TECH_REQUEST_CONTEXT	TYPE REF TO /IWBEP/IF_MGW_REQ_ENTITYSET OPTIONAL
❑▶	ET_ENTITYSET	TYPE ZCL_ZEPM_REF_APPS_PO_A_MPC=>TT_EMPLOYEE
❑▶	ES_RESPONSE_CONTEXT	TYPE /IWBEP/IF_MGW_APPL_SRV_RUNTIME=>TY_S_MGW_RESPONSE_CONTEXT
❑	/IWBEP/CX_MGW_BUSI_EXCEPTION	
❑	/IWBEP/CX_MGW_TECH_EXCEPTION	

Method	Z_EMPLOYEESET_GET_ENTITYSET		Active

Figure 10.32 Signature Method Z_EMPLOYEESET_GET_ENTITYSET

Ty.	Parameter	Type spec.
▶❑	IV_ENTITY_NAME	TYPE STRING OPTIONAL
▶❑	IV_ENTITY_SET_NAME	TYPE STRING OPTIONAL
▶❑	IV_SOURCE_NAME	TYPE STRING OPTIONAL
▶❑	IT_KEY_TAB	TYPE /IWBEP/T_MGW_NAME_VALUE_PAIR OPTIONAL
▶❑	IT_NAVIGATION_PATH	TYPE /IWBEP/T_MGW_NAVIGATION_PATH OPTIONAL
▶❑	IO_TECH_REQUEST_CONTEXT	TYPE REF TO /IWBEP/IF_MGW_REQ_ENTITY OPTIONAL
❑▶	ER_ENTITY	TYPE ZCL_ZEPM_REF_APPS_PO_A_MPC=>TS_EMPLOYEE
❑▶	ES_RESPONSE_CONTEXT	TYPE /IWBEP/IF_MGW_APPL_SRV_RUNTIME=>TY_S_MGW_RESPONSE_ENTITY_CNTXT
❑	/IWBEP/CX_MGW_BUSI_EXCEPTION	
❑	/IWBEP/CX_MGW_TECH_EXCEPTION	

Method	Z_EMPLOYEESET_GET_ENTITY		Active

Figure 10.33 Signature Method Z_EMPLOYEESET_GET_ENTITY

The ABAP code of both methods is shown in Listing 10.5 and Listing 10.6.

```
method z_employeeset_get_entityset.
   select employee_id first_name middle_name last_name phone_
number email_address employee_pic_url
   into corresponding fields of table et_entityset from snwd_
employees.
endmethod.
```

Listing 10.5 z_employeeset_get_entityset

```
method z_employeeset_get_entity.

    data: ls_headerdata     type zcl_zepm_ref_apps_po_a_
mpc=>ts_employee,
          ls_headerdata_src type zcl_zepm_ref_apps_po_a_
mpc=>ts_purchaseorder.
    data: ls_snwd_po  type snwd_po.
    data: ls_snwd_employees type snwd_employees.
    data: lt_nav_path              type /iwbep/t_mgw_tech_
navi,
          ls_nav_path              type /iwbep/s_mgw_tech_
navi,
          employee_id              type zcl_zepm_ref_apps_po_
a_mpc=>ts_purchaseorder-ordered_by_id,
          lv_source_entity_set_name type /iwbep/mgw_tech_name.

    lv_source_entity_set_name = io_tech_request_context->get_
source_entity_set_name( ).

    if lv_source_entity_set_name eq 'PurchaseOrders'.
      lt_nav_path = io_tech_request_context->get_navigation_
path( ).
      read table lt_nav_path into ls_nav_path with key nav_
prop = 'TOEMPLOYEE'.
      if sy-subrc = 0.
        call method io_tech_request_context->get_converted_
source_keys
          importing
            es_key_values = ls_headerdata_src.
        select single po_id created_
by into corresponding fields of
        ls_snwd_po from snwd_po where po_id = ls_headerdata_
src-po_id.
        select single employee_id into corresponding fields of
        ls_snwd_employees from snwd_employees where node_
key = ls_snwd_po-created_by.
        employee_id = ls_snwd_employees-employee_id.
      endif.
    else.
      call method io_tech_request_context->get_converted_keys
        importing
          es_key_values = ls_headerdata.
      if ls_headerdata is not initial.
        employee_id = ls_headerdata-employee_id.
      endif.
    endif.
    if employee_id is not initial.
      select single employee_id first_name middle_name last_
name phone_number email_address employee_pic_url
```

```
      into corresponding fields of er_entity from snwd_
employees where employee_id = employee_id.
   endif.
  endmethod..
```
Listing 10.6 z_employeeset_get_entity

Note that the coding of the `z_employeeset_get_entity` method looks a little bit complicated due to the underlying data model. Because the purchase order doesn't hold the ID of the employee, you have to retrieve this value by selecting the same using the ID of the purchase order from the database tables of the EPM demo data. As previously mentioned, you have to redefine the `/iwbep/if_mgw_appl_srv_runtime~get_entity` and `/iwbep/if_mgw_appl_srv_runtime~get_entityset` dispatcher methods so that the methods you've created manually are actually called if a GET request hits the `EmployeeSet` entity set by checking for the name of the entity set (here, `EmployeeSet`) that has been called (see Listing 10.7 and Listing 10.8).

```
method /iwbep/if_mgw_appl_srv_runtime~get_entity.

    data z_employeeset_get_entity type zcl_zepm_ref_apps_po_a_
mpc=>ts_employee.
    data lv_entityset_name type string.
    data lr_entity type ref to data.

    lv_entityset_name = io_tech_request_context->get_entity_
set_name( ).

    case lv_entityset_name.

      when 'EmployeeSet'.

* Call the method we created for the entity set

        z_employeeset_get_entity(
            exporting
              iv_entity_name          = iv_entity_name
              iv_entity_set_name      = iv_entity_set_name
              iv_source_name          = iv_source_name
              it_key_tab              = it_key_tab
              it_navigation_path      = it_navigation_path
              io_tech_request_context = io_tech_request_
context
            importing
              er_entity               = z_employeeset_get_
```

507

```
entity ).

*       Send specific entity data to the caller interface

        copy_data_to_ref(
          exporting
            is_data = z_employeeset_get_entity
          changing
            cr_data = er_entity
        ).

      when others.

        super->/iwbep/if_mgw_appl_srv_runtime~get_entity(
            exporting
              iv_entity_name           = iv_entity_name
              iv_entity_set_name       = iv_entity_set_name
              iv_source_name           = iv_source_name
              it_key_tab               = it_key_tab
              it_navigation_path       = it_navigation_path
              io_tech_request_context  = io_tech_request_
context
            importing
              er_entity                = er_entity ).

    endcase.

  endmethod.
```
Listing 10.7 Coding of the /iwbep/if_mgw_appl_srv_runtime~get_entity Dispatcher Method

```
method /IWBEP/IF_MGW_APPL_SRV_RUNTIME~GET_ENTITYSET.

  data z_employeeset_get_entityset  type zcl_zepm_ref_apps_po_
a_mpc=>tt_employee.

    data lv_entityset_name type string.
    data lr_entity type ref to data.

    lv_entityset_name = io_tech_request_context->get_entity_
set_name( ).

    case lv_entityset_name.
      when 'EmployeeSet'.
* Call the method you created for the entity set
        z_employeeset_get_entityset(
            exporting
              iv_entity_name           = iv_entity_name
              iv_entity_set_name       = iv_entity_set_name
```

```
                iv_source_name             = iv_source_name
                it_filter_select_options = it_filter_select_
options
                it_order                   = it_order
                is_paging                  = is_paging
                it_navigation_path         = it_navigation_path
                it_key_tab                 = it_key_tab
                iv_filter_string           = iv_filter_string
                iv_search_string           = iv_search_string
                io_tech_request_context    = io_tech_request_
context
            importing
                et_entityset               = z_employeeset_get_
entityset
                es_response_context        = es_response_context ).

        copy_data_to_ref(
            exporting
              is_data = z_employeeset_get_entityset
            changing
              cr_data = er_entityset
           ).

      when others.
        super->/iwbep/if_mgw_appl_srv_runtime~get_entityset(
            exporting
                iv_entity_name             = iv_entity_name
                iv_entity_set_name         = iv_entity_set_name
                iv_source_name             = iv_source_name
                it_filter_select_options = it_filter_select_
options
                it_order                   = it_order
                is_paging                  = is_paging
                it_navigation_path         = it_navigation_path
                it_key_tab                 = it_key_tab
                iv_filter_string           = iv_filter_string
                iv_search_string           = iv_search_string
                io_tech_request_context    = io_tech_request_
context
            importing
                er_entityset               = er_entityset
                es_response_context        = es_response_context ).

    endcase.
endmethod.
```

Listing 10.8 Coding of the /iwbep/if_mgw_appl_srv_runtime~get_entityset Dispatcher Method

509

Execute the */sap/opu/odata/SAP/ZEPM_REF_APPS_PO_APV_SRV_SRV/ PurchaseOrders('300000031')/ToEmployee?$format=json* URI using the SAP Gateway client to obtain the results shown in Figure 10.34.

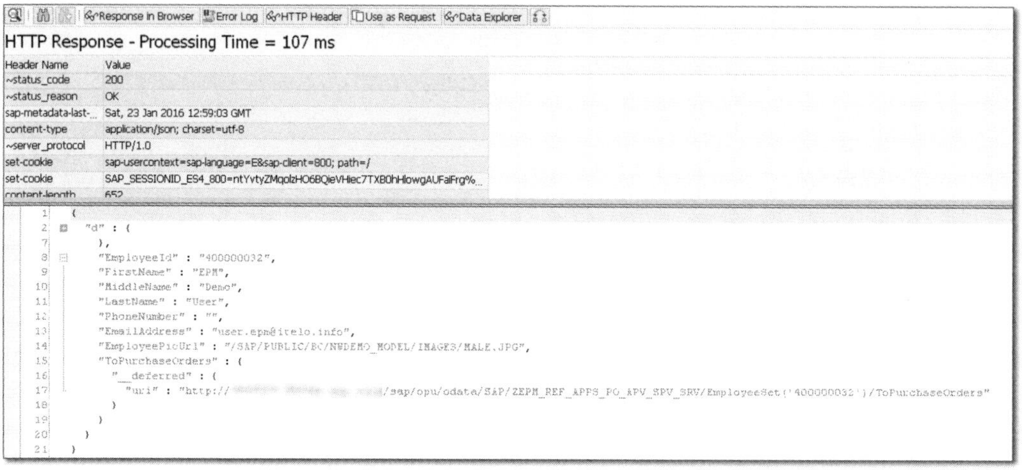

Figure 10.34 Contact Details of the Employee Who Created a Purchase Order

Having extended the OData service, next we'll look to the UI side and demonstrate what the UI developer has to do.

10.3.2 Extending the SAPUI5 Application

In this section, we'll show you how to create an extension project of an already existing SAP Fiori application (Approve Purchase Orders) on your SAP Web IDE environment and how to connect the SAP Fiori reference app to your preferred SAP Gateway system. After these default settings, we'll show you the following three extension options:

Extending SAPUI5 app

- ▶ Hide an existing UI element.
- ▶ Replace a service.
- ▶ Add new UI elements to an extension point.
- ▶ Add a second UI element to an extension point.

Create a Project in SAP Web IDE

If you don't have a SAP Fiori app, go to Chapter 9, Section 9.4, and create a project from the APPROVE PURCHASE ORDERS sample application. This will be our basis SAPUI5 app for this section.

All reference apps are delivered with the default destination RefApps-Backend, which has to be changed to your SAP Gateway system destination (Chapter 9, Section 9.2).

Log in to the SAP Web IDE, open the tree of the project NW.EPM.REFAPPS. EXT.PO.APV, and choose the file *neo-app.json.* Replace the RefAppsBackend string with the name of your already configured destination (Listing 10.9).

SAP Web IDE

```
"path": "/sap/opu/odata",
"target": {
  "type": "destination",
  "name": "ES4",
  "entryPath": "/sap/opu/odata"
},
"description": "Backend oData service"
```
Listing 10.9 Changing the Reference App Destination to ES4

Save your changes and create a new extension project. Click on FILE • NEW • EXTENSION PROJECT, and select an application. Click on SELECT APPLICATION, and choose WORKSPACE. Choose the already created project, NW.EPM.REFAAPS.EXT.PO.APV, and click OK. The default extension project name is the former project name with the word *Extension* added as a suffix. Click on NEXT to continue the wizard. Click FINISH on the following confirmation page to create the project. The extensibility pane will open and display the application. Change the display resolution in the top row to LARGE (Figure 10.35).

The application is opened in the PREVIEW MODE and connected to the configured backend system, so the application is fully running. Now you can explore the features of the preview mode. You're can also change the ORIENTATION (to emulate a mobile device). Select the OUTLINE property SHOW EXTENSIBLE ELEMENTS in the dropdown on the right side, and all extensible elements will be listed in the tree view. Click on PREVIEW MODE, and switch to the EXTENSIBILITY MODE. Now when you select an element in the layout view, the color change to pink, and the corresponding element is also selected in the tree view (Figure 10.36).

Figure 10.35 Extension Project Preview Mode

Figure 10.36 Selecting an Element in Extensibility Mode

Hide an Existing User Interface Element

UI element

You can hide an existing control element, such as the REJECT button. To do so, select the red REJECT button in the preview, right-click the element in the outline tree, and select HIDE CONTROL from the opening context menu (Figure 10.37).

Figure 10.37 Hiding the rejectButton Control

An APPLICATION CHANGED popup confirms the successful change. You can open the extension code or refresh the app. When you open the extension code, you'll notice the `visible` attribute has the value `false`.

Run the extension project as a normal application. As you can see, the reject button is gone (Figure 10.38).

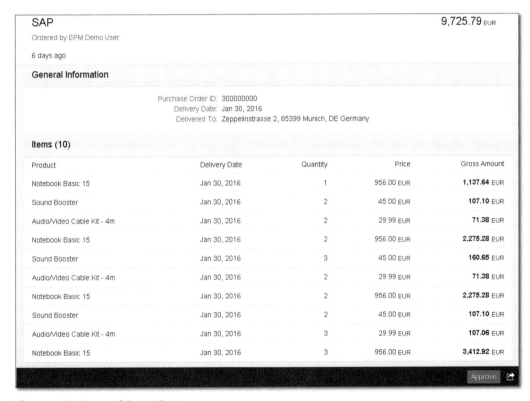

Figure 10.38 Removed Reject Button

To edit the project in the extensibility pane again, select the project, and choose TOOLS • EXTENSIBILITY PANE. The element REJECTBUTTON is now marked as hidden in the outline tree.

Replace an OData Service

Before you add a new UI element to an extension point, you need to replace the default service with our extended `PurchaseOrder` entity set. Select the project folder of the extension project, and choose FILE • NEW • EXTENSION. Confirm the selected project, and click NEXT. Choose REPLACE SERVICE from the extension selection, and click NEXT again (Figure 10.39).

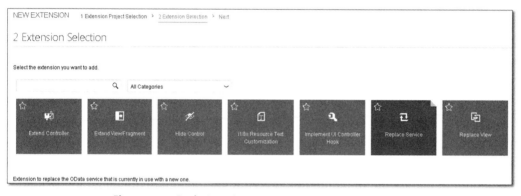

Figure 10.39 Replacing a Service

Replace OData service

Browse through the SERVICE CATALOG of the ES4 system, and choose the already extended service ZEPM_REF_APPS_PO_APV_SRV_SRV. Click NEXT to confirm your choice, and click FINISH to replace the service. The *Component.js* file will be adjusted to the newly added service.

Add a New User Interface Element to an Extension Point

Extension point

To add a new UI element to an extension point, you have to start the EXTENSIBILITY PANE (if you're not still there). In the application outline tree, select the SHOW EXTENSIBLE ELEMENTS from the dropdown. Expand the S3_PURCHASEORDERDETAILS view. All existing extension points have a screw-wrench icon with a plus to identify the extension option.

Choose EXTENSIONAFTEROBJECTHEADER, click on the EXTEND button on the bottom of the outline menu, and choose EXTEND VIEW/FRAGMENT. An APPLICATION CHANGED pop-up confirm the successful change.

You can open the extension code or click OK to confirm the successfully added extension. The element is displayed with the additional information (EXTENDED). Choose OPEN • EXTENSION CODE to open the code editor with the generated extension file (you can also view the ORIGINAL CODE). Remove the coding <!-- in line 4 and the --> coding in line 11 to display the default fields. The result with the activated coding is shown in Figure 10.40.

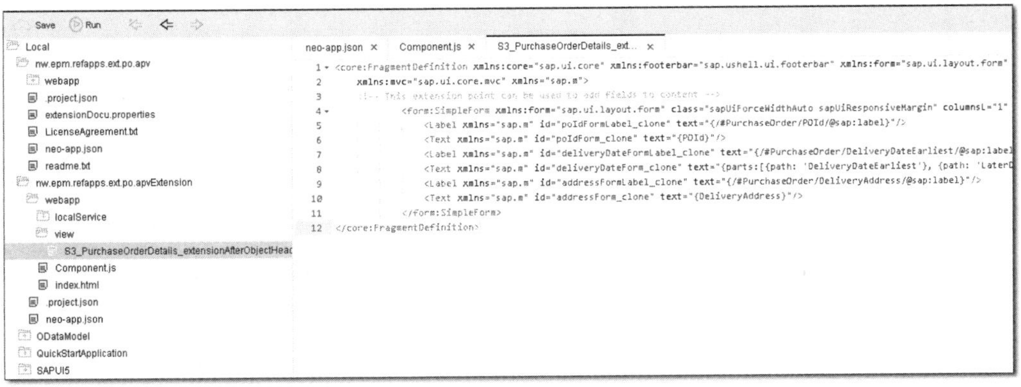

Figure 10.40 Activating Coding in the Extension File

Save the file. Now open the application, and you'll notice the general information section is duplicated. Go back to the extension file, change the title of the SimpleForm, delete all default labels and texts, and insert the newly created WeightTotal and WeightUnit fields (Section 10.3.1) from the service extension (Listing 10.10).

```
<form:SimpleForm xmlns:form="sap.ui.layout.form" class="sapUiFo
rceWidthAuto sapUiResponsiveMargin"
columnsL="1" columnsM="1" emptySpanL="5" emptySpanM="5" id="poH
eaderForm_clone"
labelSpanL="3" labelSpanM="3" layout="ResponsiveGridLayout" max
ContainerCols="2"
minWidth="1024" title="Total Weight">
<Label xmlns="sap.m" id="WeightTotalLabel_clone" text="{/
#PurchaseOrder/WeightTotal/@sap:label}"/>
<Text xmlns="sap.m" id="WeightTotal_
```

```
clone" text="{WeightTotal} {WeightUnit}"/>
</form:SimpleForm>
```
Listing 10.10 Extension Point Coding: Total Weight

Save your changes. Now you have to bind a *dataset* to the newly created view. Right-click on the view file in the workspace, and choose OPEN WITH • LAYOUT EDITOR. Select the view, and choose PURCHASEORDERS in the DATA SET dropdown (Figure 10.41).

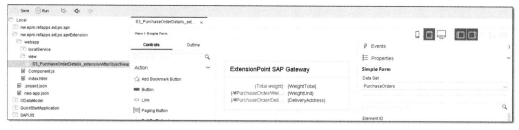

Figure 10.41 Adding a Dataset PurchaseOrder

Save your changes. In the last step, you have to extend the controller and add the two extension fields. As you've already done during the service replacement, select the project folder of the extension project, and choose FILE • NEW • EXTENSION. Confirm the selected project, and click NEXT. Choose EXTEND CONTROLLER from the extension selection, and click NEXT again (refer to Figure 10.39). Choose the already extended controller S3_PURCHASEORDERDETAILS from the CONTROLLER dropdown list, and select COPY OF THE ORIGINAL CONTROLLER from the REPLACE WITH dropdown list (Figure 10.42) to copy the content to a new file.

Figure 10.42 Extended Controller

Click NEXT and then FINISH to add the extension.

The copy, including the uncommented coding of the original controller, is shown. Remove all the comment signs "//" to activate the coding. To do so, right-click on the code, and choose TOGGLE LINE COMMENT from the context menu (Figure 10.43). Now at line 40 in the `select` statement of the controller.js, you have to add the new `WeightTotal` and `WeightUnit` fields (Listing 10.11).

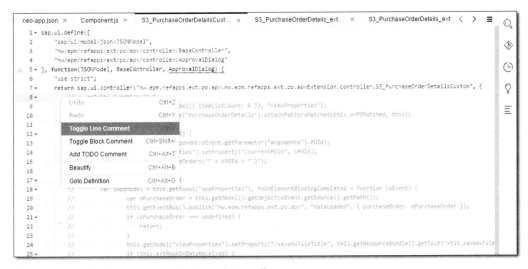

Figure 10.43 Activating Coding in the Copied Controller

```
parameters: { select: "POId,OrderedByName,SupplierName,GrossAmo
unt,CurrencyCode,ChangedAt,DeliveryDateEarliest,LaterDelivDateE
xist,DeliveryAddress,ItemCount,WeightTotal,WeightUnit" }
```

Listing 10.11 Adding the Parameter in the Select Statement

Save your changes, and start the application. The extension point with the two new parameters is displayed (Figure 10.44).

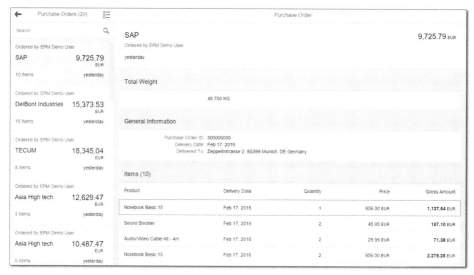

Figure 10.44 Total Weight UI Extension

Add a Second User Interface Element to the Extension Point

Besides seeing the total weight of a purchase order, you also need to look at the contact details of the employee who placed the order.

Open the coding of the extension file *S3_PurchaseOrderDetails_extension-AfterObjectHeaderCustom.fragment.xml*, and add the code shown in Listing 10.12 to add a second form to the extension point. The different data binding that you use to retrieve data in the second form, which binds the data to the ToEmployee navigation property, is achieved by adding a hidden text field <Text binding='{ToEmployee}' visible="false" /> to the form. This forces SAPUI5 to read all the data of the employee via the navigation property so that they can be addressed via statements such as text="{ToEmployee/EmailAddress}".

```
<form:SimpleForm xmlns:form="sap.ui.layout.form" class="sapUiFo
rceWidthAuto sapUiResponsiveMargin"
columnsL="1" columnsM="1" emptySpanL="5" emptySpanM="5" id="poH
eaderForm_clone2" labelSpanL="3"
labelSpanM="3" layout="ResponsiveGridLayout" maxContainerCols="
2" minWidth="1024"
title="Ordered by">
```

```
<Text binding='{ToEmployee}' visible="false" />
<Label xmlns="sap.m" id="EmployeeIdLabel_clone" text="{/
#Employee/EmployeeId/@sap:label}"/>
<Text  xmlns="sap.m" id="EmployeeId_clone"  text="{ToEmployee/
EmployeeId}"/>
<Label xmlns="sap.m" id="EmailAddressLabel_clone" text="{/
#Employee/EmailAddress/@sap:label}"/>
<Text  xmlns="sap.m" id="EmailAddress_
clone"  text="{ToEmployee/EmailAddress}"/>
</form:SimpleForm>
```

Listing 10.12 Extension Point Coding: Contact Details

Save your changes and start the application again. As shown in Figure 10.45, you now see a second new area on the screen that shows contact details of the employee who placed the order, in addition to the total weight that you added previously.

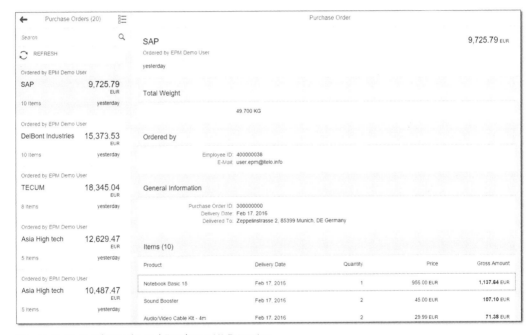

Figure 10.45 Total Weight and Employee UI Extension

519

10.4   Summary

In this chapter, you learned about using redefinition to generate a new OData service that inherits all functionalities from its base service and how to extend this service. We finished our journey with the steps that are necessary on the SAPUI5 side. You learned how an extension project can be used to extend an existing SAP Fiori application without the need to modify the original application.

In the next chapter, we'll show you how to create a hybrid app with the help of the SAP Web IDE, hybrid app toolkit add-on.

The chapter walks you through mobile application development with the SAP Gateway. You'll learn more about the required software and the technical basics for mobile development.

11 Mobile Application Development

The procession of smartphones and tablet computers in recent years has significantly affected the development of mobile applications. For example, in the early days of mobile phones, small applications such as calendars or calculators were a revolutionary part of an operating system but were permanent and not able to be removed or replaced by the owner of the device. Now, this is no longer the case. Since these early days, mobile applications have become much more flexible and now play a huge role in the consumer and business sector—and their importance continues to grow.

The change from a consumer world to a global business world, where fast changes are necessary for the success of a company, makes mobile applications more and more important. The PC market is shrinking, while the number of mobile applications downloaded rises every year by a huge amount. One of the reasons is the enormous speed of innovation inside the mobile world and the corresponding increased frequency and capabilities of mobile devices.

Before you start developing mobile applications, you should answer the following questions to make the right decisions for your future mobile applications:

First questions for mobile applications

- Do we need more than one specific hardware provider?

- Do we need OData plug-ins, or can we create our coding from scratch?

- Should we use hybrid applications, and do we have web application developers in-house?

Chapter overview   In this chapter, we introduce the topic of developing mobile applications using SAP Gateway. In Section 11.1, we discuss mobile development, including its three main approaches: native development, hybrid development, and HTML5 development. We'll begin by looking at native application development in Section 11.2. In the rest of the chapter, we concentrate on the details of hybrid development for mobile devices (Section 11.3). HTML5 isn't only for mobile applications (you can use it as a normal website for your desktop PC/Mac), so we concentrate on this special topic when we discuss SAPUI5 in Chapter 8, the SAP Web IDE in Chapter 9, and extensibility in Chapter 10).

Apple, Google, BlackBerry, and Microsoft are leading IT companies that push the market and consumers with new ideas and hardware enhancements. As a consequence, the growing options for business processes, development, and mobile device management will enable enterprises to manage and secure their mobile devices and optimize their business processes for the challenges of a globalized world.

Hybrid versus native applications   This basketful of different approaches is also one reason cross-platform mobile application development is becoming more and more important. Using this approach, you can reduce development costs and deploy functionality at the same time to many different devices. These cross-platform applications are normally web applications that run on almost every modern mobile platform in the same way but have no access to the native application programming interface (API) of the specific platform. This is the main reason that hybrid container applications, which combine the power of native APIs and the freedom of operating system choice, are becoming more and more popular in the consumer and business world.

SAP Store   The whole application market is growing every day, and every company has to decide which horse they want to saddle. SAP provides the SAP Store for all existing SAP applications that have been developed by SAP or partners.

Before a company's decision makers decide which application to buy or to develop, they have to ask themselves some questions about the use case, the existing system landscape, and the necessary devices (and, therefore, the platform).

11.1 Overview

Generally, you can distinguish between three different mobile development approaches, which are all usable with the SAP Mobile Platform:

- Native apps
- Hybrid container apps
- HTML5 apps (also known as web apps)

The major characteristics of these three approaches are outlined here:

- **Native development**
  - Reuses investments/assets from HTML/hybrid development
  - Provides access to robust device and middleware services such as database/data object store and replication services
  - Works well for applications requiring robust graphics and complex offline transactions

- **Hybrid development**
  - Provides access to native device capabilities
  - Uses encrypted/secure data store
  - Has a robust data messaging layer
  - Supports application lifecycle management (ALM)
  - Allows data integration with complex SAP and non-SAP data sources

- **HTML5 development**
  - Takes advantage of web development resources
  - Takes advantage of industry-standard development tools and tool chains
  - Allows for easy cross-platform build, support, and deployment
  - Works well for rapid development of simple applications accessing web services

Because we discuss HTML5 applications in Chapter 8, Chapter 9, and Chapter 10, in this chapter, we'll look specifically at native (see Section 11.2) and hybrid applications (see Section 11.3).

11.2   Native Application Development

Benefits of native applications

Native applications, in general, offer the best performance and options for graphic design, which is important in, for example, game development. They are based on *software development kits (SDKs)*, which are created for corresponding platforms (e.g., Apple iOS or Google Android) and fitted to the needs of a specialized developer. You have total control over the user experience and have access to the local device-specific capabilities, such as camera, GPS, or storage. The application distribution is handled in most cases over the central store (e.g., Apple App Store, Google Play).

The pros are also the reason developing native applications can be more complex and costly than developing hybrid applications or mobile websites. Native application development also involves selecting a specific platform, which will always exclude some people.

The high-level pros and cons of native application development are outlined in Table 11.1.

Pros	Cons
Good performance	Platform-specific development
Local API access	Development costs
Store distribution	License costs
Offline functionality	Application store approval

Table 11.1 Native Applications: Pros and Cons

11.3   Hybrid Application Development

Hybrid applications are a mix of web and native applications with the aim of balancing the advantages and disadvantages of both. Hybrid frameworks are usually based on web technologies and enable the development of cross-platform applications that aren't distinguishable from native apps.

Hybrid

Hybrid frameworks also offer a native container for web applications with several functions for the specific platforms. In this way, it's possible for an application to, for example, access the calendar of the specific platform or make the phone vibrate, which isn't possible within a pure web application. Using these effects, hybrid applications are compiled as "native packages" and can be offered at platform-specific app stores. To lay the groundwork for hybrid technologies, the *web view* is embedded in a native application and renders the user interface (UI) of the web application using the native browser engine.

That being said, hybrid applications can be very valuable. A connection from a web application inside a hybrid container to the native API is the key benefit of hybrid applications because developers can code their own API bridge or take advantage of existing and well-documented solutions, such as the SAP Web IDE, hybrid app toolkit add-on.

The SAP Web IDE, hybrid app toolkit add-on is an easy-to-use tool to create and deploy hybrid apps. In this section, we'll discuss how to download and install the toolkit, create your first hybrid app for Android, and test this generated app in the Android Emulator.

The toolkit includes the following three components:

- **SAP Web IDE plug-in**
  Activates the hybrid app development features in the SAP Web IDE.

- **SAP Hybrid App Toolkit Connector**
  Connects the SAP Web IDE to the local development system.

- **SAP Hybrid App Toolkit Companion**
  Enables a live preview of a web app created in the SAP Web IDE.

> **Further Resources**
>
> For more information about the SAP Web IDE, hybrid app toolkit add-on, visit *https://help.hana.ondemand.com/webide_hat/frameset.htm*.

The SAP Web IDE, hybrid app toolkit add-on needs some additional tools, which aren't part of the toolkit installer. We'll show you which prerequisites exist and where to download these tools in the following section.

11.3.1 Prerequisites

Numerous tools are required for the toolkit, which have to be installed first.

The following prerequisites must be met for the hybrid application add-on:

▸ **Latest SAP Mobile Platform SDK**
   The installation process is shown in Section 11.3.2.

▸ **Node v0.12.7**
   Download and install from *https://nodejs.org/en/blog/release/v0.12.7/*. This includes the node package manager (npm).

▸ **Kapsel command-line interface (CLI)**
   Install Kapsel CLI with the npm console. Open the console, and enter the following command: `npm install -g C:\SAP\MobileSDK3\KapselSDK\ cli`.

▸ **Latest Java Development Toolkit (JDK)**
   Download and install from *www.oracle.com/technetwork/java/javase/downloads/index.html*.

▸ **Cordova version 5.2.0**
   Install Cordova version 5.2.0 with the NPM console (Figure 11.1). Open the console, and enter the following command: `npm install -g cordova@5.2.0`.

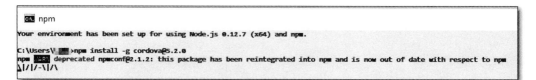

Figure 11.1 Installing Cordova 5.2.0 with npm

▶ **Latest Git client (source code management system)**
Download and install from *http://git-scm.com/*.

▶ **Latest Bower version (a package management system for Git)**
This is automatically installed during hybrid app toolkit setup.

▶ **Latest Apache Ant 1.8**
Download and install from *http://ant.apache.org/bindownload.cgi*.

▶ **Android SDK 5.1.1 (API Level 22) for Android development**   Android SDK
Download and install the latest Android Studio Package from *http://developer.android.com/sdk/index.html#Other*, and manually add SDK 5.1.1 (Figure 11.2).

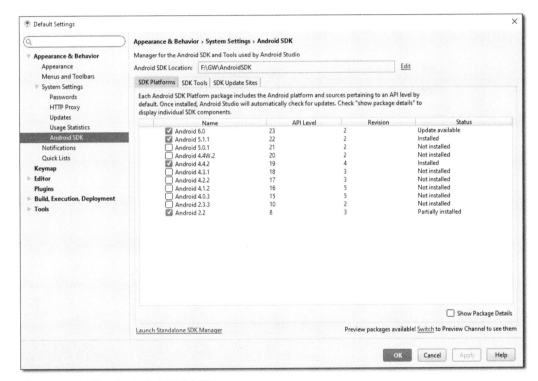

Figure 11.2 Adding the Android 5.1.1 SDK

Change the default Android virtual device TARGET to ANDROID 5.1.1 (Figure 11.3).

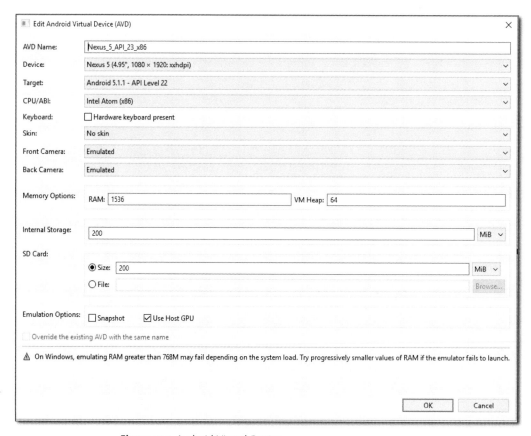

Figure 11.3 Android Virtual Device

Xcode ▸ **Xcode for iOS development**
Download and install the latest Xcode from *https://developer.apple.com/downloads/index.action,* and manually run `sudo npm install -g ios-sim` from the command line to install the simulator.

Further Resources

For more information about the prerequisites, visit the following:

▸ *https://help.hana.ondemand.com/webide_hat/frameset.htm?d2865598e67f4ddabc79e5943352b0a1.html*

▸ *https://help.hana.ondemand.com/webide_hat/frameset.htm?aa4ede549b4b4a508a9d294995707aee.html*

Now that you know what prerequisites must be in place, in the next section, we'll discuss how to download and install the SAP Mobile Platform SDK and the SAP Web IDE, hybrid app toolkit add-on. Later in this section, we'll show you how to develop your first hybrid app based on Android.

11.3.2 Download and Installation

In this section, we'll show you how to download and install the needed SAP Mobile Platform SDK to have a local development environment and the SAP Web IDE, hybrid app toolkit add-on to connect the local SDK to the SAP Web IDE.

Download the SAP Mobile Platform Software Development Kit

First, you have to download the free SAP Mobile Platform SDK trial version from the SAP Store by following these steps:

SAP Mobile Platform SDK

1. Visit the SAP Store (*http://store.sap.com*), and search for "SAP Mobile Platform SDK," or go directly to *https://store.sap.com/sap/cp/ui/resources/store/html/SolutionDetails.html?pid=0000013098*.

2. Click TRIAL VERSION to download the free SAP Mobile Platform SDK (Figure 11.4).

3. Enter your contact information in the following download popup, accept the two terms and conditions text by checking the boxes, and click SUBMIT.

4. An email with the download link will be sent to the address you entered. Open the included link. On the SAP Mobile Platform SDK downloads page, choose the download link for the operating system your development system is running on, the highest service pack (SP), and patch level (PL), and then download the installation files. Make sure you download a full version and not an update!

Further Resources

For more information about the installation process, visit *http://help.sap.com/smp3010sdk*.

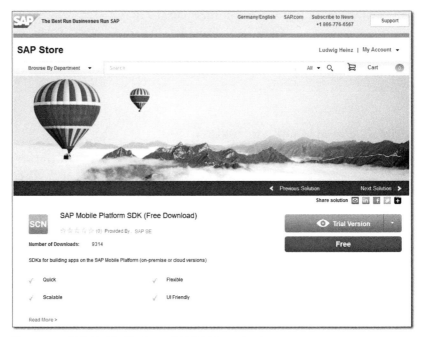

Figure 11.4 SAP Mobile Platform SDK Trial Download

5. Extract the downloaded zip file, and start the *setupAMD64.exe* installer file (Figure 11.5).

Figure 11.5 SAP Mobile Platform SDK 3.0 Installer

Follow the installation wizard to install SAP Mobile Platform SDK 3.0.

Download the SAP Web IDE, Hybrid App Toolkit Add-on

After you've installed the SDK, you have to download the free SAP Web IDE, hybrid app toolkit add-on trial version from the SAP Store. Toolkit download

Follow these steps:

1. Visit the SAP Store (*http://store.sap.com*), and search for "SAP Web IDE Hybrid App Toolkit," or go directly to *https://store.sap.com/sap/ cp/ui/resources/store/html/SolutionDetails.html?pid=0000013586*.

2. Click TRIAL VERSION to download the free SAP Web IDE, hybrid app toolkit add-on (Figure 11.6).

Figure 11.6 SAP Web IDE, Hybrid App Toolkit Add-on Trial Download

Install the SAP Web IDE Hybrid App Toolkit Add-On

In this section, we'll walk through the installation process for the SAP Web IDE, hybrid app toolkit add-on. Toolkit installation

Follow these steps:

1. Extract the contents of your already downloaded SAP Web IDE, hybrid app toolkit add-on archive to a local folder, and open the *setup.cmd* file.

2. If you've installed *Node.js* without a restart, you have to reboot your computer. The installation with the npm console starts, and the required packages are checked (Figure 11.7).

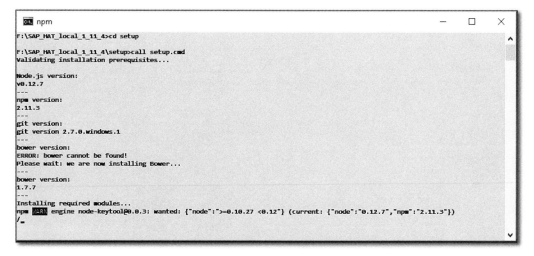

Figure 11.7 SAP Web IDE, Hybrid App Toolkit Add-on Installation

If Bower isn't installed, it will be automatically installed in the newest version.

Setup page
3. After the validation process is finished, and every base package is available, the hybrid toolkit setup page opens (Figure 11.8).

4. Read the IMPORTANT NOTES in the pop-up windows, and click the CHECK ALL button on the left side of the top bar.

5. The wizard checks the correct installation and configuration of Java SDK, Ant, Android SDK, Cordova, Android AVD, and Kapsel CLI. If the Kapsel CLI isn't installed, you can click the NPM INSTALL -G button in the error massage to install it (Figure 11.9).

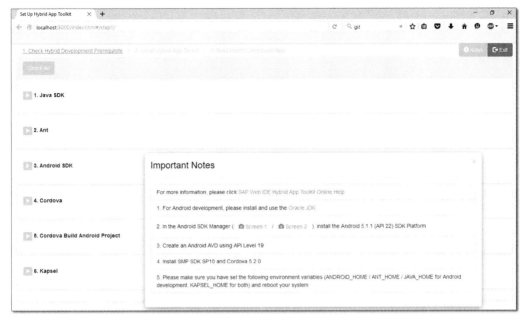

Figure 11.8 Setup Page

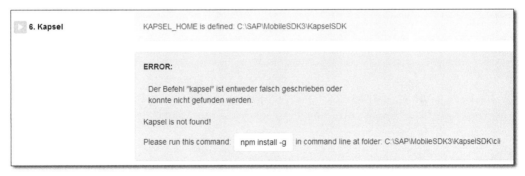

Figure 11.9 Kapsel npm Install

6. Confirm the installation in the following window, and click RUN to   **Kapsel install** finish the Kapsel installation (Figure 11.10).

Figure 11.10 npm install -g

7. Click CHECK ALL to make sure everything was installed correctly. If everything is installed correctly, you are forwarded to the next step (Figure 11.11).

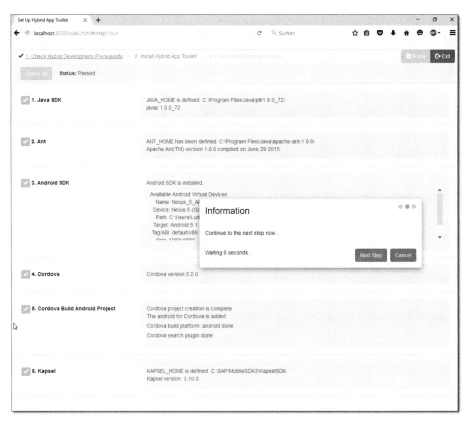

Figure 11.11 Hybrid Development Prerequisites Passed

You won't be able to continue the installation process unless you meet all requirements.

8. Click the INSTALL button, and the SAPUI5 library is downloaded and installed first (Figure 11.12).

Install hybrid app toolkit

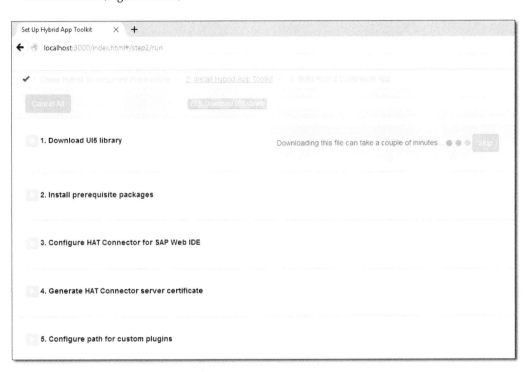

Figure 11.12 Downloading the SAPUI5 Library

9. Next, you need to configure the SAP Web IDE Hybrid App Toolkit Connector. Enter the SAP Web IDE URL to be used with the Hybrid App Toolkit Connector (e.g., *https://webide-yourusername.dis-patcher.neo.ondemand.com*). The SAP Hybrid App Toolkit Connector uses this URL to connect to your instance of SAP Web IDE. Click UPDATE.

Hybrid App Toolkit Connector

10. Enter a password of your choice twice, which is required to generate a certificate (Figure 11.13).

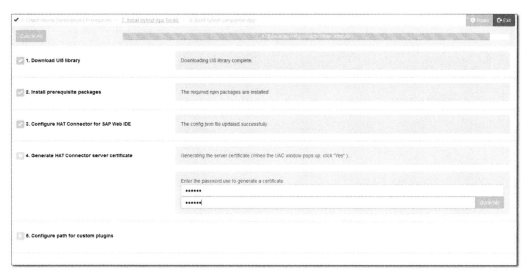

Figure 11.13 Generating a Hybrid App Toolkit Connector Server Certificate

11. Click GENERATE. The SAP Web IDE, hybrid app toolkit add-on installer generates a server certificate with your given password and installs it on your system. Accept the Windows prompt to allow the changes. We don't want to use custom plug-ins in this book, so you can skip the last step.

12. Go to the third and last step, BUILD HYBRID COMPANION APP, and click BUILD. The created companion container includes many Cordova and Kapsel plug-ins that are commonly used in a hybrid app. Retain the default values or modify the configuration parameters as required (Figure 11.14).

13. Click SAVE to complete the build. This generates the Android *WebIde-Companion.apk* file in the SAP Hybrid App Toolkit folder under *WebIDECompanion\platforms\android*. Click OK to exit setup (Figure 11.15).

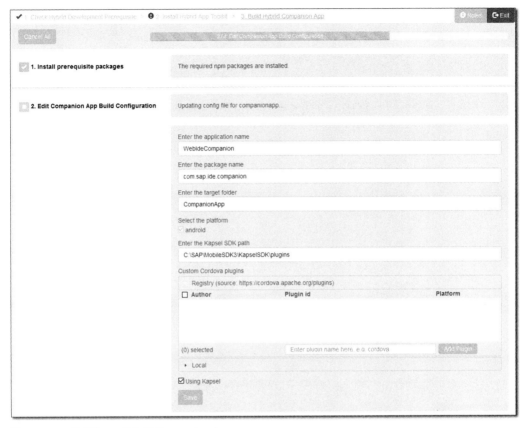

Figure 11.14 Building a Hybrid Companion App

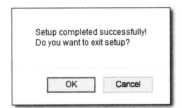

Figure 11.15 Setup Completed Successfully

Activate SAP Web IDE Plug-In for the Hybrid App Toolkit Add-On

SAP Web IDE plug-in

Next you have to activate the SAP Web IDE plug-in for the Hybrid App Toolkit by following these steps:

1. Open your SAP Web IDE, and log on.

2. Go to TOOLS • PREFERENCES, and choose OPTIONAL PLUGINS from the left menu.

3. Mark the HYBRID APP TOOLKIT plug-in as enabled, and click SAVE (Figure 11.16).

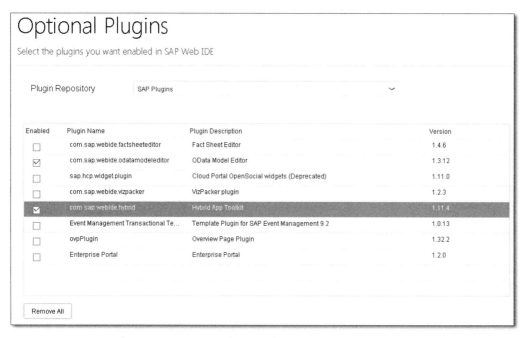

Figure 11.16 Activating the Hybrid App Toolkit Plug-In

4. Refresh the SAP Web IDE. Now you can navigate to the newly added menu entry HYBRID APPLICATION TOOLKIT (Figure 11.17).

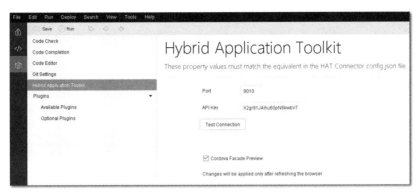

Figure 11.17 Hybrid Application Toolkit Settings

Run the SAP Web IDE Hybrid App Toolkit Add-on

You can now start the toolkit by following these steps:

1. Open the file *run.cmd* located in the Hybrid App Toolkit root folder.

2. The node *server.js* is started, and the command prompt is opened, where you have to enter your certificate password. When you enter the password, the Hybrid App Toolkit Connector is started and listening on default port 9010 (Figure 11.18).

Figure 11.18 Hybrid App Toolkit Connector Started

3. Start your default browser, enter "https://localhost:9010" in the address bar, and install/trust the security warning.

Hybrid App Toolkit Connector

> **Different Browser Configuration**
>
> When you don't know how to configure your browser correctly, visit the following: *https://help.hana.ondemand.com/webide_hat/frameset.htm?d763551065b8 4915bdd5443f0f745870.html*

4. After you accept the trusted connection, the confirmation page of your running Hybrid App Toolkit Connector is shown (Figure 11.19).

Figure 11.19 Running Hybrid App Toolkit Connector

5. With the running Hybrid App Toolkit Connector, navigate back to the SAP Web IDE, and click the Test Connection button. A message will appear that the connection is available (Figure 11.20).

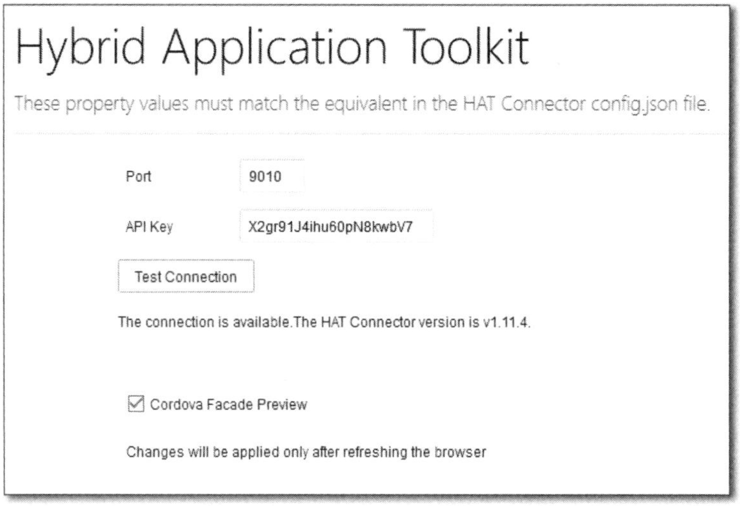

Hybrid Application Toolkit

These property values must match the equivalent in the HAT Connector config.json file.

Port   9010

API Key   X2gr91J4ihu60pN8kwbV7

Test Connection

The connection is available. The HAT Connector version is v1.11.4.

☑ Cordova Facade Preview

Changes will be applied only after refreshing the browser

Figure 11.20 Test Connection to the SAP Hybrid App Toolkit Connector

The properties are automatically inserted in the Hybrid App Toolkit Connector *config.json* file during the installation process, while the SAP Web IDE URL is provided.

We've established a connection between the locally installed SAP Mobile Platform SDK and the SAP Web IDE with the help of the Hybrid App Toolkit Connector.

For more information about the installation process, visit the following: *https://help.hana.ondemand.com/webide_hat/frameset.htm?573709669eea4 aa388e7df3856b241f7.html*

11.3.3 Create an SAP HANA Cloud Platform Mobile Service App

In this section, we'll create a new SAP HANA Cloud Platform Mobile Service (HCPms) app to securely publish the developed hybrid application to the outside world via the SAP HANA Cloud Platform (HCP).

Follow these steps to do so:

1. Log on with your credentials to the SAP HCP as already described in Chapter 9, Section 9.1.2, and click on SERVICES in the left menu.

2. Navigate to the MOBILE SERVICES entry and enable it (if not already done) (Figure 11.21).

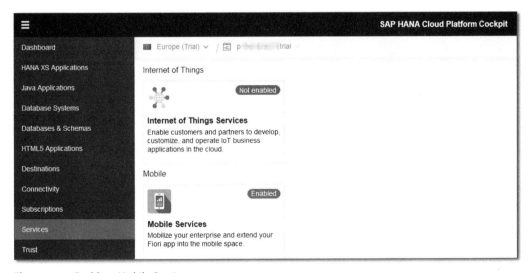

Figure 11.21 Enabling Mobile Services

3. Click on SUBSCRIPTIONS, and start the HCPMSADMIN app (Figure 11.22).   SAP HCPms

Figure **11.22** Subscribed HTML5 Apps

4. On the details screen, click on the APPLICATION URL (*https://hcpmsad-minyourusername.dispatcher.hanatrial.ondemand.com*) to open the SAP HCPms Cockpit (Figure 11.23).

Figure **11.23** SAP HCPms Cockpit

5. Click on the APPLICATIONS tile, and click the paper with a star icon to create a new app (Figure 11.24).

Figure **11.24** Creating a New Mobile Service App

Create a mobile service app

6. A new window opens where you have to enter the app details. Enter an APPLICATION ID in the format "*com.name.ending*" (e.g., "com.sapui.gw") since you have to use this app ID exactly later. Enter a NAME, choose HYBRID from the TYPE dropdown list, and deselect all checkboxes. Set the SECURITY CONFIGURATION to NONE (Figure 11.25).

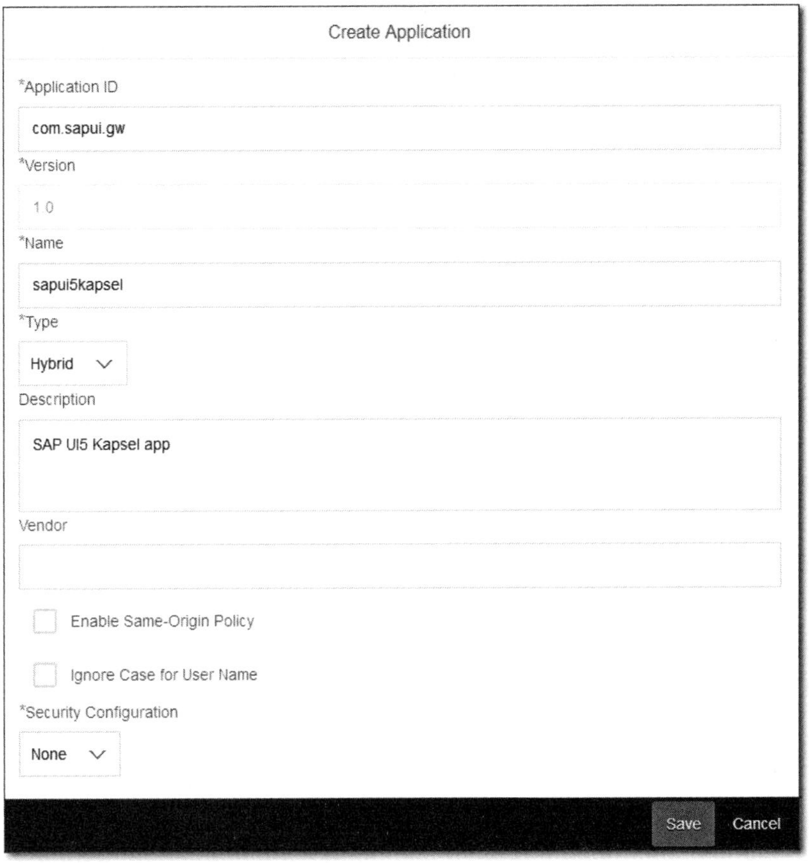

Figure 11.25 Creating an Application

7. Click SAVE to create the app.

8. Choose BACK-END in the top menu, and enter an OData service URL in the BACK-END URL field. Select INTERNET as the PROXY TYPE, and select BASIC AUTHENTICATION as the AUTHENTICATION TYPE. Enter your USER NAME and your PASSWORD (Figure 11.26).

9. Leave all the other values as shown, and click SAVE. To test the connection, navigate to the application overview, click the gear icon on the right side, and choose PING. A PING RESULT page appears (Figure 11.27).

Back-end connection

Figure 11.26 Back-End Connection Details

Figure 11.27 Ping Result

The result is successful, so you're finished with the configuration part and can continue with the development of your first hybrid application in the next section.

11.3.4 Developing a Hybrid App

In this section, we'll teach you how to develop your first hybrid app with the help of all the earlier installed and configured SAP tools. To begin, note that different project creation methods are available in the SAP Web IDE.

You can create your first hybrid app with one of the following templates:

- ▸ SAPUI5 Starter Kapsel Application
- ▸ SAPUI5 Master Detail Kapsel Application
- ▸ SAPUI5 Master Detail Kapsel Offline Application

You can also create a new project using the Hybrid Mobile Enablement feature, which can be selected in the SAPUI5 wizard. In addition, we'll show you how to consume an OData service inside your hybrid app.

For our example, we'll choose the SAPUI5 Master Detail Kapsel Application as the template. Follow these steps to create a hybrid application using this template:

1. Open the SAP Web IDE (see Chapter 9), and navigate to FILE • NEW • PROJECT FROM TEMPLATE.

2. In the opening wizard, choose SAPUI5 MOBILE APPLICATION from the dropdown list, and select the SAPUI5 MASTER DETAIL KAPSEL APPLICATION (Figure 11.28).

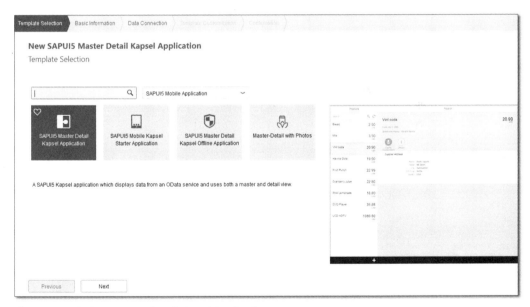

Figure 11.28 SAPUI5 Master Detail Kapsel Application

3. Click NEXT, enter a project name of your choice, and click NEXT again. Choose a service from one of the available sources such as the SERVICE CATALOG of the already created ES4 demo system (Figure 11.29).

Figure 11.29 Choosing a Data Connection

OData service   4. Select an OData service, and click NEXT. In the TEMPLATE CUSTOMIZATION area, enter a TITLE for the MASTER SECTION, and select an ODATA COLLECTION from the dropdown list (Figure 11.30).

5. Fill in the fields of the MAIN DATA FIELDS and DETAIL SECTION areas of the screen, and then click NEXT. Click FINISH to complete the wizard and create your new SAPUI5 hybrid project.

6. Right-click on your project, and select PROJECT SETTINGS from the context menu. Select DEVICE CONFIGURATION from the menu, and enter the APP NAME and the APP ID. For these two properties, enter the exact same values as registered on the SAP HCPms application (Figure 11.31).

Figure 11.30 Template Customization

Figure 11.31 Device Configuration

7. Enter a Version in the format "*xx.xx.xx*," and select the Android checkbox to choose Android as the target device platform.

Cordova API;
Kapsel API
In addition, you can select which Cordova APIs (Figure 11.32) and/or Kapsel APIs (Figure 11.33) should be available in your application.

Figure 11.32 Cordova APIs

Figure 11.33 Kapsel APIs

8. Select Logon Manager under Kapsel. Now you have to configure either an on-demand SAP HCPms host or on-premise SAP Mobile Platform for your app to log on to. It should be prefilled with the correct URL of your SAP HCPms (Figure 11.34).

Figure 11.34 SAP HCPms Host

9. Click SAVE to finish the device configuration. All these settings are stored in the *project.json* file.

You've now completed the development process and can continue with the different test options.

Test the Hybrid App with the Cordova Facade

Because the Cordova Facade is automatically activated (refer to Figure 11.20), and your application makes calls to native device APIs, you can start your newly created app inside the browser by choosing the INDEX.HTML file inside the project and clicking RUN. A new window opens where the app is displayed (Figure 11.35). **Test Cordova Facade**

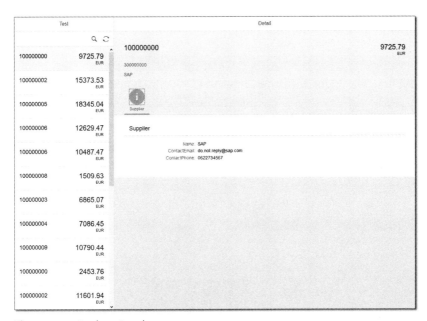

Figure 11.35 Cordova Facade

Test Your Hybrid App with the Android Emulator

You can also test the use of native device APIs inside a native environment such as the Android Emulator. To test this scenario, you have to deploy the project from the SAP Web IDE to the local Hybrid App Toolkit by following these steps: **Test Android Emulator**

1. Right-click the project, and choose DEPLOY • DEPLOY TO LOCAL HYBRID APP TOOLKIT (Figure 11.36).

Figure 11.36 Deploy to Local Hybrid App Toolkit Option

2. After the deployment is done, you can run the app on the Android Emulator. Right-click the project again, and choose RUN • RUN ON • ANDROID EMULATOR this time (Figure 11.37).

Figure 11.37 Run on Android Emulator Option

3. Select Test Key as the signing key for the Android release build, and click OK.

4. The app is packed and installed on the local Android Emulator. The process can be controlled in the SAP Web IDE console (Figure 11.38).

```
12:21:46 (hybrid-toolkit) c.\sap_aui_local_t_11_0
12:21:46 (hybrid-toolkit)
12:21:46 (hybrid-toolkit) - Packaging the SAPUI5 library to hybrid folder...
12:24:10 (hybrid-toolkit)
12:24:10 (hybrid-toolkit) THE CORDOVA PROJECT IS READY
12:24:10 (hybrid-toolkit) _____
12:24:22 (hybrid-toolkit)
12:24:22 (hybrid-toolkit) - Start to build and run app on Emulator...
12:24:22 (hybrid-toolkit)
12:24:52 (hybrid-toolkit) deploying...
12:24:52 (hybrid-toolkit) Running command: cmd "/s /c "C:\Users\▓▓\SAPHybrid\sapui5kapsel\hybrid\platforms\android\cordova\run.bat —emulator —release""
12:24:53 (hybrid-toolkit) ANDROID_HOME=F:\GW\AndroidSDK
12:24:53 (hybrid-toolkit) JAVA_HOME=C:\Program Files\Java\jdk1.8.0_72\
12:24:56 (hybrid-toolkit) WARNING : no emulator specified, defaulting to Nexus_5_API_23_x86
12:24:56 (hybrid-toolkit) Waiting for emulator...
```

Figure 11.38 SAP Web IDE Console

5. The Android Emulator is launched automatically and boots the Android operating system and later the application. This process can take several minutes because the app has to be compiled and all necessary files transferred inside the final app. After the deployment and installation is finished, you have to log on to SAP HCPms with your credentials (Figure 11.39).

Figure 11.39 Android Emulator: SAP HCPms Logon

6. Click REGISTER to continue. On the next screen, choose DISABLE PASS-CODE, and then click SUBMIT (Figure 11.40).

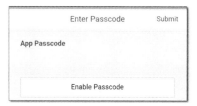

Figure 11.40 Disabling the Passcode

7. Because you've already entered your mobile service credentials in the created app, the app is directly loaded, and the main list with the data from the OData service is displayed (Figure 11.41).

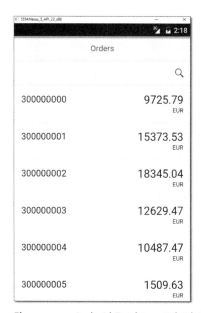

Figure 11.41 Android Emulator: Hybrid App

8. You can now click an entry and navigate to the details view (Figure 11.42).

You can now create a new SAPUI5 hybrid app with OData service consumption.

Figure 11.42 Android Emulator: Hybrid App Details View

> **Delivering and Deploying**
>
> You can find further information about the delivery and deployment process at the following: *https://help.hana.ondemand.com/webide_hat/frameset.htm?78af70cac7e444608f69b436b5391c93.html*

11.4 Summary

In this chapter, you've learned the difference between native and hybrid applications. We explained which prerequisites have to be installed for the use of the SAP Web IDE, hybrid app toolkit add-on. You've learned how to install and configure the SAP Web IDE hybrid app toolkit add-on, activate the SAP Web IDE plug-in, and create a SAP HCPms. At the end, you created a SAPUI5 hybrid app.

If you need further information, you can find more details on the SAP Community Network (SCN) or on the different manufacturer developer websites.

Social media is everywhere. In this chapter, we'll show you the available possibilities with OData for some of the biggest social media platforms in the world.

12 Social Media Application Development

We're in a data-driven economy. Web application programming interface (API) designers need to define what and how to expose data from a variety of applications, services, and stores. Even if platforms such as Facebook, Twitter, or Sina Weibo (the Chinese microblogging site and a hybrid of Twitter and Facebook) don't offer OData services themselves, this chapter explains how you can connect an OData service to any available social media platform to provide your selected data to the outside world.

Today, social media is the basis for social communication and information. Social media platforms enable people to swap ideas, exchange state of minds, or pick up information that expands beyond their own culture and society. Most people also post and tell the community about their loves and interests, so it's easy for companies that do market research to turn this information into valuable knowledge about consumers. In fact, social media is not only a platform for gathering information but also for improving services based on feedback from customers. Via feedback from social media platforms, companies can provide better products or customer-tailored services.

An effective use of social media platforms also offers the possibility of proactive contact with consumers. This is the point where SAP Gateway comes into action by providing information directly out of your SAP system and placing it into well-considered different social media channels.

> **Social Media Strategy**
>
> Remember, the goal isn't to be good at social media—it's to be good at business because of social media. You have to understand your business objectives first and then how social media can support them. You can always optimize tactics for better performance. You should pay close attention to the interests and needs of your customers and provide them with information and interactions that further support your brand.
>
> In general, a social media presence without clear business objectives isn't possible. Although this chapter shows you how to build such applications with OData service connection, how to use social media in your company is up to you.

The Hypertext Preprocessor (PHP) is the basis for any social media application development. In this chapter, you'll start by creating a PHP web page based on the OData software development kit (SDK) for PHP (Section 12.1) and use this as a basis for the subsequent sections, where you'll enhance this file and connect to the APIs of the social media platforms Facebook (Section 12.2), Twitter (Section 12.3), and the famous Chinese microblogging site Sina Weibo (Section 12.4).

12.1 PHP

PHP is a server-side scripting language designed for web development. It was created in 1994 by Rasmus Lerdorf and can be used to connect to a database or web service. Because PHP is a server-side scripting language, you need a web server that supports PHP to see the results of the developed applications in this chapter. If you don't have a web server, we recommend XAMPP. It's an easily installable Apache distribution that also includes MySQL, PHP, and Perl. To install XAMPP, you only need to download and extract a zip file.

PHP is a one of the most-used languages for creating websites and is also preinstalled on most web hosts. In the following pages, you'll see how to create an OData-consuming web page with the help of the available OData SDK for PHP.

OData SDK for PHP   The SDK enables you to easily consume an existing OData service and use the data inside your functions. The OData SDK for PHP is based on the *DataSvcUtil* file, which is used to generate a proxy class based on the metadata exposed by the selected OData service. These classes can be used later on in your PHP application to connect to your OData service and execute the available `Create`, `Read`, `Update`, and `Delete` (CRUD) methods. This makes it very easy and fast to start with your web application development because you don't need to write the code that handles the calling of the service or the data parsing. The SDK doesn't have any dependency on the web server operating system.

Getting Started with PHP

You can find all necessary download links here:

▸ XAMPP: *http://sourceforge.net/projects/xampp/files/*

▸ OData SDK for PHP: *http://odataphp.codeplex.com/*

▸ Aptana Studio: *www.aptana.com/products/studio3/download.html*.
We recommend this open-source, Eclipse-based IDE for building your web applications.

After you've downloaded the SDK, you have to install and configure it correctly. First, create a folder named *odataphp*. Extract all files and folders inside the *framework* folder from the downloaded zip file to the newly created folder. To make sure PHP can execute the SDK functions, add the path to the *odataphp* folder to the `include_path` directive in the *php.ini* configuration file. For example, you might use `include_path=".;C:\xampp\php\odataphp"`.

Next, create a variable called `ODataphp_path` in the *php.ini* file beneath the previously added line, and set it to the path where the PHP toolkit was installed, for example, `ODataphp_path = "C:\xampp\php\odataphp"`.

In addition, make sure the PHP-XML module is installed and *php_xsl.dll* and *php_curl.dll* functions in *php.ini* are enabled. If you're using XAMPP, everything is preconfigured correctly.

After the installation process is completed, you can generate the proxy class for your selected OData service. Open the command-line tool on your operating system, and navigate to the folder where your OData SDK *odataphp* folder is located. The command to create the proxy class with the help of the *PHPDataSvcUtil.php* file is well explained in the available SDK documentation.

Generate the proxy class

In this example scenario, you'll create the proxy class of your OData service in the *C:\PHPODataSample* folder, so enter the following command (replace the placeholder *youruser* and *yourpassword* with your credentials, if needed, or remove them):

```
php odataphp\PHPDataSvcUtil.php /uri= https://
sapes4.sapdevcenter.com/sap/opu/odata/IWFND/RMTSAMPLEFLIGHT /
out=C:\PHPODataSample /auth=windows /u=youruser /p=yourpassword
```

The utility file creates a proxy file in the specified output folder and provides a confirmation message in the console (Figure 12.1).

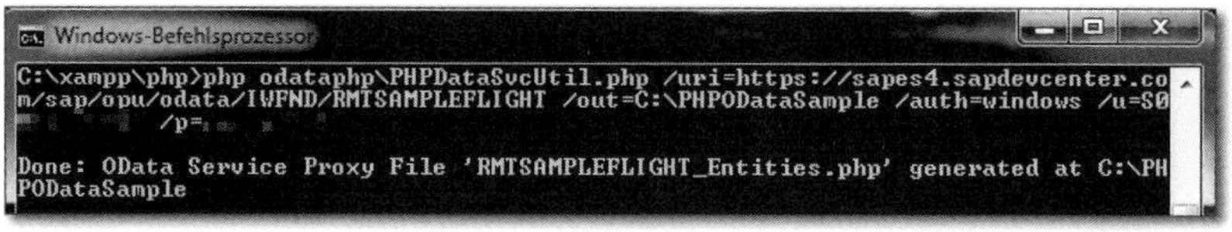

Figure 12.1 Generating the OData PHP Proxy File

After a few seconds, the proxy class for the OData service is created. The generated file contains the definition of a class that can be used to execute the available functions of the OData service.

Consume OData

You'll use the newly created proxy class file to consume the OData service in a simple list view. Navigate to your output folder where the proxy class file is now located. Create an empty *index.php* file inside this folder. Copy the complete folder to your web server (e.g., into the XAMPP *htdocs* folder). Next, the created proxy class needs to be included in your *index.php* file, for example, `require_once "RMTSAMPLE-FLIGHT_Entities.php";`.

Proxy

The field names of the proxy class are case sensitive and have to be used just as they are displayed in the metadata document. In our example, all of the key fields are lowercase, while the `PRICE`, `CARRNAME`, and `CURRENCY` fields are uppercase.

Insert the code in Listing 12.1 to consume all available datasets of the `CarrierCollection` entity and to display the `carrid` and `CARRNAME` fields. Replace *youruser* and *yourpassword* with your logon credentials.

```php
<?php
require_once "RMTSAMPLEFLIGHT_Entities.php";
// Connect
$OData = new RMTSAMPLEFLIGHT_Entities('https://
sapes4.sapdevcenter.com/sap/opu/odata/IWFND/RMTSAMPLEFLIGHT');
$OData->Credential = new WindowsCredential('youruser',
'yourpassword');
echo "------ Carrier list ------ <br/>";
try {
    $OData->addHeader('X-Requested-With', 'XMLHttpRequest');
// Execute
    $flights= $OData->Execute("CarrierCollection")->Result;
// Output
    foreach ($flights as $flight){
        echo "ID: " . $flight->carrid . "<br/>";
        echo "Name: " . $flight->CARRNAME . "<br/><br/>";
    }
    }catch(DataServiceRequestException $exception)
    {
        echo $exception->Response->getError();
    }
?>
```

Listing 12.1 PHP OData Consumption

Save your changes, and open the file in your browser. The result of our example is shown in Figure 12.2.

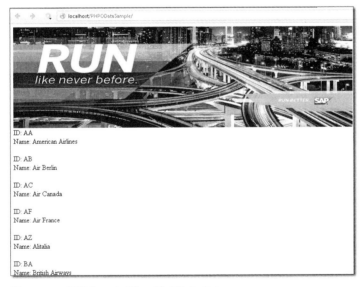

Figure 12.2 PHP Sample File with OData Data

559

Now you can implement the logic to connect to the OData service and execute the necessary functions with PHP. These functionalities are the basis for the following sections in this chapter, so it's important to make sure this works correctly.

12.2 Facebook

Facebook is the biggest free online social networking service, and it's still growing. It was founded in February 2004 by Mark Zuckerberg and some other students of Harvard University. Facebook has more than 1.5 billion active users.

Create application If you don't already have a developer account, visit *https://developers.face-book.com,* and create an account. After the creation process is finished, log in, click My Apps on the top toolbar, and click Add a New App. Choose Website, and the Create New App ID window appears where you have to enter the Display Name and choose an app Category (Figure 12.3).

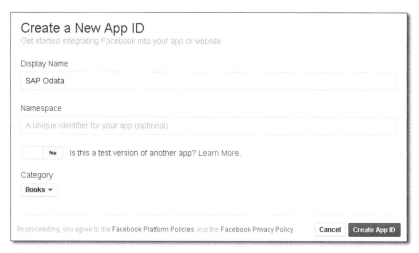

Figure 12.3 Creating a Facebook Application

Namespace Click Create App ID, enter the CAPTCHA on the following page, and click Continue again. You'll be forwarded to the Main Page. Choose Settings on the left side, and enter the Basic application settings page.

Enter a Namespace where the application will be available later ("sap-odatasample" for this example). The direct URL is *http://apps.facebook.com/sapodatasample*.

Click +Add Platform, and select Facebook Canvas to define how your application integrates or connects with Facebook. Enter your application Secure Canvas URL where the PHP files will be stored (for this example, *https://localhost/facebook/*) (Figure 12.4). Click Save Changes.

Figure 12.4 Facebook Basic Application Settings

In the next step, you need to allow the application to post new entries on your profile and add additional permissions. Click on Permissions on the left menu bar, and enter "publish_actions" in the User & Friend Permissions field. Click Save Changes, and navigate back to the Basic settings page, where the App ID and the App Secret are stored for getting access to the Facebook API.

Permissions

Next, you need to grant permissions to your app to get an access token, which provides your application with temporary and secure access to Facebook APIs. Go to *https://developers.facebook.com* and choose TOOLS & SUPPORT • ACCESS TOKEN TOOL. Grant permission to yourself (Figure 12.5).

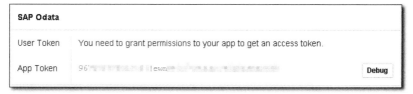

Figure 12.5 Access Token Tool

For this part of the application development, there is a Facebook PHP SDK available. (You can find a tutorial for Facebook PHP at *https:// developers.facebook.com/docs/php/gettingstarted/.*) Create an empty folder called *Facebook*, and download the Facebook PHP SDK (v5) from *https://github.com/facebook/facebook-php-sdk-v4.*

> **Note**
>
> Even if the URL points to version 4 (v4), the downloaded and actual version is version 5. SDK version 5 runs on PHP 5.4 or greater with the `mbstring` extension installed.

Extract the *facebook-php-sdk-v4-master* folder from the already downloaded *facebook-php-sdk-v4-master.zip* file, move the folder located at *src/ Facebook* into the newly created *Facebook* folder, and rename it "sdk." In addition, copy the *RMTSAMPLEFLIGHT_Entities.php* file from the created PHP folder (explained in Section 12.1) to the *Facebook* folder.

> **Note**
>
> Write permissions such as `publish_actions` can't be directly requested from the App Center for API versions after version 2.0. Therefore, you have to request them from within your app instead.

First create a new file called *fb.php*. Open the file in an editor, and enter the coding block from Listing 12.2.

```php
<?php
    require_once '/sdk/autoload.php';
    require_once 'RMTSAMPLEFLIGHT_Entities.php';

    session_start();

    $fb = new Facebook\Facebook([
        'app_id' => 'yourappid',
        'app_secret' => 'yoursecret',
        'default_graph_version' => 'v2.4',
        'default_access_token' => isset($_SESSION['facebook_
access_token']) ? $_SESSION['facebook_access_
token'] : 'yourappid'|'yoursecret'
    ]);
?>
```

Listing 12.2 Facebook API Handler File

Replace the app_Id and app_secret with your own values from the Facebook page.

Create a second file called *index.php* for the login process and the permission to post content to your Facebook wall. Paste Listing 12.3 into the created file.

```php
<?php
include 'fb.php';
$helper = $fb->getRedirectLoginHelper();
$permissions = ['publish_actions'];
$loginUrl = $helper->getLoginUrl('http://localhost/Facebook/
odata.php', $permissions);
echo '<a href="' . $loginUrl . '">Login to Facebook</a>';
?>
```

Listing 12.3 index.php File with Facebook Login

Finally, create a third file called *odata.php*, and replace the OData service user name and password with the content shown in Listing 12.4.

```php
<html xmlns="http://www.w3.org/1999/xhtml" xmlns:fb="http://
www.facebook.com/2008/fbml">
<head>
<title>SAP Gateway</title>
<?php
include 'fb.php';

$helper = $fb->getRedirectLoginHelper();
$accessToken = $helper->getAccessToken();
```

```php
    if (isset($accessToken)) {
        $_SESSION['facebook_access_token'] = (string) $accessToken;
        $fb->setDefaultAccessToken($_SESSION['facebook_access_
token']);
        echo '<h4>Access Token</h4>';
        var_dump($accessToken->getValue());
    }else{
        echo '<h4>Error</h4>';
    }
    ?>
    </head>
    <body>
    <h1 id="fb-welcome"></h1>
    <?php
    // Connect
    $OData = new RMTSAMPLEFLIGHT_Entities('https://
    sapes4.sapdevcenter.com/sap/opu/odata/IWFND/RMTSAMPLEFLIGHT/');
    $OData-
    >Credential = new WindowsCredential('username', 'password');
    try {
        $OData->addHeader('X-Requested-With', 'XMLHttpRequest');
    //  Execute
        $flights= $OData->Execute("CarrierCollection")->Result;
    //  Output
        foreach ($flights as $flight){
            echo '    <form action="" >
                        <input type="text" name="text" style="width
    :300px" value="Carrier:' . $flight->carrid . '" />
                        <input type="submit" />
                </form>';
            echo "Name: " . $flight->CARRNAME . "<br/><br/>";
        }
        }catch(DataServiceRequestException $exception)
        {
            echo $exception->Response->getError();
        }

    // Post Facebook update
    if( isset($_REQUEST['text']) ) {
        $linkData = [
        'link'    => 'http://www.sap.com',
        'message' => $_REQUEST['text'],
        ];

        try {
        $response = $fb->post('/me/feed', $linkData);
        } catch(Facebook\Exceptions\FacebookResponseException $e) {
        echo 'Graph error: ' . $e->getMessage();
```

```
    exit;
    } catch(Facebook\Exceptions\FacebookSDKException $e) {
    echo 'SDK error: ' . $e->getMessage();
    exit;
    }
    var_dump( $response );
}
?>
</body>
</html>
```
Listing 12.4 Facebook PHP OData Consumption

Save all your changes, copy all of the files to your web server, and then open *http://localhost/Facebook/login/index.php* with your browser. Click on LOGIN TO FACEBOOK to log in with your Facebook credentials, and accept the permission to write (post) to your profile (Figure 12.6).

Figure 12.6 Allow Facebook Post Permission

After a successful login, you'll be automatically redirected to the *odata.php* file (Figure 12.7).

<aside>Test application</aside>

Now you can post a new entry from the OData service data to your Facebook profile. Click one of the SUBMIT buttons. You'll see a response on the bottom of your created PHP page with information about the successful creation of your entry. Your Facebook profile will look like the screen shown in Figure 12.8.

Figure 12.7 odata.php Submit Page

Figure 12.8 Updated Facebook Profile

You're now able to directly post any content from an SAP OData service of your choice to your Facebook profile.

12.3   Twitter

Twitter is an online social networking and microblogging service founded in 2006 that enables users to send and read 140-character tweets. Twitter currently has around 650 million users. One of the reasons Twitter is so popular is the large number of developers who have built so many applications for it over the years.

To start developing OData applications for Twitter, visit *https://dev.twitter.com,* and create your personal account. Like many other social networks, Twitter has its own API that programmers can work with. You can find a complete list of all available SDKs for the different programming languages at *https://dev.twitter.com/overview/api/twitter-libraries.*

Twitter SDKs

Open *https://dev.twitter.com/apps* to create a new application, and sign in with your user credentials. Click the CREATE NEW APP button, and enter the application details such as NAME, DESCRIPTION, WEBSITE, or CALLBACK URL, which is where the user should be returned after successfully authenticating. Accept the DEVELOPER AGREEMENT, and click the CREATE YOUR TWITTER APPLICATION button to create your first Twitter application. You're redirected to the application details. Navigate to the KEYS AND ACCESS TOKENS tab where you can find the CONSUMER KEY and CONSUMER SECRET (Figure 12.9). To access your account data, click the CREATE ACCESS TOKEN button.

To make sure you're able to post messages over the API, you have to change the ACCESS LEVEL. Click on MODIFY APP PERMISSIONS, and change the APPLICATION TYPE to READ, WRITE, AND ACCESS DIRECT MESSAGES. Click UPDATE SETTINGS.

As already stated, many PHP libraries are available for Twitter. For this example, you'll use the TwitterOAuth library, which you can download from *https://github.com/abraham/twitteroauth.* Extract all of the files from the already downloaded *TwitterOAuth-master.zip* file to your XAMPP *htdocs* folder (or your webhoster), and rename the *TwitterOAuth-master* folder to "twitter." Copy the *RMTSAMPLEFLIGHT_Entities.php* file from the created PHP folder (explained in Section 12.1), create a file called *index.php*, and open the file in an editor.

Access level

Figure 12.9 Twitter Application Settings

OAuth token Insert the code shown in Listing 12.5 into the already opened editor.

```
<html xmlns="http://www.w3.org/1999/xhtml">
<head>
<title>SAP Gateway</title>
<?php

require_once 'RMTSAMPLEFLIGHT_Entities.php';
require "autoload.php";

use Abraham\TwitterOAuth\TwitterOAuth;

$consumerKey       = 'CONSUMER_KEY';
$consumerSecret    = 'CONSUMER_SECRET';
$accessToken       = 'ACCESS_TOKEN';
$accessTokenSecret = 'ACCESS_SECRET';
```

```
$tweet = new TwitterOAuth($consumerKey, $consumerSecret, $acces
sToken, $accessTokenSecret);
?>
</head>
<body>
<?php

// Connect
$OData = new RMTSAMPLEFLIGHT_Entities('https://
sapes4.sapdevcenter.com/sap/opu/odata/IWFND/RMTSAMPLEFLIGHT/');
$OData-
>Credential = new WindowsCredential('username', 'password');
try {
    $OData->addHeader('X-Requested-With', 'XMLHttpRequest');
// Execute
    $flights= $OData->Execute("CarrierCollection")->Result;
// Output
    foreach ($flights as $flight){
        echo '    <form action="" >
                    <input type="text" name="text" style="width
:300px" value="Carrier:' . $flight->carrid . '" />
                    <input type="submit" />
            </form>';
        echo "Name: " . $flight->CARRNAME . "<br/><br/>";
    }
    }catch(DataServiceRequestException $exception)
    {
        echo $exception->Response->getError();
    }

// Post Twitter update
if( isset($_REQUEST['text']) ) {
$tweet->post('statuses/update', array('status' => $_
REQUEST['text']));
}
?>
</body>
</html>
```

Listing 12.5 Twitter PHP OData Consumption

Add your OAuth tokens provided by Twitter to the `config` array as shown in Listing 12.6.

```
$consumerKey       = 'CONSUMER_KEY';
$consumerSecret    = 'CONSUMER_SECRET';
$accessToken       = 'ACCESS_TOKEN';
$accessTokenSecret = 'ACCESS_SECRET';
```

Listing 12.6 Twitter API Keys

Twitter application Save all your changes, copy the files to your web server, and open the *index.php* file with your browser. Log in with your Twitter credentials. After logging in, you're prompted to approve the application. Click the AUTHORIZE application to connect. You'll see a list of available carriers (Figure 12.10).

Figure 12.10 Custom Twitter Update Page

Click one of the SUBMIT buttons to post the content from the input form in your Twitter account. You'll see a response on the bottom of your created PHP page with information about the successful creation of your tweet. Your Twitter account will look like the screen shown in Figure 12.11.

Figure 12.11 OData Tweet

You can now directly post any content from an SAP OData service of your choice to your Twitter account.

12.4 Sina Weibo (新浪微博)

Sina Weibo (*weibo* is the Chinese word for microblog) is a Chinese hybrid of Twitter and Facebook and is also one of the most popular websites in China. It was launched by Sina Corporation in August 2009 and has more than 500 million registered users. We'll use this unique example to show you how easy it is to provide your SAP data for any available social media platform in the world.

Not every Weibo page is available in English, so we'll show you a translation for Mandarin words as necessary. You may want to use a browser with built-in page translation, such as Google Chrome. To enable the translation bar, click on the Google Chrome menu on the browser toolbar and select SETTINGS. Click SHOW ADVANCED SETTINGS, and navigate to the LANGUAGES section. Mark the OFFER TO TRANSLATE PAGES THAT AREN'T IN A LANGUAGE I READ checkbox to activate the translation feature. Because not everyone will be able to use Google Chrome, we'll show the default screen with no browser-based translation.

You need a normal Sina Weibo user account before you can create your first application. To create your new account, just open *www.weibo.com/ signup/signup.php* in your browser. Normally, the language will be automatically set to English. Otherwise, you can do this manually by opening the dropdown menu on the bottom-right corner and selecting ENGLISH (Figure 12.12).

Account

Click the 确定 (DETERMINE) button on the following message window to confirm that you want to switch to the English language.

Due to the very strict enterprise verification requirements (e.g., a signed enterprise application letter), we suggest that you create a personal account for your first test application. Enter your EMAIL, PASSWORD, and VERIFICATION CODE, and then click SIGN UP NOW (Figure 12.13).

Figure 12.12 Switch Language to English

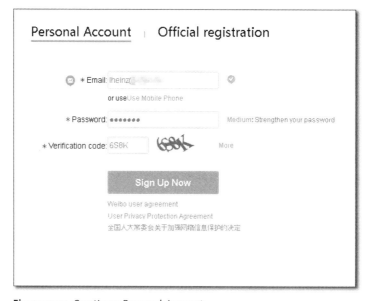

Figure 12.13 Creating a Personal Account

> **Note**
>
> Sometimes, you're prompted to verify your login data with phone verification. To avoid this, you can try the last step again with a different email address.

You're redirected to the next page, where you have to enter some further details, such as your LOCATION (美国 = USA), GENDER, and BIRTHDAY. All other information is optional. Click NEXT. You can choose up to five of your interests. Press [Enter] when you're finished. You're redirected to your user profile, where you have to click the NEXT STEP button twice and the GOT IT button once to close the WHAT'S NEW WITH YOU window. You'll see a reminder to activate your account, with an email sent to your email address. Make sure to confirm your email address.

To start, navigate to the developer web page at *http://open.weibo.com/development*, and create a new developer account. Click the 创建应用 (CREATING APPLICATIONS) button, which is the leftmost button on the screen (Figure 12.14).

Create developer account

Figure 12.14 Creating a Developer Account

If you need to log in, use your email account as the user name. Next, you have to choose the kind of application you want to create. For this example, you'll create a web application, so click in the middle on 网页应用 (the computer monitor icon).

You're prompted to enter further personal data. Table 12.1 lists the information that has to be entered.

Mandarin	English
开发者类型	DEVELOPER TYPE (个人 = PRIVATE, 公司 = COMPANY)
开发者名称	DEVELOPER NAME
所在地区	COUNTRY (美国 = USA)
详细地址	ADDRESS
邮编	ZIP
企业邮箱	EMAIL
企业电话	BUSINESS PHONE
聊天工具	CHAT TOOL
网站	WEBSITE
紧急联系人姓名	EMERGENCY CONTACT NAME
紧急联系人电话	EMERGENCY CONTACT PHONE

Table 12.1 Personal Data

Click the blue 提交 (SUBMIT) button to submit the data.

You have to confirm your email address once again by email. Confirm the opening window by clicking the blue 确定 (DETERMINE) button to confirm the email will be sent to the right address. After approximately five seconds, you should be redirected to the initial Sina Weibo user page (Figure 12.15).

Make sure to confirm your email address; otherwise, you won't be able to post anything. Check your email inbox, and activate your account with a click on the activation link inside or copy the link to your browser. A new browser window opens, and you should be redirected to the initial web page.

To create your application, go to *http://open.weibo.com/development,* and click the orange button 立即创建微连接 (Creating micro connection immediately) (Figure 12.16).

Figure 12.15 Sina Weibo User Account

Create application

Figure 12.16 Create App

Next, you have to choose the kind of application again. Click the 网页应用 (Web Applications) button, which is the third button, and fill in the form with information for your application, as listed in Table 12.2.

Mandarin	English
应用名称	NAME
应用地址	URL (application address)
应用简介	DESCRIPTION (SHORT)
应用介绍	DESCRIPTION (EXTENDED) (Enter 20 words or more.)
应用分类	CATEGORY
标签	TAGS (CHOOSE ?? –OTHER)

Table 12.2 Application Data

Keep the checkbox next to 我已阅读并接受《微博开发者协议》 to confirm that you've read and accepted the MICROBLOGGING DEVELOPER AGREEMENT.

After filling in the form, click the 创建 (CREATE) button, which is the leftmost button (Figure 12.17).

Application key and secret

Figure 12.17 Creating a Weibo Web Application

You're redirected to your application's main page. Now you need the APP KEY and APP SECRET (similar to a password token) to get access to the Weibo API. Enter the required information such as the title and description, and choose one label with your cursor as shown in Figure 12.18.

In the already opened submenu on the left side, click the 高级信息 (ADVANCED INFORMATION) button (second button in the submenu, a circle with an exclamation point) to set a redirect URL (Figure 12.19).

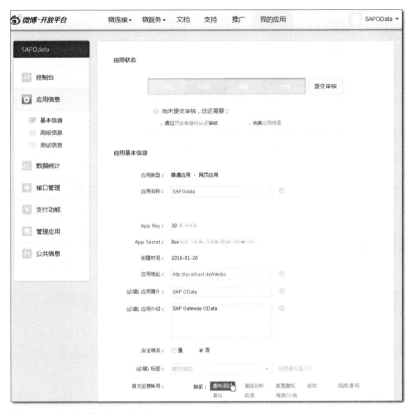

Figure 12.18 Application Settings

Figure 12.19 Creating OAuth Redirect Settings

OAuth callback page

Click the 编辑 (EDIT) button on the right side of the OAUTH2.0 授权设置 bar, and fill the two empty fields with your callback pages as shown in Table 12.3.

Mandarin	English
授权回调页	AUTHORIZATION CALLBACK PAGE
取消授权回调页	DEAUTHORIZE CALLBACK PAGE

Table 12.3 Callback Pages

Enter the authorization callback page as *"http://yourwebserver/callback.php."* Click the green 提交 (SUBMIT) button to confirm your input.

Additional test account

To create an additional test account, click on the third button 测试帐号 (TEST ACCOUNT), in the submenu that should be still open. To edit this, click on the 编辑 (EDIT) button on the right side of that bar again. Add a 用户昵称 (NICKNAME) for a new test account (添加测试帐号), and click the green 提交 (SUBMIT) button to confirm your input. Click the green 提交 (SUBMIT) button to confirm your input again (Figure 12.20).

Figure 12.20 Adding a Test Account

Now you've added a new test account successfully.

Sina Weibo SDK

Sina Weibo also offers many SDKs for different languages. You can find a detailed list at *http://open.weibo.com/wiki/SDK/en.*

Note

The Sina Weibo SDK list is partly outdated. Visit the GitHub PHP SDK, and you'll see that the shown *code.google.com* SDK isn't available anymore.

As mentioned in Section 12.1, we want to develop every social media application based on PHP, so go to *https://github.com/xiaosier/libweibo,* and download the latest version of Weibo PHP SDK.

Download the *libweibo-master.zip* file. Next duplicate the already created PHP folder (Section 12.1), and rename it to "weibo". Extract all of the files from the Weibo PHP SDK to the *weibo* folder, and overwrite the *index.php*. Start editing the *config.php* file, and insert your application key, application secret, and callback URL. Replace the information in Listing 12.7 with your created Sina Weibo application information.

```
define( "WB_AKEY" , 'AppKey' );
define( "WB_SKEY" , 'AppSecret' );
define( "WB_CALLBACK_URL" , 'http://yourserver/callback.php' );
```
Listing 12.7 PHP Weibo API Configuration

Make sure the `WB_CALLBACK_URL` is exactly the same in both the Weibo settings and the authorization callback page.

Now you have to edit the *weibolist.php* file to implement your OData connection. Open this file and replace the coding block in Listing 12.8 with the coding block in Listing 12.9.

weibolist.php

```
<form action="" >
<input type="text" name="text" style="width:300px" />
<input type="submit" />
</form>
```
Listing 12.8 Weibo PHP Block to Replace

```
<?php
require_once 'RMTSAMPLEFLIGHT_Entities.php';
// Connect
$OData = new RMTSAMPLEFLIGHT_Entities('https://
sapes4.sapdevcenter.com/sap/opu/odata/IWFND/RMTSAMPLEFLIGHT');
$OData->Credential =
  new WindowsCredential('youruser', 'yourpassword');
try {
```

```
    $OData->addHeader('X-Requested-With', 'XMLHttpRequest');
//  Execute
    $flights= $OData->Execute("CarrierCollection")->Result;
//  Output
    foreach ($flights as $flight){
        echo '    <form action="" >
                    <input type="text" name="text" style="width:
300px" value="Carrier:' . $flight->carrid . '" />
                    <input type="submit" />
            </form>';
        echo "Name: " . $flight->CARRNAME . "<br/><br/>";
    }
    }catch(DataServiceRequestException $exception)
    {
        echo $exception->Response->getError();
    }
?>
```
Listing 12.9 Weibo PHP OData Consumption

Authorize access

Save all your changes, copy the files to your web server, and open the *index.php* file with your browser. Log in with your Sina Weibo credentials. You're prompted to authorize the application accesses to your profile information (Figure 12.21).

Figure 12.21 Granting Access to Your User Profile

Post content

Click the red 授权 (Authorize) button to authorize access. The default *index.php* web page appears, in which you have to click the red Weibo login 点击进入授权页面 (Click to Enter) button. You're redirected to your callback page with an authentication code as a parameter. After authorization is complete, click the 进入你的微博列表页面 (ENTER YOUR MICROBLOGGING PAGE) link to enter your microblogging page. You'll see a list of available carriers (Figure 12.22) and a list of all related updates to your account below the carriers.

Figure 12.22 Custom Weibo Update Page

Click one of the SUBMIT buttons to post the content from the input form to your Sina Weibo account (Figure 12.23).

Figure 12.23 Sina Weibo Custom Message

You can now directly post any content of your choice from an SAP OData service to your Sina Weibo account.

12.5 Summary

Social media is important for your daily business. In this chapter, you've learned how to enable your different user groups to access and deliver data from the SAP system into the social media world via PHP and SDKs. Specifically, you've used the existing PHP SDK for OData to create a basic application with OData access. Based on this, you've created an application for Facebook, for Twitter, and for the Chinese microblogging platform Sina Weibo.

In the next chapter, we discuss our last application development example: enterprise application development.

This last chapter of Part III focuses on enterprise application development and provides examples of OData service development for Microsoft SharePoint, Microsoft Excel, and more.

13 Enterprise Application Development

Enterprise business applications are the fourth pillar of the possible options for you and your company's daily business (Figure 13.1). Although developing applications for today's enterprises is normally not a simple task, this chapter enables you to create applications on the business side with the data you need to solve your business problems on your own. Using SAP Gateway, your business can centralize data from different sources into one enterprise application.

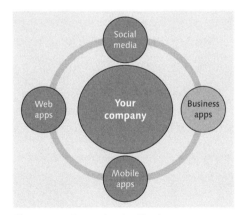

Figure 13.1 Enterprise Applications

Founded in 1975 Microsoft is the largest computer technology firm in the world, developing software and software-related services and solutions. This wide range of computing solutions makes Microsoft the most popular computing platform in the business world today. This is why some of the most common tools from Microsoft, such as SharePoint,

LightSwitch, and Excel, are used here to show you how to consume SAP-provided OData services inside your existing business system landscape.

SAP Gateway Productivity Accelerator

The tool known as SAP Gateway Productivity Accelerator for Microsoft (GWPAM) is now called SAP Gateway for Microsoft (GWM). You can find further information at *http://scn.sap.com/docs/DOC-47563*.

At the beginning of this chapter, we introduce application development with SAP Gateway for Microsoft (Section 13.1), the OData format extension for Microsoft Excel (Section 13.2), and continue with the development for Microsoft SharePoint (Section 13.3). Then we'll show you how to build a Microsoft LightSwitch application (Section 13.4), and finally help you with code snippets for Microsoft ASP.NET (Section 13.5).

13.1   SAP Gateway for Microsoft

Prerequisites   SAP Gateway for Microsoft (GWM) streamlines the consumption of SAP Gateway-based OData services in Microsoft applications. GWM integrates with Microsoft Office and other Windows/ASP.NET-based applications, which we'll discuss in this chapter.

GWM Prerequisites

Operation System (32-bit/64-bit):
- Windows 7/8
- Windows Server 2008 Standard/Enterprise

Visual Studio:
- Visual Studio 2010 (.NET 4.0/4.5)
- Visual Studio 2012 (.NET 4.5), installed Microsoft Office Developer Tools
- Visual Studio 2013 with WCF Data Service 5.6 and Visual Studio 2013 SDK
- Visual Studio 2013 Community Edition (.NET 4.5)

Microsoft Office (with latest Visual Studio 2010 Tools for Office Runtime installed):
- Microsoft Office 2010
- Microsoft Office 2013

You can find further information for GWM on the following website:

http://help.sap.com/saphelp_nwgwpam_1/helpdata/en/80/572a006e154257
99df17b5c83eb24f/content.htm?frameset=/en/53/8be0db450541e493d7b4c
2e5685ecf/frameset.htm&current_toc=/en/d8/c9a9c590ed44829bc09f04396
9cd71/plain.htm&node_id=31

In this section, we'll discuss how to install GWM.

13.1.1 SAP Gateway for Microsoft Installation

To install GWM, follow these steps:

1. Download the free GWM developer trial version from the SAP store **SAP GWM**
   (*http://store.sap.com*). You can search for GWM, or go directly to **developer trial**
   https://store.sap.com/sap/cp/ui/resources/store/html/SolutionDetails.html?
   pid= 0000013181.

2. Click the TRIAL VERSION button to download the free developer tool
   for Microsoft Visual Studio development environment (Figure 13.2).

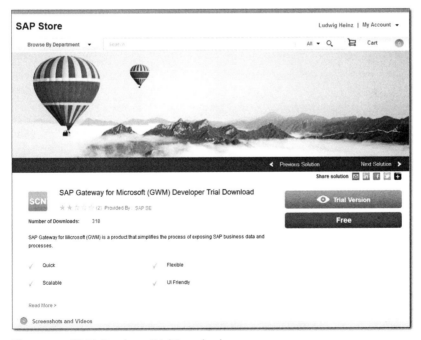

Figure 13.2 GWM Developer Trial Download

3. Enter your contact information in the download pop-up, accept the two terms and conditions by checking the boxes, and then click Sub-mit. An email with the download link will be sent to the email address you provided. Open the link, and download the installation files.

Prerequisites   Now that you've downloaded the necessary installation files, we'll show you how to install the GWM add-in while using Microsoft Visual Studio 2012 and Microsoft Office 2010. Depending on your installed software, you'll need some additional library files. Otherwise, you'll get an error stating that Data Definition Language (DDL) files are missing in your assembly cache (Figure 13.3).

Figure 13.3 Missing Library

To add the required libraries, follow these steps:

1. Download the corresponding *microsoft.identitymodel.clients.activedi-rectory.1.0.2.nupkg* nupkg package file from *www.nuget.org/packages/Microsoft.IdentityModel.Clients.ActiveDirectory/1.0.2*, open it with a zip program such as WinRAR, and extract the package to a folder. Run the Developer Command Prompt for Visual Studio as administrator, and insert the following command to add the assembly to the cache:

```
gacutil -if YOUR_PATH_TO_THE_EXTRACTED_FOLDER\lib\net40\
Microsoft.IdentityModel.Clients.ActiveDirectory.dll
```

Start installation   2. Press Enter to start, and the assembly is added (Figure 13.4).

3. Install the included *Microsoft.IdentityModel.Clients.ActiveDirectory.WindowsForms.dll* in the same way.

> **NuGet Package Manager**
>
> NuGet is the package manager for the Microsoft development platform including .NET. The NuGet client tools enable you to produce and consume packages. You can find further information for NuGet at *www.nuget.org/*.

586

4. Also install *Newtonsoft.Json.dll* version 5.0.6 (don't use a newer version) in the same way (download from *www.nuget.org/packages/Newtonsoft.Json*).

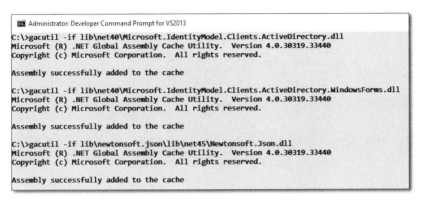

Figure 13.4 Adding the Assembly to the Visual Studio Cache

5. Open the downloaded trial file *GWM_Visual_Studio_Add-In.msi* to start the installation process (Figure 13.5).

6. On the GWM VISUAL STUDIO ADD-IN page, click NEXT. Read the copyright note, and click NEXT again.

Figure 13.5 GWM Installation

587

7. Read the terms and conditions, check I AGREE, and click NEXT to continue.

8. Choose your installation folder, and click NEXT. Click NEXT again to start the installation.

Browse SAP services

9. After the installation process is finished, close the installer. Open your Visual Studio. You can find the installed GWM extension under TOOLS • EXTENSIONS AND UPDATES (Figure 13.6).

Extension and Update Manager: GWM Missing

If the GWM extension isn't shown, close all instances of Visual Studio 2013, and download the *VsRestart.vsix* file from *https://visualstudiogallery.msdn.microsoft.com/01f0a1ae-1513-48dd-9cf0-efb38419b480*.

Open the downloaded file, and click INSTALL. After installation is finished, click CLOSE. Start Visual Studio, and the GWM extension should now be displayed in the EXTENSION AND UPDATES manager.

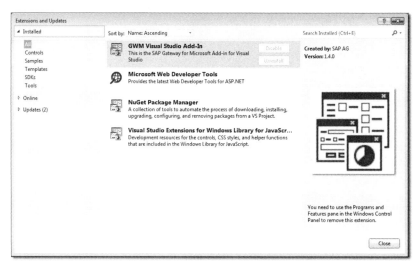

Figure 13.6 GWM Visual Studio Add-In

10. In addition, you can also browse the SAP services from TOOLS • BROWSE SAP SERVICES (Figure 13.7).

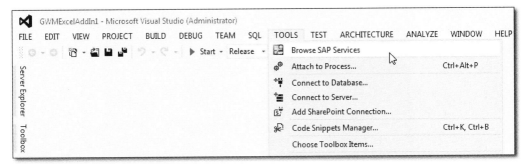

Figure 13.7 Browse SAP Services Option

11. Click on BROWSE SAP SERVICES to open the browse service wizard. Enter your SAP NW GW SYSTEM (without http or https), the PORT (default is 80), USER NAME, and PASSWORD. You can also choose the SAP CLIENT (or the USE DEFAULT SAP CLIENT checkbox) and the USE SSL CONNECTIONS checkbox. Click OK when you've entered your details (Figure 13.8).

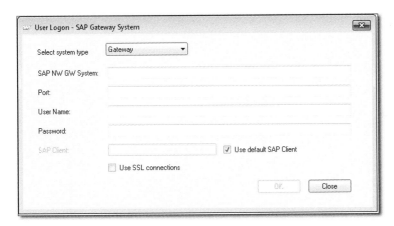

Figure 13.8 User Logon: SAP Gateway System

12. A list of all available services is displayed (Figure 13.9).

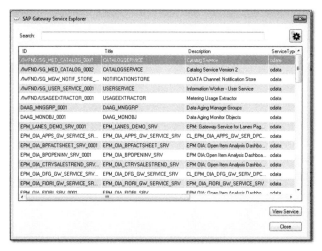

Figure 13.9 SAP Gateway Service Explorer

13. Choose a service from the list or search for a name in the search bar, select a service, and click VIEW SERVICE to see the service details (Figure 13.10).

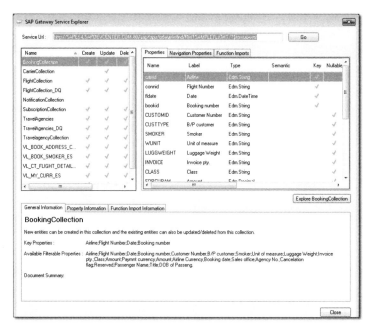

Figure 13.10 SAP Gateway Service Details

14. You'll get general information about the selected collection, the properties, navigation properties, and function imports. You can also view the first 20 records (Figure 13.11) by clicking the EXPLORE [COLLECTIONNAME] button on the right side (refer to Figure 13.10).

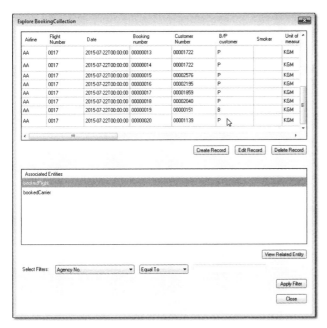

Figure 13.11 Explore Booking Collection

You can test your selected service collection from this view and explore functionalities such as creating or deleting an existing record.

In the next section, we'll walk you through how to create a Microsoft Excel project with the GWM Visual Studio Add-In.

13.1.2 SAP Gateway for Microsoft Excel 2010 Add-In

In this section, you'll create an Excel project by following these steps:

1. To create a new project, go to FILE • NEW • PROJECT, and choose VISUAL C# in the template tree on the left side. Choose GWM EXCEL 2010 ADD-IN for your next project template (Figure 13.12).

Figure 13.12 GWM Excel 2010 Add-In

Select system   2. Click OK to continue. You can select the system type from the Service System Type dropdown list with the following options: Gateway, SMP, or Azure. The default value Gateway is the right choice for this example. Enter the Service URL from your SAP ES4 sample service (Chapter 9, Section 9.3), and click Go (Figure 13.13).

Figure 13.13 Excel: Select Service URL

3. Enter your logon credentials, and click OK. If everything is correct, the following message appears: [SERVICENAME] SERVICE DETAILS WERE SUCCESSFULLY LOADED. Click NEXT.

4. Select your preferred service collection. The collection details will be displayed on the right side with the included properties from the service metadata (Figure 13.14). Click NEXT to continue.

Figure 13.14 Excel: Select Collection

5. Select the properties of your collection with the checkboxes in the first column. By default, all properties are selected. For performance reasons, you might need to deselect the unused properties (Figure 13.15). Click NEXT when you're finished.

6. Configure your service settings for the Excel sheet. You can enter the STARTING REFERENCE CELL and the MAXIMUM RECORDS TO FETCH, and then choose from the SELECT A VALUE FOR THE COLUMN HEADER dropdown. You can also enable user operation settings such as creating, updating, or deleting records (Figure 13.16).

Figure 13.15 Excel: Select Properties

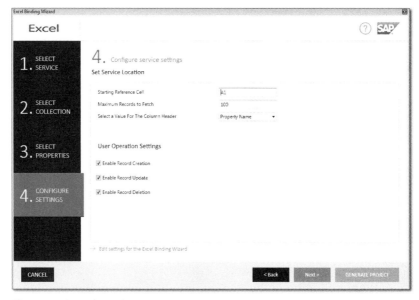

Figure 13.16 Excel: Configure Service Settings

7. Click GENERATE PROJECT to finish the EXCEL BINDING WIZARD.

8. The project is created with the settings from the wizard. The GENER-
ATED GWM PROJECT REPORT is displayed in your default browser as
HTML (Figure 13.17).

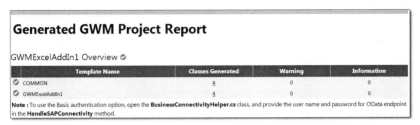

Figure 13.17 Excel: Generated GWM Project Report

9. Switch back to your Visual Studio instance. On the right side, you see
the SOLUTION EXPLORER with the created project (Figure 13.18).

Figure 13.18 Visual Studio with GWM Excel Project

Now you have to handle the authentication process for the OData service by following these steps:

1. Navigate to the *App.config* file under the *SAP Service Reference* folder. Choose from the SAP GWM authentication modes, including Basic, OAuth, or X509 (Figure 13.19).

Figure 13.19 App.config

2. Use the default mode as a base for your first app. Navigate to the Busi-nessConnectivityHelper.cs class file, and open the HandleSAPCon-nectivity method from the dropdown list (Figure 13.20).

Figure 13.20 BusinessConnectivityHelper.cs

3. Enter your credentials for the OData service in the corresponding fields (Listing 13.1).

```
switch(authenticationType)
{
case AuthenticationType.BASIC:
        webRequest.Credentials = new System.Net.NetworkCrede
ntial("username", "password");
        break;
}
```

Listing 13.1 HandleSAPConnectivity

4. Save the file, and click the START button to launch your created application. Excel opens, and you're prompted to install the created add-in. Click INSTALL to continue.

5. Switch to the GWMEXCELADDIN1 tab, and click FETCH RECORDS (Figure 13.21).

Figure 13.21 GWMExcelAddIn1 Tab

The connection to the SAP Gateway is established, and the data are fetched to the Excel sheet (Figure 13.22).

	A	B	C	D	E	F	G	H	I	J	K	L	M	N	O	P
1	bookid	carrid	connid	fldate	AGENCYNUM	CANCELLED	CLASS	COUNTER	CUSTOMID	CUSTTYPE	FORCURAM	FORCURKEY	INVOICE	LOCCURAM	LOCCURKEY	LUGGWEIGH
2	00000001	AA	0017	22.07.2015	00000114		C	00000000	00003627	P	875,90	EUR		803,58	USD	17.400
3	00000002	AA	0017	22.07.2015	00000222		C	00000000	00001957	P	803,58	USD		803,58	USD	13.400
4	00000003	AA	0017	22.07.2015	00000000		C	00000029	00004322	P	803,58	USD		803,58	USD	9.800
5	00000004	AA	0017	22.07.2015	00000104		C	00000000	00002619	P	922,01	EUR		845,88	USD	23.900
6	00000005	AA	0017	22.07.2015	00000087		C	00000000	00000324	P	829,82	EUR	X	761,30	USD	25.000
7	00000006	AA	0017	22.07.2015	00000107		C	00000000	00000132	B	571,97	GBP		845,88	USD	19.800
8	00000007	AA	0017	22.07.2015	00000111		C	00000000	00002837	P	761,30	EUR		761,30	USD	18.900
9	00000008	AA	0017	22.07.2015	00000117		C	00000000	00000095	B	737,60	EUR		676,70	USD	10.900
10	00000009	AA	0017	22.07.2015	00000109		C	00000000	00000405	P	514,78	GBP	X	761,30	USD	15.300
11	00000010	AA	0017	22.07.2015	00000111		C	00000000	00002755	P	845,88	USD	X	845,88	USD	0.000
12	00000011	AA	0017	22.07.2015	00000294		C	00000000	00001940	P	922,01	EUR		845,88	USD	21.800
13	00000012	AA	0017	22.07.2015	00000102		C	00000000	00000085	B	657,88	AUD		803,58	USD	27.100
14	00000013	AA	0017	22.07.2015	00000105		C	00000000	00001722	P	783,71	EUR	X	719,00	USD	27.500
15	00000014	AA	0017	22.07.2015	00000125		C	00000000	00001722	P	719,00	EUR	X	719,00	USD	12.200
16	00000015	AA	0017	22.07.2015	00000061		C	00000000	00002576	P	829,82	EUR	X	761,30	USD	10.400
17	00000016	AA	0017	22.07.2015	00002254		C	00000000	00002195	P	7068,29	ZAR	X	761,30	USD	0.000
18	00000017	AA	0017	22.07.2015	00000224		C	00000000	00001859	P	783,71	EUR		719,00	USD	14.400
19	00000018	AA	0017	22.07.2015	00000121		C	00000000	00002040	P	783,71	EUR		719,00	USD	13.500
20	00000019	AA	0017	22.07.2015	00003319		C	00000000	00000151	B	803,58	USD	X	803,58	USD	0.000
21	00000020	AA	0017	22.07.2015	00000117		C	00000000	00001139	P	829,82	EUR	X	761,30	USD	0.000
22	00000021	AA	0017	22.07.2015	00000103		C	00000000	00003306	P	1449,45	SGD	X	803,58	USD	0.000
23	00000022	AA	0017	22.07.2015	00000993		C	00000000	00000439	P	922,01	EUR	X	845,88	USD	0.000
24	00000023	AA	0017	22.07.2015	00000301		C	00000000	00003341	P	845,88	USD		845,88	USD	21.600

Figure 13.22 GWM Excel Data

13.1.3 SAP Gateway for Microsoft Outlook 2010 Add-In

In this section, we'll show you how to create an Outlook project by following these steps:

Microsoft Outlook
1. Go to FILE • NEW • PROJECT, and choose VISUAL C# in the template tree on the left side. Choose GWM OUTLOOK 2010 ADD-IN for your next project template (refer to Figure 13.12). Click OK to continue.

2. Select a template for CONTACTS, APPOINTMENTS, or TASKS (Figure 13.23).

Figure 13.23 Outlook Binding Wizard

3. Enter your TEMPLATE NAME, and click NEXT to continue.

4. In the SELECT SYSTEM TYPE dropdown list, select from the following system types: GATEWAY, SMP, or AZURE. Choose the default value GATEWAY for our example.

5. Enter the SERVICE URL from your SAP ES4 sample service (Chapter 9, Section 9.3), and click GO (Figure 13.24).

Figure 13.24 Outlook: Enter Service URL

6. Enter your logon credentials, and click OK. If everything is correct, the following message appears: [SERVICENAME] SERVICE DETAILS WERE SUCCESSFULLY LOADED. If you don't know the exact service URL, click on BROWSE, and enter your system data (Figure 13.25).

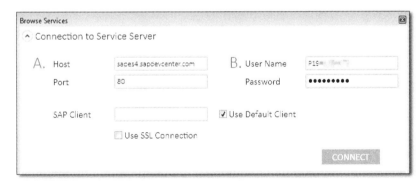

Figure 13.25 Outlook: Connection to Service Server

7. Click CONNECT to see a list of all available services (Figure 13.26).

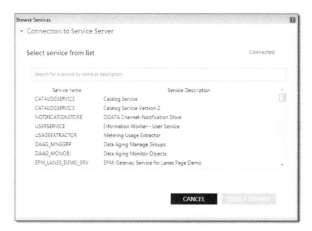

Figure 13.26 Outlook: Browse Services

8. Choose a service, click SELECT SERVICE, and click NEXT to finish.

9. Select your preferred service collection. The collection details will be displayed on the right side with the included properties from the service metadata (Figure 13.27). Click NEXT to continue.

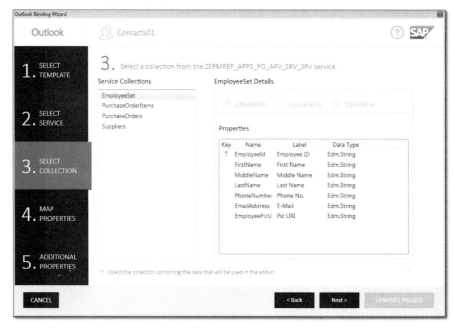

Figure 13.27 Outlook: Select Collection

10. Click Next to continue. You have to map the collection properties of the selected service to the Outlook properties (Figure 13.28).

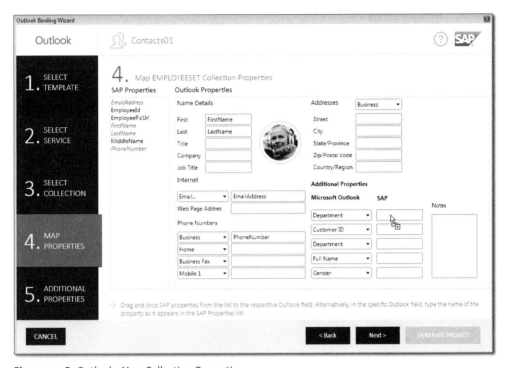

Figure 13.28 Outlook: Map Collection Properties

11. Drag and drop the SAP Properties from the service collection to the available Outlook Properties. You can also add five Additional Properties from the dropdown lists. Click Next when you're finished.

12. In the final step, Add unmapped property tabs (Custom and Associated) – Optional, enter the Custom Tab Name, and select or deselect possible associated information tabs, which contain properties from related collections in the OData service (Figure 13.29).

13. Click Next to see the Project Summary (Figure 13.30).

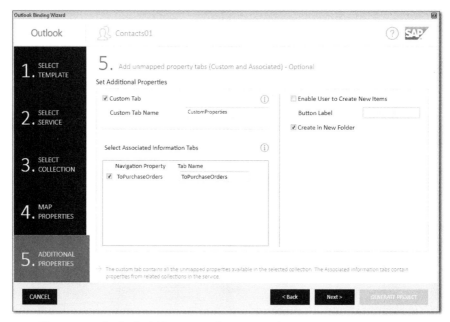

Figure 13.29 Outlook: Add Unmapped Property Tabs

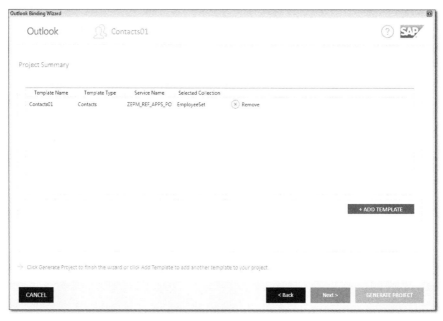

Figure 13.30 Outlook: Project Summary

14. You can add additional templates via the + ADD TEMPLATE button. Click GENERATE PROJECT to finish the OUTLOOK BINDING WIZARD.

    The project is created with the settings from the wizard. The GENERATED GWM PROJECT REPORT is displayed in your default browser as HTML (Figure 13.31).

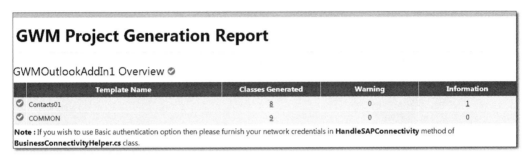

Figure 13.31 Outlook: Generated GWM Project Report

15. Switch back to your Visual Studio instance. On the right side, you see the SOLUTION EXPLORER with the created project (Figure 13.32).

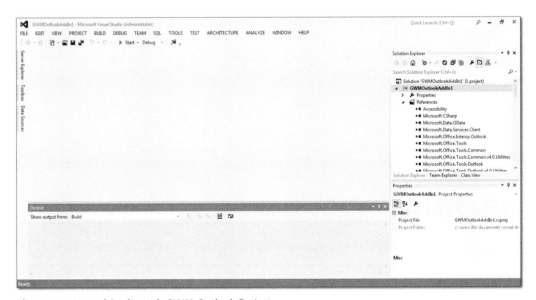

Figure 13.32 Visual Studio with GWM Outlook Project

Now you have to handle the authentication process for the OData service by following these steps:

1. Navigate to the App.config file under the SAP Service Reference folder. Choose the SAP GWM authentication mode (Basic, OAuth, or X509) (Figure 13.33).

Figure 13.33 Outlook App.config

2. The default mode is Basic, which is good for our first app. Navigate to the BusinessConnectivityHelper.cs class file, and open the HandleSAPConnectivity method from the dropdown list (Figure 13.34).

Figure 13.34 Outlook BusinessConnectivityHelper.cs

3. Enter your credentials for the OData service in the corresponding fields (Listing 13.1).

4. Save the file, and click the START button to launch your created application. Outlook starts, and the created tab is available in the ribbon row (Figure 13.35).

Figure 13.35 GWMOutlookAddIn1 Tab

5. Click GETALL, and choose the created template name. All the contacts will be fetched and created as new contacts in Outlook (Figure 13.36).

Figure 13.36 Created Contacts

Further information

You can find further information for GWM at *http://help.sap.com/nwgwpam*.

13.2   Microsoft Excel

In addition to the SAP GWM Visual Studio Add-In for Microsoft Excel, there are two other options available to consume an OData service in Excel. The first alternative option is the PowerPivot tool (Section 13.2.1) developed by Microsoft, which is also an add-in. The second alternative option is to download the OData service content with the help of the URL parameter `$format=xlsx` (Section 13.2.2), which is directly supported by SAP Gateway without any additional tools or add-ins.

13.2.1   PowerPivot

Microsoft published the PowerPivot tool to consume OData services directly from Excel. You can use the installable Excel plug-in as a data mashup and data exploration tool to create analytical reports or business graphics and update these with real data from SAP with just one click. We recommend using the SAP GWM Visual Studio Add-In to consume OData services inside Excel because it's newer then the PowerPivot plug-in and will be updated by SAP in the future.

PowerPivot: Minimum Requirements

▸ Excel 2010
▸ .NET Framework 4.0
▸ Visual Studio 2010 Tools for Office Runtime
▸ PowerPivot plug-in

PowerPivot

PowerPivot enables you and your employees to use OData to consume centralized data from different sources, such as SAP Gateway, and integrate it in one place.

You can find a detailed requirements list and the necessary download links at Microsoft's website: *https://support.office.com/en-gb/article/Power-Pivot-Add-in-a9c2c6e2-cc49-4976-a7d7-40896795d045*.

Whether to use the 32-bit or 64-bit version of the PowerPivot tool depends on the version of your installed Excel, not on your operating system.

After you've downloaded (and installed) all necessary prerequisites, you can install and configure PowerPivot for Excel. First, open the folder where you downloaded PowerPivot for your Excel version, double-click the POWERPIVOT_FOR_EXCEL_(AMD64/X86).MSI file, and follow the steps in the wizard.

After the installation process is complete, click FINISH. Start Excel, and you'll see the POWERPIVOT tab bar in the Office 2010 ribbon (Figure 13.37).

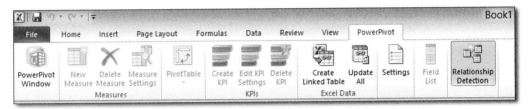

Figure 13.37 PowerPivot Ribbon

To use PowerPivot follow these steps:

1. Click the POWERPIVOT WINDOW button on the left-top corner of the bar. In the new window that appears, click on the small GET EXTERNAL DATA FROM A DATA FEED button to enter your OData service (Figure 13.38).

Consume data feed

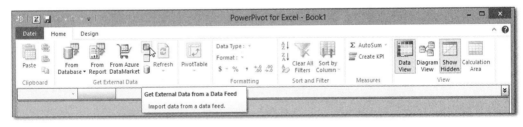

Figure 13.38 External Data Source

2. Enter your service URL in the following window, and click ADVANCED. Scroll down to the security options, and change the INTEGRATED SECURITY method, USER ID, and PASSWORD to your needs (Figure 13.39). Confirm your changes by clicking OK.

Security options

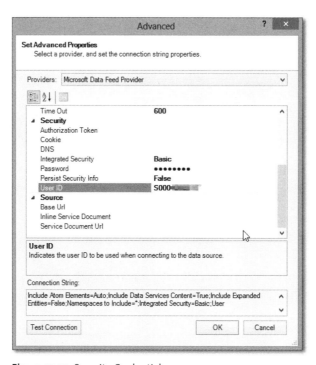

Figure 13.39 Security Credentials

3. Click TEST CONNECTION to test your settings. If the connection is successful, you can continue by clicking CONTINUE.

4. In the next screen, select the available collection, and then click FINISH to close the wizard.

OData import The PowerPivot plug-in fetches all of the data from the selected collections into Excel. You'll be informed of the number of rows for each entity received in an additional window. After the import is finished, you can close this window by clicking CLOSE. The plug-in creates a sheet for each entity collection (Figure 13.40).

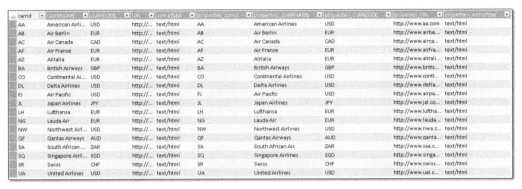

Figure 13.40 PowerPivot Data View

You can also see an overview of the entire model of the consumed   Model
OData service. Click DIAGRAM VIEW on the right corner of the Power-
Pivot ribbon. The model is displayed, including all fields (Figure 13.41).

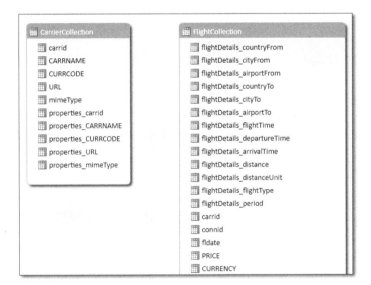

Figure 13.41 PowerPivot Data Model

Now you're able to fetch all required data directly to Excel without
copying or downloading manually from the source. You now have many
possibilities for creating analytic reports or diagrams based on your SAP
data.

13.2.2 $format=xlsx

Besides the two available add-ins by SAP and Microsoft, SAP Gateway itself already provides built-in Excel support (requires SAP NetWeaver 7.40 and SP 09 or higher) without the need of any additional tool. You can perform an OData request for an entity set with the additional URL parameter:

```
$format=xlsx
```

You can also use the following in the HTTP header:

```
accept = application/vnd.openxmlformats-
officedocument.spreadsheetml.sheet
```

If you use one of these additional parameters, the response isn't a JavaScript Object Notation (JSON) or XML file. You'll receive the binary of an Excel file (type *.xlsx*).

For example, the following call of the sample service for `CarrierCollection` with the attached `$format=xlsx` URL parameter will open an Excel .xlsx file with all carriers for download:

```
https://sapes4.sapdevcenter.com/sap/opu/odata/IWFND/
RMTSAMPLEFLIGHT/CarrierCollection?$format=xlsx
```

> **Further Information**
>
> You can find further information, including the restrictions for the included Excel support, at the following:
>
> *https://help.sap.com/saphelp_nw74/helpdata/en/a2/4c8490449041b88b789 0d299b57351/content.htm?frameset=/en/a2/4c8490449041b88b7890d299 b57351/frameset.htm&current_toc=/en/ad/612bb3102e4f54a3019697fef65 e5e/plain.htm&node_id=174*

13.3 Microsoft SharePoint/Office 365

The Microsoft SharePoint server offers your enterprise new functionalities for data access, collaboration, and document management. Developing applications for Microsoft SharePoint widens the range of possible programming languages and technology stacks, which can be consolidated with Microsoft SharePoint.

> **Note**
>
> We'll use the term *Microsoft SharePoint* in this chapter to describe the process of development for both Microsoft SharePoint and Office 365.

To start, register a new Office 365 account if you don't have your own Microsoft SharePoint server for testing purposes. There is a 30-day trial account available. You can find a how-to guide to start building your applications for Microsoft Office and Microsoft SharePoint on the Microsoft development center page: *http://msdn.microsoft.com/en-US/library/office/apps/fp161179*.

The range of options depends on the type of hosting and application pattern you choose (mixing is also possible). We show you how to create a Microsoft SharePoint application with Visual Studio 2012, retrieving data from an existing OData service. This is a very convenient option for providing your SAP data to your existing Microsoft SharePoint server, which can be accessed from the web.

> **Microsoft Office 365: Minimum Requirements**
>
> ▸ Microsoft Office 365 (trial) account
> ▸ Office Developer Tools for Visual Studio 2012
> ▸ SharePoint Client Components

To create your first Microsoft SharePoint application, follow these steps:

1. Start Visual Studio 2012, and select FILE • NEW • PROJECT.

2. Expand the VISUAL C# node, and select APP FOR SHAREPOINT 2013, which is located under the OFFICE/SHAREPOINT template node (Figure 13.42).

Settings

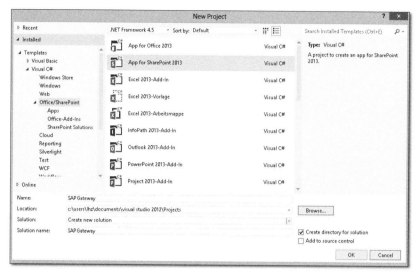

Figure 13.42 App for SharePoint 2013

3. Enter the project NAME, and click OK.

Settings 4. Next, you need to specify the Microsoft SharePoint settings. There are three different options for how to host your application, as shown in Table 13.1.

Option	Description
Microsoft SharePoint-hosted applications	All components are hosted on either an on-premise or Office 365 Microsoft SharePoint farm.
Provider-hosted applications	This includes components that are deployed and hosted outside the Microsoft SharePoint farm.
Autohosted applications	This includes provider-hosted applications whose remote components are provisioned and deployed for you on Windows Azure.

Table 13.1 Hosting Options for Microsoft SharePoint Applications

5. Enter a name for your Microsoft SharePoint application, and enter the URL of the Microsoft SharePoint server that you'll be debugging

against. The URL will be in the form *https://YOURUSERNAME.share-point.com*. After you enter the URL, select SharePoint-hosted from the dropdown menu (Figure 13.43).

Figure 13.43 Creating a New Application for Microsoft SharePoint

6. Click Finish. When the project generation process is done, a pop-up appears, and you have to enter your Microsoft SharePoint credentials.

Add OData service

7. After the validation is successfully finished, right-click on the created project, and choose Add • Content Types for an External Data Source to add a new OData service to the project.

> **Note**
>
> When using an OData service with required log-in credentials, Visual Studio uses the domain as part of the authentication header. You can add a backslash at the beginning of your user name (such as "\myuser") to ignore the domain. To avoid any problem with the authentication method on your side, we'll show the OData consumption process with the help of a free sample service from *www.odata.org* (we first introduced this in Chapter 8, Section 8.3).

8. Make sure the OData service is reachable from your Microsoft Share-Point server. Enter your OData service URL and a name for the new data source (Figure 13.44).

Figure 13.44 Specifying the OData Source

Choose entities 9. Click NEXT. In the next step of the wizard, you have to select the entities that you want to use to generate external content types. Choose the entities you want to work with by clicking on the checkbox for each entity (Figure 13.45).

10. Click FINISH to start the generation process.

> **Note**
>
> To create an external list, leave the CREATE LIST INSTANCES FOR THE SELECTED DATA ENTRIES (EXCEPT SERVICE OPERATIONS) field checked so the tools can create your external list automatically.

After a few seconds, the generation process is finished, and the tool creates an external content type and external list instances in your Visual Studio project.

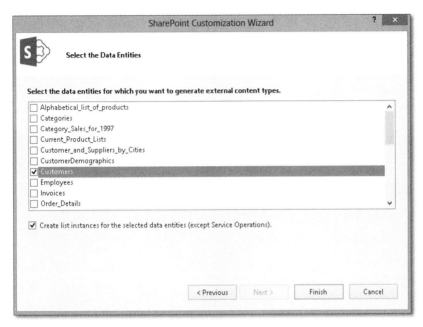

Figure 13.45 Selecting OData Service Entities

To deploy your solution, choose DEBUG • START (or press F5). Visual Studio builds the application and deploys it to your Microsoft SharePoint server (and if you change something in an existing application, the old version is automatically reinstalled). After this deployment process is finished, the default browser window opens, and you have to log in with your credentials again. Your newly created application is shown. Although you haven't configured the layout of the page, you can see some basic information, and you have to adjust the URL to show the result of the consumed OData service: */yourappname/Lists/yourentityname*. In our example, the URL will look like this:

Deploy

https://odata.sharepoint.com/SAPGateway/Lists/Customers

You can also access your application from the home page of Office 365. When you're logged in, go to the developer site, and click the SITE CONTENT link on the left side. You'll see your deployed applications in the application list (Figure 13.46).

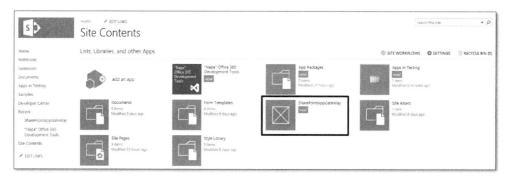

Figure 13.46 Site Contents Office 365

You'll also see your newly created Microsoft SharePoint application on the home page on the APPS IN TESTING list. As a result, you'll get a page like the one shown in Figure 13.47, including the data from the OData service in a simple table-view layout.

	CustomerID		CompanyName	ContactName	ContactTitle	Address	City	Region	PostalCode	Country	Phone	Fax
✓	ALFKI	...	Alfreds Futterkiste	Maria Anders	Sales Representative	Obere Str. 57	Berlin		12209	Germany	030-0074321	030-0076545
	ANATR	...	Ana Trujillo Emparedados y helados	Ana Trujillo	Owner	Avda. de la Constitución 2222	México D.F.		05021	Mexico	(5) 555-4729	(5) 555-3745
	ANTON	...	Antonio Moreno Taquería	Antonio Moreno	Owner	Mataderos 2312	México D.F.		05023	Mexico	(5) 555-3932	
	AROUT	...	Around the Horn	Thomas Hardy	Sales Representative	120 Hanover Sq.	London		WA1 1DP	UK	(171) 555-7788	(171) 555-6750
	BERGS	...	Berglunds snabbköp	Christina Berglund	Order Administrator	Berguvsvägen 8	Luleå		S-958 22	Sweden	0921-12 34 65	0921-12 34 67
✓	BLAUS	...	Blauer See Delikatessen	Hanna Moos	Sales Representative	Forsterstr. 57	Mannheim		68306	Germany	0621-08460	0621-08924
	BLONP	...	Blondesddsl père et fils	Frédérique Citeaux	Marketing Manager	24, place Kléber	Strasbourg		67000	France	88.60.15.31	88.60.15.32
	BOLID	...	Bólido Comidas preparadas	Martín Sommer	Owner	C/ Araquil, 67	Madrid		28023	Spain	(91) 555 22 82	(91) 555 91 99
	BONAP	...	Bon app'	Laurence Lebihan	Owner	12, rue des Bouchers	Marseille		13008	France	91.24.45.40	91.24.45.41
	BOTTM	...	Bottom-Dollar Markets	Elizabeth Lincoln	Accounting Manager	23 Tsawassen Blvd.	Tsawassen	BC	T2F 8M4	Canada	(604) 555-4729	(604) 555-3745
	BSBEV	...	B's Beverages	Victoria Ashworth	Sales Representative	Fauntleroy Circus	London		EC2 5NT	UK	(171) 555-1212	
	CACTU	...	Cactus Comidas para llevar	Patricio Simpson	Sales Agent	Cerrito 333	Buenos Aires		1010	Argentina	(1) 135-5555	(1) 135-4892
	CENTC	...	Centro comercial Moctezuma	Francisco Chang	Marketing Manager	Sierras de Granada 9993	México D.F.		05022	Mexico	(5) 555-3392	(5) 555-7293

Figure 13.47 Microsoft Office 365 Application with OData

13.4   Microsoft LightSwitch

Microsoft LightSwitch is a Visual Studio product for creating business enterprise applications. The applications are built on Microsoft platforms and .NET technologies, and the UI runs on Microsoft Silverlight and an HTML5 client, or as a Microsoft SharePoint 2013 application. It supports data sources such as Microsoft SharePoint, OData, and Windows Communication Foundation (WCF) services. The business logic can be written in Visual Basic or Visual C#, and the design of entities, relationships, and user interface screens is managed with an included graphic designer.

Microsoft LightSwitch: Minimum Requirements

▸ Visual Studio 2012
▸ .NET Framework

To start a new Microsoft LightSwitch project, follow these steps:

Create the application

1. Start Visual Studio 2012, and select FILE • NEW • PROJECT.

2. Choose LIGHTSWITCH on the left menu bar, and select the programming language of your choice. You'll create a new Visual Basic project in this example (Figure 13.48).

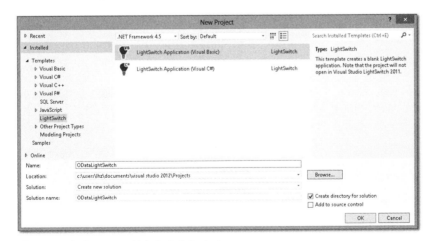

Figure 13.48 Creating a LightSwitch Project

3. Enter a project name, and click OK. After your project is created, Visual Studio opens a START WITH DATA screen.

4. Click the ATTACH TO EXTERNAL DATA SOURCE link to open the ATTACH DATA SOURCE WIZARD. First, you have to choose the data source, which is an ODATA SERVICE (Figure 13.49) in our scenario.

Figure 13.49 Data Source Type OData Service

5. Click NEXT, and you'll be asked to specify the OData service endpoint.

> **Warning**
>
> The media element data type isn't supported by Microsoft LightSwitch (this is a general issue, not an SAP-specific issue). Microsoft LightSwitch simply ignores these elements if they're included.

OData service 6. Specify the SAP Gateway service URL with the authentication type set to OTHER, and enter your credentials (Figure 13.50).

Select entities 7. Click NEXT, and the plug-in fetches the available entities and displays them in a selectable tree view. You can mark the necessary entities by clicking on their checkboxes (Figure 13.51).

Figure 13.50 Attaching the Data Source Wizard OData Service Endpoint

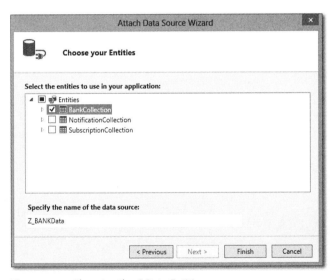

Figure 13.51 Choosing the OData Entities

8. The name of the data source is the OData service name by default, but this can be changed if you want. Click FINISH. The tool then generates the corresponding data source and shows the selected entities on the designer screen as a table (Figure 13.52).

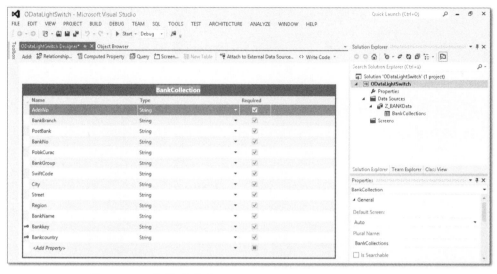

Figure 13.52 Entity Data Source

9. This table isn't a screen element, so you have to add a new screen manually to display the datasets from the OData service. Right-click the Screens folder in the Solution Explorer on the right side, and click the Add Screen button.

Add screen   10. A pop-up appears where you select the screen template Editable Grid Screen. Select your screen data source from the dropdown menu on the right side, and enter a screen name into the Screen Name field (Figure 13.53).

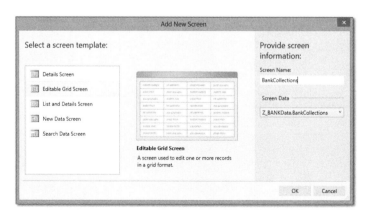

Figure 13.53 Adding a New Screen Template

11. Click OK. The ODATALIGHT DESIGNER opens with the selected collection and the default screen layout with all available attributes. Add, delete, or rearrange the attributes in the data grid row (Figure 13.54).

OData LightSwitch application

Figure 13.54 ODataLight Designer: Layout

12. When you're finished, press ⌷F5⌷ to build and start the application. The created data grid appears, and the fetched data from the OData service is shown (Figure 13.55).

Figure 13.55 ODataLight Application

621

Now you've created a simple Microsoft LightSwitch application with OData as the data source, which is the basis for further development.

13.5   Microsoft Active Server Pages (ASP) .NET

Microsoft ASP.NET is a server-side web application framework. It's part of the .NET Framework, so when coding ASP.NET applications, you have access to classes in the .NET Framework. In addition, you can code applications in any language compatible with the common language runtime (CLR), including Microsoft Visual Basic and C#.

If you're still using Visual Studio 2010, you can take a look inside SCN, where you'll find a guide on how to install and use the SAP Gateway Developer Tool for Visual Studio.

> **Warning**
>
> There is a separate standalone plug-in called SAP Gateway Developer Tool for Visual Studio available on SCN, but the tool only supports Visual Studio 2010. The statement in the SAP documentation that claims the plug-in is compatible with "Visual Studio 2010 or *higher*" is wrong.

Because the SAP plug-in for Microsoft ASP.NET doesn't work for Visual Studio 2012, Listing 13.2 shows you how to consume an OData service with any version of Visual Studio.

```
private static void GetCarrierByID()
{
    // Carrier ID for search
    string carrierId = "AA"; //American Airlines

/** SAP Gateway OData service **/
string serviceUrl = "http://<Gateway_Host>:<Gateway_Port>/sap/
opu/odata/iwfnd/RMTSAMPLEFLIGHT/";

RMTSAMPLEFLIGHT.RMTSAMPLEFLIGHT service = new RMTSAMPLEFLIGHT.R
MTSAMPLEFLIGHT(
    new Uri(serviceUrl));
    service.Credentials = new NetworkCredential(username, passw
ord);
```

```
/** Execute **/
var carrier = (from Carrier c in service.CarrierCollection
            where c.carrid == carrierId
            select c).FirstOrDefault();

/** Write result to console **/
Console.WriteLine(String.Format("Carrier ID = {0}",carrier.carr
id));
Console.WriteLine(String.Format("Carrier Name = {0}",carrier.ca
rrname));
}
```

Listing 13.2 .NET Application Code Snippet

13.6 Summary

After reading this chapter, you should be able to develop applications with GWM and provide data to consumers such as Microsoft Share-Point, Outlook, and Excel. Even if you're not a technical expert, with the Service Builder functionalities discussed in earlier chapters and, for example, the PowerPivot plug-in, you can provide and consume data from SAP by yourself. In this context, we also developed a LightSwitch sample application and gave you sample coding for Microsoft ASP.NET. The examples in this chapter explore only a small amount of possible options for enterprise application development with SAP Gateway.

PART IV
Administration

This chapter highlights a number of topics not directly linked to SAP Gateway development but still important for a production environment.

14 Lifecycle Management: Testing, Service Deployment, and Operations

Like all software developments, SAP Gateway-based software developments follow a certain lifecycle. Typically, it starts with the identification of a business need and the analysis of user requirements, which is then followed by designing a solution for the specific need with both the SAP Business Suite and the frontend specialists. Then the actual implementation, testing, documentation, and deployment of the SAP Gateway services takes place, optionally followed by the setup and configuration of SAP API Management, the rollout of the frontend developments for the different platforms, and, finally, maintenance and operations. Usually, this process doesn't stop but is incremental and looks like a spiral; as soon as new business needs come up, the process phases are executed once again (Figure 14.1). Compared with the first time, however, it starts on top of what is already there, building on the existing foundation.

SAP Gateway solution lifecycle

In this chapter, we focus on three selected SAP Gateway solution lifecycle phases: *testing*, *deploying*, and *operating* an SAP Gateway environment. The other phases (*design* and *implementation*) have been addressed throughout Chapter 5, Chapter 6, and Chapter 7. The phases covered in this chapter aren't directly related to development. However, they are very important for the success of your SAP Gateway project.

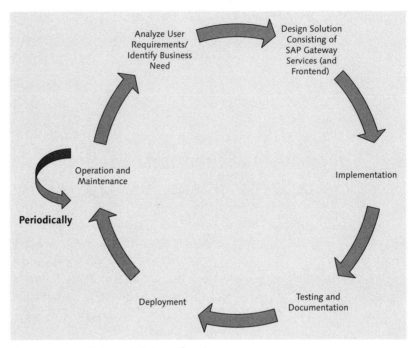

Figure 14.1 SAP Gateway Solution Lifecycle

14.1 Testing

Three-tier architecture

SAP Gateway's three-tier architecture (SAP Business Suite tier, SAP Gateway tier, and consumer tier) on the one hand facilitates testing by providing obvious and straightforward interfaces to be tested; on the other hand, it can create new challenges due to the different technologies used (ABAP, client technology) and the fact that people with different know-how who belong to different departments in the organization have to be involved.

In general, it's easy to give test recommendations for the SAP Gateway/ABAP side of things because this technology stays the same in all projects. For the client side, it gets a lot harder because the multiple possible client technologies might require different test approaches. Just think of a mobile application that should ideally be tested on the device and not only in an emulator, which could result in a bigger test setup—meaning

628

that these tests are only worth performing after the application has reached a certain maturity level. At the same time, a simple HTML5 application can easily be tested very early during development, potentially even with agile/test-driven development methods.

This is especially true for applications based on SAPUI5, which can be deployed on the SAP Gateway hub system. These applications have a lifecycle similar to OData services based on SAP Gateway because SAPUI5 applications are technically deployed on an ABAP system as a Business Server Page (BSP).

In this section, we'll introduce you to the process of testing both SAP Gateway services and client applications. We'll end the section with some general best practices for testing.

14.1.1 Testing SAP Gateway Services

Testing OData services that have been developed with SAP Gateway can be done independently of the target platform from which the service will be used. SAP provides several tools as part of the SAP Gateway platform that facilitate the testing of services. The two main tools are the *SAP Gateway client* and the *service validation tool*. Both are described in detail in this section.

Main test tools

SAP Gateway Client

The SAP Gateway client (Transaction /IWFND/GW_CLIENT) is a powerful tool that provides the freedom to test any OData service. This enables you to test your OData services proactively and run a quality assurance test before a service is used. The SAP Gateway client allows you to do the following:

- Create test cases for OData services.
- Save the created test cases and replay them at any time.
- Simulate a service at runtime to identify and resolve potential issues.
- Reproduce the runtime situations that led to a particular error.
- Run several test cases in a sequential order to test more complex scenarios of creating, updating, reading, and deleting data.

The SAP Gateway client is fully integrated with other SAP Gateway tools such as Transaction /IWFND/MAINT_SERVICE (Maintain Service) or Transaction /IWFND/ERROR_LOG (Error Log) to allow for following up on identified problems efficiently. It acts as an HTTP client and enables the testing of HTTP requests and responses as they arise at runtime. The SAP Gateway client is started using Transaction /IWFND/GW_CLIENT, and its user interface (UI) is shown in Figure 14.2.

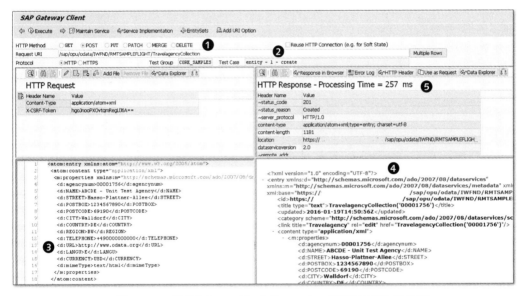

Figure 14.2 SAP Gateway Client: Transaction /IWFND/GW_CLIENT

You can perform GET, PUT, POST, PATCH, DELETE, and MERGE HTTP methods ❶. The tool provides an area for entering the REQUEST URI ❷ and a screen area for the actual HTTP request ❸. This HTTP request area can be filled with the service data (request payload) either directly or by uploading from a local file. After you've executed the request, the response is displayed in the HTTP response frame ❹. If an error arises as a result of the test, the HTTP status and value are displayed. You can then display details of the HTTP response, display the response in an additional browser window, or navigate to the ERROR LOG transaction tab ❺ to analyze and correct the error.

To facilitate repeated testing, the SAP Gateway client is integrated with an underlying database allowing for accessing request data already stored in that database or for storing your own test cases in that database. Stored test cases can then be executed repeatedly. Test cases can be grouped into test groups so that they are easier to retrieve. It's especially possible to store the expected HTTP return codes for each test case. If the return code differs from the one that has been specified as the expected one in the test case, the test case is shown as erroneous (❶ of Figure 14.3).

Test cases and groups

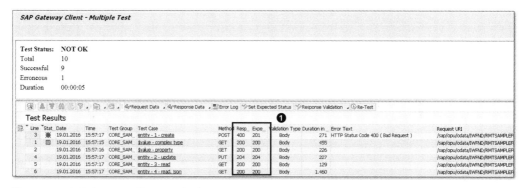

Figure 14.3 SAP Gateway Client: Multiple Test Screen

To further facilitate testing, SAP delivers the test group CORE_SAMPLES that already contains sample data for your testing. You can enable these test cases for usage by selecting SAP GATEWAY CLIENT • CREATE CORE_SAMPLES from the menu in your SAP Gateway client. Existing test cases can be adapted to your needs, or you can define and save your own.

Test cases delivered by SAP

After running your test cases, the results are displayed on the SAP GATEWAY CLIENT – MULTIPLE TEST screen as shown in Figure 14.3. At a glance, you can see the STATUS of the test indicated by a traffic light icon, the HTTP METHOD, HTTP RESPONSE, EXPECTED STATUS, descriptive ERROR TEXT, a REQUEST URI, and the TEST GROUP. In case of errors, you can jump to the error log by clicking the ERROR LOG button, and after fixing the problem that led to the error, you can click the RE-TEST button to run a retest.

> **Data Explorer**
>
> Another SAP Gateway client feature (available from SAP Gateway SP 08 onwards) is the Data Explorer. The Data Explorer allows you to display the response payload of an OData request in a user-friendly table. Remember, the response can be formatted in XML or JavaScript Object Notation (JSON) format, or for a $batch request, as a combination of these formats. Therefore, some help in making these formats even more readable and navigable is sometimes highly beneficial. To start the Data Explorer, click the DATA EXPLORER button in the SAP Gateway client. To go back to the original payload, click ORIGINAL PAYLOAD.

CSRF   The SAP Gateway client also supports you when performing WRITE operations. Here the cross-site request forgery (XSRF) token that is needed for such operations is acquired automatically. (This is opposed to the approach of using a third-party REST client. In that case, you first have to perform a separate GET request to fetch a XSRF token for any subsequent Update, Create, or Delete operation.)

Note that the SAP Gateway client requests a new XSRF token for every READ operation. As a result, the token displayed in the transaction changes all of the time, although it has a certain lifetime.

Another highlight of the SAP Gateway client is that you can access SAP performance statistics for each OData request without having to activate the Performance Trace tool. To obtain the SAP performance statistics, you can add *?sap-statistics=true* at the end of the request URL, regardless of whether it's an HTTP method of type GET, POST, PUT, MERGE, PATCH, or DELETE. Alternatively, you can enter (name=sap-statistics, value=true) in the HTTP request header.

> **Further Resources**
>
> More details on the SAP Gateway client can be found here:
>
> *http://help.sap.com/saphelp_gateway20sp11/helpdata/en/84/cdd122239d4d d0bee1da7fe4a16850/content.htm*

Service Validation Tool

Runtime validation   SAP Gateway offers a validation tool that validates the runtime for all SAP Gateway services. Runtime validation ensures that the runtime is behaving as intended with no issues (such as syntax errors in programs, RFC authorization issues, etc.). It involves executing READ and QUERY operations on the collections exposed via the service document and checking the HTTP response code. For READ operations, the tool also takes care of executing the self-links for all the collections and all the navigation properties in a recursive manner. No user intervention is required during this process.

To validate a service, go to Transaction /IWFND/SRV_VALIDATE, and enter the service document identifier. Select VALIDATE SERVICE, and choose EXECUTE. This takes you automatically to the results. After a validation run, you can select DISPLAY LAST RUN RESULTS on the main page and choose EXECUTE to look at the detailed results without needing to execute the full run again.

---

eCATT-Based Test Automation for OData Services

The extended Computer Aided Test Tool (eCATT) is one of the main tools used by customers to create and execute functional tests. Its primary goal is the automated testing of business processes in SAP. Find more information on using eCATT for the automated testing of OData services at *http://scn.sap.com/docs/DOC-64981*.

14.1.2 Testing a Client Application

Testing the client application is a complex topic because there are so many client platforms that can be used to call SAP Gateway services. Therefore, providing you with detailed recommendations on how to test your specific client application on your specific technology is beyond the scope of this book.

What is possible, however, is to look at the three main categories of SAP Gateway projects and identify commonalities of the three project categories as well as some differences that you need to take into account for your test strategies:

Project categories

▶ **Mobile**
This category contains all SAP Gateway projects in which applications are deployed on mobile devices (e.g., smartphones, tablets, notebooks) and use SAP Gateway to access SAP Business Suite systems.

Examples of mobile applications include Android applications, iPhone applications, and BlackBerry applications.

▶ **Desktop**

This category contains all projects in which an application using SAP Gateway services is developed for a stationary device, typically a PC. Examples for desktop applications include, for example, an application built using Microsoft .NET.

▶ **Web**

This category contains all projects that use SAP Gateway for web-based access to SAP Business Suite systems. Examples include Facebook applications, browser applications using HTML5 and JavaScript, and browser-based applications based on the Hypertext Preprocessor (PHP).

Most other use cases and architectures are subcategories of these three main categories. The type of an SAP Gateway project has a significant impact on its lifecycle. A lot of things can be addressed very similarly, whereas other topics differ to a major extent from one type to another. In respect to an impact on testing, the following are some commonalities of the three categories of SAP Gateway projects just defined:

▶ Clients consume SAP Gateway services and rely on their accuracy. It's hard for the client application to identify incorrect data (although not impossible). Test cases should be created in the SAP Gateway client containing all requests that are planned to be issued by the consumer applications.

▶ It's hard to decide in which direction to test. In an ideal world, you start bottom up, meaning that you first verify the accuracy of the SAP Gateway services. Only then, the client application developers start their development. Unfortunately, the world isn't perfect, and for cost or availability reasons, the work of both teams (i.e., the SAP Gateway service team and the client application team) may significantly, if not completely, overlap each other.

▶ To make things even worse, it may be that team members aren't experienced in both the client and the SAP Business Suite side, which has the potential to make communication between the two teams difficult. Fortunately, the OData protocol helps here because the entity data model serves as a contract between the SAP and the non-SAP developers. SAP Gateway certainly facilitates the process of bringing the client developers and the SAP Business Suite developers together a lot better than traditional approaches; however, there are still some gaps between these two worlds that need to be bridged.

Additional factors come into play when testing SAP Gateway client applications. These factors are project-category specific and therefore don't apply for every single client application you develop. However, if they are relevant, they have a strong impact on testing. Following are the factors to consider:

▶ **Online versus offline**
In almost all cases, web and desktop clients are used in always-online production environments. Therefore, a loss of connection should be looked at as a test case to see how your application reacts. At the same time, this will only result in a few test cases in your test plan. For some mobile applications, this might be different; that is, business-critical applications might have to run offline (i.e., when the connection is lost or the network connection is poor or unreliable). This does require additional development and testing effort.

▶ **Additional components**
Additional components or technical mechanisms can influence application behavior and need to be taken into account for tests. Examples include the use of SAP Mobile Platform together with SAP Gateway or the impact of security mechanisms for web applications.

As stated earlier, from an SAP Gateway perspective, we can only briefly mention these topics. In the end, these are development and quality assurance topics on the client side. From an SAP Gateway perspective, the main testing concern is how best to synchronize the client application development with the SAP Gateway service development.

14.1.3 Best Practices for Testing in SAP Gateway

The focus of this best practices section lies on assuring and verifying the quality of the developed SAP Gateway services and on a working setup for the development project in respect to early usage of verified SAP

Testing best practices

635

Gateway services in client application development. Consider the following best practices for testing:

▸ Before your project starts, make sure that the two development teams (client application, SAP Business Suite) talk to each other and verify that the planned SAP Gateway services deliver the right data for the client application. Unused data transferred via SAP Gateway services lowers performance levels. A missing field in the client application can result in some overhead (e.g., testing, communication). So some kind of dry testing pays off; in other words, check on whether your specifications fit both the client side and SAP Gateway side early.

▸ SAP Gateway service development usually starts first. There is no need for a major head start; a few days should be enough. Give the team sufficient time, though.

▸ Services should be grouped according to their use in the client application. Ideally, parts of the client application can already be based on developed and working SAP Gateway services. That way, client application developers can test their development against the real services at development time; there's no need for stubs on the client side, which saves time and improves quality. Overall, this results in an incremental approach. A good recommendation here in case of a tight project schedule is to use stubs on the SAP Gateway side to cater for the early consumption of services.

▸ Developed SAP Gateway services should be thoroughly tested using test tools, for example, the SAP Gateway client. When services have reached a certain maturity, these can then be handed over to the client application development. Additional tests can then be executed using the client application when it's ready to further improve the overall quality.

▸ Perform tests in the production environment early. That is, make sure that no surprises can come up with respect to the technical environment (e.g., reverse proxies, ports) or to the hardware you'll run the client application on (e.g., the development took place using an emulator only). Obviously, these early tests can't always be performed end to end at a very early stage. You can, however, run selected tests. It doesn't matter whether you call an SAP Gateway service using a browser or the client application. You detect the same problems between the browser and SAP Gateway as you would between the client application and SAP Gateway.

▶ Technically, using the `sap-ds-debug=true` query option facilitates improved testing with the browser because the XML or JSON response is rendered as an HTML page. Because of this, any browser can be used for testing, and the test results don't depend on the browser being used. In addition, using the `sap-ds-debug=true` query option shows many additional details that can be of interest during troubleshooting.

▶ Include `sap-statistics=true` at the end of your request URLs to obtain performance statistics early. That way, you can get an impression of how much your service calls cost from a performance perspective and can optimize performance early.

Overall, both OData and SAP Gateway have been designed for early and easy testing, which should result in a great service and application quality.

14.2 Service Deployment

After both the developed SAP Gateway services and the client application have reached the required maturity level, it's time for the rollout. A *classic rollout* is one where you take some piece of ready-to-use software to its future users. This type of rollout is appropriate for the client application in mobile and desktop categories, but for SAP Gateway services, this description only partially fits. The services simply have to be deployed on the SAP Gateway server or the SAP Business Suite system using the Change and Transport System (CTS). An explanation of how to roll out client applications is beyond the scope of this book. Instead, we'll focus on the SAP Gateway part, which is more of a deployment than a rollout.

As you saw in Chapter 5, Chapter 6, and Chapter 7, several repository objects, such as ABAP classes, have to be created when building an OData service. It's important to note that repository objects have to be created not only on the SAP Business Suite system but also on the SAP

Repository objects

Gateway server system. In addition to repository objects, you need to create customizing entries on the SAP Gateway server system as well. All of these repository objects and customizing entries have to be transported at the customer site using the CTS so that they can finally be used in production.

Versioning In the following, we'll take a closer look at the lifecycle management of an SAP Gateway service by first describing which repository objects have to be transported between the SAP Business Suite systems. Then we'll dive into the lifecycle management activities that have to take place on the SAP Gateway servers. Here we'll describe which repository objects have to be transported between the SAP Gateway servers in a system landscape and how customizing settings have to be transported. At the end of this section, we'll explain the concept of versioning that is supported by SAP Gateway services and investigate the different capabilities of Transaction /IWFND/MAINT_SERVICE (Activate and Maintain Services), which is used for service maintenance on SAP Gateway server systems. Versioning as a feature can be of interest if changes are performed in SAP Gateway services that aren't compatible with an already rolled out client software. In this case, multiple versions of clients and services have to be supported in parallel.

> **Deployment Options and Lifecycle Management**
>
> Of the different deployment options discussed in Chapter 4 (hub deployment with development in the SAP Business Suite system, hub deployment with development on the hub, and embedded deployment), one option needs special attention. In the case of hub deployment with development in the SAP Business Suite system, the transport of repository objects and customizing entries has to be synchronized between the SAP Gateway hub and the SAP Business Suite system—or at least you must ensure that the SAP Business Suite system transports are transported first so that the artifacts are available when registering and activating the service on the SAP Gateway hub.
>
> The other two deployment options are easier to handle because all development artifacts and customizing entries are created in and transported to only one system, where both the SAP Gateway server and SAP Gateway backend enablement components are installed.

14.2.1 Transport of Repository Objects between SAP Business Suite Systems

In this section, the backend system we refer to is the system in which the development of an OData service takes place. Depending on the deployment option being chosen, this can also be on the SAP Gateway hub system if IW_BEP is deployed or, if the hub system runs on top of 7.40 or higher, the system on which the SAP_GWFND software component is present.

As a result of the development of an SAP Gateway service using the SAP Gateway Service Builder, the following repository objects are created:

Repository object examples

- Four ABAP classes:
  - ▹ Data provider class (DPC)
  - ▹ Data provider extension class
  - ▹ Model provider class (MPC)
  - ▹ Model provider extension class
- Service object
- Model object
- Service Builder project

These repository objects (listed in Table 14.1) have to be transported into the quality and production systems, as depicted in Figure 14.4.

Short Description	Program ID	Object Type	Example of an Object Name
Service Builder Project	R3TR	IWPR	Z_PRODUCT
Class	R3TR	CLAS	ZCL_Z_PRODUCT_MPC
Class	R3TR	CLAS	ZCL_Z_PRODUCT_MPC_EXT
Class	R3TR	CLAS	ZCL_Z_PRODUCT_DPC
Class	R3TR	CLAS	ZCL_Z_PRODUCT_DPC_EXT
Model object	R3TR	IWMO	ZPRODUCT_MDL
Service object	R3TR	IWSV	Z_PRODUCT

Table 14.1 Repository Objects of an SAP Gateway Service in the Backend System

When importing these repository objects in the quality- or production backend system, the service is automatically registered in that system. To be able to consume the OData service, it has to be registered and activated in the SAP Gateway hub system. This process is described in Section 14.2.2.

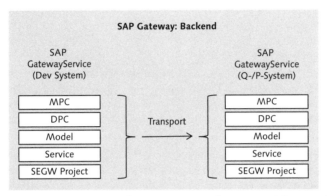

Figure 14.4 Repository Objects to Transport between SAP Business Suite Backend Systems

Transporting Service Builder project not mandatory

To use the service in other systems of the transport system landscape, transporting the Service Builder project isn't mandatory—it's enough to only transport the runtime components. You may find it convenient, however, to also have the Service Builder project available because you can then open and use it as an entry point for Transaction SEGW if needed for troubleshooting.

14.2.2 Transport of Repository Objects and Customizing Entries between SAP Gateway Server Systems

In addition to the service implementation in the backend, the service has to be activated in the SAP Gateway hub, and it might have to be registered for additional backend systems. As a result (as described in Chapter 5, Chapter 6, and Chapter 7), there are several repository objects and customizing entries created during development in the SAP Gateway hub system that then need to be transported. The administrator has to maintain some customizing settings directly in the quality and production system, however, rather than transporting them, for reasons we'll explain next.

In the SAP Gateway hub development system, only three repository objects are created:

- Service model
- Service
- Internet Communication Framework (ICF) node

In addition, the following customizing settings are created:

- System alias (which might have already existed)
- Assignment of the system alias to the activated service

These objects are depicted in ❶ of Figure 14.5. In addition, the repository objects that have to be transported are listed in Table 14.2.

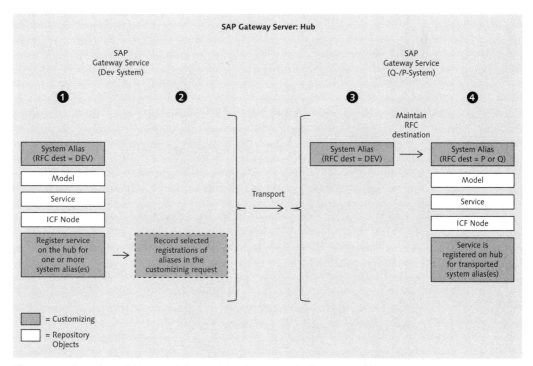

Figure 14.5 Repository Objects and Customizing Settings to Be Transported between the SAP Gateway Server Systems

Short Description	Program ID	Object Type	Example of an Object Name
Service	R3TR	IWSG	ZPRODUCT_SRV_0001
Model	R3TR	IWOM	ZPRODUCT_MDL_0001_BE
ICF node	R3TR	SICF	00O2TMQPDL0AX-GC2ZZH2Y8XW1

Table 14.2 Repository Objects of an SAP Gateway Service in the SAP Gateway Hub System

Customizing entries

The customizing entries that are created as part of the service creation process on the SAP Gateway server development system need special attention. Some customizing settings have to be manually included in a customizing request because they aren't recorded automatically. In addition, it's necessary to perform certain customizing steps on the SAP Gateway production system because these can't be transported. We'll discuss these processes next.

Transporting the Assignment of System Aliases

When using Transaction /IWFND/MAINT_SERVICE (Activate and Maintain Services) to activate a service on the SAP Gateway hub and to assign it for one or more backend systems, the customizing settings that are being created aren't recorded automatically. You have to record these settings *manually* in a customizing request instead (refer to ❷ of Figure 14.5) because it can't be taken for granted that a system alias entry does exist in other systems of the SAP Gateway system landscape.

This sometimes leads to the issue that the customizing settings that are necessary for the service to be correctly activated aren't transported. In turn, this leads to an error message in the target system if a client tries to consume the incorrectly activated service.

The transport of services usually performed by the system administrator—not the developer—so this shouldn't be an issue as long as this behavior is known to the system administrator, and the customizing settings are being manually recorded and transported. The manual recording of the customizing settings shouldn't be overlooked though.

Transporting System Aliases

In an implementation done on SAP Gateway as a hub, there is the need to access SAP Business Suite systems or third-party systems via remote function call (RFC), web services, or the OData protocol. The content provider connectivity abstracts from such protocol specifics by means of a system alias, which can be configured by the administrator to point to the desired RFC, web service, or HTTP destination. Due to their importance, the handling of these system alias entries needs special attention in a production SAP Gateway landscape.

What makes this very useful concept sometimes a little bit tricky is the fact that in development and production systems, destinations usually have different names. The reason for this is that often customer naming conventions for RFC destinations might, for example, contain the logical system name of the target system or other means that let the user conclude to which system the destination points. As a result, it's unfortunately required to maintain these system-specific settings in the system alias entries in every SAP Gateway hub system that is part of an SAP Gateway landscape (development, quality assurance, and production).

Destinations with different names

Technically, the settings for a system alias entry are stored in customizing tables that can be maintained using the /IWFND/V_DFSYAL view. Because clients in a production system are usually locked to prevent customizing changes, it's not possible, by default, to maintain the /IWFND/V_DFSYAL view unless the system is opened. Obviously, opening up a production system for this task is out of the question due to legal requirements, unless exceptional circumstances require such changes (e.g., during an upgrade). It is possible, however, to use a concept called *current settings* that has been introduced to address similar situations.

Table maintenance is started via a customizing task in the IMG, which is classified to allow such changes by having been declared as a current setting. The customizing task for system alias maintenance is configured accordingly. As a result, you can maintain a system alias if the maintenance dialog is opened via the IMG. For this, you have to start Transaction SPRO and navigate to SAP NETWEAVER • SAP GATEWAY • ODATA CHANNEL • CONFIGURATION • CONNECTION SETTINGS • SAP GATEWAY TO SAP SYSTEM.

> **Note**
>
> Note that in an SAP Gateway hub prior to SAP Gateway 2.0 SP 06, you have to change the settings in the IMG for the customizing object manually as described in SAP Note 135028: Transfer IMG Activity to Current Setting.

Using this concept of current settings, customers can now create system aliases once in the development system and then transport the system aliases to the production system. In the production system, the system administrator is able to maintain the RFC, web service, or HTTP destination that is actually used by a system alias in the target system.

14.2.3 Versioning

SAP Gateway provides versioning to keep older and newer SAP Gateway service versions separate. This is essential to enable different versions of a service to be available for consumption in parallel.

Version numbers
By default, every initial SAP Gateway service is registered and activated with version number 1. If the service is developed further, and any changes are incompatible to the consumers that already use the service, you can register and activate the SAP Gateway service with an increased version number (e.g., 2 or 3, etc.). This version number is a four-digit value, so you can potentially create 9,999 versions of your service.

When consuming this service, the consumer has to add, for example, *;v=2* to the URI to access version 2 of the service, for example:

http://<host>:<port>/sap/opu/odata/iwfnd/catalogservice;v=2/

Technically, each new version of a service is very similar to a completely new service. Each version has its own MPC as well as a DPC. This allows for keeping the entire logic of, for example, version 1 (which might be in production already) and defining everything independently for version 2.

14.2.4 Activate and Maintain Service Transaction

OData services need to be maintained and activated in the SAP Gateway hub system. To perform this task, you have to start Transaction /IWFND/MAINT_SERVICE on the SAP Gateway hub system.

On the first screen, the service catalog is displayed that contains a list of services that have been activated in the current system. Note that this list can also be retrieved using *http://<server>:<port>/sap/opu/odata/iwfnd/ CATALOGSERVICE/*.

A service can be tested by selecting it from the list and choosing either Call Browser or SAP Gateway Client in the ICF Nodes section. The Activate and Maintain Services screen lets you perform the following tasks as shown in Figure 14.6:

❶ Register and activate a new service in the hub.

❷ Start the error log for the selected service.

❸ Test the selected service using a browser.

❹ Test the selected service using the SAP Gateway client.

❺ Add additional system alias entries for the selected service.

❻ Delete the system alias assignment for the selected service.

❼ Inspect service implementation.

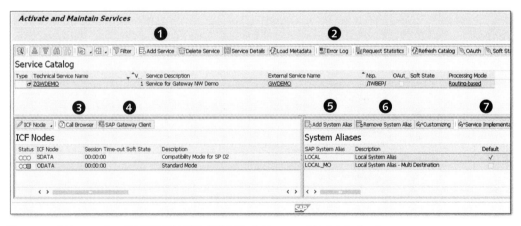

Figure 14.6 Transaction /IWFND/MAINT_SERVICE: Activate and Maintain Services

SAP wanted to make the process of activating a service on the development SAP Gateway hub system as convenient as possible for the service developer. Therefore, it's possible to start the service registration and activation on the SAP Gateway hub from within the Service Builder. You simply right-click on the SAP Gateway hub entry you want to register your service to and activate on, and then select REGISTER from the context menu.

14.3 Operations

The operations phase of the SAP Gateway lifecycle primarily consists of recurring tasks that shouldn't be neglected. Because operations isn't a one-time event but an ongoing task, operating your environment in a smart way is crucial. In this section, we'll first take a brief look at some periodic cleanup tasks before taking a deep dive into SAP Gateway-related monitoring. We'll wrap this section up with some troubleshooting best practices.

14.3.1 Periodic Cleanup Tasks

After rollout, periodic tasks need to be performed frequently to ensure that SAP Gateway runs smoothly and the performance stays optimal. Specifically, you need to use cleanup jobs on the SAP Gateway server systems that are executed on a regular basis. The frequency of running the different services depends on the load of your system and may vary.

Daily Jobs for Usage Data

When activating SAP Gateway, two daily jobs are scheduled that aggregate usage data and delete outdated usage data:

- SAP_IWFND_METERING_AGG is scheduled as a daily job that aggregates data based on report /IWFND/R_MET_AGGREGATE.
- SAP_IWFND_METERING_DEL is scheduled as a daily job that deletes data older than two years based on report /IWFND/R_MET_DELETE.

Application Log

Flag With respect to the application log, there's a flag that controls what is written into the application log (e.g., only errors or also warnings).

Make sure this flag is set appropriately. Otherwise, over time, the application log might amass a lot of entries. Nevertheless, even with limited settings, you need to periodically clear the application log. To limit the amount of data stored, the application log should only store one entry per request as a default. In addition, there's no need to store these entries for more than a few days.

In an SAP Gateway server, the application log can be cleared in the SAP Gateway IMG structure by following the navigation path, TRANSACTION SPRO • SAP NETWEAVER • SAP GATEWAY • ODATA CHANNEL • ADMINISTRATION • LOGGING SETTINGS • CLEAR APPLICATION LOG.

In an SAP Business Suite system IMG, follow the navigation path, TRANSACTION SPRO • SAP NETWEAVER • SAP GATEWAY SERVICE ENABLEMENT • BACKEND ODATA CHANNEL • LOGGING SETTINGS • CLEAR APPLICATION LOG.

It's recommended to carry out the activity, plan a job, and use Report SBAL_DELETE to clear the application log.

14.3.2 Monitoring Overview

SAP Gateway comes with an optimized set of tools to first identify issues in your SAP Gateway environment (i.e., monitoring) and then, in a second step, allow you to dig deeper into the issue to solve it (i.e., troubleshooting). This set of tools is connected in several ways to allow you to jump from one tool to another when appropriate, saving time and making it easier to follow up on potential errors. The goal is for you to be able to concentrate on finding the problem and not on the tooling.

SAP Gateway tackles the monitoring and troubleshooting topic from several sides:

Monitoring and troubleshooting

▸ **Computing Center Management System (CCMS)**
Monitors the SAP Gateway system environment and alerts the system administrator if it detects potential issues.

▸ **Error log**
Provides detailed information about SAP Gateway runtime errors and allows for root cause analysis. Use this tool to analyze errors that have

occurred and led to a termination of an OData request or notification processing (push channel). The error log can be accessed via Transaction /IWFND/ERROR_LOG on the SAP Gateway hub system or via Transaction /IWBEP/VIEW_LOG on the SAP Business Suite system.

▸ **Application log**
Enables viewing of the SAP Gateway application logs. This tool is recommended to check on more technical error details. Access the application log via Transaction /IWFND/APPS_LOG on the SAP Gateway system and Transaction /IWBEP/ERROR_LOG on the SAP Business Suite system.

▸ **SAP Solution Manager**
Monitors an SAP Gateway system landscape end to end. SAP Solution Manager delivers various monitors that raise alerts if certain error conditions are met. For example, an alert is raised if the number of errors in the error log exceeds a certain threshold.

▸ **Performance trace tool**
Offers detailed information on the performance behavior of SAP Gateway service calls. It's the tool of choice for service calls showing performance problems. You can access it via Transaction /IWFND/ TRACES.

Next, we'll discuss each of these tools in more detail. We'll conclude with some troubleshooting tips related to monitoring.

Monitoring via Computing Center Management System

Transaction RZ20 SAP Gateway is automatically monitored within the CCMS. The CCMS is provided in SAP NetWeaver and can be used immediately after installation. CCMS allows for collecting all monitoring information within your system landscape in the central monitoring system. Collected information about SAP Gateway can be viewed via Transaction RZ20. The information available here is updated on an hourly basis and includes which applications are in use and how often these are called.

Alerts are one central concept of the CCMS. These alerts are generated by the Alert Monitor if the status of a monitored system deviates from the norm. This deviation is identified by threshold values and rules. Alerts attract attention to critical situations and should be addressed by the system administrator. For SAP Gateway, this means that SAP Gateway-specific alerts point the system administrator to potential issues and greatly facilitate the monitoring of a production SAP Gateway environment.

Logging and Tracing via Error Log

The SAP Gateway error log is a very useful addition to the standard SAP NetWeaver application log viewer. We actually recommend the error log as the central point for logging in SAP Gateway. The tool can be accessed via Transaction /IWFND/ERROR_LOG. It can be used both on an SAP Gateway hub system and in an SAP Business Suite system. There you have to use Transaction /IWBEP/ERROR_LOG instead. The tool provides detailed context information about errors that have occurred at runtime by providing information in two screen areas: an OVERVIEW area and an ERROR CONTEXT area.

The SAP Gateway error log allows for identifying where exactly in the source code errors occur, seeing how often errors occur, reproducing errors, performing a root cause analysis, and, in the end, helping you fix the errors.

To facilitate this process, the error log is organized in an overview section (OVERVIEW area of the screen) and a detail section (ERROR CONTEXT area of the screen), as shown in Figure 14.7. The OVERVIEW area lists all error IDs, their attributes, and the date and time at which the particular errors occurred. Error information and descriptive error texts can be displayed to obtain more detailed information about a particular error. You can also execute searches on the error list.

Alerts

Overview and details

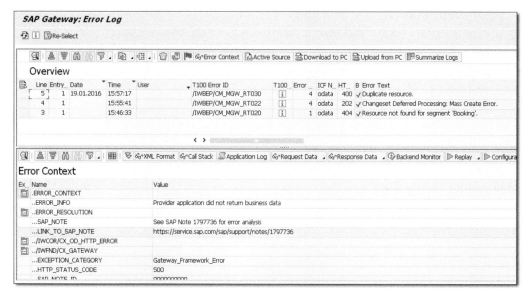

Figure 14.7 SAP Gateway: Error Log

Error context The ERROR CONTEXT area can be accessed by selecting an error in the OVERVIEW area and then double-clicking on the error information. The relevant context information about an error is then displayed in the ERROR CONTEXT area where further investigations are possible by expanding the information. The ERROR CONTEXT area provides you, among other things, with the following relevant information:

► XML FORMAT
Displays the error in context in an XML format, allowing you to see all information unfiltered.

► REQUEST DATA
Displays the request XML that was sent from an external consumer. This call contains HTTP request headers and payload.

► RESPONSE DATA
Displays the response XML sent from SAP Gateway. It contains the HTTP response headers and payload.

► REPLAY
Allows for two replay options (SAP Gateway client and web browser) to reproduce and correct errors.

► APPLICATION LOG

Allows for navigating to the corresponding entry in the application log.

Application Log Viewer

A specific Application Log Viewer tool allows you to view SAP Gateway application logs, as shown in Figure 14.8. To access this tool, go to Transaction /IWFND/APPS_LOG in the SAP Gateway hub system or Transaction /IWBEP/VIEW_LOG in the SAP Business Suite system. In the selection screen of this viewer, you can search log protocols by object, subobject, log ID, content ID, request direction, and date. The number of logs that are created can be adjusted to best serve your individual needs. This adjustment takes place in the SAP IMG in the logging settings.

Over time, the application log amasses a lot of entries, which periodically need to be cleared. As a default, it should only store one entry per request. In addition, it isn't necessary to store these entries for more than a few days.

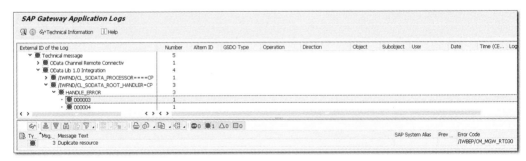

Figure 14.8 SAP Gateway Application Logs

Further Resources

More details on the SAP Gateway Application Log Viewer can be found here:

http://help.sap.com/saphelp_gateway20sp11/helpdata/en/d8/8afed0c41e4c45 93b5ecd48e8f2f76/content.htm

SAP Solution Manager

Technical monitoring in SAP Solution Manager also provides content for SAP Gateway. In addition to the content provided for ABAP systems in general, additional monitoring metrics have been added for the performance of SAP Gateway service requests and number of exceptions per time frame (5 minutes) in the SAP Gateway log as shown in Figure 14.9.

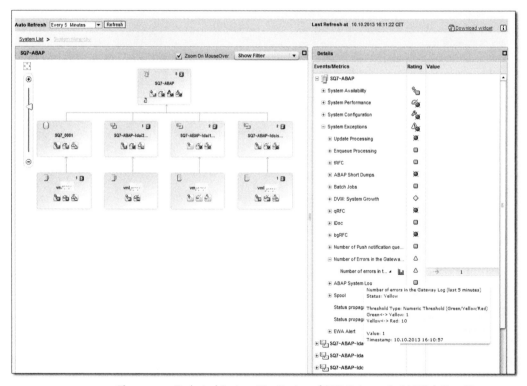

Figure 14.9 Technical System Monitoring of SAP Gateway in SAP Solution Manager

Performance Trace Tool

The SAP Gateway Performance Trace tool is a support utility for SAP Gateway that allows for monitoring system performance at a service call level. It's directed toward both developers and administrators of SAP Gateway services and enables tracing the performance of both the SAP Business Suite system and the SAP Gateway server (depending on the specific deployment).

> **Further Resources**
>
> More details on the SAP Gateway Performance Trace tool can be found in Appendix A, as well as at this link:
>
> *http://help.sap.com/saphelp_gateway20sp11/helpdata/en/9d/da3a2ceca344c f85568ae927e9858d/content.htm*

Before you can use the Performance Trace tool, you need to configure it according to your needs and activate it. To do the required configuration, go to Transaction /IWFND/TRACES (alternatively, you can go to Transaction SPRO, open the SAP Reference IMG, and then navigate to SAP NETWEAVER • SAP GATEWAY • ODATA CHANNEL • ADMINISTRATION • SUPPORT UTILITIES • TRACES). There you can configure the tool according to user name or URI prefix. **Configuration**

> **Note**
>
> To configure the Performance Trace tool for all OData service calls, enter the URI prefix "/sap/opu/."

After a successful configuration, the active trace is started and runs for two hours as a default. You can check the duration of the trace in the ACTIVE TRACE IS VALID UNTIL field. Figure 14.10 shows an activated performance trace.

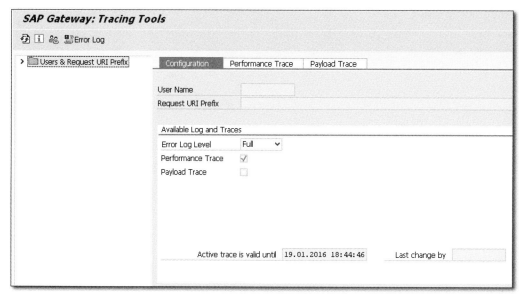

Figure 14.10 Activating the Performance Trace Tool

Tabular overview

If you now call any service according to the defined filter, the Performance Trace tool will generate information that you can display and analyze. To do so, go to the PERFORMANCE TRACE tab. You receive a tabular overview in which all service calls (after activation) are listed in chronological order.

The service call information is listed together with the ICF node, the date and time of the call, its expiry date, and the success of a specific service call execution, as shown in Figure 14.11.

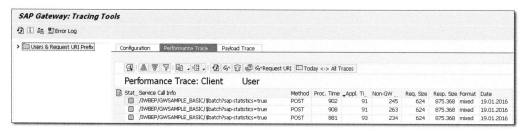

Figure 14.11 Performance Test Data

Additional information can be displayed for one or more service calls on demand. This information includes, for example, the number of sub-calls, the location of a service call (i.e., in the SAP Gateway system or the SAP Business Suite system), class, method, and—most important in a trace—the total duration and the net time of a service call (both in milliseconds).

The Performance Trace tool is well connected to other SAP Gateway tools and allows for an easy follow up on detected shortcomings. By double-clicking twice (on subsequent screens) on a service, you're taken to a detail screen where you can dig deeper into a topic. This can be done either by using SAP Gateway's error log tool or by directly jumping to the corresponding source code in the ABAP Development Workbench, as shown in Figure 14.12.

SAP Gateway: Performance Trace

Client 800 User   Status OK

Line No	Subcalls	Level	Location	Class	Method	Duration (ms)	Net Time (ms)
1	1	1	Hub System	/IWFND/CL_SODATA_HTTP_HANDLER	HANDLE_REQUEST	907	16
2				>Request Payload Size	624 Bytes		
3				>Response Payload Size	875368 Bytes		
4	14	2	Hub System	/IWFND/CL_SODATA_ROOT_HANDLER	DISPATCH	891	22
5		3	Hub System	/IWFND/CL_MED_MDL_PROVIDER	GET_SERVICE_GROUP	4	4
6	1	3	Hub System	/IWFND/CL_SODATA_ROOT_HANDLER	DISPATCH	14	7
7	1	4	Hub System	/IWFND/CL_SODATA_PROCESSOR	READ	7	6
8		5	Hub System	/IWFND/CL_MGW_PROV_DELEGATOR	GET_DATA_PROVIDER	1	1
9	1	3	Hub System	/IWFND/CL_SODATA_ROOT_HANDLER	DISPATCH	6	3
10	1	4	Hub System	/IWFND/CL_SODATA_PROCESSOR	READ	3	3

Figure 14.12 Performance Trace Data Single Request

> **Note**
>
> Performance trace log items have an expiration date. As a default, log items are stored for a duration of two days starting from the trace activation. It's possible to adjust these settings to your own needs.

Overall, the Performance Trace tool allows for an efficient and easy analysis of SAP Gateway service performance behavior and, as a result, enables you to identify time-consuming services efficiently. Using the integrated toolset, you can then follow up and improve the performance of service calls when needed.

Troubleshooting Tips

Troubleshooting is a science or an art depending on whether you take a more scientific, structured approach, or you let your experience and gut feelings guide you. To facilitate your search for the root cause of a problem in your SAP Gateway environment, consider the following tips:

▶ **Pair testing**
If your problem involves both the frontend and SAP Gateway/SAP Business Suite, it helps to choose a pair of testers that represent and know both worlds.

▶ **Incremental exclusion**
Make sure you exclude all infrastructure topics first. For example, verify using a browser that OData service calls make it through the firewall. Then exclude other potential problems one by one.

▶ **Trace the steps**
Trace the steps the service request performs by using the tools explained in this chapter. Try to find the step where the problem occurs by, for example, using external breakpoints on the ABAP side.

14.4   Summary

This chapter introduced you to the lifecycle of a typical SAP Gateway project and how to manage selected phases. You've received insights into a number of nondevelopment topics such as testing, error handling, and service deployment. Because every project is different, in most cases, you'll have to adjust and/or develop strategies for the test plan of your own SAP Gateway project or the operation of an SAP Gateway environment. The chapter has provided you a foundation that you can build on and that you can extend for your own project and specific environment.

In this chapter, we'll discuss the various security mechanisms that can be put in place to prevent unauthorized and unauthenticated use of data that has been published via SAP Gateway.

15   Security

SAP Gateway extends the reach of SAP business applications by offering easy access via the OData protocol through various channels. Of course, while taking advantage of this, it's necessary to control who is allowed to consume this data. Obviously, no CIO wants to risk the security of a company's internal or external data.

The fundamental aspects of *information security* (confidentiality, integrity, and availability) have to be taken into account for the whole lifetime of data and through all the different layers of SAP Gateway—from the OData client to the SAP Business Suite backend system. In this chapter, we provide an overview of some of the most important security concepts in SAP Gateway.

Confidentiality, integrity, availability

15.1   Network and Communication Security

A secure network infrastructure is of utmost importance when it comes to system protection. Opening up your system for easy access via OData and preventing unauthorized access to your business data have to be accomplished at the same time. A well-defined system architecture can eliminate many security threats, such as *eavesdropping*. Figure 15.1 shows SAP Gateway's three-tier architecture (business layer, SAP Gateway, consumer) together with the communication protocols that are used between the different layers.

Three-tier architecture

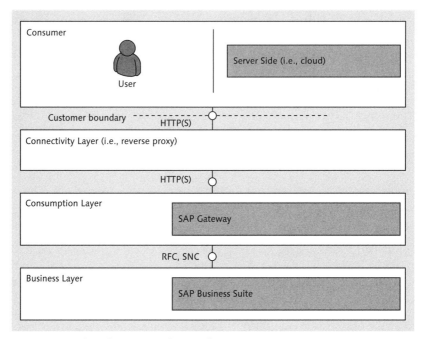

Figure 15.1 Technical System Landscape of SAP Gateway

Maintaining the security of these three different layers involves two main processes: transport protection and input validation. *Transport protection* is the process of securing the data that are transported between these layers to ensure confidentiality and integrity. *Input validation* is the process of validating input on the consumption layer before sending it to the backend system on the business layer because even if the data is secured while in transport, there are other threats based on sending the OData service malicious data. Input validation encompasses but isn't limited to validating syntactical correctness of the incoming data based on formats of OData types (length, ranges, white list values), rejecting invalid input, and so on.

We'll discuss both of these security measures in more detail next.

15.1.1 Transport Protection

SSL/TLS   To ensure transport protection for data confidentiality and integrity, the network communication between the different components has to be secured. As a standard measure, the communication between the consumer and SAP Gateway in the consumption layer is secured by means of using secure sockets layer/transport layer security (SSL/TLS).

In external-facing scenarios, a common security measure is to put a reverse proxy in between the consumers coming from the Internet and the resource that will be published to the outside world. If the HTTP(S) requests are terminated by a reverse proxy (i.e., SAP Web Dispatcher), the proxy and SAP Gateway should implement certificate forwarding in the HTTP header. (Certificate forwarding isn't an SAP proprietary approach; it's also supported by common reverse proxies.) The reverse proxy acts as a server-side proxy and is used to avoid same-origin policy restrictions.

Reverse proxy

In HTTP(S) communication, at one end of the "wire," you have an application (e.g., a browser or a native application), and on the other, you have a web server. Only the server and port number of the URL are visible on the wire, so as long as HTTP(S) is secure, you have no problem. However, a web server typically uses log files to log all of the traffic, so it's possible for someone to find the request URLs. If access to the log files isn't secured, or if you don't trust your web server system administrator, you have an issue. (Another location for spotting such information is at an intermediary server that performs HTTP termination, i.e., access logs on a reverse proxy.)

HTTP(S) isn't enough

Consider a situation where the application at one end of the wire is a browser. A browser typically stores URLs in the browser history and also sends URLs around in the Referrer header field. This is a standard behavior and can't be avoided or influenced. If you write your own native application, you can control that end of the wire. However, this doesn't mean that the entire setup is secure, which is a common assumption by consumers. While it's true that the content—the body of an HTTP request—is secured when using HTTP(S), the URL and its parameters may still be accessible via web server log files or the browser cache.

OData uses parameters in URLs quite frequently, such as filter parameters or key fields when retrieving a single entity. For the reasons we just explained, this has the potential to result in threats. For example, one possible threat is that confidential data such as credit card numbers

Problem URL parameters

might be extracted from stored URLs in the browser history on the client side, or stored as part of web server logs. For example, suppose a banking service offers a `CreditCardSet` entity set that is based on the `CreditCard` entity type shown in Figure 15.2.

Figure 15.2 CreditCard Entity Type: Unsecure

Key fields
In this case, the credit card number is part of the key of the `CreditCard` entity type. Suppose the application retrieves the credit card details using the following request:

https://<server>:<port>/<rootURL>/CreditCardSet('1234 5432 1234 6543')

In this case, the credit card number is part of the URL and can be disclosed due to the reasons outlined earlier. However, there are ways to address this problem. Specifically, transfer of confidential data as part of a URL can be avoided if the entity key fields contain values such as GUIDs, rather than using the actual data in the entity data modeling. Thus, the first step to avoid the usage of confidential data as part of the key is to change the entity set so that a GUID is used as a key field. This is acceptable from a security perspective, as shown in Figure 15.3.

Figure 15.3 CreditCard Entity Type: Secure

660

However, if an OData client sends a query to the `CreditCardSet` entity set to retrieve an entry by filtering the credit card number, the following HTTP request is sent to the server, resulting in sending the credit card number unsecured because query parameters are part of the URL:

https://<server>:<port>/<rootURL>/CreditCardSet?$filter=CardNumber eq '1234 5432 1234 6543'

Query parameters

A countermeasure against this threat is to send the query using the `$batch` endpoint. This way, the HTTP request is sent as part of a payload of an HTTP request and is thus secured by HTTP(S). This is also the reason the use of $batch is enforced by the SAP Gateway framework for OData services that are monitored using Read Access Logging (RAL). RAL is described in more detail later in this chapter.

Countermeasure $batch

In addition to the measures just discussed, it's also important that the communication between the SAP Gateway server and the connected backend systems is secured via Secure Network Communications (SNC). As of today, a trusted remote function call (RFC) is the only way to transfer user context between two ABAP systems. Trusted RFC connections are used in other scenarios as well, such as Central User Administration (CUA) and SAP Solution Manager. Because a trusted RFC connection allows the user to seamlessly connect from one system to the other system by using single sign-on (SSO), there's a threat when an unauthorized user manages to have access to the SAP Gateway hub system. The risk can be mitigated from two directions:

Backend communication

▶ Protect the access path to the SAP Gateway server via implementation of the preceding protections.

▶ Protect the backend systems by withdrawing the authorization for remote logon based on the authorization object S_RFCACL from users and functions that don't require remote access (such as DDIC, SAP*, and other administrative users).

15.1.2 Input Validation

SAP Gateway performs application layer input validations on the consumption layer. For external-facing scenarios, SAP recommends keeping systems with business functions separate from those that are used for input validation. In a production environment, as a best practice, customers can choose the hub deployment where the SAP Gateway system is installed on a separate system and not on the SAP Business Suite backend system (refer to Chapter 4 for a full discussion of the SAP Gateway deployment options). Employing this best practice means that you can monitor the communication between the hub and the backend systems, allowing any protection against overloading and attacks. In addition, if SAP Gateway is attacked, the backend systems remain safe behind the protection layer of SAP Gateway. If you choose an embedded deployment of SAP Gateway in the SAP Business Suite backend system, you must have additional systems—such as SAP API Management or a third-party product—on separate servers in front of the co-deployed system that perform the appropriate validation checks.

Next, we'll explain in more detail how SAP Gateway helps you secure your business scenario from the most prominent threats to input validation: namely *cross-site scripting* (*XSS*) attacks and *cross-site request forgery* (*XSRF* or *CSRF*) attacks. In addition to these checks, which are included as part of SAP Gateway, there are other checks that can be configured separately, for example, virus scanning systems for file verification. We discuss all of these checks next.

Protection against Cross-Site Scripting

Cross-site scripting | In an XSS attack, the trust of a user in a website is exploited (Figure 15.4). XSS enables attackers to inject client-side script into web pages viewed by other users. Although all modern browsers have implemented a "same-origin" policy, XSS attacks are still in the top 10 of web application security issues.

Countermeasures | As a countermeasure against XSS attacks, SAP Gateway offers the validation of the syntactical correctness of incoming data based on formats of OData types (length, ranges, white list values). If any invalid input is detected, it's rejected by the framework. In addition, XSS protection is achieved through escaping HTML markup (e.g., `<br>` as `&lt;br&gt;`) according to Atom content processing rules (RFC 4287).

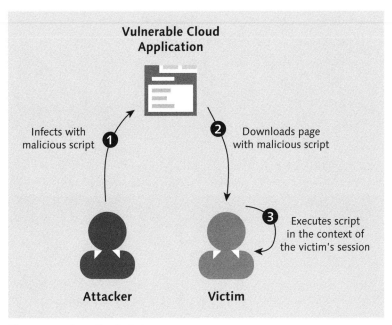

Figure 15.4 Cross-Site Scripting

Protection against Cross-Site Request Forgery

XSRF is almost the opposite of XSS. In XSS, an attacker exploits the trust of a user in a website; in XSRF, an attacker exploits the trust of a website in its consumer (Figure 15.5). In other words, XSRF is an attack that forces an end user to execute unwanted actions on a web application in which he is currently authenticated. The attack starts by an attacker luring a user to access a malicious OData service URL. The success of the XSRF attack depends on the predictability of the request URL to the vulnerable application.

Consider an example where a user is logged on to—for example—the HTML5 website of his bank that communicates to the backend using OData, as shown in Figure 15.5. While working on his bank account, suppose the user visits a different site that contains, for example, blog entries that contain unsafe content, or, as another example, he receives an email with a manipulated link.

Cross-site request forgery

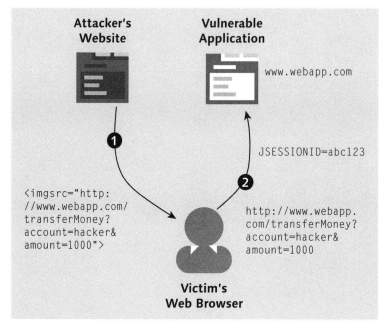

Figure 15.5 Cross-Site Scripting Forgery Attack

If the user clicks on the link in the email or clicks on a link in the blog ❶, the victim's browser follows this URL that references an action on the vulnerable website ❷ together with the cookies that are used for authentication. In other words, XSRF exploits the trust that a site has in a user's browser. Notice that the URL that the victim's browser follows points to the vulnerable site, not to the malicious site. This is the "cross-site" part of XSRF.

Countermeasure The first way to protect against XSRF attacks is to refrain from making modifications via an HTTP GET request that is in any way part of the REST paradigm. An additional way to protect against XSRF attacks is to require a secret, user-specific token if the client wants to perform a modifying request using one of the HTTP verbs (POST, PUT, PATCH, or DELETE). This XSRF token has to be retrieved by the client using a nonmodifying request that is sent to the server beforehand. Therefore, as a first step, the client has to send a GET request with the header field X-CSRF-Token and the value Fetch. In a second step, the Internet Communication Framework (ICF) runtime sends back the randomly generated XSRF token in the header field X-CSRF-Token as well as in the cookie sap-XSRF_<SID>_<client>. In a third step, this XSRF token must be included by the client in the HTTP header X-CSRF-Token in any subsequent modifying requests. Because the client also sends back all cookies, the ICF runtime can validate the XSRF token found in the HTTP header X-CSRF-Token against the token from the cookie sap-XSRF_<SID>_<client>.

Because the tokens are generated randomly, an attacker can't guess their values, and the attacker's site can't put the right token in its submissions. Note that due to same-origin policies, the attacker isn't able to read the user's tokens. It's thus not possible for the attacker to craft an HTTP request that also contains the randomly generated X-CSRF-Token.

Tokens generated randomly

To demonstrate this more practically, let's start with the following sample request:

```
HTTP GET ... /BusinessPartnerCollection('0100000002')
```

The client adds the HTTP header X-CSRF-Token to the value Fetch. As a result, the client receives the X-CSRF-Token in the HTTP header of the HTTP response. If successful (HTTP 200), you'll find an X-CSRF-Token in the HTTP response headers.

```
Status Code: 200 OK
Content-Type: application/atom+xml;type=entry; charset=utf-8
...
X-CSRF-Token: oZipsu2chxoh2YMLNo9gRg==
Set-Cookie: {client MUST store cookies set by the server}
...
```

The X-CSRF-Token then has to be sent by the client in any subsequent modifying request such as PUT, POST, PATCH, or DELETE. The update request HTTP PUT ... /BusinessPartnerCollection('0100000002') then has to contain the X-CSRF-Token in the HTTP header:

```
Content-Type: application/atom+xml;type=entry; charset=utf-8
...
X-CSRF-Token: oZipsu2chxoh2YMLNo9gRg==
Cookie: {client MUST return cookies set by the server}
...
```

In this case, the update request is successful, the HTTP response body is empty, and the HTTP header contains status code 204 (no content).

When using the SAP Gateway client for testing, as shown in Figure 15.6, it isn't necessary to first request an X-CSRF-Token via a GET request and then to send it with a subsequent modifying request because the SAP Gateway client does this automatically for you.

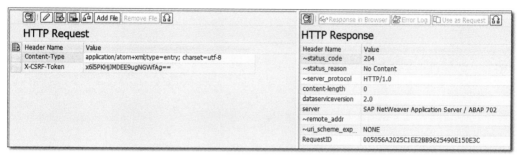

Figure 15.6 XSRF Token Handling in the SAP Gateway Client

SAPUI5   The ODataModel in SAPUI5 has a setTokenHandlingEnabled method that uses the bTokenHandling Boolean parameter to enable or disable X-CSRF-Token handling. Because the default setting of bTokenHandling is true, the SAPUI5 developer doesn't have to implement anything as the framework provides X-CSRF-Token handling out of the box.

In addition, the refreshSecurityToken method allows the developer to refresh the XSRF token by performing a GET request against the service root URL in case the token might not be valid anymore.

Virus Scan Interface

In the SAP Gateway framework, virus scanning is available for incoming update and create requests on binary data for SAP Gateway services. Binary data can, for example, be handled using *media links* as described in Chapter 6, Section 6.5.7.

The activity to maintain profiles for virus checking is available in the SAP Gateway IMG. To activate or deactivate virus checking, start Transaction SPRO, and open the SAP Reference IMG. Navigate to SAP NETWEAVER • SAP GATEWAY • ODATA CHANNEL • ADMINISTRATION • GENERAL SETTINGS • DEFINE VIRUS SCAN PROFILES. Here you can activate or deactivate the VIRUS SCAN SWITCHED OFF checkbox.

More information about the SAP Virus Scan Interface and the configuration in SAP Gateway can be found in the online documentation. Go to *http://help.sap.com/nw75*, and select FUNCTION-ORIENTED VIEW • SAP GATEWAY FOUNDATION (SAP_GWFND) • SAP GATEWAY FOUNDATION SECURITY GUIDE • DATA PROTECTION AND PRIVACY • VIRUS SCAN.

15.2 User Management and Authorizations

Because SAP Gateway is based on the SAP NetWeaver ABAP Application Server (ABAP AS), it uses the local ABAP user management. Users can be created via the standard mechanisms. To facilitate user management, the SAP Gateway server can be connected to a central user management system landscape as an additional child system, or it can be managed using an identity management tool such as SAP Identity Management. For business-to-consumer (B2C) scenarios, SAP Gateway provides a user self-service that is described in more detail in Section 15.4.7 later in this chapter.

User management

The user accounts that have to be created in the SAP Gateway hub must show the same user name as in the connected backend systems. This is because the SAP Gateway hub system is connected to the backend systems using a trust relationship where SSO is accomplished via SAP assertion tickets. If the embedded deployment option has been chosen, it isn't necessary to create users in an additional system because the users in the backend system that also serves as the SAP Gateway hub already exist.

User accounts

If an OData service is called, an authorization check is performed in the SAP Gateway server to check whether the user has the authorization to call that service, which is based on the authorization object S_SERVICE. It's thus possible to define ABAP authorization roles in the SAP Gateway system that let you use a white list approach to control access to the SAP Gateway services. If this first authorization check is successful, the framework calls the service implementation in the backend via RFC. Even if access has been granted at the service level in the hub, the SAP user authorizations in the backend are checked as well. Appropriate authorization checks should be in place in the service implementation in

Authorizations

the SAP Business Suite backend system. This is to ensure that a user won't be able to retrieve any business data via an OData call that he isn't allowed to see via SAP GUI or Web Dynpro UIs in the SAP Business Suite backend.

Because a trust relationship is used between the hub and the SAP Business Suite backend, users in the SAP Business Suite backend that will consume data via OData services must have an additional authorization based on the authorization object S_RFCACL allowing such remote calls. The backend systems have to be protected by withdrawing the authorization for remote logon based on the authorization object S_RFCACL from users and functions that don't require remote access (such as DDIC, SAP*, and other administrative users). Otherwise, it would be possible for a hacked administrative user account to log on from the SAP Gateway hub into the backend.

In certain scenarios, external user credentials need to be mapped to the user credentials used in SAP Gateway and the connected SAP Business Suite backend systems. You have to distinguish here between scenarios where mapping takes place externally and scenarios where mapping takes place internally in SAP Gateway.

User mapping in SAP Gateway

Scenarios with user mapping on SAP Gateway's side are the following:

▸ The NameID attribute value in the Security Assertion Markup Language (SAML) assertion is mapped to the SAP Gateway user name.

▸ The X.509 client certificate's subject is mapped to the SAP Gateway user name.

▸ The SAP Gateway user is mapped to an attribute value in the SAML assertion.

▸ The SAP Gateway user is mapped to the user principal name that is used as the SNC name.

External user mapping

There are other scenarios where user mapping has to be performed externally. An example for this setup is a scenario where the user name is an SAP Gateway user defined in the user store of SAP Enterprise Portal. Another example is a scenario where an Identity Provider (IdP) is configured to issue SAML tokens so that the name of the SAP Gateway user is identical to the NameID attribute value in the SAML assertion.

15.3 Single Sign-On and Authentication Options

The most efficient way to facilitate simplified user authentication in an enterprise is via single sign-on (SSO), which refers to the mechanisms for enterprise users to authenticate themselves by a single authentication authority once and then gain access to other protected resources without reauthenticating. With the SSO functionality, users only need to authenticate once and are afterwards automatically authenticated when accessing systems that trust this initial authentication.

A nice analogy to this process is the cross-boundary travel process. A German citizen receives a passport from German authorities based on an initial authentication because the citizen presented his ID card. The passport that has been issued by the German authorities is in turn accepted by the US immigration office because the US authorities trust the German authorities (Figure 15.7).

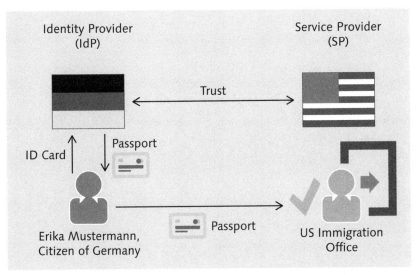

Figure 15.7 Cross-Boundary Travel: An Analogy for SSO and Identity Federation

Because the process of cross-boundary travel is easily understood, it's a great help to explain the basic terms of SSO that we'll use in the remainder of this chapter. Figure 15.8 shows the fundamental roles that participate in the process of SSO and identity federation.

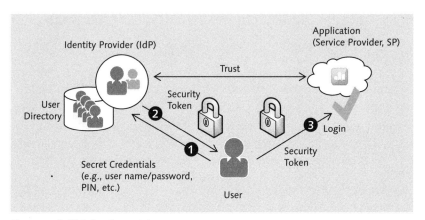

Figure 15.8 SSO Fundamentals

IdP The IdP is an authoritative site that is responsible for authenticating an end user and asserting his identity in a trusted fashion to trusted partners. For the cross-boundary travel scenario, the German authorities play the role of the IdP because they issue a passport as proof of an initial identification based on the ID card that Erika Mustermann presented to them.

Service provider The *service provider* (SP) has a trust relationship with an IdP to accept and trust (i.e., vouch for) information provided by the IdP on behalf of a user (without direct user involvement). Identity and access management are transferred to the IdP. In the cross-boundary travel scenario, the US immigrations office plays the role of the SP. The only difference here is that the traveler has to present his passport to the representatives of the immigration office, whereas in an SSO scenario, the client (e.g., the browser) presents the token issued by the IdP to the SP without bothering the end user.

For SSO to SAP Gateway, SAP Gateway plays the role of the SP. The user has to present a security token issued by an IdP to SAP Gateway, which is seamlessly accepted by the SAP Gateway server. Therefore, you must first look at the authentication options that are supported by SAP Gateway as well as the different consumers or user agents (desktop application, HTML5 application, mobile client, etc.) that are involved to decide the best way to achieve SSO for a certain scenario.

> **Note**
>
> None of the authentication methods described here provide TLS out of the box. We recommend that you use TLS mechanisms such as SSL/TLS to have increased security for the OData communication with the SAP Gateway server.

SAP Gateway supports the same authentication options offered by the underlying SAP NetWeaver ABAP runtime for browser-based communication. This is because communication via the OData protocol that is offered by the SAP Gateway hub is facilitated via the *Internet Communications Manager* (*ICM*) process using handlers in the ICF.

In this section, we explain the different authentication options that are available for SAP Gateway, including whether they enable SSO.

> **Note**
>
> Some of these authentication options require a certain release and might require additional software components from SAP or a third-party that have to be licensed separately.

15.3.1 Basic Authentication

Basic authentication is the simplest form of authentication. The consumer application just provides a user name and a password when calling the OData service in SAP Gateway. Basic authentication isn't an option that allows SSO because it requires the consuming application to store the user's credentials in a secure location and requires the application to cope with initial and expired passwords.

Using basic authentication also bears the risk that the system becomes vulnerable for distributed denial-of-service (DDoS) attacks. Users can be locked out because attackers have performed too many login attempts using the wrong credentials.

Basic authentication is, however, a valid option for the following scenarios:

▸ During design time, so developers can test their applications by using different credentials to impersonate users having different roles

▸ In B2C scenarios where user self-service is used (see Section 15.4.7 for more details about this functionality)

15.3.2 SAP Logon Tickets with SAP Enterprise Portal

SAP logon tickets are session cookies that are stored on the client browser. In the past, SAP had to rely on a proprietary SSO mechanism that is based on SAP logon tickets because common standards such as SAML or OAuth were not available at that time.

SAP logon tickets   The ticket-issuing instance for SAP logon tickets in SSO scenarios is usually taken over by the SAP Enterprise Portal system that has the role of an IdP. *SAP Enterprise Portal* (formerly known as *SAP NetWeaver Portal*) issues an SAP logon ticket to a user after successful initial authentication at the portal against a user persistence specified in the portal user management engine (UME).

Because SAP logon tickets are cookie-based, technical and security limitations apply. Logon tickets are only sent to SAP NetWeaver Application Servers that are located in the same Domain Name Server (DNS) domain as the SAP Enterprise Portal server that issued the ticket. Therefore, SAP logon tickets aren't well suited for cross-domain scenarios. However, they can be used to achieve SSO for all SAP applications inside a single domain tree using domain relaxation.

SAP Enterprise Portal itself offers SSO using different authentication options such as X.509 certificates or Integrated Windows Authentication. SAP Enterprise Portal users can thus automatically be authenticated against the portal by reusing their Windows credentials. SSO to all SAP applications and also SAP Gateway is then achieved by using the SAP logon ticket that has been issued because the user has logged on successfully using his Windows credentials.

Integrated
Windows
Authentication   Note that Integrated Windows Authentication is now also supported for the ABAP stack using HTTP access, as described later in Section 15.3.6. This is especially of interest to desktop clients that can't leverage SAP

logon tickets that have been issued by SAP Enterprise Portal out of the box.

15.3.3 X.509 Client Certificates

An X.509 certificate is a signed data structure that binds a public key to a person, computer, or organization. Certificates are issued by certification authorities (CAs). Issuing public key certificates and private keys to users and computers in an organization is the task of a public key infrastructure (PKI).

When using authentication with client certificates, each user needs to possess a key pair, consisting of a public key and a private key. The public key is contained in the X.509 client certificate and can be made public. However, the user's private key needs to be kept safe.

Key pairs

One of the major benefits of using X.509 client certificates is that they are supported by many applications. The use of X.509 certificates is a widely accepted standard, and its stability is proved in numerous implementations. X.509 certificates can be used to achieve SSO for browser-based access for the most recent version as well as for older releases of SAP NetWeaver ABAP, such as SAP NetWeaver ABAP 7.0. (Strictly speaking, this isn't a pure SSO solution because a user authenticates independently into each and every system.)

As a result, besides basic authentication and SAP logon tickets, X.509 certificates are the only authentication method that is supported for all releases of SAP NetWeaver ABAP (7.0 to 7.5) for which SAP Gateway has been released.

The one drawback to X.509 certificates is that their use usually requires customers to implement and run a PKI. Running and maintaining a PKI isn't as common as you might expect because it's seen as a cumbersome and expensive task. Fortunately, there is an alternative. Instead of implementing a full-fledged PKI, customers can implement the product *SAP Single Sign-On (SAP SSO)*. SAP SSO can, for example, leverage the Windows credentials of a currently logged-on user. Based on this authentication, which happens seamlessly, and the fact that the user has already

SAP Single Sign-On

logged on to his workstation by using his Windows user name and password, the secure login server issues a short-lived client certificate that is pushed to the user certificate store. This certificate can then in turn be used for SSO to SAP Gateway. Because you can choose very short lifetimes for the certificates, there's no need to bother with certificate revocation lists, which is necessary in a PKI.

Microsoft Active
Directory

Another way to seamlessly roll out X.509 certificates in an existing infrastructure is to leverage the auto-enrollment feature of Microsoft Active Directory. With this feature, the certificate is automatically copied to the user certificate store on a user's client. This local store is an encrypted store for certificates on Windows clients and contains personal and public root certificates.

User mapping

Whereas the initial setup in the ABAP AS is a one-time effort to accept X.509 certificates, the need to map the client certificates subject to the SAP user accounts is an ongoing task. Mapping a certificate to the end user can be accomplished automatically by using an identity management tool such as SAP Identity Management or by direct maintenance of table VUSREXTID using Transaction EXTID_DN, which also offers the option of a file upload.

15.3.4 SAML 2.0 Browser Protocol

SAML is a standard for SSO and identity federation. The SAML 2.0 browser protocol specifies a profile that describes how the different roles (IdP, SP, and user) interact if the user is using a web browser to access the service provider.

In a scenario that uses the SAML browser protocol 2.0, SAP Gateway acts as a service provider. Several IdPs that issue the SAML token based on an initial authentication are supported. Depending on the scenario, different initial authentication options can be used by the client. The advantage of using the SAML 2.0 browser protocol is that there's no need to deploy anything on the client side; this is in contrast to solutions that use X.509 certificates, which have to be distributed to the clients.

Because the SAML 2.0 browser protocol is the recommended option for various scenarios (e.g., for the SAP Fiori applications), we'll explain the authentication flow in more detail (Figure 15.9 and Figure 15.10).

The client sends an unauthenticated request to SAP Gateway via a reverse proxy server ❶. The request issued by the client refers to an external URL for the OData service that is, for example, consumed by an SAP Fiori application. The SAP Gateway server responds to the unauthenticated request with a redirect to the IdP ❷ as if to say, "I don't know who you are; go talk to the SAML 2.0 IdP server." The client follows the HTTP 302 redirect URL, and sends the request to the SAML 2.0 IdP server ❸. The SAML 2.0 IdP server challenges the client to identify itself ❹. At this point, the SAML 2.0 IdP server can be configured to use any form of authentication appropriate for the customer's system infrastructure, for instance, basic authentication against Microsoft Active Directory. The client supplies the required credentials, for instance, Windows user name and password ❺.

Authentication flow

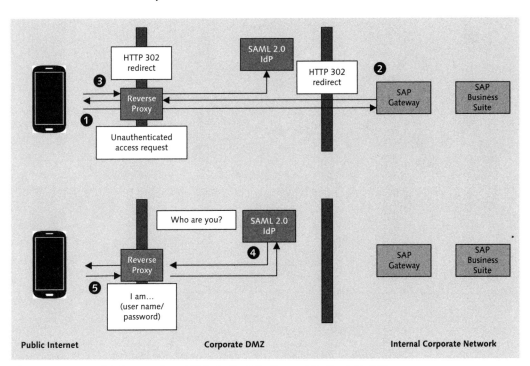

Figure 15.9 SAML 2.0 Browser-Based SSO: Artifact Binding and Redirect (Part 1)

If the SAML 2.0 IdP server determines the user credentials to be valid, it responds with another HTTP 302 to redirect the client back to the SAP Gateway server; however, this response now carries the required SAML artifact ❻ (Figure 15.10). The client follows the HTTP 302 redirect URL and, in so doing, passes the SAML artifact back to the SAP Gateway server ❼. The SAP Gateway server sends the SAML artifact to the SAML 2.0 IdP server for resolution as a back-channel web service (Simple Object Access Protocol [SOAP]) request ❽. The SAML 2.0 IdP server resolves the artifact and returns an assertion that SAP Gateway validates ❾. If validation is successful, an ABAP session is created for the now authenticated user ❿. The OData service in SAP Gateway now starts and sends data to the client ⓫.

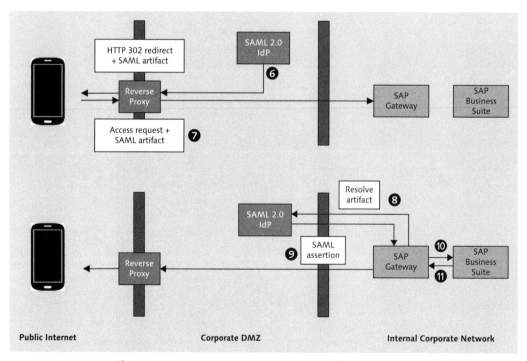

Figure 15.10 SAML 2.0 Browser-Based SSO: Artifact Binding and Redirect (Part 2)

15.3.5 OAuth

OAuth 2.0 is a protocol that allows users to grant a web-based client application access to resources that are owned by the user. The application that is authorized by the resource owner accesses the resources on behalf of the user. Strictly speaking, OAuth isn't an authentication option but a protocol to delegate authorization. From an end user perspective, however, OAuth enables SSO for a wide range of scenarios, such as mobile applications, websites, and more.

The advantage of OAuth is that it offers constrained access to services without the requirement to pass or store credentials. This makes it a good fit for cloud-based services and mobile services, where constrained access is of special interest.

One of the standard examples for OAuth, which is also used in the OAuth 2.0 Internet–Draft (*http://tools.ietf.org/html/draft-ietf-oauth-v2-10*), is a photo printing service. Assume that you've uploaded photos from your vacation on some cloud service. Now you want to print some photos and want to use another cloud service for this task. When you access the pictures, you have to authenticate by providing your user name and password. Because any access to your pictures requires authentication, this is also the case for the printing service. Obviously, you don't want to share your credentials with the printing service because you have limited trust to the printing service. Providing your credentials to the printing service allows the printing service to act on your behalf and, for example, allows it to even delete pictures. In addition, you have to change your password for the cloud service hosting your pictures to prevent the printing service from accessing this resource in the future.

Standard example

The idea of OAuth is thus to provide the printing service with a time-constrained security token that only allows limited read access to the pictures you've selected. In this example, you, as an owner of the images, fulfill the role of the OAuth resource owner.

Why is OAuth also relevant for scenarios in the enterprise? In an enterprise environment, you usually configure SSO because the systems are operated by one organization. However, even here, OAuth can make sense because it allows restricting the access to a system when being accessed via a mobile device rather than using, for example, SAP GUI. Take, for example, a mobile application for entering leave requests. When entering the data, the application only needs access to the leave

Enterprise scenario

request resources and doesn't require access to the user's payroll data. In this case, OAuth ensures that the user and the leave request application *only* have permission to access the leave request resources and don't have access to payroll resources.

OAuth is supported as part of the SAP standard as of SAP NetWeaver ABAP 7.40 and, by applying some SAP Notes, also for some releases lower than 7.40 (see SAP Note 1797103).

15.3.6 Kerberos: Integrated Windows Authentication

The most straightforward way to perform SSO in a Microsoft environment is to reuse the authentication information from Windows, that is, by using Integrated Windows Authentication, which is based on Kerberos.

When a user has successfully logged on to a Windows workstation with his credentials, the domain controller of Active Directory issues a (Kerberos) session ticket to access a resource that is offering Integrated Windows Authentication. SAP NetWeaver AS ABAP supports Kerberos with Simple and Protected GSS-API Negotiation Mechanism (SPNego) to enable authentication with web clients such as web browsers. In this case, the domain controller of the Windows domain acts as the IdP.

> **Note**
>
> To use SPNego with SAP NetWeaver AS ABAP, it requires SAP SSO 2.0 and higher as well as additional software licenses. SAP SSO 2.0 requires SAP NetWeaver ABAP 7.31 SP 06 and higher as a runtime. With SAP NetWeaver ABAP 7.40, the required ABAP add-ons are part of the standard, although usage still requires licensing this functionality.

15.4   Recommended Authentication Options

Which authentication method to use depends on the scenario and the user agent. In Table 15.1, we provide an overview of the scenarios and the recommended authentication options. In the rest of the section, we go into a bit more detail about each of these types of applications. We'll explain which of the authentication options described in Section 15.3 are feasible for achieving SSO for a specific type of application, discuss the pros and cons of each authentication option, and provide a recommendation for one or more authentication options for each scenario that is listed in Table 15.1.

Scenario	Recommended Authentication Option
Web (HTML5) Application	▶ SAML 2.0 browser SSO for extranet scenarios ▶ Kerberos for intranet scenarios
Desktop application	▶ SAML 2.0 browser SSO for extranet scenarios ▶ Kerberos for intranet scenarios
Mobile applications (direct access)	SAML 2.0 browser SSO or OAuth
SAP Mobile Platform	X.509 certificates
SAP HANA Cloud Platform	SAML 2.0 browser SSO
Web server side	X.509 certificates
Business-to-consumer (B2C)	▶ Basic authentication when using user self-service or no authentication because you're accessing a public service ▶ SAML browser protocol when mapping SAML authenticated users to service users

Table 15.1 Recommended Authentication Options for Different Integration Scenarios

15.4.1 HTML5 Web Application

The web application scenario (Figure 15.11) applies to HTML5, Internet, and intranet scenarios (other frontend technologies for web applications such as Silverlight and Flex are considered outdated and aren't recommended). The scenarios usually require a separate web server for content hosting. In the case of SAPUI5, however, the SAP Gateway server itself can be used for deployment.

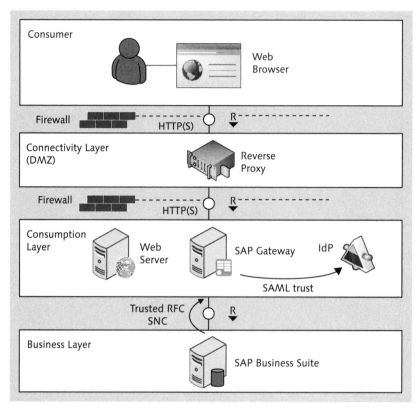

Figure 15.11 Web Application Scenario

Multiple authenti-
cation options In the web application scenario, multiple authentication options can be used. The recommended option for extranet scenarios is to use SAML 2.0 Browser SSO because it doesn't require the distribution of X.509 certificates and leverages existing user identities in a customer's identity management system. SAML 2.0 Browser SSO requires an IdP that can, for example, be based on SAP SSO or Active Directory Federation Services (ADFS).

A second option is to use X.509 client certificates that require either a PKI or the usage of SAP SSO. If the HTTP(S) requests are terminated by a reverse proxy (i.e., SAP Web Dispatcher), the proxy and SAP Gateway should implement certificate forwarding in the HTTP header. Certificate forwarding isn't an SAP proprietary approach but is supported by common reverse proxies. The reverse proxy acts as a server-side proxy and is used to avoid same-origin policy restrictions.

A third option for intranet scenarios is Kerberos. This is also the recommended option because it's the most straightforward one.

15.4.2 Desktop Application

The consumer in this scenario can be any desktop application performing direct communication with the SAP Gateway system (Figure 15.12). As a standard measure, the communication between the desktop application and the SAP Gateway system is secured via HTTP(S). From a technical point of view, several options can be used for authentication.

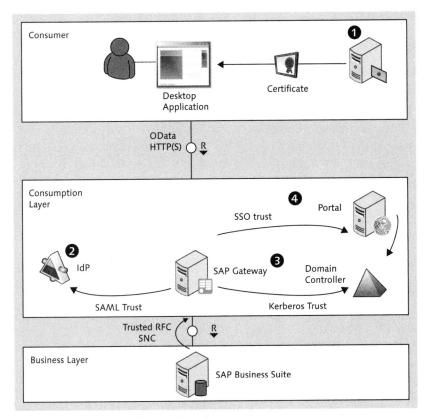

Figure 15.12 Desktop Application Scenario

The recommended option for intranet scenarios is the use of Kerberos tickets issued by a Windows domain controller ❸. The use of X.509 client certificates can also be considered ❶. This requires, however, that you have a PKI or distribute X.509 certificates using SAP SSO. The end user has direct access to these tokens.

SAML 2.0 Browser SSO ❷ can also be used because there are IdPs such as SAP SSO or ADFS that support Kerberos-based authentication. The use of the SAML tokens for SSO isn't straightforward, however. In contrast to a web application, where a browser handles HTTP redirects, parses HTML forms, and processes cookies, a desktop application doesn't support this behavior out of the box. The developer would have to ensure that the client code behaves like a browser when performing these actions. Although for extranet scenarios this is still the way to go, for intranet scenarios, Kerberos-based authentication should be chosen instead.

The same is true if you want to use the SAP Enterprise Portal as a ticket-issuing instance for SAP logon tickets that can be used for authentication against the SAP Gateway system ❹. The developer also has to deal with a proper handling of cookies (MYSAPSSO2). Although the SAP Enterprise Portal supports SSO using Integrated Windows Authentication as well as using the SPNego Login Module, it's recommended to use the native implementation of Kerberos support in SAP NetWeaver AS ABAP provided with SAP SSO 2.0 and higher. The use of SAP Enterprise Portal to achieve SSO using Kerberos for HTML5-based applications is an option, however.

When using a trusted RFC connection between the SAP Gateway server and the backend, a successful authentication against SAP Gateway allows for a subsequent SSO to the SAP Business Suite systems.

15.4.3 Mobile Application (Direct Access)

If using mobile devices, a direct access to OData services published by SAP Gateway is supported but requires additional security measures to be in place (Figure 15.13). When using SAP Mobile Platform, this is offered by the platform out of the box.

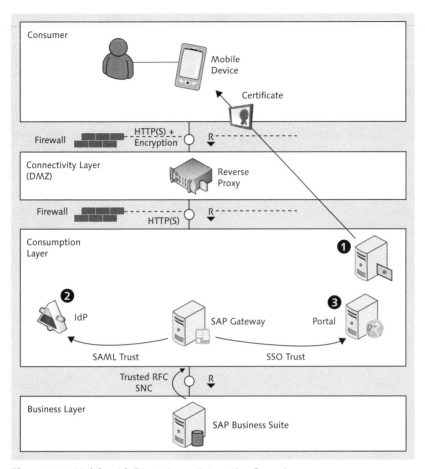

Figure 15.13 Mobile with Direct Access Integration Scenario

Communication between the SAP Gateway server and the consumer in the Internet is secured by using a reverse proxy, which is a common security measure in any data center. The reverse proxy allows restricting the access from the Internet to only certain services. As mentioned in Section 15.3.1, basic authentication isn't recommended because it requires handling and storing of passwords on mobile devices. Also, the handling of X.509 certificates can be tricky on certain mobile platforms because they don't offer an application-specific storage for X.509 certificates ❶. In addition, the rollout of certificates to the mobile devices has to be managed. Both functionalities are part of the offering of the SAP

Reverse proxy

Mobile Platform. Using SAP Logon Tickets also isn't recommended because it requires the developer to handle the request from SAP Logon Tickets manually ❸. In the end, this leaves you with either the SAML 2.0 browser protocol or OAuth 2.0 as the recommended authentication options for this scenario ❷.

The advantage of both approaches is that they don't require any installation of any additional components on the mobile device. It's possible to use an IdP, such as SAP SSO or ADFS, which offers authentication using the Windows user name and password. Using OAuth offers the additional benefit that the token issued for authentication (access token) only allows restricted access and enhances security.

Note that the code of your mobile application must behave like a browser to handle HTTP redirects, parsing HTML5 forms, and processing cookies if the SAML 2.0 browser protocol is to be used. Similarly, OAuth requires the developer to implement appropriate behavior of the mobile client.

As in other scenarios involving access by named users with SSO to the SAP Business Suite backend, any handling is facilitated via a trusted RFC connection between the SAP Gateway server and the backend.

15.4.4 SAP Mobile Platform

SAP Mobile Platform offers support for the development of mobile applications for various mobile devices based on Android, Windows 8, and iOS. It offers several out-of-the-box features that developers can implement for direct consumption of OData services published by SAP Gateway.

Out-of-the-box features
SAP Mobile Platform offers a two-factor authenticated device registration. As a result, the platform knows which user is using which device and thereby enables push notifications from SAP Gateway to the mobile device (see Appendix A for more information about this). The initial provisioning, including X.509 client certificate distribution, can be accomplished by using SAP Mobile Secure, as shown in Figure 15.14. Part of the SAP Mobile Platform is also a relay server that facilitates outside connection to the SAP Mobile Platform server. Instead of using the

relay server, customers can also use third-party reverse proxy servers, allowing a seamless integration into any existing security system landscape.

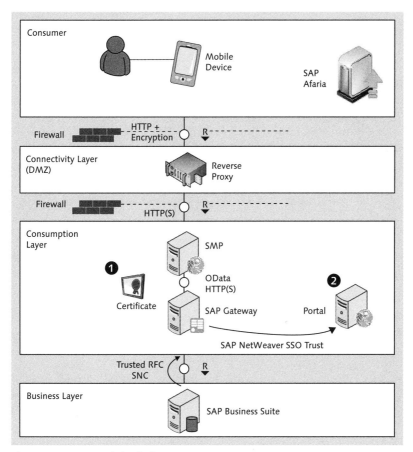

Figure 15.14 SAP Mobile Platform Integration Scenario

SAP Mobile Platform terminates client requests, handles device validation against known device lists, and offers the following two authentication options:

❶ Certificate forwarding between SAP Mobile Platform and SAP Gateway.

❷ SAP Mobile Platform request for SAP logon ticket from SAP Enterprise Portal, which is then forwarded to SAP Gateway.

X.509 or
SAP logon tickets From a security point of view, the recommended authentication option is to use X.509 certificates. However, if certificates aren't planned or can't be distributed to the mobile devices, the use of SAP logon tickets issued by SAP Enterprise Portal can be used. Note that SAP Enterprise Portal supports Active Directory as a data source for its UME. As a result, the mobile user is able to authenticate using his Windows user name and password.

15.4.5 Cloud

In a cloud-based scenario (Figure 15.15), the customer can federate user authentication from an on-premise IdP or from a public IdP to a cloud application. As an example, SAP runs such a public IdP in the cloud: the SAP Cloud Identity Service. Many social media websites can also be used; it's convenient for users to be able to reuse existing accounts from Facebook, Google, and so on. The application then accesses SAP Gateway on behalf of the consumer by leveraging one of the authentication methods supported by SAP Gateway (e.g., certificate-based logon). It can leverage an existing SAML token or request a new one from a local issuer. A reverse proxy acts as a connectivity solution for external consumers. SAP Gateway trusts the issuer of the SAML token in two authentication scenarios:

▸ Issuing a SAML 2.0 assertion for an unsolicited request

▸ Issuing a SAML 2.0 bearer assertion proving user's identity for OAuth 2.0 flow

Then SAP Gateway uses a trusted RFC connection to access services in the backend with named users.

As an example, consider a scenario based on the SAP HANA Cloud Platform (SAP HCP), which is SAP's Platform-as-a-Service (PaaS) solution for building extensions for on-demand and on-premise solutions. To securely connect from the SAP HCP to on-premise systems, applications can use a platform-provided connectivity service. The SAP HANA cloud connector establishes a secure SSL virtual private network (VPN) connection between the SAP HCP and on-premise systems. The connectivity is created by the SAP HANA cloud connector, an on-premise agent that initiates the secure tunnel from the internal network to the SAP HCP.

The SSL VPN connection supports different communication protocols such as HTTP(S) and RFC. SAP HCP supports SAML2-based user propagation to enable SSO to the on-premise SAP Gateway server.

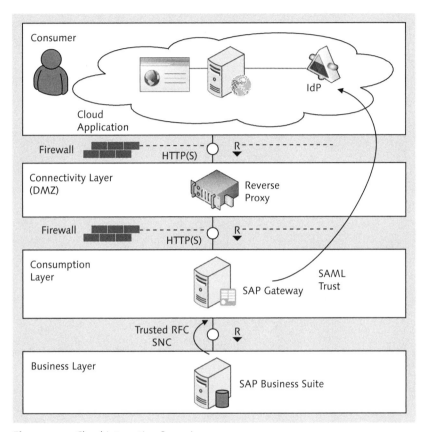

Figure 15.15 Cloud Integration Scenario

15.4.6 Web Server

In the web server scenario (Figure 15.16), the consumer has access to a web application that is hosted on a web server based on a framework such as Hypertext Preprocessor (PHP) or Active Server Pages (ASP) .NET. The application connects to the SAP Gateway server behind the scenes. Authentication can best be achieved using short-lived X.509 client certificates that can easily be generated on the fly for the current user. The user identity is part of the certificate's subject.

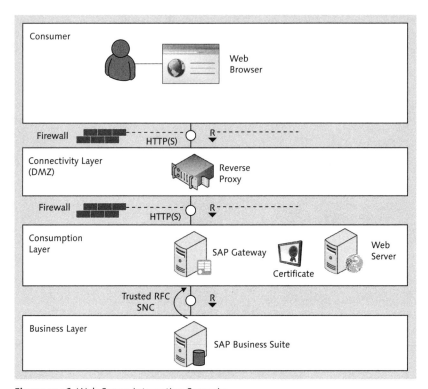

Figure 15.16 Web Server Integration Scenario

15.4.7 Business-to-Consumer Scenario

In B2C scenarios, customers access the business services provided by a company or organization that have typically no named user in the backend (Figure 15.17).

To accomplish this type of scenario, Gateway can support the following access configurations:

▶ Anonymous access

▶ User self-service to create named users

▶ Map SAML authenticated users to service users

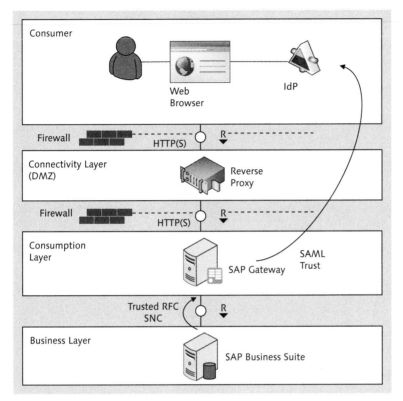

Figure 15.17 B2C Integration Scenario

Anonymous Access

The first option is that SAP Gateway provides services with *anonymous access* to all consumers. This requires some measures to be in place that prevent a denial of service (DoS) attack. An example of an application that uses anonymous access is the SAP Citizen Connect mobile app. With SAP Citizen Connect, citizens can report public-facing issues quickly and conveniently.

User Self-Service

The second option is to use the *user self-service* that allows your customers to create named users in your SAP Business Suite backend. It allows your customers to do the following:

- Create users in your SAP Business Suite system
- Manage their user profiles
- Reset their password

Using named users rather than anonymous users is very beneficial for B2C scenarios because it facilitates storage of data and controlled access to data, auditing, and troubleshooting. This is the recommended option if customers should be able to view and pay bills, as in, for example, the SAP solution SAP Multichannel Foundation for Utilities and Public Sector.

The user self-service process is depicted in Figure 15.18. The whole B2C process starts with a customer that is requesting a user ID in your SAP Business Suite and SAP Gateway hub system. The first request is calling the /IWEP/USERREQUESTMANAGEMENT service using a service user context. Here a `POST` request is performed on the `UserRequestCollection` entity set.

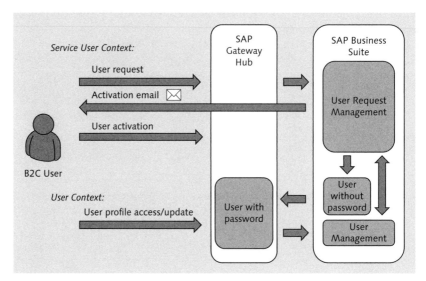

Figure 15.18 B2C Customer User Self-Service

Upon successful creation, the B2C customer receives an email notification that contains an activation URL. Here the B2C customer can enter a password that he'll use in the future to log on to the system.

B2C customers are also able to reset and change their passwords without the need to involve any manual user management.

The big advantage of user self-service is that you can leverage named users in the backend system. With named users in place in the backend system, authorizations can be checked properly using the user context of the currently logged on user. Data can be easily stored for each user separately, and, if needed, access to sensitive data can be logged using RAL, which is described later in this chapter. Also, troubleshooting is much easier because any call from a mobile device can be tracked for a user.

Advantages

If one technical user is used (as opposed to multiple named users), the application has to perform the authentication and send the backend information about the customer that is currently using the service. In addition, business logic has to be built in the backend to ensure that bookings performed by the technical user are stored in the correct context. Using one technical user is a large security risk. If, for example, the password isn't secret anymore, an attacker can access *all* customer data in the backend. When this happens with named users, only a single customer account is jeopardized.

The new self-service functionality is already used by some SAP solutions, such as the SAP Multichannel Foundation for Utilities and Public Sector. This solution allows customers use a mobile device to register, manage their accounts, and perform several actions, such as view and pay bills and report problems and outages to their supplier.

Map SAML Authenticated Users to Service Users

The third option is to map SAML authenticated users to service users. This scenario is officially called *identity federation with transient name identifiers*. In this case, SAP Gateway acts as a service provider and trusts an external IdP for performing user authentication.

Identity federation with transient name identifiers

Identity federation with transient name identifiers enables you to provide authenticated users with access to your system. However, you don't need to create named users for them in your system; you can leverage technical users instead.

In contrast to anonymous access, users first have to authenticate at an IdP as an additional security measure. (The name "transient" comes from the fact that the user name already contained in the SAML token isn't actually used in this scenario.) Instead, you only determine how the attributes contained in the SAML2 token are mapped to technical users in your system. While the IdP handles the management of the users and their authentication without your intervention, you only have to bother about mapping the rules, which is a one-time effort.

As an example for a B2C scenario that can leverage identity federation with a transient name identifier, let's take a small retail company called ITelo that sells IT equipment to its customers and thereby offers an e-procurement OData service. The employees of its customers are able to access the product catalogue, and cost center owners can place orders with ITelo through an HTML5-based application that consumes the OData service provided by ITelo.

This scenario is feasible because the employees of ITelo's customer have been authenticated by the IdP of the customer that has issued a SAML token containing the following attributes:

▶ Company name

▶ Cost center

▶ Role (cost center owner or employee)

ITelo trusts the SAML tokens that have been issued by the IdP of the customer, and ITelo's SAP Gateway hub has been configured to accept those SAML tokens. In addition, ITelo's IT department has created technical users for each cost center owner of the customer and one for all employees of the customer in the SAP Gateway hub and in ITelo's enterprise resource planning backend—rather than performing this task for each employee of the customer. (User creation has to take place in the SAP Gateway hub and the SAP Gateway backend because both use a trusted RFC connection.) Employees that aren't cost center owners are mapped instead to users in ITelo's SAP Gateway hub and backend that have only the authorization to display the product catalogue.

In our example, which is depicted in Figure 15.19, Dagmar Schulze (with the company Becker Berlin) is the owner of the cost center

10001234 and has authenticated at the IdP of her company. The IdP has issued a SAML token that contains the information about her role and her cost center assignment. When accessing the e-procurement service, she is mapped to the service user P123456 that has the authorization to place orders for the customer Becker Berlin. A normal employee would be mapped to the service user P123457, which has only read access to ITelo's backend system.

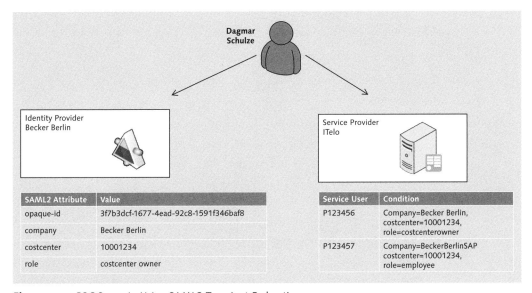

SAML2 Attribute	Value		Service User	Condition
opaque-id	3f7b3dcf-1677-4ead-92c8-1591f346baf8		P123456	Company=Becker Berlin, costcenter=10001234, role=costcenterowner
company	Becker Berlin			
costcenter	10001234		P123457	Company=BeckerBerlinSAP costcenter=10001234, role=employee
role	costcenter owner			

Figure 15.19 B2C Scenario Using SAML2 Transient Federation

The great advantage of using identity federation with transient name identifiers is that it enables you to grant controlled access to external users. Even if, for example, the role of an employee of ITelo's customer changes, ITelo doesn't have to maintain the users and rules on its side. This is especially true if an employee leaves the customer because it's the task of the customer's IT department to make sure to delete the user account of that employee.

> **Note**
>
> B2C scenarios that don't use named users in the SAP Business Suite backend require the customer to license the usage of SAP Gateway.

15.5 Read Access Logging

Read Access Logging (*RAL*) helps SAP customers stay compliant with data privacy regulations. Integrated into the SAP NetWeaver platform, RAL enables simple logging access to sensitive data to detect unwanted activities such as fraud or data theft. Using RAL, a company can track data access so that the following questions can be answered:

- Who has access to the data?
- When has the data been accessed?
- Which data has been accessed?
- Via which channel has the data been accessed?

RAL currently works for the following channels: Web Services, RFCs, Dynpro, Web Dynpro, and, as of SAP NetWeaver 7.50 SP 01, OData services. There are template roles available for business and technical administrators (SAP_BC_RAL_ADMIN_BIZ, SAP_BC_RAL_ADMIN_TEC) and supporters (SAP_BC_RAL_ANALYZER, SAP_BC_RAL_SUPPORTER) so that different type of access to the data can be allowed.

For example, RAL might be used by a compliance manager of a company after he receives complaints from one of his business partners that contact details of his employees have been misused. Unauthorized employees of the compliance manager's company used the data to contact the business partner's employees. Therefore, the compliance manager could start to monitor the access to the contact data of his business partner via an SAP Fiori application.

RAL requires $batch
In the following example, we've thus activated RAL to monitor the access to the `ContactSet` entity set of the OData `GWSAMPLE_BASIC` sample service. Several fields from the Entity Type: Contact such as BP_ID, CONTACT_GUID, EMAIL_ADDRESS, FIRST_NAME, LAST_NAME, MIDDLE_NAME and PHONE_NUMBER have been selected, so that access to the same via this OData service is now recorded (see Figure 15.20).

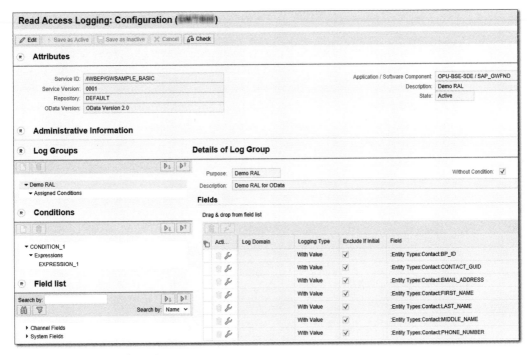

Figure 15.20 RAL—Configuration

When you try to run */sap/opu/odata/IWBEP/GWSAMPLE_BASIC/BusinessPartnerSet('0100000000')/ToContacts* in the SAP Gateway client after RAL has been activated, you'll get an error message (see Figure 15.21) indicating that access to this data is only available via $batch.

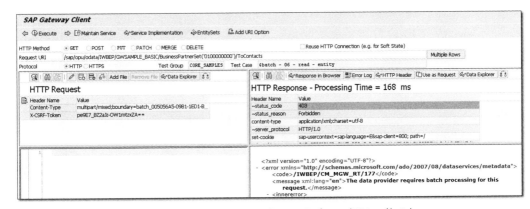

Figure 15.21 Error Stating That Access to Entities Need to Be Performed Using $batch

The reason for this error message is that after the activation of RAL, the RAL configuration is read whenever an OData service is called. If the backend runtime determines that a request is monitored via RAL, it also checks if $batch has been used. As discussed earlier in this chapter in Section 15.1.1, the use of $batch provides a higher security when using read requests. If $batch is used a GET request is sent as a part of the payload in a POST request. As a result, the complete URI, including any query parameters, is secured via HTTPS. That's why it's enforced for services that use RAL (see Figure 15.22).

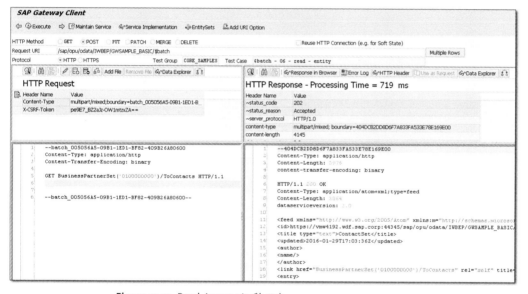

Figure 15.22 Read Access via $batch

Read access to the business partner's contacts with the Business Partner ID '0100000000' is possible via $batch (see Figure 15.22) by sending it to */sap/opu/odata/IWBEP/GWSAMPLE_BASIC/$batch* and is logged via RAL. This can be monitored, as shown in Figure 15.23.

The compliance manager is now able to prove that the details of the contact of the aforementioned business partner have been read via an OData service by a certain employee of company A.

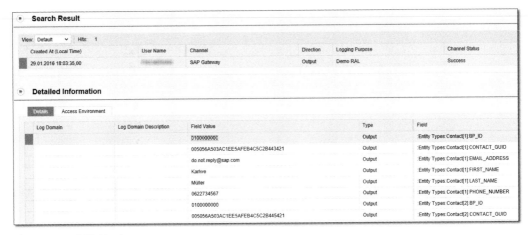

Figure 15.23 RAL Monitor

15.6 Summary

In this chapter, we've provided an overview of the most important security-related topics with respect to SAP Gateway. We touched on the basics of network-related topics and provided a sound introduction to the various authentication options, together with a recommendation on how these can be leveraged to achieve SSO. Having a better understanding about which authentication option is best suited for the various scenarios that we've outlined will help you make an informed decision for you own use case. In addition, you learned how access to sensitive data can be monitored via RAL to prevent data theft and fraud.

PART V

Roadmap

The closing chapter of the book looks at different trends that might be relevant for future developments of SAP Gateway.

16   Recent and Future Developments

By now, you should have a good understanding of what SAP Gateway is all about. With this understanding comes the realization that SAP Gateway exists in a somewhat volatile environment due to ever-changing market situations, new technology, and new business trends.

For this reason, it's necessary for SAP Gateway to adjust and grow to meet constantly changing requirements. In this chapter, we'll give you an overview of some new technologies and trends and how they relate to SAP Gateway, and we'll also look at what you can expect in the future.

> **Disclaimer**
>
> Note that this chapter is about *possible* future developments. It's an attempt to foresee some of the trends, scenarios, and technologies that will be important in the future. This chapter isn't meant to be a roadmap for SAP products. It simply offers some outlook on possible future developments based on today's information.

16.1   Cloud Computing: HCI OData Provisioning

Before we look at SAP Gateway and the cloud, let's quickly consider cloud computing in general. As we already discussed in Chapter 1, cloud computing is about effectively using resources, either hardware or software, provided by or through a network. What makes the approach special is that these resources are provided as services. In general, there are three main types of cloud services: Infrastructure as a Service (IaaS), Platform as a Service (PaaS), and Software as a Service (SaaS). (For details on the different approaches, refer to Chapter 1, Section 1.1.2.)

IaaS, PaaS, SaaS

> **BaaS**
>
> The preceding categorization is based on the classic types in cloud computing. Lately, we see additional abbreviations for different scenarios in and around the cloud. In our context, Backend as a Service (BaaS) is the most relevant when referring to scenarios in which the accessed backend resides in the cloud.

Cloud computing allows flexible, fast, and comparatively cheap access to resources on demand. The newly won agility companies achieve by moving into the cloud can be translated into acceleration of innovation cycles and increased business agility—a necessity in today's market. This becomes even more important in the age of digital transformation and the digital economy (see Appendix B for more information).

It's important to understand that most companies don't plan to move completely into the cloud; they still prefer some systems to be on-premise (e.g., due to security concerns or legal restrictions). Fortunately, systems in the cloud easily integrate with on-premise systems, and this integration allows an extension of on-premise systems that increases their value.

With respect to SAP's cloud strategy, we can distinguish different areas:

- Applications
- Platform
- Business network
- Infrastructure and lifecycle management

In the following subsections, we'll look at each of these areas.

16.1.1 Cloud Applications

Applications in the cloud are faster to deploy and easy to adopt, and they can be updated without interruption, which allows for nondisruptive innovation. SAP is offering more than 30 applications and suites in the cloud as of today. The applications focus on critical assets of companies such as customers, suppliers, and employees.

16.1.2 Cloud Platforms

SAP also offers PaaS: SAP HANA Cloud Platform (SAP HCP) (Figure 16.1). As the name suggests, the SAP HCP is based on SAP HANA, which allows the combination of the benefits of cloud computing and the benefits—and speed—of SAP's in-memory database.

Cloud platforms

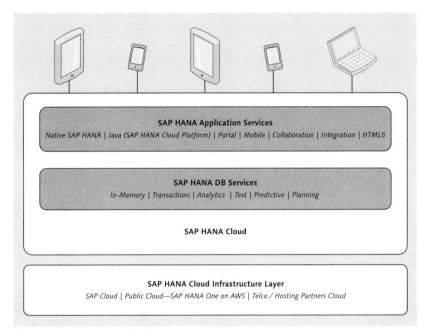

Figure 16.1 SAP HANA Cloud Platform

SAP HCP provides a standards-based development and runtime environment leveraging SAP HANA—and thus its speed—as a persistency service. It provides features such as a scalable document service or connectivity service enabling seamless integration with SAP and other systems. Furthermore, the SAP Identity Management service can be used to implement federated identity management with SAP HCP.

SAP HCP

An important aspect of SAP HCP is that it integrates seamlessly with on-premise installations through SAP HANA Cloud Integration (HCI) technology. In the context of other trends mentioned in this chapter, it comes with built-in functionality to create mobile, social, and analytical applications. Those applications can be managed and monitored via a web-based account page.

16.1.3 Business Networks

Using cloud computing as a technical solution for dedicated business scenarios is one way of leveraging the technology to save money and solve problems in specific setups. However, to get the best out of the new possibilities, going a step further makes sense. Instead of using distinguished cloud installations with no further connection, you can benefit from business networks.

SAP Ariba Network

A business network is a business collaboration community. The SAP Ariba Network connects 730,000 businesses in 186 countries around the world—all through the cloud. Not only does this network allow customers to work efficiently and cost-effectively across the complete value chain, it also allows customers to implement automated processes between companies, thus offering completely new and extended business processes.

16.1.4 Infrastructure and Lifecycle Management

SAP virtualization and cloud management solutions

One of the challenges of cloud computing is leveraging the investment made in on-premise installations. SAP provides a scalable approach to cloud computing. With SAP virtualization and cloud management solutions, it's possible to take a step-by-step approach into the cloud. This approach allows you to get the most out of existing investments while at the same time profiting from virtualization cloud computing. As an additional benefit, SAP offers the possibility to take complete existing on-premise test installations and deploy them into public clouds. With this approach, it's possible to test at a minimum cost and keep critical on-premise systems safe.

To stress the importance of flexibility, SAP HCI not only allows the integration of cloud applications and on-premise installations from SAP and third-party vendors but is also a new holistic cloud-based integration technology. SAP HCI offers both process and data integration capabilities and provides a kind of layer on top of a multitenant cloud infrastructure, creating a unified view of the data in that company. Customers who don't have an on-premise SAP NetWeaver installation can quickly get started using SAP HCI via prepackaged integration and content. In addition, new custom content can be built easily using open application programming interfaces (APIs). The deployment choice (on-premise or on-demand) remains with the customer.

Overall, it's important to note that SAP offers a very flexible approach to cloud computing. Customers who want to deploy their SAP HANA-based applications in the cloud can choose from a wide variety of hosting capabilities provided by SAP and SAP partners, offering choices of how and with whom they step up into the cloud. Furthermore, a scalable approach allows moving into the cloud with the speed the customer sees fit for his company.

How does SAP Gateway fit into this picture? For the mentioned approach, it's essential that the benefits of SAP Gateway are made available in the cloud context as well. To this end, SAP introduced *Gateway as a Service (GWaaS)*. In 2014, GWaaS was renamed as *HCI OData Provisioning*. HCI OData Provisioning is now available on the SAP HCP trial landscape and can be used to connect to SAP Business Suite systems that are SAP Gateway-enabled through the SAP HANA cloud connector. Further information can be found at *http://scn.sap.com/docs/DOC-69093*.

HCI OData Provisioning

16.2 Gamification

So what is gamification all about? It may seem a bit odd to introduce games and game mechanics in a business context, but if we take a closer look at the mechanics, it turns out the approach makes sense. (Before we do this, understand that gamification is somewhat of a new trend; that is, it's hard to predict its development and impact in the future.)

One of the main challenges companies face today is the engagement of their employees, customers, and end users in general. How can you motivate your employees to work more efficiently? How can you convince your customers to visit your product pages more often, for a longer time, and eventually buy your services? Gamification isn't the entire solution for this problem, but it may be part of the solution.

Gamification as motivation

This may seem a bit abstract, so let's briefly walk through an example of a help desk scenario involving a customer and the help desk employee. In a classic scenario, the customer calls or writes to the help desk person for assistance (e.g., "the display driver doesn't support 3D"). The help desk person then provides a solution (e.g., "update the driver"), and, eventually, perhaps after several iterations, the problem is fixed, the customer gives up, or the issue escalates.

With gamification, the motivation of the help desk employee can be increased and thus may lead to a satisfied customer. One simple way to do this is to add an experience level to help desk employees. Every piece of positive feedback from a customer increases this experience level. To enhance the effect, it makes sense to label specific levels (e.g., novice, senior, expert). Furthermore, it may make sense to introduce leaderboards or missions (e.g., solve 10 issues in a row with positive feedback). Those missions could then be combined with badges to increase motivation even further.

Depending on the scenario, the kicker might be to combine those ideas with social media, so that the players—in our example, the help desk employees—can post their achievements. (Admittedly, this is a much better kicker when customers are in the player role.)

Gamification as innovation
Before we take a look at gamification at SAP, let's consider another important aspect of gamification—as innovation. The mentioned mechanics can easily be used to increase innovation within a company. To enable innovation, motivation is essential—preferably motivation of stakeholders and involved people. Here gamification can be the difference between getting involved and not getting involved. In combination with social media and the community, it's possible to access a knowledge pool that wasn't available before. All this together may lead to a completely new level of innovation.

SAP Community Network (SCN)
SAP understood the potential of gamification quite early and was in a unique position to provide gamification and enterprise readiness with its applications. After years of using some gamification mechanics and then officially implementing them on the SAP Community Network (SCN), it's now time to offer a platform that can be used in enterprises.

Gamification has been implemented as a service in SAP HCP. For further details, visit *http://scn.sap.com/community/gamification.*

Because gamification works best when integrated tightly into your applications, it makes sense to support gamification from within SAP Gateway as well. An SAP HCP gamification service allows integration through APIs.

As of today, SAP Gateway and SAP HCP gamification services can be used to offer a flexible yet enterprise-ready approach to gamification for companies. With social media (see Chapter 12) as a kicker, gamification may be a literal game changer for engagement and innovation in companies.

16.3 Internet of Things

On a very basic level, the Internet of Things is the addition of physical objects into the Internet. For example, a lot of physical objects today are available for representation (e.g., tagged with an RFID chip), are more sophisticated and even aware of their surroundings through sensors (e.g., mini cameras), or can influence their surroundings via actuators. All of these objects communicate with their surroundings (including humans) or each other via *Machine to Machine (M2M) communication*, using communication protocols such as Internet Protocol (IP).

A basic and current example of the Internet of Things is in the interaction with end users buying consumer products. Potential buyers can use their mobile phones in combination with RFID chips (or sometimes simple QR codes) on products to get additional information on the product. (Where does it come from? Is it an original? Is it "green"?) This information can be critical for the decision of the potential buyers to buy or not to buy a product. In a more sophisticated scenario, it's even possible to imagine situations in which the product automatically changes its price to convince the buyers to buy it.

Interaction with end users

From an enterprise perspective, the Internet of Things can make it easier to track products from the production site, through shipment, to the shop, and eventually to the consumer. In addition to all of the opportunities this may offer in the production process, it can help a company identify buyer patterns and track products—in some cases, even to the individual consumer.

The business scenarios are endless. For SAP, they were reason enough to come up with a joint announcement with Ericsson at the Mobile World Congress on February 25, 2013, on a new combination of cloud-based M2M solutions to enhance enterprise efficiency. And this is just the beginning.

With solutions such as SAP HANA and its real-time capabilities, SAP HCP is in a perfect spot to come up with its own end-to-end solution—SAP solutions for the Internet of Things. The necessities to handle, analyze, and calculate with high volumes of data in real time is a perfect use case for SAP HANA.

> **Further Resources**
>
> For more information on the SAP solutions for the Internet of Things, we recommend *http://go.sap.com/solution/internet-of-things.html* and *http://go.sap.com/sk/product/technology-platform.html* .

As mentioned, the SAP solutions for the Internet of Things provides an end-to-end solution, including the integration of various devices (i.e., M2M) and tools for managing those devices. Furthermore, it provides the tools required to easily and rapidly develop applications in this context.

Although we don't yet know the details of how SAP Gateway will integrate with the SAP solutions for the Internet of Things, the applications we're talking about are for multichannel scenarios, so it's very likely to play a big role.

16.4 API Management

At the time of the writing of the first edition of this book (January 2014), we saw API management as one of the main development trends.

In light of this fact, SAP partnered with Apigee in 2014 to introduce SAP API Management. Since then, SAP began offering its own API management solution. Because this product (SAP API Management) has many ties to SAP Gateway, we dedicated an appendix to it. You can find the information on SAP API Management in Appendix B.

16.5   Summary

In this final chapter, we discussed some of the relevant trends we see in today's IT and enterprise world. We took a closer look at the different implications and possibilities related to these trends and SAP, including SAP Gateway in particular. As mentioned earlier, our intent was to outline possible future developments, as well as the importance of the role SAP Gateway might play in them. Since the first edition of our book, we saw that some of the trends became reality in the SAP world (e.g., SAP API Management).

Appendices

A   Advanced Topics

In this appendix, we'll cover some advanced topics that might be useful for your SAP Gateway project. This includes both advanced SAP Gateway features as well as advanced operations topics.

First, we'll take a closer look at scenarios in which multiple SAP Business Suite systems are connected to a single SAP Gateway server (hub) system. Then we'll look into an SAP Gateway feature that allows for sending notifications from SAP Gateway to consumers. Next, there will be an in-depth look at handling and analyzing errors and performance problems, including an introduction to the Performance Trace tool, which analyzes the performance behavior of your services and identifies potential improvement areas. Finally, we'll look into the options if you need an application to run online and offline.

A.1   Connecting Multiple SAP Business Suite Systems

Routing, multiple origin composition (MOC), and throttling are advanced and very useful features of SAP Gateway. They were introduced with SAP Gateway 2.0 SP 05 and address the use case of SAP Gateway connecting to multiple SAP Business Suite systems.

A classic example of a company that would have use for routing, MOC, or throttling is one that operates three identical SAP Business Suite systems in separate regions. Figure A.1 shows the structure of an example company with three data centers: one in America (US), one in Asia Pacific and Japan (APJ), and one in Europe, Middle East, and Africa (EMEA). We'll talk more about routing, MOC, and throttling next.

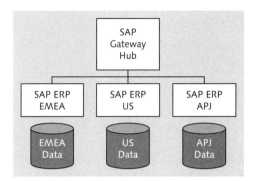

Figure A.1 Multiple Backend System Support

A.1.1 Routing

Routing is used to route a consumer request to a dedicated SAP Business Suite system if multiple system alias entries are assigned to a service. Using routing, it's possible, for example, to use a single service for all employees in a global setup that is made up of different regions. In this case, depending on user roles in the SAP Gateway hub, a system call is redirected to the SAP Business Suite system that is located in the employees' region. A US employee, for example, only retrieves data from the US SAP Business Suite system, whereas employees from the EMEA region only retrieve data from the SAP Business Suite system that serves the EMEA region.

Routing is performed in the SAP Gateway hub by the *destination finder* component. To execute the routing, it calls the /IWFND/CL_MGW_DEST_FINDER class. The destination finder performs the routing for OData services based on the customizing settings for the system aliases. For every system alias, you can maintain a user role and the hostname used by the OData client as additional optional parameters to configure the routing to a system alias entry, as shown in Figure A.2.

The destination finder compares the role assignment of the current user in the SAP Gateway hub. These settings are stored in maintenance view /IWFND/V_MGDEAM, which can be maintained via IMG by starting Transaction SPRO and navigating to SAP NETWEAVER • SAP GATEWAY • ODATA CHANNEL • CONFIGURATION • CONNECTION SETTINGS • SAP GATEWAY TO SAP SYSTEM. In addition, the value for the hostname that can optionally be maintained in the configuration is compared to the OData request's HTTP header `Host` field (e.g., 'myserver.mycompany.com: 50055'). Based on the roles assigned to a user in the SAP Gateway hub and the hostname used by the OData client, the destination finder then determines which SAP Business Suite system to call. If a service is registered to more than one system alias, as shown in Figure A.2, there must be exactly one entry flagged as default. That system alias is used for all standard requests.

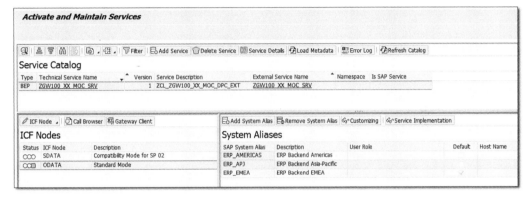

Figure A.2 Assignment of Multiple System Aliases

In some customer deployments, however, SAP roles aren't sufficient to determine the correct SAP Business Suite system. Because of this, SAP allows the implementation of customer-specific routing rules that can't be implemented via role assignment based on a Business Add-In (BAdI). Customers that want to leverage this enhanced functionality can implement the `/IWFND/ES_MGW_DEST_FINDER` enhancement spot. This enhancement spot is described in more detail in Section A.1.3 because it can also be used to shield an SAP Business Suite system from being overloaded.

A.1.2 Multiple Origin Composition

Multiple origin composition (MOC) allows a single service to connect to multiple SAP Business Suite systems in parallel and collect data from all of these systems. This data is then aggregated in the response of that single service. MOC allows for READ, CREATE, QUERY, DELETE, and UPDATE operations on this data. As a result, a single service can be made available to access data from several system aliases. For example, the CFO of the company might need to retrieve financial data from all regions.

Calling several SAP Business Suite systems at the same time using MOC obviously raises a few questions. The first question is how the result sets from the different SAP Business Suite systems can be distinguished. The framework achieves this by adding a new SAP__ORIGIN key field to each entity that is returned as an entry in the result set when the service is called using the ;mo MOC option, as shown in Listing A.1. Consequently, the service metadata document of a service that is called using the MOC option changes as well. Each entity type has an additional "SAP__ORI-GIN" key field. So, technically speaking, calling a service via MOC lets the framework create a different version of the service. For the consumption side, this has the consequence that calling an OData service with the MOC option probably requires adjustment of the client application because the OData interface has changed (if there was already an existing service without MOC).

```
Request:
/sap/opu/odata/sap/ZCD204_EPM_DEMO_SRV;mo/BusinessPartners
results": [
{
"SAP__Origin": „ERP_EMEA",
"BusinessPartnerID": "0100000000",
"CompanyName": "SAP"},
{
"SAP__Origin": „ERP_EMEA",
"BusinessPartnerID": "0100000001",
"CompanyName": "Becker Berlin"},
{
"SAP__Origin": „ERP_AMERICAS",
"BusinessPartnerID": "0100000027",
"CompanyName": "Developement Para O Governo"},
{
"SAP__Origin": „ERP_AMERICAS",
"BusinessPartnerID": "0100000028",
"CompanyName": "Brazil Technologies"}
]
```

Listing A.1 Response of a Request That Uses MOC

Performance · Another important aspect when using MOC is the impact with respect to performance. Calling the SAP Business Suite systems in a sequential order might result in increased response times that can lead to timeout errors on the consumption side—remember, the SAP Business Suite systems might be located on different continents. Therefore, SAP Gateway allows for certain settings to be made to adjust MOC in such a way that several SAP Business Suite systems can be called in parallel. You can then tailor the level of parallel calls to your specific system environment. The performance can be checked with the help of the Performance Trace tool and the statistics tool, which are discussed later in this chapter.

The MINIMUM NUMBER OF BACKEND SYSTEMS and MAXIMUM NUMBER OF PARALLEL BACKEND CALLS configuration parameters are the most relevant. Both of these configuration settings have a major effect on the parallelization of service calls, which again has a major impact on performance.

With MINIMUM NUMBER OF BACKEND SYSTEMS, you basically define whether there is parallelization. If you enter "0" for a value, no parallelization takes place. If you enter a number "n", parallelization will only be done from n SAP Business Suite systems onward.

MAXIMUM NUMBER OF PARALLEL BACKEND CALLS can be used to limit the number of parallel backend calls. This results in putting a ceiling on the use of SAP Gateway hub system resources.

As for the effect of these settings and the use of parallelization on the overall performance, keep the following in mind:

▶ For serialized calls, the duration of a service call in the SAP Gateway hub is the sum of all calls to the SAP Business Suite.

▶ For parallel calls, the duration of a service call is the duration of the single call that takes the longest.

In conclusion, configuring MOC typically results in a major performance improvement.

But reading data from multiple backend systems also raises the question of what happens if one or more backend systems aren't available. The default behavior is that the service raises an error and doesn't return any data. If a service is configured to be error-tolerant however, it would return data if one or more backend systems fail to respond. The client can retrieve the data at a later point in time by using a skiptoken, which

Error tolerance

is added at the end of the response (Listing A.2). An error is only raised if all backend systems aren't reachable.

```
<link rel="next" href=" TravelagencyCollection?$skiptoken=
MISSING_DATA_FROM__1_2" />
```
Listing A.2 Skiptoken Sent in the Response of an Error-Tolerant Service

You can configure a service to be error tolerant via customizing by starting Transaction SPRO and navigating to SAP NetWeaver • SAP Gateway • OData Channel • Composition • Flag OData Services to be error tolerant in case of MDC.

A.1.3 Throttling

Throttling helps when the SAP Business Suite system needs to be shielded from being overloaded by too many client requests. For external-facing scenarios, products such as SAP API Management or third-party tools will be used. To facilitate the implementation of throttling in internal scenarios or as an additional security measure for external-facing scenarios, SAP offers a BAdI that can be implemented by customers. This is the same BAdI that customers have to implement if they want to overrule the standard role-based routing.

The /IWFND/ES_MGW_DEST_FINDER enhancement spot serves two use cases:

- ▶ To overwrite or enhance the standard routing for a service
- ▶ To control the traffic from the SAP Gateway hub to an SAP Business Suite system to limit the load on that SAP Business Suite system

The BAdI has the following input parameters:

- ▶ User ID
- ▶ Service Document Identifier, which is a concatenated string of the technical service name and the version (e.g., ZTEA_TEST_APPLICATION_0001)
- ▶ A table of system alias entries that contains the result of the standard routing
- ▶ A list of HTTP request parameters

The output of the BAdI is a table of system aliases. The BAdI may also leave the table unchanged; in this case, the default routing is applied.

As we said, the BAdI can be used not only to implement customer-specific routing but also to shield the SAP Business Suite system from being overloaded by too many client requests. Listing A.3 provides sample code that can be used in such a BAdI implementation. This code raises an error message if a potential overload is discovered.

```
    . . .
    RAISE EXCEPTION TYPE /iwfnd/cx_mgw_dest_finder
      EXPORTING
        textid              = /iwfnd/cx_mgw_dest_finder=>backend_
load_too_high
        http_status_code = /iwfnd/cx_mgw_dest_finder=>gc_
status_service_unavailable
        system_alias     = lv_system_alias.
```
Listing A.3 Sample Implementation to Throw an Exception Due to a System Overload

When a BAdI implementation throws an exception as shown in Listing A.3, the OData client gets the HTTP error response as shown in Listing A.4.

```
HTTP Status          503 - Service Unavailable
<?xml version="1.0" encoding="utf-8" ?>
<error xmlns="http://schemas.microsoft.com/ado/2007/08/
dataservices/metadata">
<code>/IWFND/CM_COS/071</code>
<message xml:lang="en">The load on backend system 'ERP_GBC_
100' is too high. Try again later.</message>
        </error>
```
Listing A.4 HTTP Error Response

A.2   Configuring Notifications in SAP Gateway

The use of notifications in mobile scenarios is very common. Getting notified if a comment is posted on your Facebook site or if somebody replied to a tweet you posted is a must-have feature that users expect from any social media application. The important thing here is that the user not only gets notified but can also perform an action using the Facebook or Twitter client. Similar functionalities are useful in business scenarios. Managers appreciate being able to approve leave requests or purchase orders using their mobile device without having to switch to their laptop or PC after having been notified that something has happened that needs their attention.

This functionality is provided by the SAP Gateway Subscription and Notification framework, which is contained in the IW_BEP add-on or included in SAP NetWeaver 7.40 and higher. In SAP Gateway, to notify a user about a change that has happened in the SAP Business Suite system, the end user has to inform the SAP Business Suite system of which changes he's interested in and wants to be notified about via a *subscription*. For this, an entity set is marked as `sap:subscribable` in the SAP Gateway Service Builder, as shown in Figure A.3. When regenerating the project, the entity data model contains two new collections called `NotificationCollection` and `SubsriptionCollection`. These entity sets get activated after the entity set has been marked as `sap:subscribable`.

Figure A.3 Entity Set Marked as Subscribable in the Service Builder

You can create, update, delete, read, and query the `SubscriptionCollection` like any other entity set of an OData service using an appropriate URL and payload.

At this point, we now have to distinguish between push-oriented and pull-oriented scenarios:

▸ In a *push -oriented scenario*, a notification is sent from the SAP Business Suite via SAP Gateway directly to the consumer.

▸ In a *pull -oriented scenario*, the notifications are only sent from the SAP Business Suite to the SAP Gateway hub. Here they are persisted until the client pulls for the changed business objects.

If a user wants to get notified through a push notification about changes in a certain entity set, the user has to send an appropriate post request to the `SubscriptionCollection` of the service (Figure A.4, ❶, ❷). The `persistNotifications` parameter has to be set to `false`. The request for the subscription is then sent via remote function call (RFC) ❸ from the SAP

Gateway system to the SAP Business Suite system. In the SAP Business Suite system, the developer has to implement appropriate business logic, for example, in a BAdI that will check for subscriptions if an update has been performed. If a change occurred in the SAP Business Suite system, information about the change is first sent to the SAP Gateway server ❹ via a background RFC (bgRFC), where it's queued and sent to the receiving HTTP endpoint ❺ that was specified in the subscription.

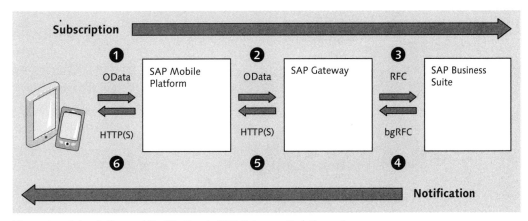

Figure A.4 Subscription and Notification in SAP Gateway: Push Scenario

In a push-oriented mobile scenario, you typically need an intermediate server as a receiving HTTP endpoint that facilitates the communication between the mobile device and the SAP Gateway server. The intermediate component recommended by SAP is the SAP Mobile Platform. Among other functionalities offered by a mobile platform, the SAP Mobile Platform holds the information concerning which device belongs to which user and is therefore able to send any notifications to the right person and device.

If the SAP Mobile Platform is used, it listens to a selected service for incoming notification requests. The information where this listener is located is sent by the mobile application to the SAP Gateway, where an appropriate HTTP destination has to be defined that points to the listener.

The intermediate server, such as the SAP Mobile Platform system, finally sends the notification to the user's device ❻.

In a pull-oriented scenario, the `persistNotifications` element in the original subscription payload `Create` request sent to the `Subscription-Collection` has to be set to `true`. The pull-oriented scenario is shown in Figure A.5. After the request has been sent from the client directly to the SAP Gateway ❶, it's sent from the SAP Gateway to the SAP Business Suite system ❷. Like in the push scenario, appropriate business logic, for example, in a BAdI, has to be implemented to check for changes in the SAP Business Suite system that will then send those changes ❸ via bgRFC to the SAP Gateway system. In a pull-oriented scenario, these notifications are then stored in the SAP Gateway system ❹.

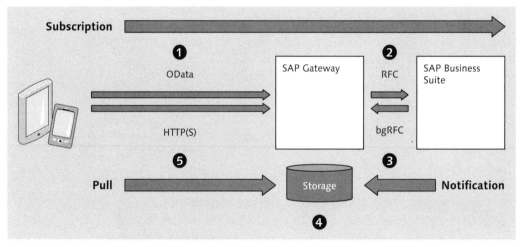

Figure A.5 Subscription and Notification in SAP Gateway: Pull Scenario

The client can pull the notifications using the `NOTIFICATIONSTORE` service provided with SAP Gateway. The notifications can actually be retrieved from the `NotificationCollection` as shown in the following `GET` request:

http://<hostname>:<port>/sap/opu/odata/iwfnd/NOTIFICATIONSTORE/ NotificationCollection

Although a pull-oriented scenario isn't a notification scenario in the strictest sense, it nevertheless helps to reduce the load on the SAP Business Suite side. Instead of querying the SAP Business Suite system for changes, this information can be retrieved from the `NotificationCol-lection` on the SAP Gateway system.

A detailed description on how to implement a service with push notifications can be found in the "SAP Gateway Self-Paced Learning" section on the SAP Community Network (SCN), together with a video on YouTube describing the process: *http://wiki.sdn.sap.com/wiki/pages/viewpage.action?pageId=318672261.*

A.3   Using the Error Log

In this hands-on section, we'll walk you through the process of analyzing an error that occurred in the SAP Business Suite system. The process flow for the error analysis is shown in Figure A.6.

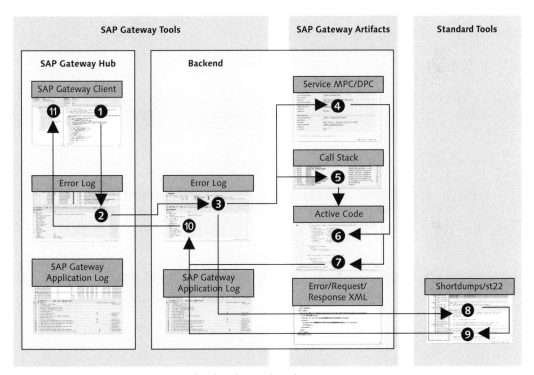

Figure A.6 Error Resolution in the Backend Coding and Replay

This process starts with a client executing a request ❶ that leads to an error. This error can be found in the error log ❷ on the SAP Gateway server. From there, the next step is to analyze the error in the SAP Business Suite error log ❸. Here you can investigate the service implementation ❹ or find the error location in the call stack ❺ to finally open the active coding ❻. The next step is then to either correct the coding or to set an external breakpoint to investigate the error situation ❼. If the error has led to an ABAP short dump, Transaction ST22 is used instead ❽, and breakpoints are set there ❾. After the error has been corrected, it's possible from within the error log ❿ to replay the request with the SAP Gateway client ⓫.

In this walkthrough, we follow, for the most part, the process outlined in Figure A.6 and start in the SAP Gateway hub. There we use the SAP Gateway client to perform an HTTP request to mimic the consumption of a service by an OData client. We use a sample service Z_PRODUCT_SRV that retrieves demo product data from the SAP NetWeaver demo data model. This sample service is intended to make the error processing visible. In this specific scenario, the requested query method hasn't been implemented so that the generated code throws an error when it's called by the service.

By executing the following request, an exception is thrown as shown in Figure A.7:

/sap/opu/odata/sap/Z_PRODUCT_SRV/ProductSet

This exception holds several details ❶ that can be inspected in the error log.

Selecting Error Log (❷ of Figure A.7) takes you to the error log. By double-clicking the error message, the error context appears (❶ of Figure A.8). Here, you can take a closer look at the system information, service information, and other details.

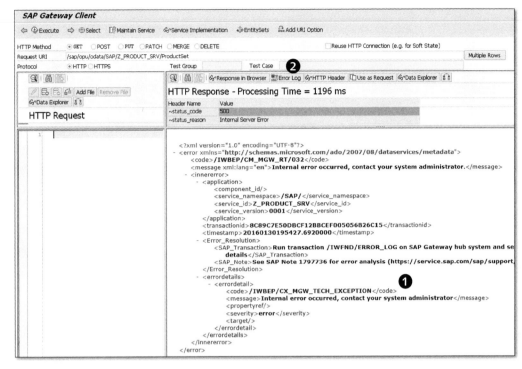

Figure A.7 Error When Calling the Z_PRODUCT_SRV Service

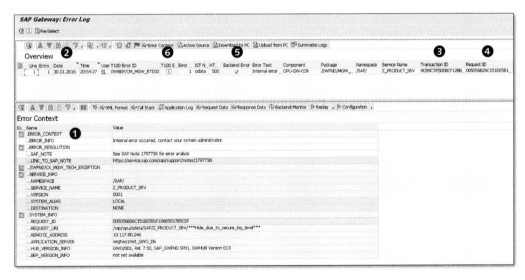

Figure A.8 Error Log

In the OVERVIEW section ❷, you can see the TRANSACTION ID of the request ❸ and the REQUEST ID of the client ❹. The TRANSACTION ID is important to know in case you want to search for this request in any standard SAP NetWeaver monitoring transaction. The TRANSACTION ID is also part of the SAP passport.

The next important information is the BACKEND ERROR flag ❺. This flag tells you that the root cause of this error appeared in the backend and not in the SAP Gateway hub system. (Backend system here refers to the system on which the implementation of the service based on IW_BEP has been performed.)

The next important information is the T100 long text, which is displayed if you click on the icon ❻ in the T100 ERROR INFO column. This long text might contain additional information about the error that has occurred, as shown in Figure A.9.

Figure A.9 T100 Error Information

When you click on BACKEND MONITOR, you're taken to the backend error log (Figure A.10) that can also be accessed using Transaction /IWBEP/ERROR_LOG on the backend system. It shows the error log in the SAP Business Suite system. This log looks very similar to the error log on the SAP Gateway server, so everything should look very familiar to you.

Now you need to find out where exactly in the coding the exception was thrown. You have two options to find this information. The first option is to select CALL STACK ❶, and the second option is to select ACTIVE SOURCE ❷. CALL STACK helps you see the flow of the application. ACTIVE SOURCE brings you directly into the coding as shown in Figure A.11.

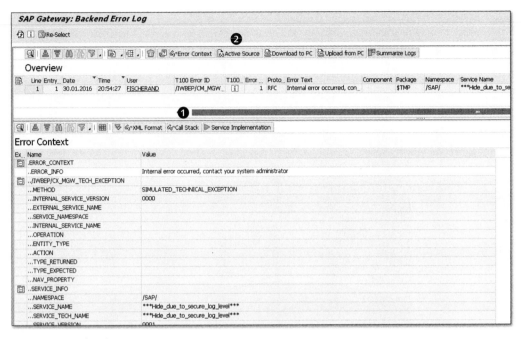

Figure A.10 Backend Error Log

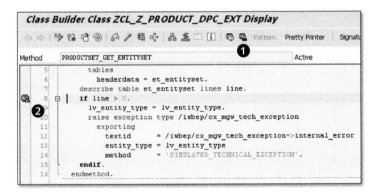

Figure A.11 ABAP Code Error Location

Here, you can set an external breakpoint (❶ and ❷). You either go back to the SAP Gateway client to perform the HTTP request again or navigate back to the error log on the SAP Gateway hub (as shown in Figure A.12) where you can choose REPLAY ❶ to run the request again.

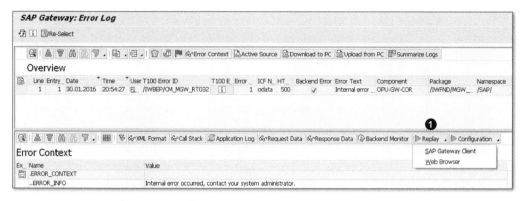

Figure A.12 Replaying a Request

The request is run in the SAP Gateway client again. In this example, however, an error message occurs that tells you a replay can't be performed due to security reasons (Figure A.13).

Figure A.13 Error Message: Secure Log Level

The error log level can be configured directly in the error log transaction. As shown in Figure A.14, from the menu bar ❶, select Error Log • Global Configuration. On the SAP Gateway: Global Configuration page, you can set the Error Log Level to Full ❷.

Run the request in the SAP Gateway client again. Because you've set an external breakpoint ❶, the system stops at the same location ❷, as shown in Figure A.15.

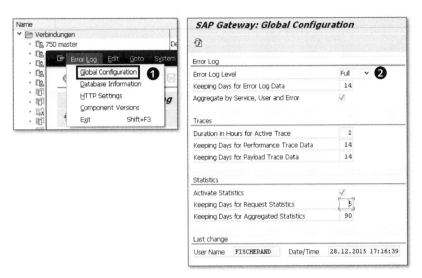

Figure A.14 Error Log Level Configuration

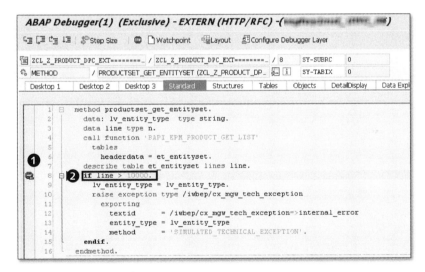

Figure A.15 Stop at Breakpoint

In Figure A.11, shown earlier, you can see that an error message was raised because the result set contains more than zero entities.

After correcting the code in the GET_ENTITYSET method in the data provider class (DPC), as shown in Figure A.15, you can try out the replay functionality again; this time, you've changed the settings of the error log as described earlier. As shown in Figure A.16, the request now runs successfully with an HTTP return code 200 ❶. The large value for the processing time ❷ is due to the fact that the request processing stopped at the external breakpoint.

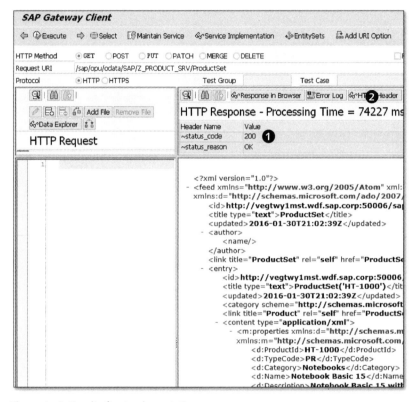

Figure A.16 Result after Implementation

If you don't know how to solve a problem, choose DOWNLOAD TO PC in the error log to download the error message to your desktop.

The XML shown in Figure A.17 contains all of the information you saw in the UI of the error log: error data ❶, error context ❷, service information ❸, and system information ❹.

```
<?xml version="1.0" encoding="UTF-8"?>
<SAPGW_BEP_ERROR_LOG>
  - <item timestamp="20160130195427">
❶ + <ERROR_DATA>
  - <ERROR_CONTEXT>
      <ERROR_INFO>Internal error occurred, contact your system administrator</ERROR_INFO>
❷    + <_-IWBEP_-CX_MGW_TECH_EXCEPTION>
     <SERVICE_INFO>
❸      <NAMESPACE>/SAP/</NAMESPACE>
        <SERVICE_NAME>***Hide_due_to_secure_log_level***</SERVICE_NAME>
        <SERVICE_TECH_NAME>***Hide_due_to_secure_log_level***</SERVICE_TECH_NAME>
        <SERVICE_VERSION>0001</SERVICE_VERSION>
        <SEC_SERVICE_NAME>Z_PRODUCT_SRV</SEC_SERVICE_NAME>
        <SEC_SERVICE_TECH_NAME>Z_PRODUCT_SRV</SEC_SERVICE_TECH_NAME>
        <MODEL_TECH_NAME>Z_PRODUCT_MDL</MODEL_TECH_NAME>
        <MODEL_VERSION>0001</MODEL_VERSION>
        <HUB_CACHE_TIMESTAMP>20160130191812</HUB_CACHE_TIMESTAMP>
❹    </SERVICE_INFO>
     + <SYSTEM_INFO>
    </ERROR_CONTEXT>
    + <CALL_STACK>
  </item>
</SAPGW_BEP_ERROR_LOG>
```

Figure A.17 Error XML

A.4 Analyzing Performance and SAP Gateway Statistics

Every HTTP request coming from an OData consumer takes a certain path in an SAP Gateway system, as shown in Figure A.18.

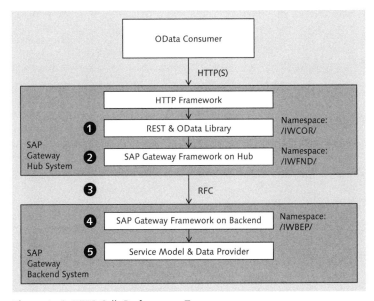

Figure A.18 HTTP Call: Performance Trace

When a request is placed, the HTTP request first enters the HTTP framework on the hub, is then handled by the REST and OData library ❶, and finally ends up in the SAP Gateway framework ❷. From the SAP Gateway framework on the hub, an RFC ❸ takes place to the SAP Gateway framework in the SAP Business Suite ❹. Finally, the application in the SAP Business Suite ❺ is called. This application consists of the service model that defines the metadata and the runtime.

From a performance point of view, you not only want to know the total response time but also what time a request takes in the different components mentioned earlier.

For a performance analysis, you want to know details about the time it took for the request to pass the SAP Gateway framework on the hub compared to the network overhead that results from the RFC from the hub to the SAP Business Suite for data transfer. In the SAP Business Suite, you want to know about the overhead of the backend framework and the processing time of the application Although it's mostly the backend implementation of a service that causes performance problems, it's also possible that a bad network connection between the hub and the SAP Gateway backend can result in bad response times.

To better understand the Performance Trace tool and statistic results, which are grouped by the namespace of the involved software components, it's good to know to which namespaces the components belong. While the REST and OData library components belong to the namespace /IWCOR/ and are contained in the GW_CORE add-on, the SAP Gateway framework components in the hub belong to the namespace /IWFND/ and are contained in the IW_FND add-on. The framework components in the SAP Business Suite belong to the namespace /IWBEP/ and are contained in the IW_BEP add-on. Note that as of 7.40, all components (GW_CORE, IW_FND, and IW_BEP) will be contained in only one add-on called SAP_GWFND, as discussed in Chapter 2.

SAP Gateway Statistics The SAP performance statistics that can be obtained by an OData client by adding *?sap-statistics=true* at the end of the request URL or by adding the HTTP request header `sap-statistics=true` that is now automatically stored by the SAP Gateway framework. The SAP Gateway statistics

Transaction /IWFND/STATS provides easy access to the statistics data described previously for requests that have just been processed by SAP Gateway.

Looking at the SAP Gateway Statistics in Figure A.19, you see data that are denoted as PROCESSING TIME, HUB OVERHEAD, RFC OVERHEAD, BACK-END OVERHEAD, and APPLICATION TIME. These time values correlate as follows to the single steps an HTTP request takes through the entire framework as noted by the callout numbers in Figure A.18:

▸ PROCESSING TIME = ❶ + ❷ + ❸ + ❹ + ❺

▸ HUB OVERHEAD = ❶ + ❷

▸ RFC OVERHEAD = ❸

▸ BACKEND OVERHEAD = ❹

▸ APPLICATION TIME = ❺

SAP Gateway Statistics

Request Statistics

Line	Cl	E	Namesp	Service Name	V	Operation	Entity Set or Fun	Exp	Batc	Processing	Hub Overhead	RFC Overhead	Backend Overhead	Application	Non-GW
1	001		/IWBEP/	GWSAMPLE_BASIC	1	read entry	SalesOrderSet			76	61	0	12	3	0
2			/IWBEP/	GWSAMPLE_BASIC	1	read entry	SalesOrderSet			76	60	0	12	4	0
3			/IWBEP/	GWSAMPLE_BASIC	1	read feed	SalesOrderSet			93	70	0	17	6	0
4			/IWBEP/	GWSAMPLE_BASIC	1	read feed	SalesOrderSet			93	71	0	16	6	0
5			/IWBEP/	GWSAMPLE_BASIC	1	read feed	SalesOrderSet			93	70	0	17	6	0
6			/IWBEP/	GWSAMPLE_BASIC	1	read feed	SalesOrderSet			103	76	0	18	9	0
7			/IWBEP/	GWSAMPLE_BASIC	1	document				123	119	0	4	0	0

Figure A.19 SAP Gateway Statistics: Transaction /IWFND/STATS

The total processing time is the sum of all five time intervals. The overhead that is caused by the SAP Gateway hub is the sum of the time intervals ❶ and ❷ that it takes the HTTP request to cross the first two layers of the SAP Gateway framework on the hub. The time for the RFC call between the SAP Gateway Hub and the backend system is denoted with ❸ in Figure A.18. Now the request enters the SAP Gateway framework on the backend system ❹ and finally calls the business logic ❺.

A developer testing a service can easily check the performance of the current service implementation. The RFC overhead time is zero in this case because we use a system with an embedded deployment.

The SAP Gateway statistics transaction also provides an aggregated view on statistics data shown in Figure A.20. This view provides a list of statistical data grouped by services, single operation types such as read feed or read entry, and finally the entity set names. For the GWSAMPLE_BASIC service, you see in Figure A.20 aggregated static data about different operations: DOCUMENT denotes the access to the service document, READ ENTRY denotes the access to a single entry in the BUSINESS-PARTNERSET entity set, and several READ FEED operations denote queries to the CONTACTSET, PRODUCTSET, and SALESORDERSET entity sets.

SAP Gateway Statistics: Aggregated Statistics

Aggregated Statistics

Line	Cl	Y	M Names	Service Name	V	Operation	Entity Set or F	E	Batch Operations	Cou	Median P	Processin	Hub Ove	RFC	Backend	Applicati	Non-GW	Parallel	Sum o
1	001	2016	1 /IWBEP/	GWSAMPLE_BASIC	1	document				1	384	384	335	0	49	0	0	0	0
2						read entry	BusinessPartnerS			3	89	285	233	0	20	32	0	0	32
3						read feed				1	511	511	206	0	194	111	0	0	111
4							ContactSet			2	247	247	172	0	43	32	0	0	32
5							ProductSet			1	352	352	128	0	100	124	0	0	124
6							SalesOrderSet			4	106	981	486	0	15	480	0	0	480
7			/IWFND/	CATALOGSERVICE		document				1	1.019	1.019	1.019	0	0	0	0	0	0
8			/SAP/	EPM_REF_APPS_P						2	81	81	75	0	6	0	0	0	0
9						read entry	PurchaseOrders			2	203	203	59	0	11	134	0	0	134
10							Suppliers			1	272	272	62	0	13	197	0	0	197
11						read feed	PurchaseOrderIt			1	688	688	68	0	30	590	0	0	590
12							PurchaseOrders			1	4.810	4.810	77	0	2.746	1.987	0	0	1.987
13				EPM_REF_APPS_PR		document				2	72	72	67	0	5	0	0	0	0
14						read feed	Products			1	13.855	13.855	137	0	7.925	5.793	0	0	5.793

Figure A.20 SAP Gateway Statistics Transaction: Aggregated Statistics

With the SAP Gateway statistics transaction, it's possible to navigate to the SAP Performance Trace tool that can also be started using Transaction /IWFND/TRACES. Using the Performance Trace tool, a trace can be started for a single user or a specific URI prefix (Figure A.21).

After a Performance Trace and a Payload Trace are activated for a user or a specific request URI, you can navigate to the trace results by selecting the PERFORMANCE TRACE tab or the PAYLOAD TRACE tab.

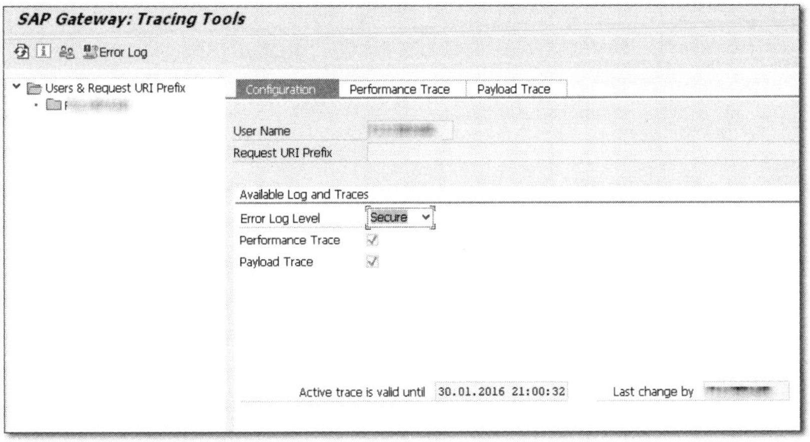

Figure A.21 SAP Gateway Performance Trace Tool

Performance Trace tool

From the list of requests in the Performance Trace tool, you can drill down to the trace details to the code that was actually executed (see Figure A.22).

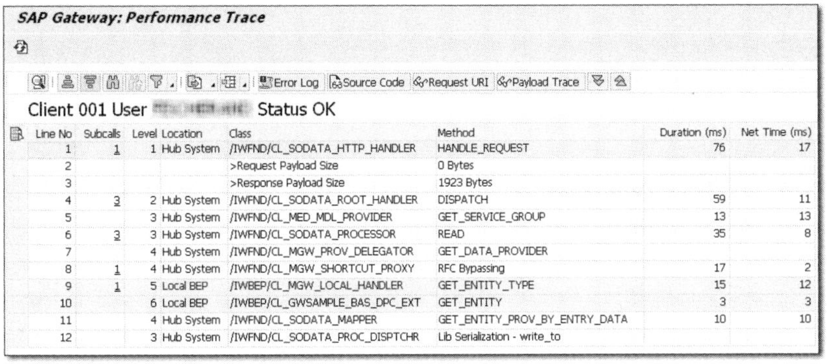

Line No	Subcalls	Level	Location	Class	Method	Duration (ms)	Net Time (ms)
1	1	1	Hub System	/IWFND/CL_SODATA_HTTP_HANDLER	HANDLE_REQUEST	76	17
2				>Request Payload Size	0 Bytes		
3				>Response Payload Size	1923 Bytes		
4	3	2	Hub System	/IWFND/CL_SODATA_ROOT_HANDLER	DISPATCH	59	11
5		3	Hub System	/IWFND/CL_MED_MDL_PROVIDER	GET_SERVICE_GROUP	13	13
6	3	3	Hub System	/IWFND/CL_SODATA_PROCESSOR	READ	35	8
7		4	Hub System	/IWFND/CL_MGW_PROV_DELEGATOR	GET_DATA_PROVIDER		
8	1	4	Hub System	/IWFND/CL_MGW_SHORTCUT_PROXY	RFC Bypassing	17	2
9	1	5	Local BEP	/IWBEP/CL_MGW_LOCAL_HANDLER	GET_ENTITY_TYPE	15	12
10		6	Local BEP	/IWBEP/CL_GWSAMPLE_BAS_DPC_EXT	GET_ENTITY	3	3
11		4	Hub System	/IWFND/CL_SODATA_MAPPER	GET_ENTITY_PROV_BY_ENTRY_DATA	10	10
12		3	Hub System	/IWFND/CL_SODATA_PROC_DISPTCHR	Lib Serialization - write_to		

Figure A.22 SAP Gateway: Performance Trace

Payload trace

The Payload Trace tool allows you to trace the exact content of the HTTP header and HTTP body of incoming requests and outgoing responses. To see all the data, the Error Log Level has to be raised from Secure, which is the default setting, to Full (see Figure A.23).

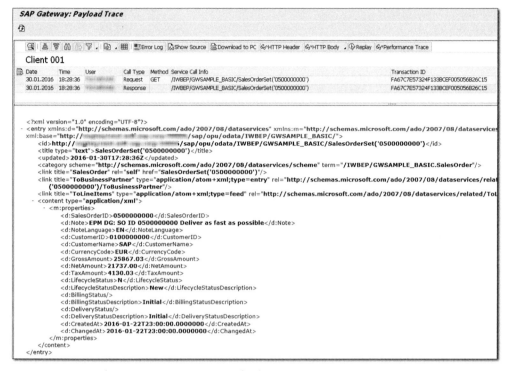

Figure A.23 SAP Gateway: Payload Trace

A.5   Delta Query Support in Offline Scenarios

The scenarios that we've looked at so far covered the use of SAP Gateway in online production environments. However, there are, of course, use cases that require an application to run offline. For this reason, SAP Gateway offers a *delta query protocol*. The delta query protocol allows a client to retrieve data from an OData service that has been created, changed, or deleted since the client last checked. The delta query protocol supports synchronizing data from a single store to multiple clients. In addition, you can submit updates from the client to the server. This provides a solution for keeping a client's local data in sync with a single store.

In this section, we'll take a look at the protocol specifics of delta queries via a sample service that is delivered as part of SAP Gateway. Then we'll describe the different options for implementing a service that supports delta queries.

A.5.1 Delta Query Protocol

The whole process starts with an initial request that is sent by a client to an entity set of an OData service that supports the delta query protocol. The server responds with a list of entities, just as a normal OData service does. In addition, a delta token link is returned at the end of the response for the entity collection.

The sample service RMTSAMPLEFLIGHT contains the `TravelAgencies_ DQ` entity set, which supports the delta query protocol. Using the SAP Gateway client, we can send the following HTTP(S) request to the sample service to retrieve all travel agencies in an initial call:

/sap/opu/odata/IWFND/RMTSAMPLEFLIGHT/TravelAgencies_DQ

Toward the end of the XML document, you'll find a relative link marked with `rel="delta"` (Listing A.5). This has to be stored by the client and has to be used for a subsequent request to retrieve newly created, changed, or deleted data.

```
<feed>
    <entry>
    ...
    </entry>
<entry>
...
</entry>
<link rel="delta" href="TravelAgencies_DQ?
!deltatoken='005056B2190B1ED396FE518A3FCB83A6_20131203081145'"
/>
</feed>
```
Listing A.5 Delta Query Protocol: Delta Token

Suppose that one or more new travel agencies have been created, or one or more existing travel agencies have been updated after the initial call. By sending the following request to the server, which contains the delta token, the client retrieves only a list of those newly created or changed travel agencies:

/sap/opu/odata/IWFND/RMTSAMPLEFLIGHT/TravelAgencies_DQ?!delta token='005056B2190B1ED396FE518A3FCB83A6_20131203081145'

If no data has been changed or created, the response of the service will be empty. In both cases, however, the response contains a new delta token link.

In addition to handling newly created and updated entities, the delta query protocol also supports the handling of deleted entities. For this, the XML response is extended with the `<deleted-entry>` tags that contain deleted entries, which are called *tombstones* (Listing A.6).

```
<at:deleted-entry ref="http://myserver.mycompany.com:50000/sap/
opu/odata/IWFND/RMTSAMPLEFLIGHT/TravelAgencies_
DQ('00001761')" when="2013-12-03T08:12:36Z" />
<at:deleted-entry ref="http://myserver.mycompany.com:50000/sap/
opu/odata/IWFND/RMTSAMPLEFLIGHT/TravelAgencies_
DQ('00001762')" when="2013-12-03T08:12:36Z" />
<link rel="delta" href="TravelAgencies_
DQ?!deltatoken='005056B2190B1ED396FE518A3FCB83A6_
20131203081236'" />
</feed>
```

Listing A.6 Delta Query Protocol: Tombstones

A.5.2 Service Implementation Options

Implementing delta query support requires the detection of changes that have been made to your business objects. There is no standard approach you can follow that works for each and every scenario. SAP currently offers two options:

▸ Use of a delta determination at request time using the *delta request log component*

▸ Use of the *Agentry SAP Framework*

The first approach calculates the deltas at request time. The second approach requires that changes to the business objects be tracked in a persistent database table, which is called the *exchange table*, with the help of the *Exchange Framework*.

Delta Request Log

When using the delta request log component, the implementation for the developer is fairly easy. Before passing the entity set back to the client in the GET_ENTITYSET method, it's passed to the framework, which calculates a hash value for each entity and stores the hash values in two application tables: /IWBEP/D_QRL_HDR and /IWBEP/D_QRL_ITM.

If the client is requesting changed data at a later point in time using the delta token in the HTTP(S) request as a query parameter, the GET_ENTITYSET_DELTA method, as opposed to the GET_ENTITYSET method, is called. (However, it's necessary to perform the same query in the backend as in the GET_ENTITYSET method, and it's also necessary to perform the same calculation of hash values.)

Based on the data that is stored in tables /IWBEP/D_QRL_HDR and /IWBEP/D_QRL_ITM, it's now possible to compare the results of the second query with the results that were retrieved with the previous call. The method will compare both result sets and only send back those entities that have been newly created, changed, or deleted.

> **Further Resources**
>
> For a detailed description of an actual implementation of a service using the delta request log, we recommend the following:
>
> *http://scn.sap.com/docs/DOC-47043*

Although the use of the delta request log component is straightforward and easy from an implementation perspective, the downside is that the load of the SAP Business Suite system isn't reduced at all. For an alternative to this method, read on.

Agentry SAP Framework

If performance is an issue, managing deltas should be handled via the Agentry SAP Framework, which uses a persistent database table to track changes. This framework is part of the SAP Mobile Platform and is implemented as an ABAP add-on. The change detection concept of the Agentry SAP Framework is depicted in Figure A.24.

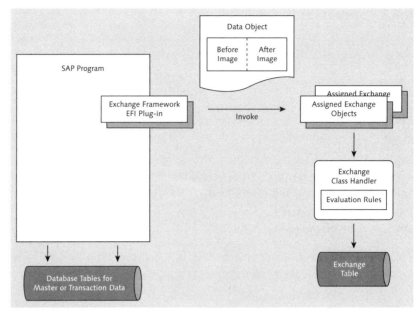

Figure A.24 Agentry SAP Framework Change Detection Concept

The changes that are detected by the Agentry SAP Framework implementation are processed by the framework in a persistent database table, the exchange table. At the very least, this table contains basic information such as last changed timestamp, change action (insert/update/delete), the user who performed this action, and—most important—the object key. In addition, the Agentry SAP Framework can store additional information such as the actual values that have been changed (to avoid additional read requests to the backend by the client to retrieve those values), and offers filtering capabilities that allow you to track only those changes that meet certain, customized filter criteria.

Further Resources

A detailed description of the Agentry SAP Framework components, an implementation guideline, and a step-by-step example of how to create a delta query implementation can be found here:

https://scn.sap.com/docs/DOC-49290

A.6   Server-Side Caching

Several business scenarios require SAP Gateway to provide more stateful behavior. Because OData services provided by SAP Gateway are stateless, the *soft state mode* was introduced. When using a soft state, a user session is held in the SAP Gateway hub and in the backend system via an RFC where the DPC can cache data in member variables. For this, the Internet Communications Framework (ICF) node of the OData service has to be configured so that it offers a certain session timeout. The length of the session timeout that is needed depends on the scenario but will usually be in the range of several seconds to some minutes. A subsequent call that is performed within a time span shorter than the configured timeout will be able to reuse the user session that then still exists in SAP Gateway.

Soft state

As a result, it's possible to reuse resources that have been loaded during the initial call because such data can be cached (see Figure A.25).

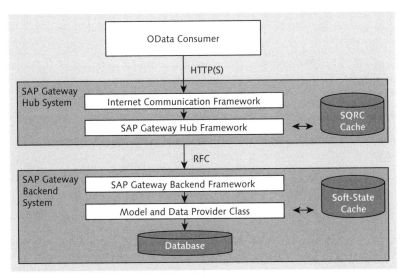

Figure A.25 Server Side Caching: Soft State

If a subsequent request is performed after the initial session has timed out, instead of throwing an exception, the framework will process the request as usual. The service implementation has to be such so that the data are read again and thus transparent for the client implementation.

The only thing the client will recognize is that the response time will be higher because the data that was cached has to be read or calculated again.

Soft state is a feature that can be useful for services that read large amounts of data or perform complex calculations such as pricing that should be available for subsequent calls while the end user is working within the application.

SQRC The soft state-based query result cache (SQRC) performs caching on the hub shown in Figure A.25. If a soft state is enabled for a service, the provider application can request the hub to cache the results of a READ_ ENTITYSET request. The goal is to speed up client-side paging. If the client is requesting additional pages using the $top and $skip query parameters, these are served by the data that are cached on the hub rather than sending these requests to the backend.

While the soft state and SQRC can provide significant performance improvements for certain scenarios, both come with a price tag because they require additional memory resources on the SAP Gateway hub and in the SAP Gateway backend. When activating a soft state for a service, the system asks you to read SAP Note 1986626 to learn about the possible impacts.

Because the use of SQRC and soft state can have a negative influence on the overall system performance, it's possible for the administrator to activate and deactivate the soft state for single services via Transaction /IWFND/MAINT_SERVICE (Activate and Maintain Services). This is possible because the services have to be developed so that a deactivation of the soft state won't break the operation of such a service. Instead, the end user will see no difference besides a reduced performance if the soft state has to be deactivated by an administrator.

A.7 Summary

This appendix has provided you with some insights into advanced topics related to SAP Gateway. Needless to say, this has been a high-level look at these topics, so consider this appendix a starting point only.

B SAP Gateway and SAP API Management

This appendix introduces SAP API Management and explains how SAP API Management and SAP Gateway work together. Furthermore, it shows some real-life examples and the basic flow behind the generation of an API in SAP API Management.

SAP API Management launch

On July 31, 2014, SAP entered a partnership with Apigee, a leading provider of API technology and services, thereby entering the world of application programming interface (API) management solutions. Built on the Apigee Edge digital acceleration platform, SAP API Management is the primary result of this partnership. SAP API Management provides central API management, governance, and monitoring as well as unified access to enterprise data. SAP API Management is available as a cloud solution on SAP HANA Cloud Platform (HCP) and also as an on-premise solution.

In this appendix, we'll take a practical approach to SAP API Management. First, we'll provide an overview of API technology and its impact on the current marketplace. Then, we'll look at SAP API Management's architecture, before showing you how to consume an SAP Gateway OData service from within SAP API Management.

B.1 Application Programming Interfaces

APIs aren't new; they are a well-known tool in programming that represents a software component in an abstract fashion. They provide a well-defined interface that allows developers to access the different entities of that software component (e.g., inputs, outputs, functionalities) in a way that doesn't require considering the implementation. Well-implemented APIs come with a self-explanatory documentation and can be easily used as building blocks for more complex applications. Those building blocks allow companies to react faster and be more flexible to market requirements, thereby enabling timely innovation.

APIs and API Management

743

To fully leverage the power of APIs, however, it makes sense to organize all—or at least all external facing—APIs through a central gateway or hub. In addition to general concerns such as security, governance, versioning, and so on, the need for an API management solution becomes more and more evident with each additional API.

Digital transformation

Taking a closer look at the market situation today, we see that companies need a digital representation. Even classical brick and mortar companies need to adapt and "digitalize" their business. This development—though very simplified here—is sometimes referred to as *digital transformation*. This is the transformation from the classic economy—based on brick and mortar businesses—into the *digital economy*.

Digital economy

The main enabler for the digital economy is the growing access to services that can be used from virtually any device, at any time, from everywhere. In this digital economy, however, services (from a technical perspective) can only be the first step. Dealing with a specific service implementation requires technical expertise. Acquiring this type of expertise takes time and money. In times of virtually infinite devices that have to be supported—preferably through the cloud—using a specific service technology simply doesn't scale.

Using open standards such as OData helps to reduce time and costs as developers can reuse their knowledge, and companies can access a large community of enabled developers. Using APIs takes this even a step further as they allow you to basically expose every function module or service to the outside world without requiring the consumer—in this case, the developer—to have to know anything about the technology or the system the function module or service is running on. The developer can simply consume the XML or JavaScript Object Notation (JSON) that is usually provided.

B.2 Architecture

Figure B.1 shows SAP API Management's infrastructure with SAP backends and third-party solutions. Note that SAP Gateway, though the perfect enabler for SAP Business Suite, is optional from an SAP API

Management perspective. As discussed in Chapter 1, SAP Process Orchestration (PO), SAP Mobile Platform, and SAP HANA Cloud Integration (HCI) come with integrated SAP Gateway functionality that can be used too. Even beyond that, any OData/Representational State Transfer (REST) and Simple Object Access Protocol (SOAP) service can be consumed.

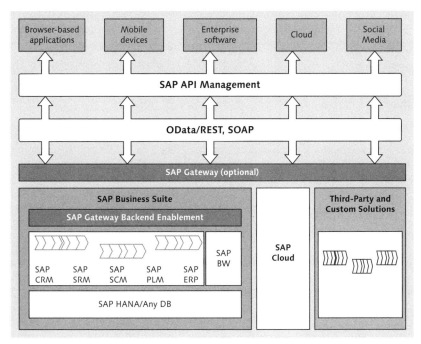

Figure B.1 SAP API Management

SAP API Management is the perfect integration layer for SAP and non-SAP solutions. In addition to an added security layer and governance solution, SAP API Management allows for the easy implementation of integration scenarios and applications. APIs can even combine services from different systems in one API.

Integration Layer

Now that you have a better understanding of how APIs fit into the new digital economy and the basic architecture of SAP API Management, in the next section, we'll provide a step-by-step approach to consuming SAP Gateway OData services with SAP API Management.

B.3   Consuming an SAP Gateway Service with SAP API Management

In the following subsections, we'll run through a simple SAP API Management scenario in which we'll consume an SAP Gateway service. Along the way, we'll create an API, a product, and an app.

API developer

The first step in every API management scenario usually doesn't start in the SAP API Management environment but in a development environment. In this environment, a developer (sometimes called the API developer) will create a function module or service that can be consumed by the API management solution in place. For SAP API Management, OData/REST and SOAP services are viable options.

We assume in the following scenario that our API developer already created an SAP Gateway OData service. Specifically, this scenario will use the SAP Gateway demo service (GWDEMO). Using this demo should allow you to reproduce the flow on your own.

> **Trial Version**
>
> With the SAP API Management trial version, you can follow the scenario and re-create our example. You can find a link to the trial version here:
>
> *http://scn.sap.com/community/api-management/blog/2016/02/02/free-trial-of-sap-api-management-on-hana-cloud-platform-is-available-now*

B.3.1   Creating an API

APIs, products, and apps

To create an API, you use the API Portal. The first step in consuming an SAP Gateway service with SAP API Management is to create an API representation. In SAP API Management on SAP HCP, this representation is simply called an API. Further down the road, you'll encounter two other important objects: the product, which allows you to publish the API, and the app, which allows you to consume the product as a developer.

> **Note**
>
> You'll notice that names are missing on some of the screens; for example, in Figure B.2, the systems don't have names. This is because we used a live system for our flow so we had to remove any references that weren't directly

related to our flow. This allowed us to provide a flow based on the latest release.

Accessing the API Portal

To create an API representation, you have to open the API Portal through the provided API Portal URL. Both portals of SAP API Management—the API Portal and the Developer Portal—are accessible through a standard web browser and a simple URL.

API Portal

> **Browser**
>
> When accessing the API Portal, we recommend using Google Chrome or Mozilla Firefox.

Identifying/Configuring a Backend System

Figure B.2 shows the standard CONFIGURE screen with system representations that are available in your SAP API Management/SAP HCP environment.

Figure B.2 API Portal: Configure Screen

This screen provides an overview of existing systems, which you can find further details on by clicking one. For our scenario, we want to access a system that isn't yet represented. Therefore, you first need to click on CONFIGURE, and then click on CREATE in the lower-left corner.

Figure B.3 shows the ADD SYSTEM screen. In addition to the title and DESCRIPTION, you can also enter the HOST, PORT, and PATH PREFIX.

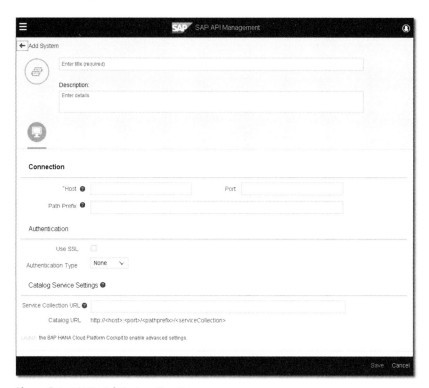

Figure B.3 API Portal: System Creation

Creating an API   In the AUTHENTICATION area, you can activate secure sockets layer (SSL) and choose from the configured authentication types. In this example system, you can choose between NONE and BASIC (for basic authentication). Eventually, you can obtain a SERVICE COLLECTION URL that allows you to provide a URL for a catalog service. Figure B.4 shows a configured system with all the relevant entries defined.

Figure B.4 API Portal: A Configured System

Note that for this example, BASIC is selected as the AUTHENTICATION TYPE in Figure B.4. To configure this basic authentication, you have to configure the destinations in the SAP HANA CONFIGURATION COCKPIT screen. To do so, click on LAUNCH, which opens the DESTINATIONS section of the SAP HANA CONFIGURATION COCKPIT of the connected SAP HCP account. Figure B.5 shows the DESTINATIONS section of the SAP HANA CONFIGURATION COCKPIT with the DESTINATION CONFIGURATION dialog already opened (to open system a configuration screen, simply click on the PENCIL icon next to it). As you can see, you can enter the USER and PASSWORD—basic authentication information—in this dialog.

SAP HANA Configuration Cockpit

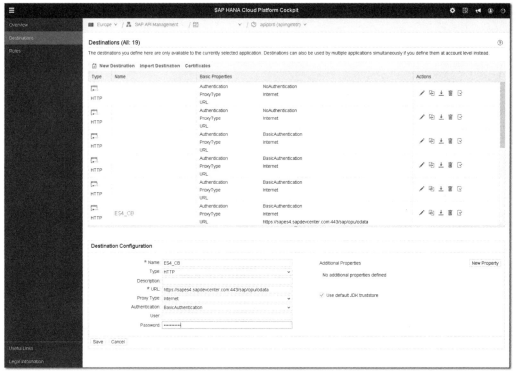

Figure B.5 SAP HANA Configuration Cockpit : Destinations and Destination Configuration

Selecting a Service

Service selection To create an API, you need to find a service to consume. To find such a service, go back to the API Portal, and open the MANAGE screen to see the existing APIs, as shown in Figure B.6.

To create your own API, click on CREATE in the lower-right corner of the screen. A pop-up will let you choose between CREATE API and IMPORT API. After choosing CREATE API, the dialog shown in Figure B.7 opens.

Figure B.6 API Portal: Manage Screen with Existing APIs

Figure B.7 API Portal: Create API Dialog

In the CREATE API dialog, you can choose the PROVIDER SYSTEM on which to locate the service you want to use for the API. You also have to provide a NAME, TITLE, and DESCRIPTION (optional) for the service, as well as an API BASE PATH and SERVICE TYPE. Eventually, you can decide if you want to fetch the documentation from the metadata of the service you're fetching. This option is only available if there is, potentially, any documentation available.

SAP Gateway
backend

If the backend system is a well-configured SAP backend system (as in our example), you'll realize three things after choosing the SAP Gateway system (in our example, the ES4_CB):

▸ A DISCOVER button will appear, which isn't there when you link, for example, to a Web Service Definition Language (WSDL) file.

▸ The SERVICE TYPE will switch to ODATA because you're connecting to the SAP Gateway system.

▸ An option to import the documentation is available.

When you use a well-configured SAP backend system, the first step in creating an API isn't to fill in the complete screen; instead, click DISCOVER and choose a service as shown in Figure B.8.

Figure B.8 API Portal: Choosing a Service

Figure B.8 shows the CREATE API screen after clicking DISCOVER and entering "GWDEMO" as a search term. As you can see in our system, there is only one GWDEMO service. As you might already have assumed, the GWDEMO service is an SAP Gateway demo service that fits perfectly into our scenario.

Gateway demo service

After you choose a service from the SAP Gateway system, the entries in the CREATE API screen are automatically filled (Figure B.9). However, it's recommended to change at least NAME, TITLE, and API BASE PATH according to your personal needs as we've done here. Using the automatically generated entries will most likely lead to duplicates and misunderstandings in the system because the entries are the same for everyone accessing the same service. After changing the entries, click on CREATE.

Figure B.9 API Portal: Create API Screen Filled

Figure B.10 shows the first representation of the newly created API. Note that to enact the creation, you still need to click on SAVE. On this screen, you see all resources of the service represented with the API, including associated operations (i.e., GET, POST, PUT, DELETE). The standard operations that make sense for a specific resource are already checked.

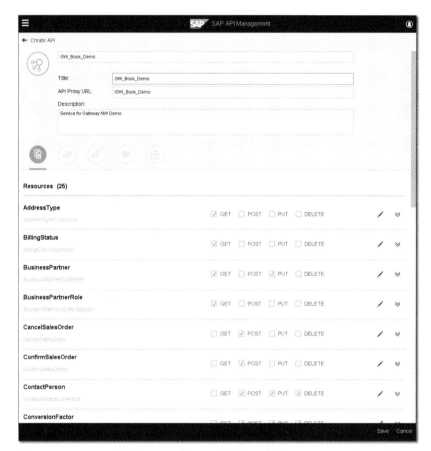

Figure B.10 API Portal: The Created API with All Available Resources and Possible Operations

If you require that an operation isn't available, you can simply uncheck it. Clicking on the arrows icon close to the resource will open the details section with the properties of the resource (see Figure B.11).

Figure B.11 API Portal: Resource with Properties

Modifying the Documentation (Optional)

As you can see in Figure B.11, the documentation was fetched from the backend system. If you want to modify this documentation simply click on the PENCIL icon, and an editor, as shown in Figure B.12, opens, allowing you to add your own information or modify the look of the documentation.

API documentation

Figure B.12 API Portal: Editing the Documentation of the Created API

After doing all this, don't forget to click on SAVE; only then is the API truly generated and accessible in SAP API Management.

Testing an API

API tests   To test an API, click on it on the MANAGE screen. Every resource has a button for the enabled methods (i.e., GET, POST, PUT, DELETE). By clicking one of these buttons, you can test the method.

Figure B.13 shows the results of invoking GET on the BUSINESSPARTNER resource. To get the XML result, you have to switch AUTHENTICATION to BASIC AUTHENTICATION and provide a user name and password. After doing so, click SEND, and you should see a similar XML response.

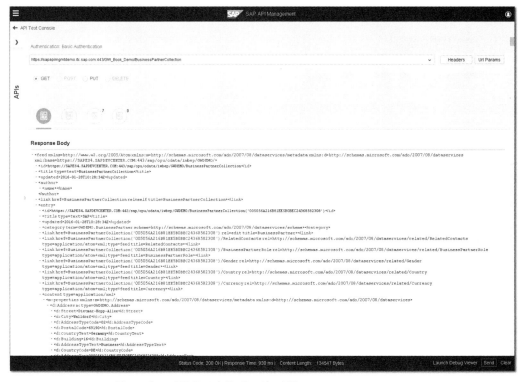

Figure B.13 API Portal: Testing the API

B.3.2   Configuring Your API

The following subsections walk through the steps for configuring your API.

Step 1: Starting the Policy Designer

One of the most powerful tools in your API Portal is the Policy Designer. You can find the policy designer in your API by clicking on the arrows icon as shown in Figure B.14. The Policy Designer allows you to define policies on all of your APIs. In our example flow, let's start with one of the simplest yet useful policies you can define: the quota policy.

Policy Designer

Figure B.14 API Portal: Launch Policy Designer

To start the Policy Designer, open your API, and click on the three arrows icon. From the list, choose LAUNCH POLICY DESIGNER. The Policy Designer opens, as shown in Figure B.15.

Step 2: Creating a Quota

To create a policy or, more specifically, a quota policy, click on EDIT in the lower-right corner. Then choose PREFLOW in the upper-left corner, and click on the plus icon close to QUOTA in the list on the right side of the screen. The CREATE POLICY dialog, as shown in Figure B.16, will open and allow you to name your policy. Make sure that the STREAM is set to INCOMING REQUEST.

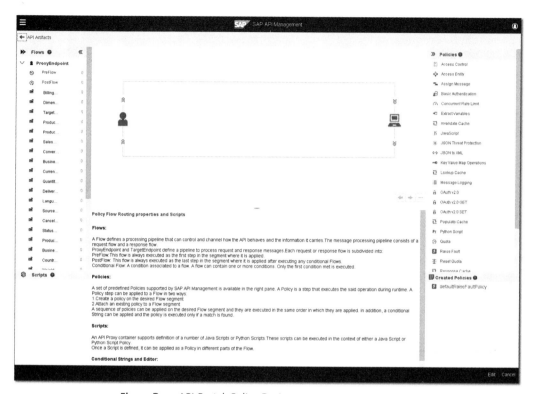

Figure B.15 API Portal: Policy Designer

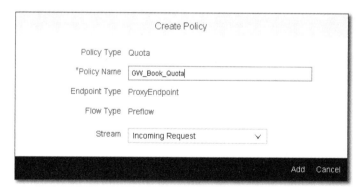

Figure B.16 API Portal: Creating a Policy (Quota)

Quota policy Figure B.17 shows the created quota policy in the Policy Designer. Note that there is some coding related to the policy. You can modify this coding to specify what the quota policy really means. ALLOW COUNT is the number of requests allowed in our example (here, 2), and INTERVAL is the time in which those requests are allowed in minutes. So, if you don't change anything, the quota policy allows two requests in a minute and then prevents any further requests from going through. Click on UPDATE and then click SAVE on the next screen to apply this policy to the API.

Figure B.17 API Portal: Quota Policy in the Policy Designer

Figure B.18 shows that you'll get a QUOTAVIOLATION error if you try to use GET three times on the API after applying the quota policy. After the time has passed, new requests will go through.

> **Note**
>
> You can apply a quota on the API and product level.

Figure B.18 API Portal: Quota Violation When Testing the API

B.3.3 Publishing Your API

To publish an API, you have to create a product. by going to the MANAGE screen and clicking on PRODUCT (Figure B.19).

Figure B.19 API Portal: Products in SAP API Management

Click on CREATE in the lower-right corner. On the screen that opens, click on the plus icon in the API section. A new dialog opens as shown in Figure B.20. Choose the API you created earlier, and add it to the product. Note that you can add more than one API to a product.

Figure B.20 API Portal: Adding an API to a Product

After clicking on OK, you can now define the other details of the product, as shown in Figure B.21. As previously mentioned, you can define quotas at the product level here too. Click on PUBLISH, and the product is officially created.

Figure B.21 API Portal: Creating a Product

B.3.4 Discovering API

To discover and consume an API/product, you switch to the *Developer Portal*. The Developer Portal can be accessed through a simple URL, similar to the API Portal. Figure B.22 shows the standard view of the Developer Portal in SAP API Management with the product you created earlier.

Figure B.22 Developer Portal: Standard View

To consume an API from within the Developer Portal, click on the created product, and then click SUBSCRIBE. From the pop-up, choose NEW APPLICATION, as shown in Figure B.23.

The resulting application screen should look like Figure B.24. Note that the product is listed in the PRODUCT area. You can add additional products to an app here. Click on SAVE to finalize the app creation.

Figure B.23 Developer Portal: Creating a New Application

Figure B.24 Developer Portal: Creating an App Based on a Product

Congratulations, you just created your first app based on SAP Gateway and SAP API Management! You'll find your app on the CONSUME screen, as shown in Figure B.25.

763

Figure B.25 Developer Portal: Success! Your First App on the Consume Screen

Testing Your API from within the Developer Portal

Optionally, to test your API from within the Developer Portal, you can either click on your app, click on the product, then click on the API, and test from there, or you can directly test the API from the TEST screen by clicking on TEST in the navigation (as shown in Figure B.25) and then click on your API, as shown in Figure B.26.

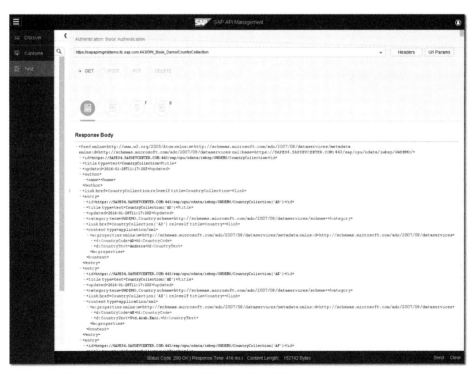

Figure B.26 Developer Portal: Testing Your API

Requiring an API Key

A standard security mechanism for APIs, although optional, is to require an API key. To ensure this for the example API, go back to the API Portal and invoke the Policy Designer. In the Policy Designer, you follow the same steps as with the quota policy, except that you choose VERIFY API KEY instead of QUOTA from the list, as shown in Figure B.27.

API key

Figure B.27 API Portal: Creating a Verify API Key Policy

Figure B.28 shows the newly created VERIFY API KEY policy. Because we want to request the API key from the header information, we have to modify the coding a little bit, as shown in Listing B.1.

Figure B.28 API Portal: Changing the Coding in the Verify API Key Policy

```
<!--
Specify in the APIKey element where to look for the variable co
ntaining the API key-->
<VerifyAPIKey async='true' continueOnError='false' enabled='tru
e' xmlns='http://www.sap.com/apimgmt'>
<APIKey ref='request.header.APIKey'/>
</VerifyAPIKey>
```

Listing B.1 Verify API Key Policy

Figure B.29 shows the testing from within the Developer Portal after you created the VERIFY API KEY policy, which will then lead to a FAILED-TORESOLVEAPIKEY error.

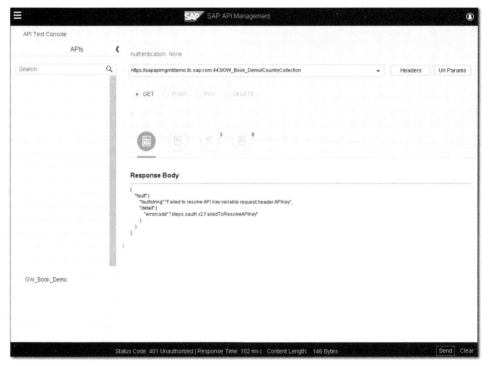

Figure B.29 Developer Portal: Error Occurs after Testing the API after Creating a Verify API Key Policy

The way the example SAP API Management is configured, the API key will be generated automatically for registered apps. Simply go to the CONSUME screen, and click on your app. There you'll see the APPLICATION KEY (i.e., the API key) that you need to access the API (see Figure B.30).

Figure B.30 Developer Portal: The Application Key among the Details of the App

In the TEST console, you can now provide this API key through the header information and access the API again (see Figure B.31).

Figure B.31 Developer Portal: Testing the API with Header Information

B.3.5   Analyzing Your API

API analytics   After implementing an API and building the products and apps, it's very important to understand how your APIs are used. SAP API Management comes with extensive analytics capabilities that can be accessed from the ANALYZE screen (see Figure B.32) for this purpose.

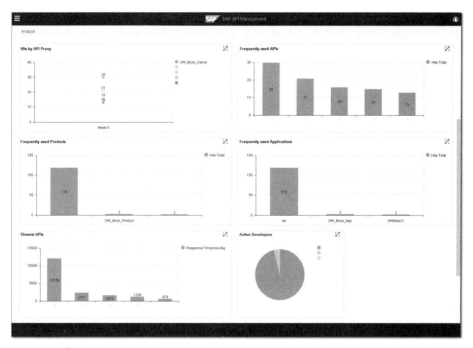

Figure B.32 API Portal: Analyzing Your APIs

B.4   Summary

In this appendix, we took a look at SAP API Management and why API management became so important in recent years. Furthermore, we saw what an SAP API Management infrastructure looks like and provided steps for consuming an SAP Gateway OData service from within SAP API Management.

While you could write a whole book on SAP API Management, this short introduction is important because SAP Gateway is a natural fit for working with SAP API Management.

C   The Authors

Carsten Bönnen received his MA in computer linguistics and artificial intelligence in Germany in 2001 and started working at SAP that same year. Initially a Java developer and trainer, he soon became a consultant and led strategic projects in the then-new field of enterprise portals. By the end of 2002, he became a product manager for SAP NetWeaver Portal (now SAP Enterprise Portal). A year later, he took on responsibility for a new product, which later became known as Visual Composer; subsequently, he managed the complete UI topic in this area. Looking for a new challenge in 2008, he joined the Microsoft Strategic Alliance Management group, which oversees the strategic alliance between SAP and Microsoft. Carsten remained in this role for four years before he joined the SAP Gateway product management team in 2012. After taking over and coordinating go-to-market activities for SAP Gateway and SAP API Management in 2015, he currently works on the new SAP API Management product management team. Beyond his business-specific activities at SAP, he founded the first SAP karate group in 2005, which he continues to lead today.

Volker Drees studied electrical engineering at Fachhochschule in Wiesbaden, Germany, and holds a degree in communications engineering (Nachrichtentechnik). He began his SAP career in 1998 in the consulting department and has experience in a number of areas: ABAP development, R/3 implementations, mySAP CRM, mobile sales, mobile asset management, and mobile infrastructure. He recently worked as a regional group expert for mobile applications in the Business User and Information Worker Division at SAP. Currently, Volker works as a product expert for SAP Gateway in the Products & Innovation Technology, Core Platform Gateway Division.

André Fischer has worked in product management for SAP Gateway since the launch of the product in 2011. After finishing his physics degree at RWTH Aachen University and Heidelberg University, Germany, he started his professional career in 1995 as a technology consultant for an SAP partner. From 1999 to 2000, he was responsible for setting up a data center as the co-managing director for a newly founded joint venture outsourcing company, and his technical expertise contributed to the company becoming a certified SAP hosting partner. As of 2002, André specialized in SAP security consulting, and, in 2004, he joined the newly created Collaboration Technology Support Center with Microsoft at SAP AG. Over the past 10 years at SAP, André has focused on the interoperability of SAP NetWeaver and Microsoft technologies, SAP Enterprise Search, single sign-on (SSO), and SAP Gateway. André is a frequent speaker at conferences, including SAP TechEd, and has published a multitude of articles and blogs on the SAP Community Network. In 2013, 2014, and 2015, he was SCN Topic Lead for SAP Gateway. He is co-author of the SAP PRESS book, *SAP NetWeaver/.NET Interoperability*. With almost 20 years of experience in various SAP technologies, André is a trusted advisor for many SAP customers and partners.

Ludwig Heinz is the CIO of the Europe-wide acting recycling company, Theo Steil GmbH. He studied business informatics at the University of Applied Sciences FHDW in Bergisch Gladbach, Germany, and has worked as an ABAP and mobile developer at itelligence AG in Cologne since 2006. Ludwig was a member of the SAP Design Partner Council for SAP Gateway from 2011 until the end of 2013. There he worked with SAP AG and other partners to improve SAP Gateway. He also took over the topic responsibility of SAP Gateway at itelligence in 2012.

In addition, he works as a college lecturer and supports students working on bachelor's theses that focus on mobile UI technologies.

Karsten Strothmann is the global head of SAP Gateway Customer and Product Success (CPS) at SAP SE in Walldorf, Germany. From Walldorf, and other locations, including Bangalore, India, and Palo Alto, California, CPS supports selected SAP Gateway customer projects, enables the SAP Gateway community, and extensively brings a customer perspective into SAP Gateway's quality assurance processes. Karsten has more than 17 years of experience in the software industry, 15 of those at SAP. Before joining SAP Gateway in 2010, he worked on diverse topics such as mobile, SAP SRM, and SAP Enterprise Portal. During his career, he has applied himself to highly varied roles in product management, development, quality assurance, and consulting, which has enabled him to acquire a holistic view of both software creation and its usage. Karsten holds a master's degree in computer science from TU Dortmund University, Germany.

Index

- ▶ Implement SAP Fiori on AS ABAP and SAP HANA

- ▶ Customize transactional, analytical, and fact sheet apps

- ▶ Develop your own apps from scratch

Anil Bavaraju

SAP Fiori Implementation and Development

Modernize your user experience with this guide to developing and implementing SAP Fiori apps! Begin by installing and configuring the system for SAP Fiori. Then, learn to implement transactional, analytical, and fact sheet apps on an AS ABAP or SAP HANA database. Customize further by creating, developing, and extending your apps using the SAP Web IDE. Are you ready to beautify your UI?

569 pages, pub. 11/2015

E-Book: $69.99 | **Print:** $79.95 | **Bundle:** $89.99

www.sap-press.com/3883

- ▶ Discover the latest and greatest features in the ABAP universe

- ▶ Explore the new worlds of SAP HANA, BRFplus, BOPF, and more

- ▶ Propel your code and your career into the future

Paul Hardy

ABAP to the Future

ABAP has been around for a while, but that doesn't mean your programming has to be stuck in the past. Want to master test-driven development? Decipher BOPF? Manage BRF+? Explore ABAP 7.4? With clear explanations, engaging examples, and downloadable code, this book is your ride to the future. After all: If you're going to build something with ABAP, why not do it with some style?

727 pages, pub. 03/2015
E-Book: $59.99 | **Print:** $69.95 | **Bundle:** $79.99

www.sap-press.com/3680

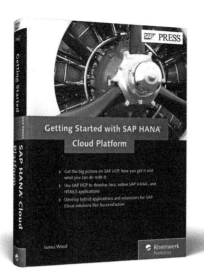

▶ Get the big picture on SAP HCP: how you get it and what you can do with it

▶ Use SAP HCP to develop Java, native SAP HANA, and HTML5 applications

▶ Develop hybrid applications and extensions for SAP Cloud solutions like SuccessFactors

James Wood

Getting Started with SAP HANA Cloud Platform

Want to extend SAP SuccessFactors? Develop a native SAP HANA application? Code SAPUI5? Guess what: SAP HANA Cloud Platform can do it all. With this book, get the basics of SAP HCP, and then take the next steps. You'll learn how to create, deploy, and secure applications, and also explore SAP HANA Cloud Portal and SAP HANA Cloud Integration. There's more to cloud than fluff—find out what it is.

519 pages, pub. 04/2015
E-Book: $59.99 | **Print:** $69.95 | **Bundle:** $79.99
www.sap-press.com/3638

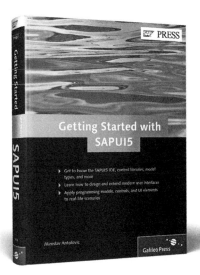

Miroslav Antolovic

Getting Started with SAPUI5

Develop next-generation UIs for responsive, versatile SAP applications. To understand the pioneering programming language SAPUI5, first walk through basic programming concepts. Then explore the development and runtime environments, tools, and plugins that you'll use throughout the design process. Learn to develop your own apps using step-by-step instructions, sample code listings, and a full-scale model application.

462 pages, pub. 07/2014

E-Book: $59.99 | **Print:** $69.95 | **Bundle:** $79.99

www.sap-press.com/3565

- ▶ Understand how SAP HANA changes ABAP for even the most experienced developers

- ▶ Enable code pushdown to move code from the application server to the database

- ▶ Get up to speed on the SAP HANA IDE and integration of native SAP HANA objects

Gahm, Schneider, Swanepoel, Westenberger

ABAP Development for SAP HANA

See how SAP HANA has changed ABAP, and learn to bring your skills up to par. This comprehensive guide uses detailed programming examples to help you design simple and advanced applications with ABAP. Learn to enable code pushdown, use Open SQL enhancements and CDS views, integrate native SAP HANA objects, and more. You'll be programming for SAP HANA in no time!

642 pages, 2nd edition, pub. 04/2016
E-Book: $69.99 | **Print:** $79.95 | **Bundle:** $89.99

www.sap-press.com/3973